# Praise for
# NEW WORLD COMING

"A groundbreaking contribution to our understanding of the culture and politics of the 1960s. Unlike most studies of the period, which focus on youth revolt, student unrest, and middle-class alienation within the United States, this collection follows a different path—tracing the many meanings of 'liberation' from Mexican rockers complicating Cuba's dominance in Latin American resistance movements to youth culture in Dakar to feminism in Palestine and Brazil."

> —**PATRICE PETRO**, Professor of English and Film Studies,
> University of Wisconsin-Milwaukee

"There is a tendency among some historians to tame the sixties, to turn a series of world-spanning uprisings into a safe nostalgic soundtrack. *New World Coming* restores the radicalism of the sixties, a period that initiated battles over power and privilege that continue to be fought to this day. The book is a model of committed, incisive, readable, and relevant scholarship."

> —**JEET HEER**, journalist and historian

"*New World Coming* is a major reinterpretation that redefines the sixties experience in a global context. Utilizing a rich, diverse, and impressive breadth of work that straddles the globe from Sarnia to Palestine and just about everywhere in between, the collection makes us rethink our most basic assumptions of place, space, and meaning when it comes to this evocative period in history. This is a significant contribution to the historiography of the time, and an important new departure in sixties studies that gives readers an original perspective."

> —**DIMITRY ANASTAKIS**, Professor of History, Trent University,
> editor, *The Sixties: Passion, Politics and Style*

全世界无产者同被压迫人民、被压迫民族联合起来！
QUAN SHI JIE WU CHAN ZHE TONG BEI YA PO REN MIN BEI YA PO MIN ZU LIAN HE QI LAI

# NEW WORLD COMING

## The Sixties and the Shaping of Global Consciousness

Edited by
Karen Dubinsky, Catherine Krull, Susan Lord, Sean Mills & Scott Rutherford

BETWEEN THE LINES
TORONTO

**New World Coming: The Sixties and the Shaping of Global Consciousness**

First published in 2009 by
Between the Lines
720 Bathurst Street, Suite #404
Toronto, Ontario   M5S 2R4
Canada
1-800-718-7201
www.btlbooks.com

LIBRARY AND ARCHIVES CANADA CATALOGUING IN PUBLICATION

New world coming : the sixties and the shaping of global consciousness / edited by Karen Dubinsky ... [et al.].

Papers presented at the conference: New world coming : the sixties and the shaping of global consciousness held at Queen's University, Kingston, Ont., June 13–16, 2007.
Includes bibliographical references and index.
ISBN 978-1-897071-51-9

1. Nineteen sixties—Political aspects.   2. Nineteen sixties—Social aspects.   3. Social history—1960–1970.   4. World politics—1955–1965.   5. World politics—1965–1975. 6. Civilization, Modern—1950–. I. Dubinsky, Karen

D848.N485 2009               909.82'6               C2009-901541-2

Cover and text design by David Vereschagin, Quadrat Communications
Cover illustration from the Ann Tompkins (Tang Fandi) and Lincoln Cushing Chinese Poster Collection, C.V. Starr East Asian Library, University of California.

Printed in Canada

Between the Lines gratefully acknowledges assistance for its publishing activities from the Canada Council for the Arts, the Ontario Arts Council, the Government of Ontario through the Ontario Book Publishers Tax Credit program and through the Ontario Book Initiative, and the Government of Canada through the Book Publishing Industry Development Program.

# contents

## Part II: Cultural Citizenship

Colour poster art related to chapter 24 follows page 276

# Acknowledgements

**This book** started life as a conference, and that's where our gratitude begins. For four days in June 2007 the staid halls of Queen's University in Kingston, Ontario, were transformed by the presence of four hundred people who gathered to debate and remember the Global Sixties. "New World Coming: The Sixties and the Shaping of Global Consciousness" brought together North American Black Power icons and twenty-something graduate students, Cuban feminists and Danish historians, grizzled Canadian new leftists and South African decolonization theorists. Scholarly conferences don't get any more eclectic, or fun.

But conferences don't organize themselves, and books don't write or publish themselves, and both of these projects succeeded because of the hard work of many people. The unflappable Linda Graham kept things on track administratively. From among the huge numbers of volunteers and advisers, we want to offer special thanks to Lincoln Cushing and Cary Fraser. We are also grateful to the Social Science and Humanities Research Council, which provided funds to both the conference and this book, as well as the many departments and administrators at Queen's that contributed.

We are extremely lucky that Robert Clarke was able to take on the demanding tasks of managing editor for this book. As well as voluminous editing tasks,

Rob kept in touch with forty contributors and five editors for almost two years; that's a mountain of email. In Canadian publishing, his way with words is legendary, for good reason. At Between the Lines we have enjoyed the support and professionalism of Anjula Gogia, Amanda Crocker, Paula Brill, and Jennifer Tiberio. Many thanks also to designer David Vereschagin for his splendid work on the inside and cover of the book.

We couldn't have done this without Susan Belyea, Sayyida Jaffer, Paul Kelley, Brian McKercher, and Anna Shea.

While we were finishing this book, Maria Lorelai Krull was born. We say welcome: another reason to make a New World.

The Editors

Scott Rutherford, Sean Mills, Susan Lord,
Catherine Krull, and Karen Dubinsky

# INTRODUCTION
## The Global Sixties

**Every locality** has a global history, but some places require digging to find it. Sometimes it is hidden in the untold stories of those on the margins, or buried under the rubble of development projects that are attempting to turn old cities into something new.

Havana, Cuba, though, is a city with a very public global history that is next to impossible to ignore. For the countless foreign visitors, it is the living story of the Cuban Revolution and the sixties that is arguably most obviously global. In the Habana Libre hotel, the iconography of revolution and the sixties is as present to the eye as a Starbucks kiosk is in any North American airport—and both can be simultaneously comforting and disconcerting. The city streets poignantly illuminate the constant collision between the histories of Empire—Spanish, American, and Soviet—and daily life: in the carnivalesque anti-American billboards along the Malécon, the multitudes of old U.S. and Soviet-era cars, Spanish colonial architecture, and the propped up bodies of Cuban men who left their limbs in Angola and now beg for pesos on Obispo in Old Havana. Ask a sixties generation Cuban how to make sense of the period—its promises, successes, lies, obvious limitations—and their nation's overdetermined place in the consciousness of First World activists and state leaders, and one phrase prefaces every answer: "It's complicated."

*New World Coming*, as its title suggests, is not *about* Havana, or Cuba, or any other single locale. It is about the shaping of global consciousness in the sixties, an era for which discussion can be prefaced with one phrase: "It's complicated." The collection has its origins in a four-day international conference held at Queen's University in Kingston, Ontario, in June 2007. That conference, New World Coming: The Sixties and the Shaping of Global Consciousness, emerged out of conversations between a group of Queen's scholars who discovered they had common interests in the history and culture of the decade. Because our collective interests in the period began with Cuba and Third World decolonization, we were having debates about the sixties that were profoundly different than the discussions found in many of the books and articles we were reading. We soon realized that we were not alone in believing that questions of race, gender, sexuality, nationality, class, locality, religion, imperialism, capitalism, colonialism, and the influence of Third World politics and culture needed to be included in an expanded understanding of the meaning of the sixties. From the conversations of several hundred participants at our conference, one theme came clearly into focus, and it subsequently guided the creation of this book: scholarship on the sixties needs to shift away from the main centres and major events that have thus far dominated representations of the period.

We would never deny, of course, the importance of familiar dramatic events of global significance that took place during the period. The Soviet invasion of Czechoslovakia, the Six Days War, the first years of the Cuban Revolution, and student and worker revolts had a profoundly global resonance, as did well-known oppositional groups such as the Students for a Democratic Society, French and Italian workers, and the Black Panthers. These events and groups (and many more) provide much of the backdrop for the articles of this book, but, with a few exceptions, they do not form its contents. *New World Coming* uncovers the full complexities of the idea of the sixties, with all its radiant possibilities and frustrating limitations. "Whose 1960s are we talking about, then?" asks Rabab Abdulhadi in the chapter that opens this book. "How might the story shift," she continues, "if we were to geographically and imaginatively shift our gaze away from the United States?"

We can expand this question—posed implicitly and explicitly by all the contributors to this collection—even further. How might the story shift if we choose new bookends for the period? Maybe the sixties begins with the Algerian War in 1954, or the Bandung conference of 1955? Maybe it ends with the Chilean coup in 1973, or the Contra war in Nicaragua in the 1980s? In other words, if the richness of the entire period is reduced to a singular chronology, or if the period is understood only as the global events of 1968, we cut ourselves off from seeing resistance as a continuing process, and instead see it as isolated events now closed off from the present. We also miss the extraordinary array of different locations, both local and international, where resistance took place.

This collection is intentionally broad, both geographically and thematically. Our goal is not to offer a representation of all the events that took place during the period. Rather, our project is at once more vast and more circumscribed. If what counts as the sixties is confined narrowly to a few major events, we lose sight of the vast array of ways in which individuals worked actively to create a new world in their homes, workplaces, neighbourhoods, and personal lives. As Alice Echols suggests, not only are traditional sixties stories Westerncentric, but they are also masculinist; "sixties studies" still bring out the boys in droves. To enlarge and enliven the debate on the who, what, when, where, and why of the sixties we can begin to grasp the period's complexities by shifting our focus to women in Havana and Palestine, youth in Dakar and Sarnia, Caribbean exiles in Montreal, and Puerto Rican workers in New York.

By bringing together this purposely eclectic collection of articles, however, we want to do more than demonstrate how the sixties played out on the terrain of everyday life, and in regions and cities outside of the main centres. While making no claim to be representative, we believe that the various voices and perspectives demonstrate the many ways in which a nascent global consciousness emerged. To get closer to an understanding of the many meanings of liberation, we need to begin by training our ears to hear these different sounds: from Mexican rockers complicating Cuba's dominance in Latin American resistance movements to a Guatemalan poet making films with a Dutch filmmaker in East Germany to the cross-currents of the Atlantic. As proprietorship of the period is increasingly contested, how will the familiar iconography and imagery change? What does the global sixties look and sound like?

*New World Coming* argues that the challenges that citizens made to dominant power structures, cultural systems, and everyday activities of their daily lives in this era were conceptualized in a global sphere. To quote veteran scholar and activist John Saul, whose own reflections on several decades of African solidarity movements grace these pages, we mark the sixties off as "a crucial moment in the birth of a distinctive and novel kind of radical and global consciousness." The local and the everyday were read through a larger transnational lens, and resistance was forged at least in part through the interaction of daily experience with an understanding of global developments.

One of the defining features of the political and cultural movements of the era was the feeling of acting simultaneously with others in a global sphere, the belief that people elsewhere were motivated by a common purpose. No matter how "local" the activity, it was often conceptualized in tandem with a larger worldwide movement. "Our perspective," writes labour activist and former Young Lord Jaime

Veve here, "was not limited to our immediate surroundings." Together, this book's articles demonstrate the extraordinary range of ways in which people in different locales imagined, contested, and lived the "global." For many in the First and Third Worlds, challenging imperialism and colonialism turned the world upside down, ensuring that the theoretical and political vanguard had moved from the North to the South. For others, images of the global—fostered through international travel, transnational cultural diffusion, migration, and media—signified a renewed understanding of the importance of local action.

Our attempt to "globalize" our understanding should therefore not be confused as an attempt to assign a singular meaning to the sixties. We are mindful of the many ways in which the idea of the global can reinforce rather than undo hierarchy and exclusion. If used unreflectively, the term can simply refer to the mapping of dominant categories developed in the West and distributed outwards into the rest of the world. Therefore the extent to which the sixties "happened" elsewhere is often reduced to an understanding of what the period means in the United States. Characterizing sixties politics and culture as youth revolt, student unrest, or middle-class alienation may reveal something about how the period played out in the United States; yet trying to read global developments through these categories obscures more than illuminates. We believe that the articles collected here, rather than following that path, demonstrate instead how transnational ideas and culture interacted with particular local conditions, generating diverse meanings. Reflecting on the Canadian sixties, contributor Ian McKay writes of a generation "lip-syncing to songs we ourselves had not written," an evocative and superbly useful image, relevant to many locales. Eric Zolov writes, for example, about *refritos*, which in Latin American contexts are literally "refried" versions or covers of the original rock 'n' roll hits. He contends: "The term's implicit associations of appropriation make it an apt label to describe the phenomenon more broadly. While some might see this as mere mimicry, we should recognize how the sheer act of performance involved the reconfiguration of foreign reference points of rebellion for a local context."

But the sixties was more than a vast array of independent initiatives, and it was more than merely thinking globally. Around the world, individuals and groups assumed an active responsibility for the societies they lived in. People worked to become the active creators or re-creators of their own lives and societies. They demanded a place as subjects rather than as objects of history; and to become the subjects of history they necessarily not only had to act, but to act in the present. The tragic problems of war and poverty, racism and sexism, imperialism and colonialism, could not wait. It is this feeling of urgency in the face of the tragedy of the present, this articulation of the creative potential and responsibility of all human beings, and this desire to challenge regimes of power and war that extended both around the world and into our most intimate relationships, that continues to draw so many of us to the period. In a particularly powerful example from the Vietnam War, Franny Nudelman cites "a landscape animated by North Vietnamese powers of renewal. Bridges destroyed by day are quickly rebuilt under cover of darkness. Easily targeted urban institutions are relocated to the country-side: schools are moved to fields, hospitals rebuilt in caves, and entire villages transplanted underground." As part of these narratives, she maintains, "Useful objects, like surgical clamps, made from spent ammunition and downed airplanes neatly figure the larger reconstruction underway in North Vietnam."

It is entirely fair for a book existing primarily as a challenge to the dominant logics of sixties memory and scholarship to be confronted with the question: why use "the sixties" at all? *New World Coming* argues that the era is in fact not one decade, but at a minimum three, implicated most obviously in the daily logics of power and resistance, and in the bodies of those who were not all young, white, or male. Moreover, we are confronted with the reality that most people in the world do not actually recognize their political and cultural alternatives as being part of the sixties generation—especially when the era is represented through the acoustics of Western whiteness. Yet we still *need* "the sixties." We need it because the dominant systems of power, in our (the editors') localities, clearly still need the sixties. Maybe Cary Fraser puts it best when he suggests, "The contemporary context of the new millennium provides ... a point from which we can examine the unresolved issues of the decade, and their impact upon global human society." The sixties retain their power to inspire, or frighten. We contend that as the sixties, a recent and powerful chapter in the history of the present, continues to inform contemporary politics and popular culture, it is also time to reimagine its cast of characters.

# The first section of this book, "Nation-Decolonization-Liberation," explores

the implications of the "nation" for various liberation movements. During the 1960s many activists and intellectuals throughout the Third World, and minority groups within the First World, imagined that the path to freedom led through anticolonial projects of national liberation. Part I also includes chapters on efforts of international solidarity, the importance of the "nation" for the new left, the reactions of the Soviet Communist Party to the events of 1968, the reception of Maoism in Mexico, and the construction of a national security state in Canada. Throughout we examine the various tensions, ambiguities, and possibilities opened up by imagining the global through the prism of the nation.

In the second part, "Cultural Citizenship," we examine the various ways in which revolution was imagined throughout the sixties. Rather than limiting the section to political ideas, authors explore the importance of a transnational cultural sphere, international travel, theatre, media and film, socio-spacial representations of urban slums, and the globalization of a consciousness of racial marginalization. All of the chapters deal with how new social imaginaries, forged in particular local spaces, connected various people throughout the world.

The third part of the book, "Mobilizing Bodies," deals with the complex politicization of bodies during the decade. Throughout much of the world vibrant second-wave feminist movements developed, and the chapters here probe the impact and meaning of that movement. Articles explore the "whiteness" of U.S. feminism, the impact that American women accompanying draft dodgers had on Canadian feminism, the masculinity of the U.S. Peace Corps, the participation of women in the Cuban Revolution, and the development of feminism in Brazil. Writers also seek to understand the "body" as a key site of resistance—looking, for instance, at transnational resistance to the use of Agent Orange, and to the complicated politics of sex reassignment surgery during the period. The chapters therefore connect the experiences of women, men, the politics of the body, and the gendered language of liberation from a wide variety of global regions and countries.

The final section of the book, "Lasting Legacies," focuses on some of the enduring political movements and cultural landscapes forged during the 1960s: the new right, the Canadian myth of peacekeeping, environmentalism, the culture of participatory democracy in the new social movements of the 1980s and 1990s, and the organization and systemization of political violence in Latin America. To wrap it all up, the Epilogue also assesses both the continued imperial legacy of Europe and the United States and the present-day consequences of Third World modernity, with specific reference to the new economic power of China. Together, the chapters argue that the political upheavals of the sixties dramatically transformed the global political landscape.

At their core, the various pieces that form this collection demonstrate that the resistance and imaginative thinking and protest movements of the sixties exhibited a heightened consciousness of global injustice. In doing so—individually and collectively—these ways of being held out a vision of the possibilities of building a new world.

Lillian Allen

# Revolution from de Beat

Revolution from de drum
Revolution from de beat
Revolution from de heart
Revolution with de feet

De riddim and the heave and the sway of the beat
De rumblings and the tumblings down
To the dream to the beat. To the impulse to be free
To the life that spring up in the heat        in the heat
In the pounding dance to be free
To burst open a window
Crash upon a door
Strip the crust of confinement
Seep truth, through cracks
Through the routing rhythms of the musical tracks     tracks

De sound of reggae music came on a wave of patter     patter
Of deeply rooted internal chatter     chatter

On wings of riddim and melodies gone free
The bass strum the heart
The bass drum the heart beat
And the Rastaman pound! Bong bong     Bong bong

And de sound all around
And the voice
Of impulse crafted into life burning darkness
Of light
Of days journeying through the night
Of riddim pulse wails and dreams
And determination to be free
Of sight
Of a vision that ignites
Of a musical bam-bam fling-down-baps, get-up-stand-up-jam
A musical realignment of the planets
A joy and a singing for those on it

Liberation impulse
Dig colonialists' graves
Crunch of the sixties
Baton carried through the Civil Rights flame
Spirit of the Hippies
Signify new ways
The Black power five
The right-on jive
Women raise banners for their rights
Communities organize
And worker struggle for human rights     for human rights

But the core of the African self
Separated by four hundred years
Ties blighted and nipped     a continental divide
And colonialist lies
A sip from the being of the African well
Uncorked the primal African self
And woo...oosh woo...oo...oosh, the well spring up
And a riddim let loose
And reggae music found us

It was the pulse in the Caribbean that echoed bright
A voice on a beat
Squashéd determination released
And the wondrous sighs of Black people once again rose high

From a little piece of rock called Jamaica
Where Arawak and Carib bones lie
Came a breath of resistance
Of peace  love  and liberation
Spread worldwide on the wings of its artists and shaman
The bass and drum prance like a winded fire
The chenke chenke chenke chenke of a guitar strum
Songs of freedom
Of spirit
Of love
Of redemption


Revolution from de drum
Revolution from de beat
Revolution from de heart
Revolution with de feet

Ah Revolution

# PART I

# NATION-
# DECOLONIZATION-
# LIBERATION

Rabab Ibrahim Abdulhadi     1

# WHOSE 1960S? GENDER, RESISTANCE, AND LIBERATION IN PALESTINE

> From Brazil to Vietnam, from the Dominican Republic to Algeria, from Mali to
> Indonesia, from Bolivia to Greece, US fleets, air force, and intelligence networks
> were undermining the achievements of the post-war period and arresting the tide of
> history. The 1960s were indeed America's decade. The 1970s shall be the decade of its
> dismantlement and complete undoing.
>
> —Leila Khaled, *My People Shall Live!*

**In her** "autobiography," published in Britain in 1973, Palestinian militant Leila Khaled argued that the decade of the 1960s was no great cause for celebration. As evidence she pointed to several spots around the world where the U.S. government had intervened against people's struggles. Assassinated leaders of communities of colour and Third World movements—people such as Malcolm X, Martin Luther King Jr., and Patrice Lumumba—would probably have agreed with her argument, if they had been allowed to live long enough to assess the decade.

At issue is the very narrative of the 1960s, which has been dominated by the discourse of the U.S. white heterosexual male radicals (in particular, members of the Students for a Democratic Society) who participated in a slice of that decade's movements and insist on owning the rights to the story.[1] Similarly, in a much-cited study U.S. feminist writer Sara Evans theorizes a single path for the emergence of women's consciousness and the feminist movement, pointing to an involvement in other movements, such as the anti-war movement, and negative experiences of ill treatment at the hands of male comrades. Other feminist commentators, such as Andrea Dworkin, Robin Morgan, and Barbara Ehrenreich—whom I call "colonial feminists"—suggest that the United States has offered the most liberating space in terms of gender justice. This dominant discourse tends to distil the specific experience of American activists and displace other—and no less significant—narratives by less powerful groups.

Although the 1960s narrative remains a contested terrain on an international as well as a North American level, nonetheless the issue became all too clear to me as I sat through the first two days of the New World Coming conference, listening to the various speakers.[2] I expected to hear references to the 1967 Israeli occupation of the West Bank, Gaza, East Jerusalem, the Golan Heights, and the Sinai Peninsula. I found it at best curious and at worst alarming that, save for one plenary speaker, the Occupation simply did not come up even peripherally.

It was curious that while several speakers theoretically cited Frantz Fanon's work on Algeria,[3] the actual struggle about which Fanon wrote and in which he participated seemed not to have seeped into the consciousness of conference participants. It was alarming that despite repeated references to the U.S. wars in Iraq and Afghanistan, there appeared to be no knowledge of the history of U.S. intervention in the Arab world, or of the resistance movements to such intervention.

Whose 1960s are we talking about, then? Should the U.S. master narrative be applied ahistorically all over the world without regard to context? How might the story shift if we stand outside the North Western Hemisphere rather than being fixed at its centre—in other words, if we were to geographically and imaginatively shift our gaze away from the United States and centre our analysis on the Arab world, named otherizingly as the "Middle East"?

Reflecting on the 1960s from that difficult to define geographical and intellectual space, often referred to as Arab/Muslim/Middle East/Central Asia,[4] I would argue against a linear, unidimensional, and singular historical narrative of the 1960s. By placing the 1967 Israeli Occupation and the Palestinian anticolonial resistance (including women's militancy) at the centre of my analysis, I intend to offer an alternative reading that contradicts the assumption that the dynamics of activism in the United States are necessarily applicable to all social movements around the world; and my focus on Palestinian women militants and their central role in the Palestinian anticolonial movement produces, in comparison to the work of Evans, a notably different conclusion about the rise of women's consciousness.

# Our 1960s

To refresh our memories, then, let me share several major developments that took place in our part of the world during the 1960s.

- The liberation of Yemen from British colonialism, which took place with the support of fighters from all over the Arab world.
- The decolonization of Algeria. While Fanon's theory of revolution

continues to be widely quoted, the writer himself seems at times to be lifted out of the context in which he acted, operated, theorized, struggled with, and negotiated on behalf of and alongside the Algerian National Liberation Front (FLN).

- Jamal Abdul Nasser and the rise of the Free Officers Movement, a group of Egyptian military officers who rose against the monarchy of King Faruq in a coup d'état that transformed Egypt into a nationalist-socialist republic.
- The founding of the Palestine Liberation Organization (PLO) in 1965. At the same time the Palestine National Council, the first Palestinian Parliament in Exile, was founded.
- The founding in 1965 of the General Union of Palestinian Women (GUPW). The insistence of GUPW that a Palestinian is one whose mother or father is a Palestinian undermines the claims of colonial feminists such as Dworkin, Morgan, and Ehrenreich who continue to maintain that Arab and Muslim women are submissive.
- Palestinians experienced the Occupation of the rest of their historic homeland and the expansion of Israeli rule over Egyptians and Syrians in addition to the Palestinians.

# Experiencing Occupation—Situated Knowledge

The sixties were my formative years. They were also when the Occupation took place. I was only twelve years old on June 5, 1967, when Israel occupied the rest of Palestine along with other Arab lands. The Occupation shaped and framed the person that I am today. Indeed, the course of life of an entire generation of Palestinians was altered in more ways than we could have imagined.

At the time of the Occupation, things that were Arab ceased to be central to our lives: road signs, currency, food labels, clothing labels, and birth certificates were now all issued in Hebrew, the official language of the Occupation. While Arabic continued to be used, documents were considered official only if they were "authenticated" in Hebrew.

Curfews were imposed, lasting at times for weeks. Jeeps full of men speaking a foreign language none of us understood would roam the streets of my hometown, Nablus. When the curfew was partially lifted we, young-girls-in-blue-and-white-striped-elementary-public-school-uniforms, were allowed to go to school. The first time the curfew was lifted after the 1967 Occupation, we arrived in our classrooms to find that Palestine was erased from geography books and its history deleted from the official Israeli-sanctioned curriculum. Palestinian teachers who returned to their jobs, however, did not accept the Israeli-imposed curriculum and instead sought to teach the younger generation of Palestinians growing up under occupation about our history and roots so that we would not forget who we were or where we came from.[5] In doing this they were risking imprisonment and other punitive measures. But it was not the first time that they defied those who ruled over us. During the Jordanian rule over the West Bank (1950–67), Palestinian teachers ignored the history that the Hashemite Kingdom of Jordan sought to impose on the Palestinian school curriculum and insisted on teaching a counterhegemonic curriculum—one that exposed the role that Jordan played in collaborating with the Zionist movement before 1948 and with the Israeli government after that.

As young girls approaching puberty we walked to school ever so carefully, seeking to avoid the stares and harassment of young Palestinian men. Later, however, we were not as successful in avoiding the jeeps positioned along the road, jeeps packed with young men in full military gear, jeeps with guns pointed at us. But the men were not speaking a foreign language now. In their broken Arabic, the Israeli soldiers were using the kind of words that our parents would never allow us to utter. Yet at such a young age we somehow knew that we could not go home and tell our parents about this sexual harassment (as we did regarding the young Palestinian men). In the face of the Occupation's military might, our parents were helpless and defenceless, thus failing at the most basic responsibility of parenthood—protecting their offsprings.

At that early age we learned what the Occupation meant and how it invaded and dominated every aspect of our lives. We excelled in understanding power relations—when some of us later read Michel Foucault's analysis of power and knowledge we recognized patterns that we had experienced growing up: the signs were all over the place even if we could not spell them out in Hebrew. We learned early on about the scarcity of resources and the harsh reality of the Occupation. We understood why we had to be careful not to let the faucets run; why water was so precious; why the neighbours' son was killed; or why their home was demolished. If we missed seeing our cousins we knew that nothing could be done; the chances of seeing relatives who lived in Amman, Cairo, Beirut, Kuwait, or Saudi Arabia were almost non-existent. The roads were closed. The bridge between the West Bank and Jordan, now controlled by the Israelis, became an international border crossing that was impossible to cross. My siblings and I lost our family's annual summer trip, the time when my parents would load the six of us into the car and take us for a week to Lebanon.[6]

## Occupation and Consciousness

We were not only aware of the harsh reality of the Occupation. It was during the sixties that we first learned of the existence of the *fedayeen* (or those who sacrifice themselves), of the Palestinian resistance movement.[7] My first experience was the arrival of my cousin Saji with a college friend at our home in Nablus. I clearly remember my mother hugging her nephew; Saji apologizing for imposing on us; and my mother waving him away and saying that she would call her sister, my aunt, to tell her that her son was safe and sound and that he would be arriving home in Ramallah-Bireh soon at his parents' home. I clearly remember Saji asking my mother not to say anything to his parents because he "was going to surprise" them. Now that I think of it, I doubt that my mother actually bought Saji's story. I am almost a hundred per cent sure that she knew he was a *fedayee* but she did not want to acknowledge it or force Saji to admit it, especially in front of little kids (the oldest was twelve) who did not know how to keep a secret and such an exciting one at that. After taking a shower and changing his clothes, Saji and his friend left for Ramallah. A few months later we learned from my aunt that Saji and his comrade, Ahmad Dakhil, had been arrested by the Israeli military.

Arrests, detention, night raids, demolition of houses, torture, and imprisonment were (and remain) regular features of the Occupation. I particularly remember the prison conditions. I used to accompany my mother and my aunt, Um Khalil, when they went to various Israeli prisons to visit Saji. Before being sentenced to seven years in military court he was tortured for several months (during which no one, including his Israeli lawyer, Felicia Langer,[8] or the International Red Cross, could see him). Midway through those seven years the Israeli authorities offered to release Saji on the condition that he would agree to being expelled from, and would never return to, the West Bank. Saji refused the Israeli offer, selecting instead to complete his sentence so that he could be released among his family and community. Then, upon the completion of his sentence, he was expelled to Jordan. "Too late" was the response of the Israeli prison authorities to Langer after she rushed to the prison where he was held (a day before he was due to be released) to show the warden the official document agreeing to release Saji to the West Bank.

Saji's story (while not exceptional) also represents the complexity and the ever-shifting Palestinian political landscape: He was arrested as a member of the Popular Front for the Liberation of Palestine (PFLP), but he exited prison seven years later as a member of the Political Bureau of the Democratic Front for the Liberation of Palestine (DFLP),[9] a group that split off from the PFLP in 1969 over ideological differences and became the third most influential group in the PLO after Fatah and the PFLP.[10] That Saji was able to understand the complete basis of the PFLP-DFLP split and thus choose sides while serving a sentence in Israeli jails attests to the extent of organizing that goes on inside Israeli prisons.

# Palestinian Women, Anti-Occupation Resistance

Around the time of Saji's arrest, word spread throughout Nablus that several women of college age had been arrested by the Israeli military: Maryam Shakshir, Amal Hanbali, and the Nabulsi sisters from Nablus, along with Rasmiyeh Odeh and Aisha Odeh from the Ramallah-Bireh area. They followed in the footsteps of Fatima Bernawi, the first Palestinian woman to be arrested after the start of the 1967 Israeli Occupation. The Palestinian women were likened to the Algerian *Jamilat*, whose participation in the Algerian war of liberation (1954–62) and refusal to confess despite extreme torture turned them into legends throughout the Arab world.[11] Following the same trajectory of the Algerian *Jamilat*, several years later, Palestinian women were arrested, tortured, and sentenced to long terms in prison.[12]

The similarities of French and Israeli colonial rule and the connection between the two resistance movements in Algeria and Palestine are extensive. For the Palestinians, Algeria was always present in their everyday reality. The Algerian struggle was a model to be followed for the Palestinians as they frequently invoked the Algerian victory to combat defeatism and a sense of pessimism: "If the Algerians could kick out the French colonists after 130 years, we too could end the Occupation after a few years." As schoolchildren we used to begin our morning routine by chanting the Algerian national anthem before starting classes. I don't recall anyone seeing this as a contradiction with the Palestinian aspirations to liberate themselves and return to the homes from which they were expelled in 1948. My elementary school, from the second to the fifth grade (when the Occupation started), was named after Jamila Bouhayred, one of the Algerian *Jamilat*.

In their guerrilla warfare, Algerian women militants pursued "passing"[13] as a strategy to escape the watchful eyes of their colonizers, as in Gillo Pontecorvo's film *The Battle of Algiers* (1966), which dramatized the Algerian war of liberation. Like their Algerian counterparts, Palestinian women militants also passed through Israeli checkpoints. This strategy could not have worked without the colonial powers' Orientalist[14] mindset that saw Palestinian women as oppressed and hapless victims of an oppressive Arab social and cultural structure dominated by misogynist males.

Contrary to the claims of colonial feminists,[15] Palestinian women were not duped by Palestinian male militants, nor were they sexually seduced by the prowess of the terrorist. In fact, they were not satisfied with playing limited roles politically, socially, or organizationally. Instead they sought to be treated equally, and they saw being included in commando missions as evidence of their equality.

Women's consciousness, then, did not, as Evans concludes, emerge as a result of negative experiences within the movement. In a series of interviews I conducted with male and female former prisoners, I found a starkly different explanation.[16] As one of the women who was a militant in 1960 said:

> We [Palestinian women members] demanded to be trained and sent on mission just like the men. We did not believe that we were less capable or less courageous. We wanted to contribute to the cause of our people in the same manner that we demanded women's liberation and treatment on equal footing with the male comrades.

The active role played by Palestinian women reflects the principles on which the Palestinian anticolonial movement was founded. The movement saw itself as part of a worldwide anti-colonization movement based in the Third World and strategically allied with oppressed people in First World countries. Not unlike other Third World anticolonial movements and organizations such as the Revolutionary Left Movement (MIR) in Chile, Tupamaros in Uruguay, and Black Panthers in the United States, Palestinian radicals drew eclectically from Marxism, Leninism, Maoism, and Trotskyism as well as anticolonial theories and indigenous practices. They read Marx, Lenin, Mao Tse-tung, Ho Chi-Minh, Che Guevara, Frantz Fanon, and they had access to literature in Arabic that is not necessarily familiar in North America—a function of the political economy of translation in a neoliberal globalized world.

The solidarities between the Palestinian and other anticolonial and antiimperialist movements around the world were evident on several levels: Palestinian guerrilla groups were training Nicaraguan fighters and militants from Iranian groups who opposed the Shah's regime. During the Black September events in 1968, aid to the "Palestinian Nation" was arriving in Amman, Jordan, where Palestinian guerrilla camps were set up, and from Vietnam, Algeria, and China.[17]

# Leila Khaled

At the centre of my memories of the 1960s emerges Leila Khaled, the most famous Palestinian woman commando and the role model for most of the young girls growing up under occupation. We did not dream of growing up to get married and play house. Instead we all wanted to be like Leila Khaled! Dreaming of becoming a militant instead of a homemaker obviously has a lot to do with the socialization of children by their environment. While it should not be surprising for a people under siege to valorize militancy or to support violence as weapons of the weak,[18] this impulse on the part of young girls undoubtedly calls for explanation, particularly given conventional assumptions about Arabs/Muslims/Palestinians

*Whose 1960s?*
*Gender, Resistance,*
*and Liberation*
*in Palestine*

and generally colonized people who fight for their liberation and self-determination, and especially given that in the United States popular culture and official statements alike have no qualms in suggesting that our people are generally bloodthirsty, Jew-hating, inclined to violence, misogynist, and irrational; those amongst us who "make it" in polite society are considered exceptions to the rule.

Leila Khaled did not escape the rule of exceptionality. Her story is constructed as an exception to the majority of Palestinian women, as the story of someone who, as a newspaper article put it, escaped "the patriarchal restrictions of Arab society where women are traditionally subservient to their husbands."[19] The accounts stress Khaled's looks—how beautiful, how glamorous, how shiny her hair; how she had wrapped the *kafiyyeh* around her neck; how perfect her features were before she had plastic surgery to disguise her appearance. Each time interviewers sat with her, the same discussion about her looks came up.

Her "autobiography," edited by and based on an interview with George Hajjar, a Canadian Arab journalist, refers to Khaled as childlike.[20] This is a deliberate discursive move on the part of sympathetic writers to endear what readers might otherwise see as a horrible hijacker. But implying that she looked as innocent as a child sends another message: that she really didn't know what she was doing, or that she was duped by their male leaders. In *Shoot the Women First* (1991), Eileen MacDonald writes that Khaled was trained by "her masters" and sent to hijack planes and commit violence.

Khaled's "autobiography" is an interesting case study in the ways in which a segment of Palestinian resistance fighters in the 1960s was represented and how the members of this group saw themselves and their place in society and history. Khaled, for example, did not want to present her life story, but she finally acquiesced because Hajjar would not stop pressing her until she sat down and agreed to the interview.

The book is introduced by none other than John Bagot Glubb, the former British Colonial Officer in Jordan. Was Khaled complicit in this decision? In other words, did this anti-imperialist fighter believe that her words could only be legitimated if a colonial figure issued his "authoritative" stamp? While it is highly doubtful that Khaled agreed, it is very likely that Hajjar sought the endorsement. This assumption is not farfetched given that accounts of Palestinians and other colonized people are not accepted as valid until and unless the colonial voices of their oppressors deem them to be "true," such as in the case of the Nakbah narrative and the New Israeli historians. Interviews with Khaled make it clear that until the book was published she had seen neither her "auto"-biography nor its translation since the time she gave the interview in the late 1960s. This is particularly interesting in this age of neo-liberal globalization and the U.S. insistence on intellectual property rights, as compared to the times of resistance (as many people who read about or were involved in the sixties may recall) when intellectual property rights were definitely not an issue to insist upon but a collective property of the people.

It is also clear that Khaled didn't want to talk about herself. She would invariably respond to interviewers' questions by saying: "Who am I? I'm just a person, why are you so interested in me? I'm not so important." In an interview with Eileen MacDonald she raised the issue:

> I was only an ordinary member of the PFLP. He [Superintendent David Frew] insisted, "No you are not. Three days after your capture, the PFLP hijacked a British plane. They flew it to Dawson's field, and they are now demanding your release for the passengers. Now do you understand you are very important?"[21]

According to MacDonald, "Leila had been overwhelmed at the news; as she commented with a faraway look in her eyes, 'A plane has been hijacked just for me.'" This response affirms that she did not view herself as an important person.

Here again, the construction of Khaled is full of contradictions. She is someone who follows her masters; she did not know what she was doing; or she was someone who was able to escape her restrictive patriarchal society. Was she duped or independent? The accounts do not provide a clue. How do we, then, read Khaled's story, in particular her statements that she was not sufficiently important to warrant having a plane hijacked to liberate her? Classical women's studies and pedagogy would offer the simplistic notion that Khaled was engaged in self-degradation. This would perfectly match the notion that women lack self-confidence and are desperately in need of higher self-esteem and that even the most militant, outgoing commanders suffer from such female malaise. As we know from women's studies, encouraging students to be motivated and speak up is a basic staple of our calling.

Voice, then, becomes a most important element of, and possibly a first step towards, liberation, while silence is seen as a sign of submission and subservience. But could there be another explanation? Is it possible to entertain the idea that what Khaled was doing was a way of deflecting individualism and self-centredness, and of refraining from self-promotion or placing herself on a higher plane than other folks—a conduct much praised in Palestinian cultural practices? Is it possible that this member of the Central Committee of one of the major Palestinian factions was just saying, *I am like everyone else, I just happen to be right now at the right place. This is the assignment that I volunteered for. I carried it out and that's all there is to it*? Isn't it possible that Khaled sought to display humility, not self-denigration?

If we take the context into consideration, the answers to this question become readily available. In a context that highly values individualism, Khaled may sound as if she is putting herself down. But if we look at Khaled in her own environment, in which people rarely use the "I" word, or cause listeners to cringe when they do, signifying that it is an inappropriate or unbecoming behaviour, we can begin to see her words in a totally different light. Imposing an analysis of one context onto a different one without accounting for the differences between them is not only highly problematic; it has serious implications for the study of revolutionary movements and for resistance studies.

# Everyday Women's Resistance

The role of women in the Palestinian struggle was not limited to commando operations or a few well-known daring incidents involving people such as Leila Khaled. I remember my mother and her activist friends passing around underground petitions. While nothing about these petitions should have been considered "illegal," given that they were simply signed by hundreds of Palestinians and directed at the United Nations, they were seen as underground activities because they were banned by the Israeli military. I remember my mother's friends coming around our home and my mother saying, "Shh, keep your voices down. The kids are sleeping." They would speak softly while passing the petitions around. "So and so has to go there," and "So and so needs to do this." We learned at an early age of the need to be discreet, and of the necessity not to say things out loud or reveal this information in public. As children living under occupation, we were constantly scared and had always to be careful. I also remember my mother and her friends organizing sit-ins at neighbourhood homes that were to be demolished by the Israelis. Sometimes I was allowed to accompany my mother and her friends to a sit-in. I remember them carrying out hunger strikes either at the neighbourhood mosque or a church but mostly at the offices of the International Committee of the Red Cross. The hunger strikes were in solidarity with prisoners on hunger strikes against the takeover of land by Jewish settlers; or to protest other Israeli violations of Palestinian rights.

In this context, then, the politics of location and situated knowledge are essential to understanding women's (and men's) activism and the diversity in experiences and lives. Notions of universality, while wonderful in their idealism, do not always reflect grounded reality. The feminist mantra of Virginia Woolf that "My country is the whole world" is an appropriate statement for women living at the heart of empire, women whose countries colonize the rest of the world. That there should be no boundaries constructed to exclude those whom we deem unlike us is correct, and so too is the implicit notion in Woolf's statement that we need to struggle against the xenophobia and chauvinism that permeate our lives. But colonized people and communities under siege do need boundaries, not to exclude others, but to protect themselves in semi-safe spaces where the hands of the colonizers do not reach. It is in spaces of this sort that the oppressed draw strength and to which they seek refuge when they flee. Those who have no country, such as the Palestinians, do not have the luxury to join Woolf's "whole world."

## Many Sources, Many Paths

My intent here has been to provide a glimpse of the 1960s by placing the Palestinian anticolonial struggle against Israeli colonization at the centre of the analysis. As such, I have delineated some of the major developments in our region (which continues to be otherizingly named the "Middle East"), including the Algerian war of liberation, which inspired the Palestinian people by offering both a live example of victory and strategies for militancy. I have drawn on the experiences of Palestinian women militants to argue that the 1960s narrative(s) must be contextualized and historicized as a corrective against applying the U.S. white heterosexual male and feminist narratives to all other areas and peoples.

My discussion of Palestinian women's experiences suggests a different reading than that offered by Evans with regards to the U.S. women's movement. Consciousness is not necessarily sequentially ordered, as Evans suggests. While such an explanation should not be excluded, a more plausible one, based on my research and experience, insists that a consciousness of gender inequality (or any other structural inequality or injustice) can supersede, accompany, or result from an awareness of other systemic oppressions. In other words, given that there are many sources of oppression, there are also many paths to consciousness and liberation.

Women who participate in anticolonial movements are not duped, as colonial feminists claim. From the Algerian *Jamilat* to Leila Khaled, and from the Palestinian women militants to ordinary mothers, teachers, and activists under occupation, the decision to participate in resisting colonialism is rational, conscious, and pro-active. And, indeed, it should be so, for how else can justice prevail?

# 2  Ian McKay

# SARNIA IN THE SIXTIES (OR THE PECULIARITIES OF THE CANADIANS)

**I was fifteen** in 1968, and from my vantage point in Sarnia, Ontario, the heart of Canada's "Chemical Valley"—just across the highly polluted St. Clair River from Port Huron, Michigan—the political universe unfolded admirably over the next three years. The French revolutionaries of 1968, the Black Panthers, and the Viet Cong were heroes, and *Ramparts*, *Win Magazine*, and *The Guardian* (of New York) our American sources of information and inspiration. My gang, oscillating between six and ten in number, sometimes ran the high school's newspaper and maintained an "Alternate Library" well stocked with Trotskyist, Maoist, and Buddhist literature. We occasionally peppered the city with pamphlets and position papers, and talked each other's ears off. We had been exiled by the school administration from a comfortable classroom to an unheated cleaning closet. We loved it. Within its spartan walls decorated with Che posters, we evolved our own miniature autonomous zone, a place from which we could critique the factory-like institution purporting to educate us and the zombies who bought into its authoritarian, inhuman regimentation. *The Student as Nigger* circulated through our little circle like a revelation.

In one dark corner the perpetually collapsing Gestetner machine—surely one of the unsung heroes of the global sixties—spat out pages that were, depending on its mood, either indecipherably faint or festooned with puddles of black ink. In another corner we might be plotting out the next step in our circuitous war of position with the school administration, whose overthrow and replacement were on at least some of our agendas. My own model, which I still maintain had some merits, ingeniously combined revolutionary anarcho-syndicalism with liberal responsible government. In essence, a student council governed by the principles of direct democracy would oversee the work of all administrators and teachers. This soviet scheme was taken so seriously at the time that the local Board of Education, under the impression that they were dealing with a mass movement and not a bunch of kids in a closet with a Gestetner machine, set aside whole evenings to discuss it.

"Why does Dow Chemical make napalm?" asked a publication put out by the head office of one of Sarnia's more controversial petro-chemical companies. Somehow the official answer, "To defeat the world communist conspiracy," seemed obscene when placed beside images of burning Vietnamese children. Some of the fathers of our group members worked for Dow Chemical. Some of the Valley's middle managers sat in my United Church, the very epitome of piety and propriety. The flares of their refineries glowed in the night sky, and the air often reeked of chemicals. Our local member of Parliament said it was the smell of good wages and comfortable homes. The local social democrats in the New Democratic Party, an unusually left-wing cadre in an otherwise mild-mannered party, were condemned as crackpots and "men of violent minds" in the local press, in part because they said—rightly, we would learn years later—that the chemical companies were poisoning the river with mercury.

The city seemed toxic to me. But before it became a place to leave, it was one to resist—blocking the Blue Water Bridge in 1970 to protest the Amchitka nuclear tests (one of the first big moments in transnational environmental activism), publicizing the first stirrings of women's liberation ("The Barbie Doll Fights Back!" was one article we reprinted in our paper), and, having learned from our Vietnamese comrades to connect with the people, placing our pamphlets on revolutionary struggle in the vestibules of the local United, Baptist, and Presbyterian churches. If it had worked with the Viet Cong among the Buddhists of the Mekong River Valley, why wouldn't it work in Sarnia, Ontario?

**It is interesting** to historicize one's own wisps of memory—to shift them from the soft-focus, sepia-toned stasis of a remembered time and place into the colder, clearer realm of analysis. If our little gang was at all typical of militants in the 1960s—and it does not seem to have been all that far removed from what I've read about, say, the high-school students who were ransacking construction sites in Montreal to get the material for their own liberation struggles—we were, well, *very young*. We did not feel privileged but alienated. We had only an approximate idea of a movement in the area. (That the famous Port Huron Statement of the Students for a Democratic Society had emerged but a few miles away was unknown to us.) We had the sense of a world afire with revolution, and a profound sense that whatever we could do would somehow matter. We had only inklings of the realms of theory and practice that might speak to this moment.

And we also had almost no sense of deep attachment to, or even an intimate knowledge of, Sarnia. We had Che's Bolivia diary in our Alternate Library. But we lacked any literature about the struggles of indigenous people right on our doorstep. If nowadays the Sarnia Reserve is famous for its skewed birth patterns, apparently pollution-induced, and Ipperwash, Ontario, for the 1995 martyrdom of Aboriginal activist Dudley George, back then one could be a teenaged leftist and never really think about First Nations issues at all. Sarnia was the site of the great Holmes Foundry struggle of 1937, one of the most violent and heroic struggles to create industrial unionism in all of Canada. But fifty years later, we youthful radicals knew nothing about it.

By extension you could apply this same critique, of placelessness and disconnection, to many of the young leftists of 1967–70. Being a radical meant shaking loose the clinging dross of merely local realities, and identifying with the more exalted struggles of a world revolutionary movement. It meant going global, not local. If you wanted to be highly critical and dismissive of us, you could say we were lip-synching to songs we ourselves had not written, emerging from places we had not been, and with meanings we had not grasped. You could say, and it would be the ultimate insult, that there was something very provincial about this yearning to be cosmopolitan, to be one small Sarnia part of the "global sixties."

# It is a critique that leads swiftly to dismissal. I want to make exactly the
opposite move. That is, when I mobilize these wisps of memory, and compare them with similar stirrings in the far more illustrious Canadian circles of the Student Union for Peace Action (SUPA) and the Young Socialists, Parti Pris and *Canadian Dimension* magazine, or the vibrant struggles at the University of New Brunswick and Sir George Williams and Simon Fraser universities, I notice *both* how derivative these inaugural moments of sixties leftism in Canada often were— how much they imported and repeated tropes from the United States and (to a lesser extent) the European new left—*and* how original and unexpectedly durable were many of their ultimate outcomes.

It is one of the "peculiarities of the Canadians"—with apologies to the shades of E.P. Thompson[1]—that since the 1890s every major left in the country has begun with transpositions of the strategies and tactics of the lefts of our various great white motherlands—Britain, the United States, and (a more pronounced trend in the 1960s) France. It is another that, after about a decade, such local derivations acquire distinctive properties. They get under the skin of the ruling order, and in doing so they change it. There is something interestingly cumulative about left politics in Canada.

One could make that point about the country's five major twentieth-century formations of leftism. The first (1890s–1920s) shared with leftisms around the world a passion for social evolutionary theory, imported holus-bolus models of labour and socialist parties from Britain and the United States, and involvement in such actual organizations as the Industrial Workers of the World and United Mine Workers of America—yet, largely because of the country's particular spatial patterns, instead of generating a socialist bureaucracy (along the lines of the German Social Democrats or the U.S. Socialists), created instead Winnipeg 1919, a system-challenging local revolt unparalleled in North America. The transnational revolutionary energies of the second left formation (1920s–1940s) were invested in revolutionary unions and parties, most notably the Communists, and led to many of the same patterns reported worldwide—yet with the significant wrinkle of substantial local legacies, in Cape Breton, Nova Scotia, and Thunder Bay, Ontario, Blairmore, Alberta, and Vancouver, B.C.—movements whose creative originality often worried the more globally-oriented, Comintern-oriented party leadership in Toronto. Among the state-building leftists who generally prevailed after the late 1930s to the mid-1960s (the third formation), once again initially following recipes cribbed from the British, Americans, and Scandinavians, we must nonetheless note the originality and continent-wide significance of the struggle of the Saskatchewan-born Co-operative Commonwealth Federation (CCF) to build socialism in one province from 1944 to 1964. In the 1960s case, in the fourth formation, when Canadians picked up the theses of decolonization and liberation, and used them to frame their movements opposing the U.S. Empire's violence in Vietnam and Latin America, they were following a global pattern—but one that would ultimately have the lastingly transformative consequence of Quebec and First Nations movements that have changed the dynamics of post-1970s Canadian politics (and ultimately led to some of the earliest articulations of radical multiculturalism). And if feminists and gay and lesbian liberations (in the fifth formation) drew primarily upon U.S., British, and French theorists and activists for inspiration, and repeated many of their ideas, the upshot of their activism was a transformed social and cultural local landscape. Each of these eras of great "leftisms" began as foreign imports. Then, as activists and intellectuals engaged with the particularities of Canada, they evinced more and more the left peculiarities of the Canadians.

Rather than dwelling exclusively on borrowing, then, we need also to study transposition. We need to notice the dual logic of ideological transposition: not just the *shifting* into Canada of global left patterns, but also their gradual *transformation* in form and content as they passed into different Canadian contexts. We need to remember both the mechanical and the musical senses of "transpose"—to remember both the ways in which Canadian leftists merely applied to their circumstances ideas and practices from elsewhere, but then often subtly changed how those learnings were activated in this peculiar domain.[2] In the powerful leftisms of Canadian history, mechanical translations and unreflecting applications have often been followed by creative transpositions and unexpected variations—certainly in the formations that have made a lasting difference in a particular context.

Essentialist and nationalist explanations of such patterns, which try to "read them back" into distant Tory origins or into inherent proclivities to statism, have proved unconvincing and ahistorical.[3] More dynamic, if challenging, explanations lie in the country's post-1840s underlying political logic—an expansive and dynamic *projection* of liberal principles of equality, liberty, and property, as exemplified by the free-standing individual.

Much of modern Canadian history can be summed up as the struggle to implant liberalism in a terrain previously organized in terms of very different social formations based on kinship or tribute. After the emergence of the mid-nineteenth-century liberal state, such a project required inventive permutations of Antonio Gramsci's triune formula of hegemony—corruption, coercion, and consent. Consequently it is no surprise to discover that, as soon as a powerful left formation begins to function within the territory claimed by the Canadian state, it is relentlessly "liberalized." Radical egalitarian visions are domesticated into piecemeal problems. Leaders are peeled away—silenced, absorbed, or even (a popular device in the 1930s) deported. Subaltern ideologies are reconstructed so that social goals become individual demands. Not much surprising about that, a well-trained Gramscian might murmur—yet in fact it is because these general hegemonic patterns have peculiar Canadian articulations that we can speak of particular Canadian transpositions. Herein lies the secret of Canadian leftists' curious persistence and influence in so liberal a dominion.

For there are substantial constraints faced by the liberal project that is Canada. Canada is a massive but thinly populated country[4] whose regions were settled at dramatically different times by distinct populations. They are now but loosely integrated into one of the world's most politically decentralized federations. Since the 1920s Marxists have debated the "Canada Questions"—colony or imperialist power? one, two, three, or a plenitude of nations?—without (to my eye) decisively resolving them. Since the 1960s the country's political elites have been caught up in a slow-burning constitutional crisis also informed by such fundamental questions of definition. (They often take the arcane and rather misleading form of debates over constitutional patriation, division of powers, immigration, land claims, and language rights.) At no time have *Canadians* declared themselves a sovereign political community, or even been given the privilege of voting in their own Constitution.

Canadian liberal order, then, is both hegemonic (in a conventional sense) and structurally vulnerable (in an unconventional sense). Generally lacking (outside the peculiar circumstances of world war) a unifying integral nationalism with which it can beat down counterhegemonic movements, or even a powerful shared sense of shared heroes, sacred constitutional documents, or unifying sites of memory—the contrast with the U.S. situation is patent—the Canadian order is perpetually on the lookout for groups and interests whose existence might either shore up its precarious legitimacy or place its future in question. Those factors that are often lamented in Canada—the weakness of official nationalism, the strength of vernacular and grassroots identities, the sheer tenacity of particular and provincial loyalties—have provided opportunities for a succession of left formations, which they have used to wrest far-reaching concessions from a liberal state apparatus.

# This is why, when we eventually do have a history of the new left in Canada, it will necessarily diverge to some extent from the master-patterns of the United States and Europe. One of the great motifs of the global new left was *decolonization*—a language of liberation whose preconditions can be found in the profound post-1945 collapse of empires, from Algeria to Cuba to Vietnam. (It was this world-historic event whose distant and muffled echoes were heard even in one high-school cleaning closet in Sarnia, Ontario.) The most promising key to the "sixties" as a global phenomenon is not generational—although undoubtedly leftism did often speak on behalf of "Our Generation"—but geohistorical. It was the time when older imperial patterns of space-time compression, as typified by formal empires, were challenged by new conceptions of a postcolonial realm of freedom and new struggles to achieve it.[5] From these struggles emerged a whole panoply of liberation struggles, which adopted and changed the language of politics in the springtime of liberation—or *liberations*, with Quebec liberation, women's liberation, and gay and lesbian liberation providing just three powerful examples.

Such languages of liberation, when imported into Canada, initially sounded much the same as they do elsewhere. Yet notice that, within a liberal order with a serious legitimation crisis on its hands, they play out very differently than

*Sarnia in the Sixties (or the Peculiarities of the Canadians)*

**29**

they reportedly did in other places. In the country as a whole they prompted the Canadian state to undertake such novel experiments in passive-revolutionary co-optation as the Company of Young Canadians and the Opportunities for Youth Program, through which more than a few radicals and revolutionaries were able to pay for their activism at the federal government's expense. New leftism and left nationalism converged in Quebec to create a profound and long-lasting crisis of the Canadian project itself. Revolutionary leftism in Montreal unfolded on what was still formally Canadian territory, but (for many participants) often in a post-Canadian, Québécois "imagined" realm of decolonized freedom. More than a few seasoned organic intellectuals of liberal order believed that the entire system had entered a revolutionary crisis in the early 1970s.

Part of the Canadian paradox is that once applied to Canada itself, with its adamantly unresolved Canadian Questions, the decolonization model entailed a profound crisis for the very Canadian state in which earlier Popular Front Communists and social-democratic state builders had invested so much of their political energies. Because of the peculiarities of the Canadians—that is, the uneven and combined development of a country that is simultaneously a colony of others and a colonizer in its own right—the challenges raised by the liberation paradigm with respect to Quebec and subsequently by the First Nations came themselves to be deeply internalized in the Canadian system. No one can understand the complexity of contemporary Canadian politics, at both the "highest" and the grassroots levels, without grasping something of the liberal order's paradoxical position, as both an age-old successful hegemonic project and a set of institutions trapped in a series of seemingly unresolvable existential crises.

In other words, the ideological weakness of the Canadian state, traceable back to its mid-nineteenth-century unwillingness or incapacity to obtain democratic legitimacy from a sovereign political community,[6] creates space within which subaltern projects of counterhegemonic democratic resistance can take shape. It is far harder to smash them, as has so often been the case in France, the United States, and Britain, with the sledgehammer of a compulsory integral nationalism. The contemporary resistance struggles of the First Nations with respect to land provide a case in point. If in one sense these are specific struggles that reach back into the murky past of the Canadian project—into its distant preconditions in Native dispossession under the aegis of the French and British Crowns—they are in another way future-oriented openings for global critiques of capitalist environmental devastation. They are intensely local—this specific uranium mine, this hydro project, this treaty, this band. They are profoundly global, fought out increasingly before a world public. In essence, they raise intense legitimacy questions for the Canadian states, above all the federal state, which seek to marginalize them and treat them as so many "piecemeal" problems. They raise questions that go to the very heart of capitalist accumulation and liberal subjectivity—to the liberal formula of liberty, equality, and property, and to the commanding figure of the possessive individual. To an extent that I doubt is paralleled in our various motherlands, the First Nations Question, profoundly energized by the 1960s, cannot be easily dislodged from the centre of Canadian politics.

So, once transposed into a Canadian context, the liberation struggles of the 1960s did not—as perhaps they did elsewhere—slowly evaporate with the end of the Vietnam War, the defeat of the Sandinistas, or the collapse of the rival superpower. Rather, they entered into the unfolding logic of the project of Canada itself, and in so doing they were themselves transformed by it. The liberal states, both federal and provincial, confronted and still confront serious wars of position, mounted by well-disciplined, historically conscious, and locally grounded movements of resistance.

Elsewhere, when people talk of the sixties, and perhaps especially in France and the United States, generation-specific declension narratives often prevail. Did "our generation" sell out? Where did the left go wrong? When did "the movement" collapse? Sometimes such questions have been plausibly put forward in Quebec and Canada, specifically with respect to specific parties and movements.[7] Yet there is a general sense in which they often miss the specificities of the Canadian situation. Here the better questions might be: "How well did that left understand and transform the liberal hegemony under which it operated? What elements of past leftisms are still alive and even flourishing in this curious archipelago of nations, regions, and peoples that we call Canada? How imaginatively and constructively did leftists develop links between struggles that by their very nature cannot be melted into one another, yet that at the same time call out, by the very similar questions they raise about liberal order, for bridge-building and solidarity? How well did the movements theorize struggles that necessarily must operate simultaneously on local, national, and world scales?"

# As for Sarnia in the springtime of liberation, it is of course true that the sixties failed to transform, in any visible or lasting way, the land that God gave to Dow Chemical. The high-school radicals dispersed, many seemingly in flight to points as far away from Sarnia as possible (Halifax in my case). The city's church-goers somehow remained unmoved by our youthful calls for revolutionary activism. When I would return to visit my parents, who in their wisdom retired to a condo right in the toxic heart of Chemical Valley, the friendly folks from the refineries would occasionally come around to urge us to shut the windows, lest our health be compromised by whatever it was they were discharging that day into the atmosphere. Some entrepreneurs even took to importing industrial wastes

from across North America for storage in nearby Lambton County, as though they were worried, despite the widely reported "Blob" of toxicity lurking somewhere down there in the St. Clair River and the less-reported holocaust of Holmes Foundry workers from occupational diseases, that my hometown might lose its reputation as Ontario's poster community for environmental devastation.

Yet some things have changed. What was considered an off-the-wall position of unhinged radicals—that the refineries and other plants should be held accountable for their polluting ways—has now become a fairly-well-entrenched part of a new common sense. Today not even a Liberal or Conservative politician would publicly sniff the polluted air and expatiate on the fine turnip-like smell of prosperity. Left achievements on other fronts have also been extraordinary, including two of the signature movements of the late 1960s and early 1970s—women's and gay liberation.

Even amid the refineries and foundries of provincial Sarnia, women's liberation was audible in the late 1960s. One of our high-school newspaper's early projects was to interview a local housewife, socialist, and feminist militant, Betty Krawczyk. She took the time to share her passionate convictions with an uninformed group of know-it-all radical teenagers. (She has gone on to become one of British Columbia's most renowned environmental activists and political prisoners.)[8] Sarnia's feminists were up against the small-town complacency that made it safe to ridicule the campaign for a women's shelter and to deride women running for office. As in so much of Canada, reading feminist literature of 1968–74 reminds us of how powerfully and integrally these activists felt themselves to be part of a North American movement. Many, like Krawczyk, were American-born; and ideas like consciousness-raising spread like wildfire from Chicago to Toronto to Montreal to New York City. A galaxy of eminent intellectuals, from Shulamith Firestone to Juliet Mitchell, inspired Canadian readers and audiences. Even our little high-school paper carried a then-shocking story about a Sarnia woman's struggle to obtain a backstreet abortion.

So much, so predictable, a transnational feminist would rightly murmur. Quite so. Yet, after a decade or so, I think the Canadian pattern of socialist feminism begins to diverge from that reported in many other countries, especially the United States. After an initial period of importing theory and theorists, Canadian feminists both transformed the theory and began to export their own more sophisticated versions of it, making Canada by the early 1980s one of the world centres of socialist-feminist theory and activism. Wherever we look—the decriminalization of abortion, the institution of employment equity, the rise of the state-funded National Action Committee on the Status of Women (NAC), the rise of a socialist-feminist trade union movement, and the emergence of feminist Marxism as a powerful current in the bourgeois academy—we see how, acting in often classically new left ways, that is, without a central committee and without one governing manifesto, this socialist-feminist formation was able to reshape both everyday life and much of the social order. If the peculiar vulnerability of the Canadian state made it extremely anxious to draw upon the feminist revolution in order to legitimize itself, a process that obviously entailed some "liberalization" of the movement, only the most uselessly abstract analysis could miss the huge transformative price that the political order was required, and ultimately ready, to pay for this privilege. Today it would take a vast counter-revolution to roll back abortion rights, affirmative action, and pay equity.

Gay and lesbian liberation is typically the Cinderella movement when we recall the sixties. It is often lumped in with the so-called "new social movements" and treated, by more conventional leftists, as the *ne plus ultra* of unity-shattering identity politics. It was when the feminists and queers showed up that "the movement" entered its sad decline, they complain. Gays and lesbians are among the low-life stoats and weasels who somehow gained occupancy of the Left Masters' Toad Hall. Whenever I read such commentaries, with their between the lines belittlements, I flash back to the various revolutionaries of the sixties and seventies, who so learnedly instructed me that homosexuality was merely a symptom of a degenerate bourgeois order, and gay and lesbian liberation a minor distraction from the real bread and butter issues confronting the working class. Why should "the left" take any position on such a distracting question?

Notwithstanding the erotic resonances of smokestacks and refinery towers, growing up gay in Sarnia presented its challenges. It is difficult now to reconstruct the consternation that the "gay issue" aroused in the mid-1960s. There were exposés on CBC radio, which generated soul-wrenching family conversations about homosexuality as something that was worse than murder. In my neighbourhood one local queer was carted off for compulsory shock therapy; another, a local doctor, disgraced himself in the local park. In 1969 the Liberals' half-assed Omnibus Bill represented a "liberalizing" strategy of trying to convert the demand for a freer sexuality into the eminently piecemeal position that the bedrooms of the nation might henceforth be considered postage-stamped-sized private realms of freedom. Christians in Sarnia circulated pamphlets depicting the faces of the degenerate damned, howling in horror as they were licked by the eternal flames of hell. One of my high-school teachers, well known for dalliances with his female students, interrupted his physics lesson for a red-faced denunciation of the bill, which was for him the beginning of the decline and fall of Western civilization.

Here, too, late sixties lip-sync eventually gave way to the peculiarities of the Canadians. Much of the rise and decline of gay and lesbian liberation in Canada would seem familiar to a U.S. or European historian: from the creative neo-Marxism of the early 1970s to the drab homo-con conformity of the neo-liberal present. At the same time, there is much that is not that familiar—trade-union caucuses and fairly general recognition of pension and other rights, state-recognized same-sex marriage, and, at least in *some* quarters, sharp resistance to the demands of some Liberal and most Conservative party members for a return to the good old days of family values. Unusually in North American terms, something different has happened here.

Why the difference? The 1982 Charter of Rights and Freedoms, good liberals would reverently proclaim. (They rather forget that gay and lesbian rights had to be "read in" to a Charter that initially excluded them.) I suspect a fuller historical treatment would say much more about the grassroots persistence of queer activists within broader left movements. In Quebec one of the less-told stories about the left is that of the prominent gay militants (Pierre Vallières, Pierre Bourgault, Claude Charron) who played key roles in the struggle for sovereignty. After the mid-1970s election of the Parti Québécois government, one of the more amusing aspects of the constitutional crisis was the competition between Ottawa and Quebec over which liberal jurisdiction was more queer-friendly than the other.

Without "Catholic" Quebec, where polls showed overwhelming support for same-sex marriage, the achievement of this fundamental human right would not likely have happened. And Quebec changed, not because the Supreme Court "read" gay rights into the Charter, but because left militants were in a position to push the issue. Rather like the Saskatchewan CCF's introduction of medicare, the Quebec left's stalwart support of gay and lesbian rights, itself a response to decades of Ultramontane repression, ramified throughout the decentralized archipelago of Canada. It has been difficult for Christian evangelicals in Canada to activate the powerful U.S. models for smashing this achievement—and not for want of trying. These days, in Sarnia, you can—it is one of those things that sometimes make me think I have checked into some implausible alternative universe—consult the "Pride Sarnia" web page, march in the annual pride parade, and marry your same-sex partner.

**The sixties** in Canada were thus both completely derivative and highly original. A hegemonic liberal order, using all the devices of passive revolution, doubtless digested and deflected many of the revolutionary energies of the left. Yet in doing so it was involuntarily forced to change some quite fundamental realities, such as the recognition of nations within Canada, of many personal and social demands of women, and even of the human rights of gays and lesbians. Moreover, lacking the pivotal instrument of integral nationalism, it could never completely absorb powerful and well-positioned movements of opposition.

There is a sense in which, in Canada, the sixties never quite ended, not even as neo-liberalism washed away many achievements in the 1980s and 1990s. The Canadian political order had to change in order to survive, and in its vulnerability on some core definitional questions it simply could not dispose of its subaltern critics. They persist to this day—as militants, political prisoners, intellectuals, and visionaries—some quietly and others noisily contesting the narrow limits that liberal order would draw around their present and anticipated realms of freedom.

*Sarnia in the Sixties
(or the Peculiarities
of the Canadians)*

# 3 Van Gosse

# MOVING INTO "THE MASTER'S HOUSE"

## The State-Nation and Black Power in the United States

**Why should** historians of the sixties turn their gaze upon the nation, let alone the state, when we have been told again and again that the essence of the sixties (or the new left, terms mixed promiscuously) was a communitarian, decentralized, localist, and personal politics that was *anti*-state, *anti*-national, even *anti*-family or *anti*-consumption? It is tempting to describe that particular ideological package, in Marx's words, as "all the old crap." The problem with such a narrowing down is its retrospective national chauvinism, as if events like the Cuban and Vietnamese revolutions were external influences, on the outside or margin of the "global sixties." That is simply wrong. Anyone familiar with trans-national radicalism in that era should know how central were those great state-making projects. Their emphasis on armed struggle, national-popular mobilization, and Third World solidarity marks the transition from "old" to "new" lefts, as figures such as C. Wright Mills, Jean-Paul Sartre, Malcolm X, and Martin Luther King Jr. recognized at the time, and we do well not to forget.

My opposition to any conception that puts Cuba, Vietnam, Angola, Mozambique, Zimbabwe, Guinea-Bissau, Chile, and South Africa outside the new left stems from my disagreement with the insistence that the new left represented a decisive break with the "old" left, a sundering of connections. The most imperative task for historians of the sixties is to ground their findings in the history of radical democratic struggles extending back to the English, French, American, and Haitian revolutions, and then forward through the long nineteenth and twentieth centuries. Only with this grounding can we achieve clarity about what was new, and what was renewed. What did it mean to call your group "the Diggers," or oneself a "communard?" Why was C.L.R. James's definition of Saint-Domingue's revolutionaries as "Black Jacobins" so powerful?

The organizers of the New World Coming conference asked us to consider whether the terms of internationalism and understandings of "the nation" had necessarily changed from those obtaining for the earlier labour-left, circa 1848–1948. Self-evidently, they had. While we think of 1945–89 as the period of the Cold War, it was equally (or even more) an era of anticolonial liberation. Rather than bookending Yalta in February 1945 and the Berlin Wall's breaching in November 1989 as the start and end of a struggle over control of the European "core," to use Thomas McCormick's formulation, we should seek other markers of change over time.[1] Equally apt beginnings become the October 1945 Sixth Pan-Africanist Conference in Manchester, England, organized by Kwame Nkrumah and George Padmore and presided over by W.E.B. Du Bois, or the moment that August when Ho Chi-Minh read the U.S. Declaration of Independence to several hundred thousand people in Hanoi. An endpoint would be June 21, 1990, when Nelson Mandela walked into Yankee Stadium, or even November 11, 1989, when El Salvador's Farabundo Martí National Liberation Front launched its final offensive, which forced the governing regime into U.N.-sponsored negotiations leading to free elections in 1994, the same year as South Africa's.

Certainly movements for self-determination, like A.C. Sandino's Army in Defense of National Sovereignty in Nicaragua, had put national liberation on the world's agenda long before 1945. The Third International's most decisive break, after all, was with the "social imperialism" practised by Second International parties, which lasted long after 1945 in places such as British Guiana and Algeria. But discourse alone tells us that something changed fundamentally after 1945. The very words "national liberation" evoke the 1950s and Dien Bien Phu, the Battle of Algiers, Mau Mau, Bandung, the Defiance Campaign, the Moncada, and so much more. As was clear at the time, to the discomfort of communists and socialists, the century-long leitmotif of proletarian solidarity had receded in favour of national self-determination in a Third World that no longer accepted European definitions of "the left."

Inevitably, this focus on reclaiming an imagined national community required that the subaltern think about not just "the nation" but, even more importantly, the state, in creative ways. This indicates Frantz Fanon's importance. In *The Wretched of the Earth* he proposed a process of state formation *first* via physical force, as a means of establishing the cultural and ideological basis of a nation *later*—a revolutionary nationalism that seems very Irish, in retrospect. The questions that ensue from such a process explain why Hannah Arendt's *On Revolution* was so prescient: would it be an existing state purified or deformed by violence—a completely new state in place of the old, at what cost? Or perhaps a polity within the state, a kind of "home rule," to quote Amiri Baraka, describing the apparatus of Black Power that he helped to build in Newark, New Jersey, after 1966? [2]

In this connection, Baraka becomes a representative figure, not as a celebrated *homme de lettres*, but in his less familiar functioning as a practical politician. My thesis for the rise of Black Power in the United States builds on Baraka's insight about Newark. It is that, regardless of where they stood on other questions, what linked almost all Black Power constituencies was a sustained commitment to boring within, replacing, or simply finding a workable modus vivendi with, existing state power. "The nation" mattered greatly to the Black Power movement, and the larger Black freedom struggle of which it was a phase, *not* as a metaphorical construct of "a nation within a nation" or a future hope, but in its immediate, practical capacities as the U.S. state-nation. Only the most marginal fractions, such as the Republic of New Afrika, actually proposed a territorial disengagement from that entity. The rest recognized that they had either to come to terms with it or displace it; in most cases, the strategy that evolved over time was to accommodate via a partial separation, as the allusion to "home rule" suggests.

To make this argument flies in the face of not just the old, vulgar assertions that Black Power equalled "separatism," but more sophisticated readings of the Black Power movement that remind one of Audre Lorde's famous dictum, "The Master's Tools Will Never Dismantle the Master's House." In this scenario, Black Power defined itself as a break with mainstream civil rights-ism through its refusal to use "the master's tools" of lobbying, legal non-violent demonstrations, voting, and insider access. But that narrative of Black Power is really all humbug, and a "new Black Power history" is rapidly rendering it anachronistic. [3] What was Malcolm X's Harlem-based Organization of Afro-American Unity but a tentative plan for local community control, using a concentrated voting bloc, and isn't that what he put on the table in "The Ballot or the Bullet"? [4] In this new direction, Malcolm was anticipating the argument made soon after his death by James and Grace Lee Boggs in the essay "The City Is the Black Man's Land," pointing to how white flight and Black voter mobilization created a historic opportunity to seize power in urban America. [5]

There is every reason to think that Malcolm and the Boggses came from a similar electoralist perspective, since, via Detroit's Group on Advanced Leadership

(GOAL), the Boggses had been central to Malcolm's move into political action, away from the Nation of Islam's political abstentionism. With the younger Black leadership in GOAL, the Boggses organized the historic Northern Negro Grass Roots Leadership conference in Detroit in November 1963, where Malcolm gave his "Message to the Grassroots." [6] Subsequently, working with figures such as William Worthy and Harold Cruse, the Boggses had attempted to organize the all-Black Freedom Now Party (FNP), as a national electoral vehicle. The FNP did not sustain itself, but it ran candidates statewide in Michigan in 1964, which was a trial run for the takeover of local Democratic Party structures by Black activists in dozens of cities over the next two decades. In 1965 the Boggses tried to convene an Organization for Black Power, another grouping of activists like those who attended the Northern Negro Grass Roots Leadership conference, and joined the Freedom Now Party, although we know very little about it because of its connections to the clandestine Revolutionary Action Movement.

Clearly, then, a considerable history predated Stokely Carmichael's and Willie Ricks's famous invocation of "Black Power" during the march through Mississippi in June 1966 to denounce the shooting of James Meredith. Carmichael's *Black Power: The Politics of Liberation in America* followed soon after, proposing to deploy a bloc vote to negotiate for inclusion and autonomy. But before outlining how the Black Power movement's main political direction in 1967–75 was the taking of power within the state-nation, via "home rule," I must move backwards, to show what the term Black Power signified long before 1963 or 1966.

When did this powerful trope enter the Atlantic world's political discourse? It originally appeared before the Civil War, with multiple meanings for antislavery politicians and editorialists in the North. Usually Black Power was an invidious synonym for "Slave Power," meaning slaveholders' dominance of national politics, which was denounced as "the black power of slavery" and the threat that "the demon of the black power, backed by General [President Franklin] Pierce, has got the nation by the throat." [7] On occasion it also signified the Haitian Revolution, as in a comment by a *New York Evening Post* book reviewer: "Our government now refuses in any way to recognize the independent black power of Hayti." [8]

Better known are the ubiquitous references by Democrats to "Negro Rule" and "Negro Supremacy" from the late 1860s well into the twentieth century, whenever the horrors of the Reconstruction period were recalled. "Black Power" thus became ubiquitous as a negative image: the murderous, lascivious but cowardly Black men in blue swarming through D.W. Griffith's movie *The Birth of a Nation* (1915), men eventually ridden down by the flower of Southern chivalry clothed in white. In this context, Black men and their white Republican allies naturally avoided any positive linkage of "Black" and "power," since their avowed goal was to maintain an interracial electoral coalition.

The modern, affirmative use of Black Power began with Richard Wright's angst-ridden 1954 book with that name, interrogating the process of state- and nation-making in Britain's Gold Coast colony on the verge of becoming the Republic of Ghana.[9] That is what Black Power meant in the 1950s—forging a state apparatus, with its own flag, ministers, army, and borders. As Penny Von Eschen reminds us, the impact was felt in visceral ways. In 1957 Carl Rowan interviewed the disgraced star Paul Robeson for *Ebony*; the mere fact of the interview was an indication of McCarthyism's limited impact within Black America. Throughout the piece, Robeson's fierce personal animus towards white supremacists such as Mississippi's Senator James Eastland, who chaired the Subcommittee on Internal Security of the Judiciary Committee, was on display. After exploring Robeson's pro-Soviet politics and the dilemma they posed for his admirers, Rowan artfully repackaged him as "a black nationalist who seems to long in his heart to see the day when the power of the world's Black men will overwhelm the whites." In its own way, this was a recuperation: while "Black nationalist" was hardly a term of approval for *Ebony*'s aspiring middle-class readers, it was considerably more palatable than "communist." In a crucial passage, Robeson suggested that his blackness trumped (or at least explained) his Redness:

> I think a good deal in terms of the power of black people in the world.... That's why Africa means so much to me.... Yes, this black power moves me. Look at Jamaica. In a few years the white minority will be there on the sufferance of black men. If they're nice, decent fellows they can stay. Yes, I look at Senator Eastland and say, "So you think you're powerful here. If only I could get *you* across the border." Although I may stay here for the rest of my life, spiritually I'll always be part of that world where the black man can say to these crackers, "Get the hell out of here by morning." If I could get a passport, I'd just like to go to Ghana or Jamaica, just to sit there for a few days and observe this black power.[10]

The next major step in naming Black Power, and its first direct application to the United States, came five years later. In 1962 Lerone Bennett Jr., another *Ebony* writer, published the first edition of his hugely influential *Before the Mayflower: A History of the Negro in America*. Its chapter on Reconstruction was titled "Black Power in Dixie." Bennett's deliberate migration of terms indicates that, just as in the new Africa, he understood Black Power to mean a visible, formal empowerment, if now within the larger frame of the U.S. state-nation. Surely Stokely Carmichael had that history in mind in 1964–65, when he was organizing in Lowndes County, Alabama, with its overwhelming Black majority and a mere handful of Black voters, the kind of Deep South place where African Americans *had* exerted some power once upon a time. His Lowndes County Freedom

Organization (LCFO) was the prototype for the all-Black electoral machines that would overturn the white democracy throughout the Black Belt.

Looking back, therefore, from the moment of its notorious proclamation in June 1966, we can thus discern a certain continuity in what Black Power meant, when used to describe what people of African descent did, or had. For both its exponents and its enemies, whether in the Caribbean, in Africa itself, or in the U.S. South, it meant control of a state. Proceeding beyond 1966, we also find continuity, even across profound, sometimes bloody schisms in the Black Power movement. Historically too much emphasis has been placed on the fault lines in Black Power, or between Black Powerites and the traditional civil rights establishment clustered in the National Association for the Advancement of Colored People (NAACP), the Urban League, the Black churches, and the Democratic Party. If we look at the movement's institutional legacy, enduring long after the death-squad murders and self-destruction of the Black Panther Party and other revolutionary groups, we see at the local, state, and national levels a systematic attempt to take power via electoral means, and to use that power to reward and defend Black constituencies. This was serious "affirmative action"—not white paternalism, set-asides, and piecemeal appointments, but an extraordinary effort to make up for ninety years of exclusion from political offices and the state, and the denial of the rights, opportunities, and status that participation in the political order rightfully confer, without which one is visibly marked as a lesser being, a colonial subject.

Consider: in 1964, when Black people in the United States cast several million votes (an estimated 95 per cent of which went to the Democratic Party, a major new development), the entire country had about one hundred Black elected officials, an infinitesimal number given the hundreds of thousands of offices spread across the many tiers of politics. Thus, the central fact of Black political life was not de jure segregation in the South, but that at every level of governance, from Boston to Birmingham, Des Moines to Dallas, Black people were represented, governed, policed, and serviced, even in their own neighbourhoods, by white people. Yet, despite the ever-growing weight of the Northern Black vote, as recognized by both parties from the 1920s on, neither Republicans nor Democrats had conceded more than a handful of elective or appointive offices in any jurisdiction. The nucleus of Black congressmen, jumping from four to six in 1964, the slightly larger number of state legislators, and the few dozen city councillors, all a-swim in the vast tide of tens of thousands of white legislators, were joined by an equally minute number of Black police sergeants and lieutenants, municipal court judges, assessors, coroners, marshals, bailiffs, and the like. From the perspective of colonial polities, the glacial process of political integration resembles the putatively colour-blind French order in Africa, where Africans deemed sufficiently "evolved" could vote, and even be elected to the National Assembly in Paris.

By the late 1960s there were three options for resolving the problem of the Black presence in the United States: incorporating Maulana Karenga's Nguzo Saba principles into a rigidly ordered communal life; a multiracial armed revolution as promoted by the Black Panther Party; or the immediate and practical possibility of confronting the disjuncture between the Democrats' reliance on the Black vote and the party's refusal to concede the principle of Black representation. That was Carmichael's core insight, as he proposed transferring his grassroots electoralist strategy to the national stage. And, as matters developed, both Karenga's most important disciple, Amiri Baraka, and the self-proclaimed revolutionaries of the Black Panther Party turned quickly to electoralism as part of a larger tide sweeping through Black politics.

The three most dramatic expressions of this entrance into the state-nation are all well known but bear repeating as central instances of Black Power taken, not just claimed:

- In just seven years, 1967–74, the conquest of city halls in Cleveland, Newark, Detroit, Atlanta, and Los Angeles, with many more to come (finally Chicago in 1983 and New York in 1989).
- The founding of the Congressional Black Caucus in 1969–71, propelled by a rapid increase in Black House members, from six in 1964 to thirteen by 1970 and twenty by 1983, and coupled with a much more assertive stance towards white power structures, whether in the Democratic Party, the Nixon White House, or even the State Department, if one looks at Representative Charles Diggs Jr.'s successful interventions in Africa policy during the 1970s.
- The National Black Political Convention in Gary, Indiana, in 1972, organized by Baraka and Diggs, which proposed a comprehensive political-economic bargaining position for negotiating with the U.S. government, as affirmed by eight thousand delegates. What is much less known is that this display of unity built upon the Congress of African People's broad "united front" strategy, which since 1970 had brought together figures as disparate as Whitney Young of the Urban League, the reverends Ralph Abernathy and Jesse Jackson, Black office-holders such as mayors Kenneth Gibson of Newark and Richard Hatcher of Gary, and leading radical nationalist ideologues.[11]

Undergirding these breakthroughs was the true Second Reconstruction, the conquest of local power by hundreds and then thousands of mayors, sheriffs, county commissioners, and administrators in the Black Belt counties and Southern urban areas with Black voting majorities, then as now the main bloc in statewide biracial coalitions in which whites exercise disproportionate power, just as in the First Reconstruction.[12] This process of democratization is hardly completed, because no Southern state has ever elected a Black senator or governor, with the notable exception of Douglas Wilder winning the Virginia governorship in 1990.

As long as we continue to mark the "firsts," however, the exceptions and breakthroughs—as in Shirley Chisholm becoming the first Black major-party candidate for the presidency (in 1972), Jesse Jackson the first who actually contended for power, and Barack Obama as the first to win a nomination and then the presidency—the work of reconstruction is hardly done, 140 years after passage of the Fourteenth Amendment. It may be that George W. Bush, in a perversely brilliant fashion, brought the politics of formal representation to a close, with his promiscuous recruitment of people of colour and women into positions of power, but it is certainly too soon to cast such a verdict.

# Achieving the Nation

The Black Power movement was always clearer than was the white new left about the imperative of engaging with the state-nation, for two closely related reasons: first, the denial of citizenship to African Americans in the South and their relegation to a caste-like status unless they fled northward and, just as before the Civil War, claimed their "state citizenship"; second, a shared consciousness of how people of African descent were *everywhere* denied equal citizenship, in the vast arc of European colonization across the Atlantic world.

Inside the United States, Black Power in 1966–76 was a phase of, rather than a break from, the larger Black Freedom Movement since Reconstruction, which in its modern incarnation developed as what Jacqueline Dowd Hall calls "the long civil rights movement."[13] That larger movement had the political goal of overturning the state apparatuses that maintain white supremacy, from Maryland's Eastern Shore to the flatlands of West Texas, in defiance of the Fourteenth and Fifteenth amendments. It was intimately bound up with the country's long, incomplete process of state construction, as Student Nonviolent Coordinating Committee chairman John Lewis made explicit in the climax of his controversial speech (the published rather than spoken version) at the August 1963 March on Washington:

> We won't stop now. All of the forces of Eastland, Barnett, Wallace, and Thurmond won't stop this revolution. The time will come when we will not confine our marching to Washington. We will march through the South, through the Heart of Dixie, the way Sherman did. We shall pursue our own "scorched earth" policy and burn Jim Crow to the ground—nonviolently. We shall fragment the South into a thousand pieces and put them back together in the image of democracy. We will make the action of the past few months look petty.

*Moving into "the Master's House"*

It is remarkable that a son of Alabama sharecroppers, schooled by the Reverend James Lawson to a devout pacifism at Fisk University, would evoke not Gandhi, not even Frederick Douglass, but rather the most ruthless wielder of power in the Republic's history, William Tecumseh Sherman, who at the peak of his massively destructive creative agency cut a sixty-mile-wide swath through Georgia on his way to the Atlantic at Savannah. At that point, after meeting with the city's Black leadership, Sherman took the nation as far towards true justice for the slaves as it would ever go. Sherman's Field Order Number 15, issued on January 16, 1865, handed over a vast coastal belt, from Charleston to Jacksonville and thirty miles inland, to the slaves who had made it productive, seizing the plantations and expelling all the whites. For a moment, then, the prospect of a "Black Belt Republic" loomed, under the auspices of a military republicanism not unlike what the Jacobin *agents en mission* promulgated across France in the early 1790s. That this experiment lasted only months, until Lincoln's white supremacist successor, Andrew Johnson, forced the army to expel the Black peasantry and restore their former masters, does not vitiate its force. Lewis's speech suggests that this Sherman, the nightmare of slaveholders, was not at all forgotten, any more than Lincoln had been, as white Communists discovered when they went into the Alabama Black Belt in the 1930s.[14] Like Malcolm X, the slaves and their descendants always knew that a revolution was about land, power, control, and force: that indeed it meant marching through countryside and city streets, tearing down and building up without remorse or delay, whether violently or otherwise.

But a century after Sherman's march to the sea, and two generations after Jim Crow was institutionalized across the South, young Black people like Lewis could situate themselves in not one but two revolutionary experiences, both "national," both unfinished. They were keenly aware of the American Civil War as an epic of failure and promises unredeemed—after all, they grew up surrounded by the sentimental apparatus of the "Lost Cause," which mocked Emancipation every day. But they were also conscious of how from the 1880s on, in lockstep with Jim Crow, the darker peoples of Africa and Asia had been colonized. They understood that the politics of their struggle, revolving around a version of the national question, was analogous to (though hardly synonymous with) the politics of anticolonial liberation in other white settler colonies.[15] Just a few months earlier, in April 1963, Dr. Martin Luther King Jr. had made this connection bitterly explicit in his "Letter from Birmingham Jail":

> We have waited for more than 340 years for our constitutional and God-given rights. The nations of Asia and Africa are moving with jetlike speed toward the goal of political independence, and we still creep at horse and buggy pace toward the gaining of a cup of coffee at a lunch counter.

Nor were these connections purely discursive or ideological. By the early 1960s, well before the rise of Black Power, African-American organizations and individuals were practising anticolonial solidarity by visiting Africa and the Caribbean, living in the new nations, and aiding revolutionary nationalists in Ghana, Algeria, Tanzania, and other countries.[16] Just as Black Power drew on a much longer tradition, Pan-Africanist anti-imperialism in the Cold War era reached back into the early decades of the twentieth century, as exemplified by Bishop Henry M. Turner and W.E.B. Du Bois visiting Africa and the Caribbean, and Marcus Garvey and many other Caribbean intellectuals and activists, and somewhat later Kwame Nkrumah of Ghana, Nnamdi Azikiwe of Nigeria, and other Africans, coming to the United States to study and agitate.[17] Black politics in the United States had always been part of a larger Atlantic world that, prior to the Civil War, was essentially British, but later became a multilingual colonial sphere—Anglo-, Franco-, Hispano-, and Lusophone—in which the fate of nations waiting to be born was always the primary concern.

The Black Power movement's focus on "the nation" was thus overdetermined, not by the rhetorical commitments of "Black nationalist" ideology, so-called, but by the lived experiences of Black people moving through political orders in which they had no guaranteed standing, and often "no rights that the white man was bound to respect." The barriers to U.S. nationhood still in place despite the Union victory in 1865, and the consciousness of colonial subalternity in systems of "separate development" privileging whites from Mississippi to Rhodesia, made a whole of many parts. The nation was thus simultaneously the problem and the solution, with the solution still incomplete and arrived at circuitously via the "home rule" evoked by Amiri Baraka and the Boggses. That this reorganization of the U.S. state-nation is still so in question, its evolution contested by engineered elections and massive suppression of the African-American vote, its fate so challenged by the appearance of an Obama, underlines how dangerous and exciting it can be to attempt to move into "the master's house."

# 4  Dan Berger

# "THE MALCOLM X DOCTRINE"
## The Republic of New Afrika and National Liberation on U.S. Soil

> Self-Determination is a wonderful thing.
>
> — Albert Cleage Jr., *The Black Messiah*

**Sponsored by** the Malcolm X Society, the Black Government Conference brought about five hundred Black radicals to Detroit's Shrine of the Black Madonna church for a weekend-long meeting at the end of March 1968. Some two years after "Black Power" had received national attention as a militant rallying cry against white supremacy, the Detroit gathering ended with a hundred of the attendees signing a declaration of independence from the United States.

Building off deep histories of Detroit radicalism and Black nationalism, the Black Government Conference was more than a next step in the burgeoning Black Power movement.[1] It brought together Black Power militants with frustrated youth, insurgent workers, fiery Marxists, and old Garveyites. While only one of many such events aiming to further such Black radicalism, it differed from the Black Power conferences held in Berkeley (1966), Newark (1967), and Philadelphia (1968).[2] Although those gatherings often drew bigger crowds, the Black Government Conference was arguably the most programmatic. Amidst the most volatile year of 1960s-era rebellion, the conference proffered a declaration of independence for all people of African descent in the United States. Out of its call emerged both an entity and an ideology.

46

The political thought and structure of the conference crystallized in the Republic of New Afrika (RNA). From the beginning the RNA put forth an ambitious program calling for self-determination. At a time when numerous leftist organizations were declaring Black people to be colonized by U.S. imperialism and white supremacy, the Republic of New Afrika declared independence from the colonial power and established mechanisms for self-rule. Borrowing from (and inspired by) the many successful revolutionary national liberation struggles then dotting the globe, the RNA attempted to forge a new nation in North America. It aimed to make concrete a homeland for those who, like heavyweight champion Muhammad Ali, proclaimed that being Black was antithetical to being American.[3] Unlike the Nation of Islam, however, the RNA platform was decidedly political, unequivocally revolutionary, and irrepressibly internationalist. In that, the RNA built on the platform pioneered by Malcolm X in the last year of his life, a strategy based on revolutionary nationalism and international law.

The RNA's history traces the contours of nationalist thought among Black radicals, providing a valuable (and understudied) case study of revolutionary nationalist organizing stretching from the late 1960s to today. Discussions of the RNA to date have been minimal and fragmentary. But without a broader focus on the RNA's attempts to establish an independent nation in the U.S. South as part of a Pan-African revolutionary movement, one could limit discussion to the group's early Detroit presence or dismiss the phenomenon by saying that "a group of RNA activists moved to Mississippi, declared the new nation, and defended their turf against local police, [but] they ultimately had little success."[4] Such a description elides the distinct contributions that the RNA made to sustaining Black Power and Pan-Africanist politics. It also overlooks the RNA's defining characteristic: in the context of pervasive Black nationalism, the Republic of New Afrika was the most explicit attempt to articulate and organize a visible and viable national liberation struggle among Black people in the United States, an attempt that refocused Black radical attention on the South and made the struggle for reparations a foundational point of concern.

# Building a Nation

The RNA was hardly the only current in the Black freedom struggle declaring itself a movement for national liberation.[5] Radicals at the 1967 Black Power conference had debated whether they should seize five, seven, or thirteen states for an independent Black Nation. At the following year's conference, many argued that an underground Black army would take over towns throughout the United States as part of liberating territory.[6] Thousands at the 1972 National Black Political Convention in Gary, Indiana—a multi-tendency conference aiming to unite the Black liberation movement in a shared program—embraced "Nation Time!" as their cry.[7] Emerging from both entrenched and burgeoning traditions of revolutionary nationalism, the RNA was an attempt to operationalize Black Power as a project of independence. Amidst such widespread nationalist fervour, RNA finance minister Raymond Willis told the *Los Angeles Times* that the Republic offered "an alternative to chaos" in a country that "is in a state of revolution."[8] Black Power was an elastic concept, allowing for everything from Black capitalism and electoral politics to Pan-Africanist revolutionary socialism. The RNA provided an alternative strategy, neither emigrationist nor assimilationist, to the widespread Black critique of U.S. nationalism, state structures, and political economy.

The Republic moved quickly and boldly in setting up the apparatus of an independent nation: the founding conference defined the five states of the Black Belt South (Alabama, Georgia, Louisiana, Mississippi, and South Carolina) as national territory. Upon its founding, the RNA "established consulates in New York, Philadelphia, Chicago, Pittsburgh, San Francisco, Los Angeles, Baltimore, Cleveland, and Washington, D.C." and began meeting with foreign governments, including the Soviet Union, Tanzania, Sudan, and China.[9]

It also elected officials to lead the Republic and developed a creed outlining its principles for self-determination. The first president was Robert Williams, then in exile for his organizing and armed self-defence as head of the Monroe, North Carolina, chapter of the National Association for the Advancement of Colored People (NAACP). Since his departure from the United States, Williams had developed his commitment to Black nationalism by building relationships with revolutionary movements from around the globe. His example, like that of Malcolm X, articulated a revolutionary nationalist politics firmly rooted in anti-imperialist internationalism. From Tanzania, the RNA president-elect issued a statement calling the Republic "one of self-determination for an oppressed people" rooted in Black nationalism, grassroots democracy, and a socialist economics.[10] Williams's high profile attracted additional attention to the RNA upon its founding, though he resigned as president in the fall of 1969 after returning to the United States following a decade-long absence.[11]

Although it declared the five Southern states its national territory, the RNA was based in Detroit for its first two years and retained a strong presence there for several years to come.[12] Founding members Richard and Milton Henry, who renamed themselves Imari and Gaidi Obadele, respectively, each had impressive track records as organizers in the Motor City. Prior to organizing the Black Government Conference, both men had already participated as key leaders of numerous groups. The pair helped start the Group on Advanced Leadership (GOAL) in 1962, the Michigan Freedom Now Party (FNP) in 1963, the Malcolm X Society in 1967, and then the RNA in 1968. Their political history and mentors are a veritable who's who of the postwar Black radical left, including Albert Cleage (whose church sponsored the RNA's founding conference), James and Grace Lee Boggs, Muhammad Ahmad—even Kwame Nkrumah of Ghana.[13] But it was Malcolm X who had the greatest impact. Three of Malcolm's most influential speeches—"Message to the Grassroots," "The Ballot or the Bullet," and his February 14, 1965, talk—were given at GOAL-sponsored events in Detroit.[14] Imari Obadele dedicated his 1966 pamphlet *War in America: The Malcolm X Doctrine* to "the Malcolmites," and an early draft of the RNA's New Afrikan creed staked its authority "by the grace of Malcolm."[15]

Setting itself up to govern an internal colony, the RNA rallied around a demand to "Free the Land." And that is what it tried to do, especially after the organization moved to Mississippi in 1970. The decision to organize in the rural South was as much for defence as ideology: based on his analysis of how ghetto rebellions were crushed in the mid-1960s, Obadele had long argued that Northern cities were strategically untenable. Even if majority Black, the cities of the urban North were surrounded by white people, making them easy to repress.[16] The post-1960s growth of suburbs only exacerbated this process of racially inflected spatial separation.[17] In the South, Obadele argued, the sizable Black rural population would provide useful cover. His position won out in a contentious struggle among the RNA top leadership. Of particular interest to the Republic was what it called "Kush," the twenty-five counties in the 15,000 square feet along the Mississippi River from Memphis to Louisiana. Kush was a prized territory in both size and historical significance. It was valued for its resources and as the only place in the United States in 1970 where Black people still constituted a majority of the population. It was therefore a strategic component of RNA plans to secure the broader Republic.[18] The Republic established its national headquarters and presidential residence near Jackson, Mississippi, in the heart of Kush.

The RNA's Southern specificity but broader U.S. and global focus distinguish the group from other revolutionary attempts. (Because the RNA still exists under a similar platform, I refer to enduring political tenets in the present tense.) As RNA organizers pushed for their own nation, they argued for the necessity of change within the current U.S. context. The organization's ongoing work around reparations and its support for U.S. political prisoners continue to call into question racial and economic injustice in the form of "national oppression." While interrogating the U.S. nation-state overall, the RNA has carved out a particular space for emphasizing the historical and strategic significance of the U.S. South; but its attention to the United States overall distinguishes the RNA's Black Belt focus from that of the Communist Party in the 1930s. Unlike the CP, the RNA defined all Black people in America as colonized, with the five states a viable solution to such colonization. Chokwe Lumumba said the five states were the

*"The Malcolm X Doctrine"*

"heart of the Black nation," but not its entirety.[19] For the RNA, the slave trade and continuing racial oppression created the Black Nation; the five Southern states provided a *solution* to the colonization that all Africans in North American faced. It was an effort to leverage the political, social, and spatial power of New Afrikans in contesting the power of the U.S. government. But the Black Nation was a salient ideological home, found wherever Black people resided.

The RNA unveiled its Anti-Depression Program in 1972, with legislative actions for securing independence. The program made three basic demands of the U.S. government: that it cede land and sovereignty to the RNA "in areas where blacks vote for independence" via plebiscite; that it pay $300 billion in reparations "for slavery and unjust war against the black nation"; and establish a negotiations procedure to determine a reparations payment.[20] This program, it was hoped, would help "end poverty, dependence, and crime," "raise self-esteem, achievement, and creativity, and ... promote inter-racial peace." Within months of its release, the program was presented to the Black Political Convention in Gary, submitted to the U.S. Congress, and approved by the NAACP-headed Mississippi Loyalist Democrats.[21]

The Anti-Depression Program was the most developed policy statement that the Republic had released to that time. Its wide circulation and sizable support among Black professional and political circles—including Michigan Senator John Conyers and comedian Dick Gregory—highlight the RNA's organizing savvy. Such petitions and programs to city councils, state governments, and the federal government expressed a serious willingness to achieve a plebiscite and cession of land non-violently. To be sure, RNA members did not hide their support of armed self-defence, guerrilla war, or sabotage, and military training was deemed compulsory for all citizens.[22] Yet the RNA never engaged in open war with the United States. Rather, the RNA has tried to establish itself under the rubric of international law.[23] As Obadele wrote from a Mississippi jail while awaiting trial, "Every step taken by the Republic of New Africa has been plotted to stay within limits generated by *their* laws and constitution."[24]

Central to the Anti-Depression plan was the development of "New Communities" in RNA territory, especially Mississippi. These communities, according to the plan, would be based on the Tanzanian socialist model of *ujamaa* and give life to the Republic's territorial claims through development and emigration. They would demonstrate New Afrikan sovereignty amidst grave repression, providing a rear base and free state for the embattled Black masses. Together with reparations, the New Communities would provide the infrastructure so that Black people who had left the South out of economic necessity or political terror could move back. Viewing these community efforts as a crucial step towards self-determination, Republic officials started the Society for the Development of

New Communities (SDNC), a non-profit corporation to raise money for Black economic development.[25]

Although SDNC was the primary grassroots fundraising mechanism, reparations remained a key strategy for developing the Republic—and for securing racial justice for all Black people in the United States. The reparations demand was not a fundraising strategy; instead, it was a strategic point of organizing that could serve as a unified rallying cry. RNA workers proved themselves quite adept at doing just that. In March 1974 the RNA held an election in thirty counties across Mississippi, where nearly 5,000 people voted for reparations and elected Obadele president of the Mississippi Black Assembly. The election was monitored by the Election Commission of the Black Political Scientists.[26] That fall the National Black Political Convention unanimously approved a resolution calling for the National Black Assembly to join the RNA and the Mississippi Black Assembly in calling for $300 billion in reparations.

# An Internationalist State

Central to the RNA's goals was to strive for international representation, as Malcolm X had encouraged towards the end of his life. This global focus was both political and strategic: RNA co-founder Imari Obadele wrote that this approach would ensure that "attacks upon us [Malcolmites] by the United States become international matters threatening world peace, and *thereby* within reach of the United Nations, *thereby* within reach of our friends in Africa and Asia who would help us." Only when Black people had clearly rejected U.S. citizenship and its civil rights paradigm, Obadele argued, could such international support blossom.[27] The RNA joined such a global framework with Malcolm's insistence on land and self-defence as key to nation-building. With the help and advice of former Communist and ex-Garveyite Queen Mother Audley Moore, this paradigm achieved practical expression through the RNA's call for reparations and for control of the five Southern states.[28] The two went together: reparations were to pay for bulking up the Black Nation's territory, similar to the way in which, Obadele argued, German reparations did for Israel.[29]

Using international law provisions against colonialism, the RNA planned to organize a plebiscite for people of African descent in the United States to determine their status. RNA officials advanced this argument as part of settling what they saw as a long-neglected aspect of the Fourteenth Amendment of the U.S. Constitution. The amendment, according to the Republic, *offers* but does not *grant* citizenship. Black people have never been given a chance to choose whether they *want* the citizenship that has been forced upon them. The *obligations* of it were bestowed while the *rights* have never been guaranteed. The plebiscite aimed

"The Malcolm X Doctrine"

to settle these questions—and move ever closer to establishing an independent, internationally recognized nation with the full consent of the governed.[30] The RNA was not the first to call for such a measure; in its Revolutionary People's Constitutional Convention, the Black Panther Party had also called for a U.N.-supervised plebiscite to determine whether Black people were citizens of the United States.[31] The two groups differed not on the demand but on the timing. As Huey Newton elucidated in a September 1969 letter to the RNA, the Panther leadership did not advocate a plebiscite until "[we] wipe out once and for all the oppressive structure of America," which would not be possible without a sizable coalition. Although he deemed the RNA "perfectly justified in demanding and declaring the right to secede from the nation," Newton feared that implementing the RNA's plans at the time would be dangerously and unnecessarily isolating.[32] The RNA, meanwhile, viewed this plebiscite both as a way of settling historical injustices and as an organizing campaign, and began working for it almost immediately. The plebiscite, argued the RNA, was fundamental to establishing an independent, internationally recognized nation—and a vital step towards securing the consent of those subjecting themselves to rule by the Republic of New Afrika rather than by the United States of America.

The principle of carving out a "Black Power state"[33] from the Southern United States emerged from what is perhaps the RNA's most interesting ideological contribution, the creation of a new political subject. At a time when national discourse was only just beginning to shift from Negro to Black or Afro-American, the 1968 Black Government Conference introduced a new political designation: the New Afrikan,[34] a Pan-African identity forged by the generations of shared oppression, language, and culture of the many African nations enslaved in the United States. It is an identity constructed through the history of slavery, rooted in the Black Belt South that slaves had built and that has always been home to a disproportionate number of people of African descent. It is an identity that carries with it a pledge of allegiance to a new and amalgamated form of social arrangements.[35] From the beginning the Republic of New Afrika did not describe an organization as much as an idea and a demand—for reparations, for independence, and for land. Since 1968 there has been an organized entity in the RNA, crafted as a state in exile and complete with elected officials. The Republic, meanwhile, defines the national territory of Black America—a vision of and a bold proposal for self-determination. Citizenship is voluntary and available to any Black person who declares it. (Yuri Kochiyama, the Japanese-American activist and stalwart comrade of Malcolm X, has been the notable exception to the RNA's African-descent citizenship policies.)[36] To distinguish between the Black Nation as a concept and its governmental apparatus, the RNA ultimately established a formal ruling body—the Provisional Government of the Republic of New Afrika

(PG-RNA). Although accepting citizenship in the Republic signified an affinity with the PG-RNA, it primarily affirmed commitment to a self-described New Afrikan Independence Movement (NAIM). For all its territorial ambitions, the RNA saw citizenship as constituting an ideological position of Pan-Africanist connection among Black people—an orientation to overturning the settler colonialism and global imperialism of the U.S. Empire.

Its focus on the (rural) South at a time when many saw Black Power as a phenomenon of the (urban) North was an attempted solution to the colonized position of all Blacks in the United States, an attempt to stitch together urban and rural resistance through the development of New Communities in Mississippi and consulates throughout the United States from which the RNA could conduct political education and organize for reparations and on behalf of U.S. political prisoners. The RNA was a call to empower the Third World within North America. Its declaration of independence defined a nation as shared culture (which it described as a way of life), shared land, and a shared government.[37] Like many other revolutionary nationalists, then, the proponents of RNA politics disaggregated nation from state: "nation" characterized the position of all Black people in the United States; "state" was a demand, consistent with the developmentalist approach of Third World liberation struggles at the time.[38]

While its demand for state power exposed the limitations of this approach—including, in the RNA's founding years, sanctioned polygamy, frontier ideology, and identity essentialism—the consecration of a new political identity located an anticolonial subjectivity while simultaneously identifying colonized territory.[39] This combination elevated the Black liberation movement's opposition to U.S. imperialism as part of a radical internationalist project. In providing a poignant interlocution of the U.S. narrative and structure, the RNA equipped the Black Power movement and its sympathizers with an ideological and physical apparatus that generated a detailed, if not widely held, vision for liberating the internal colony. The RNA's existence and its program called into question the U.S. state form itself as a legitimate political border. Nikhil Singh's description of the Black Panther Party seems especially apt in describing the RNA: it was a "projection of sovereignty" that attempted to decolonize the United States from within by asserting self-determination.[40] Establishing the apparatus of national liberation was essential to securing it. This plan called for simultaneously confronting the existing U.S. state while developing alternative institutions to replace the current social arrangements.

Formed amidst the height of state repression against Black revolutionaries, the RNA was an effort to move the Black Power struggle to a place in which it could operate on its own terms rather than from within the U.S. framework. New Afrika was the parallel to the unfolding struggle for a united, socialist Africa.

Thus it was not just the Black Power state but also the Pan-African state in North America. As such the New Afrikan was a transnational identity, making the Republic an effort in creating a diasporic Black state. Imari Obadele made an explicit connection to African national liberation movements: "For no less than they have We [sic] boldly shed the nationality of our colonizer and gone to contest for independent land."[41]

The Republic of New Afrika offered a clear program to the overarching impulse towards nationalism then characterizing many Black communities. Its strategy mirrored other stateless national liberation struggles, where establishing national identification and governmental apparatus was of primary importance. As actress and RNA organizer Colia LaFayette put it, "The Vietnamese and the Palestinians have well demonstrated to the world that even subjugated peoples can and should elect their own provisional governments. There are certain aspects of the freedom struggle that can only properly be carried out by such a popularly elected provisional government."[42]

For this reason, distinctions between "territorial" and "revolutionary" nationalism prove insufficient metrics for analyzing the RNA.[43] Beginning in a time when even detached academics described Black people in America as a colonized population, the RNA contributed to this perspective a strategic view that saw independent land as the missing ingredient for securing self-determination. Following Malcolm X, the RNA saw land and a governmental apparatus as the basis of sovereignty.[44] Its territorial claims are inseparable from the revolutionary orientation inscribed in its founding declaration of independence, which pledged New Afrika's commitment to "wage the world revolution until all people everywhere are so free." Given the declaration's support for sexual equality, collective distribution of state-owned production, and opposition to class discrimination, as well as the establishment of Mississippi communities modelled on the principles of *ujamaa*, the RNA also calls into question the corollary juxtaposition imposed between nationalism and socialism.[45]

Just as it is often positioned against socialism, nationalism is often defined as contrary to feminism—a critique with ample historical evidence. Although it is outside the scope of this article, a detailed analysis of the RNA's gender politics would be a valuable endeavour. The group's initial leaders and publicly identifiable theorists were men, though Queen Mother Moore's involvement provided a strong example of women's political and intellectual leadership. From the beginning the RNA upheld gender equality as part of its revolutionary program, which is something even the Panthers failed to enshrine in their program. As with other nationalist projects, the RNA's gender politics prized respect and equality, though saying nothing about gender roles or sexuality, presuming a heteronormative standard of relationships that still defined women as wife and mother, if also soldier and citizen. Further study of the RNA, especially in the form of oral histories, is needed to understand these and other dynamics.

## Self-Determination and the Sixties

The U.S. government did not look kindly on the RNA's efforts. The group witnessed major waves of attack in Detroit (1969), Mississippi (1971, 1981), and New York (1981). As with the Panthers, the state viewed the RNA's projection of sovereignty as a threat to its own fragile hold on hegemonic power. The RNA faced repeated battles with the U.S. state, in both Detroit and Mississippi, during an array of armed confrontations and legal challenges.[46] Such fights generated several political prisoners for the RNA throughout the 1970s. Organizing for their release, again through appeals to international law, offered another chance for the RNA to question the legitimacy of U.S. democracy by rejecting the criminalization of Black insurgency.[47]

Yet such heavy losses and legal hurdles did not shut down the Republic. The dream of New Afrika inspired ongoing action for independence, which continues to animate RNA actions. Despite its enormous setbacks, the Republic has continued organizing for reparations, against repression, and for official status. In frightening all levels of government, the RNA brought to light continuing white supremacist tensions in the Deep South. It connected Detroit's militant legacy with a strategic emphasis on the South, exposing the deep-seated hostility to Black self-determination. The RNA also placed reparations squarely on the agenda of a radical movement in the United States and as part of global Pan-African resistance. In contesting naturalized categories of nation, state, and governance, the Republic of New Afrika forces us to rethink the basic units of American political practice in the sixties and beyond.

# 5  Kimmo Rentola

# THE SOVIET COMMUNIST PARTY AND 1968
## A Case Study

**Most promising** in recent historiography on 1968 is the analytical effort to combine youth movements with Cold War history. Separately, both branches have flourished: every aspect and effect of the 1960s movements appear to have been examined, and Cold War history has experienced a vigorous revival. However, these two have seldom seriously met each other. Movement historians avoid touching dirty old men, while diplomatic or military historians neglect non-state, unruly actors. Still, youth movements and Great Power policy occurred simultaneously and affected each other deeply. For contemporaries, it was self-evident. On his first day in office, Richard Nixon ordered a CIA analysis on world youth unrest.[1]

Now the dividing wall is collapsing, as witnessed by the attention given to Jeremi Suri's book *Power and Protest: Global Revolution and the Rise of Detente*. His seducing idea of a "balance of order" pursued by world leaders of the opposite camps, who, to put it crudely, created détente and refrained from challenging each other to protect themselves against global youth unrest,[2] might need qualification, as is often the case when a new idea is put forward. Still, the point of interdependence between youth rebellion and Great Power policy is certainly sound.

My theme here is the reaction of the Soviet political elite to 1968—as a year of revolution—and the resulting Soviet ideological conclusions, which would be tested in Finland.

# 1968 as a Revolution

It is now apparent that the 1968 rebellion was primarily a cultural revolution, a revolution of the mind, of attitudes and of habits.[3] But it was seldom seen this way by the contemporary student "vanguard," who saw it instead as a prelude to a real revolution, a future seizure of power. New movements, in need of concepts to describe themselves, unable to create immediately a language of their own, often first resort to old vocabulary. Jacobins claimed the inheritance of the ancient Roman Republic; the 1968 vanguard drew on the great revolution of the century in 1917 and produced a revival of Bolshevik language and organization. Even the ever-peaceful social-democratic Sweden saw a "revival of Leninism." In 1969 new left students everywhere espoused the need for a revolutionary party. Stalin became trendy—Eldridge Cleaver of the Black Panther Party was a fan of the Soviet dictator. Anti-authoritarian origins were not enough to preclude the Milanese Movimento studentesco from chanting: "Berija, Stalin, GPU!"[4]

The brand of Leninism selected by the student vanguard in any given country or university depended on the supply available to satisfy the demand: that is, on local political traditions and on the condition of the national left wing. So there was room for competition, particularly in 1968 and 1969. This situation opened up new vistas for those claiming to possess Leninism, or created new problems for anyone accused of abandoning the original pure revolutionary doctrine. As for governments, young revolutionaries preferred the Chinese, Cubans, and Vietnamese over the Soviets. However, when young people appealed to Lenin, to 1917, and even to Stalin, that rang a bell at the Old Square in Moscow, because the position as true heirs of Lenin and Bolshevism was a key element in Soviet legitimacy. Even if there was no windfall coming, something useful could certainly be anticipated.

# The Soviets and 1968

In retrospect the invasion of Czechoslovakia in August 1968 was the point when the Soviet downtrend became irreversible. That, however, was not immediately apparent in Moscow; on the contrary, in 1968 the Soviet leaders' perception of the all-important "global relation of forces" was changing as the United States appeared to be losing ground. Strategic arms parity, the Vietnam War, and the weak U.S. reaction to the Czech occupation itself nourished the Soviet view that the balance had tipped to their favour.[5] For the Kremlin, the world tide was turning. This assessment was supported by the Western student rebellion, followed by workers' strikes, developments that revealed the surprising fragility of Western states and societies.

On the one hand, the Soviets were excessively concerned about the threat that a rival brand of Leninism, not in control or even hostile—like Trotskyism or Maoism—would take over the new movements. To watch and prevent this, in late 1968 KGB intelligence was ordered to penetrate radical Western youth movements and, in particular, to obtain even the tiniest bit of information on Maoists.[6] Of course, this was easier to say in Moscow than actually perform on the spot.

On the other hand, ideological circles in the Soviet Communist Party were impressed by the upheaval and began to consider the chances for rapid changes in Western Europe. As always, tactical needs were involved. The Soviets wanted to punish and to put pressure on main Western European Communist parties that had condemned the invasion of Czechoslovakia. One suitable method was criticism of an insufficient reaction to the *événements* and of defective revolutionary theory. In early October 1968 Vadim Zagladin, deputy head of the Soviet Communist Party International Department (MO), told Enrico Berlinguer of the Italian Communist Party that a "peaceful road to socialism" remained an exception and would not be automatically accepted. East Germans, who initially favoured the French Communist Party's handling of the May 1968 events in Paris, began to criticize the French for superficial analysis and lack of attention to non-parliamentary means of action.[7] This was reminiscent of the beginning of the Cold War in 1947, when the French and Italian Communist parties were severely reprimanded for policies initially approved or even ordered by the Soviets themselves. From autumn 1968, for a brief period, the Soviets reconsidered the prospects for a revolution in the West—prospects that they had largely abandoned by the mid-1960s, if not earlier.

By late 1968 a prominent old guard theoretician announced, "The way to socialism has become shorter than before in many countries."[8] Bright young men in MO think tanks—connected with swiftly developing Soviet Third Worldism[9]— went further. According to Anatoly Chernyaev, 1968 finally brought the postwar period to conclusion and opened up a new stage. He reasoned that a deep economic crisis or another similar catastrophe was no longer a necessary precondition for a revolution in the West. Even the revolution itself would change. A swift and open seizure of power à la Prague in 1948 was not necessary. In highly developed countries, "the revolutionary situation will apparently be 'limited' to a political crisis of short duration (and caused by most different and surprising factors), whereupon there remains only the task of picking up the perfectly ripe fruit."[10] This theory of a new kind of revolution was based on the idea that post-1968 developments would force social democracy to change. The Vietnam War would sever ties to the United States; a new generation would take over, with new ideas and aspirations, to create left-wing alliances. This potential had already been demonstrated by experience in France, Italy, Spain, and Finland. Not even the dictatorship of the proletariat would inevitably be a one-party act. For the Soviets this was indeed fresh thinking, but still, novelties were packed into traditional moulds.

This ideological current reached its apex at the end of 1969, when it was joined and interpreted by heavyweights. According to chief ideologist Mikhail Suslov, peaceful co-existence could not be reduced only to economic competition; it also created new opportunities. The year 1968 created a new room for the initiative and advance of revolutionary and progressive forces. Admittedly, it *is* odd to connect a dogmatist like Suslov with unruly youths, but he had already shown flexibility in 1962 by expressing appreciation for Che Guevara, despite the Latin American revolutionary's appearance and critical remarks. In a 1969 article a key subordinate of Suslov, MO head Boris Ponomarev, saw Lenin's definition of a revolutionary situation as no longer valid. Ordinary material complaints could turn against capitalism as a whole, and in the present relation of forces revolutionaries in any given country could be supported by socialist countries, and that made the export of counter-revolution more dangerous for the imperialists. This emphasized the "subjective factor," that is, the will of the revolutionaries to begin.[11]

This idea made it to the top level of ideological codification, the CPSU Central Committee theses on Lenin's centenary. There it was stated that, in the West, deep political crises could develop surprisingly, and minor conflicts could overflow, which meant that communists should stay abreast of momentary demands and avoid lagging behind the mass movement generating revolutionary charge. This was an attempt to translate the French *événements* and the Italian *autunno caldo* into Soviet Leninist jargon. In his Lenin centenary speech, party boss Leonid Brezhnev said that the experience of France, Italy, and Japan—and most recently the big miners' strikes in North Sweden—demonstrated that a new political situation was emerging in the capitalist countries. In this situation, it was important to find "the concrete road or 'the specific turn of events'" leading to an opening towards revolution.[12]

How seriously can such talk be taken? Even if recent Cold War research has confirmed the weight of ideology for the Soviets, we should avoid hasty conclusions. First, the talk cannot be played down as regular run-of-the-mill production. The mention of an unexpected rapid turn leading to fundamental changes in the West had disappeared from high-level ideological documents by early 1971, when the full détente approach finally prevailed in the Kremlin. Even then, MO heads still told Finnish Communist leaders: "History [shows]: when détente, swift changes possible. An active political line can retain this tendency." Second, the Soviets had a need to enhance their revolutionary credentials. There was the Chinese competition, fierce in the Third World and among Western youth; there was the need to reassure their own allies—Fidel Castro, the Vietnamese, East Germans—that the first steps towards détente with the West did not mean selling out basic ideological elements.[13]

Some beliefs were authentic. At the time, fundamental changes in direction towards the left seemed entirely believable in France or in Italy. For the Soviet reputation, it was necessary to stay abreast of these developments and to prevent them from turning into an alternative socialism. Also, Soviet ideologists genuinely believed that the repercussions of 1968 and the Vietnam War were introducing a crisis in social democracy, forcing the traditional archrival to alter its stances, particularly in Scandinavia. Olof Palme, the young new prime minister of Sweden, participated in anti-U.S. demonstrations and took the lead among Nordic social democrats in opening direct relations with Hanoi. Funded by the labour movement, the South Vietnamese Provisional Revolutionary Government opened offices in Nordic capitals. By then Hanoi was solidly pro-Soviet and approved even of diplomatic struggle, so that the Soviets were able to plan "intensification, to our benefit, of DRV [Democratic Republic of Vietnam] foreign policy activity, utilization in our interests of its certain international prestige." According to the Scandinavian department head in the Soviet Foreign Ministry, the Nordic situation was rapidly changing: "Recently a serious struggle has begun on who will influence the policy of these states, and this is actually nothing else than a reflection of the fact that this area is the theatre where two power lines [*erövonal*] meet."[14]

## The Test in Finland

The degree of seriousness and the limits of the Soviet post-1968 revolutionary ideas can be demonstrated in the case of Finland, which was used as a test laboratory by Moscow ideologists. The Finnish bulletin of the CPSU CC International Department, together with Ponomarev's article, presented a theoretical case in which reactionary forces, seeing the hopelessness of resistance, would surrender and hand over power. This was most likely to happen in a small state with a bigger neighbour that had already experienced a revolution of its own.[15] No name of the country was given, nor needed.

Why should the Soviets bother Finland, already under their heavy influence? Between the two neighbours, critical factors had emerged since 1968. Finland's foreign policy doctrine became unpalatable for the Soviets when they saw how neutrality tempted the Czechs, Hungarians, and Poles. Although the Soviets needed the European security conference (with its general recognition for postwar borders), they suspiciously eyed the Finnish initiative, seeing—correctly—a ploy to promote the Finns' own interests.[16] In addition, the Soviets were irritated by the United States' new and demonstrative warmth towards Finland. For the first time in nine years the Finnish president, Urho Kekkonen, was invited to Washington.

These factors would not have been sufficient to cause a major change in Soviet policy, had Finnish elections in March 1970 not aggravated fears of "losing" the country. The right wing won by a landslide, and the centre-left government coalition suffered heavy losses. Pro-Soviet parties and politicians were worst hit, reflecting the voters' Czech shock. KGB Helsinki chief V.S. Stepanov said to President Kekkonen that the Finnish people were no longer trusted in Moscow. Worse for the Soviets, it was generally believed that Kekkonen, soon seventy, would be retiring, and not even he was as he used to be. He had spoiled his good name in Moscow through planning to allow the right wing to take government, visiting the United States, and often following the Swedish line in foreign policy.[17]

Moscow had to act swiftly. It was a classic Cold War situation, in which "leaders can feel both very vulnerable and very opportunistic at almost the same moment of time."[18] The Finnish Communist chairmen were invited to Moscow for emergency consultations. A simultaneous right-wing election advance and leftist upsurges (youth, trade unions) made Soviet ideologists conclude that a rapid polarization was underway in Finnish society. Ponomarev saw Finland as a laboratory: "To whose benefit does time work? Should it be accelerated in SKP [Finnish Communist Party] interests?" According to him, due to the international situation, prospects for the Communists were good. The Americans were losing their grip and lacked the resources to support their clients as before, and were now plunged into a deep crisis by their invasion of Cambodia. For Ponomarev, the Kent State University shooting incident of May 1969 showed that "it is not any longer only between blacks and whites. Thus, US supporters do not have much chance [in Finland]." Even the German negotiations proved Soviet strength: "They are courting us," Senior politburo member Arvid Pelshe promised Soviet help to get communist initiatives into the platform of a renewed Finnish centre-left government.[19] This was a bold step because the Soviets usually avoided involvement in domestic affairs in full view.

An even bolder step was the appointment of Ponomarev's first deputy, Aleksei S. Belyakov, as ambassador to Helsinki. Placing an MO deputy head as ambassador was a major coup in interbureaucracy skirmishes and demonstrated the weight of the ideological factor in Soviet decision-making during the uncertain early détente.[20] The appointment reflected the "primacy of the party," controlled by Brezhnev; hitherto, in the top troika, state affairs with Finland had primarily belonged to Prime Minister Alexei Kosygin. The author of the decision was probably Suslov, who cultivated critical attitudes to bourgeois Finland. Once he was reported to have described Finnish foreign policy as "a rotten egg, the shell pure white, but the interior disgusting."[21] Now he sent a former "thaw liberal" to clean up the mess in Finland. Dark ideological currents in post-Prague Moscow made it necessary for former "liberals" to prove their credentials.

Belyakov was a specialist in revolutionary theory for Western Europe. He was the original author of the idea of peaceful advance to a socialist revolution in developed countries on the basis of existing institutions and without a distinct break; this could best happen in smaller non-militarized countries with neutralist tendencies and in co-operation with socialist states.[22] In 1965, when Finnish communists were preparing for co-operation with social democrats and participation in government, he emphasized the importance of defining the revolution "as a process and not just as an incident in a single country." In Finland the move towards "a national form of socialism" would begin to be made by *two* left-wing parties. No violence would be needed. Brezhnev explained the position in cruder terms: Finnish comrades had exceptional chances to advance the cause, having the benefit of a splendid model right over their eastern border. Brezhnev repeated this thought in 1969, when these ideas were even more relevant with the change in social democracy, the upsurge of leftist youth, and the revival of trade-union militancy.[23] Belyakov and his trusty theoretician Yuri Krasin had received first-hand experience from the Italian "hot autumn," during visits there in August and September 1969, after which the former strongly supported the Finnish Communists' resolute attitude to strikes and cherished the consequences: "The President capitulated. This was correct."[24]

**The centre-left** coalition government was reinstated in Helsinki in July 1970, and the neutrality twists were temporarily straightened out during Kekkonen's visit to Moscow. But things did not calm down. In August intelligence organizations were already reporting that the new Soviet ambassador was involved in inappropriate activities for a diplomat, such as instigating strikes and interfering in Communist Party policies.[25]

As is usually the case with intelligence materials, there were misunderstandings and exaggerations, as well as tracks left by the former crisis in modern Finnish political culture. But the reports were not baseless. The ambassador had a specific mission. He had to keep the Communist Party wings bound together by a more radical line and a stronger role in the government. He had to bring about "the permanent isolation of the right wing,"[26] as well as correct the defects in Finland's foreign policy. That was his minimum task, but there was also a maximum, a comprehensive new step, which would correct for good the Finnish Communists' vague ideas of a socialist state and their "underestimation of the issue of maintaining the power [*Unterschätzung der Fragen der Machterhaltung*]." As Belyakov saw it, the Finnish Communist Party had to choose between integrating itself as an appendage of bourgeois and social-democratic Finland, or becoming "a real party of struggle to shake the foundations of this capitalist Finland."[27]

This approach did not mean a sudden seizure of power. Rather, the idea was to follow a transition towards the left, based on the radicalization of social democracy and supported by militant strikes and the youth movement. It was another example of how "the swirling momentum of those two years" often made people turn political "somersaults in great waves."[28] The Soviets urged Finnish Communist leaders to welcome the leftist youth, despite their heresies, which time would surely correct. Communists "sometimes come late to utilize new forces—others will have occasion to manipulate." To witness it through their own eyes, politburo veteran member Arvid Pelshe and Belyakov even visited the movement haunt, the Helsinki Old Student House, where grey Russian suits were usually never seen.[29]

Perhaps it would have been sufficient for the Soviets to get only an impression of success in Finland. Having talked for five years with Ponomarev, Belyakov, and the KGB, social-democratic foreign minister Väinö Leskinen believed that "deep down the Russians don't give a damn [*ge fan i*] about their communists. For them the issue is power and state and security."[30] Brezhnev's Soviet Union was Potemkin's country: how things looked was as important as how they actually were. What Soviet ideologists primarily needed from a turn towards the left in Finland was a showpiece to influence developments elsewhere—in social-democratic Scandinavia, and then in France and Italy—to show that the *spinta propulsiva* of the October revolution was not exhausted, that they could provide a model for a leftist government of a capitalist country. Belyakov claimed that French and Italian comrades were looking at the Finnish experience "with a magnifying glass in their hand"—*they* hardly were, but *he* was, in his attempt to use Finland to impress the parties of those countries. In particular, the post-1968 French were in need of a clear identity and a convincing revolutionary project, and "revolution became once more the dominant source for legitimation" for the French Communists.[31]

As former thaw liberals, Belyakov and his comrades might have secretly cherished hopes of a two-way street: new elements could influence the traditional Soviet camp.[32]

# In analyzing the Belyakov design, we need to apply certain qualifications. First, there was time pressure. In mid-1970 the Soviet leaders were still testing

the limits of potential détente and collaboration on security.[33] After the August accords with Germany, a more positive détente approach gradually prevailed in the Kremlin. Second, disturbances were out of the question. In order not to arouse world outcry, everything had to go smoothly The Soviets believed that they possessed a powerful vehicle for this approach: hints of the Czech occupation would paralyze any Finnish resistance. In November 1968 Belyakov realized that Kekkonen was indeed afraid "that the USSR might send tanks into Finland." As ambassador, he hinted at this threat at a dinner with Finnish generals, referring to "the very small chance that the Soviet armed forces would need to come to Finland." Of course, he personally hoped that this might never be "turned into reality."[34]

There was a way of achieving a "revolution from above," because the office of the president of the republic would soon be vacant. Ponomarev and his team cherished the idea that Kekkonen would be succeeded by a sufficiently left-wing and pro-Soviet social democrat leading a left coalition.[35] Who then would have been the Salvador Allende of the North? The only one with sufficient political weight was foreign minister Väinö Leskinen, even though until his conversion in 1964 he had been a leading (and very skilful) anti-Soviet politician, and a CIA costumer. Even in 1969 Ponomarev was still suspicious and uncertain of Leskinen, "internally, genuinely." By summer 1970 Saul had at last succeeded in turning himself into Paul. Speaking of the foreign minister, Ponomarev admitted that even hardened Mensheviks like Vyshinski or Maiski had joined the Bolsheviks and distinguished themselves.[36] Leskinen did not hear this, nor was he fully aware of the Soviet designs, but as a seasoned professional he sensed a window of opportunity. He still had "wolf eyes."

The Belyakov design was not a unanimous Soviet project. At the top, Kosygin regarded sudden changes in Europe in negative terms and saw maintaining the status quo as a primary Soviet interest. But Kosygin's star was descending at the time. Most Soviet diplomats would have been content with reasonable corrections in Finnish foreign policy; the ranking one in Helsinki stressed stability and said that there were "no objective preconditions for any upheaval [omvälvning] in Finland."[37] In particular, KGB foreign intelligence mainly wanted to continue business as usual and warned that any imbalance or adventure would lead nowhere and only profit the right wing.[38] When the new ambassador was appointed, the KGB sent a new chief of station to Helsinki—Viktor Vladimirov, a veteran of presidential machinations—thus indicating its preference to continue with a favoured centre politician. Immediately upon arrival, Vladimirov began to obstruct the ambassador's designs.

The leftist design for Finland, then, was an ideological operation of the CPSU Central Committee International Department and its custodians. It might have been blessed by Brezhnev, probably on a rather vague level, but lacked the support of other important Soviet actors.

**The design** for Finland did not work out. Above all, the Soviet analysis was faulty. Youth and strike movements developed rapidly, but their effect on society was not what had been anticipated in Moscow and their nature was different from that assumed by Soviet schematics, even if there was a great metalworkers' strike coming. Social democracy did not change as wished; the anti-Soviet tradition collapsed, but instead of leftism it was replaced by Nordic reformism. In the Communist Party, the moderate majority opted for a gradual development of society and abandoned the radical turn that had risen shortly after the election disappointment. Party chairman Aarne Saarinen complained that the ambassador was "stuck on the SKP like a leech."[39]

Disappointed with the mainstream left, Belyakov in Helsinki and the Soviet press in Moscow began a heavy-pressure campaign, but the results were counterproductive. Now realizing how much the Soviets wanted, Leskinen did not comply, but instead sought protection from Sweden's four top social-democratic leaders in a hasty secret meeting in a Stockholm safe house. Having confirmed that the ambassador did not enjoy full support in the Soviet camp, President Kekkonen began a resolute counter-offensive. There would be no voluntary handing over of power. After a series of domestic and foreign moves to take the edge off the pressure, Kekkonen even complained directly to the KGB chief of station that "it is futile to imagine Finland to be in pre-revolutionary condition."[40]

Thus, no smooth transition was possible, and new problems emerged. Soviet leaders quickly abandoned the design in Finland and an open crisis was avoided. Once again, Finland proved to be "the country of unrealized catastrophes."[41] The Kremlin sent its troubleshooter, deputy foreign minister V.V. Kuznetsov, to Helsinki to tell Kekkonen that no change was on the cards, nor had such been planned in the first place. The visit was strictly secret: Kuznetsov walked over the border as the peace negotiators had done in 1944. The day before at the same border, the Soviet main negotiator in strategic arms limitation talks, V.S. Semyonov, pondered the nature of his country with his U.S. counterpart, Paul Nitze: "There are many layers in the Soviet Union: we are able to act in many ways. We are capable of extreme action; we can also be prudent."[42]

Time ran out. What seemed possible for Finland in May was no longer feasible in December. The 1968 vistas were fading, and the French and Italian cases were losing their urgency. The ratification problems of the German accords made any European disturbance undesirable. "When the Soviet Union is aiming at a European balance, then the USSR cannot foment unrest in Finland, because it could lead to a disturbance of balance in Europe," the KGB's Vladimirov explained to Kekkonen. Most importantly, considering how Ponomarev had in May linked the action in Finland with U.S. weakness, was that the Soviets changed their attitude to détente with the United States soon after Mao said, "Let Nixon come." In December the Soviets made a reasonable Strategic Arms Limitation Treaty proposal, opening the way to a breakthrough.[43]

In Helsinki the Soviet minister of defence, Marshal Andrei Grechko, heavily drunk, assured his Finnish hosts that they could live "as you please and keep your country as you wish.... We do not want to change your social system."[44] Belyakov himself now spoke against big strikes and, like a regular ambassador, tried to return to square one, but that attempt failed because he drank and talked too much and the KGB obstructed his efforts. On February 18, 1971, he left Helsinki "on official business for about one week," never again to be seen in Finland. On the same day, Foreign Minister Andrei Gromyko gave the Warsaw Pact allies a new assessment of Finnish initiatives on European security: "The Americans have several times expressed their disapproval of this policy to the Finns. Sometimes we can note dissatisfaction on the socialist side as well. It would be desirable—they say—if the Finns were more consequent. We must take into account that the Finns' behaviour is as it is, with its uncertainties. In our work we must rely on the Finns and enhance the positive features of their behaviour."[45]

The Soviets switched their basic tactics. When heavy political pressure did not yield results, they decided to prevent Finland's slide to the West by economic means, by a huge increase of co-operation. Let the money talk; that language will be understood by capitalists.

In the summer of 1971 the CPSU International Department readjusted its theories in a conference with the Finnish comrades. Belyakov was nowhere to be seen, but Zagladin explained that the European "period of release" had proved "somewhat relative, for U.S. influence is continuing." Still, he saw that détente made rapid changes possible in capitalist countries and opened up new opportunities. Yuri Krasin still wanted to incorporate the new left. "We should find means to utilize this great force," from whom the Communists could learn the necessity of action. For him, the new left was "proof of the existence of great revolutionary potential."[46] This potential was already in full swing in Finland: in the dense atmosphere of great strikes and class struggle, younger new leftists in 1970–71 joined the Communist Party, some of them after briefly visiting the Social Democratic Party. Instead of injecting leftism into the mainstream left, as the Moscow ideologists had hoped, these youths mainly selected the isolation of the Stalinist minority wing of the SKP, the fundamental opposition in the Finnish society. This was the cunning of history: you plan one thing, and get something else.

The last word in the conference was had by Boris Ponomarev. Instead of acceleration, he now praised the blessings of slowness and the need to remember "the Marxist truth: the ruling classes will not voluntarily give away the power from their hands."[47]

The spectacular results of détente lead us to think that the process was inevitable from the beginning. But 1968 introduced new and partly adversarial elements into this process; it even "reformulated the impasse of revolution or radical change in Europe, rather than putting an end to it."[48] Détente should indeed be understood as an extremely contradictory process involving various domestic, regional, and international actors, with very different and contrasting motivations. To cope with the divergent political consequences of 1968 and to accommodate them to the détente project proved to be perhaps even more difficult for the Soviet Union than for other actors. In a sense, the ambiguous actions of the Soviets can be read as a sign of them losing their grip—although for the most part that sign was not recognized at the time.

## 6

Jennifer Ruth Hosek

# INTERPRETATIONS OF THIRD WORLD SOLIDARITY AND CONTEMPORARY GERMAN NATIONALISM

I think what you have in America now of course is a concerted attempt to paint the 1960s as an aberration within American culture and to paint the kind of radical shift that we're undergoing now as a return to normalcy. I think that's what's at stake in these arguments about 1968 as a betrayal. I think '68 is basically for me connected with the civil rights movement. Now is the civil rights movement a betrayal of American culture—of Jefferson, Thomas Payne, et cetera? Certainly not. It is in the best traditions, let's say, of American liberalism interpreted in a liberal rather than an irrespective way....

And for me as a German at the time, what was so important was to learn the lesson about civil disobedience. You know, in a country that had an authoritarian mentality to understand civil disobedience as part of the practice of democracy was enormously important.

**Andreas Huyssen,** a professor of German and Comparative Literature at Columbia University, is responding here to the issue of political dissent and violent action in the atmosphere of the global protests of 1968.[1] His words challenge those of his interlocutor, conservative intellectual Owen Harries. In this 2006 ABC Radio National interview Harries had used Spanish philosopher José Ortega y Gasset's writing about the 1920s to characterize 1960s protests: "They demanded bread and their method of making their protest was to burn down the bakery." Huyssen's perspective is Benjaminian: today's zeitgeist shapes today's history. His case in point is the contemporary U.S. climate that demonizes the 1960s culture of dissent to serve contemporary political interests.

Huyssen's analysis of the U.S. situation also applies to Germany, where popular and scholarly understandings of the 1960s protests are changing in ways that delegitimize contemporary opposition and further new discourses of national identity. These discourses have been described as "normalization" narratives. In the words of former chancellor Helmut Kohl, speaking of post-1990 Germany, "normal" means a country "not 'singularized' in any question," a country that "simply" does not "stick out."[2] And, indeed, the histories of this "belated" nation and others in Europe are also now being seen as showing distinct parallels.[3] Narratives of normalization and the rise of the new right in Germany are thus being fed by and feeding new scholarship on the political dissent of the 1960s and 1970s. In this political climate, interpretations that emphasize the role of violence—including anti-Jewish violence—among activists tend to quash support for public dissent. These shifts are part of a move to the right in the wake of the unification of the Federal Republic of Germany (FRG/"West Germany") and the German Democratic Republic (GDR/"East Germany"). There is little specifically German about this political shift: it can be traced in many European and North American states. Yet the change is particularly striking in a nation marked by a notorious fascist legacy.

In both the FRG and GDR the National Socialist (NS) past led to critical and differentiated politicization among large sections of the populations. In the first decades after the Second World War, while the NATO Allies and especially the United States encouraged critical self-reflection in the FRG, the Soviet Union promoted anti-fascism in the GDR.

Each new Germany attempted to break with the traditions that had led to Nazism by creating alternatives. The Federal Republic articulated a German national identity on the basis of economic strength, social consensus, and *Verfassungspatriotismus*, a concept coined by political scientist Dolf Sternberger, picked up by politicians, and championed by left-leaning philosopher Jürgen Habermas. "Constitutional patriotism" is most striking in its appeal to rationality rather than emotion, the latter of which the Nazis had so successfully employed. The German Democratic Republic in the East based its national identity on a paradigm that linked fascism and capitalism while employing state socialism as an alternative. Germans had much occasion to experiment with leveraging their identities as critical experts in questions of pacifism and totalitarianism domestically and abroad; concepts of anti-authoritarianism became a key to this approach. Many citizens made these practices their own, so much so that today— postwar, post-1960s, and post-1980s new social movements—deep scepticism about wars of aggression and other arguably neo-colonial politics continues to shape the national identity of many Germans.

Already by the mid-1960s, though, these projects of consciousness-raising had grown beyond the terms desired by actors such as NATO and German elites.

The unification of 1990 then made critical stances doubly undesirable from the new government's point of view. The Soviet Union's dissolution brought radical shifts in geopolitical interests, including the German role in those interests. A case in point is the public outcry around German engagement in Afghanistan. The critique—scepticism and dissent—that many Germans have learned to practise as a regular part of their lives engenders resistance to the globalist geopolitics in which Germany is now to play a more active role.

At the same time, shifts attendant to German unification and the official end of the Cold War have emboldened a politics of the new right that also finds its counterparts throughout Europe and in particular in the United States. A prime example comes in the recent media and historiographic discourses on what is often called the West German student movement and, in particular, treatments of one of its most prominent spokespersons, Rudi Dutschke, a figure who became contentious enough to suffer a politically motivated assassination attempt in 1968. These contemporary discourses emphasize links between protest and violence and protest and nationalism—with nationalism being a politically charged category due to German history. The rise of a German neo-conservatism that casts dissent as being antithetical to democracy is entangled with recent Dutschke scholarship that highlights both overt politicized violence and nationalism. Such protest and nationalism, I would argue, can be adequately assessed only in a transnational perspective.

The rewriting of 1960s dissent is part of a larger pattern. As Roger Woods reveals in his work on the loosely defined new right, when extremist positions are anchored by institutional support, they aim to and do shift political debates, in this case shaping more mainstream agendas of German normalization. In his analysis Woods argues that the German new right has been underestimated and remains little understood because it has been analyzed solely as a movement engaged in the formal political system. Extremist and radical parties such as the National Democratic Party of Germany (Nationaldemokratische Partei Deutschlands—NPD), German People's Union (Deutsche Volksunion—DVU), and Die Republikaner influence and are influenced by the new right, although their precise relationships are contested. Woods emphasizes that this phenomenon is more than a matter of political organizations. It includes publishing houses, media outlets, and think tanks, that is, "institutions of ideological production."[4] So, for instance, "the far-Right political party *Die Republikaner* is associated with the journal *Junge Freiheit*; the Kassel-based Thule Seminar, a think-tank run by the journalist Pierre Krebs, publishes the journal *Elemente*; and the Institut für Staatspolitik, a think-tank founded in 2000 and run by journalist Karlheinz Weissmann and former *Junge Freiheit* editor Goetz Kubitschek, publishes the journal *Sezession*."[5] Woods argues that new right supporters believe in the importance of winning hearts and minds through culture.[6] Using Antonio Gramsci's ideas against themselves, conservative and rightist cultural institutions thus further their aims for cultural hegemony in Germany.[7] Through its activities, the new right influences normalization, and this is where reassessments of the 1960s also play out.

The normalization of German national identity involves multiple reassessments of history. What turned out to be preparations for the discursive re-creation of Germany post-unification came under public scrutiny in the 1980s, as they appeared in the political register with the visit of President Ronald Reagan and Chancellor Kohl to the Kolmeshöhe war cemetery near Bitburg, and in the realm of public intellectual discourse through what became known as the Historians' Debate. The state visit to the graves of Hitler's elite SS troops was interpreted as relativizing, even honouring, Nazi actions. The Historians' Debate involved attempts to relativize the Holocaust by suggesting that Germany's actions during World War II were primarily about fighting Soviet Communism. In recent years, normalization narratives have been characterized by an emphasis on Germans as victims. For instance, scholarship and popular culture have taken up wartime experiences such as the German flight from Eastern Europe and the Allied bombings of Dresden from the perspectives of German civilians.

How do such narratives function in the contemporary political landscape? With the passing of those generations who lived through World War II, many Germans and non-Germans may tend to agree with this move towards reinterpreting the fascist past. They may agree that this pillar of Europe should shoulder the responsibilities of a "mature" nation, including building a larger professional army that participates in military action abroad and taking a permanent position on the U.N. Security Council. They may deem it impossible for Germany to take on these roles without normalization. Others see this shift as pragmatic and voluntary and as the end of a unique opportunity engendered by the fascist legacy. They see an evisceration of the historical and constitutional frameworks that had enabled Germans to take positions that resist power politics. Moreover, without the GDR as a counterweight, post-1990 Germany has experienced erosions of the citizen welfare state and the social consensus model. Many see these shifts as impoverishments for Germany, Europe, and the international community.

The rearticulations of specifically German histories have been coupled with reassessments of German national identity. The fallout from the Historians' Debate included an appeal in 2000 by the mainstream conservative party, the Christian Democrats (CDU), for a German "lead culture" (*Leitkultur*) to which all citizens and migrants were to aspire and assimilate. *Leitkultur* is not a new idea; it extends far back into German history and is imbricated in Nazi culture.[8] Considered against this backdrop, recent statements such as those of President

Horst Köhler are striking because they reclaim notions of the German homeland (*Heimat*) as the basis of German national identity. Significantly, one of Köhler's proclamations was at the core of his *Laudatio* for the Nobel Laureate Günter Grass, one of the postwar Group 47 (*Gruppe 47*) authors commonly referred to as the conscience of Germany.[9] Köhler's speech gathered diversely left-wing and anti-fascist artists, such as another Group 47 writer, Uwe Johnson, East German luminary Christa Wolf, and New German Cinema director Alexander Kluge alongside the conservative and arguably anti-Jewish Martin Walser, under a unitary rubric of *Heimat* writers. This categorization belies the profoundly critical relationship to German national identity found in the texts of the aforementioned left-leaning intellectuals as well as in those of Grass himself. Köhler's statement is illocutionary—it seeks itself to "make *Heimat* a useable word." Immediately following this strategic classification, a self-deprecating humour coupled with a more precise articulation of Köhler's conceptual agenda highlights awareness of the risks involved in thus pushing the conceptual envelope:

> Don't worry, I don't want to declare all of the Founding Children of the German postwar literature *Heimat* writers. Moreover, the writing of literary history is not my office. Can it not, however, also be that in this literature a relationship to *Heimat* shows itself that is much stronger than is generally seen and perhaps noticed by the authors themselves? Precisely through their critical work, precisely through their often painful and merciless quarrel with the past, the word *Heimat* has become a useable word again— and also a literary motif, not less important than societal criticism and political engagement. And could not the mourning about that which has been lost have influenced the critical stance of writers and artists at least as strongly as the anger and the shame for the crimes and guilt?[10]

In Köhler's iteration, the self-examination, constitutional patriotism, and anti-fascism that so many artists developed for decades as alternatives to National Socialist nationalism is instrumentalized to posit a continuity between the traditions upon which the NS built and today's new tradition of nationalism. Köhler's recent speech at an annual "day of Heimat," a commemoration of the postwar German flight from the East that is organized by expellees themselves, called on Germans to take Poland's concerns about German claims on Polish land seriously.[11] Yet the German president's presence at the festivities can also be seen as validating the positions of the expellees. An exhibit organized by these Expellee Associations (Vertriebene Verbände) placed their miseries on an equal footing to the suffering of Jews during World War II.[12] Such rearticulations of national identity participate in the normalization of Germany. They help underwrite media and scholarly articulations of linkages between the West Berlin anti-authoritarians situated around the activities and thought of Rudi Dutschke and organizations such as the Red Army Faction (RAF) and 2 June movement—groups that killed people for political reasons.

It speaks to the divisiveness of political protest that the media reception of this student-led group has not changed significantly since 1967–68—when escalations included the shootings of protesters. Press coverage links the West Berlin anti-authoritarians to violence along lines of political orientation. Thus, for instance, newspapers and journals of the conservative West Berlin Springer publishing house were and are more likely to label student protesters "terrorists" than are more left-leaning German publications.[13] Recent debates around the renaming of Koch Street to Rudi Dutschke Street show the same trend. Belinda Davis points out that while media and government sources employed the label of terrorism strategically as early as 1967 to characterize all types of left-oriented protest actions, they demonstrated a higher tolerance for right-oriented activism. For Davis, moreover, the tendency of scholars working on left activism to hyperbolically distance themselves from their subjects points to the success of the (West) German government at "tarring 'the Left,' including Social Democrats, with the same brush, with ongoing chilling effects."[14]

The relative stability of media reporting contrasts with changes in scholarly reception. Academic work has generally differentiated between the disruptive public protests characteristic of activist movements and political violence that could promote the death of individuals. An example in the case of Dutschke is the well-respected biography by Ulrich Chaussy.[15] The relative consensus based on years of research and debate is being weakened. For instance, a long-time opponent of the new left, Gerd Langguth, now states that its violence has always been of concern for him.[16] Michaela Karl's recent Dutschke biography also directly links the student movement and violence.[17] Sociologist Wolfgang Kraushaar's move to trace ideological connections between the thinking of Dutschke and the RAF has spurred the largest quarrels.[18] It has not escaped the notice of erstwhile student movement participants and scholars that the title of a recent volume does not separate the topics even with commas.[19] Kraushaar's own misgivings about and eventual submission of his contribution for the volume at the urgings of Jan Philipp Reemtsma, his generally laissez-faire employer at the Hamburg Institute for Social Research, also remind us of material influences on the research in this area, as in other realms of scholarship.

Overall, work on the relationship between violence and the student movement has shifted in tenor from the differentiated psychoanalytic/sociological analyses of scholars such as Heide Berndt and encyclopedia historiographies (for example, by Siegward Lönnendonker, Bernd Rabehl, and Jochen Staadt), to texts that bring the dissent of the late 1960s into close resonance with armed resistance movements of the 1970s: Butz Peters's *Deathly Mistake* (*Tödlicher Irrtum*) and Wolfgang Kraushaar's *The RAF and Left Terrorism* (*Die RAF and der linke Terrorismus*) and *The Bomb in the Jewish Community Centre* (*Die Bombe im Jüdischen Gemeindehaus*), for example.[20] While *The Bomb* is in many ways the careful work so characteristic of Kraushaar and the Hamburg Institute, at certain points the argument resorts to an elision of positions that are critical of Israeli policy and positions that are anti-Jewish. Indeed, Kraushaar's is a more benign version of U.S. historian Jeffrey Herf's more recent work that labels much of the German new left anti-Jewish because of its criticism of Israel beginning in 1967.[21] These examples highlight connections between Zionist sympathies and the characterization of the West German new left as violent and anti-Jewish; they also remind us that contemporary politics writes contemporary historiography. The elision also illustrates a tendency to employ the nation-state as an axiomatic basis of identity.

Loyalties and identification are at issue here. Langguth for one states directly that his concern with dissent is its potential to destabilize national structures.[22] His position takes the nation-state as a basic societal structure independent of the relationship between governance and governed. After September 11, definitions of terrorism that categorically dismiss the possibility of state terrorism have again been importantly problematized.[23] Davis juxtaposes the characterization of extragovernmental political opposition as forms of terrorism and the German government's increasing pressure on dissenters that encouraged violent responses on the part of those dissenters.[24] She also reminds us that from the perspective of many, such political identification was much more transnational than national.

Davis's point about transnational alliances sheds light on the West Berlin anti-authoritarians who grouped themselves around the figure of Rudi Dutschke in relation to their particular interpretations of the national. Understanding their nationalism is crucial to understanding their negotiation of political violence as well as to confirming that charges of anti-Jewish sentiment are misplaced. While the anti-authoritarians grouped around Dutschke did not foreground their political sympathies with the Palestinian cause,[25] their positions on the Middle East were based on their particular conceptions of nationalism. Dutschke's sense of nationalism is fundamental. Its relevance is exemplified by his erstwhile colleague and later rival, Bernd Rabehl, who now casts Dutschke as a nationalist in terms similar to those articulated by Köhler—that is, as someone who valued a homogeneous German *Heimat* shored up by *Leitkultur* and roots extending unbroken into a long Germanic history. Rabehl's claim works to delegitimize the dissent of the anti-authoritarians and by extension political dissent more generally, for if political violence is contested, nationalism is rejected by most left-leaning Germans.

Rabehl's depiction of Dutschke as a German nationalist shores up and is informed by new-right logics. He has followed public statements in extreme right circles[26] with publication in *Junge Freiheit* and *Sezession*[27] and in a book, *Rudi Dutschke, Revolutionary in Divided Germany (Rudi Dutschke. Revolutionär im geteilten Deutschland)*.[28] For Rabehl, Dutschke's "national/ist revolutionary" (*Nationrevolutionär*) agenda rejected Allied influence in Germany and referenced an explicitly German tradition.[29] Rabehl asserts that Dutschke's vision for national emancipation involved a repeat of the revolution of 1848 for "both halves" of Germany.[30] Rabehl clearly has Germanic pasts in mind as he rehearses the history and function of national emancipation from the European feudal period to the present.[31] Further, Rabehl states that for Dutschke such "national consciousness" (*nationale Selbstbewußtsein*) was a means of overcoming the "nationalistic deformations" of "Stalinism, NS dictatorship, and the occupation of Europe" (*nationalistischen Deformationen ... Stalinism, NS-Diktatur, und die Besetzung Europas*).[32] Rabehl's alignment of these three historical situations reveals a new-right ideology.[33] Drawing on Woods's argument, we might also question Rabehl's asserted distinction between a pre-Nazi and a National Socialist national sentiment and instead consider their connections and rearticulations in new-right paradigms. Clearly, Rabehl's nationalism is not Dutschke's.

While Rabehl's contention that Dutschke was interested in traditional German nationalism is far off the mark, Dutschke did seek to redefine national identity for a reconfigured nation-state. Rabehl's narrow definition of nationalism simply precludes an adequate assessment of the nationalism that the anti-authoritarians had in mind. The youth around Dutschke rejected dominant pre-war, wartime, and postwar conceptions of German nationalism, as well as alternatives proffered by the established German new left.[34] Until recently only Wolfgang Kraushaar has seriously engaged with the anti-authoritarians' definition of nationalism, arguing that Dutschke saw it as a step towards internationalism. However, Kraushaar remains within the German context precisely where it is important to link Dutschke's nationalism with his interest in Third World solidarity.[35]

Dutschke's Third Worldism and his ideas for German and global emancipation were based on what Michael Hardt and Antonio Negri have subsequently called "subaltern nationalism," in juxtaposition to "bourgeois nationalism."[36] For Hardt and Negri, "bourgeois nationalism" is employed by an already established state structure to control its own citizens and other polities, while "subaltern nationalism" unites people in a push for national independence.[37] Dutschke's interest in Frantz Fanon, Fidel Castro, and Che Guevara was based on his sense of alliance with the Third World through subaltern nationalism; and with that connection he sought Third World models that could be legitimately employed in Europe, starting with West Berlin. Through identification across subaltern nationalism, the West Berlin anti-authoritarians could look seriously at events such as the Cuban Revolution as blueprints for change in Europe. A German engagement included careful deliberation of possibilities for translation northwards, such as visits to Cuban congresses in which such topics were discussed, and study of texts by Third World intellectuals.[38] Dutschke's attempt to map the situation in Cuba onto West Berlin demonstrates the significance that subaltern nationalism had for his vision of radical change in West Berlin. The anti-authoritarians conceived of themselves in solidarity with the bloody Vietnam struggle, yet it was by employing notions of subaltern nationalism that they could imagine a West Berlin revolution that would be as quick and reputedly bloodless as the emergence of a post-Batista Cuba.

As it is, the issue of transnational identification remains undertheorized, in part because of a tradition that studies dissent primarily within national frameworks. Broadening the scope of analysis reveals the importance of cross-border identification and its attendant strategies. In the case of Rudi Dutschke, such a transnational perspective allows us to better understand the anti-authoritarians' negotiation of violence in the opposition, as well as helping us clearly see that Dutschke's nationalism resists the (neo)conservative nationalisms with which today's Germany continues to grapple.

Gary Kinsman

7

# THE CANADIAN NATIONAL SECURITY WAR ON QUEERS AND THE LEFT

**In Canada** in the 1960s—and then into the 1970s and beyond—national security campaigns against lesbians and gay men led to the purging of hundreds of suspected lesbians and gay men from the public service and the military.[1] These campaigns, though, may have had an unexpected result. The opening up of gay and lesbian social spaces, and the queer talk in these spaces, provided the social basis for the emergence of a resistance that obstructed the progress of the surveillance. In the process queers became positioned not as "passive" victims but as active agents. Then too, in the 1970s another turnaround took place: by coming out more publicly, gay liberation and lesbian feminism directly targeted the national security campaigns against queers, again undermining the campaigns. Left activism in general also played an integral role in these developments: one of the reasons for the surveillance of early gay and lesbian groups by the Royal Canadian Mounted Police (RCMP) was the involvement of left activists in queer organizing. It was at least partly the surveillance of the left, and especially of the League for Socialist Action, a Trotskyist group,[2] that led the RCMP into spying on gay organizing.

My use of the "sixties" is not simply temporal. I reject standard definitions of the sixties as ending in 1969 or 1970 and instead take up an autonomist Marxist perspective of the sixties as defined by a global cycle of social and class struggles that includes Third World and national liberation movements, working-class insurgencies, antiwar, anti-racist, student, and youth movements, and the re-emergence of feminism and gay/lesbian movements, all of which shape and condition each other. The "sixties" is used here in relation to a particular composition of global struggle that stretched into the 1970s.[3]

Gay and lesbian organizing shifted in the 1960s and early 1970s from the homophile claim to tolerance through reliance on liberal professional experts towards a more militant approach influenced by the Black Power movements and the new left.[4] This tendency erupted in the New York City Stonewall riots against police repression in 1969, which were quickly followed by the emergence of Gay Liberation Fronts modelled on the National Liberation Front then fighting against the U.S. military in Vietnam. Gay Liberation Front activists saw themselves as part of a broader revolutionary movement. Profoundly shaped by the feminist movements, gay liberation challenged heterosexism and attempted to undermine sexism. As lesbians continued to experience sexism within gay organizations they established their own lesbian feminist groups and movement.

This early gay/lesbian organizing was not simply influenced by the left; it was also part of the broader left composition of struggle, including challenges to the heterosexism encountered in major parts of the left. A recognition of this connection makes it possible to recover links between the left and queers, thinking left and queer together. From the vantage point of our historical present, where most of these connections have been broken and much mainstream gay organizing operates in the orbit of neo-liberalism, these relationships have been actively forgotten.[5] We need, then, to work against the social organization of forgetting of the connections between the left and queers and participate in *remembering* this history. Capitalism and oppression rule in part through the social organization of forgetting based on the annihilation of our historical memories.[6] This social organization of forgetting is a crucial way in which ruling relations work in our society so that we no longer remember the struggles that won the social gains, social programs, social spaces, and rights that we often take for granted in the present. Moreover, this is also how strategies of "respectability" gain hegemony in queer communities, a process related to class formation and the emergence of new middle-class queer strata.[7] We forget where we have come from, our histories are not recorded and communicated, and we are denied the social literacy that allows us to relive our pasts and to grasp our present. Key to this is the lack of remembering of queer struggles and resistance, including the connections between our struggles and the left.

**Commie,** *pinko, fag.* These words were scrawled on my locker and used as a greeting in the halls of the high school I attended in the early 1970s. I was involved in the radical left as a member of the Young Socialists and later the Revolutionary Marxist Group, so the "commie" part made some sense to me. I never understood where "pinko" came from. The sole basis for the "fag" part seemed to be my refusal to laugh at anti-gay jokes that were all-pervasive at the school.[8] A certain type of "cutting out" operation[9] was mobilized against me as I was socially excluded from regular forms of "normal" heterosexual interaction. I was during these years beginning to explore my sexuality and starting to come out to myself and to others as gay. So I did become an anti-Stalinist "commie fag."

My interest in the national security campaigns against queers flows from my explorations of this association between commies and fags, and this association was forged in important ways during the years of those campaigns against queers and through the very real connections of some queer activists with sections of the left.[10]

The Canadian national security war[11] against queers involved not just purges but also extensive surveillance, interrogations, and the keeping of lists of thousands of names of "suspected" homosexuals. It included an attempt to develop a "fruit machine" detection technology to "scientifically" determine who was homosexual so that anyone thus so determined could be denied government employment.[12] These national security campaigns had died down by the later 1970s in most of the public service but continued at high levels of intensity in the military, the RCMP, and then the Canadian Security Intelligence Service (CSIS) until the late 1980s and early 1990s. At the same time, by the early 1960s the formation of queer networks had produced the basis for forms of non-cooperation and even resistance to the practices of the RCMP.

# The Social Basis of Queer Resistance

At first the RCMP apparently did achieve some success in getting homosexual "informants" to supply the names of other homosexuals,[13] but soon signs of non-cooperation and individual and pre-political resistance appeared.[14] In 1962–63 the Force reported: "During the past fiscal year the homosexual screening program ... was hindered by the lack of cooperation on the part of homosexuals approached as sources. Persons of this type, who had hitherto been our most consistent and productive informers, have exhibited an increasing reluctance to identify their homosexual friends and associates."[15] The subjects began to place loyalty to their friends above that of "national security." In 1963–64 the RCMP reported, "During the year the investigation to identify homosexuals employed in or by the Federal Government resulted in initial interviews with twenty-one homosexuals, four of whom proved to be uncooperative, and re-interviews with twenty-two previously cooperative homosexuals, seven of whom declined to extend further cooperation."[16]

"David," a professional and not a public servant who was involved in gay networks in Ottawa by 1964, described in part the other side of this "lack of cooperation."[17] His involvement in the security investigations began when a friend gave the RCMP his name during a park sweep of one of the cruising areas for men interested in sex with men. The RCMP would threaten to lay "criminal" charges against the men they apprehended unless the men gave the names of other homosexuals.[18] David was interrogated by the RCMP, he was followed, and his place was searched. David told us about the RCMP surveillance of bars where gay men congregated: "We even knew occasionally that there was somebody in some police force or some investigator who would be sitting in a bar.... And you would see someone with a ... newspaper held right up and if you ... looked real closely you could find him holding behind the newspaper a camera and these people were photographing everyone in the bar."[19]

David was speaking about his experiences of surveillance around 1964, in the basement tavern at Ottawa's Lord Elgin Hotel, one of the major gathering places for gay men in Ottawa. His story is also a remarkable example of resistance against police spying: "We always knew that when you saw someone with a newspaper held up in front of their face ... that somebody would take out something like a wallet and do this sort of thing [like snapping a photo] and then of course everyone would then point over to the person you see and of course I'm sure that the person hiding behind the newspaper knew that he had been found out."[20]

Rather than diving under the tables or running for cover, these men exposed the undercover agents. David's story reveals not only national security spying but also the resistance to it in the 1960s. We get a clear sense of awareness of the security campaign in the networks that David participated in. This story and other stories of non-cooperation we collected begin to flesh out the social organization of the "non-cooperation" mentioned in the RCMP texts. The response in the bar suggests that people were able to move beyond simply exposing the officer; they were also able to make fun of him and the security and police campaigns, using humour and camp as a way of surviving them. Camp was a cultural form produced by gay men during these years to manage and negotiate the contradictions between their experiences of the world as gays and the institutionalized heterosexuality they encountered. A crucial part of this cultural production was to denaturalize normality and heterosexuality by making fun of it.[21]

The social basis for this resistance came from broader forms of talk and advice in the gay networks of 1960s Ottawa. There was a clear sense that those who did give names to the security police were to be shunned and ostracized. The resistance was rooted in a sense of group solidarity in response to the attacks of the national security police and the recognition that at least some of the security strategies could be disrupted. People had enough of a sense of themselves and the networks they participated in to engage in these acts of defiance. At the same time this was a limited resistance, and individuals had little social power in relation to the RCMP. For many there were very few options if they were caught in the web of the security campaign.

# Surveillance of Queer Organizing: "Radical Lesbians" and "Gay Political Activists"

Forms of resistance expanded in the 1970s with the emergence of gay liberation and lesbian feminist movements that directly targeted national security policies, including the exclusion of lesbians and gay men from the Canadian public service and military. These gay and lesbian organizations themselves now became a target of RCMP surveillance.[22] There was a shift in the security regime response, which moved beyond a focus on the public service and military to gay and lesbian activists themselves and the new "threat" they represented.

Gay liberation developed as part of a broader left composition of struggle in the Canadian context that transformed earlier forms of gay organizing. It was based on the self-organization of queer people ourselves and the rejection of relying on liberal experts as authorities. Rejecting the relations of the closet, this activism focused on coming out and visibility. The very logic of this movement undermined the threat of "blackmail" and the pressures that the security regime had used to compel people to give them names. As many of the people whom Patrizia Gentile and I interviewed put it, the only people who attempted to blackmail them were the RCMP, who tried to force them to give the names of other gay men and lesbians. As more people came out, the threat of blackmail began to lose its effectiveness. From 1971 on the RCMP encountered a new security "threat" who was no longer afraid of being out as queer.

The RCMP was also led into the gay movement through its pre-existing surveillance of the left. In this case that work involved the Trotskyist League for Socialist Action (LSA), a group that the RCMP had infiltrated.[23] Released RCMP documents make clear that many of the first RCMP references to gay organizing come from its surveillance of the LSA. This includes the Force's initial knowledge about the August 1971 first gay demonstration in Ottawa on Parliament Hill, which was also placed under RCMP surveillance.

In the United States national security campaigns against gay men and lesbians in the 1950s and 1960s had led the Trotskyist Socialist Workers Party, to which the LSA was linked, to come to define lesbian and gay members as "security threats" to the party and to exclude queer people from membership.[24] This

response to the national security campaigns helped to produce the heterosexism that early gay and lesbian liberation activists encountered on the left. In contrast the initial response of the LSA and its youth group, the Young Socialists (YS), to the emergence of gay liberation was positive. A number of gay members of the LSA and YS in Toronto and Vancouver got actively involved in early gay liberation groups, including helping to organize the 1971 Parliament Hill demonstration. Often this involvement was undertaken without the expressed approval of the LSA leadership as these activists tried to push the organization to more active support of lesbian and gay liberation. This did not stop the RCMP from viewing the LSA and Trotskyists more generally as "infiltrating" the gay movement, implying that gay/lesbian LSA activists were not actively involved in building the movement but were trying to use it for their own purposes. "Infiltration" operated as a code word, mandating RCMP spying.

After I left the YS I became a member of the more "left" Trotskyist Revolutionary Marxist Group (RMG), and the RCMP also investigated the involvement of that group in the gay and lesbian movements.[25] The Force also explored

connections between the New Marxist Institute and the gay Marxist study group in which I was also involved.

The RCMP also engaged in surveillance of the feminist movement as a national security threat.[26] As part of this spying it quickly uncovered lesbians. RCMP surveillance of the Toronto Wages for Housework campaign, for instance, led the Force to discover that (surprise, surprise) the supporters and members of Wages for Housework included many lesbians. The involvement of lesbian activists in Wages for Housework may also have been what attracted RCMP attention. Wages for Housework was a campaign based on the importance of the domestic and reproductive labour that women do for the production of capitalist social and economic relations. It called for women to be paid for all the work that they did, including for housework. The demand for a wage was seen as a way of challenging capitalist relations and of trying to create more social and economic power for working-class women.[27]

A 1976 RCMP report on the Toronto Wages for Housework Committee (TWHC) was particularly interested in the organization because it was part of an "international network" and because the "leadership cadre within the T.W.H.C. is composed of radical Marxist feminists." The report pointed out that "there is also a high concentration of radical lesbians in the T.W.H.C. who have their own sub-group called Wages Due (WD)."[28] The involvement of "radical lesbians" is one reason cited for establishing surveillance of this group.

The RCMP account of TWHC and WD is informed by a sexist and hetero-sexist social standpoint. The report points out that the "T.W.H.C.'s membership has been described by [blanked out] as being 'Born Losers' who in appearance and attitude are both lower working class and welfare cases and involved in living alternative life-styles [blanked out]." The statement clearly indicates the class standpoint of the RCMP investigations. A following comment emphasizes the physical appearance and employment of the women: "This is especially true of the radical lesbians in W.D., who take a perverse pride in de-feminizing themselves by cultivating the dirty and unkept appearance. The general employment level of the membership is either menial office work [blanked out] the social service field ie. social workers or unemployed. Also most seem to be single and just about everyone is under 30 years of age."[29]

Here the anti-working-class and anti-poor perspective combines with a particular gender standpoint defending the hegemonic practices of the discourse of heterosexual femininity.[30] We also see a generational coding of radicalism in this text. The lesbians in WD are defined as taking a perverse pride in "de-feminizing" themselves because they construct and perform their femininity differently and engage in specifically lesbian cultural practices of gender performance.[31]

In their conclusions on the TWHC, the investigators argue that the members "do represent an excellent example of Unaligned Marxist group operating in the extremes of the Feminist Movement. Thus, our present low level of coverage is going to be maintained on this organization."[32] It is due not only to their radical feminism and Marxism but also to the "radical lesbians" in the group that the RCMP justified continuing surveillance.

The queer activists confronted by the RCMP in the 1970s were very different from the more isolated individuals that the Force encountered in the 1960s. These activists had different characteristics, and they were part of a broader left composition of struggle. In trying to comprehend and manage this new form of activism the RCMP wrote about a new group of "gay political activists" defined by their youth and public affirmations of homosexuality. A 1976 report on gay groups in Toronto stated, "Gay Political Activists are predominantly young, ranging in age from 20-25 years old, and unlike the older homosexuals they are eager to display their homosexuality through such acts as demonstrating."[33] This highlighting of the youth of these new activists is crucial; it codes this new activism along generational lines and as distinct from the gays encountered previously,

COMING

84

who most often were not "out." The politics of coming out and this movement created new problems and obstacles for the RCMP.

The same report noted, "Our interest has been in those gay groups which are controlled and directed by Gay Political Activists." This conceptualization of "gay political activists" allowed the RCMP to begin to differentiate between different gay groups in terms of their potential "security" interest. By 1976 more moderate or "liberal" groups like the Community Homophile Association of Toronto (CHAT) were no longer felt to be much of a threat, even though in the early 1970s they were closely monitored, because they were not controlled by "gay political activists." On the other hand, groups identified with "gay political activists" came under more intense surveillance. One RCMP assessment report of the Gay Alliance Towards Equality (GATE) in Vancouver even produced an argument for creating a new "liberal" gay group that could cut across the influence of that established "gay political activist" organization.[34]

"Gay political activists" were seen as being more open to influence from left groups like the LSA, YS, and RMG. One RCMP report stated: "The Gays have received little public support.... However, certain of the ultraleft groups, mainly Trotskyists, have been involved in gay groups in an attempt to radicalize them. (It has been found that those ultra left members involved in gay groups were also homosexuals.)"[35] Because of the lack of popular support, gay activists were seen as being more susceptible to influence by "ultra left" groups, especially given that these groups have gay members.

The RCMP found the "gay political activists" to be more open to a critique of capitalist social relations because of the opposition from mainstream society. Although the investigator concluded that there was a lack of popular support for lesbian and gay liberation, there was a failure to recognize the important part that state policies such as the national security campaigns play in organizing heterosexual hegemony. This lack of popular support apparently opened up a space for Marxist influence: "This in part explains why some of the gay political activists have been increasingly taking on a Marxist analysis of their position, equating homosexuals as an oppressed minority in a capitalist system. (They fail to bring up the point that in the Soviet Union and Cuba homosexuals are imprisoned.)" What the spies do not recognize is that a critical Marxist analysis of our social position might actually be a good way of grasping the social relations at the root of queer oppression. The reference to the continuing oppression of gays and lesbians in the USSR shows that the RCMP officers involved had very little understanding of Trotskyism, given that Trotskyists were critical of the undemocratic bureaucratic and family policies in that country.[36] While the Cuban example is more complex and has a different history, many Trotskyists were also critical of the Cuban regime.[37]

The report defined "gay political activists" by citing three major character-istics: their youth; being out and committed to public visibility and "pressure" tactics"; and an openness to left and Marxist ideas[38]—all of them features of the left composition of struggle that these queer activists were part of. The Force was suggesting that these activists, along with "radical lesbians," represented a "security" problem.

The emergence of gay liberation and lesbian feminist movements and the growth of public queer communities in the 1970s undermined the basis of the national security campaigns against queers. Older regulatory strategies no longer worked, as queer activists were willing to be public and open. At the same time it was not until the 1990s that the Canadian national security campaigns against queers came to an end. The campaigns would have a lasting legacy, constructing queer workers as "unreliable" and "suspect." New targets for the national secur-ity campaigns would include global justice and anti-poverty protesters as part of campaigns against "subversion" and Muslims and Arab-identified people, and other people of colour, including queers of colour, in the context of the "war on terror."[39]

The history of queers and surveillance in the 1960s and 1970s reminds us of a time when queer struggles were part of a broader left composition of struggle and when it was possible to think queer and left together. That thinking is much more difficult now in the era of same-gender marriage and gay respectability.[40] But perhaps this investigation can give us some insights into how queer activists could become part of a new left composition and cycle of struggle. The exploration also reminds us of the power of resistance. Even in the very constrained circum-stances of the 1960s, queer non-cooperation and resistance were able to force shifts in regulatory and policing strategies. In the 1970s lesbian and gay activism and community formation undermined the very basis of the national security campaigns against queers. We can continue to act to undermine national security forms of oppression and other forms of social power. We get a sense of our own power *to do*,[41] of our own capacities for change, which was a crucial resource for social transformation in the sixties and can still be so in our historical present.

Guido Panvini    8

# NEO-FASCISM, THE EXTRAPARLIAMENTARY LEFT WING, AND THE BIRTH OF ITALIAN TERRORISM

**The clash** between neo-fascism and the extraparliamentary left wing in the 1960s–1970s in Italy has never been the subject of a specific study. There is no reconstruction of this theme in journalism or in memoirs, even though writers have produced plenty about the political violence of the 1970s. References to the clash between neo-fascism and the extraparliamentary left wing are even rarer in Italian historiography, which has generally dealt very little with political violence in the 1970s. Through my research I am attempting to plug this gap. My project is to explore the reasons, the dynamics, and the aims of both sides involved in this clash, emphasizing the political cultures, representations, speeches, and violent practices of the protagonists. My initial assumption, which gradually became confirmed during the research, is that the widespread violence between the far right and far left not only produced the atmosphere within which the choice of terrorism then took shape, but also created these very conditions through a progressive *militarization* of a political struggle.

## Stages, Procedures, and Protagonists

The origins of this story can be traced back to the crisis of the centre-left government, supported by the Christian Democrat and Socialist parties, which began with the result of the general elections of May 19, 1968, and exploded in all its drama with the increasingly stronger student protest and mobilization of workers in the troubled autumn of 1969. The far right and the extraparliamentary left wing perceived this moment as a crisis in the system and intervened to radicalize the events. Violence became, therefore, a strategic choice, an instrument that both the neo-fascists and far left used to exacerbate the atmosphere of tension and make the political and social conflict degenerate.

What was put into practice was a strategy of conflict aimed at removing democratic institutions and eliminating political opponents. The far right and far left perceived each other as vanguards ready to eliminate any opponent who was on the verge of taking power: the neo-fascists saw the extraparliamentary left wing as an extension of the Communist Party, while the far left considered neo-fascists to be part of a large plan within the Christian Democrat Party and the state to carry out an authoritarian change in the country. This mutual fear caused any possible convergences, which had fleetingly brought the right-wing and left-wing youth movements closer together in the wake of the student protest, first to grow weak and then to disappear.

The polarization of the clash took place following the massacre in Piazza Fontana, Milan, on December 12, 1969, when an attack carried out by a neo-fascist terrorist organization linked to parts of the Italian secret service killed a number of people. So began the "strategy of tension" or, rather, the campaign of attacks carried out by right-wing terrorist groups with the aim not only of preventing the Communist Party from entering the government but also of stopping the advance of the social movements.

The violence took on its most dramatic forms during the regional elections of June 1970. The election campaign was tormented by neo-fascists and the extraparliamentary left wing, and for the first time both Black and Red terrorist groups intervened too, determined to influence the vote. This strategy was repeated during the local and regional elections of June 1971 and during the general election in May 1972. The toll was heavy: dozens of election rallies turned into real moments of guerrilla warfare, with the first victims of the clash coming on both sides. Rumours circulated about an imminent coup by the armed forces. News about the failed Golpe Borghese, a coup attempted by the neo-fascists and by a faction of the armed forces in December 1970, together with the worsening of the social conflict and the violent degeneration of public demonstrations, led the extraparliamentary left-wing groups and neo-fascists to adopt increasingly radical repertoires for action. With the increase in political tension, the violence became more specialized and systematic.

The early election of May 6, 1972, and the formation of a moderate, central government supported by the Christian Democrat and Liberal parties caught both the far right and far left off guard. Despite repeated attacks, parliamentary democracy remained firmly in place. A new agreement between the Christian Democrats and the Communist Party appeared on the horizon.

In view of these scenarios political extremism entered a crisis, with further radicalization of violence. This phase was marked by the assassination on May 17, 1972, of the chief of police, Luigi Calabresi, whom the extraparliamentary left wing held responsible for the death of Giuseppe Pinelli, an anarchist railway man who was accused, unfairly, of having planted the bomb in Piazza Fontana. Pinelli had fallen from a window of the local police headquarters in Milan. Another significant event was the massacre of Peteano on May 31, during which several Carabinieri died in an attack carried out by a neo-fascist terrorist cell. The extraparliamentary left-wing groups were split over the possibility of an imminent armed struggle with the state, but a part of their base had already been seduced by this prospect and moved closer to the terrorist groups with which they had shared the violent struggle against neo-fascists. Likewise, the radical right-wing groups criticized the Italian Social Movement, the most important Italian party of the far right, for not having known how to break with the democratic system; many neo-fascist militants, the youngest especially, left the Italian Social Movement and went underground, something that many of them had already become accustomed to during the clashes with the far left.

# The Organization of Violence in the Far Right Wing

Between 1968 and 1969 the Italian Social Movement explicitly adopted violence as a central political strategy. Assuming precise public responsibilities regarding the use of violence, the party formulated a strategy of conflict based on deterrence. Amidst threats of a head-on collision, what the party was really reinforcing was a position for negotiation. The use of violence was thus adapted to a fluctuating situation that would open up to different scenarios ranging from the radicalization of social conflict to the possibility of new elections. Violence became a resource that could be used in a hypothetical situation of irreversible crisis in the country. In this way the Italian Social Movement consolidated its position as a point of reference in the neo-fascist area, while simultaneously aiming to build support that went beyond its traditional voters to include a middle class frightened by the economic and social crisis.

Lastly, the centrality of violence allowed an attack on the centre-left government and the Communist Party at the same time. The Italian Social Movement underlined the government's inability to tackle the problems of public order. The government, not the police force, was held responsible for any repression of the Italian Social Movement's actions. By dragging the Communists into an area of violent action, the party intended to discredit the Communist Party as a responsible force that could be part of the nation's government, while supplying a contrasting image of the Italian Social Movement as a staunch defender of a policy of order and public safety.

The ambiguity of this strategy emerged in the neo-fascists' complex relationship with student protest, where the use of violence was revealing its most ambiguous dynamics. On the one side was a head-on collision with the extraparliamentary groups; on the other revolutionary demands were recuperated and a violent anti-system mobilization was promoted. The oddness of the Italian Social Movement's policies continued until 1972. The openings towards the Christian Democrats and other anti-Communist forces for the formation of a government that would guarantee order and stability counterbalanced an increasingly strong organization of violence that was intended to delegitimize the centre-left government and indeed attack it with increasing frequency.

From the end of 1968, on the initiative of various far-right-wing movements, in many Italian cities groups and associations had formed that were ready to intervene on the side of the police force in the event of violent incidents during public protests. In 1969 the Italian Social Movement became these groups' most important referent by promoting a rationalization and reorganization of its own internal policing services. The Italian Social Movement, moreover, invited citizens to practise self-defence, thereby questioning the state's monopoly of violence and prompting dangerous centrifugal forces. That is exactly what happened on the occasion of Richard Nixon's visit to Rome on February 27 and 28,1969: in a city swarming with police officers neo-fascists clashed with Communist Party demonstrators who were protesting against the U.S. president's visit; and they stormed the university faculties, which were occupied by students of the movement, causing the death of a student.

The mobilization of the far right, therefore, expressed itself with a complex phenomenology in which conventional mobilization was interwoven with both violence on the streets and the actions of the more radical groups. The year 1969 was marked by continuous attacks—both demonstrative and non-demonstrative—on the premises of left-wing parties and partisan associations; attacks were carried out on police headquarters and the barracks of the Carabinieri or police force. Major attacks were carried out by neo-fascist terrorist groups on institutional offices; firearms were used against political opponents; paper bombs were thrown in front of occupied schools and universities.

Furthermore, the revolutionary violence of the far right became interwoven and mixed up with the plans of the "strategy of tension" for destabilization; but as far as widespread violence is concerned, it was not rare for the Italian Social Movement militants themselves and its youth organizations to be the main participants in the most violent acts, including acts of terrorism.

# The Radicalization of Violence in the Extraparliamentary Left Wing

The extraparliamentary left wing had a long theoretical tradition that exalted violence as its repertoire of action. The myth of insurrection had sedimented in the movements—a myth influenced by the memory of the Resistance, of the days of July 1960, the experience of the wars of decolonization in Africa and Asia, guerrilla warfare in South America, the fascination with Mao Tse-tung's thought, and the urban guerrilla warfare of Black Power in the ghettos of the large North American cities. In addition, there had been the experiences of the clashes between students and the police force, like the battle of Valle Giulia of March 1, 1968. Soon publications were issued to explain to people how they could equip themselves for clashes on the streets and during demonstrations. Such publications contained information ranging from how to use sticks properly, or how to use metal marbles and nails with three tips to stop being charged at by the police on horseback or in jeeps, right up to technical instructions on how to make Molotov cocktails. Consequently, the first internal policing services, equipped with helmets and sticks, appeared at extraparliamentary left-wing demonstrations and marches.

The clash between neo-fascists and the extraparliamentary left wing was therefore asymmetric: the far left controlled the demonstrations, while the neo-fascists continued to excel in the clashes on the streets.

It was in the conflict with the far right that the use of violence by extraparliamentary groups and movements revealed its most complex dynamics. Violence was used as a defence, but it was a defence that was not aimed at maintaining the status quo. Rather, it was aimed at causing a reaction that would turn the balance of strength upside down. These dynamics were evident early on in the student protest, as, for example, on the occasion of the neo-fascist punitive expedition against the occupied faculties at the University of Rome on March 16, 1968, which ended up with the besiegers being besieged. The borderline between defensive violence and offensive violence was therefore extremely faint.

The attacks of December 12, 1969, represented an important element of radicalization for the extraparliamentary left wing, but did not immediately cause an escalation of tension between the far right and far left; the actual detonator of the violence, in fact, was the terribly bitter election campaign that accompanied the birth of the regions. The Italian Social Movement rallies often caused left-wing parties and anti-fascist associations to intervene, especially in places where memories of the war of liberation were most vivid. On the other hand the branch offices of the left wing and trade-union offices were systematically attacked in a sort of revival of the "War of the Vexilla" that had characterized the fascist paramilitary squads of the 1920s. These actions actually took the form of a "ritual of conquest" designed to eradicate political opponents.

The Italian Social Movement rallies had a similar role: the choice of "Red" cities was an attempt to challenge the left not only in its own field, in the streets, but also on its own territory in order to get possession of that territory, even if only symbolically.

The reaction of the left-wing parties was not long in coming. Added to this was the participation of the extraparliamentary left wing, determined to prevent the political access of the neo-fascists. In fact, the extraparliamentary left wing saw the regional elections as an opportunity for confrontation with the far right and as a good chance to accelerate the crisis, which it resolved to worsen through violence on the streets. At this stage, therefore, came the militarization of the internal policing services, which were by now able to withstand clashes with both the police and political opponents. The shift towards a "black" trail of the judicial inquiries into the attacks of December 12, the revolts in Reggio Calabria in the summer of 1970 and in Aquila in February 1971, the demonstrations of the "Silent Majority" and the revelations of the attempted Golpe Borghese in March of the same year caused the extraparliamentary left wing to become even more radical. It was claimed that there was an organic relationship, strategically oriented towards the same aim, somewhere between the organized violence of the far right wing and neo-fascist terrorism. At that point, on the initiative of the extraparliamentary left-wing groups, "militant anti-fascism" was born as a response to the far right-wing political tendencies that were represented as planning and militarily organizing an offensive against revolutionary movements.

This vision was consolidated by an episode in which the people's reaction to a neo-fascist demonstration was distinguished by the spontaneity and extreme violence.

On July 30, 1970, several members of CISNAL (the Italian National Confederation of Workers, an extreme right-wing trade union) came to blows with some workers outside an Ignis factory on the outskirts of Trento; shortly afterwards some Italian Social Movement activists appeared on the scene. A messy fight broke out, which ended with three young workers being seriously injured. The people responsible for the wounding were captured immediately afterwards: the workers formed a long procession and forced the activists to walk to the city centre with signs around their necks—"proletarian stocks"—which said, "We are fascists, today we have stabbed three 3 Ignis workers, this is our policy in favour of workers." It was a crucial transition: violence became a moment of revolutionary training. Exemplary actions served to arouse the revolutionary potential in the population, inviting them to rebellion. The "proletarian stocks," in fact, were used as a model and repeated, both inside and outside factories, with the clear intention of provoking a similar reaction to what had happened in Trento. The far left party Lotta Continua, for example, ideally associated the events in Trento with the executions of collaborators at the hands of various guerrilla movements in Asia and South America and to similar events during the war of liberation—in effect issuing a warning intended for both neo-fascists and members of the police force. The glorification and imitation of the "proletarian stocks" as a method for the struggle caused Lotta Continua to use violence as an exemplar of action, employing gestures that had a strong symbolic significance to push the population into taking a revolutionary stance.

# The Radicalization of Violence in the Far Right Wing

In the early 1970s the far right wing cast the country's political struggle as a tireless defence against the assault by a predominant enemy on the brink of conquering the country. This representation caused the far right wing to radicalize its repertoires of action. It generated anxiety among the neo-fascists by stressing the presence of a mimetic and omnipresent enemy. It produced its "fifth column" effect, the strikes in factories, or unrest in the workplace and in the countryside, as acts of sabotage and guerrilla warfare organized by the Communist Party on the orders of the Soviet Union. The right-wing press actually presented the scenes of social upheaval as war fronts. The resulting anxiety led to an increase in the use of violence to "get rid of" supposedly hidden potential enemies. Hence the recurrent spread, in the far right press, of appeals and requests to readers to report on left-wing militants by means of photographs: the press promised to publish the photos together with names, surnames, and home addresses. The left-wing militants would thus be exposed to the risk of violent assaults. Soon afterwards the appeals turned into practice: real files emerged containing the names, distinguishing features, home addresses, telephone numbers, meeting places, and habits of left-wing militants. This practice had already been used by the youth associations within the Italian Social Movement in 1969, and it had long been part of the repertoire of action of the neo-fascists. Such procedures were common in the most radical far-right-wing circles, where street combat instruction manuals, often based on rules followed by military commandos, had circulated as far back as the mid-1960s.

Neo-fascist violence aimed to become more and more skilled and began to be premeditated and organized, with attacks on specific individuals at demonstrations, in the streets, and in schools, universities, and workplaces. The few studies that contain statistics on episodes of political violence in those years show that between 1969 and 1974 most acts were carried out by the far right,

*Neo-Fascism, the Extraparliamentary Left Wing, and the Birth of Italian Terrorism*

whose politics, therefore, became militarized, with its youngest militants being given more and more importance. These young militants experienced fights with the far left as their initiation into violence, and this apprenticeship often led to them joining terrorist groups: secret groups that specialized in fighting against political opponents soon formed, becoming the origin of the far-right-wing armed groups that would steep Italy in blood in the late 1970s.

## The Planning of Violence in the Far Left Wing

Between 1970 and 1972 the militant anti-fascism brought about a substantial change in the use of violence by the extraparliamentary left wing: it quickly went from defensive actions to offensive actions, up to the planning and organization of operations designed to attack and terrify its opponents. This phase was marked by two particular moments: the intensification of the clashes with the far right, and the start of counter-information investigations into the attacks of December 12, 1969. The extraparliamentary groups' newspapers began to print long time-lines that listed acts of violence carried out by the right wing: these appeared in sequence, giving the impression not only of an escalation of violence but also of the contemporaneity of the attacks. The news was grouped into dossiers and published in the press, often in the form of booklets or leaflets, and reported the recurrence of violent acts carried out by fascist action squads. The posters on the walls at schools and universities fulfilled the same function: they amplified the extraparliamentary left wing's sensation of being under siege. In this way the news became a war bulletin that reported the advance of the enemy and described its guidelines and strategic aims.

The feeling of being besieged by neo-fascists was accompanied by the certainty that the far-right-wing organizations responsible for actions by fascist paramilitary squads were the same ones that planned and carried out terrorist attacks in order to reinforce the strategy of tension. This interpretation of reality had a strong repercussion on the spread of violence: any right-wing activist or supporter became a potential referent of the "*trama nera*" (black conspiracy), an expression normally used by the counter-information groups to indicate the network of power and complicity that, in their view, was behind the attacks. For this reason, counter-information and political violence were very closely linked. One consequence of investigative work was often the publication, in extraparliamentary left-wing newspapers as well as in flyers and posters, of the names, home addresses, and news concerning right-wing militants.

The neo-fascists were thus exposed both to attacks by opponents and to public condemnation if they happened to take part in attacks or terrorist actions. Public opinion was not just informed about neo-fascist activities but also made aware of neo-fascist militants' names, home addresses, and habits: in this way, right-wing extremists became the target for selective actions, and were branded as public enemies, to be tracked down and attacked.

All of these episodes show a widespread willingness within the far left to organize violence. There was, in fact, a wide dissemination of this practice, which indicates how the gathering of information, as with the far right, was often done in preparation for creating records containing hundreds—if not thousands—of files on political opponents, complete with personal details, photographs, notes taken while following the individual, remarks about personal habits, details of car licence plates, and descriptions of public places and political offices frequently visited by the individual. From this point of view, despite their many theoretical differences, the extraparliamentary left-wing groups shared most of the action repertoires adopted by the newly formed far-left terrorist groups.

In autumn 1970, for example, the Red Brigades stated that neo-fascism was a component of the "class war" provoked by the middle class at the expense of the working class. Just like the information given by the extraparliamentary groups, their leaflets began to contain the names, addresses, and phone numbers of people identified as right-wing militants or supporters and who were to be attacked. In addition all the newly formed terrorist groups started out, between 1970 and 1972, with actions that can be attributed to militant anti-fascism practices, which in this way became fundamental training for the transition to the armed struggle. In the same way it was through the fight against neo-fascists that the first secret groups emerged within the extraparliamentary left-wing groups. Part of these secret groups would subsequently join the ranks of terrorist groups. Again, it was in the area of militant anti-fascism that the process of specialization and organization of violence then began; these aspects would soon cause the internal policing service to become more and more autonomous and independent of the leadership of the groups. In the incubation period of the terrorist phenomenon, therefore, the borders between extraparliamentary groups and armed groups became fainter and fainter, particularly with reference to the organization of violence.

# Towards the Birth of Terrorism

The clash between neo-fascism and the extraparliamentary left wing represents a privileged viewpoint for interpreting the birth of the terrorist phenomenon in Italy. What emerged in the far-right-wing and far-left-wing groups, in fact, was an inclination towards the organization of violence—a behaviour that was widespread and commonly shared and was carried out by the gathering of information on their opponents, controlling territory, or carrying out violent attacks or ambushes. The habitual practice of identifying the enemy to get to know him (always "him"?), to study him, and, if necessary, attack him explains in part not just the atmosphere in which the choice of the armed struggle took shape, but also the spread, in the late 1970s, of dozens of smaller armed groups that, as a reaction to the collective movements, were structured on the model of terrorist organizations, thus helping to write one of the most dramatic pages in the history of the Italian Republic.

To study the clash between neo-fascism and the extraparliamentary left wing means, in fact, retracing the stages of the degeneration of the political struggle right up to the extreme forms of violence that authorized the *militarization* of politics itself and consequently its slide towards terrorism, which, ultimately, is the point of no return in any fratricidal struggle.

# RESISTING THE SIXTIES
## A Dutch Reaction in a Global Perspective

**Together with** the leftist radicalization and cultural revolutions of the 1960s, the Western world witnessed the emergence of counterforces to these transformations—and the most successful of those challenges was the U.S. new right movement.

Originating as a middle-class grassroots movement and inspired by Christian fundamentalism, the new right initially focused on "rescuing" American society from the libertine legacy of the 1960s. Late in the 1970s the movement allied with neo-conservative libertarians who called for the deregulation of excessive governmental controls and limits to the welfare state, together with a fierce anti-Soviet agenda. One of its nuclei was located in Orange County, California. A post-1945 immigration of middle-class Midwestern and Bible Belt conservatives had coincided with an explosive growth of high-tech defence industries, which in these modern suburban areas resulted in a strong emphasis on private development and growth as well as a sensitivity to the dangers of communism. Concerns over the autonomy of communities, the erosion of individualism, the authority of the family, and the place of religion in national life were sources for a new right agenda that was filled with attacks on liberal permissiveness, abuse of welfare, criminality, and big government. This proved to be a successful strategy, as witnessed by the overwhelming victory of Ronald Reagan as a new right presidential candidate in 1979.

The emergence of a conservative countermovement was not unique to the United States. In the late sixties and early seventies European countries such as West Germany, Luxembourg, Spain, Italy, the Netherlands, and Denmark saw the establishment of new political parties that mostly originated out of dissatisfaction with the radical left swing of the traditional social-democratic parties.

Although it is tempting to unite all counterforces to the sixties under the umbrella of a global new right movement, with a common agenda of dedication to traditional morals, law and order, anti-communism, and libertarianism, that would be a serious distortion. Due to differences in the origins, founders, and political agendas, a global new right movement with a common agenda did not exist in the 1970s. The Dutch counterforce party DS70 (Democratic Socialists '70) serves as a case study to illustrate this theme. DS70 was established in February 1970 in the Amsterdam RAI convention hall by seceded members of the Dutch Labour Party, who had become extremely dissatisfied with the increasingly dominating position of the party's New Left faction. The date and location were well chosen: the initiators were just in time for the new party to participate in the upcoming local and parliamentary elections, and twenty-four years earlier the RAI hall had also been the location of the founding of the Labour Party. Elsewhere in Europe similar right-wing secessions from social-democratic parties emerged—though none of them, including DS70, succeeded in becoming long-lasting, strong forces in their respective national political landscapes.[1]

## The Origins of a New Party

Just like elsewhere in the Western world, the turmoil of the sixties shook Dutch society and politics. The countercultural and sexual revolutions and the fast-rising stars of radical left groups were apparently successful with a substantial part of the Dutch population and met with permissive reactions from the government and most political parties. However, the protest generation and its activities also caused anger and anxiety among the Dutch. Commentaries in the populist right-wing newspaper *De Telegraaf* (Telegraph) raged against anti–Vietnam War demonstrations, the lack of a Calvinist work ethic among the long-haired radical students, and the decline of decency in sexual mores among the young generation. In July 1970 Dutch Marines spontaneously expressed their aversion to hippies by chasing them away from the national World War II memorial in downtown Amsterdam. The Marines were disgusted by the long-haired, marijuana-smoking young people who used the monument, a symbol of the struggle against Nazi oppression and of liberation from the German occupation, as a place to lounge and even to sleep. Another manifestation of rising counterforces was the publication of a successful new populist conservative weekly, *Accent*. Commentaries and articles in *Accent* were highly critical and often vicious on the events of the late sixties, anticipating the growing discontent among the "silent" majority of the working and lower middle classes, people who were often members of the social-democratic Labour Party (the country's second-largest political party).

From 1966 on the Labour Party had been increasingly dominated by the New Left faction. In fact, just like other European social-democratic parties and the U.S. Democratic Party, the Dutch Labour Party in the late sixties was torn by opposing opinions that led to endless internal, often polemical, debates and conflicts. The increasing influence of the New Left wing resulted in the formation of a more conservative group within the party. Named Democratic Appeal, the group was particularly critical of the supposed New Left sympathy with all sorts of Communist regimes (such as Cuba, People's Republic of China, and German Democratic Republic). Besides, its members feared that the New Left aimed at withdrawing the Netherlands from NATO. Two years later, in 1970, relationships within the party had polarized substantially, culminating in a heated debate on the U.S. intervention in Cambodia and resulting in the secession of the Democratic Appeal right-wing faction. Some months earlier other members of local Labour Party chapters had already quit the party out of dissatisfaction with its policy. On February 14, 1970, they founded a new party, the Democratic Socialists '70. The seceded Democratic Appeal group joined DS70 and the new party prepared to participate in the parliamentary elections of 1971. The leaders of the new party showed themselves to be remarkably self-conscious: in their eyes they were not just an incidental secession of the Labour Party, chased away by the New Left, but the answer to a new and different political situation in the Western world, something that demanded a new political party. As one of its founders, Frans Goedhart, said: "We don't want to become a party of disappointed, grumbling and homesick-ridden ex-Labour Party people. We are open to everyone who abhors fascism, communism or other forms of disastrous extremism and who wants to co-operate in the improvement of our society."[2] DS70 was presented as an institution of renewal, and its initiators refused to consider its founding as a defensive act. In their perception DS70 was to become a large, non-dogmatic, and pragmatic centre party that would be opposed to romantics and dogmatic socialists.

# Frans Goedhart: Shepherd of the Labour Party's Legacy

Even though the establishment of DS70 took place in a relatively short time (by Dutch standards at least), it was the outcome of a much longer process of dissatisfaction with the Labour Party's politics from within the party itself. In this respect its origins differed from the rise of the American new right, which did not emerge from an established party but was a grassroots movement from the beginning. Most of DS70's European sister parties were founded after a similar process (although often within different political and ideological contexts and different time slots): radicalization of the social-democratic mother party, which created resistance with the party's right wing and resulted finally in secession and establishment of a new party.[3] Electoral stagnation together with a polarized party system is said to be another condition for the founding of these rightist democratic-socialist parties.

The rise of the Labour Party's New Left faction from 1966 on had revealed that the party was divided between its older members, who had been present at its creation in 1946, and a younger generation who lacked a conscious experience of the German occupation of 1940–45. For the first group of social democrats the experience of Nazi ideology and German occupation together with the U.S.-Canadian liberation of the Netherlands in 1945 had been decisive for its postwar political outlook. For them the post-1945 economic reconstruction and the creation of the Dutch welfare state and the continuing fight against totalitarianism, or communism (and subsequently unconditional loyalty to the United States), had been their main agenda of the last two decades. It was this group that became increasingly irritated with the anti-American opinions and "Third Way" views of the New Left faction and subsequently with that faction's rise to power within the Labour Party. Most of the initiators of the DS70 party belonged to this group. The political career of one of them, Frans Goedhart (1904–90), is not just an exemplary case in this respect but also reveals a remarkable similarity to the ideological evolution of some U.S. neo-conservatives: from youthful radical leftist via democratic liberalism to neo-conservatism.

Just like so many others of his generation Goedhart was attracted to socialism during the Depression, radicalized, and joined the Communist Party of Holland in 1932. A reporter by profession, he was hired by the Communist daily The Tribune, although a conflict between him and the party leadership soon arose, resulting in his expulsion. He became a radical opponent of Stalinist communism and for a while joined a range of non-communist, radical socialist groups and splinter parties. By the end of the 1930s he had developed into a nonconformist, democrat, and independent socialist. The rise of National Socialism and anti-Semitism in Germany intensified his aversion to any form of undemocratic rule and resulted into a perception of a bipolar world in which democracies were opposed to totalitarian regimes.

In May 1940 Nazi Germany attacked and subsequently occupied the Netherlands. Goedhart went into hiding, becoming one of the major participants in the resistance movement. His choice for resistance was immediate and uncompromising: in his perception National Socialism was a severe threat to the democratic freedoms of Dutch society, and fighting this evil was the only choice that an individual could make. Together with like-minded others he published the illegal paper *Het Parool* (The motto), which became the most prominent resistance paper. He took a pen name (Pieter 't Hoen) and with his commentaries and articles became a source of hope for occupied Holland in particular because he (and others) also pleaded in favour of reform of the Dutch pre-war political system after the defeat of Nazi Germany.

In 1942 Goedhart and some of his co-resistance workers were arrested by the Gestapo when they tried to flee to England. He was sentenced to death, but miraculously managed to escape from the concentration camp, Vught, where he was held. His wartime experience had a deep impact on his perception of the postwar world—during the rest of his life he considered it his prime duty to fight every form of totalitarianism. Together with his qualities as a journalist his heroic bravery reinforced his position of someone of importance in the postwar future.

Towards the end of the war he and his partisans continued to plead in favour of a political renewal in which religious and ideological divisions would cease to be decisive in Dutch politics. However, to their regret and frustration the forces of old proved to be stronger than the urge for radical reform. Pre-1940 politics were restored and the pre-war Social Democratic Labour Party was re-established into the moderate Labour Party in 1946. As a member of Parliament for Labour during twenty-four years, Goedhart showed himself to be an ardent supporter of the West. All these years he (and like-minded friends) considered himself as the unrecognized intellectual leader of the party, and as one of the few who really knew the difference between good and evil. In his parliamentary work the fight against communism became a recurring issue, in particular during the 1950s when he was the party's speaker on international affairs. Besides his work for the Dutch Parliament and his publications in the daily paper *Het Parool*, he had advisory positions with the Council of Europe and West European Union, and participated in the boards of several international anti-communist organizations, such as Radio Free Europe. However, in the course of the 1950s and early 1960s his unconditional choice for the West was increasingly criticized by his newspaper colleagues and co-members of the Labour Party, who became more inclined towards a peaceful co-existent relationship with Communist Eastern European countries and who started to approach the United States' Vietnam policy more critically.

Goedhart remained a loyal supporter of U.S. policy in Southeast Asia, and was not afraid to say so. Several times he spoke in favour of the U.S. bombings of North Vietnam at Amsterdam "teach-ins," where his opinions were met with abuse and disapproving hissing. For him, stopping the Communist advance in all parts of the world was the only thing that counted. Regarding the manifestations of the sixties in his own country, he abhorred the countercultural Provo movement because of its anarchism, while the emergence and increasing power of the New Left faction within the Labour Party were to him a sign of growing communist influence.

His resignation from the Labour Party in May 1970 and his subsequent joining of DS70 was an example for many social democrats of his generation—people who still admired him for his role in the resistance movement during the war and for his outspoken black or white opinions that reflected the political climate of the heyday of the Cold War in the 1950s. For them—the silent members of the Labour Party—Goedhart's opposition to the forces that had turned soft on the totalitarian enemy and dared to criticize the 1945 liberators of the Dutch parallelled their own uneasiness with the recent transformations of Dutch society in general and the social-democratic party in particular. The events of 1940–45 (and how they themselves had dealt with them) and the subsequent years of fighting communism, of hard work to rebuild the country, and creating the welfare state had become the reference points of their later political opinions. The political betrayal of the young generation within the Labour Party (far more than the cultural revolutions) was their main argument for quitting the social democrats and turning to the democratic socialists. Notwithstanding the new party's credo of being a response to a new challenge and an institution of renewal, from the perspective of these supporters DS70 was a last resort. They joined the party out of status anxiety, hoping that it could restore their former certainties.

## DS70's Political Agenda: From Ambivalent to Rightist

The new party was successful in the first parliamentary elections in which it participated. DS70 won eight seats in parliament (out of 150), attracting voters from all major parties, in particular the Labour Party (32 per cent).[4] As a result of this outcome, the party was asked to supply two secretaries in the new centre-right coalition government: a secretary of science and academic education and a secretary of traffic and water affairs. The traffic and water affairs secretary was Willem Drees Jr., son of the founding father of the postwar Dutch Labour Party and designer of the Dutch social welfare state. Willem Drees Sr. had been prime minister from 1948 until 1958. No doubt the name of Willem Drees Jr. on the ballot papers encouraged voters to vote for DS70.

DS70's political program shows an evolution from moderate social-democratic goals in the early 1970s to an increasing conservatism at the end of the decade. Unlike the U.S. new right, but parallel to its European sister parties, at first DS70 didn't have an agenda in which moral issues such as family values and old-fashioned work ethics were core topics. Concerning environmental issues and women's rights, DS70 even started out as remarkably progressive. Influenced by the report of the Club of Rome, the party opposed further expansion of freeways and car mobility, and supported an improved public transformation system. Environmental and noise pollution was to be sanctioned and paid for by the polluters themselves. Legalization of abortion, contraception paid for by state medical insurance, positive action for women on the job market, and individualization of fiscal and social-economic legislation were issues on the early DS70 agenda, all of them diametrically opposed to the positions of the U.S. new right. However, in the late 1970s, due to internal ideological conflicts, the party no longer emphasized these issues and started to name "families" explicitly as the backbone of Dutch democracy: "In families the character of the nation is developed."[5] Even though in individual media performances prominent supporters of DS70 raged against long-haired youngsters—those disrespectful of the values and traditions of their parents who had worked so hard for their children's well-being and welfare—the party's priorities focused on political and economic issues. A strategy of non-dogmatism and non-polarization in fulfilling these aims was essential in the party's philosophy: "Without dogmatic judgments or prejudices, but filled with ideals," stated one of its leaders, Jan Berger, "DS70 is convinced that in a democracy the guiding principle should be to aim at balance and harmony."[6] Recent polarization on all levels of Dutch society was considered a major threat to the nation, an attack on the quality of life, worse than "stinking fumes from factory chimneys."

Just like its democratic-socialist sister parties elsewhere in Europe, DS70 considered the "democratic" in its name to be a more important issue than the "socialist." One of its core goals was the safeguarding of the existing Dutch parliamentary democracy. Ideas on establishing a direct or grassroots democracy or, even worse, a people's democracy like the ones in Eastern Europe should be fought at any cost. Threats to parliamentary democracy such as unlawful actions and disrespect for legislation should be sanctioned: maintaining law and order was crucial for the preservation of democracy. During the course of the 1970s this approach received growing emphasis on DS70's political agenda, with an explicit focus on safety on the streets and expansion of the police force. Together with its consistent and fierce anti-communist stand, such turns in focus contributed to the party's increasing rightist image. DS70's anticommunism included a refusal of political co-operation with the Communist Party of the Netherlands or even with neutralist or pacifist parties. In this respect the party followed Goedhart's guidelines: anti-communism meant absolute loyalty to the West in general

## GREECE MUST BE FREE!

### RALLY — TRAFALGAR SQUARE

Sunday, 21st April at 2.30 p.m.

**FOLLOWED BY MARCH**
**(Downing Street and Greek Embassy)**

Speakers will include:

## MELINA MERCOURI

April 21st will mark the first black anniversary of the Military junta in Greece.

Greece is still under martial law and the junta have now dropped all pretence of restoring democratic government.

The regime's plans for Greece's future as explained in their fraudulent "new" constitution amount to nothing more than the establishment of a permanent police state presided over by the Papadopoulos - Pattakos clique.

The Greek people working under difficult and dangerous conditions are developing their own resistance movements — they look to the democratic world for help!

**SHOW YOUR SOLIDARITY WITH THEM**
**AT TRAFALGAR SQUARE**
**ON SUNDAY, 21st APRIL!**

Organised by the Greek Committee Against Dictatorship, the North London Group for Restoration of Democracy in Greece and the Union of Cypriots in Great Britain. 60 Tottenham Court Road, London, W.1.

Printed by Pygmalion Press, 42 Arlington Road, London, N.W.1. — EUS 7742

Others thought differently. Handbill for a political meeting, London, England, Spring 1968.

and to NATO and the United States in particular. For the Dutch situation, membership of NATO safeguarded the protection of democracy against Soviet threats. Among other things, this tactic resulted in a strong and continuing support of the U.S. Vietnam policy as well as support of the military dictatorships in Greece and Portugal. DS70's support of these two regimes reflected its political priorities.

The party's rightist profile was further stimulated by its emphasis on the need for economy measures. Just like its international counterparts elsewhere, the party turned against the increasing bureaucracy and spendthrift nature of the administration. The creation of the Dutch social welfare state in the 1950s and its expansion during the 1960s had been attended by an ever more complex and expanding network of bureaucratic offices and regulations. From the early 1950s on, based on the principle of solidarity, successive administrations had increased the responsibilities of the state for the social security of its population—"caring from the cradle to the grave." Taxes supplied the money to pay for this. DS70 was critical of the extended social welfare state: "Sometimes social security has become a hammock instead of a safety net."[7] At first the party pleaded in favour of a strong reduction of state subsidies as a solution to the administration's rising financial problems. In the late 1970s, when inflation, increasing taxes, and budgetary deficits kept hitting the Dutch economy, DS70 turned this tendency into a pursuit of support for the introduction of the so-called profit principle: citizens who made use of certain public facilities such as universities or freeways should pay proportionally more for those goods than non-users should. In the early 1970s such a proposition was unheard of and completely against the grain of the Labour Party and Christian centre parties. On the other hand these plans were applauded by the conservative Dutch, in particular in *De Telegraaf* and *Accent*. The support of this populist-conservative press strengthened the rightist image of DS70.

# The Ebb and Flow of Global Counterforces

With a strong emphasis on budget cuts, an encouragement of economic growth, and anti–Soviet Union and law and order policies, in the late 1970s and early 1980s DS70 looked more similar to the U.S. new right movement than it did at the time of its establishment in 1970. Notwithstanding these similarities, substantial differences in ideological principles and political priorities prevented these counterforces to the 1960s from being united under one new right umbrella. The founding of DS70 originated from political discontent and was strongly related to the Dutch wartime experience of occupation and resistance and respect for intellectual leaders such as Frans Goedhart. The restoration of traditional social-democratic principles and policies was the party's main goal. This tendency was fundamentally different from the moral and religious considerations that had been push factors in the emergence of the U.S. new right movement: concerns over the autonomy of communities, the decline of individualism and the role of religion, and the lost position of the family as a cornerstone of society. Co-operation with the neo-conservatives and the Republican Party made the new right a successful power in the U.S. political landscape, while DS70's popularity rapidly declined after 1972, notwithstanding the party's increasingly rightist image. Existing differences in opinion on the party's political strategy deepened, and irreconcilable personalities clashed repeatedly, resulting in the departure of one faction in 1975. Eventually the breakup led to the cancellation of the party eight years later. Some of its supporters returned to the Labour Party; most of them dispersed among centre-right parties. Other European democratic-socialist parties experienced a similar evolution: electoral success at the start and a fast decline after a couple of years, often due to ideological differences and struggles between factions.

From the late 1960s on, most Western states witnessed the (often temporary) successful emergence of political forces that resisted the leftist radicalization and cultural transformations of the decade. As this contribution on a Dutch manifestation of these forces has shown, we can't label them all as new right. Origins, characteristics, and electoral success were too different due to their connectedness to their national past, ideology, and leadership. For the 1970s the "new right" should remain a term that strictly indicates the U.S. reaction to the revolts of the preceding decade. Clearly, the existence of the global counterforces to the radical left and counterculture calls for a new umbrella concept that is equally fitting for all and not just for one.

10  Matthew Rothwell

# TranSpacific RevolutionarieS
## The Creation of Latin American Maoism

"Do you see now? continued Mao, Thus a people's war can be started; it's not difficult.
Do you want to make war? It's only a matter of deciding to."
— Mao Zedong, speaking to two members of the
Peruvian Communist Party, December 1963[1]

**During the** 1960s the Chinese Revolution—and China's prominent place in
the revolutionary imagination of the decade—became an evocative reference point
for many Latin American revolutionaries. From the 1949 triumph of the Chinese
Revolution through the Cultural Revolution to Mao's death in 1976, thousands
of Latin American intellectuals visited China. Between 1959 and 1976 hundreds
of Latin American revolutionaries attended six-month cadre training schools held
by China for foreign revolutionaries. Chinese ideas were in the air that Latin
American radicals breathed.

Many revolutionaries would have been hard-pressed to say whether their
ideas of a peasant-based revolution stemmed more from China's Jinggangshan
or Cuba's Sierra Maestra. But a considerable, and taxonomically distinct, section
of Latin America's revolutionary left did know very well that their ideology came
from China; indeed, they embraced that ideology, which they labelled Marxism-
Leninism, Mao Zedong thought, as an all-encompassing world outlook. Typically
these Maoists were led by intellectuals who had gone through the six-month
cadre training course in China, and they consciously sought to apply Chinese
communist ideas to Latin American conditions.[2]

Travel to China by intellectuals and revolutionary activists played a key role in the creation of domestic Maoisms in Latin America. The first-hand experience in China allowed the revolutionaries to claim authority in putting forward a counternarrative against negative accounts of the Chinese Revolution and to claim privileged status in interpreting the meaning of the Chinese Revolution for their own societies. The relevance of the Chinese Revolution was often understood to lie in assumed similarities between countries in the global South. The Chinese Communist Party characterized pre-revolution China as being a semi-feudal and semi-colonial society. Many Latin American Marxists similarly saw Latin America as being semi-feudal and semi-colonial, which heightened their sense of the relevance of the experience of the Chinese Revolution to Latin America.

It was this perception of the Chinese Revolution as containing lessons for their own societies that drove Latin Americans to go to China and seek out those lessons. While China's efforts to spread and encourage the study of Mao Zedong thought were important in the overall dynamic of the spread of Maoism, I would argue that the initiative of local revolutionaries in studying the example of the Chinese Revolution was the decisive factor in the internationalization of Maoism in the Latin American case.[3] In other words, the agency of Latin Americans themselves was the decisive factor in the domestication of Maoism in Latin America.

The key elements in the formation of Latin American Maoism become clear in two distinct experiences. In Peru, one of the best-known cases of the internationalization of Maoism, the 1960s saw the consolidation of a Maoist organization, later known as the Shining Path, that would wage a protracted war through the 1980s and early 1990s, to the extent of almost overthrowing the Peruvian government. In this case direct contact with and training in China played an important role in turning the pro-Stalin, pro-armed-struggle faction of the Peruvian Communist Party into a proto-Maoist party. In Mexico, early solidarity efforts, inspired mainly by China's experience in economic modernization, had unexpected results in the formation of a radical trend that would seek to overthrow the Mexican government through guerrilla warfare.

# Peru: Direct Contacts and the Formation of a Maoist Party

When Soviet premier Nikita Khrushchev delivered his historic 1956 speech at the Twentieth Congress of the Communist Party of the Soviet Union (CPSU)—criticizing Stalin and putting forward the notion of a peaceful road to socialism—

the Peruvian Communist Party (PCP) was already in the midst of intense internal debate and crisis. In the early 1950s a popular movement had repeatedly challenged the dictatorship of General Manuel Odría, forcing the general to call elections and leave power in 1956. The most powerful expressions of popular opposition to the Odría government came in a series of uprisings and strikes in Arequipa, where the PCP played an important role in organizing student and worker participation. Despite a temporary surge in membership and its important role in the opposition movement, the PCP was unable to assimilate many of its new recruits into party life and failed in its ambition to become a more significant national political actor. This failure engendered acrimonious debate and the departure of some leading figures.

The issues particular to Peru that contributed to crisis and debate within the PCP arose more or less simultaneously to, and became intermingled with, the global debate set in motion by Khrushchev's 1956 speech. One key issue was how to evaluate Stalin's legacy and the accomplishments of the Soviet Union during Stalin's rule. While this question might seem abstract and unrelated to the immediate questions faced by Peruvian communists, Stalin had since the late 1920s been seen as the leader of the international communist movement, and his particular synthesis of Marxism-Leninism had become the theoretical basis on which parties like the PCP tried to formulate their practical policies. Additionally, the Soviet Union had long served as the society that the Peruvian communists upheld as a model for a future socialist Peru. A second major point of controversy raised by Khrushchev's speech was the possibility of a "peaceful road" to socialism. Khrushchev had revised the previous orthodoxy, which contended that violent revolution was the only way of bringing about a socialist society. This point had immediate strategic implications for Peruvian communists because it opened up the possibility of electoral alliances and work that had previously not been considered feasible.

As Peruvian communists began to argue over the meaning and validity of Khrushchev's speech, two documents produced by the Chinese Communist Party influenced one faction. These documents were "On the Historical Experience of the Dictatorship of the Proletariat" and "More On the Historical Experience of the Dictatorship of the Proletariat."[4] In 1959 China hosted a five-month seminar for Latin American communists. The official reason for the seminar was to teach the lessons of the Chinese Revolution, but it was also intended to win over adherents in the political struggle that had arisen between China and the Soviet Union. We don't know how many Peruvian communists attended the seminar, but at least three major leaders were there: José Sotomayor, Carlos de la Riva, and (later pro-Soviet leader) Jorge del Prado. We also don't know which other countries were represented, although Sotomayor does make reference to a request by the

Peruvians and Ecuadorians that the seminar cover the issue of minority nationalities in China.[5] Sotomayor describes the program of study:

> The courses covered questions that are dealt with in great depth in the works of Mao Tse tung and the Chinese leaders: The United Front, the Peasant Problem, the Mass Line, the Armed Struggle in the Chinese Revolution, the Chinese Party in clandestinity and in legality, the struggles inside the party, the philosophical thinking of Mao Tse-tung. The lecturers made a detailed exposition on each one of these subjects, in two or more sessions, and at the end gave a list of books and pamphlets that could be consulted. All, absolutely all, were works by Mao Tse tung.

In addition to the study courses, seminar participants visited major cities, factories, people's communes, cultural institutions, and schools to get a more lively notion of Chinese socialism. While the Chinese instructors repeatedly said that the Chinese Revolution could not be mechanically copied in other countries and that the courses were for the purpose of extracting general lessons, Sotomayor states, "However, the truth is that after five months of study in Peking, everyone returned with the assurance that, fundamentally, the road followed by the Chinese Revolution would be repeated in the countries of Latin America."[6]

The Chinese instructors emphasized four points in particular during the five-month seminar. First, the Chinese revolutionaries had been cut off from the rest of the international communist movement and did not follow the course laid out by the Communist International. Second, contrary to the experience of the Russian Revolution, the Chinese Revolution "followed the road from the countryside to the city." Third, the victory of the Chinese Revolution had no relationship to World War II and might have triumphed even had the war ended differently. Fourth, victory was only possible with Mao's leadership. These four points of emphasis, regardless of whether they accurately describe the history of the Chinese Revolution or not, were designed to undermine the long-standing and often unquestioned idea of Soviet leadership of the international communist movement.

Between 1960 and the 1964 China-USSR split, the PCP had a fractured internal life.[7] The split had not yet occurred publicly, and thus convinced and trained Maoists co-existed with pro-Soviet communists within the same party. The internal party dispute became public when pro-Soviet members of the PCP unsuccessfully attempted to stop the 1961 publication of Carlos de la Riva's pro-China *Donde nace la aurora* (Where dawn is born), which consequently appeared with the following dedication: "To those who made possible my trip to the People's Republic of China. To those who—"revolutionaries" or not—try to make my life impossible for having made the trip."[8] The pro-Chinese faction began directing its efforts to organizing peasants and organizing in the countryside. In July 1962 communist lawyer Saturnino Paredes took an important step in this direction when he presided over the second national congress of the Peasant Federation of Peru, but the pro-Soviet faction opposed the diversion of resources that would work in the countryside. Unsuccessful policies exacerbated the differences. The PCP's 1962 presidential candidate, General César Pando, received only 1 per cent of the popular vote, and many party leaders were arrested after a military coup annulled the elections in order to prevent the Alianza Popular Revolucionaria Americana (APRA) from coming to power.

The jailed PCP leaders were released after new elections were called (which APRA did not win). They had learned of the now public Sino-Soviet conflict while in jail. By the time the PCP central committee held its eighteenth plenary session in October 1963, the divisions had become irreconcilable. Acrimonious debate over Peruvian strategy and tactics were infused with the Sino-Soviet polemics. The central committee was divided roughly in half between the two positions. On November 14, two leaders of the pro-China faction, José Sotomayor and "Cantuarias," left Peru for China to consult with the Chinese leadership on whether or not they should form a separate, pro-Chinese party.

On November 17 Sotomayor and "Cantuarias" visited the Chinese embassy in Bern, Switzerland, where they spoke with the Chinese ambassador via a translator they had met in China in 1959.[9] The Chinese embassy took a week preparing papers for the rest of the Peruvians' trip, after which they continued on to China via Egypt, Iran, Pakistan, and Burma. This was to be the new route from Peru to China, now that travel via the Soviet Union was not an option. By the end of November, Sotomayor and "Cantuarias" had arrived in Beijing, where they were greeted by two Chinese cadres and a translator. One of the cadres was the professor who had spoken on the topic of the united front at the 1959 seminar. The Peruvians were taken to stay at the same house they had stayed at in 1959.[10]

In the second week of November they met with eight members of the standing committee of the politburo of the Chinese party. Deng Xiaoping was the main speaker on behalf of the Chinese side. Deng said that the Chinese party had been impressed by Sotomayor's speech at the 1960 Moscow conference of communist parties, and agreed with the Peruvians on the need for the PCP's pro-China faction to form its own party. Next, Sotomayor and "Cantuarias" met with Mao Zedong, who emphasized the importance of people's war as the strategy that communists should adopt for seizing state power. After receiving the Chinese imprimatur to create a new party, Sotomayor and "Cantuarias" returned to Peru, arriving at the beginning of January 1964. On January 18 the Peruvian Maoists convened the Fourth National Conference of the PCP, where they expelled the leaders of the pro-Soviet faction and elected their new national leadership.

# Mexico: Revolutionary Asynchronicity in the Guerrilla Efforts of Florencio Medrano

Florencio Medrano's efforts towards forming a base area for a Maoist people's war in Mexico from 1973 to 1978 represent a particularly noteworthy attempt at making a Maoist revolution in Mexico. While Maoist ideas had a diverse influence from the 1960s on, Medrano was a special case. A central tenet of Maoism is the idea that protracted people's war is necessary to make revolution, that "political power flows from the barrel of a gun." Of all the political forces that took a large part of their inspiration and ideological orientation from the experience of the Chinese Revolution, Medrano and his guerrillas were the only ones to make sustained efforts at creating base areas for a protracted people's war according to the Maoist model. In addition, Medrano considered Maoism an all-encompassing world outlook, unlike other communist and guerrilla groups in Mexico that were heavily influenced by Mao but believed that Maoism was only applicable to particular spheres of politics and warfare.

Florencio Medrano Mederos was born into a poor peasant family. Before becoming a Maoist he had been an activist in the Communist Party and had participated in radical peasant organizations. In May 1966 he served a month in prison for a land invasion he led in his hometown of Tlatlaya in the state of México. Between 1964 and 1966 Medrano was in dialogue with Javier Fuentes, leader of the Revolutionary Party of the Proletariat (PRP), about joining that party. After returning from a trip to China Fuentes encouraged Medrano to join another delegation that he was organizing to China. In the summer of 1969 Medrano went to China for six months (from July 9 to December 31) as part of a delegation of at least seven members of the PRP.[11]

During his time in China Medrano took the six-month cadre training course that the Chinese were offering to Latin American revolutionaries. Medrano got to see quite a bit of the country, including Beijing, Shanghai, Nanjing, Yan'an, and the Jinggang Mountains. He spent time on a collective farm and learned about Chinese rice cultivation techniques. He and his companions attended a banquet held by Zhou Enlai for foreign delegations; Medrano shook Zhou's hand. On his return to Mexico, Medrano unsuccessfully disputed the leadership of the PRP with Fuentes. Medrano believed that because the majority of the PRP's membership was from a peasant background, it should be led by a campesino like himself. This argument reflected Medrano's anti-intellectualism, which was stoked by anti-intellectual currents in China during the Cultural Revolution and heightened by the poor performance of the PRP intellectuals whom Medrano tried to train in guerrilla warfare techniques in the mountains of Morelos.

Before these conflicts between Medrano and other leaders of the PRP could lead to a split, a PRP bomb-maker in Mexico City accidentally blew himself up, setting off a police roundup of PRP cadres and leading to the arrest of Fuentes. This event left Medrano as the main leader of the PRP outside of jail. He took control of what was left of the organization, setting up a mass front called the National Worker-Peasant-Student Association (ANOCE). At the core of ANOCE was a "struggle committee" comprising thirty experienced Maoists, including some activists who knew some Chinese. The first major effort that ANOCE undertook was the occupation of vacant land (intended for luxury recreational development) on the edge of Cuernavaca.[12]

In the early 1970s, due to the crisis of peasant agriculture, poor peasants were flooding into Mexican cities, where the lack of available housing forced many of the new arrivals to join in forming new settlements on the outskirts.[13] Land takeovers were occurring across Mexico. But Medrano's March 31, 1973, land takeover in Cuernavaca was fundamentally different from other squatter struggles going on at the same time, mainly because it was launched and led with the express purpose of creating a base area for a Maoist protracted people's war.

On March 25, 1973, an assembly of poor Cuernavacans held by ANOCE set seven o'clock on the following Saturday, March 31, for the land takeover. By nine o'clock on the appointed day, after only a few families had shown up, Medrano got on his motorcycle to round up the stragglers. He rode around the poor parts of Cuernavaca, exhorting his followers to follow through on their commitment to the land seizure. By dawn on Sunday more and more families were arriving, and Medrano awarded 400 square metres to each of the first thirty families on the condition that they build their new homes and begin living on their plots within seventy-two hours. After three days some three hundred families had arrived, and the settlement was continuing to grow. To accommodate the stream of newcomers, Medrano called an assembly of the squatters to reduce plot sizes. By appealing to the need for proletarian solidarity, Medrano overcame initial resistance from the first wave of settlers and the assembly decided to reduce all plots to 200 square metres. Eventually 1,500 plots were distributed and after a few months the population reached 10,000.[14]

The squatter community was named Colonia Rubén Jaramillo (after a peasant leader who had been killed by the government in 1962). In contrast to other squatter settlements in other parts of Mexico, the way in which the Colonia Rubén Jaramillo was run reflected important themes of the Cultural Revolution as absorbed by Medrano while he was in China. To build up the settlement's infrastructure, Medrano made collective labour mandatory. When asked what materials a bridge would be built with, Medrano answered: "With the courage that we carry within," echoing Chinese propaganda about massive development projects built with little more than the will of the workers themselves. Indeed, as Medrano put it, "I want to make Colonia Jaramillo the first people's commune of Mexico." Medrano organized Red Sundays, when idealistic youths came from Cuernavaca and Mexico City and joined in on the collective labour, echoing the movement of educated youth to do peasant labour in the Chinese countryside. The hospital was named after Norman Bethune, the Canadian doctor who had died while serving in the Chinese Communist Eighth Route Army and who was the subject of one of Mao's four "always read" essays. Echoing the Cultural Revolution's education reforms, the schools built in the settlement emphasized the need for education to be connected with productive labour.[15]

By the end of 1973 the dangerous experiment of an armed, self-governing area on the outskirts of a major city was too much for the Mexican government to take, and the army invaded the settlement (which it did not leave until 1980). Medrano and the core of his armed force escaped and made their way to the countryside around Tuxtepec, where Medrano had organized some supporters. For five years, until his death in combat, Medrano and his forces continued in their attempt to adapt Mao's military and political teachings to Mexican conditions, forming a base area in a border region between the states of Oaxaca and Veracruz. In China, border regions between states had been lawless areas, and Mao Zedong took advantage of that weakness to create a relatively stable base area along the Jiangxi-Fujian border. In Mexico, while Medrano was able to use the terrain and popular support to evade the police, he was never able to create a base of operations that the police or army could not penetrate.

Medrano formed mass organizations among timber workers and peasants in the Tuxtepec region, using his armed forces in support of the demands of these organizations. Medrano criticized Mexico's Guevarist guerrillas for being disconnected from the people:

> Our movement is also the result of a series of experiences like those of the compañeros Génaro Vasquez, Lucio Cabañas, and Arturo Gámiz, who offered their lives for the sake of the people. These compañeros deserve our respect because they died for their ideals. But they also made mistakes, and we have to learn from their mistakes. These compañeros believed that a small unit of guerrillas, Che Guevara style, would be able to carry off a revolution in Mexico. That's not the way, because the guerrillas can't be disconnected from the people. A revolution has to be made by the people—that is, directed by its best children. That's why our idea is to tie ourselves to the people, so that we can teach them the ideal of struggle. They have to know their rights and know how to defend them against oppressors and exploiters and their servants.[16]

With this approach in mind, Medrano expressed his need to be close to the communities he was trying to organize, even though it meant putting his life in danger.[17] Still, despite his attempt to combine involvement in popular struggles with armed struggle, he was unable to form any sort of relatively stable base area. His party was never able to pass over from being a roving guerrilla band to become a force more deeply rooted among the people of the Tuxtepec region.

# A Snapshot of the Creation of International Maoism in the 1960s

In these two brief case studies, then, travel to China played in a key role in the creation of leaders who would have the authority and ideological preparation to launch Maoist organizations in their own countries. In the Peruvian case, Mao Zedong and Deng Xiaoping encouraged the Peruvians in 1963 to form a new party—a process that eventually led to the formation of the Shining Path in 1970. In the case of Mexico—in an example of what is called "revolutionary asynchronicity"[18]—the Latin American Maoists interpreted the Chinese Revolution as a process that could be reproduced more or less mechanically in their country. In Latin America, China and its revolution, then, took a prominent place in the revolutionary imagination—and the construction of local revolutionary strategies from the 1960s forward.

Julie Boddy 11

# ON DIGGING IT

Correspondences between Dineh Uranium
Miners and the Health and Safety Program of
the Oil, Chemical and Atomic Workers

**Following the** Allied victory in 1945 the nuclear industry, underwritten with ample public funds and benefits, stepped up production. Uranium mining, the back end of the industry—government-owned and privately operated— produced more toxic contaminants than useable ore. By the 1960s the Dineh Navajo uranium mining communities in the Southwestern United States were expanding their search for strategies to protect themselves against the harm that this activity had caused; at the same time the union that organized industries using uranium in manufactures, the Oil, Chemical and Atomic Workers (OCAW), worked out an innovative health and safety program. These separate campaigns addressed common problems, yet racialized cultural loyalties divided and diminished their sense of common ground. Still, their separate organizing efforts reveal significant similarities—qualities that were in general characteristic of sixties activism, which often drew from anticolonial struggles throughout the world.

In 1966 a theory of dialogical social relations articulated the assumptions and stratagems of anticolonial struggle. This theory, "tricontinentalism," emerged from the founding meeting of the Organization for the Solidarity of the Peoples of Africa, Asia, and Latin America, which became known as the Tricontinental

Conference, convened in January of that year in Havana. The central issue of the conference was how to organize a society that would operate on the basis of serving all its people freely rather than functioning through coercion. Pluralist in orientation, the theory envisaged decentralized networks of collaborations between various combinations of local and diasporic knowledges that might simultaneously be economic, cultural, ideological, and political, according to the particular circumstances of a time and place. Tricontinentalism aimed particularly to decentre aggressions based on race. It offered possibilities made cogent in the face of the Cold War by representing the process of gaining independence from colonial control in the mid-twentieth century, and thereby giving heft to the U.N. Declaration of Human Rights and Convention 107 of the International Labor Organization on the Rights of Indigenous Peoples. Tricontinental theory, later to become known in varying contexts as postcolonialism, can also be applied to events and issues in the United States. For our purposes it has a particular application to the similarities in choices followed by two very different groups of people in two separate places—but facing highly connected issues.

## The Dineh and Uranium Mining: Contamination at Work and at Home

The Dineh Navajo reservation is the largest in the United States; four states straddle its territory, though most of it lies in Arizona. The Dineh see themselves as a distinct political entity with treaty rights and obligations, as a people sustained by their language and culture. They were sustained as well by their wealth and skills until the recent past, when their land became degraded through exploitation of the water that fed it, curtailing their farming and prompting the government to force them to drastically reduce their herds, their treaty rights notwithstanding. "Overgrazing," the federal government had called it.

Surrounded by the United States, the Dineh Navajo might venture out of their reservation in search of occasional waged work that would allow them to return home to meet the demands of their family and kin-based livelihoods and participate in the frequent ceremonies that mark their culture. Most of the work they found was in railroading and mining, where some of them were represented by the Western Federation of Miners and later the Mine, Mill and Smelter Workers, both of them political unions with a multicultural orientation. The Dineh Navajo sold their goods as well as their labour, specializing in silver and turquoise jewellery and highly prized weaving. Many hundreds of young Dineh Navajo signed up to join the U.S. military during the Second World War. Hundreds more found work in war-related manufacturing. Thus these people became both more closely connected to the world outside their reservation and more integrated into the U.S. economy.

On the reservation, uranium deposits formed part of the landscape, revered as the culture revered everything on the land. According to tradition, uranium was something that was to be left in the ground, though sometimes people might use minute amounts of the uranium-bearing carnotite ore to make a special dye that was, as one person put it, the colour of corn pollen. Some 90 per cent of the uranium used to manufacture atomic bombs was mined on the land of a northerly people, the Dene, who lived around Bear Lake, close to the Arctic Circle, in the Northwest Territories of Canada, with supplementary sources coming from the Congo. After the Second World War the Atomic Energy Commission (AEC) in the United States began to pursue the possibilities of a domestic supply. In 1946 the U.S. government sponsored a comprehensive minerals survey. It constructed roads, promised bonuses, guaranteed prices, and established mills for what became the first federally sponsored mineral rush. With further government aid, including insurance against accidents, some of the most powerful corporations in the world became the holders of the biggest or the most uranium leases.

Deposits on Dineh land were apparently singled out for development. Although about 25 per cent of the uranium deposits discovered in the minerals rush were on Dineh land, the deposits there would furnish fully 80 per cent of all U.S. uranium mined until 1970, and they were mined by the Dineh living in the area. For absentee leaseholders this development carried huge advantages.

The Dineh themselves had no rights of ownership to the mineral holdings on their land, and no choice of mine location save for the tribal council's prerogative of endorsing a Bureau of Indian Affairs decision. The royalty cheques assigned to them were based on a much lower lease rate than were the royalties paid to others who operated mines on federal land. The difference in the lease rates corresponded to the pay differential between reservation and off-reservation miners. The remoteness of the reserve and the long-nurtured self-determination of its inhabitants seemed to invite investors' ignorance of whatever standards of construction, maintenance, and particular provision for the safety of the miners may have otherwise been in force for the mining industry at the time—which in turn meant still more savings for the mining companies. Besides, who would enforce the standards?

A series of federal policy proposals further attacked the Dineh capacity to respond to the minerals invasion. Chief among them was a termination policy. When the mineral survey was launched, a senator from Utah, one of the states partly occupying Dineh land, declared that reservations were socialistic and called for the end of federal treaty obligations and protections, including recognition of the legality of their land rights and provision of social services, such as health care and reservation schools. The act of termination transferred civil and criminal jurisdiction of the reservation to the states and gave states the right to finance their new responsibilities by taxing Indians on reservations. How were the Dineh to pay these taxes? Their way of life didn't allow for it. Some immigrated to the cities in search of full-time waged work, in a migration that was funded for a time by a federal relocation policy. Some Dineh continued to find seasonal work, when and where they could. But most remained on the reservation, even though the mining and milling of uranium there became one of the only sources of personal income available.

Many of these uranium workers were World War II veterans. Some of them, the Codetalkers, had enabled victory in the Pacific arena by using the Dineh language. A case could be made that it was the Dineh use of their own language and the inability of codebreakers to decipher it, rather than the bomb, that brought the war to a close. For these veterans, the work of mining uranium seemed a better option than leaving home again. But then, they were unaware of the particular dangers that the work involved.

With the economic losses they had already faced, the Dineh Navajo now had scant provisions for negotiating the emergencies that began on their land with a terrible blizzard in 1947–48 and continued in the repercussions of the exploitation of their minerals and water. They were persuaded to trade off land on the northwest corner of the reservation, which became the site of the Glen Canyon Dam and power plant. That must have been a hard bargain, because the beautiful canyon walls held a deeply sacred site, the Rainbow Bridge. The Glen Canyon Dam could capture two years of water from the Colorado River; while the power plant would fire the uranium mill that the Kerr-McGee chemical company was to set up nearby, and it would supply power to the major cities in the Southwest. It was not a clean operation: air pollution from the power plant became the only man-made creation visible from the moon.

Hundreds of uranium mines soon punctured Dineh land. The small ones, known as dogholes, were dug by hand. The tailings were piled up next to them or dumped down a neighbouring gulch. From there they made their way to water and ultimately through the food chain. For years the mines had no ventilation regardless of their size and the amount of dust that a blasting might generate. There was a lack of clean drinking water. The workers down in the larger mines would find pockets of water they could drink while they ate their lunches, and perhaps take some of the contaminated water home—it was plentiful and cool. They had no protective gear to wear, and no way to wash off the accumulated dust. They went home with radioactive dust on their hands and faces and contaminated clothes on their backs; home, where there was no running water, or anything like a laundromat nearby. Every few days their wives would wash their clothes by hand. The families might watch their children play in the tailings. On windy days radioactive dust was everywhere.

Deadly radioactive contamination provides no clear sensory signals for as long as twenty years or thereabouts. Who knows where chest pains, a rash, cough, headache, leg ache, nosebleed, backache, or stomach ache might come from? Doctors didn't seem to know, and in any case they very scarce and hard to visit. After all, you've been working hard; maybe you don't remember whether something might have happened to bring on the pain or discomfort. The uranium miners had to work without breaks for long hours—like slaves, some said, and it wasn't light talk either. There were no warnings that the uranium mines posed any particular danger, aside from the old, wise tradition of leaving uranium alone. And what if there were a problem, what could they do? Some workers submitted to repeated tests from the Public Health Service. They were given a clean bill of health.

Some miners saw the veins of uranium-bearing ore as looking something like menacing serpents. Some saw the milled ore as the colour of corn pollen, and since the land couldn't support corn anymore, or for whatever reason, they might bring some of it home to add to a holiday celebration. The Public Health Service had published a report about the dangers of radioactive contamination in the 1940s, and had urged the AEC to warn the miners (to no avail). It had given miners repeated health screenings, without telling them why. The American Cancer Institute had published something too, but had not informed the miners. Nobody in officialdom had made the leaseholders observe precautions. But truth will out, and by the early 1960s the cancer epidemic had announced itself. It eventually killed all of men who had entered the mines in Cove, Arizona, where the first uranium mine had been opened on Dineh land.

# Mobilizations

The widows of the men who died began to come together. Throughout the reservation they started to talk about their husbands' deaths at regular meetings. Meeting together must have been hard, if only for the regular workloads that the widows sustained, where water and fuel for the stove had to be carried and travel was most likely to be on foot. Nor were there telephones at hand. Nevertheless, the meetings went on, and so began the long campaign for compensation for their losses. In Colorado, Dineh and non-Dineh women formed Widows against Radiation (WAR) and sought the help of the Oil, Chemical and Atomic Workers International Union.

Earlier, anticipating troubles near the end of the war, the Dineh Navajo had begun to organize intertribally. In November 1944 they had taken part in the founding convention of the National Congress of American Indians (NCAI), described by

some as a United Nations of Native peoples. This group, representing over one hundred First Nations peoples, aimed to protect treaty rights, to claim prior consultation in any federal policies that affected Native peoples, and to receive grants-in-aid on the basis on their economic self-sufficiency, and so to mount an effective opposition to the problems brought on by minerals invasions and the termination of rights, which was at that time apparently in the wings, though not yet announced.

They corresponded with Washington and travelled there repeatedly, and eventually achieved a measure of the effectiveness they sought. In 1967 Stewart Udall, as secretary of the interior, submitted the Indian Resources Development Bill to Congress. The bill offered funds for development, but based them on mortgaging Indian land. For the Dineh its terms were especially unwelcome. Vine Deloria, president of the NCAI, called on President Lyndon Johnson to issue credit without jeopardizing Indian land. Johnny Belindo, Kiowa-Navajo and Washington, D.C., director of NCAI, helped to defeat the measure. Udall had introduced it, and he was in some ways very much a friend.

The threats to Dineh sovereignty and self-determination were so manipulative, and the consequences so dire, that for a time the tribal government refused inducements of any kind from the United States that didn't treat them as equal partners in the arrangements. The Dineh banned union-organizing twice, once in the 1950s and once in 1968. They turned down OCAW overtures and instead formed their own work-based association, which operated without imposing dues or hierarchical relationships. They began to explore with other First Nations the possibilities of broader networks that specifically addressed the invasions of extractive industries.

In the 1950s, using their precious oil royalties, the Dineh elders set up a scholarship fund for thirty-five students. Between 1950 and 1960 high-school attendance more than doubled, and the number of college students grew from three dozen to four hundred. The new students at the University of New Mexico faced a huge gulf between cultures. They addressed this problem by organizing the Kiva club and beginning their meetings with war dances. The discussions at thse meetings would lead to the formation of the National Indian Youth Council at the community centre in Gallup, New Mexico. The club members had invited their elders to the meeting and began a dialogue with them. Herbert Blatchford, one of the youth, spoke first:

> We, as Indian students, have been deeply indoctrinated to the importance of education many times and by multiple measures. We have been educated to affirm one

proposition: American cultural education. On the other hand, we have, under false pretenses, been encouraged to obliterate our own cultural values. Our problem is: How can we as young people, help to solve conflicts between cultures? What happens when a person graduates from college?"[1]

As the story goes, the elders replied: "Education is necessary. We will support you, if we can. Come home when you are educated in the white man's ways. Your people need to know what you know."

Additional influences unvoiced in the reported dialogue were the civil rights, Black Power, and Chicano movements. The first direct action taken, modelled on the approach of Black student activists, was to organize fish-ins on the lower Columbia River. Blatchford, as executive secretary of the Youth Council, declared that it was the first full-scale, intertribal action since the defeat of Custer at Little Big Horn. He then went to Washington to claim unpaid Dineh royalties that were under custody in the capital, along with $200,000 in interest that the royalties had been accruing.

The National Indian Youth Council began to involve itself in off-reservation issues such as voting rights and litigation against unfair labour practices. In 1961, along with representatives from some one hundred other nations, members of the Youth Council joined the march for the Test-Ban Treaty in New York City organized by Women Strike for Peace. The Youth Council was the First Peoples' co-ordinator for the Poor People's march, the interracial campaign headed by Martin Luther King Jr., before his death, to bring an end to poverty.

On the reservation Raymond Nakai, a cultural radical, was elected tribal chair. Nakai had become well known to listeners of the Dineh language radio station. As tribal chair he lent his weight to the creation of a community-controlled college, the first of its kind, and saw to the relegitimization of the Native American Church, itself an early supporter of the American Indian Movement. On and off the reservation he gave speeches on civil rights and the meanings of tradition in the present. The youth among the uranium miners, including Thomas Benally, Phillip Harrison, Harry Tome, and Esther Yazzie, began to spread their messages near and far.

Photos (and, opposite page, logo) from the files of the National Indian Youth Council, University of New Mexico Center for Southwest Research, Special Collections.

*On Digging It*

# Long Island Cosmetic Factory Workers:
# Finding a New Purpose

In 1953 workers at the Long Island, New York, Helena Rubenstein factory—members of Local 149 of the United Gas, Coke and Chemical Workers Union, soon to merge into the Oil, Chemical and Atomic Workers International—chose Anthony Mazzocchi, a native of Bensonhurst, Brooklyn, to represent them. Mazzocchi was a streetwise war veteran who knew his way around the neighbourhoods and docks of Brooklyn. About 85 per cent of the Rubenstein plant workers were women. Women ran the factory production line, and men worked at either end of it supplying materials and clearing the line. A considerable pay gap existed between male and female job classifications, and as a candidate for the Local Mazzocchi had promised to reduce that pay gap as the first thing he would do in office. He continued to give priority to shop-floor democracy by paying attention to informal work groups and work group leaders. In less than two years he went from chief steward of the Local to Local president. When he won a big wage increase, he won it across the board rather than as a percentage increase, which meant that everyone would benefit equally.

"I learned my politics at the kitchen table," Mazzocchi told his friend and biographer.[2] The culture of that kitchen table included a diverse group, starting from kinship and ethnicity but not bound by it. Mazzocchi's family welcomed difference, and shared food and the pleasure of lively conversation, much of it about politics. Mazzocchi had benefited from the GI Bill of Rights to educate himself as a dental technician before taking a job the Rubenstein plant. There he quickly became known for his ability to fix bridges and dentures and his willingness to do it. His biographer tells us: "He talked. He charmed. He showed respect. He played on the baseball and bowling teams. He spoke up at every meeting." As Mazzocchi later recalled, "Sometimes I said good stuff, sometimes I didn't. But basically I got up and talked at meetings about the shortcomings of the contract. I mean they were obvious, and a lot of people felt them, but couldn't give voice to it."[3]

By the 1960s the workers at the Helena Rubenstein plant were the best paid in the industry, with a benefit plan better than anything that existed, including the first dental plan ever, a year's maternity leave, and a credit union. What's more, according to Barbara Garson:

> The most important benefit from the past struggles in this factory, and from the impartial rotation systems, has no official recognition. There is no clause in the contract that says that the workers shall have the right to laugh, talk, and be helpful to one another.

Nor is there a formal guarantee that the workers can shrug, sneer or otherwise indicate what they think of the supervisors. But most of the women at Helena Rubenstein are helpful to each other and they present a solid front to the supervisors. The right to respond like a person, even while your hands are operating like a machine, is something that has been fought for in this factory. And this right is defended daily, formally through the grievance process and informally through militant kidding around.[4]

Local 149's militancy included vigorous support for civil rights, a well-demonstrated willingness to go out on the picket line whenever the need arose, even if it represented unfriendly unions, and a willingness to organize small, mob-run plants, wresting them from control of the mob. Workers from the area consulted Mazzocchi with a variety of problems, and he was invariably willing to help. Local 149 soon represented workers at more than thirty plants and had a membership of nearly fifteen hundred. It became so well recognized that even national politicians sought its endorsement. The husbands of the Helena Rubenstein workers had long taken notice.

While returning Dineh veterans might turn to uranium mining, veterans from the New York City area might take up work in one of the defence plants on Long Island and use their GI credit to buy one of the tens of thousands of tract houses being built there. Between 1952 and 1967 the Atomic Energy Commission licensed the Sylvania plant in Hicksville on Long Island to manufacture nuclear fuel rods for weaponry. The plant processed and milled Uranium-235 and thorium, then machined and ground it and incinerated the leftovers before burning the sludge to recapture whatever uranium remained. Although unauthorized to do so, the plant burned uranium on site in fifty-five-gallon drums, as a three-shift, seven-days-a-week operation until 1960. Not surprisingly, there were accidents. Sylvania workers asked Mazzocchi for his help. Increasingly he observed the subordination of safety to productivity in the maintenance of workplaces, with the result that workers who kept their jobs did so despite increased health risks. These nuclear workers, like the uranium miners, preferred not asking questions to the possibility of losing their jobs.

As on the reservation, contamination clearly became both a community and a workplace problem on Long Island as the unhealthy conditions at a plant began to have an effect not just on its own workers but on adjoining communities. As Mazzocchi saw it, the cancer business itself was slated to become a leading growth industry. When cutbacks in employment arrived on Long Island, Mazzocchi addressed the cutbacks and contamination together. Acting through the Long Island Federation of Labor he prepared a detailed proposal for a pilot program to convert federal funding from defence contracts to public works programs, which he then submitted to President Johnson.[5]

A further source of alarm about the nuclear contamination reaching Long Island came from the use of stockpiled uranium turned into bombs deployed for above-ground testing. Bikini atoll had been the site of the first such peacetime tests. It was also the site of the most bombs tested, as well as the biggest, messiest, and most lethal, but territory in the United States did not lag far behind. During the first three months of Mazzocchi's twelve-year tenure as president of Local 149, Operation Upshot-Knothole exploded eleven thermonuclear devices in Nevada, basically in Indian Country. Wind blew the fallout across the country.

With support from Local 149, by now recognized as militant voters by the Long Island Democratic Party, Mazzocchi expanded his involvement in politics, specifically in antiwar and anti-nuclear issues. He became a founder of the Committee for a Sane Nuclear Policy. Inspired by the privileges enjoyed by the professionals he met there, he initiated the Joe Hill scholarship that year and proposed paid workers' sabbaticals. Through his new connections he gained a hand in forestalling the construction of Ravenswood, slated to be the largest nuclear power plant in the world, in New York City. His involvement in anti-nuclear issues led to one battle after another against contamination, to the point where he entered public consciousness. In New York City people responded by electing him chair of the first Earth Day. Along the way to becoming an anti-nuclear activist he forged links with public-oriented scientists such as Barry Commoner and René Dubos. Mazzocchi continued to be so trusted by the members of Local 149 that they gave him their babies' teeth to be used as definitive evidence that strontium-90, a by-product of nuclear testing, established itself in bones—thus building the case for the Limited Test-Ban Treaty.

In the second half of the 1960s Mazzocchi continued to move up through union channels. As legislative director of the Oil, Chemical and Atomic Workers Union he was able to put health and safety issues on the national agenda. At the 1967 OCAW convention he took the lead in passing a health and safety program to be implemented by educational, collective-bargaining, and political action projects. The convention resolution led to the formation of a community/labour coalition that was instrumental in the passage of the Occupational Health and Safety Act of 1970. It was a bitter labour-management fight, relying, as Mazzocchi was wont to do, on the testimony of union members to drive its point home and continuing for over two years, culminating in the federal occupational health and safety legislation that created the Occupational Safety and Health Administration, and then the National Institute for Occupational Safety and Health (NIOSH), the body responsible for enforcing the legislation. It was considered the most pro-labour legislation in fifty years. OCAW was the first union to file a complaint under the act and the first to request an imminent danger inspection. In the process OCAW developed in-house expertise and structured programs known for their innovation, allying everyone from academics and public health scientists to students and environmental activists in the process. Interning physicians worked with OCAW members to permit on-site training of occupational physicians, and a broad program trained worker educators to inform fellow workers about on the job hazards and regulatory mandates. The entire program was grounded on the reality that workers learn best from other workers. The trainers were health and safety union members called OSHECS (Occupational Health and Safety Education Coordinators). They aimed for a program to transform health and safety issues from reaction to prevention, focusing on inherent safety systems such as maintenance and warning devices, with training programs and full-time health and safety representatives at every plant.

# Dineh-OCAW Connections

The Dineh and OCAW made forays into each other's provenances. Dineh widows had approached the OCAW, and the OCAW had approached the Dineh miners. In a terrible sense the Dineh had led the way towards mutual involvement by entering the mines before Local 149 had begun its renewal. By the time the OCAW Health and Safety program was up and running, death had been on the rampage among uranium workers. The technicians at the uranium mines and mills may well have been OCAW members, and they were white and provided with showers and adequate drinking water. They stayed only brief intervals at the mine, had cars or trucks to take them where they wanted to go, and they didn't share any of these privileges and benefits.[6] Perhaps they were among those OCAW members who believed that they had a hand in shaping the nuclear industry. After all, the OCAW leadership included business unionists and CIA agents, along with echoes of the Industrial Workers of the World (IWW), the Mine, Mill and Smelter Workers, and Local 149.

But what if the spirit and substance of Local 149 and the IWW had prevailed, and the Local's recent triumphs of shop-floor democracy were extended to the uranium millers and miners, whether they joined or not: with standards for wages and hours, including paid overtime, along with health and safety standards, transportation to work if needed, and health insurance, maybe a big across-the-board raise? It would be a start, but even so there would be problems arising from the centralized and standardized terms of OCAW policy. For instance, mine vents, which the union was later instrumental in having installed, channelled radioactive gases and dust next to the Dineh houses and play areas of their children.

The Dineh would have to have a voice in the planning of any undertaking that affected them. It seemed as though that was not in the cards, then, if judging only from Mazzocchi's 1967 testimony before a Congressional hearing, where he spoke eloquently on behalf of inclusion of Dineh miners in public health statistics to give a truer picture of the dangers involved in working with uranium. True to form, he had brought witnesses with him to make their case, but none of them were Dineh.

As it was, both Local 149 and the Dineh uranium miners had the advantage of a perspective from the margins of the labour market. Many of the Helena Rubenstein workers had, for instance, been seasonal, and the Dineh had long looked on their labour-market involvement as supplementary. Both had a broad sense of justice, as well as of community, which they sought to fortify by reaching out to civil rights and right-to-know-based networks and alliances. The Dineh were to continue these associations into the twentieth-first century, as their global dimensions came more powerfully into play through organizations such as Abolition 2000, the International Indian Treaty Council, the Indigenous Mining Campaign Project, and the Indigenous Environmental Network. Otherwise, both groups benefited each other just by doing what was important to each of them. Certainly the relatives or friends of off-reservation Dineh could receive whatever benefits might come from the OCAW health and safety program, which included a booklet on sexual harassment, and from the Occupational Safety and Health Act, which had been designed with all workers in mind. Both the OCAW and the U.S. public were beneficiaries of the Dineh insistence on maintaining their way of life and of the unmistakable proof that their struggle gave of the hazards posed by uranium mining and milling, especially when coupled with the dangers of government indifference and deception and the reluctance of operators to respect the well-being of the people who worked for them.

Perhaps the closest the two sides got was on the political front. Both the Dineh and Local 149 were represented at the international march for a Test-Ban Treaty in 1963, where Abolition 2000, the international anti-nuclear network, began to take shape. Certainly the treaty benefited them jointly. Though, as far as we know, they had not come upon any other ways of working together by the close of the 1960s, the seeds were there.

John S. Saul    12

# LIBERATION SUPPORT AND ANTI-APARTHEID WORK AS SEEDS OF GLOBAL CONSCIOUSNESS

## The Birth of Solidarity with Southern African Struggles

**This book** seeks to mark the 1960s off as a crucial moment in the birth of a distinctive and novel kind of radical and global consciousness.[1] Excavating such origins, we can hope that those living and active in the present-day world—ensnared as it is in the toils of a brand of globalization that is now largely driven and defined by contemporary capitalism—can find inspiration, while also learning some useful lessons in terms of which to better define our present practice. Thus we look back to the 1960s to see the first flickering signs of environmental awareness and cultural innovation and also a wide range of novel solidarities being manifested around the world. In Southern Africa, for example, the 1960s signalled something quite distinctive and important, not only because of the launch of liberation struggles in various territories there but also because of advances in the worldwide mobilization of energies and support to which that struggle would increasingly give rise. Here was, in fact, one forerunner of the kind of globalized consciousness now made more familiar to us in our own day in various manifestations of the mobilization against capitalist globalization that have occurred.

There is, however, a question about this earlier "anti-apartheid" mobilization (using the term "anti-apartheid" loosely to include the struggles against all forms of white minority rule in Southern Africa) that demands consideration right at the outset. For the struggle for liberation in Southern Africa must be assessed at two levels, having much to do with the meaning to be attached to the very notion of "liberation" itself. Certainly we must not underestimate the importance in the region of a liberation from white political domination per se—whether that be the palsied colonial Portuguese variant, the white settler hegemony of Rhodesia's Ian Smith, or the mining- and industry-driven but also racist-defined overlordship of South Africa's apartheid version. For this was to be the end of unapologetic racism-in-power, ranging from its most exploitative economic forms to the grim reality of police bashing through the doors of Black people at four in the morning to terrorize the inhabitants. Self-evidently, political freedom from such enormities of authoritarianism and racist tyranny is no small thing. Thus each of the five territories that came to be at the centre of the "thirty years war for Southern African liberation" constituted the last major fronts, on the continent and more generally, of unapologetic white minority rule.[2]

In fact, the Black American scholar and activist W.E.B. Du Bois had predicted, in 1905, that the chief issue facing the twentieth century would be "the colour bar," while also suggesting in 1917 that "the 'dark world'—Japan, China, India, Africa and the Negroes in the Americas—might [now] wage war upon the 'white world'" in a "world movement of freedom for coloured races."[3] Of course much else was to happen in the twentieth century beyond this, yet there can be no denying that the global rollback of formal colonialism constituted some such victory. And the "war for Southern African liberation," which persisted dramatically over several decades (especially between 1960 and 1990), must be considered a kind of final and particularly salient campaign in that particular global contestation.

Yet—a second level—any truly liberated future should also be one open to the hopes of people, all of the people, for a fundamental betterment of their material and spiritual condition more generally. Henning Melber has put the relevant point neatly, suggesting:

> The anti-colonial movement's proclaimed goals and perspectives were not only about fighting the oppressive and exploitative system of apartheid colonialism. The liberation struggle was at the same time about creating conditions for a better life after apartheid—not only in terms of political and human rights but also with regard to the inextricably linked material dimensions to human well being and a decent living of those previously marginalized and excluded from the benefits of the wealth created (to a large extent by them).[4]

Moreover, this latter sentiment—implying a much expanded, even socialist, definition of liberation—was verbally professed by virtually all of the ultimately victorious liberation movements in Southern Africa. True, during the liberation struggle itself some, like the present South African president, Thabo Mbeki, were at some pains to distinguish the African National Congress's aspirations for "freedom" from socialist ones: "The ANC is not a socialist party. It has never pretended to be one it has never said it was, and it is not trying to be. It will not become one by decree or for the purpose of pleasing its 'left' critics" ("Just call me a Thatcherite," he later added).[5] Still, such an a-socialist ethos was not the one that the ANC had generally evoked in the past. Moreover, there were very many in South Africa who felt confident that, despite Mbeki, there were just too many contradictions, given voice in the actions and intentions of the Congress of South Africa Trade Unions (COSATU) and other social movements, that were pulling people (and pushing the ANC) beyond "merely" racial contestation and towards class-consciousness and class action.

There was another premise at play here as well: that Southern Africa, like the rest of the continent in this respect, was and is unlikely to be liberated in any meaningful and adequately expansive sense under the aegis of capitalist globalization or along neo-liberal lines. Add to the dubious moral claims made on behalf of a full-blown capitalist, market-centric option (it is, after all, a system premised on aggressive individualism and inequality) the doubtful developmental claims made for such an option and the case seems clear: the fact is that Southern Africa simply cannot compete successfuly with the more powerful capitalist centres at playing the global capitalist game that such central players themselves invented and continue to control. Small wonder that Colin Leys and myself could state more recently that "marginalization" is at least as salient a likelihood for Africa as is its continued exploitation and that the continent's fate, on its present trajectory, seems to be

> relegation to the margins of the global economy, with no visible prospect of continental development along capitalist lines. Population growth has outstripped production growth; the chances of significantly raising per capita output are falling, not rising; the infrastructure is increasingly inadequate; the market for high-value-added goods is miniscule. Global capital, in its constant search for new investment opportunities, finds them less and less in Africa. Which does not mean that nothing is happening, let alone that no alternative is possible. It simply means that Africa's development, and the dynamics of global capitalism, are no longer convergent, if they ever were.[6]

A hard truth, especially when writing at a time when the commonsensical acceptance of global capitalism's overriding writ is so widespread throughout the West—and in official circles in Southern Africa. For, as suggested, in Southern Africa itself the promise of a liberation from inequality and exploitation, local and worldwide, was indeed one of the ostensible premises of those engaged in struggles. And yet precisely the same parties that brought "freedom" in the first place and that are still in power have now largely subordinated themselves to global capitalism.[7] Of course, even in the 1960s it was difficult enough, in Western countries, to make credible the argument that "the problem" for the mass of the people in Southern Africa was both one of entrenched and institutionalized racism and one of capitalist exploitation, domestic and worldwide. How, then, to now discuss an outcome in which racism-in-power, in its most straightforward and unapologetic sense, has been banished from the region, while capitalism, driven by the interests of both whites and (some) Blacks but at the expense of any broad realization of the hopes and aspirations of the mass of the population, reigns victorious? Clearly, it behooves us, looking back, not only to acknowledge some of the ambiguities of the liberation struggles themselves—struggles that could produce such startling and, in many ways, anti-climactic outcomes—but also to assess the role played by the worldwide anti-apartheid and liberation support movement more broadly defined in facilitating the settling for such a relatively modest outcome.

**For the force** of "common sense," not least the "common sense" of worldwide capitalist hegemony, is not self-evident; it must be *created*. For, however seductive it may prove to be to those few who stand to gain by it, it is merely to be imposed upon the many for whom it offers no real promise. Such *imposition* is, for example, quite precisely what happened in the case, just prior to the 1960s, of one of the original and most impressive of Western anti-apartheid movements, the movement amongst U.S. Blacks led in the 1940s and early 1950s by people such as Paul Robeson, Alphaeus Hunton, and W.E.B. Du Bois. The importance of this radical movement is painstakingly documented by Penny Von Eschen in her exemplary book *Race Against Empire: Black Americans and Anticolonialism, 1937–1957*—but equally revealing is her grim account of the Cold War repression, led by the likes of President Harry Truman and Senator Joseph McCarthy, of any such radicalization.[8] True, Von Eschen does see the 1960s, and especially the 1970s (no doubt fuelled in part by simultaneous mobilization against the Vietnam War), as a period of recuperation—although only to a limited degree—of the ideological ground lost to Cold War machinations. Yet she also underscores the long-term costs to the Black community in the United States of the siege by the right against "anti-imperialist understandings" and against any expressions of scepticism about capitalism. For this ultimately affected negatively, she argues, even its own domestic agenda, since, as "the inequitable social relations of empire rebounded back home they eventually eroded the situation in the industrial and public sectors where African-American workers had made significant gains."[9]

True, the assertions of the 1940s left positive residues. For example, as Von Echen writes, "The global vision of democracy developed by Malcolm X, in the 1960s and just before he was slain, embraced anti-imperialism," and Malcolm X "also joined forces with the Student Nonviolent Coordinating Committee (SNCC), explicitly linking his internationalism with the fight for civil rights in the United States."[10] Moreover, if, by the end, Malcolm X had become ever more radically anti-imperialist in both race and, increasingly, class terms, so too did Martin Luther King Jr. Yet King's fate—as he moved in the 1960s to radicalize the terms of the link that he continued to assert between African (and other international) struggles and that of Blacks in the United States—is even more instructive as to the limits of the acceptable in Cold War America. This too is extremely well documented by Von Eschen: "As King attempted to reconnect the international and domestic politics that had been so thoroughly severed during the Cold War, he was increasingly isolated and chastised, abandoned by both white liberal and Black establishment allies." In sum, "The intellectual and political culture and the forms of institutions and alliances necessary to sustain his vision ... had been lost in the early Cold War."[11] Moreover, this history is essential to our understanding of the strength and limitations of the anti-apartheid movement in the United States—and elsewhere.

Of course, it was sometimes difficult in those days to disentangle anti-imperialist sentiments and understandings from pro-Soviet ones—although in retrospect it is quite evident that they were very far from being the same thing. Yet the Trumans and the McCarthys were working overtime to blur the lines of this distinction (manipulatively eliding anti-imperialist consciousness exclusively with "Soviet-lining") in the interests of their own reactionary political and economic ends. As a result, as the anti-apartheid movement regrouped for action in the 1960s, it did so on an ever more congealed Cold War terrain and in the context of an ascendant capitalism that made the raising of more systematic anti-imperialist claims neither credible (to most) nor viable—despite their absolute appropriateness. For two things were happening simultaneously as regards the anti-apartheid movement throughout this period, evoking, in fact, two storylines about anti-apartheid work that both warrant narrating.

One such narrative does demonstrate the building, slowly but surely, of a global movement, from the 1960s, directed against the enormities of racist hegemony in Southern Africa. In this regard 1960 was itself a crucial year. It was during that year, and in the immediately succeeding ones, that movements in Southern Africa itself either repositioned themselves (the ANC in South Africa) or were created (Frelimo in Mozambique) in order to take up armed struggle as a necessary component of their pursuit of liberation—this initiative constituting an important escalation of the struggle. But it was also the year that the United Nations, in a General Assembly resolution, declared colonialism to actually be illegal.[12] The stage was thus set for some further internationalization and expansion of the constituency in support of the struggle for freedom in Southern Africa that has been well documented elsewhere.[13]

Thus, in the United States there began to flower in the 1960s and much more fully than previously a new kind of national movement, one that found voice not only amongst Black Americans but also in the white community. The American Committee of Africa, based in New York, was a strong example of this focusing of new energies. So too were the first expressions of diverse initiatives at the local level, something that would grow impressively in the following decades. Indeed, it is hard to quarrel with the burgeoning record of assertive discord that those who saw the importance of the apartheid issue were able to sew in diverse ways—including a wide range of tactics of demonstrations and other modes of exposé and pressure upon banks and corporations caught with their hands in the cookie jar of South Africa's apartheid exploitation.[14]

At the same time, the "reformist" approach to U.S. capitalism that many of these corporate-focused activities embodied may also suggest the wisdom of the old adage that the better is enemy of the best: "improving" capitalism is scarcely the same as breaking the logic of its inordinate power. In fact this may seem to be particularly the case given that many reform undertakings actually had very little impact—as Gay Seidman persuasively argues was the case with the celebrated Reverend Sullivan–inspired "Code" designed to guide and monitor corporate conduct.[15] Of course, in creating the climate in which a more full-blown sanctions initiative could ultimately emerge from Congress in the 1980s, such actions did play a real part. But by then capital itself had successfully begun to move to adjust, in its own interests, its tactics—the better to control both the ANC itself and the overall shape of any post-apartheid settlement. In other words, the strength of capitalism, both as fount of power and of cultural predilection, was so strong in the United States as to rule out—beyond relatively confined circles of radical action and understanding—belief in any real alternative to (at best) mild reform. Such "reform" did, in fact, encompass something as significant as the reversal of formalized white minority rule: half a loaf is thus better than none, some might be tempted to say. Unless, that is, you happen to be amongst the vast numbers of people in Southern Africa who have been left, by post-apartheid capitalism, with the non-existent other half of that loaf.

True, by the 1970s the anti-apartheid movement was, as Francis Njubi Nesbitt writes, "also rejuvenated by what Ron Walters calls the 'new' or 'modern' pan-Africanist movements that emerged in the diaspora," as many "African-American youths began to explore their cultural heritage in Africa and to adopt a Black/pan-African identity."[16] Indeed, Nesbitt further notes the continuing importance in this decade of African consciousness of Malcolm X and the Black Power movement, suggesting that already, by 1967, "the SNCC and the Black Panthers had become anti-imperialist and Third Worldist." The stage was thus set for diverse activities on this front, actions ranging from the growing role of the Congressional Black Caucus (important to the eventual passage of the "Comprehensive Anti-Apartheid [Sanctions] Act" of 1986 over President Ronald Reagan's veto) to the sports boycott and other related high-profile actions led, principally, by Black American athletes such as Arthur Ashe, Tommie Smith, and Lee Carlos. And these actions were crystallized, in the late 1970s, in the emergence of such organizations as TransAfrica that grew out of "the sustained mobilization of African-American groups through the 1960s and early 1970s, combined with ... dramatic successes" in Africa itself.[17]

There was promise here, then, but it is also true that the actual degree of "liberation"—in any suitably broad sense of that term—achieved in Southern Africa was to be severely limited. What was realized was the overthrow of formal racist rule, no small accomplishment. Yet corporations national and multinational, and not least U.S. ones, that had such a horrific track record of collaboration with apartheid over the decades proved quite capable of switching horses as the prospects for the continuance of unapologetic racist rule waned in the 1970s. What then emerged, in the context of capitalist globalization and more strongly asserted American imperial hegemony, was, arguably, a virtual recolonization of the newly "liberated" countries of Southern Africa.

Meanwhile, most white proponents of anti-apartheid work have drifted away from Southern Africa–centred support work and into other fields, not lingering to support those who still struggle, often against the very liberation movements that are now in power, for progressive outcomes in the region. Indeed, as Bill Fletcher regretfully notes, some Black Americans even continue to support Zimbabwe's aging dictator, Robert Mugabe, and his wholly opportunist "anti-imperialist" charade.[18] As Fletcher infers, the risk is that—as also in the case of continuing Black American support for the ANC's meek acceptance of global capitalism's writ in South Africa—race will continue to trump class in the liberation equation, when in fact both race and class stand as active and essential dimensions of the plight of the oppressed in Southern Africa, just as antagonism towards both racism and class oppression should be keys to any genuinely liberatory politics of support. In short, an adequate history of the U.S. anti-apartheid/liberation support movement, in considering the 1960s and after, must spring from anti-imperialist premises that give due consideration to class-cum-capitalist realities as well as those of race.

A similar story can be told elsewhere. In Great Britain, an emergent left anti-apartheid consciousness began less dramatically than it had with Robeson and Du Bois (and did not, therefore, have to be crushed quite so dramatically). Indeed, amidst a plethora of anti-apartheid activities, slowly growing in the 1960s but becoming more marked in the next couple of decades, there operated—as the leading scholar of the anti-apartheid movement itself notes—an admirable "moral imperative" that was central to Britain's Anti-Apartheid Movement (AAM), as it was formally named. At the same time, notes Roger Fieldhouse, this was something that did lead to a division between those who "regarded the campaign against apartheid as a single moral issue [those "more inclined to see apartheid simply as evil, immoral and abhorrent"] and those saw it as part of wider political struggle," with apartheid seen by them as "a particularly nasty manifestation of the much wider problem of human exploitation." Moreover, it was the former of these two tendencies that established itself as hegemonic, the key being the victory of "liberalism" within the official AAM (and within the broader mobilization against apartheid more generally), as Fieldhouse spells out very clearly indeed.[19]

The AAM, it is worth emphasizing, was from the outset preoccupied on two fronts. Certainly, the AAM looked upwards towards the holders of power. Yet under neither the Conservatives nor Labour was there much likelihood of shifting the weight of capital-logic as the driving force of the economy and polity, and AAM positions tended to reflect both this fact and, more pervasively, the "commonsensical" imperatives of capitalist considerations. It was therefore drawn easily towards the adoption of "reformist" tactics and strategies, with "apartheid" in consequence looming very much larger as a target than "capitalism." But the movement also looked "downwards," towards a potential constituency available for some significant degree of popular mobilization. And this was a constituency that might, on occasion, also manifest the beginnings of an even more radical brand of consciousness.

Here both the organizational centrality established by the AAM itself and, paradoxically, the effective work of cadres of both the South African Communist Party (SACP) and the Communist Party of Great Britain (CPGB) within it helped to reinforce a more moderate line and a more moderate approach. After all, the ANC that the Communists, South African and British, actively supported was itself protagonist of a two-stage theory of struggle that placed "national liberation" firmly in the forefront of its goals. And the AAM itself was itself quite content, by and large, to avoid any "wider political objectives." Left challengers were merely driven back, the movement's drive for control and centralization merely "inhibiting alliances that should have been welcomed" and imposing an "almost overbearing centralized control" (in Fieldhouse's words)—a kind of "control-freakery" that distorted "the national office's attitude to AAM's own local, regional, student, professional and specialist groups, including the women's and Black and ethnic minorities committees." A movement, in short, became more than ready to accede to the least revolutionary of outcomes to the anti-apartheid situation, including the moderate outcome that the ANC itself was quick, when the opportunity arose, both to accept and to present it with.

As for Canada, this country in the 1960s had neither the large and increasingly mobilized Black population of the United States nor the inescapable sense of a colonialist past of Great Britain (our own history as regards our approach to the First Nations being at that time scarcely visible or worthy of note to many Canadians). We thus possessed a context that would see only a slower emergence of popular action on the Southern African question. There was, of course, the memorable moment of Diefenbaker at the Commonwealth Heads of State meeting in 1961 helping "drive South Africa out" of that body. Even if his role in this respect was less crucial than some at the time presented it as being, it was not an ignoble one. But it was one that, for the moment, still found only relatively muted echoes within the broader society—although some voices were beginning to be heard within both Canada's white and Black communities (with the Black community in particular being still relatively small but increasingly active, especially in Halifax and in Toronto).

Only towards the end of the 1960s did articulate anti-apartheid voices really begin to make themselves heard, especially in the churches, in ways that demanded increased attention from a broader public, and giving rise, but only at the beginning of the 1970s, to two documents that would provide benchmarks for what was to follow. One was *The Black Paper: An Alternative Policy for Canada Towards Southern Africa*, a carefully argued and principled 1970 response to the rather bland passages on Southern Africa found in the government's own White Paper, *Foreign Policy for Canadians*.[20] The initiative for the *Black Paper* emerged from a meeting held at Carleton University, Ottawa, and from the more or less simultaneous formation of a group calling itself the Committee for a Just Canadian Policy Towards Africa, whose membership included "churchmen, officials of voluntary organizations, trade unions, businessmen, academics, and returned CUSO volunteers." The Committee in turn asked four of its members to prepare the response that immediately became a part of the (admittedly limited) public discussion of the time.[21] Its conclusions were stark and indeed would become axioms for the broader "liberation support" movement that would begin to surface in the 1970s.

Of similar saliency and also reflecting the previous decade's slow growth of concern—principally church-centred—about Southern Africa (and also as regards Canadian corporations' largely negative role there) was *Investment in Oppression*, a document produced by the Study and Action Committee of the World

Relationships Committee of the YWCA of Canada on Canadian Links with South Africa. Tracing both the multiple trends towards an ever firmer entrenchment of apartheid policy in South Africa and the failure of the Canadian government to stay the hand of Canadian business interests from getting in on the wrong (though temporarily most profitable) side of the polarization of forces there, the report concluded, in stern if not precisely revolutionary terms: "Individual and institutional shareholders should be prepared to publicly sever their connections with firms which remain unresponsive to such requests and fail to meet the minimal code of ethical employment practices."[22]

Fortunately, Renate Pratt, a principal architect of the YMCA report, was soon to become co-ordinator of the Taskforce on the Churches and Corporate Responsibility (with Garth Legge serving on its board for some years), which carried on a worthy critique of the multiple (and largely negative) activities of Canadian corporations—although no real critique of Canadian capitalism per se—from the 1960s and for many years.[23] Meanwhile, the other authors of the *Black Paper* were not to remain especially active in advancing the anti-apartheid struggle (although Cranford Pratt remained an important critic of Canadian foreign policy for many decades; and Linda Freeman, research assistant to the authors, was to become in time the principal academic chronicler of official Canada's unworthy long-term record vis-à-vis the unfolding Southern African situation).[24] Nonetheless, their initiative became one inspiration for the emergence of a range of anti-apartheid (broadly defined) organizations. For by the mid-1970s (and indeed right up to the last, waning days of the apartheid dispensation in South Africa), it was still accurate to argue that "Canada's role has changed hardly at all from that correctly described and condemned by the authors of the Black Paper several years ago." Indeed, as I continued at the time:

> Such a pattern of policy is not due to any mere lack of information or sympathy on the part of Canadian decision-makers. Rather it is the inevitable by-product of the structure of Canada's economy and society, and the country's own colonial status [vis-à-vis the United States] and domestic capitalist imperatives virtually determining subservience to imperial demands within NATO and the worship of established trade and investment patterns at the expense of any discernible principle. Indeed, it could be argued very convincingly that the primary contribution of Canadians to the African cause would be to carry on their own "liberation struggle" at home.[25]

Of course, as an anti-apartheid activist in Canada myself during those years, I was well aware of the contradictions in our approach. Most of us in the activist group TCLPAC/TCLSAC (Toronto Committee for the Liberation of Portugal's African Colonies/Toronto Committee for the Liberation of Southern Africa)

Police remove demonstrators from the ground during cricket match featuring a South African team at Toronto Cricket, Skating and Curling Club on Saturday.

—Globe and Mail, Derek DeBono

# 31 charged in protest against South African cricket team

The author (in the middle, with a cop on top of him), at a Toronto demonstration. From *The Globe and Mail*, front page, July 12, 1976.

were of radical disposition, as much opposed to global (and Canadian) capitalism as we were to apartheid per se. We would even jokingly refer to ourselves as part of "the foreign policy wing of a new left movement for Canada in-the-making," and we sought—in our popular Cinema of Solidarity series, in our direct actions against Canadian banks implicated in bank loans to South Africa, in the exposure of the Hudson's Bay Company's tawdry role in the karakul fur trade in Namibia and of Gulf Oil Canada's involvement in laundering "stolen" Angolan oil for the U.S. market, in exposure of the grisly actions of Falconbridge and other Canadian mining companies throughout the region, and in our various publications—to keep the flag of radical criticism and radical practice flying. But in the end there was no really plausible larger movement for "a socialist Canada" that we could easily be a part of. True, we sought to keep a radical analysis of Southern Africa going long after formal freedom there had been achieved, principally through our magazine *Southern Africa Report* (published until 2000), since we were firmly convinced that Southern Africa was still very far from being "liberated" in any fully meaningful sense. But energies and interests began to drift elsewhere, with some former comrades moved by the misguided sense that Southern Africa was now free while others moved on, more plausibly, to other fronts of the "anti-(capitalist)-globalization" struggle.

More immediately, to return to the 1960s and 1970s, it seemed appropriate to focus, as the Taskforce would also increasingly do, on the contradictions of Canada's policies as summarized in Prime Minister Pierre Elliott Trudeau's celebrated response to his own challenge (quoted in the *Black Paper*) regarding

*Liberation Support and Anti-Apartheid Work as Seeds of Global Consciousness*

**137**

Canada's Southern African policy: "It's not consistent.... We should either stop trading or stop condemning."[26] Of course, on Trudeau's watch Canada continued to do both: to condemn and to trade. As a result, by the latter part of the 1970s and into the 1980s many groups in English Canada—TCLPAC/TCLSAC, Canadian Anti-Apartheid Movement, Canadians Concerned About Southern Africa, South African Action Coalition, Southern Africa Information Group—began, along with other organizations in Quebec, to surface alongside that active church constituency to sustain a progressive Southern African agenda. In short, the overall liberation support/anti-apartheid movement in Canada was becoming as visible and potent as was the case elsewhere. It could thus lend a sense of solidarity to those struggling for freedom on the ground in Southern Africa itself while also providing a brand of resistance that forced holders of governmental and corporate power to be a little more circumspect than they might have otherwise been as to the import of their actions. Of course, it was the shifting balance of political power on the ground in Southern Africa and the consequent implications of this shift for the profitability of Canadian corporations that focused the attentions of power-wielders more forcibly than our own efforts. Still, moral suasion and our political actions must have provided some countervailing force to both the dreadful illogic of racist rule and the grim logic of profit: so most in the anti-apartheid movement hoped and thought.

Of course, in the positive efforts made by all these movements to resist racist oppression (if not global capitalism!) they were also part of a much broader global set of activities.[27] If this was just beginning to take shape in the 1960s, it would soon become a major social force on a global scale and certainly contribute to the end of formal apartheid. Such, to conclude, is the forceful case made by two recent writers on this broader subject.[28] Hakan Thorn, for one, convincingly describes this force as "a 'transnational social movement' comprising national components but linked internationally by new media, new global movements of people (including from Africa) and new global institutions such as the United Nations developing at a time of 'political globalization.'"[29] Less convincing, however, is the strong support that Thorn lends to the first of two possible narratives regarding anti-apartheid work. For his is a positive, an unqualifiedly benign and liberatory reading, of such work. The reality of continuing capitalist hegemony and ongoing mass immiseration—the touchstone to a second narrative, one that explores the tragic shortfalls of the actually-existing anti-apartheid movement both in Southern Africa and more globally—is never fully discussed. The second author, Peter Limb, seeks, to his credit, to balance the two narratives more carefully—and is left in the end with a dilemma with which he visibly struggles: the ANC in South Africa, for example, both is, and is not, part of the capitalist globalization problem that confronts the mass of the population there.[30] Nor is he wrong to emphasize the continuing strength of the global capitalist framework in dictating such an outcome. Nonetheless, I would judge that he lets self-interested domestic elites in Southern Africa (beginning with South African president Thabo Mbeki) off far too lightly. Still, I suspect that he and I would agree that there is still a great deal of work to be done in Southern Africa to fully realize a genuine "liberation" there.

For the fact remains that the story of the post-apartheid phase of the Southern African liberation movement, one that seemed in so many ways to be a triumph, has proven, at another level, to represent a profound anti-climax, even a severe defeat for the poorest of the poor. For it will already be apparent that the "second story" regarding the nature and import of the anti-apartheid movement has come to the fore, this being the story of a movement that came to narrow its agenda so narrowly to challenging primarily race and "apartheid" that it neglected to emphasize the importance of any simultaneous struggle against class and capitalism (both domestically and internationally). Perhaps it could be argued that this was merely a judiciously circumspect tactical approach under the prevailing circumstances. But it was also most certainly (as we have seen Fieldhouse argue) a fatefully narrow one. Nor was such a reformist approach[31] merely a result of intense ideological pressure wielded by those deploying Cold War mantras—although, as we have seen, such right-wing forces have certainly been in action. Nonetheless, a great deal has had also to do with the comfort of populations in the relatively affluent centres of the global capitalist system, a situation that continues to polarize populations on a global scale much more dramatically than it does at home. This has, of course, further worked to weaken the voice of the left in the imperial centres. In fact, deeply felt anti-capitalism was quite simply not to be on the long-term agenda there even of many (most?) of those in "the West" who could nonetheless bring themselves to act against institutionalized racist rule.

# But this is also true in Southern Africa itself where, unfortunately, there has been no very positive outcome to the various liberation struggles either in economic or even in political terms. Thus, in my paper "The Strange Death of Liberated Southern Africa"[32] I felt moved to pose the question as to "who really had won?" the struggle for Southern African liberation.

We know who lost, of course: the white minorities in positions of formal political power (whether colonially in the Portuguese colonies or quasi-independently in Zimbabwe, and also in South Africa). And thank fortune, and hard and brave work, for that. But who, in contrast, has won, at least for the time being: global capitalism, the West and the international financial institutions, and local

*Liberation Support and Anti-Apartheid Work as Seeds of Global Consciousness*

**139**

elites of state and private sectors, both white and Black? But how about the mass of Southern African populations, both urban and rural and largely Black? Not so obviously the winners, I would suggest, and certainly not in any very expansive sense. Has it not been a kind of defeat for them too?

Admittedly this is a sobering conclusion to have to draw. And, of course, a struggle does continues against the recolonization of Southern Africa by a "new empire" driven by global capitalism and its local minions. However, the unfortunate fact remains that Thabo Mbeki, Sam Nujoma, and even Nelson Mandela have merely become—much like Colin Powell and Condaleeza Rice did, closer to the imperial heart—junior ministers in a system of global governance centred in the boardrooms of global capital, in the World Bank and the IMF, and in the councils of the G8. In fact, only an anti-imperialist perspective could serve to complement a righteous and rightful indignation towards racist rule with a conscious rejection of global capitalist domination and thus contribute to turn liberation into a reality. In the long run, for all its importance and for all its accomplishments, "anti-apartheid" tended to muffle a necessary understanding of global realities rather than serve as a step towards it. The result: scarcely a whimper is now heard either here or from local power-holders there. Yet as Southern Africans begin, from the ground up, to launch a new struggle for liberation, we can, as students of the 1960s still living in "the belly of the beast," also learn from that moment—learn how, more appropriately, to support the poorest of the poor there while also expanding effectively the terms of our own struggle to realize, in some post-capitalist (especially post "neo-liberal" capitalist) world, a better future.

# PART II

# CULTURAL CITIZENSHIP

# UPON THE LONG AVENUES OF SADNESS
## Otto René Castillo and Transnational Spaces of Exile

It only struck me, Teresa, that the gesture of disapproval is horribly like the gesture of capitulation. I've often read that people who wash their hands in innocence do so in blood-stained basins. And their hands bear the traces.
—Pedro Jaqueras, from Bertolt Brecht, *Señora Carrar's Rifles*

**A white screen** gives way to a photograph of the smirking poet standing before the Brandenburg Gates in Berlin. After a few brief introductory words, the title of the film appears in German: *Erinnerungen an Otto René Castillo* (Memories of Otto René Castillo). The documentary short film, produced in 1979 by DEFA—the former state-owned film company of the German Democratic Republic—examines the cultural activism of the eponymous subject, a committed Guatemalan poet and filmmaker who studied in Germany and Cuba before being murdered by the Guatemalan state in 1967 for participating in his country's communist-affiliated guerrilla movement.

The film—itself an example of the prevalence of internationalism—offers glimpses into the transnational world of the 1960s inhabited by Castillo, and revolutionary activists like him. From this obscure cinematic relic of the Cold War we bear witness to images of a life interrupted by the politics of the era. Still-photographic frames appear on the screen as the young Guatemalan manifests multiple identities in different locales: Castillo as an aspiring student of letters in Leipzig; Castillo as a troubled poet and filmmaker in Berlin; a coy-looking Castillo before a white wall decorated with the tricoloured Cuban flag and the seal of the Unión de Jóvenes Comunistas (Young Communist League), complete

Otto René Castillo as guerrillero, c. 1967. A film still from Karlheind Mund, *Erinnerungen an Otto René Castillo*, DEFA-Studio, German Democratic Republic, 1979. (Used with the permission of DEFA-Stiftung.)

with the profiles of Cuban revolutionaries Camilo Cienfuegos and Julio Antonio Mella; and, finally, Castillo as a bearded *guerrillero* in rural Guatemala. These personal glimpses into an individual's life implicitly suggest that anti-imperialist action in the 1960s did not just have many methods of combat; it also had many theatres of struggle.[1]

The life of Otto René Castillo was the epitome of the cosmopolitan intellectualism that characterized social activism in Guatemala and throughout Latin America in the 1960s. The lives of such proprietors of revolutionary thought and culture were marked by the transient nature of forced or voluntary exile, itself moulded by the geopolitics of the Cold War. Within a five-year span commencing in 1954 with the overthrow of President Jacobo Arbenz of Guatemala and the reversal of that country's October Revolution, the cultural terrain of the Caribbean Basin altered fundamentally for Latin American socialists as their fortunes rose and fell. While Guatemala quickly became a bastion of Cold War reaction, with the military cementing its grip on power, the struggles of Fidel Castro's 26th of July Movement prepared to morph the politico-cultural landscape of the region. For many Guatemalan intellectuals, the Cuban Revolution of 1959 refocused the prospects for revolution back to the Caribbean and away from Eastern Europe, which had heretofore served as ideological inspiration for much of the hemisphere's left.

Certainly this is not to negate the importance of the Soviet bloc to the Latin American left, as Otto René Castillo's life itself demonstrates. But the Cuban Revolution provided a new template for revolutionary struggle, and it also functioned as a liberated cultural and ideological space—a "free territory of the Americas"—for radicals persecuted in their own countries. With the rapid consolidation of Castro's regime after January 1959, the Cuban Revolution served as a catalyst for many aspiring revolutionaries and inaugurated many of the social, political, and cultural trends that characterized the Latin American 1960s. Exile to the socialist world sharpened protest by providing evidence of alternative forms of social organization; it also offered pedagogies of resistance that enabled engagement in such protest, from literary vocation and the craft of filmmaking to guerrilla training.

Born in Quetzaltenango in April 1934, Otto René Castillo came of age amidst the social and political upheaval of the "ten years of spring," Guatemala's decade-long experiment with representative democracy. Arguably the defining moment of modern Guatemalan history, the period was initiated with the October Revolution of 1944, which ousted the remnants of the old military guard that had ruled Guatemala since the early 1930s. A coalition of civilians and junior military officers formed a junta and within months allowed for the country's first elections. A university professor named Juan José Arévalo was voted president by an electorate limited to men and literate women. Arévalo's government took steps to make the country's political life more inclusive: adopting measures to reduce illiteracy, expand suffrage, improve working conditions, and encourage popular participation in national culture, measures continued by Jacobo Arbenz, who was elected Arévalo's successor in 1950.[2]

Arbenz legalized the Guatemalan communist party—after 1949, known as the Partido Guatemalteco de Trabajo (Guatemalan Workers' Party or PGT)—which, in different incarnations, had remained clandestine for much of its history. Many members of the PGT, including Castillo, who associated with the party's youth faction, were involved in political and cultural activities. The relaxation of restrictions on association and assembly and the lack of press censorship allowed social-democratic culture to flourish. Left-wing adherents from across the hemisphere flocked to Guatemala City to relish in the revolutionary atmosphere.[3] Indeed, the governments of the period promoted an affiliated cultural front to reflect state policy through its artistic creation and synchronize indigenous themes with the dominant national culture.[4]

In 1952 Arbenz's administration passed Decree 900, an agrarian reform bill that virtually confiscated unused lands from large *fincas* and plantations and called for its redistribution to petitioning communities. Opposition to these measures soon percolated from a series of sources. With Arbenz having mobilized and empowered rural dwellers through government-associated committees, military officers increasingly became concerned that "the revolution in the countryside" was growing unruly and that the military itself was losing its traditional place as the primary institution of the state in rural zones. Meanwhile, reactionary university students—the sons of middle-class planters—began a vicious propaganda campaign against the perceived communist inspiration of the reform and Arbenz's close association with the leadership of the PGT. Finally, the U.S.

State Department under President Dwight D. Eisenhower vocalized its opposition to Decree 900, which had jeopardized the interests of the Boston-based United Fruit Company. The intimate ties between the Eisenhower White House and the banana company, as well as the anti-communist atmosphere of the McCarthy era, compelled the president to activate the Central Intelligence Agency to ally with domestic opposition forces in Guatemala to topple Arbenz.

Tensions came to a head in June 1954, when a CIA-trained "liberation army" entered Guatemala with the intention of sparking a popular uprising. While poorly armed campesinos loyal to Arbenz stopped the invasion force, high-ranking military officers launched a coup d'état. Despite the efforts of Arbenz supporters, including the adolescent Castillo, who helped organize ill-equipped brigades for the defence of the constitutional government, the president, desiring a cessation of bloodshed, had limited options. Having lost the confidence of the military brass, Arbenz resigned, and—after a series of diplomatic manoeuvres—a new regime was installed under Colonel Carlos Castillo Armas, effectively ending the October Revolution.[5]

Through the summer of 1954 a brutal counter-revolution purged those associated with the land reform process. The October Revolution's cultural front was vanquished and many of its members fled the country. Faced with certain imprisonment, Otto René Castillo joined the torrent of exiles, settling in neighbouring El Salvador. There he befriended Roque Dalton, who later rose to international prominence for his poetry and would also pen the most detailed biography of his Guatemalan comrade. Together Castillo and Dalton shared the 1955 Central American Poetry Prize and joined Salvadoran writers and cultural workers in a series of radical literary groups, eventually forming a circle known as the Generación Comprometida—the Committed Generation. The essence of the group's cultural philosophy was that literature must perform a social function for the betterment of humanity, while emphasizing that co-optation by the state in its existing form was not an option. Only with the overthrow of the state and the establishment of socialism could a nourishing culture be attained, an end to which the committed poets dedicated themselves. Moreover, their struggle was not determined or limited by national boundaries; internationalism was a central tenet of the writers.[6] Thus, by the late 1950s a younger generation of Central American writers had rejected the prospects of state reform, replacing it with political and cultural militancy. Yet until the Cuban Revolution, the strategies of the radicals would remain undefined.

In Guatemala civil liberties were curtailed after the assassination of Armas in July 1957, a fitting eulogy for the president's brutal reign. For months prior to his death, civil society had pressured the military to expand freedoms. The Asociación de Estudiantes Universitarios (University Students' Association, or

AEU) at the Universidad de San Carlos de Guatemala, for example, demanded the right of opposition parties to function freely, and the AEU's newspaper, *El Estudiante*, petitioned to allow for the amnestied return of all exiles.[7] Only following Armas's murder and the temporary state of siege did Guatemala enter into a brief period of political openness.

With the respite from political persecution, Castillo returned to his homeland. Using the experiences garnered from his exile, he became a founding editor of a Guatemalan monthly, *Lanzas y letras*, in 1958. Representing a radical departure from its contemporaries, the review published poetry, essays on a variety of political and social themes, and served as a local cultural guide. Castillo's participation in the project was short-lived because he was awarded a scholarship from the AEU to study at the Karl Marx University of Leipzig in the German Democratic Republic. For the next four years Castillo remained in the Eastern bloc on a scholarship that became a de facto exile as the brief political aperture in Guatemala closed.

In terms of revolutionary strategy, while Castillo was in Europe countervailing trends emerged that would divide leftist movements in Latin America throughout the 1960s. On the one hand, parties like the Guatemalan PGT exercised continued adherence to the Stalinist popular front strategy of the Kremlin as the dominant mode of struggle for international communist movements. On the other hand, new forms of revolutionary praxis were being forged in the Cuban Sierra Maestra. Indeed, through the summer of 1958 Castillo's *compañeros* in the AEU began to forecast a Castro victory and applauded the armed efforts of the Cuban people against the "treasonous Cuban army."[8] That the Cuban Revolution disrupted existing orthodoxies hitherto accepted by much of the Marxist revolutionary left in Latin America is beyond dispute. While Guatemalan revolutionaries had certainly considered the possibilities of revolutionary armed struggle prior to 1959, the success of Castro's 26th of July Movement and the Rebel Army ignited a firestorm of enthusiasm for replicating the guerrilla heroics of Cuba from the Guatemalan sierra.

In Europe Castillo engrossed himself in German studies as a student of letters, graduating in the summer of 1961. He soon began writing poetry in his acquired language. With student newspapers in Leipzig providing a medium, his work expressed solidarity with the Algerian war against French colonialism.[9] Like many poets of his generation, Castillo exhibited a sense of solidarity noted for its transnational motif and personal identification with foreign resistance against imperialism. His mastery of German opened up new avenues of struggle, beyond committed literature. In late 1961–early 1962 East Germany hosted the prestigious Fourth Leipzig International Film Festival. A Cuban delegation from the Instituto Cubano de Arte e Industria Cinematográficos (ICAIC, or Cuban Institute of Cinematographic Art and Industry) was selected by Cine Cubano to attend the festival. One Cuban delegate, Octavio Cortázar Jiménez—who later directed the classic Cuban short film *Por primera vez*—was nominated to serve as a juror for the festival. In an interview years later Cortázar explained that because he did not speak German he "was introduced to a young man with glasses, not very tall, and with a Latin American accent: it was Otto René Castillo who was going to act as my interpreter during my stay at the Festival."[10] At the film festival Castillo mingled with the likes of filmmaker Roman Karmen and screenwriter Kurt Stern. Most significantly, he met the great Dutch documentarist, Joris Ivens.

By the early 1960s Ivens had already won international acclaim for three decades of documentary filmmaking. Among other projects, Ivens had worked in partnership with Ernest Hemingway on *The Spanish Earth* to document domestic Republican resistance during the Spanish Civil War. He had also worked alongside photographer Robert Capa in China for *The 400 Million*. In 1960 ICAIC invited Ivens to Cuba, where he produced two documentary films about Cuba and the Revolution's struggles against counter-revolutionaries. He taught for two months at Escuela Frank País, a film school created by ICAIC to teach documentary filmmaking to members of Castro's Revolutionary Armed Forces. Ivens fused diverse elements of internationalism; while remaining dedicated to European socialism, he was inspired by the contemporary anticolonial struggles in the Third World that generated new avenues of revolution.[11]

In this spirit, under the auspices of DEFA at its film studios in East Berlin, the Dutch filmmaker created the so-called Joris Ivens Brigade, which consisted of aspiring Latin American filmmakers from El Salvador, Guatemala, Haiti, and Venezuela. The idea was that following intensive technical and paramilitary training these artists would film revolutionary armed struggles in their respective countries. Technological innovations in cinematic reproduction in the early 1960s transformed the nature of documentary filmmaking. Early in the decade, for example, Ivens heralded the development of new 16-millimetre film that recorded in shoulder-carried cameras, freeing the filmmaker from the strictures of sets and permitting the production of a new film aesthetic.[12] While the technology liberated the documentarist, the prospect of filming guerrilla movements for popular consumption in Latin America—a region plagued by high levels of illiteracy—possessed great revolutionary potential. It is no surprise then that a recurring metaphor during the period was the transformation of the film camera into a weapon as the lines between insurrection and revolutionary culture were blurred.[13] Joining the Brigade, Castillo was enlisted for two years by DEFA Studios in February 1962.

The vocational training—aimed at documenting armed rebellion—was a unique opportunity afforded to the exiled Castillo, and it came at a fortuitous period as an embryonic guerrilla uprising was maturing in Guatemala. The guerrilla movement grew out of an aborted November 1960 military revolt, and its leaders came to ally themselves ideologically with the PGT. The relationship, however, was fraught with tensions as internal dissent fermented within the party over its endorsement of armed struggle and outward shift from popular frontism. By 1964 the Fuerzas Armadas Rebeldes (Rebel Armed Forces, or FAR) was Guatemala's largest guerrilla movement under the command of Luis Turcios Lima, who also headed up the FAR's Frente Guerrillero Edgar Ibarra (Edgar Ibarra Guerrilla Front, or FGEI). The FGEI operated in the Sierra de las Minas of Zacapa, a department in eastern Guatemala, where it regularly engaged the Guatemalan military.[14]

In the spring of 1964, following his film training at DEFA, Otto René Castillo returned to Guatemala. Armed with the knowledge acquired in exile, he formed a Brechtian-inspired experimental theatre troupe in the capital city and organized clandestinely with the PGT. Soon Castillo was making plans to document the activities of the FAR on film. Before the project fully developed, however, he was arrested and imprisoned for over a month and then exiled to Mexico. The next several months of his life were a whirlwind. He was nominated as the Guatemalan delegate to the Organizing Committee of the World Youth Festival to be held in Algiers in July and August 1965. But his preparations for the festival in Algeria—the country whose people he had paid homage to in verse three years earlier—were broken up and the festival put on hiatus following the overthrow of Algerian president Ben Bella in June 1965. His plans changed, Castillo returned to Germany and travelled through much of Eastern Europe before making his way to Cuba.[15]

The Cuban Revolution altered the geopolitics of the 1960s. In liberal and conservative discourse in Guatemala—and throughout Latin America—the Soviet Union no longer served as the principal Red menace, threatening to pervade the body politic by feeding social discontent. Rather, after 1959, Cuba was placed at the vanguard of the revolution in Latin America as the political lexicon of the period swung from the prospect of the Soviets establishing a beachhead in the region to the peril of Cuba exporting Castroism from the Caribbean.[16] Although the Cuban state censored certain cultural expression that it denounced as "counterrevolutionary," it also endorsed radical thinking so that the ideology of revolution reached the proportions of a historic bloc; revolution, as an identity of a collective cultural and political being, permeated most aspects of Cuban life.

The emergence of a socialist state in Cuba generated new options for Latin America's exiles. While repressive states disrupted organic left-wing organizing, the hemisphere's exiles were able to re-forge socialist communities in new guises and with broader international perspectives in Cuba. Indeed, for many Latin

American intellectuals, the Cuban Revolution provided a safe cultural space in which artistic expression could be shared, contrary to the restrictive state policies of their home countries. Further, Cuba also offered a cultural infrastructure that cultivated socialist modes of analysis and cultural practice. Through presses like the Casa de las Américas—and later, Tricontinental publications—a hemispheric literary space was opened in which emerging and established left-wing authors had a forum to publish and promote their works. Such organizations catered to communities of exiles and domestic intellectuals alike, concentrating diverse but like-minded groups to develop new forms of cultural expression.

With its ideological and theoretical contributions to revolutionary thinking—emphasizing the importance of personal agency and popular armed struggle—the Cuban Revolution challenged the assumptions of Soviet peaceful co-existence through expressions of transnational solidarity. By early January 1966 Otto René Castillo found himself in Havana during the proceedings of the first meeting of the Organization for the Solidarity of the Peoples of Africa, Asia, and Latin America (OSPAAAL)—the Tricontinental Conference. In retrospect, the conference was in many ways the apogee of militant Cuban rhetoric and internationalism during the 1960s. It served as the denouement of several years of effort by the Castro regime to integrate Cuba—and Latin America—into the global solidarity networks that had emerged with the process of decolonization in Africa and Asia.[17] With accord established between organizations, movements, and various governments of the three continents, anti-imperialist perspectives that had emerged over the preceding decades were formalized in the founding of *Tricontinental Magazine*.[18]

The Guatemalan delegation at the founding meeting of OSPAAAL identified with many of the theoretical positions highlighted by the conference. Representing Guatemala, Turcios Lima echoed Cuban rhetoric, contending that the FAR was fighting to attain Guatemala's second and true independence from the trappings of neo-colonialism.[19] For his part, Castillo had espoused the armed example that Cuba presented to the people of Guatemala and Latin America well before the conference. In a Guatemalan student publication from 1964, he published a poem entitled "*Comandante Cuba*." Dedicating his poem to the people of Cuba, Castillo praises the armed resistance of Cuban fighters against the incursions of reactionary forces. The poet's imagery is militant, composed of references to weaponry and his willingness to self-sacrifice for the perpetuation of the revolution. Moreover, in revolution Castillo sees the future for the rest of the hemisphere, contending that Cuba is the "example of the day's sojourn/ you are the commander of America up in arms."[20] Acting on similar motivations, Castillo used the occasion of what became known as the Tricontinental Conference to interview Turcios Lima in preparation for his eventual return to Guatemala and enlistment in the FGEI under Turcios Lima's command.

After the conference Castillo enrolled alongside other trainees for guerrilla instruction provided by the Cuban government. Present at the military training was the French intellectual—and student of Louis Althusser—Régis Debray, the author of the polemic *Revolution in the Revolution?* Debray was to join Ernesto Che Guevara's ill-fated guerrilla band in Bolivia.[21] Castillo took the guerrilla exercises seriously and spoke extensively to Debray, then regarded as a major theoretician in the art of armed struggle.[22]

When Castillo returned to Guatemala, he did so with the intent of establishing himself as a combatant in the FGEI, moving beyond the advised role of an intellectual. Nonetheless, while in the guerrilla underground, he did find time to translate Bertolt Brecht's *Señora Carrar's Rifles* from German to Spanish. The one-act play—set during the Spanish Civil War as fascist armies advance on Republican positions—follows a heated discussion in the house of Señora Teresa Carrar about social responsibility, sacrifice, and pacifism in the context of national strife. Pedro Jaqueras, Señora Carrar's brother, insists that to defend the town she must permit her sons to arm themselves with her rifles, equating neutrality with acquiescence and capitulation to fascism. As the essence of the Committed Generation's thinking, these themes reverberate in Castillo's literary works, especially in his exposition of the "apolitical intellectuals" of Guatemala.[23] Such similarities explain Castillo's desire to bring Brecht's work to a Guatemalan audience. He believed that the play mirrored conditions in the left's insurrection and would clarify the poet's decision to personally take up arms.[24]

Otto René Castillo immersed himself in the armed struggle of the FGEI in November 1966. Recognized for his intellectual capacity, Castillo was designated chief of propaganda and education in the Eastern Region. To this end, he committed himself to a literacy campaign for both FGEI combatants and the local population in the FAR's zone of operation, as well as staging cultural events with ideological subtexts in the jungle. But Castillo integrated into the guerrilla movement at a time when its fortunes were on the decline. Comandante Turcios Lima had been killed in an automobile accident the month before Castillo's arrival in the Sierra de las Minas. Although the FGEI's second in command, César Montes, assumed control of the FAR, the Guatemalan army and its proxy forces immediately commenced a campaign of terror and violence that systematically dismantled the social infrastructure of the guerrilla initiative. The countryside, invaded by the army, was quickly embroiled in a brutal anti-insurgent conflict that targeted suspected leftist sympathizers. While previous military campaigns against the guerrillas had yielded no significant results, the army offensive from October 1966 until the summer of 1967 effectively decapitated the FGEI, and the FAR ceased to function as a rural guerrilla movement in Eastern Guatemala. Otto René Castillo was among the casualties. Ambushed in March 1967, he and his comrade Nora Paíz Cárcamo were taken prisoner, interrogated, tortured, and murdered; their bodies disappeared, leaving their families unable to gather their remains.[25]

Far from his homeland of Guatemala, Castillo once wrote that "exile is a long, long avenue where only sadness walks." Despite this, the poet added that should the exile not lose heart, his enemies will never succeed in killing "the powerful strength of his heart's storms."[26] For socialist thinkers during the 1960s, exile brought transformations in subject positions, complementing and fortifying the ferocity of desire, described by Castillo, to modify the social structure. While exile profoundly interrupted the lives of political outcasts during the Cold War, major shifts in geopolitics such as the Cuban rebel victory altered the socialist spaces of resistance against Western imperialism. Cuba provided not only a renovated model for seizing power and socialist state-building but also a safe cultural and political space for the hemisphere's exile community to gather and share their experiences. Indeed, in terms of the major ideological, theoretical, and cultural upheavals that exemplified the politics of the decade, the Cuban Revolution of 1959 served to inaugurate the Latin American 1960s.

While lamentable, the transience of exile brought new methodologies of social analysis and modes of struggle. In a sense, international perspectives served as a catalyst to accelerate revolutionary change in specific localities. Still, as in the case of Otto René Castillo—who received language, filmmaking, and guerrilla training abroad—after returning to their home countries, left-wing activists were often regarded by their governments as a greater threat than before to national well-being. Regrettably for Castillo, the pretexts of transnationalism and international solidarity served as justifications for harsher punishment by the state.

María Caridad Cumaná González 14

Translated by Jesús Quirós Maqueira and Danielle Nobriega

# CUBAN FILM AND THE BURDEN OF REVOLUTIONARY REPRESENTATION

**The political** landscape of Latin America in the 1960s was characterized by the philosophy of liberation, the development of popular and independence movements, the Cold War, a bipolar world, and U.S. military interventions to impose economic and political dependence. International imperialism and national oligarchy were understood as being responsible for misery, underdevelopment, and poverty, and many if not most intellectuals postulated the subsequent liberation of oppressed people from these conditions. Their arguments were based on a faith in the moral and revolutionary background of people as a mass and the possible establishment of societies without class antagonism. Concrete results of these tendencies were seen in a strengthening of the Cuban Revolution of 1959, an expansion of liberation movements throughout the Third World, and the emergence of youth movements in cities and guerrilla activities in rural zones.

At the same time the deeply rooted anti-imperialist and anticapitalist rhetoric began to express itself through the merging of the aesthetical and political avant-gardes, and particularly in the art of cinema. In a variety of countries filmmakers took up radical projects grounded in an opposition to the hegemonic mode of representation advanced by the commercial cinema—projects that were, in turn, in favour of creative and industrial decentralization.

In Cuba one of the dreams that came true in the 1960s was the organization of a modest film industry that was based in the country's cultural institutions and able to respond to the technical requirements of a style of filmmaking that would complement the new socialist system. In March 1959, only three months after the triumph of the Revolution, the government passed its first cultural law, creating the Instituto Cubano de Arte e Industria Cinematográficos (ICAIC), an organization that would manage film production in the country for the next fifty years, and continuing.

A key issue at the beginning of ICAIC was the absence of a wide pool of experienced, and trained, film professionals who could put the country's cinematographic goals into practice—a pool of personnel who could be entrusted with the rising production of the Caribbean film industry. A partial solution was to bring in experts from around the world—people who sympathized with the Cuban Revolution and could offer workshops and help to train the future filmmakers. ICAIC thus contracted foreign documentary directors, photographers, scriptwriters, actors, fiction directors, animators, and technicians to organize workshops and various activities related to film practice.

The production methods of Cuban cinema were forged, then, in the heat of the experience of an influx of documentary, fiction, and avant-garde filmmakers. These artists included, in the documentary field, Joris Ivens (Holland), Roman Karmen (Russia), and Theodor Christensen (Denmark). They included French avant-garde members of the SLON (Société de Lancement des Oeuvres Nouvelles) group, Agnès Varda and Chris Marker, French fiction filmmaker Armand Gatti, Mexican José Miguel García Ascot, and the Puerto Rican Oscar Torres. Later, in 1963, the Czechoslovakian Vladimir Cech, the Russian Mikhail Kalatozov, and the German Kurt Maetzig all arrived.

The fiction filmmakers Armand Gatti, José Miguel García Ascot, Oscar Torres, Vladimir Cech, Mikhail Kalatozov, and Kurt Maetzig contributed very different aesthetic approaches. The work of Russian cinematographer Sergei Urusevski, who filmed Kalatozov's *Soy Cuba!* (I am Cuba! 1964), stands out as a fundamental contribution due to the courage of his spectacular camera movements and shots, which demonstrated a vigorous command of cinematography—an artistry that over time made a large contribution to film techniques in Cuba. Chris Marker and Agnès Varda were the spiritual carriers of the Nouvelle Vague (New wave), Roman Karmen brought with him the styles and preoccupations of Soviet film, and Joris Ivens exemplified, in his great body of work ranging through a large number of different countries and contexts, the art of making social documentaries as a means of presenting "truth" in controversial situations. Theodor Christensen posited that the narrative structure of documentaries had to come from the dramatic force offered by reality; he stressed the art of filming with imagination in a way that would effectively communicate with the spectator.

The visit to Cuba of Italian scriptwriter Cesare Zavattini proved invaluable. As a member of the neo-realist school, he had collaborated with Vittorio de Sica (*The Bicycle Thief*, 1948, *Miracle in Milan*, 1951, and *Umberto D*, 1952) and others. He came to Cuba in large part because of a close friendship with Alfredo Guevara, the founding president of ICAIC.[1] Guevara offered him a contract to write two fiction scripts, and the final result was *El joven rebelde* (The young rebel, 1961), which was made into a film by Julio García Espinosa. Zavattini's presence meant that students encountered the neo-realist influence not just at the theoretical level, but also through lessons delivered by one of its more distinguished figures and representatives. Of course, this influence did not come without meeting some reservations on the part of Cuban filmmakers, who expressed objections to neo-realist artistic practices such as an insistence on the use of non-professional actors and a certain rigidity in the use of the camera—with a predilection to long, contemplative takes. It was a film style, they found, that for the sake of narrative clarity left only a small space open to experimentation.

Indeed, many of the more experienced Cuban filmmakers had already previously worked in a neo-realist style and were now in search of a new language. For example, Tomás Gutiérrez Alea, with sagacious lucidity, had discovered already in 1960, during the shooting of *Historias de la Revolucion* (Stories of the revolution), that the photographic style created for him by the Italian Otello Martelli (who worked regularly with Federico Fellini and was cinematographer for Roberto Rossellini in his 1946 film *Paisa*) did not respond to his expressive necessities:

> I wanted a more dynamic image, looser mise-en-scène, with photography of high contrasts, harsh, dramatic. Nevertheless, the result was a static mise-en-scène, reinforced by camera movements that were much too cautious and a soft lens where everything is seen. From this technical point of view his work was perfect, but it was in contradiction with the desired aesthetic.[2]

Hence, on the one hand, the search for another referent was almost an obligation; but, on the other, Cuban cinema had to find its own way, to be authentic: "released from petty chains and useless servitude."

Cuba, as represented by Varda in her documentary short *Saludos Cubanos* (1963), is the steadfastness of a people in revolution. Varda's statements to the journal *Cine Cubano* offered an inspiration for Cuban directors when she referred to her first film (*La Pointe courte*, 1954), a mix of fiction and documentary: "This is what always has interested me: the mix of what surrounds us and the interior life, which sometimes is much more imaginative but nourishes realities."[3] Varda's aesthetic influence in Cuban cinema was seen most notably in *Memorias del subdesarrollo* (Memories of underdevelopment, 1968), by director Tomás Gutiérrez Alea.

Still, despite all of this input from abroad, most of the Cuban filmmakers of the first ten years of the Revolution were self-taught; they learned while filming shorts, newsreels, and documentaries. The Latin American Newsreels division of ICAIC, headed by documentary filmmaker Santiago Álvarez, became a training school, and the production of a weekly newsreel (which continued from 1960 to 1990) fostered the rapid education of technicians and specialists who were then ready to film narrative features and longer documentaries. Not surprisingly, though, more than forty years after the birth of ICAIC as co-ordinating centre of the cinematographic movement in the island, British scholar Michael Chanan would write: "Many of the principles evolved in the course of development of the social documentary in the new Latin American cinema, and especially in Cuba, have strong parallels with positions that were taken up within radical film practices in Europe and North America over the same period."[4]

As with every emerging industry, the work of Cuban cinema from the beginning of the 1960s passed through different stages. During the first years of production it focused on:

- a denunciation of the social problems of the neo-colonial past—in documentaries such as *Esta tierra nuestra* (Tomás Gutiérrez Alea, 1959); *La vivienda* (Julio García Espinosa, 1959); y *El negro* (Eduardo Manet, 1960); and narrative features such as *Cuba Baila* (Julio García Espinosa, 1960) and *Cuba 58* (José Miguel García Ascot and Jorge Fraga, 1962).
- the state of society at the triumph of the Revolution—in the documentaries of Nicolás Guillén Landrián, *En un barrio viejo* (1963), *Los del baile* (1965), and *Retornar a Baracoa* (1966); the narrative features *Las doce sillas* (Alea, 1962), *En días como estos* (Jorge Fraga, 1964), and *La muerte de un burócrata* (Alea, 1966).
- and revolutionary achievements in different fields—including *Muerte al invasor* (Alea and Santiago Álvarez, 1961), *Historia de una batalla* (Manuel Octavio Gómez, 1962), *Reportaje* (Nicolás Guillén Landrián, 1966), *En la otra isla* and *Una isla para Miguel* (both Sara Gómez, and both 1968).

Another tendency of the young Cuban film industry was to challenge the political discourse on national history by creating films emphasizing the viewpoint of revolutionary principles. Within this stream came a great number of documentaries, including *Historia de un ballet* (José Massip, 1962); *Cimarrón* (Sergio Giral, 1967), and *David* (Enrique Pineda Barnet, 1967). Narrative films reviewed Cuban history since its beginning with Alea's *Historias de la Revolucón* and continued with García Espinosa's *El joven rebelde*, *Cuba 58*, *Soy Cuba*, *Manuela* (Humberto Solás,1966), *Aventuras de Juan Quin Quin* (Julio García Espinosa, 1967), *Tulipa* (Manuel Octavio Gómez, 1967), *Lucía* (Humberto Solás, 1968), *Memorias del subdesarrollo* (Alea, 1968), *La odisea del General José* (Jorge Fraga, 1968), and *Girón* (Manuel Herrera, 1968). The decade closed with the release of one of the most remarkable experimental works of the Cuban cinema, *La primera carga al machete* (Manuel Octavio Gómez, 1969).

It is in *La primera carga al machete*, the third narrative feature by Manuel Octavio Gómez, that we find crystallized the main characteristic of the films from this decade: the strong influence of documentary on fiction films, evidenced in so many early works such as *Historias de la Revolución*, *Las doce sillas*, *Las aventuras de Juan Quin Quin*, and *Memorias del subdesarrollo*. One of the many creative challenges assumed by Gómez was to adapt the modern interview technique of news reporting to a fictional narrative. *La primera carga al machete* has actors playing the role of historical characters who are supposedly being interviewed in the present—whether on a street or on a battlefield—and thus introduces elements that starkly reveal the contradictions of the colony and the metropolis in the nineteenth century. Furthermore, considering the wide range of opinions arising from the film, the audience could and must reconstruct its own version of the historical events. This productive and intense interactive process between the film and its audience followed the theoretical assumption of the time that saw the only possible cinema as "the one that promoted reflection."

Some filmmakers—Tomás Gutiérrez Alea, for example—dared to theorize with regard to the way in which a film audience should be educated. In his book *Dialéctica del espectador* (Viewer's dialectic), Alea writes:

> If we want film to be good for something more (or for the same thing, but more profoundly), if we want it to fulfil its function more perfectly (aesthetic, social, ethical, ideological ...), we ought to guarantee that it constitutes a factor in spectators' development. Film will be more fruitful to the extent that it pushes spectators towards a more profound understanding of reality and consequently to the extent that it helps a viewer live more actively and incites them to stop being mere spectators in the face of reality. To do this, film ought to appeal not only to emotion and feeling but also to reason and intellect.[5]

In many of these films the Revolution assumes anthropomorphic qualities in that characters, through their fictional worlds, contest everything that does not demonstrate unconditional loyalty to the ideology of the new social regime. In this way, cinema as a means of artistic expression revealed an extreme existing ideological polarity in Cuba,[6] which was displayed not only in what was happening on screen but also in ideas about what should be represented or not.

Basically the big-screen fictions brought to life characters that were closely related to the country's history, beginning with the rebels themselves who made the Revolution. The first narrative feature, *Historias de la Revolución*, illustrates through its three stories the main actions that led to the revolutionary victory during the final stage of revolutionary struggle. *El joven rebelde* devoted itself to telling the story of a young man who goes off to join the troops of the Rebel Army. This thematic line—the ideological legitimation of a history immersed in the vision and principles of the recent Revolution—was widely adopted by national film production during the next four decades of ICAIC existence.

The fight for independence—its leaders, slavery, the colony, and neocolony—served as a theme of many fiction films and even of a wide number of documentaries. The greatest aesthetic achievement of this thematic was Solás's *Lucía*, which expressed the concepts of nation, identity, history, fatherland, and society through three feminine characters whose actions revealed the complex interaction between historical destiny and individual experience.

Another thematic line that brought to life characters of the social environment of the time was one reflecting the attitudes of expropriated capitalists (called *siquitrillados*, because they were constantly overwhelmed by a pessimistic state of mind) in the new context. It was a theme embraced by films such as *Las doce sillas*, *Tránsito* (Eduardo Manet, 1964), and especially *Memorias del subdesarrollo*. In these three films, the Revolution became an ideological counterpart to the actions of resentful capitalists. Public places became tribunals to condemn acts of the past, and publicity billboards in open spaces turned into political propaganda. More than one film established a controversial interaction between the dialogue and the advertisements on the billboards.

This work of intertextual dialogue between billboards and context was excellently developed by the documentary filmmaker Nicolás Guillén Landrían, from his first piece of work, *En un barrio viejo* (1963), continuing in *Ociel del Toa* (1965) and *Reportaje* (1966), until in his master work, *Coffea Arábiga* (1968), the use of graphics suggests a dysfunctional rarefied relationship between the public, to which the propaganda was addressed, and the propaganda itself.

For many years the commitment of documentary to reality was considered unquestionably true, as long as it was considered an exceptional witness of certain moments of social development. Today we know, after years of research, that documentary, like fiction and all other forms of media representations of reality, has been always permeated and manipulated by the director's subjectivity. Nevertheless, during the 1960s, the prestige of documentary as a "realistic" approach to historical, political, economic, and social events was in many senses a premise for the development of the poetic narrative of the ICAIC documentary filmmakers. Based on this aesthetic assumption, a considerable part of the Cuban documentary production of the period devoted itself to recording the most important events of the national and international scene, such as: the announcement of the socialist character of the Revolution (*Asamblea general*, 1961, Tomás Gutiérrez Alea); the cultural roots of the nation (Massip's *Historia de un ballet*); African heritage (*Abakua*, 1962, Bernabé Hernández); the literacy campaign (Octavio Gómez's *Historia de una batalla*), the roots of Cuban music (*Nosotros la Música*, 1964, Rogelio París); natural disasters (*Ciclón*, 1963, Santiago Álvarez); racism in the United States (*Now*, 1965, Álvarez); the Vietnam War (*Hanoi, martes 13*, 1967, and *79 primaveras*, 1965, both by Álvarez); the death of Ché in Bolivia (*Hasta la victoria siempre*, 1967, Álvarez); the everyday routine of the Havana and countryside societies (Guillén Landrián's *En un barrio viejo* and *Ociel del Toa*); and, finally, the aspiration of the new social project to the formation of a "new man" (Gómez's *En la otra isla* and *Una isla para Miguel*). Sara Gómez's documentary work constitutes one of the most interesting areas of film production in the 1960s—on one hand, because she was the only woman able to create extended work during this period, and on the other hand, because of the authentic way in which she was able to demonstrate a sense of national identity in the crossroads of the African, Spanish, and Creole heritage.

Sara Gómez's filmography, with a total of fifteen works, includes seven documentaries made in the 1960s. At least two of them were interested in revealing the Cuban rhythmical essences: *Iré a Santiago* (1964) and *Y tenemos sabor* (1967). Another work, *Guanabacoa: crónica de mi familia* (1966), with its autobiographical character, explores the feminine side of her family—the grandmother and aunts, Black women—and the social practices of the time they lived in. Their testimonies provide evidence of the racial discrimination experienced by Black people in the Cuba of the 1950s, as well as Cuban women's confinement within the domestic space.

Gómez's work from the second part of the 1960s decade is grouped in what is known as the trilogy of La Isla de la Juventud (Island of youth, the biggest island of the Cuban archipelago), the place selected by the state for the training and re-education of the future "new man," whose ideal should agree with the revolutionary process. The triad comprises *En la otra isla, Una isla para Miguel,* and *Isla del Tesoro* (1969). *En la otra Isla*, dedicated to Michelle Firk,[7] investigates the life of nine youths, five women and four men, who express what it means to them to participate in the momentous project of the Revolution in La Isla de la Juventud. The interviews raise questions related to racism, marginality, the risks of setting goals in cultural work, sexuality, and other concerns of the Cuban youth of those years.

*Una isla para Miguel* examines the life of a rebellious youth who is sent to the island to be re-educated according to the values of the new society. In her analysis of his upbringing in a marginal neighbourhood, within a family living in poverty, and his difficult insertion in the universe of values advanced by the Cuban Revolution, Gómez emphasizes the psychological. This documentary would become an essential reference for Gómez in the following decade, influencing her work on her only fiction film, *De cierta manera* (1974). In that movie she presents a clash between the marginal principles of the main character, Mario, and the goals of the revolutionary project, but complicates matters with a story open to multiple levels of reading and further enriched by reflections on the role of women in the new society—their work, education, male chauvinism, and the eradication of ideas rooted for centuries among economically oppressed segments of Cuban society.

The 1960s were a building platform for Cuban society. On that platform the consciousness of the need to explore social conditions and point out the dynamics of a slow process of social integration prevailed, along with a desire to document the constant mutations endured by the country—to articulate a revolutionary society on the constant move, with an identity of its own and a cultural discourse that would contribute to confirm the aspirations of socialism. The Cuban cinema contributed to this process with a great variety of representations: in the case of fiction films, with a particular tendency to the epic and the prevalence of the collective over the private; and in the case of the documentary, with a tendency to reflect the social changes and their impact on the dreams and aspirations that revolved around the construction of a new society.

Without doubt, since the 1960s globalization has illuminated cultural processes in the West. In Cuba this illumination began with the great influx from other countries of specialists who left their mark in works that attempted to catch the spirit of the largest West Indies island. Some of these films turned out to be less memorable than others, but they all contributed to the apprenticeship of the native talents who joined in their making, anxious to practice and to learn. The freshness, topicality, and boldness with which these filmmakers, using different approaches, reflected on screen the conflicts of the social fabric inherited by the Revolution transcend the frontiers of the historical time and space to which they belonged. In doing so they allow us a better understanding of what has been, and what still today is, the essence of Cuban society.

Kyoko Sato 15

# THe Japanese sixties
## Kon Ichikawa's "Tokyo Olympiad"

**Held in** the midst of rapid economic growth, the 1964 Tokyo Olympics were celebrated as a marker of Japan's miraculous postwar recovery and full reintegration into the international community. Commissioned by the Japan Olympic Committee, Kon Ichikawa's 1965 film *Tokyo Olympiad* was to become a historical documentary record of that seemingly celebratory moment in Japanese history. But for "the Japanese sixties," and in particular as read against the background of the rise and the fall of the movement against the U.S.-Japan Security Treaty, which was renewed in 1960, and the subsequent development of antiwar movements in the 1960s and the 1970s, *Tokyo Olympiad* can also be seen as representing something quite different: Ichikawa's critical intervention into a state-sanctioned historical narrative of postwar Japan.

The argument here takes up and works towards what I think of as a periodizing hypothesis. As Kojin Karatani observes:

> Periodization is indispensable for history. To mark off a period, that is, to assign a beginning and an end, is to comprehend the significance of events. One can say that the discipline of history is, to a large extent, fought out through the question of periodization, for periodization itself changes the significance of events.[1]

161

For Karatani, periodization obscures interrelational structures and creates an illusion of "a single, autonomous, discursive space" while nevertheless illuminating "certain relational structures" that exist within that discursive space.[2] Karatani's observations are pertinent to an examination of how the internal relational structures of the discursive space of 1960s Japan relate to exterior factors—that is, to the multiple, simultaneously existing, and interrelated discursive spaces within a "global sixties." Within certain structural limits a whole array of responses and creative energies were released in Japan—and those conditions illuminate what was, and continues to be, meaningful about the "Japanese sixties."

## When Was "the Japanese Sixties"?

Fredric Jameson suggests that a Third World 1960s began in the late 1950s with the decolonization movements in British and French Africa, leading to the independence of Ghana and the Battle of Algiers in 1957. Owing much of their politico-cultural models to Third Worldism, the "most characteristic expressions of a properly First World 60s," such as the formations of counterculture, the rise of a student new left, and a mass antiwar movement, emerged later with "the first sit-ins in Greensboro, North Carolina, in February of 1960"—an event that Jameson considers a kind of decolonization movement "at home."[3] For Jameson, then, it is the birth of decolonization movements that marks the beginning of the sixties.

In the case of Japan, Jameson's Euro-American-centric model does not quite capture the significance of the period, precisely because of the Euro-American interests in the geopolitics of Japan in the post–Asia-Pacific War era. The inaugural year of the 1960s in Japan was a time of intense struggles over the renewal of the U.S.-Japan Security Treaty (Anpo), which was the legacy of Japan's problematic independence from U.S. and Allied forces. Signed in September 1951, immediately following the signing of the San Francisco Peace Treaty, which virtually ended the occupation of Japan by the U.S.-dominated Allied forces, the U.S.-Japan Security Treaty was initially the United States' plan for a separate peace treaty that, in the words of Victor Koschmann, "would include only those former enemies of Japan whose governments would be willing to accept a U.S.-Japan security treaty."[4]

In the context of the Cold War, the Security Treaty integrated Japan into the capitalist camp. It also placed the country under the firm grip of the U.S. military strategy to contain communism in East Asia because it obliged Japan to provide military bases for the United States.[5] The everyday consequences for local residents—including noise pollution as well as rapes and murders perpetrated by U.S. soldiers with apparent immunity—became a source of opposition to the military bases and Security Treaty. Moreover, for Japanese citizens the U.S.-Japan Security Treaty represented the continued—and, in effect, permanent—subordination of their country to the United States. Some also feared that Japan would be further implicated in the U.S. wars.

In addition, the Security Treaty became a focal point of a peace movement that was formed in the late 1940s among intellectuals who, according to Koschmann, were "generally sympathetic to the early postwar ideals of peace, democracy, and modernity."[6] This movement "represented the anti-imperialist nationalism that animated the Communists." Specifically, they sought to find "the form, terms, and timing of a peace treaty that would bring an end to the Occupation."[7] Even though the outbreak of the Korean War in June 1950 caused some members of the movement to sway their opinions momentarily, the group was generally in agreement on opposing the Security Treaty. The peace movement eventually won support from the newly formed General Council of Trade Unions of Japan (Sôhyô). The peace movement was able, Koschmann says, to relate "international issues to domestic ones in a manner that marked the beginning of the broad coalition among renovationist (kakushin) forces that reached its apex in the struggle against renewal of the U.S.-Japan Security Treaty in 1960."[8]

The original term of the much-contested Security Treaty was to expire in June 1960 unless the U.S. Congress and Japanese Diet ratified a renewed treaty, which by early that year had already been worked out between them with nominal revisions.[9] When the deadline for the Security Treaty renewal approached, divergent groups—socialists, student groups including the All-Japan Federation of Student Self-Governing Associations (commonly known as Zengakuren, founded in 1948), women's groups, and even some members of the ruling Liberal Democratic Party (LDP)—converged on the streets of Tokyo to oppose its renewal.

It was not until Prime Minister Kishi Nobusuke rammed through the renewed treaty in the Diet late at night on May 19, 1960, that the anti–security treaty movement reached a mass level. In the wake of the ratification, massive demonstrations in ever-increasing numbers of participants surrounded the Diet for several weeks and compelled Kishi to cancel U.S. president Dwight Eisenhower's scheduled visit to Tokyo for a grand signing. It was estimated that the largest protest numbered over two million demonstrators.[10] Indeed, it was Kishi's draconian tactics and what they symbolized to the Japanese that turned the Anpo struggle into a mass movement. Kishi was a Class A war criminal who, as a young bureaucrat during the heyday of Japanese imperialism on the Chinese continent, led the industrial development of Manchuria and later served in the Tôjô administration. Yet in a matter of twelve years after the conclusion of the Asia-Pacific War Kishi climbed up the political ladder and became prime minister. His autocratic manoeuvring in the Diet thus became an uncanny reminder, according to Yoshikuni Igarashi, of "the monstrous qualities of the repressive pre-1945 Japanese political system" and helped to simplify "the complicated issue of the treaty's revision" into a binary opposition between the "democratic present" and an "autocratic past."[11]

Moreover, in the eyes of the Japanese masses, Igarashi writes, "Kishi was a stand-in for the military regime, against which the Japanese should have collectively fought but did not before the defeat of Japan, as well as for the humiliation that this regime brought to Japan." Furthermore, "By affirming the subservient position of Japan to the United States in the new Security Treaty, Kishi served as a reminder of the earlier drama in which Japan had been defeated and tamed into a subordinate client state." Thus the anti–U.S.-Japan Security Treaty movement "became the unresolved past in postwar Japan." The forcible ratification of the new treaty by the Kishi government therefore shifted the focal point of the anti-security treaty movement "away from the international ramifications of the treaty to domestic democratic order in postwar Japan." What many saw as the return of the dark forces thus conjured up a sense of nationalism that had been brewing in postwar Japan, and the anti-security movement became an outlet for many Japanese to express "nationalistic feelings embedded in past experiences and emotions" vis-à-vis Kishi. Indeed, as Kishi, taking responsibility for the political turmoil, resigned from his post, "Many who had participated in the antitreaty rallies went ahead and enjoyed economic prosperity under the aegis of the Security Treaty itself."[12]

Originating at least in part in the postwar intellectuals' guilty conscience—to make up for the failure to resist war and advocate peace in the pre-1945 era—the anti–U.S.-Japan security treaty movement was, perhaps, a moment of opportunity to finally realize a "missed opportunity" to resist war in defence of peace and a postwar democratic order. At the same time, the Anpo struggle brought closure to the lingering legacy of a pre-1945 Japan. Instead of becoming a moment at which a critical reflection on Japan's own colonialism and imperialism of the past and the present could begin, the Anpo struggle of 1960 became an occasion on which Japan could finally put to rest, once and for all, its unpleasant memories of the nation's past and move on as a newly democratic—and modern—nation. Incidentally, Japan in the 1960s witnessed a resurgence of ultra-nationalist movements as well as popular and state-sponsored right-wing nationalisms. In addition, Koschmann points out, "The new self-confidence that accompanied high growth rates and levels of consumption was also expressed in increased attention to 'modernization' and the possible uses of the Japanese experience as a model for developing economies."[13] It was against this background of a newly confident populace and mass historical amnesia in the wake of the Anpo struggle that the Japanese sixties unfolded.

The leftist movements such as the Peace in Vietnam Committee (commonly known as Beheiren, formed in the wake of the U.S. bombing of North Vietnam in 1965), new left youths, and a radical student movement known as the Zenkyôtô (university-wide joint struggle councils, founded in 1968) all turned increasingly against what Oda Makoto called "a banal nationalism" that apparently lacked critical self-awareness.[14] The Tokyo Olympics in no small measure exacerbated the rising unself-critical nationalism as it turned a new Japan's postwar economic miracle, modernity, and successful modernization in all its newly found innocence into a spectacular: yet, it was precisely for this reason that the Tokyo Olympics became a site in which Ichikawa's critical intervention into the Japanese sixties could be made.[15]

# Tokyo Olympiad

Even before being released in 1965 *Tokyo Olympiad* had been attacked by both sides of the political spectrum. It was hated by the emperor Showa, and the Japan Olympic Committee, which commissioned the work, insisted on recutting the film before it could be released. The government officials complained that the film presented too few Japanese athletes, Japanese flags, and shots of the newly built stadium. The political left, in turn, alleged that it used too many shots of the sun. Certainly, the film does not focus on Japanese athletes or the Japanese flag, although it does show, with considerable sense of empathy, the involvement of Japanese labourers and the masses in the making of the Olympics. Indeed, *Tokyo Olympiad*, at first glance, appears to avoid direct reference to Japan other than the shots of the "rising sun." But what the formal and narrative strategies deployed in the film do is gesture towards questions of the Japanese nation-state at that particular moment in history.

Ichikawa's obsession with individual athletes, particularly with the minute details of their bodies and how they move, is one such strategy. The long takes of body parts stoically examine the machinery of the body; but this scrupulous examination of athlete's bodies appears amidst the manipulation of time and space. In his representation of the 100-metre race, for instance, Ichikawa chooses to show the end result of the event (with athletes dashing across the finishing line) before going back to the very beginning, to the time even before the athletes are in the starting position. The camera closely follows the athletes as they prepare for the race in absolute silence and isolation. As viewers, because we have already seen how the race ends, we know that one of the featured athletes is destined to lose. The silence and isolation at the beginning of the race contrast starkly with the roar of the excited audience at its end. By going against chronological time, Ichikawa urges us to consider the process to form an understanding of how the race ended in the way it did, or to imagine how the race could have ended differently.

The film's treatment of time crosscuts the spatial representation of the Tokyo Olympics. In the cycling event, to take another example, the viewers go outside the stadium for the first time and are brought to the outskirts of Tokyo. While the stadium, downtown Tokyo, and the emerging middle class who congregate in those spaces all epitomize Japan's postwar success story, the rice patties, the farmers, a young woman with a baby strapped onto her back, and the old folks who sit on milk crates by the edge of a freshly paved country road reveal the other side of the nation's success story.[16]

Incidentally, part of the then prime minister Ikeda Hayao's celebrated "income doubling plan," implemented in 1960, was to emphasize industrial over rural development in order, in the words of David Apter and Nagoyo Sawa, to "reduce the size of those sectors of the economy that were relatively inefficient and to divert the labour force into needed and better paying occupations," primarily in the urban centres.[17] This cabinet decision presumably made possible Japan's postwar economic recovery in less than twenty years, but came at the expense of the rural economy and the environment. Japan's postwar capitalist economic development exacerbated the formation of class society and the widening discrepancy between town and country, environmental destruction not withstanding. Read against this background, *Tokyo Olympiad*'s formal strategy— to unsettle a teleological understanding of temporality and to juxtapose urban and rural spaces—was to cast light on the negative spaces of what was visible, namely the historical processes in the production of the Japanese nation-state as we know it. In *Tokyo Olympiad* the camera's gaze upon the machinery of athletes' bodies was an integral part of the film's attempt to draw our attention to the machinery at work at a moment of production.

Despite the apparent lack of references to Japan itself, the film consistently calls into question the formation of the Japanese nation-state. The film does not fail to capture the flag-raising moments at which athletes are interpellated as national subjects.[18] Such scenes appear as typical Olympics moments of the sort that are all too familiar in television broadcasting. However, in *Tokyo Olympiad*, these scenes are all shot in an identical composition: three medalists on the podium are shot from the sides so that they can all be seen at once; as they look up the camera cuts to a shot of flags going up the poles. Throughout, the film repeats this pattern over and over. The repetition emphasizes the banality of the supposed moments of "glory" of the nation, and it calls into question the category of the nation-state and its modes of governance and belonging at the precise moments of interpellation. What is more, the film demystifies the connection between individual athletes and the nation-states represented: the symbols of the nation-states come into being if, and only if, the athletes look up to see them. In other words, while the medal-granting ceremonies are an occasion for the nation-states to interpellate individual athletes as national subjects, this event cannot take place unless the potential subjects grant the nation-states the right to exist. It is here that *Tokyo Olympiad* threatened to break open, once more, the debates over the question of the Japanese nation-state that were submerged under the postwar economic miracle and the gradual consolidation of nation and state.

By the mid-1960s global relations of power were evidently being transformed, as the forces of decolonization that reached their height in the early 1960s begat numerous newly independent nations in Asia and Africa. The anti-war and anti-imperialist movements that developed in Japan from the late 1960s onward had strong affinities with anticolonial struggles elsewhere, and, certainly, the participation of newly independent nations from Africa in the Olympics might have been seen as a sign of hope. However, the future of those nations was not yet determined, and perhaps the focus on the loneliness of an athlete from Chad, as represented in Ichikawa's film, gestures towards the fragility of such hope.

Moreover, the formal strategy of *Tokyo Olympiad* powerfully articulates the fictitiousness of "world peace" and "humanity" by formally turning the Tokyo Olympics into a fictional narrative. The film does this, first, by juxtaposing its own scripted narration and the narration of television news coverage, with the TV news being also structured through the film's narration; and, second, by the insertion of photographic black and white shots in an otherwise entirely colour film. The film credits are also set against the black and white background of the shots of the legendary marathon runner Bikira Abebe of Ethiopia and the Japanese women's volleyball team, both of which had been previously presented in colour in the body of the film. For a moment, viewers are impelled to wonder if even Abebe was, after all, a fictitious figure.

While exposing the fiction of the Olympics, the cinematic language of *Tokyo Olympiad* speaks to the ideal of world peace and humanity. In the famous and controversial shots of the "rising sun" that begin and end the narrative, the opening shot of the sun is quickly cut to the wrecking ball. Many viewers interpreted this effect as a symbol of the destruction of old Japan; but it can also be seen as a signal of the beginning of a new story *of* the Olympics—situating that story in a circular narrative that opens and closes with the sun. The sun here is represented as a source of fire, an element sanctified in Greece as the purpose of the Olympics. The sacred fire is then passed along and travels from Greece to Japan via many countries and places that were previously excluded from the itinerary of such travels. At the end of the film the sacred fire returns to the sun. Unlike the sacred fire (whose itinerary is dictated by the world politics of the day), the sun is simultaneously the origin and the telos of a circular narrative of human history regardless of the specific itinerary of any given travel. In this sense the sun in *Tokyo Olympiad* is benevolent and ubiquitous: it does not belong to any one nation or individual because it belongs to all of humanity. Whether the sun is rising or setting is therefore irrelevant. Such a question has become a point of dispute or fetish only in the eyes of Japanese nationalists or modernists. *Tokyo Olympiad* thus imagines a kind of utopia in which nations and nation-states do not exist: everyone is equal under the sun.

# A New World in the Making

Tokyo Olympiad dreamed of a future utopia in a way that was possible—and seemed imperative—in the historical context of the mid-1960s, before what I call "the Japanese sixties" came to an end in the early 1970s. Has the dream of *Tokyo Olympiad* materialized? Or has it turned out to be humanity's worst nightmare? Or, perhaps, if the future utopia had been imagined differently in the maturation period of the Japanese sixties, could the future world in which we now live have been different?

To be sure, the utopian future—a nationless and stateless world—that Ichikawa had imagined in his characteristically liberal-humanist mode in the mid-1960s has returned to present-day Japan with a vengeance. In the wake of the economic bubble bursting in the early 1990s, a neo-liberal regime took hold, leaving the Japanese nation-state utterly unaccountable for the social and political disasters that are now consuming Japanese citizens.[19] While paying lip service to neo-nationalism, Junichirô Koizumi, the controversial former prime minister of Japan, and his successors pursued the road to remilitarization as part of their larger aspiration to stake out Japan's place in a U.S.-led empire by working closely with—and for—Washington.[20] At this juncture, a "millennial Japan" structurally resembles the inaugural moment of the Japanese sixties.[21] And if Karatani's periodizing hypothesis carries any significance in understanding a "millennial Japan" in relation to the exterior, then, what we are witnessing today in Japan is symptomatic of the current moment in global discursive space. Without a clear road map, how can we imagine a future that is dictated neither by neo-liberalism nor by neo-nationalism—or that does not simply become a battle between the two discourses? A renewed exploration of the Japanese sixties urgently calls for a radical rerouting of our critical paths, leaving us open to imagine another new world coming.

Andrew M. Ivaska 16

# CONSUMING AND CONTESTING "SOUL" IN TANZANIA

**In a 1970** issue of the *African Communist*, the London-based journal of the South African Communist Party, a Ghanaian university student named J.K. Obatala chronicled his reaction to the news that the Tanzanian government under President Julius K. Nyerere had banned soul music a few months previously. "At first," wrote Obatala, who had lived most of his life in the United States but was now studying in Ghana, "Nyerere's actions appeared to me to be a deliberate slap in the face to the Afro-Americans, alas, an indication that Tanzania was relapsing into a self-induced coma of ultra-reactionary nationalism."[1]

Puzzled by why one of the continent's most "progressive" leaders would take such an apparently reactionary step, Obatala described how he had discovered the answer in observing students on his dormitory floor watching a James Brown concert on Ghanaian television one night. Lured away from his research by "pandemonious outbursts coming from the students' lounge," the normally studious Obatala "decided to go and see what it would be like to catch 'J.B.' in Africa." What he saw—James Brown "sliding over super-slick floors, flinging off one diamond studded cape after another" to the delight of a "packed" student lounge—convinced him of the "destructive" influence of soul in Africa, for its "propagation of the myth of Afro-American affluence" to young Africans who relished soul only as the latest American capitalist craze and knew little of the truth of African Americans' struggle for justice. "I felt," he recalled, "as if I had been given a one hour lecture by Julius Nyerere himself on 'Why I banned Soul Music from Tanzania.'"[2]

Soul had indeed been banned in Tanzania—on November 12, 1969, to be precise. But contrary to Obatala's account, it was not on President Nyerere's initiative, but on that of the coast regional commissioner, Mustafa Songambele, who on that day was meeting with a group of primary-school teachers in the capital city, Dar es Salaam, to discuss student participation in an upcoming rally. Presented with the teachers' complaints that "this type of dance ... was a cause of bad manners in the country's youth," Commissioner Songambele agreed and promptly declared soul music "banned from being played in Dar es Salaam," effective immediately.[3]

With the announcement apparently coming as something of a surprise even to his colleagues, the official reaction to Songambele's statement was slow in coming. Although the government did back its commissioner's initiative, its support was made public only a full week later in the rather unusual form of a letter to the editor of *The Standard* by the director of information services, A.A. Riyami. Citing the corruption of "our young girls, especially school children," the presence of a network of Dar night clubs, and the imperative to preserve the national culture against destructive "foreign" influence, Riyami tried to assure the public that "the Regional Commissioner has not made a hasty decision but one which was well thought out."[4]

In the meantime, the ban attracted a flurry of reactions from Dar es Salaam residents, not least in the letters to the editor pages of *The Standard*, where tens of letters opposing the ban were published before the editor decided to close the correspondence in the wake of official government support for Songambele's initiative.[5]

It was not the first time that Tanzania's capital had seen the banning of a global cultural genre. Indeed, the move was one in a series of campaigns against a range of cultural practices deemed antithetical to a prominent, if contested, national cultural project that was at its height in the late 1960s and early 1970s.[6] One year prior to Songambele's announcement, a high-profile ban on miniskirts was hotly debated in Dar es Salaam. Wigs, Afros, bell-bottoms, cosmetics, and beauty contests would also be outlawed, and they were joined, somewhat ironically, by other forms of culture, including Maasai traditional dress, that officials saw as embarrassingly "primitive" and unworthy of inclusion in an explicitly "modern" national culture. Enforcement of these bans was often placed in the hands of the ruling party's Youth League, whose sometimes violent campaigns succeeded more in sustaining a whirlwind of visibility for the "operations" than in ridding the capital of any banned fashion. Each campaign generated massive public debate, in many cases shattering records on the already lively letters to the editor pages.[7]

Ostensibly launched in reference to an ideal of national culture, most of these campaigns (the soul ban included) were explicitly targeted at *urban* populations and, most specifically, Dar es Salaam. As the government's statement of support for Songambele's initiative suggested, it was the city's network of "soul clubs" and their alleged popularity with schoolgirls that topped the officials' concerns. Much as with the campaign against certain kinds of dress, the soul ban showcased the articulation of official anxieties about perceived unruly practices among urban youth ("bad manners," in the paraphrased words of Commissioner Songambele) centred on particular urban spaces (in this case, the nightclub). Even though during the colonial period many of Tanzania's nationalist political elite had been among those asserting an urban identity against British colonial efforts to deny the possibility of an "urban African," after independence they consistently deployed rhetoric vilifying the city. An official ideology valorizing the rural as the appropriate sphere for the performance of citizenship only grew in importance in the late 1960s as the state moved towards the enforced "villagization" policies that would dominate the 1970s.[8]

The national cultural campaigns were crucial for the portrait of the city being painted: a site of spoiled femininity and decadent consumption, the ugly foil against which a healthy and productive rural idyll could emerge. But in the heated debates that swirled around these campaigns, this discourse was challenged by other imaginings of the city and its possibilities—possibilities linked to a view of the city as a site of transnational networks of style. In the case of the ban on soul, the debate was further complicated by the other, competing transnational networks, agendas, and visions that brought African-American diasporic politics and the Tanzanian state's own commitments to international liberation movements into the mix. In these various ways Tanzania's national cultural project was complicated by Dar es Salaam's competing sixties cosmopolitanisms.

Visible signs of the people, politics, and styles of Black America made a significant impact in Tanzania—and particularly in Dar es Salaam—in the late 1960s and early 1970s. Especially after the military coup that overthrew Ghana's Kwame Nkrumah in 1966, Tanzania became arguably the premier African destination for Black diasporic intellectuals and activists seeking to develop personal and political linkages between civil rights struggles in North America and liberation movements on the African continent.[9] Often inspired by the political project of President Nyerere's *ujamaa* socialism, these visits took various forms, ranging from speaking engagements at the University of Dar es Salaam, which was a major centre of pan-African and Marxist thought at the time, to more permanent

*Consuming and Contesting "Soul" in Tanzania*

stays for thousands of African-American visitors and expatriates, some of whom settled in rural areas as self-styled *ujamaa* pioneers.[10] Moreover, the activist networks that brought figures such as Angela Davis, Malcolm X, Stokely Carmichael, and Eldridge Cleaver to the country were only part of the landscape of Afro-Americana in Tanzania in this period. Throughout the late 1960s and early 1970s, the sounds, fashion, images, and icons of African-American popular culture also made their appearance on the capital's landscape, to be consumed, engaged, and reworked alongside other transnational influences. Particularly after the 1968 performance of blues star Buddy Guy in Dar es Salaam, the capital's most popular bands began incorporating soul numbers—defined broadly and often reworked with Swahili lyrics and Congolese musical influences—into their repertoires. As one local journalist described the mix in 1969, "This can be soul, blues, cha-cha, samba, the latest local crazes—'sukusu,' 'kirikiri,' 'toyota,' and for good measure, the old dances like the tango."[11] Played by bands such as the Rifters, the Sparks, and Air Bantou in the city's small circuit of downtown bars, nightclubs, and hotels, "the hottest music in town" in 1969 generated the dance style that would be dubbed "soul" and provoke the consternation of Songambele and his audience of teachers.[12]

Obatala's contribution was not the only intervention that assessed the soul ban in relation to an Afro-American political scene. Amidst the wave of correspondence to Dar es Salaam's press came a letter from Bob Eubanks, an African American writing from the campus of the city's University College. Addressing "those who would say that soul music is foreign music to Tanzanian Wananchi [citizens]," Eubanks discussed Afro-Americans' roots in Africa, the destruction of their original culture under slavery, and their continuing cultural separation from white America. Cleverly appropriating vocabulary from the national cultural discourse of the ruling party Tanzania African Nationalist Union (TANU), Eubanks argued that in light of this history:

> Soul music, soul dancing, blues music and jazz music are … the Afro-Americans'
> Ngoma ya Taifa [national dance]. They are no more foreign to Tanzania than music
> from the Congo or from Zambia. We understand that each nation has to make sure
> that its own Ngoma ya Taifa comes first before other music…. But, to ban soul music
> and leave the music of the oppressor to be heard … brothers and sisters of Tanzania
> do not forsake your ancestors who died in that strange and foreign land of America;
> and we, the Afro-Americans of today are their children. All Power to the People,
> A Soul Brother.[13]

Although they held opposing opinions on the political valence of the soul ban, both Obatala and Eubanks suggested that Tanzania's position on soul music had everything to do with a correct (Obatala) or incorrect (Eubanks) assessment and appreciation of the bond that united the struggles of Tanzanians and Afro-Americans. However, both the Tanzanian state and the letter writers protesting the ban engaged soul—and Afro-American culture in general—rather differently.

From the moment that Commissioner Songambele's remarks to the school teachers were made public, there was some confusion over what exactly was being targeted, and why. Was it the music or the dance, several letter writers asked. "Can he [Songambele] give a precise definition of 'soul' anyway?" queried an unsigned letter.[14] The initial report of the commissioner's statement specified that the music was banned, but hinted that what Songambele and the teachers found unacceptable was the "type of dance" accompanying soul, and its effect upon young people in Dar es Salaam. Director Riyami's letter announcing government support for the ban confirmed that the intended target was the public performance of soul music in nightclubs, particularly because "investigations" revealed the participation of "young school children" in that nightlife.[15] Most letter writers seemed to interpret the ban as being directed at a specific style of dance associated with music by particular Afro-American artists like James Brown, Wilson Pickett, and Buddy Guy (at least one letter writer credited Guy with launching, in his performance in Dar just a year earlier, soul's ascendance as a "very popular dance" there).[16] For his part, Eubanks suggested that Dar's music lovers were mistaking truly "foreign" music by the Beatles, Monkees, Jim Reeves, and Elvis Presley, for soul.[17]

Young fans of soul in Dar es Salaam took a number of different tacks in opposing the ban. One was to directly challenge its national cultural basis. Recalling official reasoning that had been deployed in the campaign against miniskirts the previous year, many letter writers argued that soul music was no more "indecent" or promoting of "bad manners" than was much officially sanctioned Tanzanian popular culture. Referring to traditional dances performed at national holiday celebrations, "Fairness" wrote:

> He [Songambele] should attend the coming Idd and Jamhuri festivals to witness how worse Chakacha is to Soul Digging. It is a pity to see our parents including young children mouth-open clapping hands at and even giving "tuzo" [tips] to the actor or actress who performs sexual play (buttock shaking) properly. To this, Mr. Songambele says, "Go ahead."[18]

"Ungando" echoed this sentiment, devoting his letter to enumerating the "hooliganic" elements of the Mkwaju ngoma dance of the Zaramo. He concluded: "There is no point banning soul music which expresses the feeling of fellow Afro-Americans and does not show hooliganism or insult. We should leave out some of our local ngomas [traditional dances] which clearly show that hooliganism is part of its elements."[19] Still others pointed to the Kirikiri, the Sekuse, and the "naked ... Kiluwa" as evidence of a perceived official double standard when it came to establishing measures of decency in national culture.[20]

Alongside those attempting to question the assertion that soul was any more indecent than dance styles recognized as indigenous, other critics of Songambele's action simply refused altogether the common official characterization of soul as a foreign dance. However, rather than foregrounding a shared history of racial oppression, as Eubanks did, these letters from Tanzanians in Dar es Salaam instead revolved around celebrating "keeping up with the changes" and situating soul in a long line of successive dance styles to hit the capital. As Mike P. Francis wrote:

> I will just give some examples of dance styles which were once popular but have now faded or are just on the point of fading away! These were, Mnenguo, Rock, Samba, Twist, Rhumba, Waltz, Bollero, Monkey, Chacha, Shake, Pachanga, A Go-Go Rama, and others.... These are now being replaced by new ones like, Likembe, Kirikiri, Toyota, Chikuna, Soul, Tetema, Apollo and the like. Why is the "soul" then not left alone for a while?[21]

Such lists chronicling the coming and going of new dance styles appeared in over a third of the letters on the soul ban.[22] In some ways they resembled theories of modern fashion—the value of "the latest," the ephemeral nature of any particular style, the premium placed upon, as one letter writer put it, "keep[ing] up with the changes of life."[23] Perhaps more challenging to a discourse of national culture, these interventions collapsed any easy distinction between the foreign and the indigenous, instead mixing styles originating in Congo, Tanzania, and abroad as part of the aesthetic landscape of a desirably cosmopolitan city.

Running through these letters describing the new dance called soul was evidence of the development of vocabularies articulating a new, subcultural scene and a particular teenage, urban, cosmopolitan identity. Talk of downtown "soul sessions"[24] as forums for "digging" this new art form jostled with statements hailing the "protest generation."[25] Commenting that "soul ... has doubtlessly been the most appreciated, particularly here, downtown," one enthusiast asked:

> Does it mean a Saturday night out in a night club is already deprived of this one type? That we will have to go soul-less? How about our stocks of soul records at home, do they have to go in ashes? Does the law ... bar me from digging it within my own apartment, and does the importation of an "I am Black and Proud" type render me possible for prosecution? Please advise and clarify.[26]

And as one letter writer proudly signed his submission "Soulman," another lamented the conflation in some quarters of his "fellow youngster's" "soul digging" with the label "bangi [pot]-smokers."[27]

Indeed, many young writers claimed soul as their own, associating it approvingly with "the teenagers," "the youth," or "youngsters." One writer, "Ungando," complained about the ban on soul digging: "To me and all the teenagers this has brought a tremendous oppression which cannot be expressed. And, one unpleasant thing to note about the banning of soul is that it has reduced a great percentage of happiness to many young Tanzanians living in Dar es Salaam."[28] More than a few personalized their attack on the ban, ridiculing Commissioner Songambele as hopelessly out of touch with the times. "It appears to me that Mr. Songambele doesn't like soul music. May be because he doesn't know how to dig it," wrote Maganja-Stone Chimlo.[29] "Pilly" agreed: "Perhaps Mr. Songambele was annoyed when he saw one of his children 'souling' to the music from the radio. Teenagers should be allowed to go on with their soul."[30] Gai Mwashinga advised the commissioner to "keep cool," and A.J. Kanoni urged, "Those who do not know [how] to dance and who do not keep up with the changes of life in the way of music let them keep away from dancing places."[31]

These elements of opponents' critiques of the ban—their arguments about the ephemeral nature of style; their derision towards "aged people"[32] like Songambele "who do not keep up with the changes"; and their articulation of a stylized, urban identity expressed through new vocabularies and organized around a network of nightclubs—all came together to make up a position on the city that was particularly charged in the context of late 1960s Dar es Salaam. The Arusha Declaration of February 1967, which signalled Nyerere's and Tanzania's turn towards quasi-socialist economic policies, also marked a ratcheting up of an official discourse of "modern development" and an emphasis on "hard work" as a primary condition of good citizenship. The declaration also featured lengthy exhortations on the need to "value more highly the rural peasant" and to realize that "development will be based upon farming," positions that would become central policy planks for the decade to come.[33] With this intensification of a stress on the rural as the appropriate scene for national development and civic duty, the city became more than ever the foil for the village, with city dwellers becoming symbols of parasitical sloth.

More specifically, Nyerere (who authored the Arusha Declaration) singled out in the document two categories of Tanzanians as obstacles to the new work ethic: "village men" and "city women." Raising village women up as examples of the kind of hard workers that the nation needed, Nyerere lamented the loss of "the energies of the millions of men in the villages and thousands of women in the towns which are at present wasted in gossip, dancing and drinking."[34] While such condemnation of the village men would prove to be rare (indeed, the figure of the ideal peasant-citizen ended up being quite consistently represented as male in the years after the Arusha Declaration), the stigma attached to city women was an enduring and constitutive element of the vilification of the city and city dwellers in general. For it was not only that city women were represented as the worst of the city's unproductive masses. More fundamentally, the city itself—as the site of excess, consumption, illicit leisure, and thus as the target of the new politics of frugality and hard work—was gendered feminine.

Situated in this context, interventions by opponents of the soul ban ran counter to an official ethic and aesthetic of frugality, rural hard work, and peasant citizenship that was becoming increasingly important to the state's legitimacy at the time of the ban. The letter writers' articulation of an ethic of consumption valuing the latest craze and connecting them to the appropriation of stylistic elements of an imagined, global youth culture challenged state discourse. It did so not because of the strident cosmopolitanism of the celebratory statements about soul, but rather because this transnational imaginary was quite different from the internationalist connections invoked by TANU around a network of socialist or Communist states. Furthermore, the defence by self-identifying teenagers of the nightclubs, public halls, and dancing places in which soul was enjoyed reversed the polarities of the rural/urban dichotomies of official policy-making. Indeed, in the political climate of post-Arusha Declaration Dar es Salaam, soul digging in clubs to which schoolgirls were reportedly lured represented a kind of conspicuous consumption by a prominent urban problem category: young people refusing the proper vanguard role of "youth" for the ideologically suspect one of "teenagers."

Obatala's assessment of African young people's consumption of soul as "not [being] rooted in any genuine appreciation of the historical, political, and economic ties that bind us [Africans and African Americans] and make us a common people with one destiny" may not be directly contradicted by the Tanzanian soul debate.[35] But neither does his characterization capture either the personal or political meanings of soul for young Tanzanians in the context of official attacks on an urban style that did not conform to either a rural aesthetic or a "respectable" urban one; and there is a similar disjuncture between Obatala's and Eubanks's concerns on the one hand, and the motivations of Tanzanian officials in banning soul on the other. The motivations of the officials were informed by anxieties over the mobility and sexuality of urban, particularly female, youth, not by allegiance to, or neglect of, political affiliations and commitments to an African diaspora. Such affiliations did exist for TANU, but they were played out in ambiguous ways when it came to official positions on Afro-American culture in Tanzania.

Official ambivalence towards Afro-American culture and politics was perhaps most apparent in the visits of the noted African-American personalities—

visits that captured considerable public attention. The week-long official visit of Angela Davis, for instance, coincided with the buildup to a new TANU campaign to ban "indecent dress," and both events featured prominently—indeed, competed for space—in the October issue of *Nchi Yetu*, a cultural magazine published by the government's Department of News and Information. Gracing the issue's cover (a space typically featuring state-sanctioned models of national femininity) was a portrait photograph of Davis sporting her large, trademark Afro and dangling hoop earrings, and wearing a stylish, white pantsuit, the trousers of which were obscured in the cover photo. The magazine cover's brief text box, though, alerted readers to what was to be the main story of the issue and the subject of its page one editorial: "*Mavazi ya heshima*" [Respectable or dignified dress]. On turning the page, readers encountered the two stories side by side yet again—this time with Davis's miniaturized image vacating centre stage to make way for the editor's condemnation of "shameful dress." Lauded in the photo's caption as that of "a daring revolutionary and fighter for justice ... worldwide," Davis was represented in an image that competed with the editor's exhortations against "wantonly dressing up and imitating people of other nationalities."[36] Inside the magazine, full-length articles on each story followed. "Respectable Dress" attacked banned dress in terms of national cultural and singled out several specific styles for special condemnation: among them, the trousers (known locally as "Pekosi") "worn especially by the internationally-famous soul musician called James Brown"; wide belts; women's short skirts and tight pants; and the practice, popular among both men and women, of doing one's hair "to look like African Americans."[37] The biographical article on Davis—"A Fighter for Equal Human Rights"—was accompanied by photos from her visit to Arusha District. Dressed in the pantsuit outfit featured on the cover, this time sporting large, round sunglasses, Davis was portrayed "showing clearly that she has African roots" as she tasted some roasted maize offered by residents of a *ujamaa* village, and chatting with the Arusha regional commissioner at his office.[38]

Although the writers and editors of *Nchi Yetu* at the Department of News and Information scrupulously avoided any textual mention of Davis's sartorial style, readers of the issue could not have helped noticing her Afro, sunglasses, pants, and jewellery—all markers of a cosmopolitan style that, when displayed by Tanzanians, was under attack as indecent, foreign, and shameful to the nation. One of the visual examples of unacceptable dress accompanying part two of the "*Mavazi ya heshima*" article was striking in its affinity with the photos of Davis the month before.[39] That *Nchi Yetu* made no comment objecting to Davis's appearance can, of course, be attributed in part to her being not a Tanzanian, but rather a foreign guest of honour. But what the curious juxtaposition of these two events and reports suggests more than anything is that official campaigns against Afro-American culture in Tanzania were not launched in reference to the way in which such culture enabled or disabled a Black struggle worldwide, as Eubanks and Obatala argued respectively, but were, rather, based upon concerns over decency and the city. This is not to contend that Tanzanian officialdom was blind to diasporic politics or an internationalist agenda—indeed, the piece on Davis alone, not to mention the wider record of Tanzanian international alliances and commitments, strongly indicates the contrary. What it does suggest is that the state consistently tried to frame the two issues as entirely independent, as distinct and separate: in official discourse, banning soul or the Afro had nothing to do with hailing radical, Black diasporic politics, and the two positions could be articulated side by side for precisely this reason.

This finding, then, allows us to see the correspondents' interventions on the issue—those of both Tanzanians and expatriates like Obatala and Eubanks—in a new light. For if state discourse showcased efforts to disentangle, and maintain as distinct, its own support for Black liberation causes internationally from its assault on indecent, urban others at home, many letter writers repeatedly undermined such distinctions. Letter writers appealed both to ways of being modern that were at odds with official visions of modernizationist development, and to vocabulary and imagery drawn from international youth cultures. These appeals fed claims to particular urban identities. In highlighting the uneven encounters and disjunctures between these multiple positions on the soul ban, this discussion responds to recent calls to produce transnational histories of "Black cultural traffic" that, to paraphrase Kennell Jackson, loosen our views of the paths that Black popular culture takes.[40]

Such histories, as the work of Brent Hayes Edwards, Paula Ebron, and Catherine Cole compellingly demonstrate, must be attuned to the disjunctures, no less than the solidarities, that emerge along these routes.[41] As the negotiations around African-American culture in 1960s Dar es Salaam suggest, soul music or the Afro travelled not with a fixed set of meanings, but rather as forms that were susceptible to passionate reappropriation, reworking, and revaluing along the way.

# EXHIBITING a GLOBAL BLaCHNESS
## The First World Festival of Negro Arts

**Thumb through** any *Jet* magazine from the spring of 1966. Mixed with ads for hair products and skin lighteners selling "beauty at half price" are updates on developments within the realm of African-American politics— "Trio Handed Life Terms in Death of Malcolm X." Among the inside scoops on Sidney Poitier's new film, readers will come across serious debates on war and U.S. foreign policy— "Not Right for 3 Sons in Vietnam Says Mom, 1 Killed." And among these accounts you will inevitably encounter stories about Africa—evidence of the increasing interest of African Americans in the continent and its newly independent nations.

Dakar, Senegal, in particular, dominated headlines in 1966 with its ground-breaking First World Festival of Negro Arts. Arguably the most ambitious cultural project of its time to be hosted by an African nation, the festival brought together Black artists and intellectuals from around the world to participate in displays of dance, music, literature, and drama. It also presented exhibitions of contemporary visual art and traditional African art. Followed closely by both *Jet* and *Ebony*, in addition to a number of Black academic journals, this international festival came to embody the shifting political and artistic ties between independence-era Africa and its diaspora.

For Senegal, the host nation, the First World Festival of Negro Arts presented an opportunity not only to explore and display a new national identity in an international arena but also to put forward the philosophy of Negritude upheld by Senegal's poet-president, Léopold Senghor. For many artists and performers of African descent living in the United States, it represented an opportunity to examine the position of African-American art within their own country and internationally. Further, for the artists participating in the festival, as well as those who merely followed the event through news reports, it was an occasion to reassess their own relationships to Africa.

The festival and its presence in the annals of U.S. Black popular media reflected an increasing interest in examining the global reach of what was then known as Negro identity. Within the explicit goal of presenting the genius of the "Negro World" to an international community, both the festival's organizers and participants worked under the assumption of a unifying Black identity—one that reached across the geopolitical boundaries of nation-states and through the historical rifts of the middle passage and colonialism to connect all peoples of African descent. Yet it is difficult to chart the qualities that constitute a unified Black identity; a blackness or *africanité* that bonds all people of African descent into a global community. While it was the mandate of the First World Festival of Negro Arts to demonstrate and define Black identity through its cultural exhibitions, the diversity of ways in which blackness was imagined in the exhibition betrayed fractures and slippages in the constitution of a global Black subjectivity. As it turned out, in the exhibitions of contemporary visual art (my focus here), art works were created and mobilized in various ways around a debate about Black identity in the national and international contexts. The conflicting political and cultural goals presented by the exhibition organizers, African-American participants, and observers reveal that the concept of blackness held by African nations such as Senegal functioned quite differently than did the concept of blackness as held by diasporic artists in the United States.

# The exhibition's emphasis on the arts as a means through which peoples
of African descent could connect to a global Black community was not misplaced. Art, and other cultural expressions, are essential in the building of communal identities. To regard identity as constructed through culture helps to explain the importance of the global cultural event. It allows us to think beyond a model of Black identity that is presumably rooted in a stable, innate quality to consider instead how such identities are imagined and created in art exhibitions. As Stuart Hall notes, identity, rather than being a stable fact, is inherently mutable. Further, art and other forms of cultural production are essential tools in the constitution and calcification of identities. Hall writes, "Instead of thinking of identity as an already accomplished fact, which the new cultural practices then

represent, we should think instead of identity as a 'production' which is never complete, always a process, and always constituted within, not outside, representation."[1] The First World Festival of Negro Arts, then, can be seen as an attempt to produce a global community through a shared blackness. The contemporary contexts of the exhibition, more than any universal connection, informed the conceptions of a global blackness for the festival's participants.

Countries throughout Africa, South America, North America, Europe, and the Caribbean were invited to send delegations of artists and performers to represent their Black populations. In addition to the cultural and arts displays, the festival was preceded by a nine-day colloquium, "Function and Significance of African Negro Art in the Life of the People and for the People," in which artists and academics alike explored the weighty topic of "Negro art" through speeches and presentations. These proceedings were created to serve four official goals, as set down by the organizing committee: to establish interracial and international bonds, to provide an international forum for Black artists, to demonstrate the vital contributions to humanity made by the arts of Africa and its diaspora, and, lastly, to promote Negritude.[2]

The most explicit of those goals was to promote Negritude—to present an international display of the genius of the "Negro World." The complexities in achieving such a goal were a focus of great debate in the colloquium and throughout the media coverage of the festival. For Senegal, it was clear that the favoured path of Negritude posited a unity among all Black people through a metaphysical *africanité*. This quality made people of African descent both distinct from Europeans and able to sit at the table of humanity as equal to them. Negritude was central to Senegal's national identity because the country's first president, Senghor, was a major contributor to the formulation of that philosophical position. As Senghor stated in his opening address to the festival, "In a word, if we [Senegal] have assumed the terrible responsibility of organizing this Festival, it is for the *defense and illustration of négritude*."[3] For Senghor, the festival presented a forum in which to broaden what had largely been a literary movement into a full-blown political philosophy; Negritude was the main strategy for him and many francophone thinkers in imagining a modern, independent Africa. Speaking at the colloquium on the possible roles of Black art in the future, Cameroonian writer Engelbert Mveng proclaimed, "That technical civilization in which Africa claims to take her place must be built in our own country on the rock of Negritude," which, he said, "must furnish the basis of a concept of Man, and of a political, economic, and social organization which respects the peculiar genius of Black Africa."[4]

If Negritude was to be adopted as the philosophical model that would unify a postcolonial Africa and its diaspora, Senghor saw to it that Senegal would be the model country for this new Black world. Negritude was Senegal's solution to mediating the difficulties of its emergence as a postcolonial nation by mitigating the problems of colonial history, political rivalries, and economic disparities within the country with a discourse that unified identities. Senghor's Senegal expanded the existing network of cultural institutions to give material form to Negritude, creating national art schools that would act as proponents of a distinct visual vocabulary developed around Negritude's ideas of *africanité*. Art historian Elizabeth Harney has written extensively on the emergence of the first generation of post-independence artists, known as the École de Dakar, who flourished under the considerable support of the Senegalese government.[5] Artists such as Papa Ibra Tall and Ibou Diouf created works that tended towards abstracted forms, with an interest in African motifs and an emphasis on colour and rhythm. These artists visualized the rhetoric of Negritude to create a distinctly modern art movement based on an *aesthetique negro-africaine*.[6]

The festival's exhibition of contemporary artists, "Tendencies and Confrontations," included artists from around the globe but was largely imagined as an international debut for the artists of the École de Dakar.[7] Through the exhibition Senegal was able to exploit a vision of a modern African nation for the consumption of an international market of potential investors. As Harney observes, in addition to the overtly stated intentions behind the organization of the Dakar festival, implicitly the festival functioned as a mode of expressing an image of the ideal African nation in order to foster international relations for the relatively young nation of Senegal.[8] Rather than inviting individual artists to participate in the festival, the Senegalese organizing committee only accepted contributions by national entities. Each nation had control over the organization of its own delegation, including the selection of artists and performers as well as the raising and distribution of funds. Thus the show became as much an opportunity for the Senegalese government and other governments in Africa to nurture international relations through cultural networks as it was an opportunity for fostering a reconnection between Africa and its diaspora.

If the Senegalese contribution to the festival was meant to demonstrate the possibilities of Negritude in unifying its citizens under a global Black culture, the contribution from the United States was somewhat less confident in this rhetoric of universal blackness. Most of the U.S. contributors and observers did not readily accept Negritude as a philosophical model. As Lloyd Garrison reported in *The New York Times*, Negritude elicited a range of responses and critiques: "It has been praised by many, denounced by others as 'Black nationalism' or simply shrugged off as being merely the private mystique of Senegal's poet-President, Leopold Senghor."[9] Many U.S. observers objected to the idea of applying the term Negritude to work that was as amorphous and diverse as their Black identities. Choreographer Katherine Dunham asserted, "I see no reason for putting any particular label in front of what we are doing that requires an elaborate explanation. The Negroness that we are is there. There's no way to get out of it."[10] Others were able to take the term and give it an alternate definition through exploring American equivalents. Langston Hughes, for example, found a correlation between Senghor's notion of Negritude and "what younger American writers call 'soul.'"[11]

How, then, does one create a criteria for the representation of African-American artists in an international festival based on the assumption of a shared Black identity? The African-American artist Hale Woodruff considered this question in his foreword to the catalogue *Ten Negro Artists from the United States*, the U.S. contribution to the contemporary arts portion of the festival. "For the answer," Woodruff wrote, "one must look first to the interacting forces which shape the artist and his art and, in the process, guard against over-simplification, for these forces are far more complex than they seem."[12] Woodruff thus attempted to embrace a notion of Black identity that is inherently complex and contextual against the essentialist notion of Negritude. The visual arts component of the U.S. participation attempted to address the onerous task of representing contemporary African-American visual artists in light of this complexity.

Because of the official role played by nations in the organization of the festival, the U.S. contribution to the First World Festival of Negro Arts was overseen by the U.S. State Department. Participation on the part of the United States was born into controversy with the appointment of white philanthropist Virginia Innes-Brown as chair of the general committee for the U.S. delegation. However, the contemporary visual arts section of the exhibition was chaired by the well-respected Woodruff. Originally, it was the wish of the visual arts committee to exhibit some seventy-five to eighty works by about forty living artists, thus presenting a representational cross-section of contemporary African-American art.[13] This plan proved too ambitious, as a list of factors eventually reduced the number of artists to ten. For one, the exhibition space allotted by the festival's organizers was significantly less than had been hoped. Further, the funds available to the committee were not enough to financially support a large presence. Eventually six artists withdrew their contributions to the festival in protest of broken promises on the part of the organizing committee.

In the resulting exhibition the ten included artists displayed what might seem a surprising aesthetic diversity. Many of the exhibited artists—Barbara Chase, Sam Gilliam, Richard Hunt, and William Majors, for example—created completely abstract work. Others, such as Jacob Lawrence and Charles White, worked in more figurative, social-realist modes. The stark contrast between the work of White and Majors in particular provides a good example of this diversity.

White's exhibited work, *Birmingham Totem* (1964), is a naturalistic ink drawing on paper. The piece depicts a Black youth stooped atop a huge mound of splintered wood that dominates the lower half of the drawing. The crouching youth's downcast eyes and solemn face express determination as he focuses on the task before him. He reaches down into the chaos of wooden shards, carefully picking up the pieces. The work is a reference to the notorious 1963 bombing of an African-American church in Birmingham, Alabama, in which four teenagers were killed, and it exemplifies White's dedication to social realism. It mirrors a number of works in which he made social commentaries on political issues important to African Americans.

Majors's *Ecclesiastes V* (1965) is a work of pure abstraction. Revealing no explicit connection to his identity as African American or to the political movements of the time, Majors's etching is a study of shape, line, and movement. Rather than the political project embraced by White, Majors imagined his artistic project as one of technical innovation and aesthetic experience. Nor did Majors assign much validity to the Negritude philosophies of the First World Festival of Negro Arts. As he asserted in an article about the Spiral group, to which he belonged, "I don't care about going to Africa ... I just work."[14]

These two examples alone reveal both the diversity of aesthetic styles used by African-American artists and the conflicting attitudes towards the role of Black identity in African-American art. Since the Harlem Renaissance, artists in the United States have grappled with the notion of working in an artistic mode that is distinctly Black. Some artists believed that Black art should be reflected by the incorporation of African-derived aesthetics. For White, the incorporation of politically engaged themes that communicate the lived experiences of African Americans reflected the notion of Black art. Yet for Majors the notion of identity was entirely irrelevant to his own artistic practice. Still, both artists engaged with or were mobilized into a discourse on blackness.

White's work posits a completely different model of blackness than that imagined by the proponents of Negritude. It is a blackness built on the notion of a shared Black experience. In many ways this model of Black identity counters the metaphysical elements of Negritude, whose emphasis in the primordial "African personality" was a point of much debate.[15] One can question how the experiential model might translate into a global blackness when the experiences of peoples of African descent vary so drastically; but notions of identity as experience have created communities geared towards political empowerment. For instance, definitions of blackness upheld in Britain during the 1980s emphasized a shared experience of oppression over racial or cultural affiliation and allowed Britain's Asian population to identify as "Black Brits."

The Black rhetoric behind Majors's example is somewhat more ambiguous, if it can be said to be found within the work at all. Still, despite the artist's assumed position against the identity-focused organization of exhibitions like the

First World Festival of Negro Arts, Majors's etching won the Grand Prize for print-making and illustration in the festival. The Grand Prize for painting also went to an artist working in abstraction, British artist Frank Bowling, which raises the question of how such work could be chosen as exemplars of an identity-driven exhibition. The festival's interest in an undefined universal quality that could be drawn upon to create a Black avant-garde might begin to explain the favouring of such modern works. The exhibition's identity-focused frame could itself create the possibility of reading Negritude philosophies onto the otherwise purely abstract works. Both pioneering in its modernity and essentially Black, works like that of Majors allowed for an image of Negritude as projected into the new world.

Another possible force at work in framing the contributions made by Majors and other abstract artists was the image that the U.S. government was attempting to put forward through the show. Majors's aesthetic concerns existed at the time of abstract expressionism's pre-eminence in the American art world. Thus his work can be seen as demonstrating Black participation in the United States' dominant artistic paradigm. Because of the State Department's role in organizing the U.S. delegation to the festival, the prominence of abstract art may support the arguments about abstract expressionism's connection to the Cold War posed by art historians such as Eva Cockroft and Serge Guilbaut. They assert that abstract expressionism was promoted internationally by U.S. governmental agencies to fight the Cold War on the cultural front through a discourse of artistic individuality and freedom of expression.[16] Majors, then, provided a distinctly Black model of artistic freedom against the spreading threat of socialism in Africa.

Certainly, Cold War tensions provided an interesting subtext to the U.S. media coverage of the Dakar festival. Most of that coverage concerned the loan of a Russian cruise ship that helped to fill the increased demands for lodging. Writing for *The New York Times*, Garrison offered the following account: "As guests sip their vodka on the main deck, they are also treated to an exhibit extolling Russian-Negro brotherhood. Several display boards highlight the fact that the Russians never engaged in the slave trade, while guess-who did."[17] Easily absorbed into the rhetoric of Negritude upheld by Senegal and an anticommunist rhetoric for the United States, Majors's work might well have been offering a chance for each government to put forth its own agenda.

The organization of the festival in relation to nation-states is central to the major critiques of the U.S. delegation. As would be expected, given that its committee responsible for organizing a delegation to a festival dedicated to Negro arts was not only under the control of the State Department but also headed by a white person, the U.S. effort met with a great deal of criticism within media and Black cultural circles. Described in *Jet* magazine as "a white wealthy woman who supports 'charities,'" Innes-Brown was the only white committee chairperson out of all the participating countries.[18] Her appointment was not made because of the lack of Black interest in the organizing of the festival. Pianist and arts organizer Robert Pritchard was a vocal opponent to her chairmanship from the moment the appointment was announced. He told *The New York Times* that he had reached the understanding that he and other African Americans would be involved with overseeing the U.S. committee following early correspondences with the Senegalese organizer, Alioune Diop. Somewhat later Diop made clear the official Senegalese position. As the *Times* reported, "The World Festival of Negro Arts was being organized by governments and [Diop's] mission would deal only with governments. He said that Mr. Pritchard's group had his approval, but as it was not a branch of the United States Government, it could not have an official mandate from the festival."[19]

Because of the central role given to nations by the organizing committee of the festival, the U.S. delegation was overshadowed by the constant possibility of government censorship in the selection of artists who would represent the country. One main critique of the show offered in the media was that the participation in the exhibition was so closely tied to the State Department that no controversial artists were allowed to participate. Certainly, many younger artists who were associated with the visual arts components of the Black arts movement were not represented in the festival. It is difficult to say whether their exclusion was the result of censorship, but their politically engaged works, which often worked outside of established art-world venues, would later become emblems of African-American art in the 1960s and 1970s. For many within the context of the United States, blackness expressed itself in the works of artists, musicians, and writers who were marginalized by mainstream America. In his critique of the festival Hoyt Fuller wrote that such producers "are likely to be among the Negro artists who could bring to a world festival the essence of Negro experience in America."[20]

In the end the contested notion of blackness revealed by the exhibition illustrates how the African-American delegation managed to make its distinct contribution to the discursive goals of the First World Festival of Negro Arts. Despite the lack of any explicit Black aesthetic or political agenda, the work hinged on the very notions that defined an exhibition like the Dakar festival—by exposing its own ambivalence to the possibility of a unified and defining Negritude. Rather than being situated outside the rhetoric of racial unity put forward by Negritude, the diversity of the works in the U.S. delegation mirrored the larger space of the exhibition as a site for a dialogue about the possibility of creating a global blackness.

Marilisa Merolla 18

# ROCK 'N' ROLL, POLITICS, AND SOCIETY DURING THE ITALIAN ECONOMIC BOOM

**The "Italian miracle"** exploded in the mid-1950s, transforming in a very short time the young and rural Italian Republic into one of the most industrialized countries in the world. From the middle of the 1950s both old and new media actively, and vitally, combined to make a decisive contribution to the radically changing face of an Italy on the road to modernization; and through the birth of teen and women's magazines, the diffusion of cinema and rock 'n' roll music, and new radio and television formats—all of them as both symbols and vehicles—new consumer trends, coming largely from across the ocean, were spread across Italy.

The irresistible diffusion of the "American way of life" and its impact on Italian reality began with the arrival of the U.S. troops during the years of the Liberation and took a firm hold during the mid-1950s. As a result of the sudden and powerful economic boom, goods and technologies that were only a short time before considered luxuries—the refrigerator, the washing machine, the compact car—became accessible to the masses. In the following decade the Italian political class played its part in this by attempting to use the mass media for the purposes of producing a national identity for the very young Democratic Republic. For the government, led by the majority party of Christian Democrats, which throughout the 1950s and 1960s controlled all the radio and television broadcasting and part of the music industry, the media provided the main instruments that could be used to guide modernity and adapt it to a national tradition. But, ironically, the media also provided the very instruments that, even if controlled, would decisively influence a major change in Italian lifestyle.

For the traditional political parties—Christian Democrats, Socialist Party (PSI), and Communist Party (PCI)—a key priority became the necessity of controlling the effects of the sudden and explosive economic "boom," and especially its impact on the young. The perceived threat was the laicization or secularization of youth—an emerging condition for a generation of young people who had not actively participated in World War II, who grew up during the civil war between Italian fascist and Italian antifascists, and who were now experiencing the founding of a new democracy. This generation sought to emancipate itself from a fidelity to traditional political ideologies that in the postwar period, as a consequence of the Cold War, were splitting Italian society in two, with Catholic and Atlanticist on one side, and Socialist and Communist on the other. As an effect of the new consumerism and new customs that came with the economic boom, Italian teenagers began to adopt the standardized identities and lifestyles of the young generations in other Western democracies. Just as important, along with increased consumption came the unification of the generation in the form of demands for civil rights, social emancipation, and freedom in their attitudes and lifestyle.

The history of the years preceding and accompanying the Italian economic miracle—roughly from the mid-1950s to the mid-1960s—has been thoroughly discussed by scholars in terms of political, economic, and social conditions. Only recently have historical studies introduced a new perspective on this period, not only looking at the history of consumption as a result of the industrial evolution of the country, but also assessing the effects of consumption on the Italian population's attitudes and values. The consumption of music in particular had effects that were not only immediately visible, but in fact disruptive to the "look of Italy," starting precisely with the young generations who would be the future leaders of civil and political life. The arrival of rock 'n' roll music in the Italian landscape well expressed the young Italian Republic's parable of modernization. It was a modernization that strongly pushed the Italian population to conform to the conditions of the advanced Western democracies, but it nevertheless occurred in the context of a country that, in the 1950s, retained, for its majority, the characteristics and peculiarities of an agricultural society.

Rock 'n' roll music, with its transgressive charge, accelerated the teenage takeover of the music industry and, in a striking contrast with the melodic tradition that was still prevalent, marked a cultural discontinuity; because the political class saw this break as a threat they tried to devitalize it by promoting a mass-produced "Italian way of rock 'n' roll" that would be in many ways harmonious with the national musical tradition—a sort of "provincial" rock that had little echo abroad but found success among Italian consumers. The arrival of rock 'n' roll music in Italy is, then, a kaleidoscope through which it is possible to read the contradictions, the hopes and the fears, the anxieties and the enthusiasm, the leaps and the resistance of a society that pushed towards emancipation through the spread of wealth and its totems, yet largely remained strongly tied to tradition and was not willing to change its skin to interpret the changing world.

The new media of the mid-1950s were examples, interpretations, and at the same time agents that amplified the desire of the Italian people to forget the pain and the fatigue of the long postwar period and run towards prosperity and well-being. The symbols of this prosperity resonated through the old and new forms of mass communication. In his celebrated 1958 song "Il blu dipinto di blu"—better known as "Volare"—Domenico Modugno perfectly interpreted the mood of many Italians. Ready to leave behind the difficult economic sacrifices of the reconstruction years, Italians were now euphoric and eager to "fly" towards prosperity—possibly at the helm of a Vespa and Lambretta or a new Seicento (the economy car) just off the Fiat assembly line. These new mobile commodities were launched into the race to traverse the new, long tracts of highway that made their way to vacation villages; they were dreamed of through the images of cinema and television, but were now no longer unreachable myths.

More than anyone else it was the teenage girls and boys who grew up during the hard years of the economic reconstruction of the country who felt the impact of modernization. Unlike their parents and older siblings, they had not experienced the traumas of the Second World War and the civil war that, between 1943 and 1945, had split Italy in two between the fascists and antifascists. In many cases these young people passed part of their childhoods in the athletic and recreational organizations of the parishes or the political parties, but still, for the most part, on the outside of any militant party organizing. They had not absorbed the culture of ideological conflict between communists and anticommunists that poisoned the Italian political atmosphere during the 1940s and 1950s. These young people, who came of age in a more democratic Italy that offered them the novelty of freedom of thought, were more open to accept the myths of the new prosperity synthesized in the "American way of life."

This myth would be a symbol of the collective imagination until the end of the 1950s. It wasn't only the mirage of better living and working conditions, but also the sparkling images and the new sounds, projected by the old and new media, that irresistibly encouraged thousands of young people to leave the agricultural and socially backward south of Italy to reach the north of Italy, the land of industrial development and modernization, or to emigrate to the richer European countries.

In Italy, rock 'n' roll music landed in 1954, with the arrival of American marines in the Naples AFSOUTH (Allied Forces Southern Europe) Base, installed two years before in Bagnoli Bay. Through the myriad of bars and nightclubs that gathered along the port area and in the city area of Campi Flegrei, the rhythms of music characterized by Afro-American roots fascinated the middle-class young people as well the Neapolitan "*scugnizzi*," the Neapolitan little boys and girls who belonged to the poorest families. In both cases these youth lost no time in making this rhythm part of their own culture, music, and lifestyle. From here the contagion spread throughout the national territory, thanks to record companies and indirectly to the movies that imported the American model. Through the diffusion among the young people of the new jukeboxes, of the gleaming new covers of the 45 rpm records and of the coloured portable record players, rock 'n' roll became the soundtrack of the "great transformation."

On May 18, 1957, the first Italian rock 'n' roll festival took place at the Palazzo del Ghiaccio in Milan. Debuting with the song "Ciao ti dirò" were the I Rocky Boys, a band formed by the young and, at that time, totally unknown Italian singers Adriano Celentano, Enzo Jannacci, Giorgio Gaber, and Luigi Tenco. The show was concluded by the violent intervention of the police, who were totally unprepared to face the imposing number of boys and girls who came through the gates. In October of the same year, the precursor of the so-called "*urlatori*" (shouters), Tony Dallara, produced his first single, provoking shock and dismay among the musical critics of the time. With this new way of singing (characterized by his famous "hiccup"), the conventional canons of the beautiful melodic Italian song, belonging to the tradition of Claudio Villa, Luciano Tajoli, and Nilla Pizzi, were totally disrupted. The traditional repertoire passed through a deep crisis, overcome by rockers, "shouters," and singer-songwriters, who gave a strong provocation to the sales of records, ensuring the triumph of the new 45 rpm vinyl record (and the demise of the by now retrograde 78s). In 1957 the total number of records sold was 11,137,700, and just over 3,000,000 of them were 45s. Only one year later the total number of records sold reached 16,875,200; more than 10,000,000 of them were 45s.

The increase in record production played a decisive role in the change of tastes and of the typology of Italian musical consumption, which at the same time gave a strong impulse to the expansion of the music market, generating a continuous circle. Still, in the immediate postwar period the companies that constituted the Italian phonographic industry could be counted on the fingers of one hand: the VCM (Voce del Padrone-Columbia-Marconiphone); the Cetra, a public institute constituted in 1933 by the fascist government and tied first to the fascist radio broadcaster EIAR (Ente Italiano Audizioni Radiofoniche) but after the Second World War to RAI, the public radio and television broadcaster controlled by the government; the Fonit (Fonodisco Italiano Trevisan); the Durium, which appeared in the market in the 1940s, producing fairy-tale records for children; and a handful of others. When the futuristic establishment of the multinational colossus RCA Corporation opened its doors in Rome in 1953, it was evident that the music business had arrived in Italy.

The result was the sudden decline of the traditional musical publisher. This professional figure—who had previously controlled the decision to launch a song in the market and who represented the only point of contact for the composers— was now replaced by the much more aggressive figure of the music agent, whose task was not only to launch a bestseller, but also, first of all, to promote a particular teen idol according to the new rigid rules of marketing. In this way the production and promotion of records assumed an importance hitherto unknown in the Italian market; but the true novelty was that the singer began to be identified with a particular song. Even when performed by other voices, a song always evoked the figure of the original artist, recalling that person's look, tonal qualities, and stage movements. The success of the product depended now on image, not just on the song. In Italy the era of the star system had begun.

In 1958, on the occasion of the 150th anniversary of the birth of its musical editions, the prestigious music publishing company Casa Ricordi in Milan turned itself into a modern record industry: Franco Crepax, the Italian cartoonist whose first engagement as an artist was designing record covers, and Nanni Ricordi were called upon to manage the department of light music. Ricordi, and another firm, Music, created by the Guertler brothers, were the first phonographic companies to profit from the great transformation in the field of Italian song, generating the first Italian teen idols such as Adriano Celentano, Giorgio Gaber, and Ornella Vanoni.

As true precursors of the Italian record industry the new companies understood the many economic implications of the explosion of myths and symbols associated with the consumption of light music. Beginning with the jukebox, "the sonorous box that produces happiness," to quote Adriano Celentano, and continuing with the first coloured portable record players, the same 45 rpm vinyl records had to change their look, starting with the packaging. The transparent wrap with the hole in the centre in which the record was traditionally contained was substituted by a much more appealing cover displaying the title of the song, the singer's photo, and flashy images that visually anticipated the exciting rhythm of the content.

With this new look, the records were sold not just in traditional music shops, but also, in a new flexi disc format enclosed in some magazines, as, for example, with the music review *Il Musichiere*, which was linked to the television show of the same name. By the end of the 1950s the flexi record was also appearing in the family games magazine *La Nuova Enigmistica Tascabile*, and subsequently in *Big*, a new teen review. Even the major Italian weekly news magazine *Espresso* couldn't resist the temptation to include in its pages the magic plastic record, in this case containing some historical songs.

Around the same time *Selezione dal Reader's Digest* started getting good results selling records by correspondence. Consequently a large diversity of prices appeared in the music market, causing havoc. Different music companies sold records at different prices, and produced different record formats: 33, 45, 45EP (Extended Play, with four songs), and 78 (although this last format was near extinction). In the years from, roughly, the mid-1950s to the early 1960s, the cost of a vinyl record was around 4,000 liras (excluding taxes) for 33 rpm, 1,300 liras for the 45EPs, and 700 liras for 45 rpm singles.

Not surprisingly, after the uncontrollable boom of the 45 rpm vinyl, the government hastened to add music records to the "goods and luxury" tax, creating an immediate price hike and making vinyl records much more expensive for the consumer.

Nevertheless the huge economic success of music records also appealed to other forms of media. Intensifying its relationship with cinema, and following the stream of new music films for teenagers that had recently exploded overseas, Italy also started to produce the so-called "*musicarelli*"—as inspired by the film that launched this phenomenon in the United States, *Rock around the Clock* (1956), riding on the great success of Bill Haley's rock 'n' roll hit. The same song had already been featured in the soundtrack of the "generational breakup" film *Blackboard Jungle* (1955). Shortly after that the movie *Jailhouse Rock* (1957) captured the disruptive sex appeal of Elvis Presley. In 1959 *Go, Johnny, Go!*—its plot inspired by Chuck Berry's rock 'n' roll hit "Johnny B. Goode"—was introduced in Italian cinemas with the title *Dai, Johnny, Dai*. In the same year the Italian rockers and home howlers started to play the role of professional actors: Celentano, Mina, Dallara, Betty Curtis, Joe Sentieri, Fred Buscaglione, and other singers became the protagonists of movies with such exciting titles as *Jukebox urli d'Amore* (Jukebox cries of love), *Ragazzi del Juke-box* (Boys of the jukebox), *Sanremo la grande Sfida* (Sanremo festival, the great challenge) and *Urlatori alla sbarra* (Shouters at the gates).

This revolution in the music industry was a sign that the citizen's lifestyle—until now anchored to the traditional cultures of the Catholic Party, Socialist Party, or Communist Party—was radically changing. People in general were now involved in the exploding process of modernization and laicization, as thoroughly spread by the new media.

This enormous economic, social, and cultural change forced the major political party, the Christian Democrats, to modify the governmental balance of power, beginning its dialogue with the Italian Socialist Party. The objective was to create the first government with the participation of socialist ministers, increasing the base of political support to include the working class, the real protagonists of the great transformation caused by the Industrial Revolution, of which the Socialist Party was considered one of the most important representatives.

The road towards the first centre-left government was long and thorny and destined to conclude only in 1963. This was because the Italian Socialist Party, in contrast to other Western European socialist parties, was tied until 1956 to the Italian Communist Party, with whom it shared a loyalty to the Soviet Union and a political opposition to governments led by Christian Democrats.

Nevertheless, in the mid-1950s, in the new context of economic prosperity, along with the "Red Scare" came a new concern about the threat that the society was modernizing too rapidly and that by so quickly breaking the many ties with the past the citizens risked being separated from traditional values. This concern was demonstrated with the riots of 1960 against the threat of the establishment of a reactionary centre-right government led by Fernando Tambroni. Those who protested against this political development in the piazzas across Italy were not only the "Reds"—the Communists and the Socialists—but also many teenage boys and girls who grew up in the new climate of prosperity and democracy and who did not intend to return to the past. In addition to their political identity with the left, they were united by clothing style and musical taste. The press of the day referred to them as "the kids with the striped T-shirts."

Not surprisingly, then, the government took prudent measures to control the spread of these new consumers' trends and rhythms—the symbols and soundtracks of disruptive modernity—attempting to contain them within traditional roles. What made this cultural policy operation possible was the governing Christian Democrats' monopoly of the radio and state-run television, a control that also seemed to extend to the diffusion of the new styles of music. The public corporation RAI-TV found itself in the controversial position of having to reconcile the unstoppable push of modernization that arrived from the U.S. media with the more reassuring conservative national traditions.

This cultural policy operation was carried out through radio programs that focused on civil and cultural education, on the promotion of national unity and solidarity, and on linguistic standardization of the Italian population. The activity was also carried out through the newborn medium of television—introduced to Italy in 1954—which RAI used to promote a linguistic, historical, and territorial Italian identity, based on democratic values. Indeed, it launched a cultural policy of media innovation and tradition that would define the "*via italiana alla televisione.*" Thanks to this "Italian way of television," the U.S. formats were readapted in a version that valued Italian culture and traditions. The most significant example was that of the U.S. quiz show *The $64.000 Question*, which was transformed into the famous Italian version, *Lascia o raddoppia*. This quiz show brought to the screen contestants coming from diverse parts of the national territory. In this way previously unknown places were revealed, strongly symbolic in the eyes of the viewers, offering images and situations that were Italian but not necessarily part of daily experience. Through TV, the Italian population could finally recognize itself and feel directly represented in a live program.

During the early 1960s, in the launch of the new centre-left station's season, television revealed more fully its role as the true unifier of the social reality of the country. At the beginning of 1961, when a second television channel was introduced, the culture and information valued in the area of programming policy were those that adopted models not only of the cultural rubric—social investigations and reflections of actuality—but also of historical reconstruction. This approach contributed to the definition of a corpus of knowledge that was a reference point for the Italian people. In 1961 *Tribuna Politica*, a program promoted with the aim of providing political information to the general public, was introduced. It was the first televised debate in which exponents of the ruling party and the opposition would face each other in front of all the Italian people.

The aim of RAI-TV was best expressed in the area of musical programs that looked to reconcile the unstoppable push of modernization with the more reassuring national musical traditions. As proclaimed explicitly by *Radiocorriere TV*, the official RAI-TV magazine, the program review of the second radio channel referred to "a public in movement, people that listen to the radio in the car, while they go from place to place for business affairs or small errands, housewives that hurry to do the chores, continually moving from one room to another."[1] The strong points of the listings were the new musical formats, starting with the cult program *Discobolo*, which presented the major international successes in five-minute daily segments. The programs wanted to evoke dynamism, euphoria, and enjoyment,[2] which was evident in their titles—*Musica sprint, Ping pong, Flash*. The reach of radio went even further, arriving to listeners on vacation throughout the national territory. Direct from Italian beaches, vacationers could select their favourite hits from a large jukebox connected to the RAI stations.

Television fashioned an especially privileged relationship with the record industry, starting with Fonit-Cetra—a music label established in 1957—which was also controlled by the government. The programs featuring singers multiplied in those years, from the already famous *Festival di Sanremo* to the newer *Il Cantagiro* and *Il disco per l'estate*; and variety television and musical quiz shows— *Il Musichiere, Canzonissima, Giardino d'inverno* e *Studio Uno*—were popular. All of these many programs ensured a feedback between public television and the song market. RAI-TV had the ability, on one hand, to exercise the role of talent scout and, on the other, to control and manage the sweeping musical revolution, accepting the challenge of modernity. One significant example of its role was the music program *Alta pressione*, which was geared towards young people without the traditional pedagogical context of original Italian TV, but offering the small screen as a dance hall for a teenage public spellbound by the chance to dance together with already famous singers.[3] After all, it was dancing and not just music that fascinated the Italians, now hypnotized by the small screen. Thanks to the new syncopated musical rhythms, teenage boys and girls gyrated and twirled in the Twist, the Madison, the Surf, the Hully Gully, and the Yé Yé.

The new media not only transmitted the exaltation of prosperity and all its benefits, but also revealed a dark side. As underlined in the very songs that interpreted Italy's first Golden Age as it became an industrial power, this dark side started with the sentimental relationships that consumer goods, freedom, ample time, and even wealth did not make easier or happier. Actually, it almost seemed as if the likes, understanding, loves, and desires of the time were becoming more complicated, more difficult, and more unreachable. The existential malaise already surfacing among the younger generation was gathered through songs that spoke of anguish, waiting, parting, abandonment, and unhappiness—and, for the first time, of sentimental relationships as possible escapes from a world that was no longer shared. It was especially the new Italian singer-songwriters who signalled this fracture in the triumphant optimism of the late 1950s and early 1960s. It was an ethos destined to become larger and more disruptive with the passing of this magical decade. In the enduring mood of the sounds there was an echo of the French chanson, but also evident in the emotional tension and melancholic vein in verse, melody, and harmony was the influence of jazz and blues from across the ocean.

This apparent dark side was one of the first indications that the challenge to modernity, which had for a time been effectively contained by the political and governing class through the deliberate use of old and new media, would be difficult to overcome. This dilemma would be demonstrated a few years later with the crisis of 1968, which exploded in the entire Western world as a generational crisis. It would also be demonstrated in Italy with a crisis of the traditional parties, which the younger generation accused of not being capable of representing the new social situation. It was a crisis destined to become even more dramatic in the 1970s.

19    Stefan Backius

# POPULAR CULTURE AS A TOOL FOR CHANGE

## Rural Working-Class Theatre in Sweden

**A salient feature** of the global sixties was the marked politicization of cultural activities. In case after case during the 1960s aesthetic expressions became united with societal utopian perspectives to create a new mix of political and cultural activism. Politics often took the form of performances, of cultural expressions and activities; culture, manifested through both popular and avant-garde aesthetics, was seen as a vehicle for political and social change—to the extent of sometimes providing not only the anthems of certain movements but also performances—or repertoires—that were within themselves a form of political action.

Swedish historical scholars have tended to handle questions related to the politics and cultural experiences of "the sixties" by focusing on national perspectives, looking at the issues as they appeared within political parties or traditional institutions. Many scholars have emphasized the personal experiences surrounding or embedded in left-wing political quarrels of the period, to some extent bringing historical research together with an increasing amount of attention to the conflict on what Tom Hayden calls "the battlefield of memory."[1] Perspectives on the period as a "cultural revolution," which focus mainly on changes in lifestyles, norms, and values, still need to be expanded.[2] The image of the sixties as being founded on the logics of Cold War dualism and challenges towards established political parties needs to be completed by more in-depth studies of cultural activities and how those actions reinforced or altered political conditions. As recent research is revealing, innovative cultural activities were a central feature of the 1960s period—and with an effect that continued long past the 1960s proper. Avant-garde acts and other unusual performances—combined with unconventional modes of organization—often in the realm of a youth culture, were crucial aspects of rebellion, protest, and activism. One study, for instance, focuses on the role of intellectuals and artists as instigators of social activism, with examples from the Situationists, Beat poets, and the Amsterdam Provos countercultural movement, maintaining that cultural rebellion played an important part in the shaping of "the spirit of 1968."[3] The anthology *1968 in Europe*, with its aim of representing the protest movement of the 1960s and 1970s, cites subcultural and mass-mediated occurrences as examples of the transnational roots of the 1968 protest movement, arguing that global popular culture inspired by new aesthetics, alternative lifestyles, and countercultures became a crucial mobilization resource all over Western and Eastern Europe.[4]

In the case of Sweden, perhaps one of the lesser known outcomes of sixties activism was the introduction of radical theatre programs in rural industrialized villages. In Sweden the influences of the transnational cultural movement were closely connected to, indeed blended with, political and cultural activism generally—and specifically in amateur labour theatre activities in a small blue-collar industrialized Swedish village. This occurred during a time when the national cultural debate and a new cultural policy encouraged activities that involved working-class participation, especially in the rural areas; and when, in the 1970s, frequent wildcat strikes fuelled a general sense of solidarity towards marginalized and oppressed groups. It was, indeed, a political and cultural movement that managed to challenge the ruling Social Democratic Labour Party on a national level.[5] What happened, then, when the established traditions met aspects of the cultural activism of the sixties?

# The Strike Theatre in Bergslagen

On Monday morning, December 15, 1975, people in the small village of Norberg, in the "iron belt" of the Bergslagen region, could read in the local newspaper about a public meeting that had happened the day before in the labour movement assembly hall. About fifty people had gathered, representing local organizations and associations with an extensive membership: unions, the rural folklore society, popular education organizations, and, above all, the municipality. The headline said (in translation): "Total unity about strike theatre. Everyone in meeting wanted to take part."

The meeting was the result of preparatory work that had started a couple of months earlier when a professional theatre director and a few cultural activists from the Norberg area had gone to an international amateur theatre conference in the residential city of Västerås. All of them had a firm background in the cultural and political settings of the sixties; some had personal experiences from both the antiwar and the free theatre group movements. The director had been influenced by a summer amateur theatre project in rural Finland, where professionals and amateurs had worked together in politically and socially committed projects. He now wanted to try similar ideas in Sweden. At the theatre conference, when a strike among miners in the Bergslagen area in the 1870s was mentioned, the matter was settled: that would be the subject of a new play they would develop. After returning home, they started preparations for the project.

A few days later the initiators formalized a project group and decided to invite all of the organizations in Norberg to a meeting. The group saw two contacts in particular as being key: first, the culture council of the local municipality, which was asked not only to participate but also to finance all the invitation letters that had to be mailed out; and, second, the Norberg Alternative Culture Association, a group of youngsters who had been involved in the anti–Vietnam War movement as well as exemplifying the youth spirit of the sixties through the progressive music movement. After a period of hesitation these youth joined the association, with some of them becoming active and influential members. The financing of the project was an early issue; initial attempts to get funds through the newly formed Ministry of Culture were rejected.

A couple of months after the December 15 meeting participants formed a new organization: the Association for the Play about the Strike in Norberg 1891–92 (Föreningen för spelet om Norbergsstrejken 1891–92). This formal association, open to everyone, would manage all the practical issues, such as financing, the employment of professionals, and other necessities. The membership would not just be single individuals but also other associations and organizations. The Association would follow a traditional organizing principle of the popular movements in Sweden: once a year or so representatives would attend meetings, but everyday decision-making and practical task-solving would be done by an executive committee. In June 1976 the municipality of Norberg also became a member of the new Association, contributing a large amount of money. Finances gradually were improved with the help of labour unions and neighbouring municipalities. During that first year the Association achieved a strong base of support in the local society.

Except for three persons—the director, who throughout the project was employed by the regional theatre, the musical composer, and the scriptwriter, who was employed on a freelance basis—all participants were engaged as local

A strike scene staged in front of the pit, Norberg. Photo by Arne Andersson.

amateurs. The writer started to work on the theme of the play: the political conflict around the strike in the mines in Norberg 1891–92, where workers had fought for better working conditions and against the attempts of the mining company's managing director to reduce wages. In his preparation the writer, questioning the older historical narrative, did historical research out of the oral tradition among local people and in the archives of the labour movement. The strike had previously been represented as a defeat for the workers in Norberg and described as a disappointment for the awakening Swedish labour movement; but in the realm of the new play the story became one of victory—the positive one of an awakening emotion of solidarity among the workers.[6] In August 1976 the first outline synopsis was tried out and rehearsals began.

Within the Association a number of different work groups took up a variety of cultural tasks: for example, stage design, properties, rehearsal organization, information (PR), merchandise, and documentation. In time other groups were formed with tasks oriented towards public activities in the wintertime. These developed as activities around exhibitions, bringing in theatre groups from outside the village, local history events, and study circles focusing on

A rehearsal: directing amateurs performing roles based on their own labour history. (From the Archives of the Swedish National Foundation of Amateur Theatre.)

labour history and other theatrical issues. An editorial group produced a newsletter with information, debates, and practical information directed towards all members. In 1979 an office was opened in a central old historical building in Norberg.

The strike play in Norberg was a huge success and continued as a large summer event for five years. It was well covered by national newspapers and national TV and radio. A movie and an LP recording were also produced. Its audiences came from all over Sweden, and soon the Ministry of Culture awarded financial support. The notion of creating something new in the theatre field was strong. Yearly seminars were arranged out of these experiences, and people from Norberg travelled to other centres to inform other groups. The work was soon followed by the formation of similar projects, and a national labour theatre surge occurred more or less on the pattern of the Norberg project. The influences spread from projects in small or middle-sized industrial cities from 1977 to 1981 to larger cities, mainly in suburbs, in the following years.[7] The labour theatre projects played an important role in local mobilization and social identity-forming processes during the 1980s.

The labour theatre projects had a number of distinctive traits.

- The focus of the plays was a historical event closely connected to strikes or conflicts that were central to the labour movement's own conception or interpretation of the history.
- Local associations handled formal and practical issues, such as employment of professionals, marketing, fundraising, and finances.
- Participants were mainly amateurs, or perhaps not even that because many of them had never been on a stage before.
- The performances often took place in closed-down mines or factories, or places that represented everyday circumstances, often closely connected to mobilizations around the closing down of mining operations in the 1980s.
- Many people were involved, both on stage and with practical tasks and a strong commitment and devotion to both the plays and the local community.
- Political aspects were prominent, with a distinct class perspective and focus on the harmful consequences of capitalism.
- Ideas, experiences, and modes of action were exchanged and spread through seminars, networks, and the development of national amateur theatre organizations.

Meanwhile, the old and established popular education organization ABF (Workers' Educational Association), closely connected to the Social Democracy party, was following the development of the Norberg project, and its spread to other places, with a keen interest. It analyzed the project's methods of working and the participants' affiliation to the Social Democratic party. Given that experiences of earlier projects had often resulted in criticism against the party, the ABF members noted that all the amateur groups were depending upon cultural activists who, with their knowledge of how to create theatre projects, were able to engage a large audience and contribute to forming public opinion. They also saw reduced possibilities for controlling the emerging associations through the representative system. When all of the other popular education organizations, together with the Swedish National Touring Theatre (Riksteatern), formed a political independent national organization for amateur theatre in 1977, the ABF saw the new body as a threat. It thus began a process with the fixed purpose of introducing its own organization, and hoping to include the labour theatre surge in the social-democratic movement. In 1982 ABF formed its own national organization for amateur theatre. Its main task was to educate leaders for amateur groups within the labour movement nationwide.

# Cultural Activities and Political Action

The strike theatre project in Norberg was an important event that revealed what could be achieved with amateurs in a rural working-class setting in Sweden. Both the leftist independent theatre groups and the social democrats within ABF were active in this regard for many years, the former initiating new projects in different areas and the latter trying to control the movement by incorporating it within the institutional framework of the party. Something akin to a power struggle occurred around the question of which group would be able to control the initiative. These efforts underline the intricate interplay between traditional political parties and cultural activism generally. The cultural activists acted both inside and outside the institutions and the political parties, and also to some extent outside of the left-right dichotomy of the traditional political landscape.

The idea of cultural activities as a means for political action had played a prominent role in the transnational communist movement before World War II. From the American point of view, within the Popular Front of the 1930s and 1940s a radical culture was taking shape, which resulted in a political imprint on both high and mass culture. The proletarian avant-garde of the Depression was, for a brief moment, formed through cultural activities within literary clubs, workers theatres, dance troupes, film and photo leagues, and magazines. This cultural front, consisting of a generation of working-class intellectuals allied with European anti-fascist emigrants and an older generation of American modernists, triggered a deep and lasting transformation—a "labouring" of American culture.[8]

During the 1960s these earlier ideas and practices came once again to the fore, but this time with a wider implication. There was a growing certitude about the role of political theatre in helping to bring about societal change. In Germany the early 1960s brought a rediscovery of the theatre traditions from the Weimar Republic, with famed director Erwin Piscator returning to prominence in 1963 with a documentary play (*The Deputy*) and a reissue of his 1929 book *Das politische theater*. There was also a renewed interest in the works of Bertolt Brecht, who had previously been subject to a boycott. His work was now performed with the Marxist perspective that had earlier been removed—serving as an example of how the postwar winds were about to change direction, blowing all over Europe. These changes, though seen mainly in independent theatres, also influenced more traditional institutions.

The uprisings of 1968 caused a rethinking about the relationship of theatre to society and a revival of the notion of cultural activities as a means of political communication. Although the works displayed in European independent theatres in the 1960s were all shaped by different national political circumstances,

The Norberg cast
members who
appeared in a new
interpretation of a
historical political
conflict. Photo by
Kenneth Sundh.

the contents and form were more or less universal. Numerous transnational interchanges occurred through travelling groups, festivals, and conferences. The widespread intention was to seek new audiences and transcend class barriers—with work often geared towards folkloristic culture—with attempts to produce a theatre that was more closely related to everyday life. These universal trends included didactic approaches, with audiences expected to consider their own moral and political responsibilities, combined with a critical attitude towards commercial and traditional theatre. Practitioners within both traditional institutions and independent theatres, taking up ideals of equality and collectivity, questioned hierarchal managerial structures.

These anti-authoritarian ideas resulted in a different perception of the role of the director; independent groups functioned more as co-operatives in which writers, directors, actors, designers, and other workers enjoyed equality of status. The desire for more decentralization nationwide influenced traditional national institutions, to a varying degree in different countries. Visiting U.S. touring companies also made a large impact on the Europeans in the 1960s. The repeated visits of New York's Living Theatre (founded 1947) were on the one hand shocking, with their hippie tendencies, communal lifestyle, and physical confrontations with the repressive attitude of authorities, but they also rapidly received the status of a cult and made disciples wherever they went. Another U.S. company, the Bread and Puppet Theater, caused a sensation with a Vietnam protest piece performed in 1968 together with street theatre shows. The influence of U.S. radical theatre in Europe in the 1960s paved the way for new groups seeking to give back to the theatre its social function; agitprop-inspired forms questioned both traditional ways of acting and production methods.[9]

# A Public Debate: The Context

The cultural activism of the 1960s—exemplified here by the political theatre movement—had strong connections to the upsurge of the new left and student radicalism. But what about the context into which that action was blended? In postwar Sweden an economic-efficiency and growth-oriented social policy ideology held a strong position. The support for the Social Democratic party was closely connected to its capability to deliver social reforms. With the country staying out of World War II, a heavily facilitated industrial capacity and economic boom led to a long-lasting power regime, rhetorically socialistic but with capitalism as an indispensable foundation for social reforms. The ruling party's policies were carried out in the name of improving equality between classes, and the party gradually achieved a hegemonic position.[10] The economic expansion and material welfare did result in a view of the country as a democratic, social, and economical ideal— "the Swedish model"—a view to a high extent formed by U.S. and Western European perspectives.[11] Within Sweden this ideal, coined as the famous *folkhems* (The people's home) model, represented an image of a national cross-class solidarity including everyone and not just the working class. Social welfare originated more out of the idea of a universal social policy and less out of individual needs. From the Social Democratic perspective, the model and the material welfare circumstances pointed to the successful political achievements of the party during the past century.[12]

Until the economic transformation, boosted by the global capitalism starting in the 1970s, the industrial villages of Bergslagen were seen as symbols of the well-organized society. These were small rural mill towns that originated out of old iron estates, which in the course of time had developed into dominating companies in almost total control of natural resources, the production process, and the labour force. Here small, local pre-democratic "welfare states" emerged, framed by hierarchical social relations, patriarchal ideals, and continuous economic growth. After World War II the social service system, which was first developed by the companies in an industrial management strategy, piece by piece, was handed over to municipalities. This development was a parallel to the national postwar welfare expansion, also mainly hosted by the municipalities, all of them having a fairly high degree of autonomy against the state. The local authority in the industrial villages of Bergslagen slowly shifted from the iron master to the social-democratic "big wig," starting with housing, roads, and infrastructures and in the 1980s also covering cultural issues and local economic policies. These villages, based upon economic growth and a pattern of behaviour emphasizing a mutual understanding between workers and capital, were seen as the core of the Swedish model. Norberg and other similar villages in Bergslagen became something like models of the model.

During the 1960s these tendencies began to be questioned. The spirit of the sixties embraced a criticism of hierarchy and authorities, of central planning, of the shortcoming of the welfare state and the limited extent of the democratic system. The early advocates of this new spirit were writers who during the 1950s had more explicitly engaged in international societal topics, such as the colonial emancipation and the racial question, mainly in South Africa and the United States. The movement against plans for a Swedish atom bomb were soon transformed into a more international-oriented organization inspired by the British organization Campaign for Nuclear Disarmament. International issues became a centre of attraction, and the issue of governmental Third World aid was rising. During the first half of the 1960s this mainly liberal questioning was transformed into a wide intellectual leftist movement, including discussions about the relations between political, social, and moral commitments and artistic quality and expression. Being an intellectual became synonymous with being a leftist; the establishment of the new left and the upsurge of Vietnam protests were important, but not crucial, in this process.[13]

The public debate in the 1960s about culture emerged out of initiatives by individual intellectuals with a background in cultural work and popular education—often people who had access to media as journalists, writers, musicians, and artists. Through radio, TV, LPs, and paperbacks, new ideas and perspectives became widely circulated, often connected to the search for new aesthetical expressions and boundless art forms. Even though the discussion about culture included only a minority of the population, it had important effects on the general political climate in Sweden.[14] The cultural sections in Swedish newspapers expanded, and the cultural debate moved from a peripheral position in the 1940s to an arena in which leading politicians in the 1970s took a greater part.[15] Statistical surveys certified the notion of inequality in cultural participation among different classes and highlighted the income and employment conditions of cultural workers. Activists saw solutions as coming out of the state as a vehicle against underlying unequal social and economic circumstances. In another argument functioning as a criticism of the capitalistic system, the state could also be a vehicle against commercialism, which needed to be controlled.

A further example of the effects of the movement came with the establishment in 1968 of a new government commission, the State Culture Council, charged with preparing a new national cultural policy. When the final government bill passed the Swedish Parliament in 1974, after being referred for consideration by several groups and organizations within the cultural field, it was accepted by all political parties, and culture policy thus became an established organizational field in the country. The bill contained eight goals, including the protection of freedom of speech, steps to counteract the negative consequences of commercialism, decentralization of activity and decision-making, and fulfilling the needs and experiences of disadvantaged groups. One goal emphasized the exchanges and ideas across language and national borders. A Ministry of Culture was created for the overall handling of issues outlined and the new modes of financing.[16] The policy was aimed at improving equality within culture consumption and shifting the focus of cultural activities from attendance to participation.[17] The cultural field was now formally an urgent priority of the state characterized by the notion of culture as a tool for societal change.

Even though left criticism of cultural policy and practice was prominent, the Social Democrats were also influenced by the growing right-wing critique that developed into the neo-liberalism of the 1980s with its new interpretation of the role of the state—moving away from an approach that saw the state as a vehicle for equality and economic security to a view that saw the state as something that prevented liberty by, for example, making people addicted to social welfare and, as was said, destroying their ability to take initiative. In this perspective the 1970s become a transition period, with the emphasis on small-scale projects and decentralization, and a rural ideology. The change in political direction was noticeable in the 1976 election, when the former peasant party, the Centre Party (Centerpartiet), captured the prime ministerial appointment, ending a forty-four-year-long period in which the Social Democratic party had continuously held power.

# The Politicization of Cultural Activities: New Influences and New Initiatives

The narrative of the Swedish sixties mainly includes the anti–Vietnam War movements, the green movement with its emphasis on going rural and recognizing folk culture, changes connected to sexuality and gender roles, and the frequent wildcat strikes of the 1970s. This view is fairly similar to other European national narratives. Perhaps the exception was a relatively weak student movement, which was involved mainly in only one small innocent incident in Stockholm, and the absence of prominent flower power elements. But the antiwar movement was strong, and set the political agenda both through its content and action repertoire. It developed into two competing organizations, one closely connected to the Social Democratic party, carrying out activities aiming primarily at institutions; and the other, more closely associated with the left, doing more public-oriented street performances and distributing pamphlets.

The politicization of cultural activities in 1960s and 1970s Sweden was particularly important in the theatre and music fields. The powerful progressive musical movement, which became highly successful in the 1970s, had its own recording and distributing companies and a deep influence on certain music styles, concert forms, and recording and distribution companies that were conceived of and discussed in political terms.[18] Within the field of theatre, political perspectives were even stronger, especially in its influence on other art forms, and actors and issues emanating from this sector played a strong role in the public debate about culture. The free theatre group movement emerged in the environment of 1960s cultural activism, in which avant-garde and experimentation blended with political perspectives. Formed by young actors, these groups developed outside traditional theatre institutions. They were based on a strong collective ideal in which artistic, organizational, and economic issues were decided upon equally by all participants. Both the progressive music and free theatre group movements formed their own networks concerned with distribution, lobbying, and producing journals, activities gradually funded in many ways by the Ministry of Culture. These new influences created independent groups within traditional theatre institutions, leading to a more direct democratic decision-making process and a more collective-oriented creative process, often including a questioning of the domination of the director.[19]

Among these utopian future-oriented perspectives a paradoxical interest in history developed, mainly geared towards labour history. In 1978 a widely distributed book issued a call for amateurs to produce their own history.[20] This work developed into an extensive activity nationwide, often organized within popular education organizations and trade unions, focusing on labour history. These "digging projects," as they were called, developed out of a local perspective and often took place in villages in which factories were threatened with closure, or had already been closed down. A change in the way of looking upon heritage occurred as well. Within the established national cultural heritage field, industrial buildings, industrial work, and the proletarian culture were focused on to a much greater extent.[21] A notable effort in this regard was the Tent Project, a musical theatre production that toured Sweden in 1977 with its interpretation of Swedish working-class history performed in a big circus tent. The project represented a collaboration between the best-known progressive music groups and free theatre groups in Sweden at that time, and it contained a profound critique and generated reactions from many social democrats. The project had a big impact through national newspapers, TV, and an LP, but also through local supporting committees in the places that the tour visited. Out of tasks such as selling tickets and handling practicalities connected to the show, the participants also initiated working-class history projects locally, often organized as popular education projects, resulting in exhibitions, study circles, and theatre projects.[22]

Through the strike play in Norberg, then, a mode of action developed and spread throughout Sweden, resulting in performances that highlighted, through both the action repertoire and substance, a societal critique of capitalism and the hegemony of social democracy. As was the case with the global cultural activism, these politicized aesthetic expressions fuelled by aims of societal change were performed in Swedish suburban and rural settings. Solidarity and alternative historical interpretations were carried out within associations and "digging projects." Through different labour theatre projects, large groups of amateurs were staging their own role as a part of an identity process interwoven with a local community perspective. Cultural activists were an important catalytic group in introducing important aspects of the action repertoire and to some extent defining the problems of society and thereby also the desired attitudes or actions for improvement. These activists had a particular position in the political institutions, with ideas consisting of a mix of aesthetical and political/societal utopias. With a well-developed ability to organize, communicate, and artistically express and interpret these ideas, they had an extensive influence—thus making the performing arts field a crucial part in building an understanding of this dynamic and radical period.

Angela Bartie 20

# A "BUBBLING VOLCANO"
## Edinburgh, the Festivals, and a Cultural Explosion

**Since their** mutual beginnings in 1947, the Edinburgh International Festival and Edinburgh Festival Fringe have made the city an important site of cultural expression and creative exchange. This was particularly true of the 1960s, by which point the Festival City had developed into a significant site of cultural contest—a contest that, when examined, reveals the growing challenges to then-existing concepts of "culture" and "the arts" as fuelled by international developments such as the folk song and Beat movements and new trends in the visual and performing arts. Together, the Edinburgh festivals and other cultural ventures located in Edinburgh provided an important nursery and laboratory for many of the individuals and ideas symbolic of "the sixties." A number of the links that formed that motif of "cultural revolution"—and in particular the London-based counterculture—were established in Edinburgh in the early years of the decade.

Certainly, to build an understanding of how the development, transmission, and cross-fertilization of ideas were working simultaneously at grassroots national and international (in its broadest sense) levels in what we think of as "the sixties," we need to turn our attention to tracing the routes of particular individuals, groups, and ideas—essentially cultural networks—to map the journey and development of the ideas and practices that have come to symbolize that decade. Edinburgh, as host to an international festival, offers a unique illustration of how new ideas and practices were communicated during the early years of the 1960s. Furthermore, it offers an opportunity to critically analyze the impact of these ideas, individuals, and ventures. We can ask, for example, how far their rhetoric of liberation worked in practice, or how effectively it reached beyond the original, predominantly avant-garde participants.

## The Festivals as a Stage

As historian and cultural critic Robert Hewison noted, during the 1960s, "More than at any other time in our history, the arts were a battleground for the conflicting forces of social change."[1] It was not just models and forms of culture that were being confronted—and transformed. Challenges were made, in the words of Arthur Marwick, "within more dispersed spaces around issues of gender, class, race and generation" and to a range of ideas, values, institutions, and forms of authority.[2] As Marwick argues, the early part of the 1960s represented a "contested beginning" that "led directly and with accelerating speed towards the great transformations by the end of the decade."[3] By the end of the decade, and especially after the events of the "international" year of 1968, these transformations would become global in scope.

Still, to comprehend these transformations on a global level we need to understand the expression and communication of the ideas that shaped them at an earlier point and on more local stages. As the editors of the journal *The Sixties* put it, "The part may be the key to the whole."[4] Indeed, in the case of the Edinburgh festivals, the activities of specific individuals and cultural initiatives reveal early manifestations of key themes associated with the decade: assaults on authority, the creation of subcultures, the formation of new social and cultural relationships, living theatre movements, permissiveness and sexual liberation, social and cultural protest and activism, and the blurring of boundaries between cultural forms, art and life, and the public and the private.

Although many of these themes were global in impact, the nature, pace, and form of their expression and influence were uneven across different local (Edinburgh), national (British), and international (North American and Western European) contexts. The restrictive conception of the term "international" as used in the following pages is unfortunate but necessary. In the 1960s Edinburgh was still establishing itself as an "international city," and at the time the majority of those performing, engaging with, and visiting the festivals and related initiatives were more European and North American than truly "global." Yet "international" was commonly used to mean worldwide. The discussion here is therefore one small part, a building block, in constructing a knowledge and understanding of the circulation of ideas and practices and the shaping of the "new world" from different national and transnational perspectives.

# Exploring Edinburgh

Unlike its current reputation as an exciting, cosmopolitan, and liberal city, the Edinburgh of 1947, seat of the Presbyterian religion and with a reputation for religious conservatism, was an unlikely choice of location for a festival of the arts. Still, very quickly the Edinburgh International Festival defined itself as an "interpreter of the arts," as a site that presented the very best in music and drama as performed by the very best artists that the world had to offer. It thus established its status as a provider of so-called "high" culture right from the outset. Indeed, in its early years the festival reflected much of Matthew Arnold's conception of culture, with its emphasis on "the best which has been thought and said in the world."[5]

With its solid commitment to high culture the festival also immediately attracted a cultural challenge, and in 1947 the "Fringe" was born when eight theatre groups appeared and performed in Edinburgh at the same time as—but not as part of—the official festival. A key motivation of the Fringe festival was to challenge the exclusion of Scottish artists and material from the International Festival program. This was an issue that provoked (and continues to provoke) cultural protest, and led to the establishment of the short-lived Edinburgh People's Festivals, instituted from 1951 to 1954 by organized labour groups, Scottish folk singers, and nationalists—out of which the Scottish folk song revival of the late 1950s and early 1960s arguably grew. This concept of cultural protest gained wide currency in the late 1950s when the new left took shape. It was a movement that historian Dennis Dworkin has argued was pivotal in creating "cultural Marxism," which fused cultural and political protest and sought to redefine the social struggle in the light of social change, with culture at the "very heart" of the project.[6]

At the time the festivals began, culture (used here in reference to the arts) was perceived of as hierarchical, with what was termed high culture seen as the pinnacle of cultural production. A key shift that occurred in the 1960s surrounded the deference accorded to "culchah" (a mime word that came out of the association between culture and class distinction, with culture hitherto being the preserve of the "grand masters"). That deference was broken down, and new ideas were offered about cultural expression and participation, about the place of the arts in society.[7] The growing influence and impact of more contemporary art and its creators became more keenly felt; it became clear that members of a young radical avant-garde were mounting a challenge to traditional barriers in "culture" and

Jim Haynes and "Big Chief" in the doorway of the Paperback Bookshop, Edinburgh, c.1959. Copyright Handshake Editions, All Rights Reserved. (From Jim Haynes's personal collection.)

between different art forms. Of course, in Edinburgh (as elsewhere) this phenomenon was not limited to the avant-garde; intellectuals, folk singers, and community activists such as Helen Crummy (who created the Craigmillar Festival of Drama, Music and the Arts for people living in one of Edinburgh's poorest housing estates) were also keenly involved in challenging such barriers.[8]

As writer Joyce McMillan noted of Edinburgh around 1960: "Paralysed in dour provincial respectability from September to August, it was nonetheless galvanised, for the three weeks of the year, by what was then quite unrivalled as the world's greatest and most exciting arts festival."[9]

It was this galvanization, this energy, that one young American counter-entrepreneur in particular sought to extend all the year round in Edinburgh. Jim Haynes had arrived in Edinburgh in October 1956 as part of his national service (undertaken in a nearby British-American air force base), and three years later, in autumn 1959, he opened the Paperback Bookshop in Edinburgh's university district.

Reflecting the outlook of its owner, the store had an international focus from the beginning. Its name was displayed on the outside of the shop in twenty-five languages, and Haynes's business card described it as "Europe's new international book-shop, coffee-cellar and gallery."[10] Not surprisingly, the Paperback attracted individuals and media attention with the range of paperback books it sold, its relaxed atmosphere and soft background music, and free coffee and tea—features that shocked the conservative local book trade and were almost unheard of in bookshops more generally. It quickly became a popular meeting place for a range of people in Edinburgh; it was casual and drop-in, much like the style of San Francisco's City Lights Bookstore, which had been established by poet Lawrence Ferlinghetti not long before, in 1955, and had become famed as a home of the American Beat movement.[11]

During the late 1950s Edinburgh had become a popular stop on Britain's Beat trail, a place for like-minded people to meet and exchange ideas, often via the medium of poetry, as part of an "on the road"–inspired movement of creative energy around Britain. Mike Horovitz, perhaps Britain's leading beat poet and in 1959 founder of the influential poetry magazine *New Departures*, ran "New Departures" poetry nights in Edinburgh. Another leading poet, Spike Hawkins, recalled the "constant movement" of poets around Britain's towns and cities in an effort to communicate their ideas and establish new centres.[12] Small venues like these were crucial to the cross-fertilization of ideas and practices from different cultural forms in the early 1960s, providing meeting places, experimental spaces, and atmosphere conducive to the exchange of ideas and the formation of new networks.

The Paperback functioned as one such cultural centre, hosting poetry readings, folk-song nights, art exhibitions, and theatre productions that sought to actively engage the audience by blurring the lines between them and the performers. It attracted individuals from all over Britain, and some of the people who visited, and often met there—including Jeff Nuttall and Barry Miles (known simply as Miles)—would become key figures in the counterculture movement of the later sixties.[13]

Together with others, London publisher John Calder and Haynes, who had met through the Paperback, introduced a Writers' Conference to the official Festival program in 1962 and a Drama Conference in 1963. These conferences proved to be important in relation to the development of the London counterculture. Hewison argued that certain gatherings, which he saw as becoming increasingly "tribal" in nature, were what signified the growth of the counterculture in sixties Britain. He traced these events from the "prophetic utterances" by William Burroughs and Alexander Trocchi at the Edinburgh Writers' Conference of 1962, to the poetry reading at the Albert Hall in 1965, and then through to the Dialectics of Liberation conference at the Round House in London in 1967.

The Writers' Conference took place over five days in August 1962 and featured a lineup of writers that included Burroughs, Trocchi, Norman Mailer, and Henry Miller, to name only a few of the seventy or so who attended. The writers were mainly from the United States and Western Europe, although Israel, Ceylon, India, and some Eastern European countries were represented (the Cold War and associated travel and visa obstacles prevented a number of Soviet, Polish, and Hungarian authors from attending). Despite the Western bias in attendance, various political issues—alongside the broader concerns that authors of many nationalities were tackling in their writing—were well represented during the course of the conference: East-West relations, South African apartheid, forms of oppression, the nature of commitment (to national and international ideas, politics, values), censorship and propaganda, and human identity and the human

*A "Bubbling Volcano"*

condition, for example. A clear theme throughout the conference was how such issues transcended national borders. One writer asked that all authors "make it quite clear that we belong to an international society, even without wanting to."[14]

Controversially for both the time and the place, various references to homosexuality and drug-taking were made, issues not commonly discussed in public anywhere at that point, let alone in Edinburgh on the official Festival stage. In the early 1960s, remember, censorship was still routinely applied to references to sex (and particularly homosexuality), and homosexuality was still a criminal offence in Britain.[15] One correspondent for *The Times* newspaper commented: "Even fairly worldly journalists at the press conferences held by writers have signified that they have been disturbed by the repetition of these themes."[16] Events like these—high profile, in front of a large audience, and with media attention from other parts of the world—brought issues of changing attitudes to morality, and especially that shift from public to private decision-making symbolized in the term "permissive" (which remains a potent emblem of social change in the 1960s), to public attention and consideration.

The conference also launched beat writers Burroughs and Trocchi onto the British stage. On the last day Burroughs explained his "fold-in" technique of writing to an intrigued yet puzzled audience, while Trocchi coined the famous expression (later associated with Burroughs) "cosmonaut of interior space" to describe the importance of exploring "the individual self."[17] Trocchi, Scottish by birth, had spent most of his adult life in Paris (where he had edited the influential literary journal *Merlin* and been a founding member of the Situationist International) and the United States (where he had spent time in the New York and San Francisco beat scenes).[18] During the 1960s Trocchi became more widely known both through his novels (one of which, *Cain's Book*, was the subject of an "obscenity trial" in 1964) and the expression of his growing belief that old categories and boundaries were defunct—as expressed in his famous essay "The Invisible Insurrection of a Million Minds," first published in June 1962. His thought became an international phenomenon in the form of his *Sigma Portfolios* (begun in 1964), newsletter-style publications sent to a network of people in an attempt to build a strategy for cultural revolution. Although they never achieved the aims that Trocchi hoped for them, and had fizzled out by 1967, the newsletters demonstrate the international countercultural network being established in the early to mid-1960s (which led to more fruitful developments) and, in the words of famed Scottish poet Edwin Morgan, the "paradigmatic Sixties phenomenon, with its emphasis on revolt, liberation, alternative lifestyles, anti-universities and worldwide cultural networking."[19]

During the Drama Conference of 1963, an avant-garde demonstration called a "Happening" took place—essentially, a pseudo-theatrical event intended to shake the audience's sense of reality and make them realize that, as John

Calder put it, "The world is an uncertain place where anything can happen."[20] Organized by Americans Allan Kaprow and Kenneth Dewey, with input from Charles Marowitz, alongside Scot Mark Boyle, the Happening represented a new direction in the world of drama. Developed out of concepts from the visual arts (like the Boccioni and Italian Futurists, Bauhaus artists, Dadaists, and Surrealists) and first incorporated into experimental theatre by American avant-garde composer John Cage, it evolved during the 1950s and 1960s (with Kaprow a key figure) in the United States and Europe.

The Happening in Edinburgh in 1963 aroused interest in the form in Britain. London-based venues began to create and host happenings in the mid-1960s, while *Encore Magazine* called it one of the "portents" of a radical shift taking place in the arts—what the conference itself had "ominously" referred to as "the death of the word."[21] As Barry Curtis, a professor of visual culture, writes:

> The generation of the sixties had new ways of using culture. Deploying everyday ideas, objects and experiences as creative sources and materials indicates a rejection of Matthew Arnold's formulation of culture as an uplifting model of the best. The popular culture of the sixties saw a re-evaluation of transformative notions that drew on ... an engagement with art as a model for everyday life.[22]

The festivals became, Tom Normand points out, "a forum for experimental and neo-conceptual art, much of it centred upon a confluence of drama, performance and the visual arts."[23]

A significant influence in this regard was the Traverse Theatre Club, which opened its doors in January 1963. Its name came from the layout of the tiny studio theatre, with its seating for an audience of sixty traversed by a two-sided stage. Within a year of opening, the Traverse had gained international recognition and brought the attention of theatre critics to Edinburgh outside the three weeks of the festival period. A key ingredient in its success was a commitment from very early on to *new* material and writers. Haynes, its chairman and public face, was quickly deluged by playwrights and artists keen to work with a theatre that actively encouraged new and experimental work. It showcased plays that sought to challenge conventions, ideas, values, and attitudes, and because it was established as a club it could also play a part in challenging the existence of theatrical censorship in Britain. Until 1968, when censorship was finally abolished, partly as a result of the pressure generated by theatre clubs (many of which took the Traverse as their model), all plays in Britain had to be licensed by the Lord Chamberlain except those presented in clubs. The assault on censorship in all its forms was a cause that was global in the 1960s, although with varying degrees of success across categories of censorship and nationality.

An important concept developed by the Traverse was that of an "artistic open house" in which, as Haynes stated, "Drama does not exist in a capsule, but becomes part of the fabric of what has been called the quality of life."[24] This idea of the all-encompassing world of the arts, a breaking down of the demarcation between art and life as symbolized by the Traverse, was developed and expanded later in the decade. The kinds of challenges to theatrical traditions that the 1963 Happening and the Traverse program mounted in both form and content were clearly evident in countries around the world in 1968, a year in which avant-garde theatre was seen to be "flowering everywhere."[25] Crucially, social activism and political protest utilized elements of avant-garde theatre, blurring and redefining the boundaries between the personal and the political to produce a new and more potent form of protest: the personal quite simply *was* political, and individual actions could coalesce to produce powerful social and political statements. From 1968, avant-garde touring groups seeking to find a new theatre language by exploring radical departures in form—groups such as Open Space, the Freehold, the American Theatre Project, and the People Show—found a base and a venue in the Traverse. Marwick later described the Traverse as both "one of the most important subcultural developments of its time" and also "a perfect miniature of the semi-capitalistic, non-dialectical interrelationships which are central to an understanding of the sixties."[26]

In 1966 Haynes relocated to London, where he co-founded the underground newspaper *International Times* (*IT*), followed in 1967 by an influential alternative arts space, the Arts Lab. Later he moved his attentions to Amsterdam, where he co-founded *Suck*, Europe's first "sexpaper" (in 1969), and the international Wet Dream Film Festivals (held 1970–71). In London the Arts Lab was the culmination of the sixties ethos—an experiment in "art-and-life-style" that hosted multimedia events, films, drama, and all manner of artistic experiments, including many of Yoko Ono's earliest works. In the space of the one year in which it was open the Arts Lab had, in the words of Catherine Itzin, a writer on experimental theatre, "an enormous impact, capturing the spirit of the counter-culture, presenting the first of a new generation of writers, actors and directors who were rejecting the structures of conventional theatre institutions."[27]

# A Bubbling Volcano

By the end of the 1970s Britain had over 140 arts centres, many modelled on Jim Haynes's Arts Lab, which had its roots in the Paperback, the Traverse, and the energy created around the annual festivals in Edinburgh. Indeed, as Itzin asserted, "Edinburgh in the sixties, and on into the seventies, was an important area of fertilisation for alternative theatre—in the annual Edinburgh Festival with its showcasing and coming together of British and international fringe theatre, and in particular with the Traverse Theatre."[28] Still, while many writers on the sixties, particularly those writing about theatre and the arts, have made mention of Edinburgh, no one has hitherto tried to identify and examine what was happening there in any detail, or explore its relationship to the cultural revolution of the sixties. Surely what was the biggest international gathering of the arts—at a time when the arts were seen as a crucial space for challenge and confrontation—deserves more attention from cultural historians?

After London's Albert Hall Poetry Reading of 1965, and with the launch of the alternative magazines *IT* and *Oz* in 1966 and 1967 respectively, as well as the opening of "underground" clubs like UFO and Middle Earth, individuals and groups came together in London and produced the remarkable output of cultural styles and artistic innovation that have dominated the histories of sixties Britain's culture, and especially counterculture, ever since. As writer Shawn Levy emphatically wrote: "London was where youth culture finally cemented its hold on all forms of expression, and made itself loudly and exuberantly known."[29] But Edinburgh, as host to an international festival of the arts and a number of exciting artistic ventures, also played a vital, so far largely unacknowledged, part in the cultural ferment of the sixties. Edinburgh had been an important location for experimenting and for establishing connections between people, particularly through the opportunities presented by the Fringe and the Traverse, a theatre that had inspired and informed theatre clubs all over the world and had (like the Fringe) provided an important nursery and laboratory for many significant directors, playwrights, and actors and actresses, including the influential directors Peter Brook and Charles Marowitz. If London was host to a "cultural explosion," Edinburgh was, in the words of Jim Haynes, "bubbling away but it hadn't exploded." The explosion had occurred, Haynes said, "in London with the Beatles and the Rolling Stones

*Oz* magazine cover, March 24, 1968. Cover by Martin Sharp.

*A "Bubbling Volcano"*

**217**

and '68, certain art colleges were taken over by the students and, you know, it exploded in London whereas it hadn't exploded in Edinburgh when I was there." As he put it, "Edinburgh was just like a small little bubbling away volcano."[30]

**At the beginning** of the 1960s, the key features and movements that we recognize as symbols of the global sixties were beginning to form, but there was no sense of "shared consciousness" or organized challenge to the prevailing attitudes or authorities. As Calder commented of the early sixties: "They were very exciting times . . . but we had no way of knowing then how things would turn out and what the 1960s would become. We were just discovering these fantastically big ideas and sharing them with young people."[31]

As Marwick has repeatedly stressed, the 1960s was a period "characterized by the vast number of innovative activities taking place simultaneously, by unprecedented interaction and acceleration." They were activities that spectacularly converged in 1968 to produce the global understanding of the sixties so familiar to us today.[32]

Sean Purdy 21

# CONSTRUCTING PARIAH SPACES
## Newspaper Representations of Slums, Ghettos, and Favelas in São Paulo and Chicago

**Favela** in Brazil, *poblacione* in Chile, *villa miséria* in Argentina, *cantegril* in Uruguay, *rancho* in Venezuela, *ghetto* and *slum* in the United States and Canada: countries in North and South America have developed distinct terms to label marginalized neighbourhoods in large cities.[1] In North America, "slum" is most frequently applied to poor tenement neighbourhoods in the inner city, places that existed from around the end of the nineteenth century well into the first half of the twentieth. In the post–Second World War period slum also became applied to public housing projects located in both inner cities and suburbs. "Ghetto" is now employed to delineate neighbourhoods with a clear ethnic or racial identification, whether they are areas of private-market housing in Black, Latino, and other minority communities or housing projects with disproportionate numbers of people of colour.[2] In Latin America, the various terms for marginalized urban neighbourhoods refer to the tenements of the inner city and the squatter settlements that proliferated in the 1950s and onwards in the major cities.

Generally identifying extremely poor areas in which jobs are unstable and poorly paid, unemployment is high, and life conditions are miserable, all of these terms also have wider cultural and social meanings in state, media, and public discourse: the "marginal" spaces of North American cities are not solely seen as areas of poverty; they are regarded as sites of socially and culturally disorganized populations characterized by dangerous social pathologies. Marginality is thus simultaneously constructed as a *representation/identity* and a *structure/place.*[3] Since the 1960s, marginalized spaces—from North American public housing projects to Latin American shantytowns—have been disproportionately important touchstones for wider debates around urban renewal and planning, crime, "race," the "underclass," and urban social movements.

In the last thirty years, rich ethnographic, sociological, and, to a much lesser extent, historical studies of squatter settlements in Latin America and North American slums and ghettoes have thoroughly exploded the notion that the poor have always been disorganized, socially isolated from the rest of the city, and passive "objects" of history.[4] Nevertheless, theories of "marginality" or of the "culture of poverty," and their modern counterparts—the "underclass" thesis in North America, for example—have had widespread and continued purchase in media and popular representations and attract new adherents among every generation of scholars.[5] In the 1960s in particular—a key period in the material and ideological consolidation of such "pariah spaces"—the print media underrepresented the reality of life in slums, ghettos, and favelas. My analysis here—focusing on the cities of São Paulo (Brazil), and Chicago (United States)—concentrates on what the newspapers neglected to cover or only treated in a truncated fashion, including the appeal made to social-scientific legitimacy by frequently citing one-sided government and academic studies and neglecting alternative interpretations made by social movements. I would argue that these nefarious representations were initially based on the *undercoverage* of urban social realities.[6]

It was in this very period that favelas and Black ghettos and slums in Chicago, for example, became visible social "problems." By 1960 one-quarter of Chicago's population consisted of African Americans, many of them living in dilapidated tenement housing or public housing projects in racially segregated neighbourhoods.[7] In São Paulo, while favelas only constituted 1.1 per cent of the Paulistana population in 1973,[8] they were located in highly visible sites along the new expressways and/or near older middle-class neighbourhoods. In both cities they constituted significant areas of public policy and engendered social struggles, such as the civil rights movement in Chicago, and various social service organizations working in the favelas in São Paulo. Yet the media constructed a "primary definition" of urban problems that ignored the lives, struggles, and perspectives of the urban poor and the root reasons for poverty, focusing mostly on the sensationalist and often distorted interpretations of "moral defects" and "unsavory behaviour."

The primary sources for this preliminary investigation are the principal mainstream daily newspapers of these cities, reflecting both "liberal" and "conservative" viewpoints, including the *Chicago Tribune* (hereafter *Tribune*), *Folha de*

*São Paulo* (hereafter *Folha*), and *Estado de São Paulo* (hereafter *Estadão*). These newspapers had a largely middle-class and upper-middle-class readership and originated in long-standing family businesses with close contacts to the elite.

# Theoretical and Methodological Considerations: Media Representations of Urban Marginality in the Transnational Context

São Paulo and Chicago, of course, belonged to very different social and economic formations. Urbanization in developing countries did not follow the historical route of the industrialized nations of North America. In the United States, industrialization and urbanization occurred more or less simultaneously, creating a substantial working class in the growing cities by the early twentieth century.[9] In the developing countries of Latin America, dependent industrialization created an incomplete "proletarianization" and resulted in a rapidly growing urban population with a relatively small industrial sector, a disproportionately large commercial-service sector, and a large informal urban economy.[10] The two countries also had different experiences relating to "race": while Brazil and the United States are distinguished by a long-standing legacy of slavery, racial relations were framed in distinct ways in the twentieth century by political and economic developments. In the 1960s, in particular, while the United States, with a consolidated and strong state structure, was fitfully expanding its welfare state under the pressure of the Black civil rights movements, Brazil suffered through a military dictatorship whose repressive apparatus and state-directed economic development exacerbated the dependent industrialization of the country and the anarchic growth of urban areas. Finally, political and judicial structures and cultural traditions developed in unique and divergent ways.

Nevertheless, the large industrial cities of Brazil and the United States in this period shared similar characteristics. While patterns of economic development and urbanization proceeded at different times and in different ways within an increasingly global economic environment, both cities were among the premier industrial cities in their respective countries. In the post–Second World War period, national and local states in both countries initiated interventionist economic and social policies to restructure the urban fabric to foster capital accumulation. Internal migration of Southern Blacks to Chicago, and agricultural labourers from the interior and Northeast of Brazil to São Paulo, played an important role in the formation of urban populations. Favelas and ghettos also showed relatively similar levels of socio-economic deprivation within their respective contexts. Most

*Constructing Pariah Spaces*

importantly, shared notions of social and economic "modernization" shaped the social and cultural attitudes of ruling-class and middle-class elites and their counterparts in the media.[11]

Critical media scholars and historians have conducted considerable research on the external, often racialized, depictions of "marginalized" spaces in North America, showing that their substance and rhetoric revealed more about distinctly white, middle-class notions of what was a proper neighbourhood and requisite behaviour than about the actual physical, social, and cultural environments of the poor and minorities.[12] Brazilian historians, too, have begun to look at how representations in film, photographs, and other media are "documents" that help us understand the "invention" of the favela (as analyzed in particular by the doyen of favela studies in Rio de Janeiro, the sociologist Licia Valladares).[13] Despite the clear differences in the nature and origins of ghettos and favelas,[14] scholars in both countries are increasingly attuned to the role that the mass media played in the social construction of "moral panics," characterizing such marginalized areas in the city and their inhabitants as "deviant," "threatening," and "troubling" to the social order and responsible for a host of social ills such as crime, deviance, and social and cultural immorality. As Steve Macek argues, the media provided politicians and elite decision-makers with "influence and social weight"[15] for urban policies based on repression of the marginalized, the discrediting of adequate social welfare policies, and the depiction of social and economic problems as "natural" and "immutable" and, therefore, as the fault of the very victims of social and economic exclusion rather than being caused by the social and economic problems inherent in capitalism. While television news increasingly played a central role in these social constructions, newspapers, at least in the 1960s, maintained a dominant role in the formation of the elite opinion that guided the key political decision-makers. Yet if newspapers in Chicago and São Paulo developed in tandem—with similar commercial outlooks and shared socio-economic and cultural diagnoses and interpretations of the urban moral crisis supposedly engendered by marginalized urban neighbourhoods— this preliminary analysis demonstrates clearly that differing political, economic, and cultural factors also shaped the discourses of marginalization.

# Underrepresenting the Reality of Life in the Ghettos and Favelas

**São Paulo:** Until the 1960s the Paulistana press frequently commented on the problems of favelas in the rival Brazilian metropolis of Rio de Janeiro, reflecting a long-standing city-boosting pride in São Paulo's pre-eminent position as the industrial centre of the country. Indeed, one of the first comprehensive social-scientific studies of favelas in Rio de Janeiro, "Human Aspects of the Carioca Favela," was commissioned and published as a special supplement in São Paulo's *Estadão* in April 1960.[16] If, as Brian Owensby has argued, the principal characteristics of middle-class Paulistana identity were education, occupation, race, dress, hygiene, and consumption patterns,[17] then the growth of favelas would constitute a significant social problem for the press and local government. Indeed, a 1968 editorial in *Estadão* on the growth of favelas accentuated this city pride: "The simple report of these facts has arisen as an aggression to the eyes and ears of the *paulistano*, proud of their state and its riches."[18] Unlike the relatively hidden poverty of the tenement house (*cortiço*), common in São Paulo throughout the twentieth century, the favela was a highly visible mark on the urban and social landscape, and it noticeably worried the Paulistana elite and middle class.

Yet coverage of favelas in the Paulistana press in the 1960s, including references to government and academic studies, rarely concerned itself with the socio-economic origins of the massive internal migration to Brazil's large cities—a migration caused by poverty in the countryside and shifts in productive activities on the land, shifts that resulted in fewer opportunities for rural labourers. Instead, those who wrote for the press assumed that rural poverty was natural and that migration to the cities for work was irrational. Nor was there any acknowledgement that migrants from the interior of the Southeastern states and the Northeastern states provided the requisite cheap labour force for São Paulo's massive industrial and commercial expansion in the period. Indeed, as Nabil Bonduki argues, "Investments in the official city and for the creation of infrastructure for industrial expansion ... were only possible thanks to the abandonment of the periphery and to the reduction of the cost of the reproduction of the labor force."[19] Finally, the press almost entirely neglected the anarchic and inefficient state of the housing market and the woeful shortage of affordable housing.

What the two Paulistana newspapers did focus on was what they saw as an alarming increase in the numbers of favelas and favela dwellers in the 1960s and the inefficiency of the state in ensuring that favelas would be eradicated. Much ink was spilt on attempts to accurately identify the numbers of favelas and their inhabitants, with almost no contextual and background information on why there was an increase or not. In the 1950s both newspapers hailed the importance of transnational social-scientific theories of urban planning. While ignoring the "push" and "pull" factors for internal migration, one rigorous 1957 study drew on the latest statistical and planning theories from the United States and Britain, commissioned by the city of São Paulo and conducted by the Sociedade de Análises Gráficas e Mecanográficas Aplicadas aos Complexos Socais (Society for the Applied Graphic and Mechano-Graphic Analysis of Social Complexes,

SAGMAS), an institution created and managed by the French priest Louis-Joseph Lebret. The study found 141 nuclei of favelas, totalling 8,500 shacks and 50,000 people,[20] shocking numbers for the proud Paulistanas. Lebret directed the international movement, Economy and Humanism, an attempt to create a Third Way political theory and practice in city planning by eliminating the worst excesses of capitalism and thereby preventing communism, which was seen as particularly attractive in the underdeveloped world.[21] Such managed, scientific, and anti-communist reform was particularly in the interests of the Paulistana elite, the very readers and backers of the two principal newspapers.

In fact, throughout the 1960s both newspapers searched, often in vain, for the social-scientific legitimacy needed to justify the eradication of the favela phenomenon. A 1966 editorial in *Estadão*, for example, criticized the underestimation of the number of favelas by a prominent state commission, citing studies by academics and community groups working in the favelas that the numbers were rising and highlighting that the size of two prominent favelas had more than doubled.[22] In a January 3, 1968, article in *Folha* the welfare secretary of the city of São Paulo stated that the city had 250,000 to 300,000 favela dwellers, representing 5 per cent of the total population. Wilson Abujamra of the social service and charity organization Movimento das Organizações Voluntárias pela Promoção do Favelado (Movement of Voluntary Organizations for the Promotion of the Favela Dweller, MOV) disputed this figure, saying that there were only 30,000.[23] Some eight months later *Estadão* cited MOV figures indicating that there were only 25,000 favela dwellers.[24] In a November 1970 article, citing MOV without question, *Folha* suggested that the numbers of *favelados* had decreased in the past two years, from 25,000 to 15,000.[25] We know from recent statistical studies that the favela population in São Paulo in 1973 was about 1.1 per cent of the population, or about 72,000 people.[26] The number of favela dwellers had increased somewhat from the 1957 SAGMAS figures—certainly not to the extent cited by the welfare secretary of São Paulo, yet significantly higher than the numbers claimed by the newspapers.

Both *Folha* and *Estadão* regularly cited, sometimes with scepticism but often without question, dubious official figures from the city or state government and more frequently reports from MOV, whose director, Abujamra, was a former state official and later a business leader in São Paulo. MOV was active throughout the 1960s and, along with its charity work and job training programs in the favelas, was a staunch advocate of abolishing the favelas—and of finding existing housing opportunities for favela dwellers or transporting them back to their cities and states of origin.[27] Abujamra even insisted in 1967 on blocking the highways and trains entering São Paulo to prevent further internal migration from the poorer areas of the country.[28] Another group that the newspaper appealed to before the 1964 military coup, but seldom afterwards, was the University Movement Against Favelas (Movimento Universitário para Desfavelamento, MUD), which shared MOV's position about eradicating the favelas completely, but whose more progressive university student membership, loosely linked to the reform programs of the deposed government of João Goulart, did extensive charity work in conjunction with the favela dwellers.[29] Its progressive background probably led to a neglect of this organization after the 1964 coup, when the Paulistana newspapers treaded on egg shells in relation to official censorship by the military government.

Confusion about the actual extent of the favela "problem" in São Paulo in newspaper coverage may have stemmed from various factors. First, due to a lack of resources and expertise in such endeavours, and especially since São Paulo's population growth in these years was highly anarchic and incredibly rapid, state organs were clearly unable to accurately accompany the growth of favelas. Sloppy journalism may also account for the wildly different figures reported in the press. But they may have also resulted from the two newspapers' political tendencies to exaggerate, on the one hand, as *Folha* did until 1970, the extent of the problem to force the population and city authorities to tackle the problem. On the other hand, in underestimating the numbers, *Estadão* was demonstrating that efforts by the state (which succeeded in eradicating various favelas in this period) and organizations such as MOV were actually on the right track even if its writers continued to criticize the overall failure of government action. In both cases, however, the appeal to statistics and hard social science revealed the subtext that the poor, ignorant hordes of favela dwellers represented a potential threat to social order, economic progress, and the cherished image of the city among the Paulistana elite.

**Chicago:** As in São Paulo, the mainstream newspapers in Chicago saw themselves as ardent city boosters and defenders of the city's image. The wretched housing conditions and racial segregation in Chicago were frequently downplayed, if not denied, by the *Tribune*. In 1964 a front-page article on Mayor Richard Daley's visit to students at Harvard University praised his efforts in urban renewal in Chicago, something quite at odds with the tumultuous social conflicts engendered by housing policies in the city.[30]

Chicago's principal mainstream newspaper also frequently cited government and academic reports and surveys and, as was the case in São Paulo, provided little contextual information as to why tens of thousands of U.S. Blacks had migrated from the South to metropolises of the North, where they found few affordable housing alternatives and were forced to live in ghettos in substandard houses and apartments, often owned by white slumlords. Moreover, the *Tribune* consistently discredited or ignored statistical studies by Black organizations such as the Urban League and Martin Luther King's 1964 Poor People's Movement, which demonstrated the extent of racial discrimination in housing and the wretched housing conditions of the city's Black population.

In 1963, for example, the *Tribune* openly defended Mayor Daley's ludicrous statement that Chicago had "no ghettos."[31] Despite widespread criticism from the Black community and the overwhelming evidence of residential segregation, which was sometimes mentioned in the paper, a *Tribune* editorial (strategically putting "ghetto" in quotation marks in its headline), stated:

> It is getting tiresome to read the numerous references to Negro "ghettos" in Chicago and other northern cities. The implication is that each of the cities has intentionally set up quarters like those which formerly existed for Jews in Europe.... There are no walls or gates in Chicago or Los Angeles.... Nobody herded the Negroes into West Garfield park or any other Chicago "ghetto." On their own volition they came to Chicago by the hundreds of thousands because they hoped to find better jobs and better living conditions here.... Most of the Negro families are not locked in slums. Many live in elegant residences. It is inaccurate and unfair to imply that all Negroes live in "ghettos" and that this is an explanation for the misbehavior of a small minority.

An earlier 1962 story on charges of conscious "redlining" and the refusal to provide mortgages for Black homeowners in non-Black areas similarly framed the statements as being only a "claim" by Black groups. With the phrase "dual market," a claim by a Black real estate official referring to racist practices in housing, the front-page article openly cited Black civil rights officials and their criticism as well as stringent denials of the existence of racism by white real estate agents. What is missing is any acknowledgement of the well-documented racial segregationist practices of the Chicago real estate sector. Even the language used is revealing. While the white real estate officials are assumed to be legitimate representatives of their industry, the *Tribune* cites one Black, Warren Lehman, who called Chicago the most segregated city in the North, adding that he "said he is a housing specialist for the Chicago Urban League." Black "experts" were not even accorded legitimacy. While purporting to be neutral, the newspaper subtly and not so subtly showed its readers its support for the status quo and suggested why they should not accept the outrageous claims of the "civil rights" movement. Putting "civil rights" in quotation marks aimed to question the very legitimacy of the movement. The paper framed arguments and studies by the Black movement as mere "accusations" with no authenticity, and/or buried such stories in the back pages.[32] Not only *undercovering*, but *denying* the existence of conscious racial segregation by the white community, the city government, and the public housing authority, the *Tribune* sought to discredit the efforts to overturn racism in Northern cities.

By the same token, in a front-page article in the newspaper much was made of the results of a bizarre report on New York, Chicago, and Los Angeles commissioned by a Senate Subcommittee on Executive Reorganization in 1966. Specifically citing the advanced social-scientific methods of the research, in which local Black researchers were trained to do interviews, the report contradicted almost everything claimed by the civil rights movement over the past decade, almost every study done by academics and other government agencies, and even recent events demonstrating widespread Black anger about socio-economic conditions. According to the study, "Most Negroes living in the ghettos live in near-anarchy, and instead of being concerned about police brutality, want more police protection." The average Black person "cares little for civil rights laws, rejects school integration, and is much more interested in their schools teaching basic discipline, manners, and personal hygiene, and strongly dislikes welfare programs, believing current welfare programs are largely responsible for the separation of families." A highlighted subtitle in the article claims that "[Police] Brutality not mentioned." Such claims defied logic, especially because they were made soon after a series of community rebellions had occurred in Black communities across the country, events often sparked by acts of police brutality and rooted in anger over socio-economic conditions.[33] They also contradicted much of their very own reporting[34] and even the half-hearted, but clear, admission by other editorials in the *Tribune* that indeed Blacks did suffer from racial discrimination.[35]

# Transnational Newspaper Coverage

Newspapers in Chicago and São Paulo during the 1960s, then, shared similar elite perspectives regarding certain aspects of urban poverty. The print media in both cities saw themselves as city boosters, demonstrating considerable pride in prosperous economic development and viewing poor urban neighbourhoods as dangerous "blots" on the urban landscape. They also presented almost no information on the structural socio-economic conditions that shaped living conditions in the city, such as demographic and economic changes (internal migration in both cases), the anarchic nature of industrialization (in São Paulo) and deindustrialization (in Chicago), or residential segregation by race and class (in both cities). Newspapers in both cities did not question poverty, assuming it to be largely the result of individual failures. They never considered systemic and structural reasons for housing hardships, remaining very much within the fold of mainstream critiques of governance. Even reports discussing community efforts to resist stigmatization or community development projects were firmly situated within an underlying scaffolding of "abnormality," which reinforced the branding of marginalized urban areas by obscuring the totality of the realities of the life of the poor and downplaying structural explanations for poverty. They both appealed to social-scientific legitimacy to highlight the severity of problems and/or the efficiency of state efforts to eradicate urban problems. Nevertheless, they selectively cited such academic studies and/or discredited alternative explanations from social movements that veered from the status quo.

Yet the transatlantic circulation of similar ideas about the economics of poverty, social movements, and urban cultural propriety was inserted in specific national and local contexts. The very size of the Black community in Chicago, the existence of a militant Black civil rights movement, and the expansion of the welfare state forced the *Tribune* to contend with alternative explanations of the urban crisis. In São Paulo, the relatively small proportion of favela dwellers in relation to the city's population as a whole (which would increase dramatically in the 1970s and 1980s); the widespread support among the elite and among nascent social movements for the eradication of favelas instead of urbanization and regularization; the safety valve of irregular lots for self-construction of houses on the periphery; and the circumscribed options for alternative policies and strategies in the context of a repressive military dictatorship: all of these factors shaped the nature of underrepresentation in the newspapers. Regardless of a set of shared ideas between newspapers in São Paulo and Chicago, therefore, local social relations and political-economic structures were ultimately more important in translating such ideas into practice—or not.

Colin McCullough  22

# "NO AXE TO GRIND IN AFRICA"

## Violence, Racial Prejudice, and Media Depictions of the Canadian Peacekeeping Mission to the Congo, 1960–64

**On November 28, 1960,** two daily newspapers in Toronto—the *Daily Star* and *Globe and Mail*—ran stories from the Associated Press about the Opéra-tion des Nations Unies au Congo (UNOC). As an AP article, the same story would have run in newspapers across North America. Arriving at a time when the mission faced increasing challenges on the ground, the stories did not discuss the work that was being done by both the United Nations and the Congolese in an attempt to sta-bilize the country in the face of troop mutinies and separatist movements that had plagued the Congo since its declared independence from Belgium in June 1960. Rather, the articles chose to invoke images of the Congo from the colonial past and discussed the growing threat of cannibalism in the newly independent nation.

The *Globe* article's headline was "Cannibalism Making Comeback," and it appeared on page seventeen underneath several photos of the festivities at the annual Grey Cup football championship. In the *Star* that same day the front cover carried the headline "Congo Cannibals Eat U.N. Troops," with a much lar-ger and more dramatic story awaiting the reader below.[1] Using language that seems to have been stolen from a horror movie of the time, the article notes: "Human flesh is again being eaten in secret tribal rituals—not as a delicacy or for nourishment, but for the magic properties of a dead enemy's limbs and organs.

The heart brings courage, the brain intelligence and the legs speed, according to the witch doctors."[2] Neither of the papers challenged the use of "witch doctors" as a source; they apparently saw this reportage as unproblematic. Indeed, as readers who went beyond the headlines soon found out, the real story involved the disappearance of a single Irish soldier from a group of eight U.N. soldiers who had been ambushed and killed, and there was no concrete basis for believing that he had been eaten. His body was not recovered, and it would seem that the word "cannibalism" was invoked to make his disappearance a front-page story.

Newspaper articles such as these complicated the role that Canada would attempt to play in the decolonization of Africa. Rather than depicting the Congolese in terms that might be used to describe Canadians, both the *Star* and the *Globe* tried to familiarize their readers with events taking place in the Congo by using the inaccurate and racially prejudiced language and imagery that for centuries had been associated with Africa. The papers were demonstrably open to the idea of Canada as being "more civilized" than the Congo. What makes articles like these especially important is that they were often the only source of information for many Canadians about the Congo, its independence from Belgium, and what Canadians were doing there as part of the U.N. mission.[3]

Both the *Star* and the *Globe* featured extensive coverage of what was occurring in the Congo from 1959 through to the early months of 1961. But, while the Congo was the location for the stories, the real subjects were Canada and its peacekeepers who were sent overseas. The Congolese were presented as nameless men and women in a backwards land; the Canadians were given names and identities as peacekeepers and granted the selfless goal of giving succour to a distant continent.

In their attempts to make the unfamiliar more familiar, in addition to taking stories from the AP and other wire services, both the *Star* and *Globe* sent reporters to the Congo for "on the spot reports." These male reporters were supposed to be objective members of the press, but they inevitably brought their own cultural biases to their writing, particularly emphasizing the exotic and inferior aspects of the Congo for their Canadian readers. Many reporters also encountered difficulties gaining access to U.N. officials in Katanga, a southern province of the Congo, which often led them to use questionable sources for reasons of expediency.[4] The deadlines of the newspapers, and the desire to get any story out, made the reports that came out of the Congo more inaccurate than they might otherwise have been. The sources also tended to be critical of the U.N. and its mission, and as a result the language and imagery used often gave a negative twist to stories about the efforts in the Congo.[5]

According to a long-standing belief, widely accepted by scholars, Canadian participation in the UNOC was undertaken in large part because the Progressive

Conservative government of John Diefenbaker experienced pressure from the Canadian press and vernacular culture.[6] If indeed the press did play an important role in pressuring the Diefenbaker government to take part in the UNOC, and the reporting of the mission then presented the efforts in an unfavourable light, the press historiography of the mission to the Congo necessarily needs to take that factor into account—and especially the language used by newspapers to describe Canada and its peacekeepers, and the Congo as a destination. Still, despite that central role, newspapers were not solely responsible for the opinions adopted by their readers. Given a wide range of readers, a story could be interpreted in a variety of different ways, all of them at the audience's control.[7] Simply putting a story on the pages of a newspaper did not give even influential publishers like the *Globe* or the *Star* a direct influence on how readers understood that story. The media's role in influencing how the Congo was conceived in the minds of Canadian vernacular culture in the 1960s was, then, central but not all-encompassing.

In a recent exploration of the role that decolonization played in influencing the actions of both the Canadian Department of External Affairs and the Canadian military forces sent to the Congo, Kevin Spooner argues that the Canadian government was wary of the problems of race and decolonization when it considered whether or not to participate in the U.N. mission.[8] A divide existed between the opinions of the Department of External Affairs and the press. Foreign Affairs officials recognized that the situation in the Congo was likely to break out into a conflict that would be difficult to contain thanks to the animosity that they believed would be a legacy of the terrible conditions of Belgian colonial rule; the rapid and unorganized Belgian exit would be another potential source for disorder. The Canadian media and reading public had a different way of seeing, of imagining, the people they were writing and reading about; images and language of an inferior and essentially uncivilized Congolese people became widespread. Much of this puzzle can be explained through the framework of postcolonial theory; for it can be argued that even though Canada itself never had colonies, postcolonial ideas are pertinent to Canada's past. For Albert Memmi, for instance, colonial relations did not stem from individuals alone; rather, they existed before the first Europeans came to North America, or Africa, in the realms of imagination, books, and the theatre.[9]

Edward Said's *Orientalism* also stresses that, at some point, "An assumption had been made that the Orient and everything in it was, if not patently inferior to, then in need of corrective study by the West."[10] In these differences Said identified a constant relationship to weakness: a region such as the Orient or, in this case, Africa, was seen as being inferior because it was so different to Europe.[11] Through this weakness, the people who lived there "were rarely seen or looked at; they were seen through, analyzed not as citizens, or even people, but as problems to be solved or confined or taken over."[12] Said also saw novels, artistic works, and other cultural creations as the vehicles that allowed racially prejudiced understandings of the "Other" to be perpetuated and spread.

The image of the Other in the Congo, as presented by the *Globe* and *Star*, was exaggerated and simplified in most cases. While leading actors such as Prime Minister Patrice Lumumba were given names, and pictured wearing suits and travelling to the West to appeal for aid, that was not how most of the Congolese were described. The Congolese people who were given coverage tended to be male, but were often pictured (or featured in cartoons) wearing "traditional" clothing such as grass skirts. From 1959 to 1961 only rarely did stories about the Congo in either the *Star* or *Globe* have a Black woman as subject or as eyewitness. The newspapers used the overly male and simplistic Congolese man to create links to the older, familiar imagery of Africa. The Congo was depicted as an exotic place that was full of dangers for women. Moreover, the imagery illustrated how modernity had failed in Africa.

With a daily circulation of around 350,000 readers at this time, *The Toronto Daily Star* was one of the larger newspapers in Canada. Politically, its editorials also supported the Liberal Party, and Lester Pearson occasionally wrote a column for the paper. In the year leading up to the independence of the Congo, the *Star* published several editorials, including one on January 9, 1959, which suggested that "forces are loose in Africa that even the enlightened Belgians could not control."[13] The editorial went on to say that the Congo "was to be an example to all other colonial powers on how to civilize a backward, savage people and make them industrious, prosperous, and contented."[14] The backwardness of the Congolese people and the noble intentions of the Belgians framed the Congo as a place in which Western enlightenment had tried, and failed, to create a modern society.

Echoing Memmi's contention that no Westerner could ever understand the plight of the colonized, the editorial ends by stating, "It would be unfortunate if political unrest should slow the Congo's really remarkable economic development, but apparently the Congolese are willing to pay that price for more freedom."[15] Economic development was incredibly uneven in the Congo under Belgian rule. While whites could make their fortunes trading in primary resources such as copper, the Black population was not allowed such possibilities.[16] The *Star* failed to see that the economic development it valued was inherently tied to the colonial system, and that this system had to be removed for the Black population to improve its standard of living.

When the Congo gained its independence on July 1, 1960, violence broke out. This garnered a series of front-page headlines—a typical headline was "New Congo Terror; Two Whites Slain." The white Belgians—their safety and escape—

became the focus.[17] On the *Star*'s front page nine days later, an "on the spot atrocity report" detailed the struggles that white women had encountered in the country since independence.[18] While the experiences of these women were awful, the paper's emphasis on the fifty-four white women who remained in Lulabourg is telling: thousands of Black women were experiencing similar conditions. Once again, too, the Congo was portrayed as a place completely unlike Canada; women did not have to "walk warily" down the streets of Toronto in fear of Black mobs.[19]

While the *Star* continued to print stories about the struggles of the white Belgians in the Congo, it also devoted a considerable amount of space to discussions of Canada's role in the conflict. An editorial on July 7 stated: "It is Canada, with her non-colonial history and her record of disinterested aid to the have-not countries in Asia that is among the best qualified to help the young African nations."[20] The *Star* had come out against colonialism as a policy in its editorials in November 1956, when the British and the French had tried to exert their influence in the Suez region.[21] In that case the *Star*'s editorials supported the efforts of Lester Pearson and the United Nations to introduce a legal and responsible international force that would promote peace. In the editorials about the crisis in the Congo, they reaffirmed that commitment to the United Nations and peacekeeping as having a higher legal and moral authority than any reintroduced occupying force from Belgium could have, which the Belgians and some other commentators had been suggesting as a solution. These sentiments were restated four days later in another editorial, which argued, "It should not be a white man's army sent to put down the black man's revolt.... Canada—which has no interest in the Congo save that of peace—could play a vital role."[22] The *Star*'s portrayal of Canada as a country without a past tied to the colonial system allowed the situation in the Congo to be presented as uncomplicated: peacekeepers were needed and Canadians were peacekeepers. Such ideas occasionally emerged from the men in the Department of External Affairs, and yet many others in the department did not believe, as the *Star* did, that the matter of sending troops who were white was so uncomplicated.[23] Any such reluctance expressed by government officials was never printed in the *Star*, and the daily articles on the independence of the Congo gave the newspaper a louder voice on the matter.

The *Star* placed the Canadian aptitude for peacekeeping alongside the Cold War and Canada's interests in preventing the spread of communism as reasons for the deployment of UNOC. On July 7 an article argued, "The want and turmoil in Africa must not be allowed to continue indefinitely, for they present fertile soil for the spread of the Cold War."[24] A July 13 editorial saw Canada's participation in this force as being vital to its role in the nuclear age.[25] The *Star* envisioned this force as restoring order and "depriv[ing] the Soviets of an excuse to turn this into another Cold War battlefield."[26] The independence of the Congo became a story that had less to do with decolonization than it did with international politics and the struggle between the West and the Soviet bloc. The plight of the Congolese people was sidelined, and any offers of assistance that the Soviets made towards the Africans were seen as being insidious and provoking a possible war.[27]

Cold War politics also mingled with stereotypes. In a *Star* story from June 3, 1960, Smith Hempstone wrote, "Belgium's act of abdication after little more than half a century of colonial rule has caught the Congo, which is eight times as large as Italy, with its loin cloth down."[28] The image of the savage wearing a loincloth played into the long-standing tropes associated with Africa in the West.

A similar use of stereotypes occurred on August 28, 1960, in a story by reporter Ron Haggert about two Canadian soldiers. Under the headline "'Thought They Would Eat Me Alive' Canuck Tells Haggert,"[29] the article, like others written by Haggert, put the Canadian forces into the role of the heroes in a strange land and suggested that the soldiers were not getting the respect they deserved. Haggert wrote about the arrest of Charles Bernier: "The soldiers set up a pot of boiling water in the military compound. Some of them made lip-smacking eating motions with their mouths and fingers. It was a cruel joke ... rather than a real threat of cannibalism."[30] Although recognizing that the incident was a practical joke on the part of the Congolese, Haggert did not bother to place the joke in a broader context: if such a joke were to be attempted in another part of the world, or in Canada, it would never have been taken seriously. The news angle, apparently, focused on attaching ideas of cannibalism to the Congo so that readers would pay attention to the story, no matter how inaccurate it was.

Despite supporting the Conservative Party on most political issues, *The Globe and Mail*, like its competitor the *Star*, also saw Canada as being a nation that could be engaged throughout the world because it did not have a colonial background.[31] This engagement was best realized through peacekeeping operations, and the paper pressured Prime Minister Diefenbaker to send troops to the Congo in 1960.[32] In language strikingly similar to that used by the *Star*, a *Globe* editorial argued, "What the Congo upheaval requires is a pacifying force sponsored by and drawn from nations that clearly have no axe to grind in Africa, no interest save that of protecting human lives, black and white. Canada is such a nation."[33] There was no conflict between Canada's links to the British government and its entry into the Congo, because of the differences between the colonizers. Indeed, an editorial of August 2, 1960, argued that Canada had recently undergone a similar experience of moving from colony to nation. Thus it had a duty to help. The argument, ignoring the differences between a white settler colony and a conquered colony, misrepresented what was taking place in Africa at the time.[34]

The *Globe* also found it increasingly hard to separate the people of the Congo from the cultural stereotypes existing in the West. When the Belgians were told to leave the country, an editorial asked, "Who will run the country if and when the Belgians go?"[35] The editorial writers apparently never considered the possibility that the Congolese could run the country themselves; the only options were the Belgians or United Nations.[36] A cartoon embedded within a August 2, 1960, editorial also perpetuated ideas of Black inferiority by carrying the caption, "Bingo, bango, bongo, I don't wanna leave the Congo!"[37] Behind a white Belgian figure were two Black figures who were shown stepping out from the brush. Their features were ape-like. They wore loincloths, were naked above the waist, and had exaggeratedly large heads and facial features. Given the *Globe*'s penchant for citing the simplicity and "backwardness" of the Congolese people in its articles, the cartoon served as a visual reminder of its opinions.

The cartoon was originally published in the *Indianapolis Star*, which raises the question of whether it was included simply to fill the space on the page, or if it was seen as being funny and topical. Newspaper content is often dictated by the margins and column widths of the paper, but this cartoon was not the only one available to the paper at the time. The same page included a much larger cartoon by an in-house artist, which suggests that the paper could have called on its own people to come up with a cartoon on the Congo for that issue. The inclusion of this cartoon made a visual statement about how the *Globe* and its editorial staff thought the Congo should be portrayed. They did not seek accuracy in such images, but rather chose to reference the well-trodden cultural stereotypes that were appearing in popular works such as Herge's *Tintin au Congo*.

Similar imagery appeared in another cartoon on July 20, 1960.[38] The caption for the cartoon was "Clothes don't make the man." Again, the cartoon featured a dark and semi-clothed figure with exaggerated and ape-like features, this time surrounded by clothes with the word "independence" written across them. This cartoon, originally published in the *Moncton Daily Times*, was implying that Blacks in the Congo were not ready, or capable, of governing themselves. It was also suggesting that because Blacks could not govern themselves, the job of running the Congo was best left to a larger white figure who was presumably the previous owner of the clothes.

The cultural biases in the *Globe* went beyond cartoons. Columnist Donald R. Gordon, who later pondered the media's role in the failure of the mission, also wrote a series of articles on the newly independent Congo in 1960, including one on August 17, headlined "Primitives Loose in Technology's China Shop."[39] In that article, beyond the obvious prejudice of calling the people of the Congo "primitives," Gordon did much more to make clear the differences between white Canada and the Black Congo. First, he relied heavily on a single white "agricultural specialist" for information. He quoted that man as saying: "Africans don't think the same way we do and they can't be judged by our standards. They're people alright, but they are people on a different level.... There are educated ones, some able ones, too, but with most of them it's like living with children. They're friendly, happy, loyal in their way and brave enough, too. But they'll never be able to run a decent farm, let alone a country."[40] Gordon does not contradict the man's opinions at any point during his article. Instead, Gordon states, "They [the Congolese] have never been able to even begin to approach European standards of knowledge, competence, or intellectual ability."[41] While Gordon would later blame the U.N. for not granting reporters more access to its officials, he himself used prejudiced sources without questioning their accuracy or challenging their ideas.[42] Rather, the news printed supported the opinion that the Congolese people themselves were responsible for their plight, and not the oppressive Belgian regime that had ruled prior to 1960.

The language and use of stereotypes of the *Globe* and *Star*, with their large and diverse audiences across Central Canada, cannot be considered exceptional. The Canadian press had access to millions of readers every day, and the regular and prejudiced content on the Congo helped to shape the opinions that many Canadians had of the mission. At the same time, as postcolonial theory suggests, newspapers used familiar language and imagery, despite the inaccuracies and racial assumptions that such ideas carried over from the colonial past. The assumptions had dangerous consequences on the ground during the work of the UNOC, in which, as Spooner states, it was "clear that racial differences were apparent, at times problematic, and perhaps suggestive of colonialist assumptions."[43] In this regard, given the language and imagery being presented by the *Globe* and *Star* every day, the Canadian forces were not alone.

Peacekeeping as a policy was also hurt by the debacle in the Congo. Both Liberal and Conservative members of Parliament and the newspapers that supported either party were in favour of the UNOC mission in 1960. The press did not publish stories that looked at the colonialist assumptions of the peacekeepers who were sent to the Congo, as they would for similar events in Somalia thirty years later. At the same time, many articles did portray the Congo as a place in which the West had failed because of the innate inferiority of the Congolese themselves. The mission's failure, combined with the expulsion of the Canadian contingent of the United Nations Emergency Force at the request of Egypt's president Gamal Abdel Nasser in 1967, made many scholars and government officials question the utility of peacekeeping.[44] To this day, despite continuing efforts to publicly commemorate Canadian peacekeeping missions, the same consensus around the country's foreign policy has never again been achieved.

Franny Nudelman   23

# TRIP TO Hanoi
## Antiwar Travel and International Consciousness

**On his second** wartime visit to Hanoi, student activist Rennie Davis toured an underground hospital in the village of Thanh Tich. In the operating room a nurse showed Davis and his companions "several pieces of hand-made equipment," including a surgical clamp that had been crafted, she explained, "from the wing of an F-105." In his essay "Behind Enemy Lines," Davis celebrates the remarkable energy and ingenuity that the North Vietnamese bring to the reconstruction of their homes, villages, and institutions. In this context, the surgical clamp, an instrument of destruction refashioned to heal the wounded, conveys the power of the North Vietnamese to turn the tide of the war. Describing the country as a "moonscape," subject to "more tons of explosives than the combined European, African, and Asian theaters of World War II," Davis marvels at the ability of the North Vietnamese to build a new society underground. Like other activists who wrote about their experiences in North Vietnam, Davis venerates useful objects, made out of U.S. weapons, that manifest the ability of the North Vietnamese to withstand destruction as they prepare for "total victory."[1]

Davis was one of nearly two hundred Americans who travelled to Hanoi during the U.S. war in Vietnam.[2] In the tradition of direct action, these trips were highly theatrical public gestures that involved a significant degree of risk. Courting physical danger, government persecution, and emotional harassment, travellers demonstrated their solidarity with the people of Vietnam. Defying the U.S. government's restriction on travel to North Vietnam, these activists challenged a Cold War geography that divided the globe into capitalist and communist spheres.[3] Keenly aware of the ideological nature of the geographical divide, they saw travel as a means of developing what Tom Hayden and Staughton Lynd called "international consciousness."[4] Travellers to Hanoi flouted passport restrictions not only to demonstrate their opposition to the war but also to liberate themselves from ideological constraints on thought and feeling that they believed made war inevitable. They hoped that travel might produce new forms of knowledge that would foster solidarity between Vietnamese anticolonialists and the American left.[5]

The trip to Hanoi generated a large body of writing—essays, poems, letters, books—as returning travellers used their experiences and insights to influence public debate over the war. In keeping with the antiwar movement's interest in reshaping perception, those who wrote about the trip often describe it as an inward journey, examining the experiential complexities that attend such acts of political bravado. This essay surveys narratives about the trip to Hanoi, arguing that activist writers strained against journalistic conventions as they tried to find ways of recording change that takes place at the level of consciousness. Their attempts to cultivate innovative forms of documentary description reflect efforts in the activist counterculture and, indeed, the culture at large, to redefine observation and its relationship to social change.

Specifically, I situate narratives of the trip to Hanoi along a continuum, comparing those that embrace the conventions of reportage to those that abandon objectivity in favour of a meticulous attention to subjective experience. Many people travelled to North Vietnam in order to gather reliable information about the war; their narratives use factual evidence to produce detailed and convincing accounts of North Vietnamese suffering. Even writers that aspire to impartiality and comprehensiveness, however, show signs of self-doubt: is it possible, they ask, for an American visitor to perceive, let alone reproduce, the reality of North Vietnamese experience? If some of the narratives I examine question the reliability of recorded fact, others reject a journalistic approach altogether. Those writers least confident in their ability to capture the reality of North Vietnam choose instead to record the process of introspection as it unfolds under the pressure of cultural difference and wartime trauma. In these texts the ability of the North Vietnamese to put the detritus of war to new uses provides a model for the writer's own efforts to refashion consciousness.

**In the context** of government misinformation and public complacency, conventional reporting on conditions in North Vietnam served a vital function. When the United States began bombing North Vietnam in 1965, most Americans knew little about the war. The Pentagon insisted that it was striking only military and industrial targets, and the mainstream press tended to accept these claims. In the early years of the war, Americans travelled to North Vietnam in order to see the consequences of the bombing campaign for themselves.[6] In December 1966, *The New York Times* reported that Patricia Griffith and three companions were "going to Hanoi to see whether the United States was bombing military targets only and to find out how the people had been affected by the war."[7] Many "reports" from North Vietnam, published in the antiwar press, document widespread devastation in an effort to refute official misrepresentations of the conflict.

Banking on the authority of direct observation, these reports are largely descriptive and adopt a neutral style. Harrison Salisbury, the first U.S. journalist to report from North Vietnam, travelled to Hanoi in December 1966. His trip resulted in a series of reports to *The New York Times*, as well as a book-length narrative, *Behind the Lines–Hanoi*.[8] Early in his narrative, Salisbury invokes the infamous "credibility gap" that plagued the administration of President Lyndon Johnson, noting, "People no longer believed what their government told them."[9] He steps into the gap, hoping to provide a credible assessment of U.S. military policy by examining the aftermath of the bombing of Hanoi on December 13 and 14. Throughout, Salisbury takes pains to describe himself as an open-minded investigator who carefully weighs evidence and gives his government the benefit of the doubt. In Hanoi, Salisbury finds ample evidence that homes, schools, and civilian neighbourhoods have been decimated. He manages to come up with a range of excuses for discrepancies between the government's stated aims and what he witnesses in North Vietnam: pilots are given assignments that are beyond their capability and, as a result, make mistakes; reconnaissance equipment is faulty; the military is lying to President Johnson.[10] It is only when he sees the devastation in the "ghost city" of Namdinh, where he can find no military targets, that Salisbury reluctantly concludes that the U.S. government may be targeting civilians.[11]

In his *Liberation* article "North Vietnam: Eyewitness Report," peace activist David Dellinger writes as an outraged witness, shaken by his encounters with children who have lost limbs, mothers who have lost children, and survivors who have lost entire families. Even so, like Salisbury, he carefully weighs evidence and avoids jumping to conclusions: when Hanoi residents describe the "'deliberate bombing' of residential areas, schools and hospitals," Dellinger tries to keep an "open mind and raise questions." Visiting the bombed village of Phuxa, Dellinger decides that the damage does not provide "conclusive evidence of civilian bombing as governmental policy," but may be attributed to "enraged or frightened" pilots. This restraint strengthens his ultimate assertion: "I reluctantly agreed with the

Vietnamese that the United States has consciously and deliberately attacked the civilian population in a brutal attempt to destroy civilian morale."[12]

Avoiding polemics, these reports establish the credibility of the eyewitness and offer evidence of North Vietnamese victimization that, presumably, speaks for itself. Visiting Americans describe the destruction of the landscape, the built environment, and the human body, and provide documentation to support their observations. In "Report from North Vietnam," John Gerassi notes, "Never, in the 2,000 miles that I traveled in North Vietnam, did I escape the sight of bomb damage."[13] In Salisbury's book this damage provides evidence of a military policy that is at odds with the U.S. government's stated aims. For Dellinger, flattened buildings and gutted thoroughfares can only hint at the "real impact of the bombing"— the greater, irreversible damage done to human bodies.[14]

These reports provide documentation to support their observations and intensify their impact on the reader. Dellinger's "Eyewitness Report" includes extended excerpts from his interviews with maimed children and bereaved parents. Indeed, many texts about the trip to Hanoi include long, unassimilated passages of North Vietnamese testimony. While undermining the flow of the narrative, these passages prove the narrator's commitment to exactitude, and involve the reader in the process of interpreting documentary evidence. Photographs also testify to the accuracy of these eyewitness accounts. Dellinger's essay, for example, includes photographs of Dellinger himself wandering through the rubble and holding wounded children in his arms, as well as photographs of dead children that corroborate the stories of surviving relatives.

Reports from North Vietnam privilege direct experience as a means to reliable information, and view travel as a vehicle for fact-finding. They assume that by going to North Vietnam and observing conditions there first-hand, individuals can learn the truth about U.S. military policy. Using fact-based description, supported by documentary evidence, to expose official misrepresentations, they attempt to inform Americans and arouse their consciences. Embracing the assumption, long vital to the documentary tradition, that the exposure of hidden realities will activate an ignorant but well-meaning audience, these reports challenge the mainstream press without questioning the value of objectivity or the reliability of reported fact.

# By the mid-1960s, however, objectivity was under assault from various quarters. A popular new journalism, which explored the journalist's subjective impressions, and a robust alternative press, which mocked truth claims altogether, expressed both a distrust of (and boredom with) conventional reportage and an interest in experimenting with new ways of producing and interpreting knowledge. This critique of objectivity implied not only a growing scepticism

about the reliability of mainstream news and government propaganda, but also a growing concern that accurate knowledge might not lead to principled action. As Marilyn Young observes, "Living in America increasingly meant having guilty knowledge of the war and of the government's lies about it."[15] Disturbed by the realization that people might know a great deal about what was happening in Vietnam and still fail to care, antiwar activists addressed themselves to the problem of consciousness. In step with the counterculture's commitment to a politics of perception, some visitors regard the trip to Hanoi as an opportunity to produce a profound, and potentially transformative, disorientation. These travellers interrogate—and at times abandon—direct observation as the basis for their documentary ventures.

At the conclusion of *Hanoi*, Mary McCarthy reflects, "My own avowed purpose in going to the North was to judge, compare, and report back.... I counted on the public to believe me, as it had believed Harrison Salisbury."[16] McCarthy travels to Hanoi to collect knowledge that will be of use to the antiwar cause. Her intentions are undermined by her repeated failures to communicate effectively with the North Vietnamese, and her gradual recognition that she cannot penetrate, let alone transcend, barriers of language, culture, and, especially, circumstance.[17] Many visitors, like McCarthy, found themselves frustrated by such obstacles. Travellers routinely chafe against the tightly controlled and carefully scripted nature of these government-sponsored tours. They describe being bored to tears by long lectures from Vietnamese officials, and irritated by the propagandistic language of their hosts. They struggle with the language barrier and the cumbersome process of translation. In the face of these difficulties, some conclude that accurate observation is impossible.

Frequently, these conditions prompt self-examination. As Paula Rabinowitz observes, those who set out to report on "the effects of America's war on the people of Vietnam" often ended up recording "the Vietnamese people's effects on them."[18] McCarthy's *Hanoi* narrates the "identity crisis" that results from her growing awareness that her desire to collect knowledge is not disinterested and that her initial intentions—to judge, compare, report back—belie an imperialist's sense of superiority. During her stay in Hanoi, McCarthy finds herself steering conversation towards the neutral ground of natural history, hoping to learn something about "the native trees, flowers, birds, folk remedies, how the rice seedlings were transplanted, the difference between Vietnamese tea and Chinese tea." McCarthy may long for some disinterested terrain that she and her North Vietnamese companions might share, but she quickly recognizes that

> to be so concerned about the names of flowers and trees ... was a luxury typical of
> a capitalist author, who could afford the pedantry of nomenclature, just as if North

Vietnam were still Tonkin ... and Frenchmen in tropical helmets were still exploring the upper reaches of the Mekong, looking for the shortest route to China.[19]

Finding their access to North Vietnam limited in various ways, travellers focus instead on what the journey can teach them about themselves and where they come from. As Grace Paley observes, "If my understanding of Vietnam was imperfect, my understanding of my own country was growing daily."[20]

**Narratives,** like McCarthy's, that question travel as a means of comprehending a foreign, wartorn country, shy away from descriptions of deprivation and suffering. Instead they paint a nearly surreal scene of industry and well-being: despite significant differences in structure, style, and purpose, many accounts of the trip to Hanoi stress the tranquillity of North Vietnam, and the resourcefulness of its people. Noting the brevity of his stay in Hanoi and his inability to speak Vietnamese, Noam Chomsky cautions, "My impressions are necessarily superficial.... The reader should bear in mind the limitations of what I am able to report." In the next breath he observes, "For a country at war, North Vietnam seems remarkably relaxed and serene."[21]

Anticipating a heart-wrenching encounter with suffering and victimization, some visitors are surprised to discover a thriving North Vietnam in which the will to survive is expressed in countless ways. They describe the high morale of the North Vietnamese people, who appear to draw superhuman energy from America's military onslaught. Rennie Davis recalls that he expected to find "a population inflicted with napalm scars, steel-pellet wounds, amputated arms and legs, broken spirits." Instead, he discovers "roads . . . thronged with Vietnamese carrying rock for roads, wood for bridges, manure for fields, and food for markets." Davis offers an especially radiant, though not atypical, portrait of the Vietnamese people, who not only survive but also seem strangely fortified by incessant bombing. He remarks that the bombs dropped, in "massive quantities," on North Vietnam have had "little military impact." Neatly separating violence done to the built environment from violence done to human bodies, Davis writes, "Signs of massive military assault were everywhere on the physical environment, but the people showed no signs of it."[22]

In place of the dead and wounded bodies that populate eyewitness reports, these writers describe a landscape animated by North Vietnamese powers of renewal. Bridges destroyed by day are quickly rebuilt under cover of darkness. Easily targeted urban institutions are relocated to the countryside: schools are moved to fields, hospitals rebuilt in caves, and entire villages transplanted underground. In these narratives, useful objects, like surgical clamps, made from spent ammunition and downed airplanes neatly figure the larger reconstruction under-way in North Vietnam. In *Trip to Hanoi*, Susan Sontag describes the North Viet-namese craft of reuse in some detail:

> Each plane that's shot down is methodically taken apart. The tires are cut up to make the rubber sandals that most people wear. Any component of the engine that's still intact is modified to be reused as part of a truck motor. The body of the plane is dis-mantled, and the metal is melted down to be made into tools, small machine parts, surgical instruments, wire, spokes for bicycle wheels, combs, ashtrays, and of course the famous numbered rings given as presents to visitors. Every last nut, bolt, and screw from the plane is used. The same holds for anything else the Americans drop.

The North Vietnamese demonstrate a "principle of total use" that stands in stark contrast to the destructive wastefulness of Americans. This utilitarianism acquires mythical proportions in these narratives as the North Vietnamese appear "some-how to nourish themselves on disaster."[23]

These writers call on figurative language, rather than documentary evi-dence, to stress the surreal qualities of what they witness in North Vietnam. McCarthy describes the "vast metamorphosis" underway in rural North Vietnam as "a delightful magic show, complete with movable scenery, changes of costumes, disguises."[24] Rennie Davis uses bleaker post-apocalyptic imagery to describe the underground society in which he and his companions "glimpse the outline of a possible future, should life on the earth's surface become untenable."[25] In place of documentation and fact-finding, these narratives describe a scene that strains credibility and provokes the traveller to a greater awareness of what lies beyond her field of vision and understanding. Travelling to North Vietnam, these writ-ers encounter a spectacle of resistance that demands an alternative approach to documentary description. As Sontag puts it at the conclusion of *Trip to Hanoi*, "In the end, of course, an American has no way of incorporating Vietnam into his consciousness." Instead, it continues to "glow in the remote distance like a navigator's star."[26] Intensifying the distance between the writer and her subject—North Vietnam—these writers develop a mode of description designed to convey the impact of this larger-than-life spectacle on the visitor's consciousness.

# Narratives that extol the ingenuity and resourcefulness of the North Viet-namese demonstrate the tendency, widespread on the American left during the 1960s, to romanticize anticolonial movements abroad. As Michael Renov observes in his discussion of antiwar documentaries, the "will to solidarity, to the forging of a shared identity, resulted in the construction of a Vietnam of

radical imagination." It is tempting to dismiss these idealized portraits as naive projections or, in Renov's words, evidence of the "Left's collective daydream."[27] Indeed, the American depictions of North Vietnamese resistance, characterized by significant omissions and exaggerations, have a dream-like quality. I would contend, however, that these distortions were essential to antiwar discourse. On the one hand, they reflect the very misconceptions that consciousness-raising was meant to address, and, on the other, they express the movement's utopian aspirations. For some activists the process of idealization was deliberate and strategic—a means of casting light on the shortcomings of the status quo, and envisioning a better future. Sontag, for example, would readily agree with Renov that antiwar activists constructed Vietnam to suit their purposes. She writes, "Vietnam offered the key to a systematic criticism of America. In this scheme of use, Vietnam becomes an ideal Other."[28] Sontag takes the imagined nature of the American activist's North Vietnam as a given. In her view, however, representations of Vietnam are not meant to be truthful—they are meant to be useful. In *Trip to Hanoi*, Sontag narrates the agency of her own imagination as, through a complex process of trial and error, it "constructs" (or fabricates) a politically viable description of North Vietnam.

In the opening paragraph of *Trip to Hanoi*, Sontag notes that she went to Hanoi "with the pretty firm idea that I wouldn't write about the trip upon my return." She is not a journalist, and doesn't believe that she can improve on accounts already published by Salisbury, Hayden and Lynd, and McCarthy. Instead, she travels to Hanoi in order to change herself. "Unless I could effect in myself some change of awareness, of consciousness," she writes, "it would scarcely matter that I'd actually been to Vietnam."[29]

As the title *Trip to Hanoi* implies, Sontag sees her journey to Hanoi as a consciousness-raising experience, akin to a drug high. Indeed, experiments in distorted perception provided common ground for the various subcultures, including the antiwar movement, that made up the counterculture of the late 1960s. Advocates of the counterculture claimed that experiments in consciousness, and the new forms of self-expression that resulted, would pave the way for revolution. Drugs, in particular, offered a surefire method for cultivating new perceptions. In his *Essay on Liberation*, Herbert Marcuse remarks on the relationship between the drug trip and radical politics:

> Today's rebels want to see, hear, feel new things in a new way: they link liberation with the dissolution of ordinary and orderly perception. The "trip" involves the dissolution of the ego shaped by the established society—an artificial and short-lived dissolution. But the artificial and "private" liberation anticipates, in a distorted manner, an exigency of the social liberation: the revolution must be at the same time a revolution

in perception which will accompany the material and intellectual reconstruction of society.[30]

Hallucinogenic drugs allowed people to recognize that perceptions, like objects, were subject to transformation, and to practise moving between perceptual states. The language of drug use—"tripping," "getting high," "coming down"—figures these transitions in spatial terms, suggesting the relationship between geographical dislocation and consciousness-raising that Sontag's narrative explores. Forgoing a descriptive narrative of the trip—what she observed in Hanoi—in favour of a meticulous rendering of her inward journey, Sontag illuminates the degree to which activist travel participated in the counterculture's fascination with altered states of consciousness.[31]

*Trip to Hanoi* theorizes activist travel as a means of cultivating the uncertainty that allows for radical self-transformation. Sontag records this process in excruciating detail. Early in the narrative she reproduces extended excerpts from the diary she kept in Hanoi. These record her extraordinarily limited perspective on Vietnamese culture—putting her ethnocentrism and impatience with cultural difference on display. She then proceeds to use these diary excerpts as evidence of the degree to which her own point of view has been shaped by the excesses of consumerism—excesses that she believes are at the root of the U.S. assault on North Vietnam. Taking her own private writing as a form of evidence, Sontag investigates her complicity in the war economy.

In this text the object that must be deconstructed and rebuilt is the traveller's own consciousness: *Trip to Hanoi* narrates the difficult process through which a new self is produced by taking a trip. Incorporating private writing—writing that she herself finds embarrassing—into her narrative, Sontag recycles writerly waste in an effort to reshape her own attitude. Reusing her occasional writing, rather than throwing it away, Sontag sets up a contrast between her early and subsequent impressions and, in doing so, dramatizes the process of self-transformation as an act of reconstruction. Employing her own resistant consciousness as an object—and the North Vietnamese craft of reuse as a model for remaking it—Sontag uses a minutely detailed language of introspection to lend a sense of materiality to the internal landscape as it is reshaped through a difficult encounter with a remote country.

As a result of strenuous self-criticism, Sontag comes to enjoy North Vietnam, and to celebrate the virtue and equanimity of the North Vietnamese people. "I found, through direct experience," she writes, "North Vietnam to be a place which, in many respects, *deserves* to be idealized."[32]

Narratives of the trip to Hanoi are marked, on the one hand, by glowing descriptions of North Vietnamese resourcefulness and, on the other, by a sharp turn towards introspection. While these attributes reflect the antiwar movement's commitment to consciousness-raising, they are also the result of cross-cultural collaboration. The trip to Hanoi was a performance staged jointly by North Vietnamese and American participants. The North Vietnamese used speeches, statistics, ceremonies, and museum exhibits to demonstrate their capacity to rebuild and prosper. Reciting growth statistics or offering their guests rings made out of U.S. airplanes, North Vietnamese guides and officials asserted their determination to win the war. In response, the American visitor demonstrated her capacity to be altered by this spectacle of fortitude and resistance; her participation in the North Vietnamese struggle depended on her willingness to change herself.

In some narratives, the North Vietnamese craft of reuse provides a vehicle for the American visitor's programmatic self-reform. Many of those who travelled to Hanoi describe the trip as a form of labour through which the traveller retools her own habits of thought and feeling in preparation for a better future. To this traveller, deracinated and bewildered, objects, typically known from a distance and through the lens of established knowledge, appear strange and distorted. Travel produces a state of psychic vulnerability that allows the voyager to recognize her own perceptual habits and, ideally, to alter them; like other states of consciousness in which the familiar reappears in an ideal form—hallucinations and dreams—the trip reveals quotidian objects and routine experience in a new light, suggesting that both self and circumstance can be remade with the beautiful spectacle of North Vietnamese endurance in mind.

The utopian prospect of "international consciousness" required idealized objects. It would be a mistake, however, to overlook the instrumental nature of such idealizations or to assume that they negated North Vietnamese realities. Considered in its entirety, trip to Hanoi literature suggests that "a Vietnam of radical imagination" offered an alternative to the present that was unavailable in journalistic renderings of the war. Indeed, reports of widespread victimization could not convey the possibility of North Vietnamese victory—the improbable outcome of the conflict.

In an effort to make real the capacity of the North Vietnamese to resist the U.S. military, writers describe a country that thrives in the midst of war. In this setting, rebuilt objects give form to the processes of transformation, demonstrating the resourcefulness of the North Vietnamese, figuring the material nature of self-transformation, and confirming that the social world can be systematically reconstructed. Despite vast differences, antiwar activists and their North Vietnamese hosts shared a common enemy and a common goal. They made use of the resources at hand in an effort to survive: a radically reimagined North Vietnam gave reality, however briefly, to the hope that the world might rid itself of the threat of U.S. militarism.

Lincoln Cushing    24

# POLITICAL GRAPHICS OF
# THE "LONG 1960S"

**Posters are** among the significant ephemera of the long 1960s. Synonymous with rebellion and visual wit, these fragile documents were densely packed cultural viruses capable of transmitting such abstract concepts as "solidarity," "sisterhood," or "peace" all over the world.

Political posters did not blossom as a cultural form until the mid-1960s. In the United States the chilling effect of the Cold War and McCarthyism during the 1950s made it too dangerous to produce political content for public spaces. The socially conscious graphic artists had turned inwards, continuing to create limited-edition prints shared among friends and displayed in shows, and only occasionally did something agitational make it to the streets. The civil rights movement imagery was limited to a few placards, such as the iconic "I AM A MAN"—characterized by use of simple type and without illustration. Berkeley's 1964 Free Speech Movement, vibrant though it was with song, poetry, and theatre, did not produce a single poster. It was not until the rock and counterculture posters exploded on the scene in the San Francisco Bay area that public appetite for these visual expressions spread to political posters. Similarly, the visually radical new imagery from the Cuban film institute ICAIC inspired the other Cuban political publishing agencies to push their own design work in new directions.

Although these documents were often produced in the thousands, social neglect and physical impermanence have reduced their numbers to a ghost. Huge voids in scholarship remain to be filled. A handful of community-based archives and special collections—most notably the Center for the Study of Political Graphics in Los Angeles and Michael Rossman's AOUON Archive in Berkeley—have taken on the huge task of drawing these artifacts out of the woodwork, arranging them, cataloguing them, and making them accessible to scholars and the public.

The images chosen for this book are a sampling of this enormous genre.

**Note:** For posters 1, 2, 3, 4, 7, 8, 10, 12, see the colour insert after p.276.

## 1. May Day 1961

Artist: Hugo Gellert
Publisher: 1961 Labor and Peoples Committee for May Day
1961

With the Liberty Bell and subtitle "Made in USA" in parentheses, this poster telegraphs the struggle for public legitimacy sought by the Communist Party U.S.A. at the end of the 1950s. The members of the organizing committee were forced to host this hallmark radical memorial in New York's Washington Square instead of the preferred Union Square because they were denied a permit; they were also refused the use of loudspeakers because the sound might interfere with classes at nearby New York University. Although beautifully hand-lettered and illustrated by lifelong activist illustrator Hugo Gellert, the simple two-colour poster nonetheless remains locked in a design aesthetic that was little changed from the posters of the Works Progress Administration (WPA) of the 1930s.

## 2. Viet Nam Day: May 21 & 22

Artist: unknown
Publisher: [Viet Nam Day Organizing Committee]
1965

Although broadly similar in general design to Gellert's 1961 May Day poster—both are illustrated two-colour announcements—this early antiwar movement piece displays characteristics of many new left outreach documents. Most likely designed and produced by an amateur, it is composed of a main title created with hand-applied commercial transfer lettering that has been artistically "cracked" to highlight the crisis of the situation. The smaller text was produced on a typewriter; Jerry Rubin's home phone number was listed as the contact. The illustration carries no artist's name, which is typical for a creation ethic that considered personal credit for political work to be antithetical to the collective values of the movement.

## 3. Stop the Draft Week Rally

Artist: Frank Cieciorka
Publisher: [Stop the Draft Week Organizing Committee]
1967

Stop the Draft Week was a nationwide antiwar initiative, and the demonstration at the Oakland Induction Center was the largest yet held against U.S. involvement in Vietnam. The popular antidraft slogan "Hell no, I won't go" had been deliberately expanded to reflect the "we" collectivity of the resistance. Massive presence by police almost guaranteed that this demonstration would escalate into a riot, and indeed it led to the beating of hundreds and several arrests. A subsequent set of rallies in January of 1968 for the defence of the "Oakland Seven" resulted in a poster with the stylized clenched fist clipped off, highlighted as the only graphic element—giving birth to the iconic "new left fist" later adapted by Students for a Democratic Society and many other groups.

## 4. Resolutely Support the Anti-Imperialist Struggle of the Asian, African, and Latin American People

Artist: Zhou Ruizhuang
Publisher: Shanghai People's Fine Art Publishing House
1967

China's Great Proletarian Cultural Revolution (1966–76) has been called "the largest social engineering effort in the history of mankind." Posters generated during this period were defined by several guiding political principles, among them avoidance of Western and classical Chinese styles, support for artwork from previously disenfranchised social strata and regions, and rejection of "art for art's sake." Although most of the posters were intended for a Chinese audience, many were broadly distributed around the world and sold through solidarity bookstores and political groups. The iconographic and textual messages they expressed were issues that resonated with activists across the world, people working on issues such as women's rights, international solidarity, and anti-imperialism.

## 5. Soutien aux usines occupées pour la victoire du peuple

(Support the factory occupations for a people's victory)
Artist: unknown
Publisher: Atelier Populaire No. 1 (École Nationale Supérieure des Beaux-Arts)
1968

In May 1968 Paris was gripped by a general strike that paralyzed the city. Students at six colleges joined in to produce a massive outpouring of silkscreen posters expressing the spirit of the strike in more than five hundred distinct designs—challenging the police, the de Gaulle government, and the nature of bourgeois society itself. The two most prolific *ateliers* (workshops) were the École Nationale Supérieure des Beaux-Arts and the École Nationale Supérieure des Arts-Décoratifs. The creative flood of these graphic works stands as a milestone in the history of revolutionary art. The students adopted a medium that was unfamiliar to them—screen printing—because it was cheap, fast, and could be done with available supplies and volunteer labour. The pressure to generate numerous titles over a short period was accomplished by a design aesthetic of relatively simple, monochromatic images that nonetheless succinctly captured the spirit of the moment.

## 6. Libertad de Expresión

Artist: Adolfo Mexiac
Publisher: Taller de Gráfica Popular (Mexico)
1968

This image of a gagged citizen was one of the most dramatic posters to come out of the Mexican student movement. Ten days before the opening day of the 1968 Summer Olympics in Mexico City, during a protest against the military occupation of the National Polytechnic Institute, hundreds of students had been killed by army troops in the Plaza de las Tres Culturas in Tlatelolco. This poster was printed by Mexico's pre-eminent political graphics workshop, Taller de Gráfica Popular (TGP), founded in 1938.

The graphic was "recycled" from an earlier TGP election handbill of 1958, with the addition of "Made in USA" on the padlock. According to TGP artist Alberto Beltrán in conversation with Carol Wells of the Center for the Study of Political Graphics, the 1958 version itself originated in an even earlier version done in 1954, when a CIA-supported military junta overthrew the democratic Guatemalan government of Jacobo Arbenz.

## 7. Day of Solidarity with Zimbabwe

Artist: Faustino Pérez
Publisher: Organization in Solidarity with the People of Africa, Asia and Latin America (OSPAAAL)
1970

OSPAAAL, based in Havana, Cuba, is a non-governmental organization recognized by the United Nations, with a board of representatives from all over the world. It is the primary producer of international solidarity posters in Cuba. Among its many activities has been the publication since 1967 of *Tricontinental* magazine, which at its peak had a circulation of 30,000 copies, produced in four different languages and mailed to eighty-seven countries. Most issues included folded-up solidarity posters, thus establishing the most effective international poster distribution system in the world. Cuban artists were particularly adept at expressing abstract concepts in succinct visual form; this poster elegantly represents the triumph of indigenous resistance to colonialism.

## 8. Don't Be a Silent Part of the War Machine: Speak out against Cambodia

Artist: unknown
Publisher: [U.C. Berkeley student poster workshop]
1970

After the antiwar student demonstrations and killings at Kent State, Ohio (May 4, 1970), and Jackson State, Mississippi (May 14, 1970), there was a massive upswelling of resistance culture in the United States. Political poster workshops blossomed all over the country (including the California College of Arts and Crafts in Oakland, the University of Southern California's School of Architecture, and the Poster Factory in Minneapolis) to express public outrage. At the University of California, Berkeley, faculty at the College of Environmental Design encouraged the use of campus facilities for a short-lived workshop that created an estimated 50,000 copies of hundreds of works. Although most of these were about the war, numerous other issues of the day were examined—such as the role of higher education under capitalism, student self-determination, police violence, and the Nixon presidency. Many of these exhibit the same design characteristics as those of Paris 1968, and were clearly influenced by that body of work. This example was produced on discarded tractor-feed computer paper.

## 9. Free Our Panther Sisters

Artist: unknown
Publisher: unknown
circa 1970–71

Although the best-known posters of the Black Panther Party were illustrations by Minister of Culture Emory Douglas or the iconic photo of an armed Huey Newton in a wicker chair, many other images were produced concerning the wide range of issues surrounding the party. This poster addressed efforts to liberate incarcerated Panthers—seen as political prisoners in proto-fascist America—as well as the struggle for recognition of the contribution of women in the movement. The Panther 21 were arrested April 2, 1969, and charged with conspiracy to plant bombs at several New York public sites. On May 13, 1971, after the longest political trial in New York's history, they were acquitted of all charges after less than an hour of jury deliberation. In the case of the Connecticut 14, also known as the New Haven 14, Panthers were charged with the murder of an alleged police informant, but were eventually acquitted (the charges proved to be based on COINTELPRO malfeasance).

# 10. March for Peace: April 24

Artist: unknown
Publisher: National Peace Action Coalition, Labor Support Committee
1971

During the 1950s, having purged most of the left-wing critics of U.S. foreign policy, organized labour benefited greatly from the Cold War economy and was almost universally supportive of U.S. government military actions. As historian Philip Foner noted, "Labor spoke with a Neanderthal voice. In May of 1965, George Meany declared that the AFL-CIO would support the war in Vietnam 'no matter what the academic do-gooders may say, no matter what the apostles of appeasement may say.'" But as the war ground on, and working-class soldiers came home in body bags, support began to crumble and labour began to change. First, independent locals spoke up, and in 1969 the Alameda County Central Labor Council (CLC) came out against the war, the first CLC in the country to do so. The following year trade unionists ran full-page ads in the *Washington Post* and *San Francisco Chronicle* against the war. The April 24 demonstration in San Francisco, even though not endorsed by the CLC, was a groundbreaking show of antiwar solidarity by major trade unions.

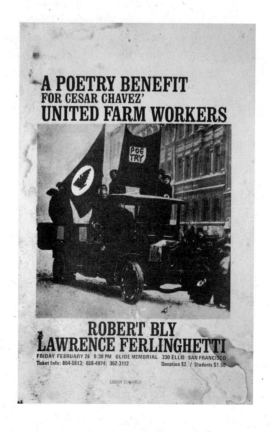

# 11. A Poetry Benefit for Cesar Chavez' United Farm Workers

Artist: unknown
Publisher: [unidentified United Farm Workers support group]
1971

The grassroots organizing and boycott campaigns of the United Farm Workers deliberately and dramatically involved the massive participation of community organizations. This poster, announcing a benefit by popular poets at a well-known progressive San Francisco church, displays a vigour and whimsy that was not typical of the rest of organized labour. By the mid-1960s beat poetry had moved beyond the confines of cafés and bars, and this reading reflects a convergence of the counterculture and the activist migrant labour community. The source image—complete with snow and fur hats—was whimsically modified from a 1917 Bolshevik Revolution photograph.

# 12. Newsreel Presents the Woman's Film

Artist: unknown
Publisher: San Francisco Newsreel
1971

Efforts to develop alternative media—tools to document, analyze, and disseminate the issues not covered critically or at all by the mainstream channels—were an integral part of the new left. This poster publicizes a woman-made film from San Francisco Newsreel, a west-coast office and distribution centre amplifying the work of the original Newsreel founded in New York in 1967. Additional Newsreel offices were active in Detroit, Boston, Kansas, Los Angeles, Vermont, and Atlanta. After many internal political struggles over the years, the work continues. There is a Third World Newsreel in New York and a California Newsreel in San Francisco. The Vermont Newsreel Archives maintains their historical records and footage. This film was a collective effort involving the women behind the camera as well as those being documented, a deliberate effort to challenge conventional artist-subject roles.

## Sources

1. Special Collections Research Center, Syracuse University Library.
2. Michael Rossman AOUON Archive, Berkeley, Cal.
3. Lincoln Cushing Archive (gift of Ann Tompkins), Berkeley, Cal.
4. Ann Tompkins (Tang Fandi) and Lincoln Cushing Chinese Poster Collection, East Asian Library, U.C. Berkeley.
5. Holt Labor Library, San Francisco.
6. Center for the Study of Political Graphics, Los Angeles.
7. Lincoln Cushing Archive, Berkeley, Cal.
8. Michael Rossman AOUON Archive, Berkeley, Cal.
9. H.K. Yuen Archive (item not yet accessioned, bulk of collection at U.C. Berkeley).
10. Holt Labor Library, San Francisco.
11. Michael Rossman AOUON Archive, Berkeley, Cal.
12. Lincoln Cushing Archive (gift of Ann Tompkins), Berkeley, Cal.

# PART III

# MOBILIZING BODIES

# 1968: SPRINGBOARD FOR WOMEN'S LIBERATION

**The growth** of women's liberation is often assumed to have represented a complete break with existing forms of radical politics. While it is true that the feminism of the late 1960s and early 1970s was innovative and iconoclastic, there is a danger in regarding it as standing apart from any wider political context, for this feeds into a fixed conservative stereotype of women as a purely moral force outside theory and somehow outside political currents. In fact many of the ideas and underlying assumptions that were taken for granted in the early days of women's liberation derived from the left movements and culture of the time. These roots and interconnections help to explain why a particular kind of feminism was to appear.

In my school exercise books we were taught neat lists of "causes" of the French Revolution or of Chartism, which we would learn by heart for exams. But as you get older you realize that causes are always contested and depend very much on your point of view and where you look. Why social and political movements arise and why they take the shape that they do are difficult historical conundrums. As women's liberation movements were to sprout in quite dissimilar places over the course of the 1970s, not simply in Europe and North America but in India, Mexico, and the Philippines, for example, tidy generalizations are hard indeed. I have taken a narrower focus. I want to consider why a women's movement appeared in Britain in 1969 in the wake of the upheavals of 1968. In looking at a particular movement, I hope that wider resonances and insights will be evident.

The macro changes occurring within British society over the course of the 1960s seem like the obvious place to look for causes. Relative prosperity, the expansion of administrative and welfare services, the new technologies of contraception, a decline in the older religious codes and a more liberal social framework; all of these had a significant bearing on the lives of young women. While higher education still reached only a minority, there were, nonetheless, women as well as men from families in which no one had been a student going to university. Historically education has always been a key factor in encouraging aspirations of emancipation among women, for it has secured a degree of economic independence along with greater self-esteem. In the late 1960s higher education encouraged the expectation that opportunities would increase for everyone to live a fuller life.

It is frequently not those who are most downtrodden who rebel, but those who have been led to expect more than society can deliver to them. Young educated women in the late 1960s were no exception. The shock of motherhood in weary isolation would dash many hopes, while the apparent sexual freedom enjoyed by women who belonged to the in-between strata of the educated middle class would turn out to be complicated by undertows of double moral standards, fear, and contempt.

While social and economic shifts clearly influence individual lives they cannot satisfactorily *explain* why individuals act personally or collectively. People living through such changes rarely say to themselves, "I am now part of a structural change and hence will form a movement." So while it is true that education has been a vital precondition historically for feminist protest, it has tended to be education and a sense of expanding possibilities *plus* a specific set of political circumstances that have acted as catalysts. Radical movements like anti-slavery in nineteenth-century America have swept women into moral causes that contributed to a new sense of themselves as women individually and collectively.

Movements enable women to experience acting in concert and to acquire habits of organizing. They also carry within them jostling ideas that can foster rebellion, so, when women participate in movements posited on democracy and equality, they can gain the confidence to question assumed social divisions, including those of gender. Moreover the incongruence between the rhetoric and day-to-day practice within radical movements has often sharpened an awareness of the subordination of women as women. The beginnings of women's liberation as a movement in Britain followed this pattern. In creating an autonomous women's movement, we challenged and rejected both the overt and implicit sexism of the male-dominated left—from wolf whistles when we spoke in public to the assumption that we would type the leaflets.

It has been quite common to simply leave it at that. The women's movement of the late 1960s is often said to have arisen in response to the left's sexism. Yet that is only part of the story. While it is true that the libertarian rejection of old left formal institutional structures took the chivalric gloves off in power relations between men and women, the personal interconnections were not simply conflictual, for alongside the rows and the anger went love and comradeship. Similarly, as 1968 turned into 1969, the theoretical legacy continued to be entangled, for many radical political ideas and cultural assumptions were translated and reshaped by feminists. We new feminists might have wanted to distance ourselves from the revolutionary bombast that wafted around 1968; nevertheless we carried bits of that extraordinary year with us, including its heady utopianism.

In periods when the possibilities of changing society for the better seem slim, utopianism is well-nigh incomprehensible and is inclined to acquire a crazed glint. However, the late 1960s and early 1970s were years when the process of transformation seemed to be accelerating and new ways of being and relating appeared to be possible. So many young people had found themselves with a freedom inconceivable to the earlier wartime generation. New terrains of political action had opened up in movements such as civil rights in the United States, while Black Power was contributing to a new political language that defied cultural subordination. In Britain a broad social-democratic and liberal conservative consensus favoured sexual tolerance, extending opportunity, and ending poverty. In the summer of 1968 women sewing machinists went on strike, putting equal pay onto the trade union and Labour Party agenda. Our high hopes of equality, democracy, and freedom in all aspects of political and social existence might have been ambitious, but in the context of the optimistic times they did not seem off the wall. We were simply determined to go faster and further than the liberal mainstream. Having grown up in an era of relative affluence and expanding expectations, the radical young could remember neither the Depression nor the deferred dreams of the war years. Being in our twenties we possessed a great deal of energy and we had no experience of defeat. Consequently we accommodated without difficulty to the emphasis on human agency characteristic of the 1960s libertarian left and duly transported it into the women's liberation groups that began to form during 1969.

Along with the stress on agency went a faith in democracy. Representative democracy appeared to be woefully inadequate. Indeed we were inclined to take it for granted, oblivious to older leftists' warnings of the danger of fascism. Instead we imagined an extensive participatory democracy with women, as well as men, actively deciding their destinies. An important influence was the American student movement and the experience of our own student occupations during 1968, in which direct democracy had been put into practice. But other sources of ideas had been accruing over the decade. In Britain from the mid-1960s the Institute for Workers' Control had been resuscitating early twentieth-century anarcho-syndicalist ideas of workplace democracy, and, when the Campaign for Nuclear Disarmament splintered, it generated many community projects that mixed direct action with self-help around homelessness, transport, child poverty, alcoholism, racial discrimination, single mothers, and disability. This do-it-yourself politics might be about specific reforms, but its approach could be grafted onto the more sweeping idea of liberation. Like the movement for workers' control, community action linked empowerment with extending democracy into daily life.[1] In 1968 work and community came together when the wives of Hull trawler men protested against the unsafe ships that had resulted in the death of fishermen. This protest from women who had previously had no public voice was profoundly inspirational.

The radical stress on human agency, empowerment, and direct democracy was also to inform the processes of political resistance and organizing. In the late 1960s the Vietnamese defiance of the U.S. government provided an example of a small, ill-equipped movement fighting against a seemingly invincible force. They became the embodiment of the active agents that liberation movements extolled. Within the United States itself over the course of the 1960s the civil rights movement and later Black Power were reconfiguring the meaning of democracy by claiming symbolic space in the segregated South and by developing a language to express resistance to how people were seen and defined. While this cultural awareness of subordination had been implicit in the working-class movement in previous decades, U.S. Black politics during the 1960s made it *explicit*. Democratization evidently involved a contest within the differing wings of radical movements themselves as well as against capitalism. This approach provided an important insight for the burgeoning women's movements.

The militancy of the Black movement made a dent in the Marxist assumption of the primacy of the workplace and class. The examples of civil rights and Black Power suggested that space was to be taken in everyday life and that identity could be historically asserted by human beings in action. Feminists would take up the concept of a politics of identity, emphasizing in some cases a multiplicity of oppressions and in others an alternative pre-eminence of gender.

A sense of empowerment also came from the May events in France, in which intense, direct participation and realization through rebellion in the streets had figured so dramatically. A language of subjectivity was the crucial innovation of the wall posters in Paris; students and young workers brought the body and desire on to the barricades that spring. The Situationists fused with Jean-Paul Sartre, Frantz Fanon, and Aimé Césaire in a whirl of defiance and revolt in which the micro-world of the subject interacted with a dream of social revolution. By the summer it had been swept away; nevertheless, briefly, the French state had wobbled uncertainly—a moment that many of the young participants could never quite forget.

Although the connection between subjectivity and the social manifested itself most dramatically in May 1968, it constituted a long-term theoretical project. The year before, for instance, in London at the Dialectics of Liberation conference at the Roundhouse, Black Power activist Stokely Carmichael, Marxist philosopher Herbert Marcuse, and the anti-psychiatrists R.D. Laing and David Cooper, among others, had tussled over the links between inner and outer forms of oppression.[2] Despite angry, often painful conflicts, it had felt as if the search for the synapses between micro- and macro-experience was underway. Anti-psychiatry, with its emphasis on the oppressions of the family and the coercion of the insane asylum, seemed to suggest that personal experience could be surveyed through a new and illuminating lens. The Dialectics of Liberation went on for two weeks in July 1967 and contrived to etch itself into the memories of several women who later went into the women's liberation movement, even though women speakers at the event were notably absent.

During the late 1960s new ways of thinking about politics were coming across the Atlantic from the American new left, which contained a much stronger emphasis on prefiguring the future within the present than was customary in Britain, where old left attitudes had survived. The American new left had its roots in a moral radicalism that preceded the 1960s, but it found an activist organizational expression in the Students for a Democratic Society (SDS). The activists in the SDS drew on the sociologist C. Wright Mills, the anarchist Paul Goodman, and French existentialist Albert Camus.[3] Warned during the McCarthy era of the dangers of Stalinism, the new left activists were adamant that the end did not justify the means. On the contrary, they sought to be ultra-democratic in their practice—in the words of Greg Calvert, "While fighting to destroy the power which had created the loveless anti-community, we would ourselves create the community of love—*The Beloved Community*."[4]

Several women from the U.S. new left, including Sue Cowley (later O'Sullivan), Sheli Wortis, Karen Slaney, and Lois Graessle, brought these approaches to politics into the early women's liberation groups in Britain. The small consciousness-raising groups we adopted on the American model stressed how democracy, respect for individuality, and collectivity must be part of the process of organizing. This was a politics that turned away from the strategic suggestion that politics was the art of the possible as well as any idea that the

*1968: Springboard for Women's Liberation*

means were justified by the end. The process of politics was assumed to influence outcomes. We must prefigure in order to sustain a movement.

The politics of prefiguration thus set the stage for the slogan "The personal is political." Their interconnection not only enabled the early women's liberation groups to expose how the actual practice of male-dominated leftism was falling short, but also made it possible to extend "politics" into the everyday realms of housework and child care as well as into sexual relationships and the representation of the body. Wini Breines has argued that the reasons for this occurring were partly because "economic, political and cultural changes" were politicizing what had been demarcated as "personal."[5] Some forty years on it is hard to convey just how startling this "new politics" seemed at the time. In retrospect there is a certain irony in how feminists' assertion that men should share the babysitting was scornfully dismissed as "utopian" by the same young men who were proposing revolution!

The late 1960s was an intense and heady period in which ideas seemed to be spinning in the ether and events occurred at a pace that overtook any space for contemplation. Initially new ways of seeing arrived literally "in movement," through snatched conversations and hasty reading between demonstrations and meetings. There was no time to work out where they were originating or to sort them out and follow them through. The theoretical search to assimilate and comprehend came later; in the first half of the 1970s socialist feminists in Britain would turn to the works of Henri Lefebvre, Antonio Gramsci, and Louis Althusser for insights about everyday life, culture and hegemony, and ideology. Similarly those of us interested in history began to discover women in the revolutionary past and in feminist struggles. As "women's history" grew in scope we would learn, to our surprise, how so many of our "new" discoveries had surfaced before and been forgotten.

Two women who provided the inspiration for early feminist discussions were Simone de Beauvoir and Doris Lessing: de Beauvoir because she asserted that femininity was created through culture, and Lessing because her novels, and *The Golden Notebook* (1962) in particular, explored the interaction between the personal and the political. Their response to women's liberation differed: de Beauvoir hailed the new movement while Lessing deplored it. Many of us admired Lessing's work nonetheless.

In 1967 my interest in the history of left psychology had led me to Karen Horney's *Feminine Psychology* (1926), which raised the impact of male cultural dominance on how femininity was experienced psychologically. I also came across the writings of the French sociologist Evelyne Sullerot on women's position as workers. Similarly influential was the wonderful French historian Edith Thomas, whose own experience in the Resistance had alerted her to the manner in which participation in grassroots movements affect women's consciousness. In the early 1970s, when I was writing *Women Resistance and Revolution* (1972) and *Woman's Consciousness Man's World* (1973), the perspectives that these writers suggested would be crucial in helping me to orientate my thinking.

These were the influences of which I was aware at the time. However, when I came to write a memoir of the sixties, *Promise of a Dream* (2000), I realized how my questioning of the conventional maps of femininity had arisen partly out of the culture around me, which I had simply taken for granted as I was growing up. I suspect similar implicit attitudes were also affecting other young women of my generation. Over time feminists have gone back to interrogate seemingly unlikely aspects of popular culture, from Hollywood icons of 1950s womanhood to the girl groups of the early 1960s, for underground traces of subversion. Still, a visual culture of women defying convention existed closer to home in British films, from Shelagh Delaney's Salford teenage mother in *A Taste of Honey* (1961) to Nell Dunn's rebellious outsiders in *Up the Junction* (1967) and *Poor Cow* (1967); while from the mid-1960s thoughtful television dramas, written, directed, and produced by David Mercer, Ken Loach, and Tony Garnett, were portraying women who were prepared to question the status quo. At the same time the novels of Margaret Drabble and Penelope Mortimer provided an uneasy literature of female alienation and disconnection.

Embedded sets of assumptions were lodged too within prevailing structures of feeling. While difficult to discern at the time, these assumptions nevertheless exerted considerable influence. Early in the 1960s enthusiastic folk revivalists had sought "authenticity," while in the middle of the decade the quest for the "real" continued in the gritty docu-dramas that enlivened television. Both shared an emphasis upon experience, and "experience" in a different guise reappeared in the second half of the decade, carrying with it a powerful impulse to open and extend consciousness through mystical illumination. These apparently dissimilar sides of the 1960s were connected by a shared distrust of reason. Spontaneous intuition was seen as the key to understanding, and was valued over theory. So, on hearing about the U.S. women's liberation consciousness-raising groups, radical young women in Britain were ready to entertain the idea that by releasing and sharing individual experience it would be possible to understand the wider nature of subordination and find a political alternative.

Another key conviction, the release of suppressed voices, had predated the 1960s. From the late 1950s the folk singer Ewan MacColl and the BBC radio producer Charles Parker collaborated on a series of "Radio Ballads" that explored the lives and feelings of railway workers, labourers, and miners through the spoken word and in song.[6] Oral history began outside the academy as an attempt to catch ways of life that had been neglected by polite upper-middle-class culture. This search for the marginalized contributed to the idiom of authenticity and spontaneous insight that helped to shape a cultural valuing of experiential knowing.

During the late 1960s the History Workshop meetings that Raphael Samuel started at the trade union college, Ruskin, in Oxford brought this approach into radical history by encouraging working-class students to base their research on topics close to their work, communities, and families. Aptly the initiative for what would be the first women's liberation conference at Oxford came out of the 1969 Ruskin History Workshop. There would be close continuing links between future History Workshops and an early group of feminist historians such as Sally Alexander, Anna Davin, Barbara Taylor, and myself.

The adoption of the term "workshop," first by the Ruskin meetings and then by the London Women's Liberation Workshops, has interesting roots. The idea of a workshop originated in both 1930s American radical drama and the experimental theatre work done by Joan Littlewood with Ewan MacColl during the 1930s and 1940s.[7] In 1953 Littlewood moved her Theatre Workshop to Stratford East, a working-class area of London.[8] The collaborative, unscripted approach that she advocated would influence both Ken Loach's and Mike Leigh's filmmaking, and the workshop idea was also adopted by radical artists in the mid-1960s. In the visual arts it not only expressed a commitment to co-operative, non-hierarchical ways of working but also suggested an openness to fluidity and flux that was evident in the sixties zeitgeist.[9] Early women's liberation groups assumed the same ethos of being open-ended and continually in the making, allowing space for co-operative reshaping. Any person's contribution could be partial and unfinished; but after being handed on to the group it could be thought about, worked over, and recrafted. When this process went well it brought the confidence to articulate tentative thoughts and resulted in an innovative political creativity.

The radical movements of the late 1960s and early 1970s were intensively collective while also being passionate about self-expression and development. It has been the individualism that has persisted in popular memory, but that is to miss the point. The powerful impact of the era arose from the *combination* of self and collectivity. The women's liberation movement contained the same convergence. The assertion of individuality has been vital for women who are expected to sink their identities into the needs of others. Yet individualism on its own leaves women isolated at times of vulnerability. The collectivity of sisterhood brought sustenance and allowed for individual creativity.

Capitalism, of course, proved sturdier and niftier on its feet than we had thought, while over the course of time snags became apparent in the "new politics." The consciousness groups were not always open to the free expression of individuals, nor did they prove a miraculous way out of political conflict. The participatory democracy we espoused could be indecisive and as subject to manipulation as other forms of democracy. Declaring the personal to be political could be moralistic and restrictive rather than prefigurative and liberatory, while the emphasis on experience could lead to an anti-intellectualism that reinforced the idea of female irrationality. The notion of identity proved to be particularly fraught, and it would often divide rather than unite as intended when it was taken to be a fixed category rather than an active historical connection to others.

Notwithstanding the setbacks, an innovatory approach to politics *did* appear in the late 1960s; and it did question how means affected outcomes and struggled to connect to much wider aspects of life and consciousness than social democracy or the old left had done. Vitally it brought together individual freedom and collective action and imagined how human relating might alter. The hope of 1968 flowed outwards into women's and gay liberation in the early 1970s. Since then it has had an impact all over the world through many different kinds of movements. Perhaps this is why the radical implications of that year are still so passionately contested. The dialectics of liberation have taken much longer to work themselves out, and the grand transformation was not to be, yet the utopian energy of 1968 galvanized women and men to keep on struggling for that loving community glimpsed amidst the turmoil of a time when desire and reality seemed to merge.

## 26

Joana Maria Pedro

# GROUP CONSCIOUSNESS IN BRAZIL
## Appropriation (1964–89)

> During those days when we had our discussion group going, if I were to say, "I've never come [to a climax]," the woman next to me would also say that she hadn't either, and how could that be so? And in a group right here, in Rio de Janeiro, a friend of mine showed me how to remove the top of the shower head and let the water pour over my clitoris, and that's how I had my first orgasm.
>
> — Branca Moreira Alves

**The testimony** of Branca Moreira Alves of Rio de Janeiro registers a kind of experience that belonged to the "*grupos de reflexão*" or "consciousness-raising groups" that were common throughout Brazil around 1972—and the statement comes from a research project into the experiences of Brazilian women who became involved in feminism and the women's movement between 1964 and 1985.[1] The consciousness-raising groups were adaptations of a methodology applied by Brazilian women who had in turn learned about it during time spent in the United States and Western European countries. The groups formed in the United States and Europe can be considered part of a project for cultural change that envisioned consciousness-raising as the first step towards the elimination of hierarchies between men and women.

Between 1966 and 1967 in the United States and European countries, as part of the second wave of feminism that had begun in the middle of the decade, urban middle-class women initiated a practice that would have international repercussions. They formed what came to be known as "consciousness-raising groups" made up entirely of women. In order to change how they thought about themselves, and how they lived, women sought to revise the dominant images, myths, and prejudices that portrayed them in diminished terms, as weak of intellect, physically fragile, and generally incompetent, and also as naturally inclined towards remaining within the confines of the home. Furthermore, they sought to spread this new consciousness, and to this end they cultivated the idea that each member of a consciousness-raising group should go on to form another group.

These practices, initiated within the ranks of what came to be known in the United States as "radical feminism," soon spread out to other parts of the world, including Brazil—although it took more time to appear there, and emerged within a different political context. In Brazil it was a period during which the military dictatorship that had begun with the 1964 coup made it difficult—if not impossible—to carry out any type of political militancy within the country, and much less organize major mass demonstrations like those going on elsewhere in the world. The Brazilian women who started consciousness-raising groups had the advantage of access to literature that was coming out abroad but was not readily available in Brazil in translation.

The Western groups came together through informal meetings that were usually held in people's homes, although they were not necessarily restricted to that location. They could also take place in offices, church basements, and cafés. Together they constituted the basis of the women's liberation movement of the late 1960s and early 1970s, and they had their roots in the student movement, the Black movement, and the counterculture. They were made up of small groups, usually consisting only of women and with somewhere between six and twenty-four in attendance.

Conversations began with the women's own experiences. Some of the sessions developed a methodology that focused on different stages in the life cycle—childhood, the first menstrual period, youth, marriage, abortions, childbirth, relationship with spouse, menopause, and so forth. Such conversations were referred to as "life lines." No aspect of women's lives was ignored. The underlying principle was that "the personal is political." In other words, as Amy Erdman Farrell put it, "Every woman's personal life is politically structured through visceral power struggles."[2]

This practice, according to Juliet Mitchell, was "copied" from the consciousness-raising groups of Chinese peasants of the pre-revolutionary period. Just as the peasants had done, the women believed that speaking up and making their demands heard would be a way of creating a new image for themselves, of exorcising the "low self-esteem" that was a common problem. The goal behind organizing these groups was "to unite women, in order to establish close ties of friendship and solidarity among them." They were also meant to become "revolutionary collectives." Thus, activity was expected to move forward from "personal consciousness" to "group consciousness, from the personal to the political."[3]

A large number of the women who took the initiative of putting these consciousness-raising groups together had participated, along with men, in the diverse social movements that fought against racism, for civil rights, and against the Vietnam War and the arms race. In their accounts, within these movements their words and opinions had been belittled or ignored. It was precisely to get away from such attitudes that they began to put together groups in which each woman was encouraged to speak and her words would be respected.

Within these consciousness-raising groups women could reformulate a self-image that to a large extent had previously been negative. They were able to overcome stereotypes and prejudices, creating an identity of which they could be proud—in which they could begin to feel "proud to be a woman." In their under-standing, this meant that they were discovering their "real identity."

As they spread, the groups pushed beyond boundaries and put together a veritable international network, disseminating activities through books, maga-zines, debates, conferences, theatre, cinema, and music. They expressed them-selves through demonstrations, struggles to change laws, and the publication of newspapers that might—coincidentally or not—have a similar name, such as *Nós Mulheres* (We women, a São Paulo newspaper that circulated between 1976 and 1978), *Nosotras* (in Chile and México), *Nos/Otras* (in Spain), or *Noi Donne* (in Italy). Many of these newspapers were produced by a "Women's Collective" or repre-sented a "Women's Circle." Thus, what we are able to perceive here is the common reference to collectives, circles, and the like, terms that represent elements of the ways in which the consciousness-raising groups themselves were organized.

In Brazil it was in this context that in 1972, in the city of São Paulo, the first meetings took place of a group made up of women who were university pro-fessors with ties to leftist political groups. Their ages ranged from thirty to thirty-eight years of age. Most had been members of political parties or were relatives, daughters, or wives of people involved in resistance to the dictatorship.

Maria Odila Leite da Silva Dias was one of them. She was born in 1940 in São Paulo, and today she lives there and teaches at the Catholic University of São Paulo (PUC/SP).[4] Her first contact with consciousness-raising groups came in the 1960s when she was working on her Ph.D. in history at Yale University in the United States. The groups there were the product of the feminist movement that had been gaining ground on the streets and in the media in general, throughout different countries. Back in Brazil she became, in 1972, one of the organizers of a consciousness-raising group called Conscientização Feminista. The books that the women devoted themselves to reading had been brought into Brazil in the suitcases of several group members who had spent time abroad, particularly in the United States and France. In Brazil the activity of these women represented a novelty. This first group lasted until 1975.

Another group, created by Branca Moreira Alves, was formed in Rio de Janeiro as of 1972, lasting until 1973. Branca Moreira Alves had studied in Berkeley, California, where she had first come into contact with feminist consciousness-raising groups. The Rio group, however, rather than referring to itself as a consciousness-raising group, chose to call itself a "*grupo de reflexão*" (a "group for reflecting," in literal translation), so as not to be confounded with "political activism."[5]

Several of the Brazilian women interviewed for this research spoke of how their identification with feminism sprang from their participation in one of these groups. This, for example, was the case of "Santinha"—the nickname of Maria do Espírito Santo Tavares dos Santos—who participated in one such group in Rio de Janeiro. Santinha was born in the city of Bacabal, Maranhão state; today she lives in Rio de Janeiro and is a member of the State Health Council (Conselho Estadual de Saúde do Rio de Janeiro). Like other women, she had been an activist member of leftist parties fighting against the military dictatorship. In her case it was the Brazilian Communist Party, which designated her for participation in the Rio feminist movement.[6] When she began her participation in a consciousness-raising group, her initial intention was to "win over" new members for her party. Yet she ended up identifying so completely with feminism that it soon became her most important political commitment.

Nonetheless, not all women who came into contact with these consciousness-raising groups experienced that same initial affinity. Suely Gomes Costa, born in Rio de Janeiro in 1938, found her identification with feminism during the 1970s, under the influence of Maria do Espírito Santo. She said that following an initial invitation to participate in one of these groups, her first reaction had been one of discomfort. In her view, the women were referring to a form of domination that she had not experienced. At that time, she was "more involved in leftist struggles." It was only some time later that she came to understand the importance of the groups, when she herself began to experience marital strife.[7]

As well, many women who identified with feminism in Brazil related their participation in these small groups in books, articles, and testimonies.[8] They said they had discovered an "identity" through the group, that they came to a "better self-understanding." In other words, rather than the group constructing an identity for them, it was through the group that they were able to "discover" an "essential truth." Furthermore, they went on to form veritable international networks; and it was through such networks that a number of women who participated in these groups in Rio de Janeiro were able to obtain U.N. sponsorship to hold a meeting, in 1975, at the headquarters of ABI (Associação Brasileira de Imprensa–Brazilian Press Association). That conference, "Women's Role and Behavior in Brazilian Reality," came to be considered the founding landmark of second-wave feminism in Brazil.[9]

Significantly, then, the groups were in effect reproduced through those who took part in them. Felix Guatari, in a 1982 visit to Brazil, referred to this type of organizational practice as a "rhizome."[10] This was certainly a pertinent designation. In the interviews that we carried out, we could easily come to understand how these groups multiplied and recognize the contacts that they provided at local, national, and international levels. In the southern state of Santa Catarina, for example, during the 1980s (rather than the 1970s) there were two feminist groups, Amálgama and Vivências. The first one functioned as a consciousness-raising group and was formed in accordance with North American ideals. The sociologist Julia Silvia Guivant, of Florianópolis, Santa Catarina's capital city, was born in 1952 in Argentina and did her Master's and Doctoral degrees in Brazil at the UNICAMP (Campinas, São Paulo state). She has been a professor at the UFSC (Universidade Federal de Santa Catarina) since 1980. But she became a member of one of these groups in Campinas, a city near São Paulo, and she took the idea from there back to Florianópolis. She then went on to form the Amálgama group in Florianópolis.[11] In turn, the Campinas group was made up of women who had taken part in this type of group in the United States. Marisa Correa was among them. In this regard, the women were reproducing experiences that they had been through abroad.

In the city of Rio Branco, in the state of Acre, nestled into the far northeastern corner of the country, two women known as feminists—Júlia Matias de Albuquerque and Mara Vidal—also reported that their identification with feminism began through their participation in a consciousness-raising group that used the "*linha da vida*" (life line, or life cycle) approach. Júlia Matias de Albuquerque was born in Seringal in the state of Acre in 1960, and in 1973 moved to Rio Branco. She has been an activist through CDD (Católicas pelo Direito de Decidir–Catholic Women for the Right to Decide–Brazil)[12] since 2001. Mara Vidal, born in 1964 in Mogi das Cruzes, São Paulo state, began her activism as a member of youth segments of Catholic Church movements, which was where she came into contact with feminism. She moved to Acre in 1986, where she began working in the church's Pastoral Committee on the Land (Comissão Pastoral da Terra). Today she is secretary of policies for women for the state of Acre. These two women told me that Teresa Mansur, who today lives in Vitória, in the northern state of Espírito Santo, was responsible for putting these groups together.[13]

Various adaptions of this type of group formation came to my attention in the interviews. In São Paulo, Maria Amélia de Almeida Teles related her experiences co-ordinating consciousness-raising groups in eighteen different "mothers' clubs."[14] She would go into different neighbourhoods carrying issues of *Brasil Mulher*, a newspaper that circulated between 1975 and 1980. This was her appropriation of the methodology of consciousness-raising groups, with the difference that she put herself in the position of "taking consciousness" to groups of women who would otherwise "not have it." Maria Amélia was born on October 6, 1944, in the city of Contagem, state of Minas Gerais. She was an activist in the Brazilian Communist Party (PC do B–Partido Comunista do Brasil) and was twice imprisoned during the years of the military dictatorship. It was there—in prison—that she came into contact with feminism. Today she lives in São Paulo, where she is the head of a non-governmental organization.

Another adaptation emerged from the narrative of Sônia Weider Maluf, an activist during the 1980s in the southern state of Rio Grande do Sul.[15] Sônia Weider Maluf was born on October 3, 1960, in the city of Santana do Livramento, in that same state. She moved to the city of Porto Alegre at age seven, and it was there that she became active in the student movement, in the Socialist Democracy (Democracia Socialista) tendency of the PT (Workers' Party) and within the feminist group Liberta. She obtained a degree in journalism from the UFRGS (Porto Alegre) and has taught since 1986 at the UFSC (Florianópolis, Santa Catarina), where she is now a professor of anthropology. She said that both men and women participated in the groups that were organized—an unusual occurrence given that one of the main characteristics of the groups that formed during the 1960s was their tendency to have an exclusively female membership. For the most part women believed that men's participation in the meetings would inhibit women's speech and initiatives, and to avoid inhibition of this sort, feminist movements ordinarily did not let men into the meetings.[16]

Another important point is that those who participated in these consciousness-raising groups believed that the new type of discussion group that they were implementing also represented the invention of a new type of relationship between people and collective work. They said that the groups enabled them to avoid the emergence of "leaders" and "spokesmen" or "spokespersons." They argued that, rather than a vertically organized structure, they were putting together horizontal organizational forms in which no one would be seen as having a monopoly on truth, and in which no one would be able to "dominate or not take part during the time allotted to discussions." Meetings were not to be chaired or, where a chair was to be had, women were to take turns assuming the role, as part of a new feminist way of organizing. Attempting to work as collectives with no chairs or leaders was thought to be a way of avoiding "competitive relationships" among women, of the sort that abounded in the society in which they lived and the likes of which they meant to reject.[17]

At the time these groups were subject to numerous criticisms. They were often considered merely "benign," and some people argued that their lack of hierarchical structure could be seen as a kind of "authoritarianism without rules."[18] Some argued that although self-awareness served as an organizing principle, it organized women "around no purpose" at all. Some of their critics advocated, instead, an activism that promoted women's demonstrations and marches, "bra-burning," and the organizing of support and health centres. Still others believed that concrete social change was contingent upon changes in the law.

Among members of the Brazilian left, the major criticism directed towards consciousness-raising groups was that they were a sort of "afternoon tea" for wealthy women who "had nothing better to do." Or, at best, they were considered a waste of time that could be better employed in a "greater" and "wider" project such as the struggle against the dictatorship, or for socialist revolution. Thus these groups were seen as divisive—as if rather than bringing people together, they promoted conflict within families and within the left as a whole.

Still, this practice of group consciousness or "reflection" became so common that it was even adopted in theatre by Cidinha Campos and other actresses, such as Marilia Pêra. In the play *Homem não entra* (No men allowed), written in 1975,[19] Cidinha Campos engaged her audience in a sort of "consciousness-raising group." Action took place within the audience, rather than on stage. Only women were allowed; men remained outside, and children were cared for by people left in charge of them. Just as in actual consciousness-raising groups, women narrated their life stories and made their complaints heard. The military regime banned the play, which was accused of "being sexist." To a large extent the play was part of a trend adapting theatrical events from the United States—the same thing that happened much later with Eve Ensler's *The Vagina Monologues*.[20]

Intimate matters were not only discussed on stage. In 1979 Marta Suplicy, at that time a well-known sexologist and today a member of the Brazilian government, directed a segment of the television program *TV Mulher* (TV for women) in which she talked about orgasm and sexual pleasure, and even encouraged women to masturbate. Rose Marie Muraro, in her book *Memoirs of a Defiant Woman* (*Memórias de uma mulher impossível*) mentions the shock she experienced in seeing the program after returning to Brazil from the United States around the beginning of the 1980s.[21] The program, broadcast during the morning, was meant for an audience of housewives.

Today such "consciousness-raising" groups no longer exist. In their place, perhaps, are "workshops" organized and developed by non-governmental organizations[22] and given by "specialists." The groups even cause some embarrassment to women who have recognized trajectories as feminists.[23] Today, people no longer believe that through discussing personal issues women's "real identities" can be found. In fact, we no longer even believe that "real identities" exist. Identities, using contemporary lingo, are "under erasure"; that is, identity is transformed through the ways in which we are discursively interpellated or represented. Identification can be gained or lost.[24]

Yet there was a time in which in which the transformative power of change through small consciousness-raising groups was a firmly held belief. Evidence to this effect enables us to think about the changes that occurred during the 1960s, which did not lead in the direction that we had dreamt they would—and, furthermore, leads us to realize that many of the changes that have since taken place were neither planned nor intended.

## 27

Amanda Third

# REFRAMING THE "WHITENESS" OF U.S. FEMINISM

The Protest Movement, Radical Feminism, and the Abjection of Whiteness

**Histories that** track the rise of second-wave feminism frequently note that the U.S. women's movement, in both its active constituents and the conceptualization of its aims, remained overwhelmingly white until well into the 1970s, when "the difference debate" gripped feminism. Whilst it has become customary to acknowledge the whiteness of late 1960s/early 1970s U.S. feminism, and evidence demonstrates that the initial phases of second-wave feminism were indeed profoundly shaped by a blindness to the circumstances of women of colour, what is rarely interrogated are the very conditions that produced this "whitewashing."

Second-wave feminism comprised a spectrum of groups with widely divergent understandings of women's subordination, and an equally divergent set of strategies for putting cultural and political change into effect. However, in the late 1960s a small number of women's groups who identified either as "politicos" or "feminists"—those now labelled "radical feminists"—came to dominate the political scene of feminism.[1] Todd Gitlin suggests that radical feminism had its origins in the transformations taking place within the broader social protest movement towards the end of the decade: "From the embers of the old movement, a new one rose scorching—sisterly, factional, wild, egomaniacal, furious with insight and excess, the voice of millions of women, *living survivors of the death and transfiguration of the New Left.*"[2] In the following pages I consider this relationship between the emergence of radical feminism in the late 1960s and the changing nature of the North American social protest movement. In particular, I track the origins of "white" feminism by situating radical feminism's blindness to differences of colour in relation to the problematic currency of whiteness within the broader context of the larger social protest movement.[3]

# Sketching the Movement:
# Eschatological Temporality and Despair

"The movement" here refers to the broad constellation of left-wing issue and/or identity-based groups calling for radical change, including political organizations affiliated with the civil rights movement, the antiwar movement, the free speech movement, the Black Power movement, and the North American counterculture. Although the movement comprised diverse groups with varying agendas, these groups frequently understood themselves as sharing political ground. Broadly speaking, they embraced a Marxist critique of society. They defined their particular interests in terms of "class oppression" and outspokenly condemned a nefarious "system" that continued to thrive only at the expense of subaltern groups.

No single central organization co-ordinated the activities of these disparate groups. Yet organizations such as Students for a Democratic Society actively worked to construct alliances between the movement's various groups and to provide overarching leadership. But, as Sara Evans states, "Above all the term 'movement' was self-descriptive. There was no way to join; you simply announced or felt yourself to be part of the movement—usually through some act like joining a protest march."[4] Whilst affiliations with the movement were often informal, nonetheless, for much of the 1960s there was a sense, however illusory or transient, of unity. According to Evans, "Almost a mystical term, 'the movement' implied an experience, a sense of community and common purpose."[5] As John Muncie states, in the "spate of university sit-ins, marches and demonstrations of 1968 . . . the strange agglomeration of black militants, students, drop-outs, draft dodgers, mystical hippies and women's liberationists seemed to be momentarily united."[6]

The various camps of the movement historically sought to downplay their differences to promote an image of a large and diverse mass movement with unified interests. By the late 1960s, though, despite synergistic moments, the movement's sense of unity, potential and actual, was rapidly disintegrating under the pressure of increasingly incompatible factional demands. Its members had become excessively preoccupied with the demarcation of boundaries of dissent. The contradictory forces that had given the movement vibrancy and legitimized its claims

*Reframing the "Whiteness" of U.S. Feminism*

to embody the blueprint for a new and inclusive society could no longer be subordinated to a notion of unity and had radically undermined its already tenuous cohesion. Amongst certain segments of the movement, despair began to set in.

Various commentators argue that the movement "disappeared," or "self-destructed," or that it was "killed off" at the end of the 1960s.[7] But rather than disappearing, it transformed. In the late 1960s a fundamental change in the conceptualization of the ideal leadership of both the movement and the future society emerged. The civil rights movement had metamorphosed into the Black Power movement. Often with the support of white radicals, this new movement began to claim that Black people, as a group whose history of oppression gave them a unique insight into the "human condition," would lead the way forward.[8] In this process, white activists, many of whom had previously considered themselves, alongside their Black counterparts, to be the vanguard of the revolution, found that they were not just alienated but often excluded from that same revolution.

Since at least as early as 1967, white constituents of the movement had a sense that their whiteness was increasingly problematic. As radical journalist Andrew Kopkind put it:

> To be white and radical in America this summer is to see horror and feel impotence. It is to watch the war grow and know no way to stop it, to understand the black rebellion and find no way to join it, to realize that the politics of a generation has failed and the institutions of reform are bankrupt, and yet to have neither ideology, programs, nor the power to reconstruct them.[9]

Prior to this moment whiteness, a marker of privilege for mainstream America, had been almost entirely invisible. However, the emphasis on Black self-determination crystallized the demarcation of racial identities; increasingly whiteness within the movement became a more visible category with highly pejorative connotations. White radicals' feeling of exclusion was compounded by a relative lack of success in organizing "the ghettos of the (white) poor" in the Northern United States, as compared to Black radicals working to mobilize Black constituents around the issue of race. It was compounded also by the often open antagonism of Black leaders towards white radicals.[10] Young white men and women thus found themselves in an increasingly ambiguous relationship to the movement. Their place, not only in the movement but also in the dominant vision of the new society, seemed radically uncertain.

For white participants, the movement appeared to be committing a form of metaphorical *genocide*—an erasure of whiteness—that marked "the end of the interracial 'beloved community.'"[11] At times the movement's "genocidal" impulse was articulated in highly explicit terms. For example, at the 1967 National

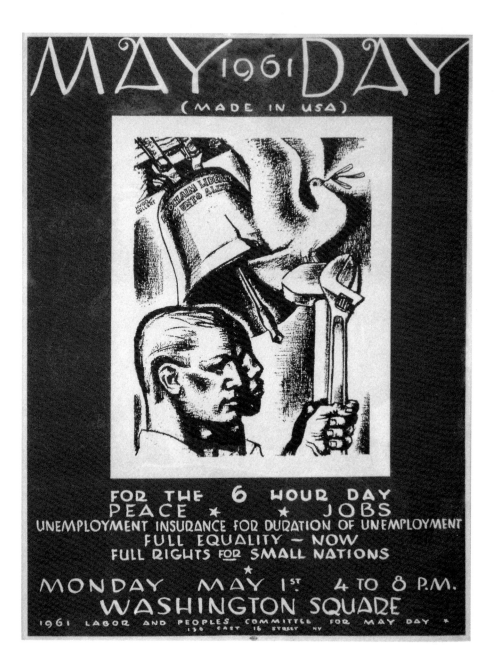

**1. May Day 1961**,
United States,
1961.

# VIET NAM DAY may 21 & 22

A COMMUNITY MEETING

A 30 HOUR EDUCATIONAL PROTEST SPONSORED
BY A. F. T. University of California (Berkeley)
Faculty Local 1474 ● A. F. T. University of California
(Berkeley) Employed Graduate Students Local 1570 ●
Faculty Peace Committee (University of California
at Berkeley)   STARTING AT NOON MAY 21 ON THE
BERKELEY CAMPUS

SPEAKERS AND ENTERTAINERS INCLUDE: ● ●
U.S. SENATOR GREUNING ● I.F. STONE ● BOB
PARRIS (BOB MOSES) ● BOB SCHEER ● PAUL
KRASSNER ● WILLIAM STANTON ● SI CASADY ●
"THE COMMITTEE" ● DAVE DELLINGER ● M.S.
ARNONI ● COLIN EDWARDS ● S. F. MIME TROUPE ●
PAUL POTTER ● DR. BENJAMIN SPOCK ● NORMAN
THOMAS ● KENNETH REXROTH ● BARBARA DANE ●
PROFESSOR STAUGHTON LYND ● FELIX GREENE ●
JAMES ARONSON ● and many others ● IF YOU WANT
TO HELP CALL: Jerry Rubin  848-3158

*The S. F. Mime troupe will present benefit performances of Bertolt Brecht's
play "The Exception and the Rule" at Garfield High School in Berkeley on
May 14, 15 and 16.  Tickets are available at Campus Records in Berkeley.
Proceeds to help finance Vietnam Day.

2. **Viet Nam Day:
May 21 & 22**,
United States,
1965.

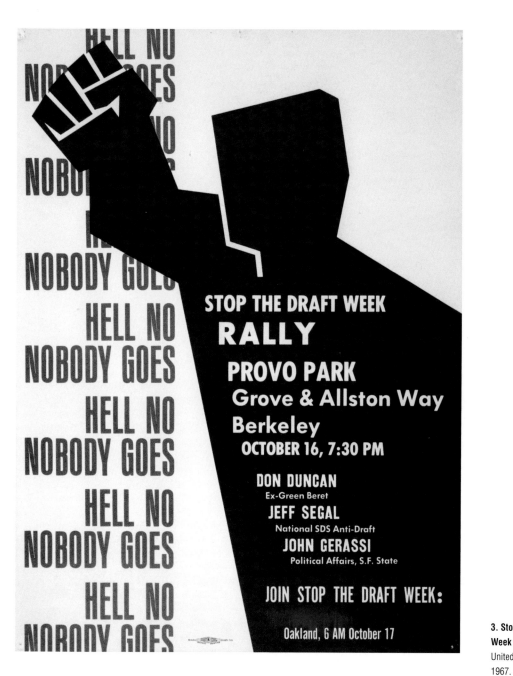

3. **Stop the Draft
Week Rally**,
United States,
1967.

**4. Resolutely Support the Anti-Imperialist Struggle of the Asian, African, and Latin American People**, China, 1967.

JORNADA DE SOLIDARIDAD CON ZIMBABWE (17 de marzo)
DAY OF SOLIDARITY WITH ZIMBABWE (March 17)
JOURNEE DE SOLIDARITE AVEC LE ZIMBABWE (17 mars)
أسبوع التضامن الدولي مع ثيابنا مر ضد الغاشية ١٩ مارس

7. Day of
Solidarity with
Zimbabwe,
Cuba, 1970.

**Don't Be a Silent Part of The War Machine**

**Speak out against Cambodia**

8. Don't Be a
Silent Part of the
War Machine:
Speak out against
Cambodia,
United States,
1970.

10. **March for Peace: April 24**, United States, 1971.

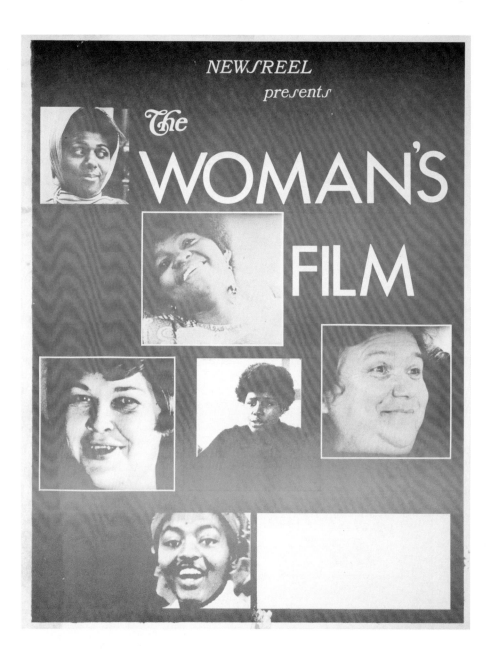

NEWSREEL

presents

The

WOMAN'S

FILM

**12. Newsreel Presents the Woman's Film**, United States, 1971.

Conference for New Politics, whose agenda was to nominate a presidential ticket for the 1968 elections, "Black delegates shouted: 'Kill Whitey!'"[12] In that call we have an example of how the discourse of genocide—extermination on the basis of race—was used to police the racial hierarchies of the movement. As whiteness became increasingly problematic, white radicals' responses varied. A significant number of young white men and women embraced increased militancy, formed organizations such as the Weathermen, and promptly went underground to carry out their version of "the revolution." The alternative for young white radicals was to "drop out" and join the counterculture; they did so in droves. Whilst often leaving out of despair, these white radicals were in a sense complicit with the genocidal drive of the movement in that their dropping out made possible the further erasure of whiteness from the movement.

Importantly, the white radical sense of despair at a movement that sought to erase whiteness was gendered in that it was particularly acute for white men. Alice Echols notes, "White men ... wondered what role, if any, they could comfortably play in the struggle."[13] But for white women, whilst a number of them joined revolutionary terrorist groups, and many of them moved into the counterculture's communes, a third option existed. White women, Gitlin notes, "could take refuge, find community and political purpose in the women's movement."[14] It was amidst this atmosphere of white chromatic anxiety that the women's liberation movement began to assert its position as a legitimate force of left-wing political dissidence. As Echols suggests, radical feminism erupted just as "the movement was ... becoming a less congenial place for white women."[15]

# A White Women's Movement:
# Radical Feminism and the Idea of Genocide

Radical feminism from the outset, then, was a predominantly white movement framed by a racial anxiety. This was not a racial anxiety about the "purity" of the white ranks of the movement—not the kind of anxiety that, deriving from a desire to reproduce a position of *dominance*, has characterized white colonial history more generally.[16] Rather, white feminists were anxious about *their own exclusion* from a burgeoning movement poised to overthrow society. This internalized *terror* of white impotence, although rarely articulated, still haunted the edges of the feminist project and was a key motivating factor in formulating radical feminist aims and objectives. To make this claim is not to deny that feminism responded to the injustices inherent in the material conditions of women's everyday existence. Many radical feminists explicitly positioned their feminism as a direct response to their lived experiences of sexism, particularly of living and working with the male left.[17] However, they were incensed not only about their experiences of sexism, both in and outside the movement, but also about the movement denying them a place in the revolution on the basis of their skin colour.

Indeed, radical feminism was a notoriously angry movement. For Evans, radical "feminism had tapped a vein of enormous frustration and anger."[18] The white women who made up the majority of the participants in early radical feminism were doubly outraged—furious about their experiences as women and, therefore, as second-class citizens, and also about their exclusion from a movement in which their whiteness was increasingly shunned. As such, the discursive practices of women's liberation, the language of the feminist movement's struggle, and the conceptualization of its tactics of resistance and overthrow were framed, sometimes paranoiacally, by the politics of race.

Radical feminist texts frequently spoke in apocalyptic language of decimation and destruction, often deploying the idea of genocide to encode their political message. Drawing analogies between the everyday lives of ordinary women and that quintessential (post)modern figure of human suffering, the Nazi concentration camp inmate, radical feminists painted women's suffering under patriarchy in terms that invoked the spectre of genocide. Shulamith Firestone spoke of the "massacre" of women. Valerie Solanas constructed man as a being whose "proving [of] his manhood is worth [to him] an endless amount of mutilation and suffering, and an endless number of lives." Ti-Grace Atkinson charged that "*men neatly decimated mankind by one half* when they took advantage of the *social* disability of those men who bore the burden of the reproductive process.... The original 'rape' was political, *the robbing of one half of Mankind of its Humanity.*" Roxanne Dunbar railed against "a system which *systematically destroys half of its people.*"[19] For radical feminism, then, the genocide of women under patriarchy became an important ground for their rallying cry. Deploying the descriptor of genocide in relation to the subordination of women parallelled the tactics of other groups within the movement—like anti–Vietnam War activists—who were simultaneously emphasizing the genocidal tendencies of dominant U.S. thought and practice in relation to the Third World and, thus, translated the struggle of women into terms with political currency.[20]

Yet, radical feminists also used the idea of genocide to convey the means by which women should redress their history of subordination. Perhaps the most striking example is Solanas's *The SCUM Manifesto*. Whilst often remembered for her near-fatal attack on Andy Warhol in 1968, Solanas also authored one of the most angrily outspoken texts of U.S. radical feminism. In parodic style, she deployed the modern discourse of eugenics to argue that "the male is a biological accident" whose continued existence was no longer justified.[21] The manifesto advocates a violent and clandestine politics that renders the extermination of the male species as the only plausible solution to the age-old problem of women's subordination.[22] Envisaging a world in which the possibility of sexual difference has been erased, Solanas invokes genocide to articulate her feminist agenda—a genocide based on sex, or what we might call "sexocide." Textually, this is foreshadowed by her allusions to the most infamous of the modern technologies of genocide: Nazi gas chambers. She beckons the day when "the few remaining men can ... go off to the nearest friendly suicide centre where they will be quietly, quickly and painlessly gassed to death."[23]

Irate and incendiary, in many respects Solanas's manifesto epitomized the spirit of late 1960s radical feminism and circulated as a key inspirational text. Dunbar, for example, proclaimed the manifesto to be the "essence of feminism." Atkinson heralded Solanas as "the first outstanding champion of women's rights" and attributed her own radicalization as a feminist to the influence of the manifesto.[24] For these radical women of the feminist movement, Solanas's genocidal vision resonated with their own developing feminist beliefs. Their formative work echoes Solanas's manifesto in both tone and content. Reinterpreting Solanas's call for sexocide as a metaphor for the obliteration of the system of culturally ascribed "sex roles," this small but highly vocal group of women argued fiercely for the "elimination" of sexual difference and the "annihilation" of the structure of gender relations that underpinned Western culture. For example, in 1970, in what was to become a landmark text of second-wave feminism, *The Dialectic of Sex*, Firestone argued: "The end goal of feminist revolution must be, unlike that of the first feminist movement, not just the elimination of male *privilege* but of the sex *distinction* itself."[25] For these women, the radical feminist struggle was about "gen(der)ocide," as opposed to a literal sexocide. Thus, the idea of genocide—whether sexocide or gen(der)ocide—was key to the structure of radical feminist thinking. To understand why and, indeed, to make better sense of the anger with which radical feminism proceeded, it is necessary to turn to the psychoanalytic tradition and its concept of "the abject."

# Abjecting Impossible Whiteness: Feminism and the Call for Gen(der)ocide

In the view of prominent radical feminist Robin Morgan, to be both white and radical in the late 1960s provoked a very *visceral* response:

> My white skin disgusts me. My passport disgusts me. They are the marks of an
> insufferable privilege bought at the price of others' agony. If I could peel myself

inside out I would be glad. If I could become part of the oppressed I would be free. I must do something, something far more confrontative of the system than I've done so far. Besides, I believe the oppressed are going to win—and I want to be on the winning side.[26]

Morgan's description of her "disgust" at being white is the kind of response that Elizabeth Grosz says characterizes a subject's reaction to the abject: "The subject's reaction [to the abject] is visceral; it is usually expressed in retching, vomiting, spasms, choking—in brief, in *disgust*."[27] For Morgan, the recognition of her embodiment as a white subject produces this sense of disgust. It is her white corporeality that she experiences as impossible—it is the thing that defines her as an outsider to the movement, the thing that stands between her and being "on the winning side."[28] She is painfully aware of her whiteness (as never before). She is helpless to remedy it, and its denial is problematic. (How to claim that one is not white when it is "obvious," "verifiable," that one is? How to deny whiteness when the label is not yours to apply? When your whiteness is inscribed on your body by others? How does one claim, or more importantly prove, that one is *not white on the inside*? "Impossible.") It is this condition that she must transcend, but which is also *impossible* to transcend. Deeply stigmatized by the larger movement, Morgan's whiteness is simultaneously irrefutable and abhorrent. Thus Morgan abjects her whiteness. As Grosz suggests, "Abjection is a reaction to the recognition of the impossible but necessary transcendence of the subject's corporeality."[29]

For Julia Kristeva, reworking the concept from Freud, the abject is "something rejected from which one does not part."[30] The abject, that is, is not an object; it is not an entirely differentiated Other but, rather, simultaneously Same *and* Other, simultaneously within, or a part of the subject, and outside, rejected by the subject. As Grosz says, "The abject is that *part of the subject* (which cannot be categorized as an object) *which it attempts to expel*."[31] There are two key points here, both of which can be related to the formation of the (white) radical feminist speaking position.

First, the abject is an Otherness *within* the self that produces a sense of terror; a terror of inescapability. For Kristeva, the horror of abjection is strongest when the subject, "weary of fruitless attempts to identify with something on the outside, finds the impossible within; when it finds that the impossible constitutes its very *being*, that it *is* none other than abject."[32] If we consider this understanding of the abject in relation to the movement, it becomes clear why whiteness should provoke such intense revulsion. It is white radicals' discovery that the enemy—previously coded as the "oppressor" or "capitalism" or "the bourgeoisie," but now coded as "whiteness" or "honkiness"—lies within; that white people *themselves* constitute the enemy. Hence Morgan's statement, "If I could peel myself inside out I would be glad."

Second, the response to the terror inspired in the subject by their discovery of the abject residing within is to attempt to annihilate the abject, to radically exclude the abject through its obliteration. Whilst the subject can never eradicate the abject, nonetheless the desire to do so perseveres. Importantly, for both Kristeva and Grosz, the process of subject formation is bound up with the process of abjection. Grosz states, "The ability to take up a symbolic position as a social and speaking subject entails the disavowal of [the subject's] modes of corporeality, especially those representing what is considered unacceptable, unclean, or anti-social. *The subject must disavow part of itself in order to gain a stable self.*"[33] Grosz speaks of individual identity formation. But in the psychoanalytic understanding, as Freud himself made clear, the production of collective or social subjectivities mirrors the production of individual subjectivity.[34] Through the abjection of whiteness, then, and via a process of sublimation, radical feminism, as the voice of a collective of white women, emerges as a temporarily "stable" speaking position.

If we accept that for white radicals, whiteness constitutes the abject, then we can understand the emergence of radical feminism as a response by radical white women—a translation, a sublimation—of the process of abjecting whiteness. As the abject, whiteness threatened the very possibility of claiming a place, an identity, within the movement. As such, whiteness had to be sublimated. It had to be named as something else—*objectified*—for it is through the process of sublimation, a process of objectification, that the terror of the abject can be managed. For Kristeva, "Through sublimation, I keep [the abject] under control."[35] Thus the abject-ness of whiteness translates into a radical feminist conceptualization of (white) men as the enemy. Objectified, men stand in for the unnameable abject whiteness that must be removed. Now it is (white) men that must be obliterated. For this reason a genocide against men, as called for by Solanas, or a metaphorical gen(der)ocide that will destroy the system of binary oppositions that establishes women's subordination, as proposed by radical feminism's reinterpretation of Solanas, begins to resonate with the white women of the movement. In this move, radical feminism is called into being. Understanding the place of abject whiteness in the rise of radical feminism also makes sense of the anger for which the movement was renowned. The anger of radical feminism was not only directed at the injustices suffered by women collectively, or not just a straightforward anger at the erasure of whiteness, but also an anger *fuelled by the energy of abjection.*

This abjection of whiteness proceeds in a bipartite manner. On the one hand, the abjection of whiteness is projected onto (white) men, who are now defined in opposition to (white) women. This process converts the abject into an object against which a defence can be mounted, holding it, temporarily, at bay. In a limited way, this enables the abject to be mastered, producing subjectivity. On the other hand, the distance produced in this attempt to objectify the abject is always about to close. Kristeva writes: "From its place of banishment, the abject does not cease challenging its master."[36] The abject never disappears—it hovers, threateningly close, still "within" the space of the subject.

Radical feminism responds to this terror with its own form of terror—a call for genocidal annihilation (of men or of the system of binary representation) that is none other than abject whiteness in its sublimated form. But this response is only possible if whiteness is continually, obsessively, disavowed. Thus radical feminism continues to emphasize the "meaninglessness" of race, to insist on a sisterhood based on women's fundamental sameness regardless of other acknowledged but downplayed differences of race, class, sexuality, and so on. Abject whiteness is held at arm's length, and radical feminist subjectivity is established, by the dual processes of objectifying abject whiteness by projecting it onto (white) men and disavowing women's difference by invoking their sameness.

In this process we have, then, a disavowal of the movement's politics of racial exclusion. Or, rather, the displacement of the white experience of Otherness within the movement by radical white women constitutes a disavowal of the racial parameters that construct the movement's exclusivity/inclusivity. In this sense, the radical feminist construction of a genocide against women operated not only to legitimize the feminist cause by encoding it in the language of the larger movement, but also to relegitimize, and hence recuperate, *white* female activism. Yet, this recuperation of white female activism, based on a disavowal of the importance of the difference of whiteness in shaping the direction of the movement, depended upon repudiating whiteness. Indeed, this denial of racial difference remained a trademark of radical feminism until it was contested hotly in the mid-1970s.

Many radical feminists argued vehemently for women's right to control their own bodies, principally via access to abortion, contraception, and child care. However, the framing of the radical feminist agenda in terms of these demands marked radical feminism as a *white* women's movement that resonated very uncomfortably for many Black women.[37] Towards the end of the decade, certain leaders of the Black Power movement suggested that the increasing availability of the pill and other forms of contraception was part of a carefully orchestrated government strategy, veiled by the language of sexual freedom, to commit the genocide of Blacks. As such, they advocated "Black matriarchy" and the duty of Black women not to use birth control.[38] In this context, much of the (white) radical feminist agenda seemed to Black women, at best, irrelevant and, at worst, part of a wider conspiracy to eliminate Blacks once and for all. As such, radical feminists inadvertently played into Black women's fears of a (Black) genocide.

Thus, in many senses, radical feminism's deployment of the discourse of genocide undermined white women's claims to be organizing on behalf of *all* women, and helped to consolidate the impression that radical feminism was an exclusively white women's movement. In this way, radical feminism—a movement forged by and embedded within the racial politics of the movement more broadly—ultimately, and paradoxically, operated to reproduce those same politics.

# 28

Sonia Enjamio Expósito, Lourdes Pérez Montalvo, and Inés Rodríguez Pedroso

# CUBAN WOMEN AND THE TIME OF TRANSFORMATION

**Just ten years** long, the decade of the 1960s was of great historical significance. Within the confines of the Cold War it was suffused by the division of the world into two opposing social, economic, and ideological systems. It was a decade of great wealth in Western countries, but in the post-colonial world there were struggles for national liberation. Both that world and capitalist countries also saw the rise of social movements in favour of social justice. The time in general was justly characterized as a "decade of ideology," "a decade of turbulence," and "a decade of questioning."

In Cuba the 1960s actually began on January 1, 1959, with the revolutionary triumph of Fidel Castro and his followers. As a political revolution to realize social justice for the more humble classes, this triumph initiated profound change and transformation for all levels of Cuban society. From the beginning, the popular character of the Moncada program—a plan laid out by Castro during his trial for the 1953 attack on the Moncada barracks—reflected a gradual transformation of Cuban society. "History will absolve me," Castro said at his trial. Denouncing the existing situation in Cuba, he cited the main problems facing the country—industrialization, unemployment, health, education, and housing—and outlined measures to overcome them that would become the basis of national economic, social, and cultural policy after 1959. The essential feature of the program was the identification of the interests of the majority with the social project, and the implementation of those interests by new laws and policies.

For Cuba, this was a decade not exempt from ideological confrontation: the mercenary invasion of Playa Giron and other terrorist actions fabricated with exterior help; conflicts such as the Cuban Missile Crisis; and the ending of relations with the U.S. government and the imposition of an economic blockade, which continues today. The decade also produced a definition of the socialist character of the revolutionary process. Thus, as one of the most significant decades in Cuba's history, it is the litmus test for understanding the reality of our present time.

With the revolutionary triumph of January 1959, structural changes were established in the Cuban economy that permitted conditions for an underdeveloped country to open the door to socio-economic development. If the economic changes that took place had not been accompanied by a profound cultural revolution that liberated the vast majority of the Cuban population from ignorance, Cuban society would not have been able to attain the high levels of technical and professional education and scientific preparation enjoyed today. The transformation of Cuban society included women. Changes that occurred in the status of women during the 1960s did not occur at the margins of an ethical debate about the position of women; they were and are an expression of the transformation of historical attitudes and stereotypes rooted in Cuban society. Although there are still goals for Cuban women to achieve, the first important steps occurred with the success of the Revolution and the social, economic, and political changes of the 1960s.

# Some History: The Role and Place of Women in Cuban Society

Cuba lived through four centuries under the control of the Spanish empire. At first, from the arrival of the conquerors until the end of the sixteenth century, Cuban communities were populated by Aboriginal people—at least until the brutal slavery to which they were subjected practically destroyed the whole population. Indigenous women suffered the same fate as men. Despite the disappearance of these communities, archaeological investigations and the contemporary Spanish observations provide a glimpse of their life. For instance, Christopher Columbus, the explorer who discovered the island, related how indigenous women performed diverse work of great importance and held important positions in that society.[1] But the genocide of the indigenous population meant that the Spanish colonists had to find a substitution for Aboriginal workers, and they went on to seek cheap labour in Africa. Black slave workers were extracted by force, initiating an era of slavery. The Spanish colonists were interested in extracting Cuba's wealth and mindless of the suffering of those whom they exploited.

The role of women in colonial Cuba is important. Archival documents show that slave women, even those who were pregnant or had just given birth, were forced to work in sugar fields without consideration of their circumstance. The strength of these women, as well as the strength displayed by the male slaves, surprised their masters.[2] Of course, the patriarchal culture of Cuba's colonial period saw all women live in an extremely disadvantaged condition relative to men. Yet despite social norms some women broke their imposed limitations and achieved access to public spaces usually occupied only by men. Some women belonging to the upper reaches of colonial society were involved in cultural activity; others from the exploited classes had poorly compensated jobs doing domestic manual work. In the end, the fight for national independence, which began in earnest in 1868, gave Cuban women the possibility of showing that supposed innate feminine qualities such as dependency, fragility, and submission had been socially constructed. By the late nineteenth century, many Cuban women were active participants with men in the struggle against the Spaniards. In their history of Cuba, Eduardo Torres Cuevas and Oscar Loyola Vega write: "At this time women began [both] the patriotic work of women and the roles as nurse, cook, cleaner, teacher and many other indispensable occupations for the pursuit of the labour revolution."[3] Women who became exiled in the struggle to defeat the Spanish were not immune from the norms of a society immersed in a patriarchal culture. Far from their homes, many of them consciously assumed the responsibilities of the life they were given, including performing roles for which they were not prepared:

> Women were responsible for taking care of their children, their elders and themselves. According to their extraction of class and their readiness, the Cuban woman was a singer, a master chef, a maid, a seamstress, an ironer, a tobacco worker, an agriculture worker and many other things.[4]

Cuba's pseudo-Republican stage lasted from 1902 to 1958. In this half-century only a few situations permitted women to build their own place in the island's society. For some middle- and upper-class women, for instance, limited access to education, admittedly within a sexist framework, allowed a degree of social and economic progress. But working-class women experienced a greater diversification of labour in comparison to the colonial period, albeit a significant increase of compensated work without the abandonment of domestic duties. The majority of women's jobs were in low-wage positions—and the wages were lower than those of working-class men—a painful process to break identity norms deeply rooted in society for centuries. Statistics from the 1953 census point to the circumstances that distinguished women's access to work beyond their domestic duties. In the agriculture sector, men comprised 47.4 per cent of the active labour force of the country; women just 5.8 per cent. In the industrial sector, 20.4 per cent of employees were men and 19.7 per cent women. In the business sector, the proportion between men and women was, respectively, 18.2 versus 9.5 per cent; while the service sector saw 13.4 per cent male and 64.7 per cent female workers.[5]

Although the 1953 census shows the majority of employed women toiling in the service sector, it does not adequately show the scale of female presence in the workforce as a whole. In agriculture, for example, because of their miserable earnings women took on additional responsibilities like washing the clothes of sugar-cane workers during harvest time. Some cooked for temporary labourers employed in the fields; others worked the land, tended cattle, and picked beans with a single objective in mind: to cover basic necessities for themselves and their families.

For poor women who immigrated from the village to the city, two destinies awaited them: being a maid in richer homes or prostitution. The majority, those who became maids, were exposed to a medieval style of servile work and were taught to sew, embroider, and cook without being compensated. Their employers considered that providing food and allowing them to learn domestic skills was recompense enough. For many women, an option for alleviating this situation was marriage. Yet marriage produced dependency on husbands, and in many cases the women were poorly treated and humiliated. Prostitutes inhabited the bottom rungs of society, and the chances of a woman breaking from this aberrant situation were practically non-existent. Working-class life also had a racial dimension. Black Cuban women suffered not only for being female but for being Black. Because of racial discrimination, they were denied access to selected public institutions and state-owned premises. Deeply rooted in Cuban society, such prejudice inherited from centuries of slavery constituted a bitter calamity.

For poor women, domestic work conspired against their physical and intellectual integrity. Many were able to seek wage employment only if they could rely on social services that allowed them to go out of the home to participate in the working sector. With those services being scarce, some left their children in the care of family, siblings, and neighbours; or as a final solution, they simply left their children home alone. The laws supporting women, and especially women employed outside of the home, covered just 30 per cent of registered workers. Home workers, for example, did not receive any social security. Yet, even with these restrictions, some women obtained jobs that were almost exclusively male: intellectual activities, and art, science, sports, and political activism. Moreover, mirroring the late nineteenth century, some women participated in the difficult struggle against the Machado and Batista dictatorships, even surrendering their lives for these causes.

## Changes with the Revolutionary Triumph

Those Cubans most vulnerable to discrimination and marginalization during the pseudo-Republican era were women and Blacks. After January 1959 the development of a popular process for revolutionary change required citizen participation on the part of sectors of society with a high interest in political, social, and economic change. The 1960s were difficult years in the sense that they combined two big objectives: defending the new society and, equally important, transforming the lives of average citizens. Defending the new society, cardinal to the survival of the revolutionary nation, not only meant vigilance against the growing hostility of the displaced ruling classes; it also meant alertness towards the emerging hostility of the U.S. government, which supported Cuban counter-revolutionaries. The transformation of everyday life generated policies and programs designed for the whole population. But that Cuban women before 1959 were discriminated against by class, race, and gender conditioned the implementation of specific programs for them, based on the hope of reducing social inequality.

The economic and social transformation of the first few years of the 1960s aimed to break up the previous neo-colonialism system and establish better and more responsive political structures. In terms of social policy, the focus centred on creating conditions that would allow Cubans in all social spheres to enjoy the benefits of the Revolution. The new political system took up this task; and not only did it try to do so by national legislation, it fostered the creation of local programs to achieve social improvements that could not be assumed by the central government. To this end, mass social organizations emerged, fulfilling an essential role by securing popular participation in the application of programs. In time, this process led to a close identity between the leadership and the people.

The changes guaranteed a substantial growth in basic services and the rise of better living conditions in the humbler sectors of society. During the early 1960s, strong national programs for the general benefit were developed— for example, the literacy campaign, anti-polio vaccination programs, and the training of people to work in the child day-care centres, among others.[6] For this, organizations like the Federation of Cuban Women (FMC) were formed, and these social networks helped create direct citizen intervention.[7] Cuban women were the main beneficiaries of the changes, with each woman experiencing her own

transformation. This process was not easy. The historical road travelled was full of gender inequalities that
touched their public and private lives, both spheres
suffused by a strongly rooted patriarchal culture. Still,
how could Cuban women progress in the Revolution
without integration into all the walks of social life? For
this integration the first step was to join the different
women's associations.

The unifying process began in 1959–60 with the
integration of key women's organizations. Some groups
were created during the revolutionary struggle; others
rose after. One of these bodies, Women's Revolutionary Unity, was formed clandestinely in 1956 as the
United Oppositional Women to fight against the Bat-
ista tyranny. Under its own direction, activities, and distinct campaigns, it supported the revolutionaries; after 1959, it helped with national defence. Another
group, established in February 1960, was the National Orientation and Integration movement, which advocated a national secretary of women affairs and "a
practical consecration of equality for all Cubans."[8] Supporting the Revolution,
Catholic women created a feminist assembly, "With the Cross and the Country."[9]
While keeping within the traditions of the Catholic Church, their purpose was to
safeguard the general interest of the Revolution through co-operation with the
government. After the First Inter-American Congress for Women, in November
1959, and between May and August 1960, important meetings of all women's
organizations took place; to ensure women's rights, they agreed to meet collectively in a general assembly. On August 23, 1960, just prior to a general assembly,
the leaders of the different bodies agreed to dissolve their organizations and create a single association to unify their efforts to incorporate women into public life.
As a result, four national and six provincial groups integrated to form the Federation of Cuban Women.[10] Its principal leader was Vilma Espín Guillois, who had
fought with the rebel army against Batista. Its primary goal was "to strengthen
the unity of Cuban people, around their revolution, and especially of women, not
excluding the nature of politics, religion, or race types, with the end result to
achieve an integrated improvement for women and children."[11]

Vilma Espín Guillois was elected president of the national executive, while
Dr. Elsa Gutierres and Delia Echevarria assumed vice-presidential roles. With its
principal objective being to integrate women into the public sphere, the FMC had
two fundamental aims: ensuring women's cultural and ideological progress; and
constructing networks to resolve problems relating to home and family. Working
with other institutions—the Cultural Council, National Sports and Recreational

Cuban youths participating in the literacy campaign, Dec. 22, 1961, around the time of the declaration that Cuba would be an illiteracy-free territory. Woman Editorial Centre Archives, Havana.

Institution, National Leadership Children's Circle, National Plan for Scholarships, and Cuban Radio Broadcast Institute—the FMC was successful in achieving its objective.

A unique aspect of these years was the opening of spaces for and opportunities of mass popular participation through organizations like the FMC. This situation occurred as a response to the revolutionary government's request for assistance in carrying out programs of social justice. In the process of integrating women into different social organizations, and taking into account their individual skills and work, women contributed to the process of social improvement. Policies were developed to support marginalized sectors: rural women, women in domestic service, and prostitutes. Such policies were necessary to begin to eliminate cultural, ideological, physiological, economic, and social constraints that kept these women in subordinate conditions. During the first ten years of revolutionary power, a series of educational programs were developed and experienced significant growth. With the Women's Leadership Program, founded by the Ministry of Education to aid in elevating women's cultural status, the FMC was at the forefront of many of these programmes. By the end of 1960 the School of Revolutionary Instructors, "Conrado Benítez," was founded. Night schools for domestic workers were organized, and, specially designed for youth from the countryside, the Ana Betancourt school system was created. The first six hundred instructors combined their studies with teaching and were required to organize night school for domestic women, as well as provide courses designed specifically for young rural women.

A transcendent element of the initial years of social transformation in Cuba was the Literacy Campaign developed in 1961; it benefited not only illiterate women, but also the more than 50,000 participating teachers. For these teachers, on the whole young, urban, and in general without previous work experience, the campaign became a landmark in their lives—they were not only educators but carriers of the cultural transformation of Cuban life. For many sent to rural areas, the Literacy Campaign provided the opportunity to understand a part of society unknown to them. In the majority of cases, these teachers, men and women, had never been away from their families; thus they were isolated and unfamiliar with life in the countryside: the dynamics that supported family relations; religious practices; recreation and artistic desires; how to dress; living without electricity; rustic housing with minimal sanitation; different eating habits; and difficult means of communication. In contradistinction to patriarchal

Graduation at Ana
Betancourt school.

understandings, beliefs about the alleged innate fragility and dependency of women began to crumble during the campaign. Women teachers dealt with difficult living conditions. Undertaking the same activities as men and provoking a huge shock in gender stereotypes, they became promoters of progressive social change. The Literacy Campaign allowed women to break the dogma that limited their possibilities of being incorporated in activities outside of private space.

In urban areas, a vast development of school programs for domestic workers occurred. These centres provided primary schooling and, through revolutionary instruction, discussion of day to day problems in society. The schools had consistent enrolment; and for those who obtained a high level of education, acquiring better jobs, especially office work, was a possibility. For example, many domestic workers were able to get jobs as National Bank employees, filling a gap because a significant number of bank workers had gone to the United States after 1959. There were about one hundred such schools, with, in times of high enrolment, 10,000 students. These schools were developed until 1967 throughout the country; after that other education programs for adults were set in place.

At the same time a massive program was developed for rural women, where the initial focus was the teaching of sewing, hygiene, and first aid. By 1963, although initially optional, these courses were already in the primary school

Cuban women at work, 1960.

curriculum. Enrolment was fixed at 10,000 students. Those women who demonstrated interest in continuing their education were given direct enrolment in the next course, and vacancies were filled by new students. Gradually in this decade, student enrolment rose not only at the primary school level but in high school and beyond. Of the approximately 150,000 women coming from rural areas who studied in the Ana Betancourt plan, many stayed as teachers and others completed university studies. As a true expression of equal opportunity and opening new horizons, courses to become agricultural machinery operators were developed and women had the opportunity to do work traditionally not designed for them. Furthermore, they acquired technical knowledge following the increased mechanization of agriculture. Women driving taxis and working as lathe, milling machine, and industrial operators contributed to a profound change in female identity.

In 1961 a program to rehabilitate prostitutes began with a census to determine the number of women in this profession. In Havana, roughly 5,000 women were surveyed, and a rescue process began whereby they could go to special schools to learn a different way of living. This project was then extended throughout the whole island. More than five hundred women voluntarily joined these schools and integrated themselves in regular life: many found work on their own, others returned to their place of origin, and some left the country. In those schools, primary studies were combined with other activities like self-employment skills, crafts, and sewing. The fundamental objective of these schools was to pre-pare these women through basic studies and trades training to be incorporated into the new society and enter the workforce with a different perspective on life.[12] Night schools were created for those unable to attend during the day, in which mainly humble women of colour enrolled. This decision allowed these women to obtain jobs in banks, stores, and other places previously denied them. Their presence in the workforce contributed to the elimination not only of sexual dis-crimination, but also of racial discrimination. Their audacity broke the barriers that had kept them situated in the most degraded social stratum.

Homemakers also sought new perspectives. Taking advantage of eighty-five night schools for women, 20,000 homemakers prepared themselves for office work as typists, stenographers, accountants, and secretaries. School hours were set to allow the participation of women who were doing domestic work, which largely took place during the day. Even though their family responsibilities were not over, night classes gave them the possibility to leave their homes for a few hours. In 1962, 300,000 homemakers finished night school studies up to Grade 6; and of these women, 144,000 continued their studies to Grade 9.

Another aspect, no less important, was the infrastructure created so that women could integrate into public life and finish their education. The cre-ation of the Children Circle in 1962 allowed for day-care centres throughout the island for children until age five. In 1962, more than 100,000 scholarships were awarded; a scholastic timetable was established according to workforce schedules; and lunch was guaranteed in schools. Similarly, lunch also began to be provided for the workers. During the course of 1962–63, school councils were formed to promote parental contributions to the educational direction and control in each school. The Fathers and Mothers for Education movement was created to stimulate both parental participation in the full education of their children and their decisive influence in the formation of the values that the new society demanded. In this process, the state converted itself into being the guarantor of rights and the social provider. This transformation had great influ-ence on families and the dynamics of everyday life. New family strategies were assumed, and adjustments in everyday schedules, decision-making, and the rise of new roles emerged. Many grandmothers took responsibility for looking after grandchildren so that young women could take on outside jobs. There was also a change in the attitudes of men, who discreetly started to get involved in the "support" of women and began participating in household chores and looking after children. Yet this process had an ironic twist. It became important in the erosion of stereotypes concerning work and home care; but it also gave weight to the "double income" syndrome that even today falls on women as an unjust cultural and ideological inheritance.

In the 1960s the educational and cultural breakthrough achieved by Cuban women opened their way to the worlds of science, technology, and politics, raising their importance in all social aspects and, consequently, breaking social stereotypes regarding their supposed "incapacity" and "inferiority." Women themselves started to understand that their capacity to produce, educate, create, and investigate were infinite when social conditions existed to develop their aptitudes. The public sphere opened and, instead of being the compliant beneficiaries of social politics, women transformed themselves into active citizens with an impact on the strategies of social development. Clearly, the rationale that underscored the formulation and implementation of social politics in the 1960s was inspired by attaining equality of opportunity and the real exercise of human rights.

## Social Politics in Its Fundamental Directions

Although the social' politics developed by the revolutionary government during the 1960s through plans, programs, projects, and other mechanisms covered distinct social spheres, the objective was the well-being of society as a whole. The fundamental elements of social politics focused on health, education, employment, and social assistance. In the health sector, there emerged free, guaranteed services, better coverage and quality, the development of preventative programs specifically directed to women, a rise of health indicators, greater female participation within the sector, the education of specialized medical personnel, and more. In education, free admission, easy access, equality, and non-discrimination were all starting points. Courses to improve the training of teachers were developed, and new classes as well as new school centres, reforms to curricula, and teaching programs commenced. In addition, the necessary conditions to guarantee the continuation of studies to the highest levels of education were created. In this context the 1959 Decree Law for Integrated Teaching Reform was approved, and 10,000 primary classrooms were opened in the rural zones of the country. A goal of 4,000 teachers was authorized, and police quarters were converted into schools. Establishing new jobs with better conditions, guaranteeing equal pay for equal work, and providing subsidies to allow individuals from the most vulnerable sectors into the workforce—the disabled and single mothers—were all social policies directed at employment. A reorganization of the whole system of social security and assistance was initiated to include all workers of different sectors and activities and ensure total coverage. Workers' compensation covering illness and common accidents, plus pensions and retirements, was created and funded by the national government. A plan to assist people in need or without family assistance was established, as was paid maternity leave.

Ensuring social rights and equality of opportunity for women has been a struggle and consistent priority for the Cuban project. Access to knowledge made possible the personal achievements necessary both for women and men. The FMC played an essential role in achieving the progressive transformation obtained in the female consciousness, establishing guidelines to define the problems and needs of women and formulating the political proposals that followed. The challenges then and since have been many and great; and while much was accomplished in the 1960s, there is still much to do. The Cuban female identity continues to overcome myths and stereotypes and, in this way, ensure the transformation of the socio-economic, political, cultural, and ideological dynamics that have characterized the country. But while many women in the world in the first decade of the twenty-first century seek to acquire those same rights and equality of opportunity, to a great extent Cuban women achieved those same goals in the 1960s. It cannot be disputed that Cuban women constructed a "revolution within a revolution."[13]

# 29 Michael Egan

# SHAMANS OF THE SPRING

## Environmentalism and the New Jeremiad

**Two things** distinguish 1960s American environmentalism from the rise of other social movements during the decade. First, the vanguard of the movement consisted of scientists, a branch of professionals who, after World War II, were typically seen as entrenched in favour of unmitigated technological progress. This phenomenon produced a novel kind of scientific public intellectual. Prompted by the resounding popular response to Rachel Carson's *Silent Spring* (1962) and the emergence of a charismatic generation of environmental scientists, the environmental movement gained widespread credibility by deferring to scientific expertise. This first distinction led to the second: the production of a new vernacular science designed to inform the public about the severity of the environmental crisis. To gain a wider audience, this accessible science was paired with a new rhetoric reminiscent of the biblical jeremiad, so prominent a feature of Revolutionary America. Like its predecessor, this new jeremiad warned of doom and destruction, but urged ecological—rather than spiritual—awakening.

Here, in providing a thumbnail sketch of the culture and politics that combined scientific and environmental activisms in the 1960s, I intend to examine the intersection between these environmental shamans and their jeremiad. Both were unmistakable products of 1960s society and culture. For its part, though, the new jeremiad ultimately undermined the scientific authority of its practitioners, hindered the continuing success of the environmental movement, and fostered distrust in science.

**During the** 1960s American environmental concerns shifted focus from a heavy concentration on land management to a considerable emphasis on new hazards, transforming the movement from a special interest group to one that sought to redefine how society assessed risk. In effect, risk was the kernel of 1960s (and subsequent) environmental consciousness. In his groundbreaking work on the social dynamics of risk analysis, Ulrich Beck identified an intimate relationship between the technological expansion that occurred during World War II and the introduction of a variety of hazards that defied easy solution. As a result, Beck argued, society had changed its point of emphasis from the production of goods to the management of those hazards and the social controversies that ensued. Frederick Buell, summarizing Beck's discussion of the creation of a "risk society," put it this way: "No longer does society need to deal only with social conflict resulting from the unequal distribution of environmental goods; it now has to cope also with the tensions and conflicts that come from the inequitable distribution of environmental bads."[1]

Concerns arose over radioactive fallout from aboveground nuclear weapons testing and the threats associated with synthetic chemicals used in the new fertilizers, pesticides, detergents, and plastics that proliferated after World War II: these were risks, and they introduced public health as a new environmental priority. At the same time, however, the extent or gravity of these new threats was frequently unclear, or scientific findings were uncertain at best. If scientists disagreed as to the potential hazards confronting the public, how could citizens make independent decisions?

What was becoming clear, however, was that the dynamics of environmentalism were undergoing a stark change in the 1960s. Fuelled by concerns over nuclear fallout during the late 1950s, environmentalism shifted from a movement geared towards conservationism to a movement that increasingly put human health and welfare front and centre. In short, the human body became an ecological landscape worth protecting; human health was more fully recognized as a product of the larger ecology. Thalidomide, foam streaming from taps, polluted water systems, and poor air quality all found their ways into humans and the food chain. That these new environmental hazards were the products of new technological systems that emerged during and after World War II only contributed further to the popular anxiety that postwar technological progress was poisoning humanity.

In conjunction with these new environmental problems wrought by new technologies, the 1960s witnessed the emergence of public scientists or scientist-activists. The new environmental hazards required a more specific kind of expertise, and politically concerned scientists entered into public politics to share their expertise and relay scientific information to the public. Experts concerned about new threats did much to galvanize the public. According to historian Donald Worster:

> The campaign against technological growth has been led not by poets or artists, as in the past, but by individuals within the scientific community. So accustomed are we to assume that scientists are generally partisans of the entire ideology of progress ... that the ecology movement has created a vast shock wave of reassessment of the scientist's place in society.[2]

Similarly, Joseph Petulla observed, "Ecological science ... provided the intellectual basis for and a predominant role in the leadership of the contemporary environmental movement."[3]

Scientific concern added weight to the growing sentiment that a human-made environmental crisis was in full swing, and a big part of the scientist-activists' successes stemmed from the authority associated with their professional training and standing. Carson's bestseller *Silent Spring* had warned millions of the hazards presented by synthetic chemicals. Although a relative outsider in scientific circles, Carson offered an adept combination of fluid prose and scientific evidence that proved a lightning rod not just to a concerned public but also to activist scientists who adopted her approach in their own subsequent activism. The anthropologist Margaret Mead and biologist Barry Commoner had begun similar work in the late 1950s to raise awareness about the radioactive hazards inherent in aboveground nuclear testing. In the 1960s, following Carson's lead, they honed this activism to address multiple environmental issues.

Reflecting on the significance of *Silent Spring*, Commoner observed that Carson's book offered "the first evidence that there was a wide affinity for environmentalism among the American public."[4] His own book *Science and Survival* (1966) explicitly linked science and technology with environmental issues, while also articulating the role of scientists as key social actors in the larger political discussion of risk. Also following Carson's lead, in *The Population Bomb* biologist Paul Ehrlich wrote powerfully about the calamitous environmental impact of human population growth.[5] The French-American microbiologist René Dubos, perhaps best known for coining the environmental motto "think globally, act locally," also wrote passionately about the deep connection between ecological health and the preservation of civilization. His 1968 book *So Human an Animal* may not have captured the popular imagination (or sales figures) in the same way as *Silent Spring* or *The Population Bomb* did; but it did win the 1969 Pulitzer Prize for non-fiction—a moment suggesting both the mainstream recognition of the environmental movement's message and the scientists' place at its vanguard.[6]

As they stepped outside the cloistered walls of the academy and into the public debate over environmental protection, these scientists lent their authority and expertise to activists and warned the public about the hazards they faced. Their reception propelled them even further into the popular mainstream; whereas the scientific community had been referred to as a priesthood, the scientist-activists became the shamans of the spring. Their message was clear. "In view of the large and unknown risks involved in multiple insults to the integrity of the environment," Commoner warned the National Industrial Conference Board in 1966, "prudence suggests the withdrawal from our surroundings of as many synthetic pollutants as possible."[7] Commoner's plea for prudence was the primary environmental message during the first half of the 1960s and was consistent with his creation of a science information movement. As important as the message itself, the method in which it was transmitted was equally critical. In their work to raise awareness about aboveground nuclear testing, Commoner and his colleagues avoided taking a political stand. They preferred to let the public interpret their scientific findings.[8]

For Commoner and many of his colleagues, maintaining the appearance of an objective science was critical. While scientists possessed a special kind of expertise that led to a deep understanding of new environmental hazards, they did not have any moral authority to determine what constituted acceptable risk for the public. The scientists' role, as Commoner outlined in *Science and Survival*, did not involve encouraging citizens to "leave it to the experts," but was, rather, quite the opposite. "The notion that ... scientists have a special competence in public affairs is ... profoundly destructive of the democratic process," he wrote. "If we are guided by this view, science will not only create [problems] but also shield them from the customary processes of administrative decision-making and public judgment."[9] More than a decade earlier, Carson had made a similar appeal in her 1952 acceptance speech for the National Book Award: "We live in a scientific age; yet we assume that knowledge of science is the prerogative of only a small number of human beings, isolated priestlike in their laboratories. This is not true. The materials of science are the materials of life itself. Science is part of the reality of living; it is the what, the how, and the why for everything in our experience."[10]

These sentiments, which gained ground in the 1960s, constituted a marked departure from the emphasis of the Progressive Era on efficiency and expertise. The public needed to be more involved. And this was more than just a warning. Commoner insisted that misuses of science and technology were so pervasive and the technical nature of information so inaccessible to non-scientists that there already existed an "apparently insuperable barrier between the citizen, the legislator, the administrator, and the major public issues of the day."[11] Scientists of the 1960s sought to address this disconnect between experts, policy-makers, and the public. Their main conduit was the science information movement, with its overriding focus of translating technical science into a vernacular language that could be interpreted and understood by citizen groups.

Building off his success in disseminating nuclear information during the late 1950s and early 1960s, Commoner founded the Center for the Biology of Natural Systems in 1965 at Washington University. The Center, whose expanded mandate addressed a host of environmental issues, was the prototype for this new kind of scientific institution. The creation of a new scientific school engaged in collaborative research aimed at analyzing and criticizing the ecological damage caused by new technologies—and other schools like it that followed—constitutes one of the most significant and underestimated developments in twentieth-century U.S. science. In addition to carrying on their standard research programs, scholars looked to publish work in less technical language in more mainstream venues. Moreover, scientists were in regular demand to give talks to various lay audiences. Again, they avoided taking positions, but rather sought to lay out information. The science information movement grew rapidly; in addition to the Center for the Biology of Natural Systems, small scientific research centres sprang up around the country. In 1963, Commoner, Dubos, Mead, and others had developed a larger network called the Scientists' Institute for Public Information (SIPI), which served as an umbrella organization for nuclear fallout information groups across the country. As the 1960s progressed, SIPI contributed to the development of further environmental centres and helped co-ordinate their interests and findings.

This vernacular science was built upon a very simple, yet crucial, premise. Providing the public with the information necessary for participation in political debates about environmental and technological decisions was a form of social empowerment and central to the core tenets of democracy. Commoner advocated a formidable alliance of scientists and citizens. Working together, they needed "to learn how the objectivity of scientific investigation and the judgments of public opinion ... brought [nuclear] contamination to a halt."[12] Similarly, Carson had very methodically outlined the hazards associated with synthetic pesticides and pointed to the foibles of relying heavily on the petrochemical industry, but *Silent Spring*'s prose and rhetoric—while powerful and persuasive—were measured in their tone. Carson's primary intent was to inform.[13] Ehrlich was also effective in reaching a wide audience with his message. In addition to the popularity of *The Population Bomb*, Ehrlich was also a regular guest on *The Tonight Show* with Johnny Carson. He was witty and charismatic, and handsome, and he possessed a deep and strong voice. He spoke clearly and convincingly to a popular audience about the dangers of human population growth.

As the environmental message entered the mainstream, however, the rational pitch and faith that accurate public information would improve political decision-making seemed to run against the grain during a decade in which political decisions tended to spark bitter divisions. Competing for attention with other social concerns—the war in Vietnam, the civil rights movement, the women's liberation movement—the environmental message began to become more urgent and shrill in tone. As more scientists and citizens flocked to environmentalism, the direction of the movement became muddied; questions about priorities stalled much of its success.[14] Another feature of the environmental movement's efforts throughout the 1960s had been the building of links with movements for social equality, for peace, and against nuclear weapons and war. Many of these new allies had difficulty adopting the more restrained rhetoric of public information, and very little desire to do so. Their more inflammatory language infused the environmental movement with greater passion, but also represented a step away from a strategy that had previously served them well.

In January 1966 a group of Boston-area scientists took out a full-page advertisement in *The New York Times* in their opposition to the use of chemical weapons in Vietnam. Regardless of whether or not the agents were poisonous, the scientists contended, the use of such weapons was "barbarous," and "a shocking deterioration of our moral standards."[15] Whereas the earlier science information movement might have pointed to the dangers associated with chemical weapons and left the public free to determine their position, this new tone galvanized a new kind of environmental rhetoric based largely on scientists making moral evaluations. The Harvard biologist George Wald offered a decidedly bleak picture of the future. He estimated that "civilization will end within fifteen or thirty years unless immediate action is taken against problems facing mankind." At a talk at Swarthmore College just before Earth Day, Kenneth Watt warned, "We have about five more years at the outside to do something."[16] By 1970 Barry Commoner had appeared on the cover of *Time* magazine and was hailed as "the Paul Revere of ecology," the revolutionary hero who had warned of imminent danger.[17]

In the same article, Commoner and his scientific colleagues were also labelled the "new jeremiahs." The jeremiad—a term that appeared as a common form of American rhetoric—had always been a part of the environmental message—how could it not have been? The jeremiad form foretold decline and doom, and was a popular method of revitalizing the social and spiritual mission. But as the more alarmist intonations began to take hold, the jeremiad seemed to supercede the more practical efforts of the science information movement. Just as the original Jeremiah's dire predictions warned of the destruction of Jerusalem, the new jeremiahs prophesied the destruction of the Earth's ability to sustain life; both lamented the human fall from grace and saw the human condition and attempts at redemption as almost hopeless. *Almost.* In the jeremiad's rhetoric, there lingered a glimmer of hope to which audiences were meant to cling. The environmental jeremiad aimed to lead their audiences to despair, but then redeem them through the narrowest of hopes.

This kind of tone slipped into Commoner's *Science and Survival*:

> For the benefits of powerful pesticides we pay in losses of birdlife and fish. For the conveniences of automobiles we pay in the rise of respiratory disease from smog. For the widespread use of combustible fuels we may yet be forced to pay the catastrophic cost of protecting our cities from worldwide floods. Sooner or later, wittingly or unwittingly, we must pay for every intrusion on the natural environment.[18]

In traditional jeremiad form, Commoner brought his audience back from the abyss: "We are still in a period of grace, and if we are willing to pay the price, as large as it is, there is yet time to restore and preserve the biological quality of the environment."[19]

Garrett Hardin lamented the "tragedy of the commons," in which natural resources were being depleted with no chance of being replenished. Ehrlich had begun *Population Bomb* with the stark statement, "The battle to feed all of humanity is over." According to Ehrlich, famine and devastation were inevitable. Rigid population control, he argued, was not only necessary, but needed to be implemented immediately.[20] Ehrlich, in particular, was adept at offering such cataclysmic warnings, both in his writings and in his public speaking engagements. According to journalist Stephen Fox: "Ehrlich—with his thundercloud visage and deeply resonant voice—seemed the very personification of the Voice of Doom."[21] Even Carson adopted the jeremiad. Her vision of a silent spring was, due to the invasion of chemical pesticides, one without birdsong. One cynical review blamed Carson for creating "a big fuss ... to scare the American public out of its wits."[22]

Of course, this was the devil's bargain. The jeremiad unquestionably drew attention to and stressed the urgency of environmental issues, but the shamans adopted it only at the cost of moving away from the rational scientific claims that grounded their discourse. Moreover, many jeremiads overreached in their rhetoric, forecasting ecological doom before the end of the decade. The jeremiad itself began to wear thin. As their predictions proved to be off the mark, they hurt their professional standing. Scientists were tuned out as popular culture adapted to or resisted the alarmist rhetoric. Frederick Buell described the transition as "from apocalypse to way of life."[23]

Distrust in science was the result of a series of other factors, too. To a certain extent, the culture of anti-authoritarianism that was pervasive through much of the 1960s played a role; scientific expertise implied a kind of authority against which the counterculture railed. Still, this explanation is not wholly satisfactory. The shamans of the spring, after all, were instrumental within the leadership of U.S. environmentalism; moreover, many of them enjoyed audiences of thousands at the first Earth Day.[24] But this anti-authoritarian sentiment was pervasive, and led to an oversimplification of science and scientists into a single fraternity or cabal that stressed progress and was intimately connected to the military-industrial complex. Some radical environmentalists were reluctant to see scientists as anything more than government-funded advocates of technological progress. This kind of sentiment was a by-product of U.S. scientists' prominent role in the early Cold War arms race; their reputation was tarnished by the discovery of fallout from nuclear weapons, and they were associated with the tensions of the Cold War in general. In some circles Commoner, who criticized the means of production and technological decisions, was derided as a technocrat.

# The environmental 1960s were bookended by, at the beginning of the decade, the emergence of a new kind of environmentalism that interested itself in the pollution of the human body and, at the end, the mass celebration of the first Earth Day, April 22, 1970. The 1960s then played a crucial role in the history of U.S. environmental consciousness. However, in its rise into mainstream politics we might also perceive and understand environmentalism's continuing failings. While the jeremiad was instrumental in garnering attention to the environmental cause, it also moved the environmental movement away from the scientific evidence that might have helped to advance its claims in both popular opinion and in legislative change. Its warnings of doom and destruction were less effective over time and clearly proved themselves to be incompatible with the new hedonism that swept American cultures in the 1970s. The energies and activisms that drove environmental concerns in the 1960s wore thin during a subsequent decade in which the ongoing war in Vietnam, the oil embargo, and economic stagflation commanded more attention and fractured the links that brought together would-be allies.

What had started as a movement of scientific shamans who inspired an "Age of Ecology" and offered hope through ecological progress devolved through the 1960s into a series of gloomy and increasingly alarming prophecies of ecological apocalypse. The positive message, which empowered the public through information, was replaced with something more negative. The most alarmist predictions of that message never did materialize, thus alienating many of those concerned from the authority that had served as an early bulwark of the new environmental movement.

# 30 Edwin Martini

# More Dangerous Than Bombs or Bullets

## Agent Orange, Dioxin, and the Environmental Imaginary

**On January 7, 1971,** Operation Ranch Hand flew its final official herbicide mission in Vietnam. Over the previous decade the United States and its South Vietnamese allies had dropped over 72 million litres of chemical agents on two and a half million acres to defoliate the jungles and limit the access of the National Liberation Front (NLF) to local food supplies. Of that 72 million litres, about 62 per cent was made up of Agent Orange, a herbicide that by 1971 was known to contain often dangerous levels of dioxin, a potentially deadly poison.[1] By late 1970, largely due to growing health concerns about the presence of dioxin in herbicides used in the United States as well as in South Vietnam, President Richard Nixon ordered his military commanders to phase out all herbicide operations in Vietnam. Nobody told Russell Bliss.

Bliss was a waste-oil hauler operating in rural Missouri, about thirty miles west of St. Louis. Around the same time Operation Ranch Hand was being phased out, Bliss contracted with the Independent Petrochemical Corporation to remove "still-bottom" waste from reactors at a trichlorophenol plant in Verona, Missouri. Although in 1971 the plant was owned by Independent Petrochemical, some of the still-bottom waste had been in the tanks since the early 1960s, when the plant was owned by Hoffman-Taff, one of several major chemical companies contracting with the U.S. government to produce Agent Orange. Over time the dioxin content in these still-bottoms had risen to levels of thousands of parts per million (ppm), far higher than the normal concentrations found in the herbicides used in Vietnam.[2] In addition to seeing to waste-oil disposal, Bliss contracted with local constituencies to spray his oil products as a dust-control agent. Over the next several months Bliss mixed the still-bottoms from Verona with other waste oils, which he then used to spray dusty horse stables, farms, and dirt roads in and around Times Beach, Missouri. The spray that Bliss used contained between 306 and 356 ppm, a total of between 12 and 14 pounds of heavily concentrated dioxin. By 1974 the Centers for Disease Control (CDC) had been called in to investigate the cause of the human health problems and the deaths of dozens of animals in Times Beach. They eventually found soil samples containing well over 30 ppm dioxin.[3]

Reactions to chemical exposure both abroad and domestically thus came from two very different communities: members and former members of the National Liberation Front for South Vietnam and the residents of Times Beach, Missouri. Clearly, these subjects and their communities were exposed to dioxin in markedly different manners. Still, despite this most obvious difference, the responses to Agent Orange and dioxin showed several similarities. In the face of uncertainty about the effects of exposure to these chemicals, the two constituencies each questioned both state-based and scientific authority.

The reactions also reveal the ways in which the people involved contributed to what Christopher Sellers and others have termed the "environmental imaginary" that emerged during the 1960s. In this formulation, citizens and activists used local-global geographic conceptions and a focus on the human body as environmentally threatened to develop various forms of ecologically-oriented politics. While this social formulation had become fairly stable by the end of the 1960s, the legal and policy formulations for which "environmentalists" had fought came to valorize objectively measurable scientific effects on "nature" over subjective and experiential effects on the body. Later events such as the Love Canal disaster in New York, Sellers concludes, helped lead to the reimagining of a "naturalistic human ecology beyond the pale of the biologically provable."[4] The reactions to chemical exposure in Vietnam and Times Beach reveal both that this reimagining of the environment occurred across cultural and geographic divisions and that, in both cases, the populations involved framed these formulations in response to the perceived inadequacies not only of scientific knowledge but also of the state authorities that were disseminating that knowledge.

# The NLF, the Village War, and "The Spray"

Interviews conducted in Vietnam by the Rand corporation provide one of the few written records about the reactions of the people there to the defoliation and crop destruction programs undertaken by the United States and Army of the Republic of Vietnam (ARVN) in the early years of the war. The interviews reveal that the NLF (often referred to in the interviews as "VC," for Viet Cong) was fairly effective in preparing villages for the occurrence of chemical missions as the frequency of herbicide missions increased after 1964.[5] Front cadres attempted to explain to villagers, accurately, that the United States was using different types of chemicals for different types of missions, distinguishing between defoliation (which would have used primarily Agent Orange) and crop destruction missions (which would have normally used Agent Blue, a cacadylic acid compound containing arsenic).

NLF cadres, according to several interviewees, told the locals that if they did not cover their mouths and noses they would have difficulty breathing and could perhaps even die, a claim that villagers became increasingly sceptical of as the war went on.[6] In fact, aside from a handful of interviewees who claimed "minor medical concerns," there are few accounts of immediate and short-term health problems resulting from exposure to "the spray." Former Front members said that on occasion they experienced fever, dizziness, or nausea, but that the symptoms quickly faded. These claims were just as common as those who had "heard stories" of health problems, including fatalities, but had not themselves witnessed any such incidents. There were no mentions of serious skin rashes, like chloracne, recognized by scientists, doctors, and epidemiologists as hallmarks of high levels of dioxin exposure. This is not to suggest that the sprays in question were not chemical agents, or that, in the case of Agent Orange missions, they did not contain dioxin; only that the scientific knowledge being dispersed by the Front often did not match the experiential reality of the villagers. As one subject put it, "People worried about the chemicals until they saw no one died."[7]

While the effectiveness of the Ranch Hand missions in limiting the Front's movement and its food supply was much debated among military commanders at the time, the Rand interviews suggest that the most significant threat to the NLF posed by the chemical war came not when the Front's food supply began to erode, but when the basis for its propaganda about the program began to erode. Over time villagers in several provinces began to realize that the spray was not as dangerous (at least in the short term) as the Front claimed, and, moreover, that the presence of the NLF in their area was exposing local villages to repeated chemical attacks, which were in turn undermining their way of life, their food supply, and their economic lifeblood. Just as the presence of the Front in an area would lead to U.S./ARVN patrols through local villages and increase the likelihood of air attacks and civilian casualties, that presence could also draw "the spray," increasing the likelihood of crop destructions. As the chemical war escalated after 1965, many villagers began to question the Front through the lenses of scientific and political authority.

As a civilian near the village of My Tho put it: "When the chemicals were first sprayed, the people were all excited and frightened. Thus, when the Front called on them to protest to the government of Vietnam (GVN) against the sprayings, they agreed and responded enthusiastically." But later on, the same figure noted, "As they saw that nothing happen [sic] and nobody was going to die, they stopped thinking about the chemicals."[8] An education cadre familiar with the program concurred:

> Before the aircraft sprayed chemicals, the people had heard a lot from the VC about how the Americans sprayed chemicals to kill the people and destroy the crops. After the sprayings the people found that only the crops were destroyed and that the people weren't affected. They realized that the VC's propaganda was only partly true; that is, the chemicals only destroyed the crops and didn't kill the people.[9]

The explanation from local Front leaders was not that they had intentionally misled the local population about the possible health effects of the chemical agents, but rather that their own studies had led them to believe that the spray could have potentially deadly effects. "The documents which we studied said the chemicals could be deadly for the people," explained a Front education cadre. "In our studies, we learned that the chemicals were very dangerous to our health and that they could kill people. But actually I didn't find them very harmful to men and animals."[10]

The set of responses that best reveal experiential concerns about bodily harm from the intrusion of chemical agents into locals' lives came from a question asked near the end of every interview: "In your opinion, which is more dangerous, the chemical spraying or bombings?" Given the level of bombing that many of these same areas were experiencing during this period, this is not an insignificant comparison. Despite the claims in most of the interviews that people had come to believe that the sprays were less harmful than they were originally told, the majority of the interviewees expressed their belief that the spray remained more dangerous than bombings because of its intrusion on their bodies and their land.

One interviewee found the spray "much more dangerous than bombs and bullets. You can avoid bombs and bullets by hiding in underground trenches, but you cannot protect yourself against the spray, especially when the operation is carried out at night. Furthermore, the spray destroys crops and causes much damage. Bombs and bullets can't destroy crops to that extent."[11] A defector from the Front responded, "We would rather be killed by bombs than be poisoned by chemicals or starved to death." In his opinion, he noted, "Spraying is like a bomb—a bomb with a delayed fuse."[12] Another former member of the Front summed up the general local reaction to the spray, and to the war in general, when he replied to the question asked of every interviewee: Whom did [the villagers] blame? "They blamed both sides, he noted. "They blamed the VC for their own presence which brought damage to the crops. They also blamed the GVN for not taking people into the consideration before spraying. They, the innocent villagers, were caught between and were hurt.... I think the bombs and shells hurt the VC forces most. Most of the victims of the chemical spraying were innocent people. Myself, I'm scared of them all."[13]

Aside from demonstrating the strains of war for the Front and local villagers, these stories also reveal how Vietnamese villagers and soldiers negotiated the new agents in their villages, bodies, and everyday lives. The chemical agents destroyed crops and defoliated forests, actively altering the landscapes of the region. They added to the fears of villagers already caught in the midst of an increasingly deadly war. Indeed, even when villagers did not experience the harm predicted by the NLF, many still found that the spray was feared more than the bombs from U.S. planes. The erosion of the Front's authority on scientific matters appears to have been a factor in challenging its larger political authority in the countryside, but it also demonstrates how Vietnamese villagers were imagining the long-term implications of the chemical war.

The NLF and local villagers were discovering first-hand what scientists from around the world would come to learn several years later: that Agent Orange and other chemical agents deployed by the United States and ARVN forces resist a great many forms of scientific analysis and simplification. Whether in the field or in the laboratory, Agent Orange and its associated dioxin, along with the other chemicals used by the United States, have long stumped experts in a number of fields to the extent that they cannot definitively answer the types of questions that South Vietnamese villagers were asking of the Front. Years later, U.S. doctors at the Veterans Administration and epidemiologists at the Environmental Protection Agency (EPA) would be in similar predicaments; the responses they received from their constituencies echoed many of the concerns offered by Vietnamese villagers in the 1960s.

# "Ignorance Is Bliss:" Agent Orange and the Times Beach Dioxin Disaster

After Russell Bliss sprayed his dioxin-infused waste oil and the initial investigations revealed the soil to be contained with dioxin, the Centers for Disease Control, which was leading the investigation, recommended that the contaminated soil be removed and either buried or incinerated. The matter eventually died amidst the infighting between various state and federal bureaucracies; much of the contaminated soil was left in place, though particularly contaminated spots were cleaned; and the lawsuits from cases against Bliss were settled out of court.

Yet two events conspired to keep the story going. First, as part of an ongoing Environmental Protection Agency investigation into health concerns in Missouri, a former employee at the Verona plant where Agent Orange had once been produced, and which many in the area believed to be source of the dioxin problems, revealed to EPA investigators that nearly 100 drums of chemical waste, later found to contain over 2,000 ppm dioxin, had been illegally buried at several sites around Missouri. Second, while the EPA investigation and assessment continued into the fall of 1982, the town of Times Beach, which sat on the edge of the Meramec River, flooded. The EPA tests at Times Beach, completed on December 3, confirmed the persistence of heavy amounts of dioxin in the soil. The Meramec overflowed its banks on December 4, leading to concerns that the dioxin was now spread across the entire area, making Times Beach uninhabitable. Although the actual hazards posed by staying in the area would be debated for several more years, the federal government and the state of Missouri eventually bought out the town, leaving a potentially toxic ghost town where Times Beach once stood.

By the time the Missouri dioxin episode began to unravel in the early 1980s, the war in Vietnam had been over for several years, but attention to Agent Orange and dioxin was growing due to the claims of U.S. veterans of the war that they had been exposed to the chemical and were suffering serious health problems as a result. While the Veterans Administration (VA) and the federal government continued to deny that most veterans had been exposed or that such exposure was harmful in the manner in which veterans were suggesting, the issue of Agent Orange became the subject of litigation when a class action suit of veterans launched what would become the largest tort liability case in history.[14] Commenting on another case involving Missouri railroad workers exposed to dioxin after a railway accident, Dr. Gary Spivey, who was leading the Agent Orange study being conducted by the VA, argued, "The fear which is generated by current publicity is very likely to be the most serious consequence of Agent Orange."[15]

As was the case in Vietnam, the uncertainties faced by Times Beach residents were a function of the extent to which dioxin pervaded their everyday lives and their immediate surroundings. Confusing and conflicting statements from various authorities further complicated this realization. Particularly after the flood damage, Times Beach residents were forced to choose among many possible risks. "We are afraid of the chemicals, but we are worried about the rats and snakes first," local resident Donna Mansker told *The New York Times* on Christmas Day, 1982. "We must put our fears in order. Surviving is the bigger problem."[16]

After the government revealed that the dioxin had actually been contaminating the area's soil for nearly a decade, many residents adopted a fatalistic attitude that rested on assumptions about the authority of the state and scientific knowledge. Many felt that if indeed they had been exposed since the early 1970s, the damage was already done. Local bartender Faron Rowen explained this position: "Why, if it's so dangerous, did the government wait ten years to warn us? I figure anyone's who's been contaminated done been contaminated. Why put your tail between your legs and run now after you've been living with it for so long?"[17] Or as Donna Mansker, discussing the vegetable garden in her exposed backyard with a "nervous laugh," put it, "We ate lots of dioxin."[18] Another local resident ridiculed the invisible but seemingly ubiquitous nature of the dioxin threat in their surrounding landscape, joking with his neighbour that "he thought he had seen 'a dioxin' run under" his front porch.[19]

Everyday objects that had long been taken for granted in Times Beach began to induce fear. "I used to cut wood for my stove right over there at City Park, " Ernest Hance Jr. told a *Times* reporter. Several articles noted the fear that vacuum cleaners, and the dust inside of them, were striking in the hearts of local homemakers after the EPA released a memo noting that samples from vacuum bags had registered unsafe levels of dioxin.[20] The concerns of many residents revolved around the elusive nature of the threat. "You can't see it, taste it or feel it," the owner of a local trailer park told a reporter. "It's fear of the unknown."[21] An epidemiologist at the CDC confirmed this sentiment: "Under no circumstances would I want to raise a family in Times Beach. There are too many unknowns at this point."[22] Just as Vietnamese villagers were unable to confirm experientially the supposed dangers of "the spray," the residents of Times Beach were unable even to confirm that they had been exposed to the agents in question.

Also like villagers in Vietnam, the people of Times Beach were given conflicting and confusing information from various agencies and authorities about potential harm from chemical exposure. By the time of the Times Beach episode, dioxin was well established as a carcinogen and teratogen (causing birth defects in fetuses) in laboratory animals. The cases of horses and livestock in the areas sprayed with contaminated waste oil reinforced these claims. Despite the claims of veterans of the Vietnam War, many environmentalists, and anecdotal evidence from Southern Vietnam, links between dioxin and medical issues in humans were less definitive. The complex issues of determining risk, exposure, and harm in Times Beach were often oversimplified in public debates, and media coverage of the events did little to help clear up debates over the science of dioxin.

While many pieces demonstrated that the effects of the chemical were debatable (*Times* headlines included "Dioxin's Peril to Humans: Proof Is Elusive"; "Concern Growing over Unclear Threat of Dioxin"), those articles often quoted wildly differing statements from scientists and government officials. "It gets me that some scientists are saying that dioxin is the most deadly chemical known to man," said Rita Lavelle, a high-ranking EPA official dismissed in February 1983 in part for her mishandling of the Times Beach case. "That's not true. It depends on the concentration. In the right concentration, table salt is just as deadly."[23] While Lavelle's statement was *technically* accurate and stated in the context of explaining the difficulties presented by attempting to determine accurately the extent of contamination and exposure in Times Beach, it was the sort of statement that sent mixed messages to the public.

As was the case in villages throughout Southern Vietnam, questions about the uncertainties of the risks related to chemical exposure and about conflicting information from authorities readily translated into questions of who was to blame for the situation. Many initially focused their blame on Bliss, unpersuaded by his argument that he was unaware of the poisons present in his waste-oil product.[24] A popular bumper sticker at the time showed a tanker truck with the word "Dioxin" written on the side next to the phrase, "Ignorance is Bliss." An *Economist* editorial under the same title ran in February 1983. The more common target of criticism, though, was the U.S. government. Some residents of Times Beach used language that was virtually indistinguishable from that used by U.S. veterans claiming problems from exposure to Agent Orange during their service in Vietnam: "We feel betrayed by the U.S. government."[25]

The problem was that none of them—the government, the chemical industry, or independent scientists—had easy answers. Just as the National Liberation Front had provided villagers with the best information available, the U.S. government attempted to do the same. As difficult as it was for Missouri residents to understand at the time, dioxin provides no easy answers. Although Rita Lavelle certainly mischaracterized the potential harm by equating dioxin with table salt, the reality was that determining the levels of dioxin present throughout the affected communities and the potential harm for local residents even *before* the area was ravaged by flooding was a painstaking process likely to result in less than definitive answers. Similar to the growing distrust of the NLF among Vietnamese villagers for its failure to provide accurate information about the nature of "the spray," many citizens of Times Beach and the surrounding areas exposed to dioxin chalked up the government's response to simply being another way, in the wake of the Vietnam War and Watergate, in which their government had let them down.

# Towards a Global Environmental Imaginary?

On the cover of its retrospective on the Missouri dioxin episode, the St. Louis *Post-Dispatch* featured a photo of an abandoned garage in Times Beach, spray-painted with the message, "Gone and Forgotten by the U.S. Government." The spectre that looms over the picture, that which is gone and forgotten, is that of those human bodies, irrevocably altered by their chemical encounters regardless of what soil tests, blood samples, or "parts per million" might reveal.

From Missouri to the Mekong Delta, the millions of bodies that encountered Agent Orange and the other chemical agents developed, disseminated, and deployed during the war in Vietnam have indeed been largely forgotten. The global lawsuits that continue to be waged over the human impact of the chemical war make clear that the regulatory apparatus in the United States continues to privilege scientifically measurable effects over experiential bodily trauma.[26] While the chemical companies that produced Agent Orange and the U.S. government that ordered its deployment are the targets of these attempts at justice and regulation, the longer histories of contested scientific knowledge and state authority are also an important element of these battles.

Vietnamese villagers, veterans of the war from around the world, and residents from polluted areas near chemical manufacturers have all faced uncertainty and frustration as they encountered the global reach and local realities of the chemical-industrial complex. Regardless of specific similarities and differences, these case studies can contribute to our understanding of human negotiations of a world increasingly mediated and overrun by a variety of chemical agents, and to the role of scientific knowledge and state authority within those negotiations. By considering Agent Orange and dioxin as part of that larger story, we can contribute to a greater understanding of global responses to chemicals and the environment—in multiple nations and localities at different historical moments.

Kristin Ireland     31

# SEH REASSIGNMENT SURGERY IN ONTARIO
## Adrift in a Political and Cultural Climate

**Canadians** tend to see themselves as essentially liberal, peace-loving, tolerant, diverse, and civilized. As Sherene H. Razack writes: "A Canadian today knows herself or himself as someone who comes from the nicest place on earth, as someone from a peacekeeping nation, and as a modest, self-deprecating individual who is able to gently teach Third World Others about civility."[1] Thus, in a period such as the 1960s, generally considered ideologically and sexually liberal, in a country thought to foster liberalism, one might believe that the history of transsexuality in Canada would be located within a narrative of liberalism. However, as sex reassignment surgery (SRS) became somewhat obtainable during the late 1960s and early 1970s, the right to *choose* that treatment was, from the point of view of medical professionals, almost non-existent.

The history of SRS in Canada did not follow a single path. Health care is under provincial jurisdiction, and those seeking such medical procedures in different provinces and territories have had quite differing experiences. The first Gender Identity Clinic (GIC) opened its doors in Canada at the Clarke Institute of Psychiatry in Toronto in 1969, three years after the first clinic in the United States was established.[2] A clinic at the Montreal General Hospital began operations in 1971, and a clinic was set up at the Vancouver General Hospital in

1985.[3] Individuals residing in other areas of the country had to travel to these clinics, or to other parts of the world entirely, to receive this type of medical care.[4] Until 1985 the Clarke Institute in Toronto, according to Stephanie Castle, "held virtual sway over the medical aspects of the Canadian gender scene, by reason of the fact that it had been the pioneer and had gathered around it the biggest group of specialist medical caregivers in the country."[5] The history of sex reassignment surgery took shape in Canada, then, under particular circumstances and for particular reasons, and it was a history that differed distinctly from the U.S. experience. Canadian transsexual and transgendered activists and their allies must understand these differing histories as they explore whether or not to embrace U.S.-based activist goals as universal principles. The liberal ideology of choice is a key theme in this experience: amidst the political and cultural climate of the 1960s, concepts of liberalism were put into play—to be used and/or rejected— by both transsexual individuals hoping to attain SRS and the medical or mental health professionals working in the sector.[6]

In the historiography on transsexuality in North America, most of the literature has focused on the United States, with the implied, if silent, assertion that the conclusions drawn there can be transplanted easily to the Northern side of the border. But Canada's health-care system differs from that of the United States in fundamental ways. In 1957 the passing of the *Hospital Insurance and Diagnostic Act* allowed funding from the federal and provincial governments to cover hospital stays and diagnostic treatments. By 1966 Prime Minister Lester Pearson and the federal Liberals had passed the *Medical Care Act*, which extended health-care coverage to include doctor services. Consequently, when the University of Toronto decided to fund a study on transsexuality so that those who passed all of the diagnostic criteria would be able to obtain SRS, the Ontario government covered the cost.[7]

Canadians became familiar with the concept of sex change after December 1952, when an American, George Jorgensen, achieved celebrity status after returning, as Christine Jorgensen, from SRS in Denmark.[8] In 1955 the Vancouver humorist and newspaper columnist Eric Nicol published a collection of articles, *Shall We Join the Ladies?* His argument was that living as a male was undoubtedly more gruelling than doing so as a female; hence, if given the option, men would ostensibly rush to SRS and thereby avoid things like shaving and paying gas bills.[9] He wrote: "If enough more of these boys take the easy way out of baldness, tight collars and last chance at lifeboat, the H-bomb won't be needed. We'll be closed on account of alterations."[10] Nicol was not commenting on the experience of being transsexual but, rather, on the decision to obtain SRS. Yet, in his mind, it seemed clear that such decision was a personal choice made regarding one's body—without interference from outside sources.

At the time that Nicol's work was published, Canadian medical professionals were not yet performing SRS, and thus the assumed impediment faced by those seeking surgery was the availability of money needed to travel to countries in which the operation could be performed for a fee. The liberal assumption, especially pervasive as an ideal in postwar Canada, that all individuals begin on an equal playing field assumed that all who desired SRS had an equal opportunity to obtain it—that personal finance was based on one's hard work and fortitude. Nearly eight years after Jorgensen's first public appearance, on October 25, 1960, a number of clinicians met at the Toronto Psychiatric Hospital—later the Clarke Institute of Psychiatry—to discuss the topic of transsexuality.[11] They intended to determine what could and should be done about transsexuals in Canada; and to understand who could be counted as a *true transsexual* and how best to cure them. Based on a limited number of cases, these doctors made a number of generalizations about *the transsexual*.[12]

Almost a decade later, in October 1969, the University of Toronto announced plans for "a pilot study of the phenomenon of trans-sexualism and related problems of gender identity."[13] Its original purpose was to "learn more about the phenomenon,"[14] not to advocate sex reassignment surgery. By October 1970 the resultant Gender Identity Clinic closed its waiting list for the study: eighty-eight patients had been referred to it—seventy-four male-to-female (MTF) and fourteen female-to-male (FTM).[15] In Stage I of the study, eleven individuals did not fill out the questionnaire about their life history and were, thus, considered "dropouts."[16] A further eleven dropped out after completing Stage I by declining appointments or stating that they were not transsexual. After completing Stage II about one-third were rejected "as being unsuitable for further evaluation."[17] At this point seven additional individuals also dropped out.

Stage III was considered to be an extension of Stage II, in which "the family, spouse, and/or lover are interviewed in order to cross-check the information given by the patient."[18] In Stage III, four more patients were rejected and three patients dropped out. The final phase, Stage IV, consisted of a demanding ten-day evaluation. By this point, fifteen of the original eighty-eight cases were still active, and four more were still in the process of evaluation. The psychiatrist in charge of the study, Dr. Betty Steiner, explained that by the time her report was partially published in 1973: "Eight patients [had] undergone surgical sex reassignment, four male-to-female and four female-to-male (bilateral mammectomy and pan hysterectomy only). Three patients [were] waiting approval for surgery, and one [was] in long-term follow-up and was operated on in 1971."[19]

By restricting who was deemed to be a *true transsexual* and, consequently, who could or could not obtain SRS, the Ontario medical profession limited the bodily autonomy of transsexual people. Individuals who approached the GIC had to take a number of tests before they were allowed to officially enter into the program. For example, doctors assumed that a transsexual who was born with male genitalia but identified herself as a woman should be attracted to a man. Consequently, admitting an attraction to women for MTFs or attraction to men for FTMs could call into question the transsexual diagnosis needed for their access to sex reassignment surgery. Kurt Freund, a doctor involved in the study at the University of Toronto, developed a phallometric test to determine an individual's sexual preference. At the Second Interdisciplinary Symposium on Gender Dysphoria Syndrome in 1973, he explained that the first fifty-seven MTFs who applied for SRS at the Clarke Institute were given a sexual deviation questionnaire; this automatically excluded five subjects because they admitted to being attracted to women and thus were deemed "transvestitic and heterosexual."[20] However, he feared that some subjects who denied being attracted to women were untruthful and applied the phallometric test that recorded penile volume changes while observing various pictures.[21]

In her memoir, Dianna, the first transsexual to obtain SRS in Canada, described her disgust with this particular test:

> The most distasteful test was when I had an apparatus attached to my penis. It consisted of a condom within a test tube that fitted snugly over my penis, this in turn was hooked up to a pressure gauge and the results were recorded in an adjoining room. As part of the test, I was shown a series of anatomical pictures of naked and clothed men, women, and children. When I realized just how personal, prying, and, in my estimation, degrading this was, I flung the contraption from my body, put on my clothes and, stomped from the room.[22]

She explained that Steiner advised her that because she was a volunteer participant in the test, she was not required to partake in anything that went against her wishes.[23] However, we can assume that many subjects did not feel that they were elective participants.

The FTM transsexuals who applied for SRS at the Clarke Institute were judged less on their sexual object preference, perhaps because there was no equivalent phallometric test, and more intensely on their desire to take on the role of husband to heterosexually-identified women. In a video, *Transsexual and Lesbian Couples*, Steiner and Dr. Daniel Paitich interviewed a number of FTM transsexuals who, with their female partners, had approached the clinic requesting SRS. One of the participants, twenty-one-year-old Dusty, was deemed to be transsexual based on his statement that he had an aversion to his own genitalia and abhorred his partners touching them. Dusty remarked, "When she's satisfied I'm satisfied."[24] In comparison, Paitich and Steiner concluded that another couple, Derek and Betty, were homosexual. They explained that Derek had legally changed his name but was ineligible for SRS because both partners "enjoy sex and touching of the genitalia."[25] After interviewing other couples, they concluded, "The lesbians allow genital touching—but in the transsexuals they orgasm from body friction and don't let the partner touch them."[26] The possibility that FTM transsexuals could be attracted to other men was not even broached.

In addition, in deciding who was suitable for SRS the gatekeepers also took into consideration the ability of transsexuals to live successfully in their desired gender role. One report resulting from the 1960 Toronto Psychiatric Hospital meeting praised MTF transsexuals who possessed what they considered to be feminine characteristics and criticized those who did not. For instance, one subject was described as "slender and graceful, *his* skin is smooth with scanty hair, *his* face mobile and expressive."[27] In comparison, another was described as having "an almost delusional belief that *his* figure is almost worthy of Marilyn Munroe [sic] and that, if given the chance to live properly, *he* would be a dark Spanish beauty. One suspects that this is *almost psychotic and those who have seen him and read his correspondence concur.*"[28] The study concluded, "If the total re-registration is not possible with all that may result from it, then operative treatment should not be considered at all."[29]

In comparison, the GIC established in 1969 determined the ability of transsexuals to pass the *real-life test* by requiring them to work, go to school, or volunteer full-time as their desired gender for a one-to-two-year period before being considered for surgery. The clinicians who published the results from the University of Toronto-funded study reported that their subjects were more than happy to wait the allotted time. In one reference video, a transsexual woman named Ali told the viewing audience: "The climax part is living successfully as a woman before surgery."[30] To clarify, Steiner asked, "So you don't regret the fact that you did have to wait and that you did have to establish your cross gender identity very firmly before you had surgery?"[31] Ali replied, "No I don't regret that."[32] However, Canadian researcher Viviane K. Namaste tells a much different story. One of the biggest complaints that arose in her interviews with transsexual people who approached the clinic was the requirement of the real-life test.[33]

The possibility that SRS could be conceptualized as a choice, similar to a cosmetic procedure, was evident in discussions among Toronto medical experts as early as 1960. One of the doctors involved in the Toronto Psychiatric Hospital discussions asked the group, "What do you think of the parallel of the patient who asks for an operation on the nose and insists on having it done?"[34] His question remained unanswered. At no point during the 1960 study did the medical professionals articulate SRS as a viable individual *choice*. In fact, the general conclusion seemed to be "that *one cannot cure these people (in the ordinary sense) so why not treat them surgically and thereby remove their frustration, bitterness and uncertainty,* thus making them happy and better adjusted citizens."[35]

Although conceptualizations of SRS as a legitimate choice were not present among medical experts in Ontario in the 1960s and 1970s, that did not stop transsexual people themselves from imagining that choice existed. During this era, groups like ACT (Association for Canadian Transsexuals) and FACT (Foundation for the Advancement of Canadian Transsexuals) emerged. Clearly frustrated by her inability to obtain SRS, one anonymous ACT member wrote a letter enquiring, "Has society or the medical profession any 'right' to deny us a sex change?" The seemingly rhetorical answer was: "I think not."[36] Imagining SRS as an individual choice generally entails comparing it to cosmetic procedures. But if individuals could choose SRS in the same way that they could, for instance, choose to alter their noses, the power invested in the GIC would obviously have to be completely overhauled. The gatekeeping procedures could potentially diminish, and the hoops through which individual transsexual people have had to jump might be altered. In this context, requirements such as mandatory counselling and the real-life test could potentially be eradicated.

The principal concern with the conceptualization of SRS as choice is that it has the potential to create a consumer model of health care that perpetuates class privilege. The demedicalization of transsexuality would make surgery available only to those with the deepest pockets. In 1973, for instance, a private clinic was opened in Jacksonville, Florida, under the direction of Dr. Ira M. Dushoff. At the Second Interdisciplinary Symposium on Gender Dysphoria Syndrome in 1973, Dushoff explained that there was "no loading of the fee because of the unusual nature of this surgery."[37] Still, it is easy to imagine that overcharging could easily result.

In Ontario individuals who passed the diagnostic tests at the Gender Identity Clinic between 1969 and October 1998 had their surgeries financed by the provincial government. In 1998 the Conservative government in Ontario stopped funding SRS, choosing instead to redirect the money to cardiac care.[38] In May 2008 Ontario's Liberal government confirmed that it would resume coverage of SRS under the province's health insurance plan. While many in transsexual and transgendered communities did not embrace this announcement with adulation, arguing that returning to the policies that existed in 1998 will actually help only very few people and will subject many more to invasive and degrading treatment, others saw the move as a step—however small—in a positive direction.[39]

The surprising reality is that, although during the 1960s and 1970s and until our present day, many transsexuals have utilized liberalist ideologies based on individual sovereignty to campaign for access to SRS, it may have been the denial of such discourse by the legal and medical professionals that allowed SRS to be paid for by the government. In some ways it may be argued that not resisting the medicalized model of transsexual identities and campaigning instead for publicly funded SRS is a way of *using the master's tools* to *dismantle the master's house.* By the close of the twentieth century in Canada, historian Ian McKay writes, liberal assumptions had become "successfully and massively diffused through the population"—so much so that it was now "difficult to see" them.[40] In essence, talking about liberalism for Canadians is like some imaginary fish talking about water—it is invisible, it is everywhere, and it is seen as self-evidently good. While transsexual individuals used liberal arguments based on freedom-of-choice ideology to obtain SRS, the medical experts involved did not agree, which may have helped to have SRS, or at least certain procedures, funded by the government.[41]

On the Southern side of the U.S.–Canada border the experience of changing sex has been somewhat different. In the U.S. context of privately funded health care, the government will probably never pay for sex reassignment surgery. Even though the technology has been around for decades, the majority of insurance companies and health maintenance organizations categorize SRS as an experimental procedure and refuse to include it in their coverage.[42] Thus, while some argue in favour of maintaining the pathologized understanding of transsexual identities in the hope that SRS will someday be reimbursed by private insurance companies, many others have decided that the damage is not worth the potential benefit.

On this side of the border, in the 1960s, a period most often characterized by its liberal attitudes, and in a country in which liberalism has been "akin to a secular religion or a totalizing philosophy,"[43] transsexual people were not granted complete sovereignty over their own bodies.[44] Certainly, for all of us, understanding how these arguments have worked in the past is a valuable key to understanding the directions that future activism might follow.

32    Molly Geidel

# AT THE POINT OF THE LANCE

## Gender, Development, and the Peace Corps

**From the moment** of its inception in 1961, the Peace Corps captured the liberal imagination in the United States, inspiring hundreds of thousands of applicants and countless speeches, books, and articles lionizing its staffers and volunteers. By 1968 Frank Zappa's song "Who Needs the Peace Corps?" could take for granted the organization's reputation as the embodiment of heroic action. In his parody of the counterculture, Zappa pitted the hypocrisy and laziness of "phony hippies" who "drop out and go to Frisco" and buy "books of Indian lore" against the instantly recognizable stoicism, heroism, and genuine intercultural understanding of America's young Peace Corps volunteers.[1]

Although Zappa posed his question parodically, here I intend to take it seriously, closely examining the cultural ethos of the 1960s Peace Corps interventions in Latin America, including operations in two Andean communities. In an era of widespread social unrest, the Peace Corps performed crucial ideological work for its architects, staffers, and volunteers, as well as for its constituents in the United States and overseas. It shaped a discourse that would paint the rugged U.S. corpsman not only as an altruist, but also as a partner in the postcolonial struggle for self-determination. In particular, the 1960s Peace Corps' vision of global modernization through heroic action faced two challenges from the Andean communities—challenges that point to the dialectical relationship between discourses of liberal modernization and revolutionary nationalism. Both of those discourses in turn subordinate women's subjectivity to competing narratives of transformation to modern masculinity and patriarchal utopia.

Modernization theory both charted and facilitated the United States' postwar ascension to global dominance. At the 1944 Bretton Woods Conference, as European empires crumbled, the United States formed global governance organizations whose mission was to conscript the entire world into an integrated economy, replacing the old colonial order with an even more ambitious and violent modernization project. Modernization theory asserted that before a nation could integrate fully into the global economy, its indigenous rural population had to undergo a spiritual shift, transforming from tradition- and community-bound villagers into rootless, individuated labourers.[2] Sociologist Daniel Lerner, in his 1958 work *The Passing of Traditional Society*, argued that U.S. policy could contribute to rise of the "mobile personality," which would lead each individual to make "a personal choice to seek elsewhere his own version of a better life."[3] Economist and Peace Corps adviser Walt Whitman Rostow further elucidated the nature of the individual metamorphosis that modernity required in his 1960 *Stages of Economic Growth: A Non-Communist Manifesto*. Rostow suggested: "More generally—in rural as in urban areas—the horizon of expectations must lift, and men must become prepared for a life of change and specialized function."[4]

The violence required by modernization doctrines, as well as the gendered nature of the transformation they prescribe, appears vividly in founding Peace Corps director R. Sargent Shriver's 1964 manifesto, *Point of the Lance*. Shriver, in his introduction, states that he borrowed the book's title from a "revolutionary-minded" Bolivian official. Though *punta de lanza* translates simply as *vanguard* or *forefront*, Shriver makes the phrase his central metaphor for Peace Corps philosophy and policy. He employs the mythology of Camelot and phallic, militaristic language to articulate the Peace Corps strategy of eroticized foreign intrusion in the service of peace, freedom, and development. Speaking of a Peace Corps official, he writes that he saw the organization

> as the human, cutting edge of the *Alianza para el Progreso*, as the sharpest thrust of the United States policy of supporting democratic change in Latin America. Our Volunteers, he said, are penetrating through all the barriers of protocol, bureaucracy, language, culture and national frontiers to the people themselves. "They are reaching the minds and hearts of the people." The point of the lance is lean, hard, focused. It reaches its target.... Since 'there is no alternative to peace,' this is the most effective power we have.[5]

Appropriating and elaborating on the "revolutionary-minded" official's formulation, Shriver frames the "protocol, bureaucracy, language and culture" of other nations as barriers to be penetrated in succession by the "lean, hard, focused" lance. Protocol and bureaucracy, more commonly understood as barriers to intercultural understanding, cede naturally to language, culture, and nation, instantiating the logic, made familiar by experts like Lerner and Rostow, that the Peace Corps must eviscerate everything around the people it serves in order to develop them anew.

The push to worldwide modernization, and its attendant opportunities for rugged development work, helped to soothe the anxieties of white American men, who in the postwar era confronted the psychic trials that accompanied a newly managerial, mechanized, mass-consumption-fuelled existence (ironically, the very modernity that the United States sought to impose on the rest of the world).[6] The early Peace Corps, and the frontier iconography and rhetoric that characterized it, responded to this crisis of white masculinity by creating tough, seductive American heroes who could persuade individuals worldwide to enlist in the development enterprise. Peace Corps discourse combined elements from the mythical Old West with elements from the new Hollywood: volunteers and staffers could be muscular men bonding through strenuous living in the wilderness, but they were also charismatic personalities who turned their constituents into adoring fans.

Both of these Western elements shaped Shriver's relationship with another Peace Corps stalwart, Jack Vaughn. On December 7, 1961, Shriver wrote to President John F. Kennedy (his brother-in-law) to "urgently recommend" that the president take Peace Corps official Vaughn on his next trip to South America. Shriver told his brother-in-law that Vaughn "knows all the officials in both Venezuela and Colombia ... and is considered very 'sympatico' by the Latinos." He went on: "I make this recommendation with only one red flag. NO ONE IS TO BE PERMITTED TO HIRE VAUGHN AWAY FROM THE PEACE CORPS." The letter closes with a postscript: "Vaughn went 6 rounds against Sugar Ray Robinson 10 or 15 years ago and subsequently was coach of the University of Michigan boxing team."[7]

Vaughn remained at the Peace Corps until 1964, when President Lyndon Johnson temporarily hired him away to repair diplomatic ties with Panama. The United States had massacred twenty-six Panamanians who had been peacefully protesting U.S. control of the Canal Zone; Johnson called Vaughn to the White House and asked him to "sneak in there and get things back in shape."[8] Shortly after his arrival in Panama Vaughn wrote Shriver lamenting his "basically untenable position" there. But he devoted most of the letter to praising his mentor and friend. "I wanted to try to tell you of my profound gratitude for all the guidance, support and kindness you gave me all the while I was part of your great organization," Vaughn wrote. "I have frequently puzzled over whether it was you or the idea of the Peace Corps which was the greater. Finally decided it was you." After pledging his loyalty to Shriver, Vaughn declared: "I would love to have a signed, glossy, unretouched photo of you one day." He then returned to his current troubles: "I really thought I was leaving the Peace Corps until Saturday, the day after I arrived, a Volunteer said 'down with the Canal Zone Company.' How do you stop Volunteers from holding press conferences?" He closed with "Please accept, excellency, the assurance of my continuing and red hot interest in the Peace Corps."

Although he was not able to silence the volunteers, whose opposition to U.S. militarism strengthened as the decade progressed, Shriver did honour Vaughn's request, sending him an eight-by-ten photo inscribed, "To my good friend, *El Rubio*, with many thanks for all he has done for the Peace Corps."[9] Vaughn prevailed in Panama, earning a reputation in the U.S. government as the "*campesino* ambassador" by re-establishing normal diplomatic relations in only a few months. He would later recall that he "didn't do anything brilliant. It was just like a lovers' quarrel in which you realize that the pouting and vituperation don't accomplish anything. I arrived in Panama just when they were ready to kiss and make up."[10] Vaughn stayed on as ambassador for nine months, and in 1966 succeeded Shriver as Peace Corps director.

The letters and events suggest that the arena of U.S. foreign policy in the 1960s allowed its architects to express desire for one another—a desire made acceptable through both references to violence (here to boxing and suppressing volunteers) and the exchange of women, both literal (Eunice Kennedy Shriver) and symbolic (Panama).[11] In the letters between R. Sargent Shriver and Vaughn, Latin America functions like a *Playboy* magazine left sitting on a coffee table. It allows them to enact their homosocial desires through shared fantasies of conquest while remaining resolutely heterosexual. Imagining Panama as a pouting, vituperative lover, Vaughn attempted to win back the country by summoning Shriver's charm—both his charismatic and talismanic power. The physical presence of the dashing Peace Corps idol helped Vaughn imagine the utopian frontier space that the 1960s Peace Corps was attempting to create: a space of violent male bonding in the service of securing feminized territory.

Third World territory had to be secured, according to Peace Corps logic, to transform the men of rural indigenous communities from silent passivity into active modernization. That transformation would make the communities more properly patriarchal. In *Living Poor*, the only 1960s Peace Corps memoir still in print, Moritz Thomsen writes that the Andean society he encountered was "matriarchal by default, and secretly," and that its men were "not working models but something decorative . . . to beautify the beach, to hang indolently from the windows of houses, and to brighten up the shady places."[12] Thomsen's figuration of foreign, racialized matriarchy reads not only as a reiteration of the Cold War logic that constructed women outside of capitalist societies as grotesquely unfeminine, but also as a flowery transhemispheric application of Daniel Patrick Moynihan's diagnosis of African-American culture as a pathological matriarchy.[13] Just as Moynihan suggests that the survival and "progress" of Black America depends upon its ability to conform to patriarchal norms, Thomsen attempts to develop this deviant community by enriching his local counterpart, Ramón. Although he ultimately acknowledges that he has isolated Ramón and failed to change the village, he maintains that "the Peace Corps exists as a vehicle for acting out your fantasies of brotherhood and, if you are strong enough, turning the dream into a reality."[14]

Fantasies of reforming deviantly gendered indigenous communities through heroic, unequal brotherhood also shaped U.S. development work in the town of Vicos, Peru, a community that expelled thirteen Peace Corps volunteers in March 1964. Vicos had been of interest to the United States since 1952, when Allan Holmberg and his team of anthropologists from Cornell University bought the village from a Peruvian *patron*. "Millions of Indians still sit in their mountains waiting for history to begin," proclaims Walter Cronkite in *So That Men Are Free* (1962), a short film on Holmberg's project. "But in Vicos, history has begun." By 1962 the town had become a potato-growing enterprise with an annual income of $20,000. Cronkite reports that the anthropologists' "gringo magic" (seed, fertilizer, insecticide) "initiated the "great leap for [the Vicosinos] into the twentieth century world of science, commerce, and cash.... The Indian in modern clothes, speaking Spanish, thinking like a modern Peruvian, becomes *mestizo*, as modern immigrants became American."[15] *So That Men Are Free* reiterates the all-encompassing logic of development, promising indigenous communities freedom and wealth as long as they follow the example of the "modern immigrants" and leave behind cultural identities that Cronkite links to passivity, antiquity, and misery.

Despite the film's title, Cronkite assures the audience that Holmberg has also brought equality to the women of Vicos, specifically by teaching them how to make and sell lace instead of working in the fields and weaving "rough cloth" as they had done before. Holmberg also urged the men of Vicos to serve in the army, after which, according to the film, they would return "speaking Spanish, with new ideas of a wife, one who can sew modern clothes, things both to wear and to sell.... Suddenly an industrial revolution has everything to do with the deepest desires of a woman." Although no indigenous women, or any indigenous Peruvians, are interviewed in the film, Cronkite, the filmmakers, and Holmberg alike assume that the women's deepest desires are for containment: to stay home and make lace while the men join the army and return to the town as modern entrepreneurs and political leaders. The film declares the Vicos experiment a success, "a model for the U.S. Peace Corps, Peruvian agencies, the United Nations." The last scene depicts the Vicosinos celebrating "their independence day ... the greatest fiesta Vicos has ever seen," while Holmberg smiles benevolently down from a balcony.

When the Peace Corps arrived in 1962, the Cornell team stayed, "carefully measur[ing] every aspect of Volunteer life over a period of two years." After the Vicosinos voted to expel the volunteers, Holmberg and two other Cornell anthropologists prepared a 329-page report to uncover the reasons for the expulsion. The anthropologists conclude that the volunteers fell out of favour with the villagers by flaunting their wealth and engaging in other faux pas. "Allan," a Harvard-educated volunteer, behaved particularly egregiously. He "tried to use a new method of castrating a friend's donkey, and the donkey died, angering the friend's father and causing the friend to run away from home." He also "knocked down a pedestrian with his vehicle in nearby Huaraz, and incurred the wrath of police when he tried to 'arrange' the consequences of the accident." The report attributes Allan's behaviour to carelessness and cultural unawareness, but concludes that the "psychological gulf" created by the inequality of wealth is most clearly to blame.[16]

The anthropologists are less forgiving with the female volunteers. They argue that the "physical narcissism of young females," played a role in the expulsion: "Physical behavior by a few young Peace Corps Volunteers that proved provocative to others created a certain number of inefficiencies among other Volunteers and in relationship with male Peruvians." The report finds one volunteer's behaviour especially egregious: "The physical message of sexual promise this Volunteer conveyed to another Volunteer was so great compared to the reality of fulfillment that this frustration, combined with cultural shock and other factors, rendered the male Volunteer completely unfit to work in Peru." Although the two female narcissists competently taught home demonstration courses and sewing classes, the research team concludes that while "the classes made 'distinct gains' for the women in Vicos, the people affected represented a relatively small portion of the total population."[17] The report illuminates how the Peace Corps' anti-domestic orientation crowded women out of its official vision of American altruism; what looked like necessary charisma in male volunteers became narcissism in the women.

In the end, Peace Corps officials succeeded in framing the Vicos incident as a success story. Latin America director Frank Mankiewicz put a positive spin on the expulsion, calling it "a great triumph for community development." Radical journalist Andrew Kopkind took Mankiewicz's triumphant gloss at face value.

In a February 1966 *New Republic* story Kopkind wrote: "So effective was the organization, and so determined were the volunteers to get the Indians to think and act for themselves, that one of the villagers' first acts was to kick the Peace Corps out of town. Officials in Washington couldn't have been more pleased." The usually sceptical Kopkind credulously inferred from the official account that the Peace Corps had adopted a "daring new look." The agency, he said, was learning from social movements at home how to "promote social revolution abroad."[18] Kopkind's attribution of revolutionary status to the Vicos delegation indicates the Peace Corps' facility at appropriating the language and the look of revolution. The volunteers were able to convince leftist observers at home of their commitment to Third World peoples' self-determination.

Despite officials' attempts to frame resistance to the Peace Corps as minor, scripted rebellions, the Vicos expulsion signalled the beginning of a large-scale trend. Between 1966 and 1971, Indonesia, Ceylon, Libya, Mauritania, Gabon, Somalia, Turkey, Tanzania, Bolivia, and Malawi all expelled their Peace Corps volunteers. The most famous case of expulsion occurred in Bolivia, where the Peace Corps inspired one of the best known and most militant films of the New Latin American Cinema movement. *Blood of the Condor*, made by Jorge Sanjinés and his radical Ukamau collective, was based on the accounts of indigenous women who reported that they had been forcibly sterilized by the Peace Corps (called the Progress Corps in the film). *Blood of the Condor* was suppressed by the Bolivian government until massive popular demonstrations forced its release in 1969. It was eventually seen by more Bolivians than any film before, domestic or foreign. In 1971, as a result of evidence gleaned from official and journalistic investigations, Bolivia expelled the Peace Corps.

The film, a crucial text of anti-imperialist cultural nationalism, demonstrates that modernization theory did not just undergird new global governance organizations but pervaded the very movements that resisted those organizations. Maria Josefina Saldaña-Portillo argues that the idea of development as personal transformation—of individual maturation into masculine subjectivity as a prerequisite for national modernization—not only enabled the ascendancy of new global hegemonic structures after World War II, but also pervaded the thinking of anti-imperialist revolutionaries, policies, and programs in the postwar-era Americas.

*Blood of the Condor*, like the texts that Saldaña-Portillo reads, enacts its vision of revolutionary subjectivity under the influence of development discourse. For example, the film opens as if it intends to tell the story of Paulina, a young Quechua woman. But as it turns out, Paulina's subject position must be evacuated to make way for the story of the journey, to modernity and back, of Sixto, her brother-in-law. The movie and Sixto's quest end with his reabsorption into indigenous society even as he uses the lessons of his journey to the city to spur that indigenous society to revolution.

Early in the film the camera follows Paulina as she rides into La Paz with the wounded body of her husband, Ignacio—local officials have shot him because he had discovered that Peace Corps volunteers were sterilizing unwitting indigenous women. The film tracks the urban landscape through Paulina's increasingly fearful, alienated perspective. The looming gleaming buildings literalize the terror of whiteness, while the electric whine and gnashing machinery speak the violence of the global capitalist system that seeks to absorb her. But we soon find out that the story is already not entirely Paulina's. From the start, the movie depicts women as little more than vessels for indigenous identity and cultural knowledge.

Paulina brings her wounded husband to Sixto, Ignacio's assimilated brother, who casually reaffirms the place of women in his first scene, a scuffle depicted as a routine brush with racism. "I'm not an Indian, dammit!" he tells his antagonist. "Did you see me being born?" In this early scene Sixto not only rejects his indigenous blood but also imagines that it is carried and transmitted entirely by mothers. Likewise, when Paulina speaks she tells her story collectively, alternating between narrating her family's story and the story of her whole community. "We had three kids. People liked us. Then the plague came and death shadowed our children's faces," Paulina tells Sixto, still able at this early moment in the film to both narrate and diagnose the crisis. "I think the evil arrived with the foreigners," she says, and the film cuts to a flashback of her first encounter with the Progress Corps volunteers.

The flashback scene none too subtly allegorizes the secret task that the volunteers perform inside their shining white health centre: the forced sterilization of Bolivian women in the service of cultural eradication, modernization, and global capital. As Paulina walks by, the volunteers detain her, demanding that she sell them "all the eggs" in her basket "for the centre." After her initial refusal, the volunteers attempt to interpellate, or incorporate, her into the modern global social order by hailing her in slow Spanish. "You are Paulina. Paulina Yanahuaya," the male volunteer says, offering her the opportunity to exchange her eggs for modern individuation and subjectivity.

After the first few flashbacks, the film abandons Paulina's narrative frame and splits into two stories, interlacing Ignacio's earlier attempts to determine why the village women are not having children with the story of the narrative present, in which Sixto embarks on a search for blood to save his wounded brother. Because Sixto has rejected his own indigenous blood, the correctly indigenous Ignacio rejects it too; Sixto is not a match (neither, of course, is the incorrectly female Paulina) and so must either buy or beg blood from whiter, wealthier friends and doctors. The flashback structure reiterates the trajectory of development in its move from the rural-communal past to an urban narrative present. The film mirrors and mocks the path through "mobile" personhood and modernization in its depictions of Ignacio's horror and Sixto's despair, both of which increase as each travels alone along the prescribed course from superstitious rural subjection to informed, assimilated, liberal urban citizenship.

But for the film to tell the story of development as alienation and genocide, Paulina must remain underdeveloped. First she is silenced in the hospital, where a young boy must interpret for her because she does not speak Spanish (upon hearing Ignacio's prognosis, she silently cries). Then she relinquishes her narrative to the two male protagonists. By allowing the narrative to slip away from Paulina, the film dramatizes the gendered personal transformation prescribed by modernization discourse, the spiritual shift away from a feminized communal identity to a masculine subject position that must take place before a nation is able to assume its place in the global economy.

Just as development logic underlies and enacts both imperialism and the revolutionary push to reject it, the women's failure at ensuring cultural survival figures at once as the central tragedy of the film and the impetus for the men's heroic drive to revolution. The elders' prayers "that fertility makes our women blossom" go unanswered because the village women are swindled by the foreign messengers of global capital. Although Paulina refuses to sell them "all the eggs," the foreigners obtain them anyway and transform her against her will. She ceases to function for the good of her community, and the men must thus take over as both modern revolutionaries and preservers of indigenous life; the women's failure allows them to destroy the old nation and give birth to a new one. In the end Sixto, in Quechua clothing, returns to lead his people; Ignacio's death has restored him, transfusing him once again with indigenous blood. Paulina, a small and shadowy presence, begins the final scene alongside him but walks entirely out of the frame, re-enacting the numerous evacuations that the film performs. The last frame depicts rifles raised in the air, spurring the community to violent revolution.

The film did inspire uprisings in Bolivia, if not the complete social transformation envisioned by its creators. Sanjinés writes that even before the Peace Corps's expulsion, "As an immediate result of the film's distribution, the North Americans suspended their mass distribution of contraceptives, recalled all the members of the organization who had been working in the three sterilization centers, and received several staff members' resignations."[19] Sanjines' equation of sterilization with the distribution of contraceptives elaborates the film's argument that in a revolutionary society, men will embody and control both virility and fertility. Even as *Blood of the Condor* reveals the racial eradication that necessarily underlies the development imperatives of making Indians into *mestizos* and communities into profit-making ventures, Paulina and the other unnamed Quechua women in the film remain caught between a narrative of development that entails their culture's annihilation and a cultural nationalist vision in which they become little more than vessels for cultural preservation and witnesses to men's transformation into modern revolutionary subjects.

Today, amidst a war justified by images of oppressed Third World women and buoyed by a resurgence of liberal interventionism—and at a moment when the United States seems to be turning to 1960s liberalism for vision, rhetoric, and concrete policy ideas—we might well pause to reconsider the ethos of the Peace Corps. In the 2008 presidential election, Barack Obama energized voters with his calls for increased volunteerism and particularly his plan to double the size of the Peace Corps. He argued that his country's "security and moral standing depend on winning hearts and minds in the forgotten corners of this world." Obama further invoked 1960s liberalism when he stated, "All it takes is one act of service—one blow against injustice—to send forth that tiny ripple of hope that Robert Kennedy spoke of."[20] But a closer look at the Peace Corps demonstrates that service and injustice are hardly incompatible, that the rhetoric of service, like the language of development, forecloses ethical questions about empire and exploitation by rendering inequality natural and inevitable. Those interested in a revival of the left should not continue to confuse commitments to heroic service, cultural eradication, and economic integration with struggles for social justice.

# 33

Jaime Pensado

# STUDENT POLITICS IN MEXICO IN THE WAKE OF THE CUBAN REVOLUTION

**The rebellious** spirit of the Cuban Revolution, as represented by the iconic images of the young revolutionaries Fidel Castro and Che Guevara, played an important role in shaping a new global consciousness of social protest and anti-imperialism throughout the 1960s. In Mexico in particular this key international event, with its social and economic programs that promised to build a more egalitarian society, led to the explosive rise of a new culture of contentious student politics. Inspired by the Cuban example—though eventually disillusioned by some of its contradictions concerning democracy—new and more democratic student organizations arose to challenge Mexico's own revolution as institutionalized by the state in the 1940s and 1950s; student activists embraced a new culture of global protest to denounce the authoritarianism of the Mexican state. These events included my subject here: the radicalization of leftist students who created new spaces of contestation at the National Autonomous University of Mexico (UNAM) during the early part of the decade.[1] Although this phenomenon has received relatively little attention, I would argue that it marked a defining moment in student politics.

Collectively, the new student organizations that emerged helped to crystallize a moderate new left that would determine the political tone, structure, and articulation of the 1968 student movement.[2]

# The Radicalization of Leftist Student Politics

The radicalization of the National Autonomous University of Mexico during the early 1960s was particularly notable, of course, among the student organizations that broadly identified themselves as "leftist." Despite various attempts at unification, however, these organizations never did constitute a homogeneous front. Rather, the left that radicalized student politics in Mexico during this period consisted of at least three factions.

One group that managed to create a temporary but nonetheless crucial base inside UNAM was what could be described as "the traditional old left." This group was distinguished by a close relationship with the Mexican Communist Party (PCM), which, following the Cuban Revolution, began to increase its presence inside the university.[3] Initially the demands made by these student organizations were broadly characterized by a general (and often vague) support of the Cuban Revolution in which "national sovereignty," "economic development," and "anti-imperialism in solidarity with the Latin American people" became the most common slogans. With time, as these organizations grew in numbers and in importance, the demands became more specific and echoed requests by students of the 1950s, including an "end to political violence," "reincorporation of the dormitories and subsidized cafeterias," "scholarships for student with low incomes," and "better schools."[4]

The PCM's support for students in general bore fruit in 1963 with the emergence of the National Central of Democratic Students (CNED). Originally conceived of as a broad student front, CNED aimed to unite all the different national student organizations that identified with the left. To this end it organized three national congresses at which representative delegates from all schools were invited to present their grievances. The first and most important of these congresses took place in Morelia in 1963, with the estimated participation of more than 100,000 students. At the congress a group of students presented a manifesto, "The Declaration of Morelia," which came to define the political tone of CNED as well as that of many other student organizations of the 1960s. In this declaration students presented an analytical critique of the principal problems in higher education, called for "greater national unity," and argued that "only the creation of a truly democratic student movement' would put an end to police brutality and political imprisonment at the hands of corrupt authority figures. In addition, the declaration stated that in order to bring such a movement into being, students would have to make a stronger effort to "incorporate the voice of the people" by reappropriating (from the state) the older banners of the Mexican Revolution, including "popular education," "agrarian reform," "democracy," and "workers' independence."[5]

The life of the CNED was relatively short. In 1966 it began to lose many of its most vocal members to other organizations that found its leadership "too close to the government in power." In 1968 student activists went as far as to accuse the leaders of having "sold" their organization to the state.[6] Still, CNED did play an important role in the rise of student politics. The congresses offered a forum that students used to denounce transgressions on the part of the governing elite—transgressions otherwise ignored by the media. In addition, the delegates' insistence on reinforcing national student unity transformed CNED into a political mass movement that forged new political circles and a new leadership that would play a central role in the 1968 student movement.

In addition to the front endorsed by the PCM, the leftist presence inside UNAM during the early 1960s included a broad range of groups that began to challenge the older generation of leftists. This heterogeneous group included representatives of the progressive wing of the government, supporters of former president Lázaro Cárdenas (1934–40), and militants of the youth wing of the PCM who briefly put aside their differences for a variety of reasons. Some factions joined together to support Ignacio Chávez (rector of UNAM, 1961–66, and sympathizer of the Cuban Revolution) with the common goal of leaving conservative authorities with limited control of the schools. Others united to support the policies of the National Liberation Movement (MLN), a broad populist coalition committed to defend Third World liberation movements, and to promote a better understanding of the Cuban Revolution. With time, this coalition—including a growing number of young intellectuals who became involved in student politics but did not necessarily identify themselves as "communists," but rather as "independent thinkers"—would be identified as Mexico's "new left."[7]

With names such as Nueva Izquierda, Patricio Lumumba, and Movimiento II Declaración de la Habana (among many others), these new organizations challenged the hierarchical, authoritarian, and orthodox structure of both the state-sponsored youth federations and the student organizations associated with the old left. Furthermore, this new generation of leftists looked at recent historical events to underscore the importance of their movement and define its political tone in a more specific way than previous activists had done. They spoke of issues concerning students worldwide, including the accomplishments (and contradictions, to a lesser extent) of the Cuban Revolution, the liberation movements in Africa, the Black Power movement in the United States, and the U.S. invasions of Latin America and Vietnam. But above all, the student organizations of the new left were primarily concerned with the local issues that *universitarios* (UNAM students) believed had a much more concrete impact on their lives, including police brutality and the lack of democratic spaces inside their schools.

To present their demands these student organizations made use of both new and old strategies of struggle. In a more relentless and public fashion than that practised by the older generations of students, universitarios of the early 1960s distributed informational bulletins throughout the city and led numerous torchlight parades in front of their schools. They organized marches to the central plaza of the city and created self-defence brigades to prevent attacks by *agent provocateurs*. A notable innovation was the holding of student assemblies (*asambleas*) in school auditoriums in which students discussed a variety of issues and made important democratic decisions. In addition, reflecting an increasingly violent and aggressive stance, universitarios of the early 1960s made the hijacking of transportation buses and the strategic blocking of streets common tactics of struggle. They became known for erecting barricades inside the schools; and small groups of universitarios would momentarily take over the radio station to inform the public about their movement. Others made a habit of breaking into publishing houses to print their copious manifestos (which proliferated following the Cuban Revolution). Some activists became famous for organizing festive acts of protest involving the reappropriation and/or destruction of recognizable symbols hitherto practised during cultural and civic celebrations. The most common of these defiant acts included the burial of the Mexican Constitution and the denigration of widely recognized "symbols of repression," such as "Uncle Sam figures."

Finally, leftist activity inside UNAM during the 1960s also included more radical groups, which, armed with orthodox Marxism and greatly influenced by the writings of José Revueltas, a prolific Mexican writer and important political activist, sought revolutionary changes with a capital "R" as the prelude to the implementation of a socialist system. In particular, the "R"evolutionary students of the new left were influenced by Revueltas's piercing critiques of the Communist Party for having failed to take a leading position during the labour strikes of the late 1950s; the students, in agreement with their mentor, saw these strikes as the most important confrontations led by the working class against the bourgeoisie up until that time. But especially resonant for these students was Revueltas's critique of the "moderate" new left, and of what he interpreted as the new left's misguided assumption that the solution to the proletarian problem could be found in the Mexican Revolution.[8] "R"evolutionary students noticed that Revueltas not only echoed in his writings what many intellectuals during this period were contending, namely, that the "Mexican Revolution was dead," but, with more resonance, that neither the Revolution's nationalist tendencies nor ideological tones were relevant to the interests of the working class.[9]

Broadly self-identified as "Maoists," "Trotskyites," and "Guevarists," these student organizations were characterized by self-criticism and ideological experimentation. In contrast to the moderate groups of the new left, they represented only a small minority. Like comparable student organizations elsewhere, they believed that revolutionary consciousness was a struggle in which only a few students were capable of engaging. To acquire the proper state of consciousness, they welcomed heated debates regarding a variety of issues that ranged from the Cuban Revolution to the writings of Revueltas, Mao Tse-tung, Che Guevara, and Régis Debray.

The majority of these "R"evolutionary organizations shared a common dislike of students affiliated with the Mexican Communist Party. They saw the authoritarian leaders and practices of the Communists as "anachronistic." In particular, they rejected the hierarchical structure that characterized the student organizations affiliated with the youth wing of the PCM. They accused their members of elitism, calling them "defenders of the excesses of Stalinism," "puppets of the bourgeois government," and "opportunists who only cared about their personal political ambitions." In addition, they dismissed the idea put forth by the moderate new left that all young people were capable of bringing about revolutionary change. They instead argued that "only the radicalized students who had achieved a true understanding of Marxism-Leninism" could lead a proletarian revolution.

Some attempts were made to unite the different "R"evolutionary groups; but those groupings never achieved the popularity of the student organizations affiliated with the PCM—and much less so if we were to compare them to the reformist student organization of the moderate new left. Many universitarios dismissed these "R"evolutionary groups as "provocateurs," while the majority of student activists grew increasingly impatient with their "verbal attacks."[10] By the end of the long 1960s, disillusioned by their failure to forge strong political alliances with the working class and further convinced of the violent nature of the state—as demonstrated by student massacres in 1968 and 1971—many of these "R"evolutionary students moved to marginal neighbourhoods in Guadalajara, Cuernavaca, and Morelos or to isolated mountains in Chihuahua, Sinaloa, and Southern Mexico to join guerrilla armies.[11]

The leftist activism that came to dominate student politics inside UNAM during the early 1960s, then, experienced the same factionalism that had divided the left at the national level for several decades. Yet each of these factions offered innovative spaces of political contestation; and all of them substantially radicalized the student body of the university. Indeed, the demands made by the majority of universitarios demonstrate that the most important faction of the left that emerged inside UNAM during this period was the moderate new left.

## The Principal Demands of the New Left

The form of the left that came to dominate student politics during the early 1960s was represented by moderate students who, echoing the concerns of a rising generation of young writers and intellectuals, also became part of Mexico's new left. This new generation of leftist students took issue with the ideological contradictions of the traditional old left, and in particular they rejected the "sectarianism," "authoritarianism," and "outdated rhetoric of revolutionary nationalism" that characterized the old left—especially as epitomized by what they saw as the "anachronistic images" of Vicente Lombardo Toledano (the most important labour leader in Mexico during the first part of the twentieth century) and the Mexican Communist Party. For them, these institutions not only lacked "a practical language" and "more direct action," but also were part of the same repressive system that characterized the government in power. Instead, the new left that emerged in the early 1960s supported the political efforts of popular leaders who refused to be subjugated to the revolutionary family, such as Othón Salazar in the teachers' movement, Demetrio Vallejo in the railroad workers' movement, and José Revueltas, who in his bold way was more pertinent to their own movement. In 1959–60 these politicized students of the new left would find a more coherent voice through the Cuban example and other national liberation movements. They would adopt new *heroes*, including Che Guevara, Camilo Cienfuegos, and Patrice Lumumba.

Above all, these representative students of the new left spoke of the necessity of transforming the university into a genuinely democratic space, where the importance of political freedom, dialogue, liberty of ideas, society's main concerns, and economic and social justice as guaranteed in the Mexican Constitution could be articulated without the fear of repression. In particular, the students presented a series of demands that would reappear on banners throughout the decade and would eventually be articulated at the national level during the 1968 student movement. The most common of these demands included:

1. the firing of the Federal District police chief, whom students believed was largely responsible for incorporating violent mechanisms of mob control;
2. the immediate disbanding of the *granaderos* (riot police);
3. the obliteration of the "social dissolution" provision from the criminal statutes, which students argued was "unconstitutional";[12]
4. respect for the autonomy of the university, with numerous references to "no more intervention in cultural institutions on the part of government secret agents, provocateurs, reactionary politicians, or the Federal Army";
5. immediate freedom for all political prisoners.

For students of the new left, therefore, the *villains* of this ideological Cold War that characterized the 1960s in Mexico in the wake of the Cuban Revolu-

Student Politics
in Mexico in the
Wake of the Cuban
Revolution

tion were primarily the corrupt authority figures whom the students believed had abused their political and economic power. Rejecting the Cuban model—yet inspired by its rebellious spirit—the new generation of universitarios demanded the opening of greater democratic spaces, independent of state control.

To combat the different forms of political repression, student representatives of the new left expressed the need to take a more active role in social politics inside the university. Convinced that the Mexican Revolution had been betrayed by the state, increasingly disillusioned by the promises of the so-called "economic miracle," and inspired by the social and economic programs of the Cuban Revolution that promised political independence from the United States and a more egalitarian society, they urged students to come together to revive the constitutional rights of all Mexicans, to democratize their respective schools, and to assume a more vanguard approach in relation to the people.[13]

However, unlike most outspoken intellectuals, the new generation of students who identified with the new left refused to see the Constitution of 1917 that emerged from the Mexican Revolution as a panacea for the nation's social problems. Instead, looking at UNAM as a microcosm of the modern world, they argued that democracy could only be achieved inside their schools when students were exposed to as many different ideologies, alternative ways of life, and aesthetic forms as possible. To this end—and with the support of professors and school authorities sympathetic with their struggles—universitarios of the new left founded new magazines and organized an unprecedented number of conferences, roundtable discussions, workshops, film festivals, music concerts, art galleries, and literary contests. For example, with the support of teachers and intellectuals, universitarios pressured the rector to add new courses on Marxism to the university curriculum and organized provisionary seminars on the writings of Marx, Lenin, Stalin, Mao, Guevara, and Gramsci. In addition, with the active participation of various international editorial houses, such as Progreso in the Soviet Union, Pueblos Unidos in Uruguay, and Fondo de Cultura Popular in their own country, students were introduced to a significant number of classic texts on Marxism in Spanish, and at affordable prices.

With the backing of progressive intellectuals, a new generation of young talented writers who questioned the paternalistic and authoritarian nature of the revolutionary state also gained an opportunity to publish work with the editorial houses affiliated with the university. Some examples included José Agustín, Gustavo Saínz, Salvador Elizondo, and Sergio Pitol, who in their writings described a sharp division between what they (and most young students) saw as two very distinct worlds: the authoritarian, moralistic, traditional, and conformist world of the adults, on the one hand, and the exciting and adventurous world of young people seeking new ideologies, alternative ways of looking at life, and fun on the other.[14]

A group of young writers benefited tremendously from the new opportunities offered by the editorial houses of the university, including Carlos Monsiváis, Roberto Escudero Castellanos, Paquita Calvo Zapata, Miguel Álvarez, and many others. They came together to create their own student magazines, including *Linterna*, *Combate*, and *Nueva Izquierda*, and would eventually be given an opportunity to present their concerns to a wider public in *Siempre!*, *El Día*, and similar publications that became obligatory readings for all activists. Collectively, these students used their magazines to put together a series of events inside the university with the intention of promoting "revolutionary consciousness" in general and a better understanding of Marxism, the Cuban Revolution, the liberation movements in other parts of the developing world, and freedom of academic expression. For instance, besides writing articles, they organized literary contests, conferences, roundtable discussions, workshops, and seminars.

Of particular importance were the courses organized during the winter and summer breaks. Prominent international authors such as André Gorz, Erich Fromm, Irving Louis Horowitz, Serge Mallet, and C. Wright Mills (among many others) were invited to discuss a variety of issues related to "the crises of industrialized societies," including the poor distribution of work and wealth, the structure of power, and the role of the media in authoritarian societies. Especially memorable was the visit to UNAM by Herbert Marcuse in February 1966. Invited to talk about his book *One-Dimensional Man*, Marcuse addressed universitarios with a dual critique of capitalism and the Soviet model of communism of which Cuba had become a part. What was most enduring, a student present at the time remembers, were the words highlighted by "Marcuse regarding the need for students and intellectuals to become agents of social change."[15]

# The new left that came to dominate student politics inside UNAM during the early 1960s, then, created new spaces in which activists could speak of "revolution." Still, with the exception of a smaller minority (the "R"evolutionary group), these students did not propose bringing down the government in order to implement a socialist system, as had happened in Cuba. Instead, the new left welcomed different ideologies (including Marxism) in a much more inclusive and reformist spirit and celebrated (and eventually critiqued) the Cuban Revolution to highlight the contradictions of Mexico's own revolution.

The new left created new subcultures and spaces of contestation that allowed students to critique the traditional mores institutionalized by the paternalistic state and introduce alternative lifestyles, but the majority of students were not ready to create a counterculture in the strictest sense of the word. For instance, inspired by the spirit of the Cuban Revolution, universitarios spoke

Student Politics
in Mexico in the
Wake of the Cuban
Revolution

of the need to become "agents of revolutionary change" by creating "an alternative society," but the majority aspired to get jobs in institutions affiliated with the "establishment." They celebrated new sexual mores and promoted gender equality, but most student organizations remained overwhelmingly composed of young men who believed that revolution was a man's job. A women's liberation movement (much less a gay movement) did not emerge from the student conferences or university halls during the 1960s in Mexico. Similarly, the universitarios made "social inequality" and "constitutional rights" their most important symbolic heroes, but unlike other movements of the new left they turned a blind eye to the issue of racial bigotry in Mexico. Instead, the key issues raised by the new left included paternal authoritarianism (on the part of the state as well as of the old left), police brutality, and the lack of democracy. These issues would come to the fore at the national level during the 1968 student movement.

Lara Campbell 34

# "Women UNITED AGAINST THE WAR"

## Gender Politics, Feminism, and Vietnam Draft Resistance in Canada

**An estimated** 100,000 Americans, a majority of them female, immigrated to Canada between 1965 and 1974 to protest against the war in Vietnam or avoid the draft. Despite the large number of women involved, historians have tended to focus almost exclusively on men—on their experiences as "dodgers" or resisters, and their participation in antiwar activism and draft resistance[1]—while marginalizing the crucial roles that these U.S. women played in both initiating immigration and building community in Canada. What is most often missing in the story of resistance to the Vietnam War, then—and what I am attempting to redress here—is the story of the sexual politics of draft resistance, of a prevailing gendered politics.[2]

Antiwar protest, like most forms of protest in the 1960s, was understood to be a quintessentially male endeavour. This point of view was particularly notable within the draft resistance movement, which is not surprising given that only men could be drafted against their will into the U.S. military. Activism that focused on publicly, and illegally, burning a draft card or going to jail as a political statement against the U.S. military machine was activism that placed men at the centre of war resistance. While women still participated, they often did so in a supportive role; their presence in the movement was seemingly secondary to that of men. And while some women enjoyed participating in draft resistance regardless, and made antidraft and antiwar work their central priority, many of them felt that their secondary status was rooted in the underlying sexism that ultimately shaped all women's experiences in North American society.[3]

# Women's Liberation and Antiwar Work

Women's liberation was deeply connected to the work of antiwar organizing in the Vietnam era, both in the United States and in Canada. The development of the women's liberation movement in Canada was partly connected to the political development of the new left and to antiwar activism, and while it is difficult to state whether there was a direct correlation between women's involvement in antiwar politics and the development of feminist consciousness, a rich but ambivalent relationship existed between the two. In the language of the many manifestos and memos of the late 1960s, radical women attempted to push their male colleagues towards an understanding of female subordination.[4]

The flourishing underground press of the sixties provides many examples in which the early women's liberation movement used the revolutionary language of the student and antiwar movements to critique the hypocrisy of male-dominated left-wing politics. Antiwar and activist women in both Canada and the United States made it clear that "left wing objectification is still objectification," as one woman wrote in 1969. The only way of rejecting such oppression was for women to embrace feminism, to be "love guerrillas," reject marriage and "traditional gender roles," and "embrace complete autonomy and communal socialization of children."[5] The expectation that women in sixties-era social movements would remain satisfied with their secondary status, making coffee and filing papers instead of organizing protests and writing policy, led many women to publicly critique progressive men and to name that oppression as sexism. For example, the Montreal Pan Canada Deserter and Resister Conference in 1970 was largely devoted to a discussion of the continued tendency for women to do the "shitwork" for the movement and of the characterization of women who accompanied male draft dodgers as "baggage brought by men."[6] Even an organization like the Vancouver Yankee Refugee group, which prided itself on its progressive politics in all areas, was quite tentative regarding the formal politics of female equality. Noting that in other antidraft groups women did all the traditional labour, such as cooking, one woman stated, "Well, our group tried to at least keep women's liberation in mind."[7]

The problem was that many within the antiwar community understood women's liberation as being separate from and less important than ending the war in Vietnam. Women's groups and feminists within antiwar organizations worked hard to place women's concerns within the framework of antiwar activism, to guarantee that women sat on local antiwar committees, or to ensure that women's groups marched under their own banner in parades and protests.[8] Furthermore, while many of the leading activists in antiwar work in Canada were married couples, the husbands in these relationships often had a greater public profile, even though women played crucial roles in distributing draft evasion and immigration material, or in helping U.S. immigrants find housing and employment. It was antiwar activist and feminist Naomi Wall, for example, who arranged for the publication and distribution of the infamous *Manual for Draft Age Immigrants,* and who set up a job program to aid male dodgers. But in a 1967 article in Toronto's *Globe and Mail* she was simply described as "Mrs. Martin Wall," "wife of a psychology professor at the University of Toronto, who finds work for dodgers."[9]

Yet preliminary evidence for Vancouver suggests that the majority of volunteers in antiwar groups were women, many of whom insisted that women's oppression and the making of war in Vietnam were connected.[10] For example, the broadsheet "Women United Against the War" written by Nancy Knox for the Vancouver Vietnam Action Committee noted that a "society oriented toward war and death, toward maximizing warmakers' profits, is not a society which can meet the real needs of human beings. Women suffer particularly from this evil, because we have been so long denied the realization of our human potential."[11] Women's liberationist groups tried to make connections between their own liberation as North American women and the suffering of women in Vietnam; they demanded a space in which they could make connections between U.S. imperialism overseas and women's oppression at home in North America. In antiwar parades they chanted slogans like "child care not warfare." They sponsored antiwar meetings in which they showed the suffering of pregnant women under conditions of war and occupation, and they publicized images of children and babies disfigured from napalm bombing.[12] They also used the language of sisterhood and of universal gender oppression. For example, the Vancouver Vietnam Action Committee showcased the link between militarism and women's oppression, arguing that the funds spent on war-related causes were needed for Canadian women, mainly in the areas of child care, birth control, and abortion clinics. But they also made global links between women by critiquing Canadian government complicity in the war: "Our hard earned money is contributed by the government of our 'just society' to support an imperialist war which brings rape, hunger, mutilation, bereavement and death to our sisters in Vietnam."[13]

This evocation of sisterhood is understandable, and it is true that Canadian feminists were aware that racism and poverty divided women in North America and worldwide. As they pointed out, "There is a qualitative difference in women's

*"Women United Against the War"*

**341**

oppression.... A genuine sisterhood has to be struggled for and cannot be universal while racism and class differences exist."[14] But any assumptions about universal gender oppression were problematic, insofar as these assumed deep connections and similarities based on gender and women's experiences; connections that were not necessarily felt or understood similarly by women within North America, let alone women suffering under conditions of war, occupation, and imperialism in Vietnam. Many of these tensions would surface dramatically in 1971 at the Indochinese Conference in Vancouver, where questions of war, feminism, racism, and imperialism dominated the proceedings.

Tensions existed between feminist women as much as between antiwar activists and women's liberationists. Earlier women's peace groups such as Voice of Women (VOW) in Canada and Women Strike for Peace (WSP) in the United States did not fit easily within the politics of the women's liberation movement. For example, VOW groups in Canada developed boycotts of goods manufactured by companies that also built weapons used in Vietnam—they called it a "buying with conscience" campaign—and they held public panels discussing how Canadian women might help support war objectors upon their arrival in Canada.[15] The well-developed contacts of VOW and WSP in the global peace movement led to the 1971 Vancouver Indochinese Conference, where women from the United States and Canada intended to engage in dialogue with a group of female delegates from Vietnam. But the groups struggled to find a common women's position on the war, and the delegates ultimately could not agree on a program or agenda. Tensions ensued, with women's liberationists accusing VOW and WSP of fearing public association with more radical women and women of colour. The conference soon devolved into arguments over whether women should prioritize ending the war, ending colonization, or ending women's oppression.[16] As one participant later remarked, the conference ended up in a "who is the enemy game," played with "much shouting and bitterness."[17]

Tensions within the women's movement also emerged alongside nationalist conflict between U.S. and Canadian women. The Canadian-U.S. border was "permeable," allowing Canadian and U.S. activists to move back and forth, sharing ideas, strategies, and even engaging in shared activism. As Americans moved north, many expressed longing and hope for a safer, kinder, gentler country.[18] As many Canadians pointed out, this glorified a country that had serious socio-economic inequality, including civil rights violations and the practice of segregation in restaurants, urban housing, and movie theatres, extremely high levels of Aboriginal poverty, and single mothers and children living in poverty. The influx of large numbers of Americans also led to increasing tensions within the Canadian left. Many leftists resented the media attention paid to Americans, and some were protesting the Americanization of Canadian culture.[19] In the case of the Indochinese conference in 1971, Canadian feminists accused their U.S. counterparts of "U.S. chauvinism," claiming that the Americans took too many delegate spots and knew nothing about Canadian politics and history. Canadian women's concerns about U.S. women echoed those of women within the new left in general. They accused U.S. women of allowing Canadian women to get "stuck with all the shitwork" at events, for example.[20] These nationalist concerns would only continue to grow in the 1970s with the continued critique of U.S. domination of Canadian culture and institutions.

# Bodies and Activism

Both men's and women's bodies were at the centre of antiwar activism and the politics of draft resistance.[21] Within the sexual revolution, women's bodies and women's sexuality were offered as the "reward" of activism for male radicals. When, for example, *The Globe and Mail* interviewed a group of young male draft dodgers in their hostel in Toronto, one man expressed his loneliness by remarking that what he missed most in Canada was "the girls." Clearly, his was not the only complaint. To fix this problem, the Toronto Anti-Draft Program (TADP) held a party specifically for men to meet women. The invitation read: "A revolutionary action group has been set up to round up girls—or bring your own."[22] As the famous "Girls say yes to boys who say no" poster suggests, women showed their loyalty and commitment to radicalism, or showed that they were "hip," by freely having sex with men. As one Vancouver woman complained to the local counterculture newspaper, *The Georgia Straight*, men "say to us . . . my first commitment is the movement, baby . . . it is your duty to the movement to screw with me."[23] The bodies of heterosexual women were expected to serve men—with the women, for example, marrying dodgers or deserters in order to help the men stay in Canada. In Vancouver in 1970, *The Georgia Straight* began publicizing the campaign of Mike, a U.S. war deserter who was seeking asylum in Canada. Desperate to find a "Canadian girl" willing to marry him as an "act of human kindness," Mike became increasingly frustrated by the unwillingness of women to make this much-needed sacrifice. He publicly criticized Canadian women as "parasites" and hypocrites, especially the "politically aware, libertine, existentialist, hip, women's liberationist shit chicks."[24]

But the bodies of men were also at the centre of antiwar activism; the category of masculinity itself was called into question by the act of draft evasion. The body of the draft dodger occupied a complicated space, and rested in a position of both masculinity and cowardice, which created a seemingly unsolvable paradox. Could a real man retain his masculinity by fleeing his country? Or was immigration to Canada a heroic sacrifice of home, family, and nation for a larger cause? Equating masculinity with the courage to fight, and feminizing resistance to military service as cowardice, have a long historical tradition. Therefore, it is not surprising that during the Vietnam era, the rhetorical battle over how to characterize draft dodging largely centred on arguments over the courage, bravery, and masculinity of draft resisters.

To critics on the right, in leaving his country behind, the draft dodger was a coward; to those on the left he was a "cop-out."[25] Many critics condemned draft resistance as the cowardly act of middle-class youth who fled and left the most marginalized to fight in their place. Dodgers were not unaware of this issue, and they knew that leaving for Canada would mean being labelled cowards. Nor were they unaware of the class privileges that allowed many of them the option of Canadian exile. As one man remarked, many feared being seen as "hopelessly bourgeois middle class brats."[26] Some contemporary commentators and later writers tended towards a hagiographical perspective, celebrating the heroic narrative of courageous men who fled the draft for the "moral grandeur" of fleeing to Canada.[27] Those who deliberately placed dodging the draft in the category of heroism put great emphasis on men's bravery and sense of moral and ethical convictions.[28] In contrast, some prominent draft resistance advocates in the United States counselled a principled resistance based on challenging the criminal justice system. From this perspective, draft dodging was "running away" from effective political action or authentic political engagement; resisters with "real courage" remained in the United States and accepted the risk of imprisonment.[29]

Contemporary Canadian observers called these men "cowards," "slackers," and a "passive breed," or "zombies marking time, knowing that they are going nowhere, doing nothing."[30] To others, draft dodging was an easy way out of "the demands of citizenship."[31] These criticisms were not necessarily wielded by conservative nationalists but were often viewpoints held by those who were at least somewhat sympathetic to principled war resistance or even pacifism. For many, political change occurred through active engagement as a citizen within one's own country, and the move to Canada would not result in significant political change in the United States. Dodging the draft, according to this perspective, was selfish, ineffective, and ultimately passive—qualities that marked one's political commitment, and also one's masculinity, as deeply questionable.

For conservative Canadian nationalists, the judgment against draft dodgers was even more vitriolic. Most of the concern seemed to focus on the belief that such men were not just "slobs" or "slackards," but cowards who would "run out of Canada by the back door" if they were asked to uphold their masculine duty to defend the nation.[32] This kind of rhetoric marked draft dodging as passive and apathetic, and the men who engaged in it as fundamentally emasculated.[33]

# American Women: Creating Community

Yet despite these tensions between men and women, and between Americans and Canadians, women who emigrated from the United States became central figures in the establishment of new communities in Canada. Although the experiences of U.S. female immigrants have been marginalized by the almost total historical focus on men, preliminary work and oral histories have suggested that women initiated immigration, were critical of U.S. foreign policy, actively sought contact with Canadian supporters, and were political resisters or conscientious objectors in their own right.

Surviving letters to activists living in Canada offer a glimpse of the concerns and internal conflicts as Americans struggled to balance a commitment to social change with an increased sense of political impotency.[34] Virginia Kanter of Ohio wrote a series of letters to B.C. minister and activist J. McRee Elrod complaining that her university-professor husband did not have the same urgency to leave the United States, nor did he share her strong desire to protest the war. But her "moral opposition to the way this country is run" led her to feel Canadian "in spirit."[35] The letters reflect a range of American women's concerns as the war continued. Some wrote pre-emptively, in the fear that their young sons would eventually be drafted. Other felt deep frustration regarding the seemingly endless war, and the deeply alienating U.S. political landscape. Claire Hurwitt, a widow with two young children in Scarsdale, New York, wrote that she was "torn between staying here to put up the best possible fight against the policies of the government and leaving because there seems to be no effectual way in which to fight."[36]

The process of draft evasion and immigration was experienced in different ways by men and by women. Many women felt like appendages to men in the movement, even though they too had given up friends, family, and work in the United States. Some women came as political protesters in their own right and not with men. They did so due to their own ethical and political beliefs, and resented that this was not understood by the media or by fellow activists.[37] Many such women saw themselves as "political refugees." They were frustrated, as one activist noted, that "the media would come in, ignore the women completely. . . . [It was] hard to live with, especially when you share all the decisions, the work, the pain, the uncertainty, the consequences of exile."[38] The strain that immigration placed on relationships was difficult, and only increased due to isolation from friends and family, and the growing hostility to U.S. immigration in the early 1970s. Janiel Jolly, wife of a war resister in Vancouver, noted the very "difficult" position that women were placed in. Their absence from the United States made little political impact because women could not be drafted, but staying in the United States meant abandoning their partners. She, along with many women, believed that emigration from the United States was essentially a "non-choice."[39]

In addition, the struggle to re-establish families, community, and work opportunities and lives in Canada often fell to women. For example, because men could not travel freely over the border once they had evaded the draft, women became responsible for maintaining links to friends and family back home, or for taking children back to visit grandparents. Loneliness, isolation from friends and family, and difficulty finding jobs created deep strains within relationships.[40] The experiences of draft and war resistance, and also of immigration to Canada, were therefore deeply shaped by gender.

**Efforts to** examine draft resistance within both a transnational and feminist perspective will, I hope, deepen the story of 1960s activism. Gender politics, women's secondary status within antiwar activism, the growing influence of the women's liberation movement, and concerns over masculinity all shaped the experiences of men and women as they moved to Canada. With the ongoing U.S. "War on Terror" and the NATO intervention in Afghanistan, the divisions in North American society over the relationship between antiwar activism and patriotism, and debates over the meaning of war service, are still very much alive.

These debates were played out in the international news media when a group of residents in the town of Nelson, in the interior of British Columbia, announced plans to build a peace monument and host a conference in July 2006 to honour the various contributions of Vietnam draft resisters to Canada. When the story was picked up by the international media, and particularly by Fox News, the response was largely hostile. The city received emails and letters from outraged Americans who characterized war resisters as dishonourable cowards and disgusting criminals. The letters written embraced the image of U.S. patriots as tough men, willing to "kick your [cdn] inbred ass." The outrage grew so loud that the conference was moved to the nearby city of Castlegar, and the statue has yet to find a public home.

Clearly, memories of the sixties continue to play a central role in attempts to re-energize a modern antiwar movement—though without a historical attentiveness to gender, the long decade will only retain its mythical aura, belying a far more complex period of time.

# PART IV

# LEGACIES OF THE SIXTIES

George Katsiaficas 35

# THE GLOBAL IMAGINATION OF 1968
## The New Left's Unfulfilled Promise

**Beginning with** the global insurgency of the 1960s, grassroots movements continue to be activated by principles of direct democracy, autonomy, and solidarity. These now seemingly universal desires stand in stark opposition to the entrenched system of capitalist patriarchy. With these unifying aspirations, social movements today remain globally connected, and spontaneously synchronized actions are increasingly international.

Even when they appear to be constrained within the apparently particularistic forms of "new social movements," grassroots organizing for change after the sixties often contains universal elements. Just as we understand that African-American music is universally appealing, so should we comprehend that women's liberation is in all our interests and not simply a particularistic concern of one fraction of humanity. Movements for peace and nuclear disarmament, for global economic justice and against the "real axis of evil"[1]—the World Trade Organization, International Monetary Fund, World Bank, and the multinational corporations they serve—all overtly contain aspirations that benefit all of humanity. This universality of species interest, an integral dimension of the new left, remains the movement's most important feature and is carried into contemporary struggles against war and neo-liberalism.

Insurgencies like the new left are often portrayed as purely negative, that is, as fighting only for *freedom from* poverty and disease, *from* racism and sexism, or *from* imperialist domination and capitalist exploitation. When we empirically examine the actions of millions of people during new left general strikes (such as May 1968 in France or the U.S. movement's apex two years later), the new left's ideals—what it *fought for*—are brought into high relief:

1. direct democracy—forms of decision-making in which people participate in making rules themselves and determining the content of society's direction;

2. autonomy—self-management; politics of the first person independent of governments, politicians, and hierarchical parties;

3. eros effect—international solidarity; the erotic cathexis of energy that forms among people around the world as they struggle for freedom (regardless of race, gender, nationality, age, and other such unimportant dimensions of our human essence).

In my books I offer empirical analysis of the actions of millions of people in order to distil these dimensions of aspirations-in-action. In the eighteenth and nineteenth centuries Kant and Hegel developed German philosophy's conception of truth and beauty using a method similar to much left theorizing today: speculating about ideas. Turning such idealism into historical analysis of the unfolding logic of freedom struggles requires comprehending the concrete evolution of the planet's greatest natural resource: human beings' need for freedom.

## New Left General Strikes

During climactic new left eruptions, millions of peoples' actions revealed their innermost aspirations. Take the case of the now legendary May 1968 events in France. What began as students seeking an end to same-sex dormitory regulations escalated without warning far beyond anyone's dreams (or nightmares). After a few males spent a night in a women's dormitory, they were chased into a crowded lecture hall by police who, in their quest to punish the rule-breakers, beat anyone wearing blue jeans. Student government leaders from all of France gathered in Paris to voice opposition to the violence, but they were all arrested, leading to further protests, against which the government called in the nation's hated riot police. Nights of barricade fighting activated the people of Paris. The Sorbonne was occupied; workers from factories learned of the struggle; they decided to join. Soon the entire country was engulfed by an insurrectionary wildcat general strike of more than ten million workers. Revolution seemed to be the order of the day. No one appeared to understand how to proceed. Seeking legitimacy, the Communist-dominated trade unions negotiated a stupendous wage and benefit package, but when they smugly presented their settlement, workers threw their lunches and bottles at them. People demanded qualitative changes in their daily lives. They did not want to spend their best years as appendages to machines in factories and offices in exchange for the meagre offerings of consumer society. They rejected racism, hatred of foreigners, and blind patriotic pride; they wanted to run their own affairs and have lives worthy of being called free.

Some two years later the high point of insurgency in the United States came from May to September 1970 when a popular upsurge again prefigured a whole different kind of society. This period marked the closest the United States came to a revolutionary situation in the twentieth century. After killings of college students at Kent State and Jackson State universities during protests against the expansion of the Vietnam War into Cambodia, the largest strike in the history of the United States was organized: a national uprising of more than four million people on the nation's campuses paralyzed the system of higher education, traumatized the country, and spelled the beginning of the end for yet another U.S. president who failed to pull out of Vietnam. The strikers did not demand lower tuition or better conditions on campus, but peace, an end to the murderous repression of the Black Panther Party, and the conversion of U.S. universities from Pentagon research facilities into socially responsible institutions. Across the country, more than 35,000 National Guard troops were called out in sixteen states to bloodily suppress protests. From Kent and Jackson to Buffalo and Albuquerque, more than a hundred people were killed or wounded in the ensuing violence. The acute phase of the crisis that finally resulted in President Richard Nixon's ouster lasted for five months, and before calm was restored the nation was irrevocably changed.

During the five months from May to September, the United States endured a crisis of a depth and intensity to which only its Civil War can compare. *Business Week* warned about the danger of a revolution, as every social movement in the country intensified its activities and reached a climatic peak. In this period, in addition to the student/faculty strike, the National Organization for Women called for a general strike of women (and the modern symbol of feminism was born); Vietnam veterans organized against the war; entire army companies in Vietnam refused to follow orders; more than five hundred GIs deserted every day of the week in May; the first Gay Pride Week was celebrated; the Chicano Moratorium against the war drew 100,000 marchers in Los Angeles before it was viciously attacked by police; and Federal Employees for a Democratic Society formed—an organization credited with the capability to "operate as a shadow government."

This remarkable series of events culminated in the Black Panthers' Revolutionary Peoples' Constitutional Convention (RPCC) in September, when, despite police and FBI terror, over 10,000 people converged on Philadelphia to write a new constitution. Breaking down into participatory workshops, people drafted a revolutionary "Internationalist Constitution" that far surpassed the reformist program of the Black Panther Party. As an indication of how much existing social antagonisms were transcended, one of the most spirited and well-received groups came from the newly emergent gay liberation movement. Declaring an International Bill of Rights and promising reparations to the people of the world, the RPCC ratified proposals drafted by working groups of women, Black nationalists, street people, ex-prisoners, veterans, students, health workers, and artists—all of whom outlined how their constituencies viewed a free society.[2] With the bitter and bloody internal feud that tore the organization—and the movement—apart, the new left's aspirations remained unconsummated.

There are many remarkable features to the RPCC. In the process of the self-formation of the human species through struggles for freedom, the last should come first; in Philadelphia that is precisely what transpired. The most oppressed united all subaltern constituencies and facilitated the precise, written formulation of aspirations. Produced by thousands of people in the midst of a tumultuous historical moment, these documents are uniquely situated to answer the question: "What did the new left want?"

## Historians' Blind Eye

Despite the significance of the Philadelphia gathering, scarcely anything is written about it. Veritable libraries of books have been produced about the movement, but historians have almost completely neglected this event and only superficially treated the movement's 1970 high point. This blind eye speaks volumes about the nature of historiography and the idealism of contemporary theoreticians. Even from the left (which should know better), we have ideologues like Antonio Negri who offer vacuous "proletarian" pontifications, or, on the other extreme, annalists (including many former activists) who pay close attention to (auto)biographical details. Political axes may be ground, but even a basic understanding of the movement's concrete history gets obscured beneath the narcissism of me-first culture and me-be-better-than-you politics.

One of the great myths of the history of the new left is that the early phase of the movement was characterized by a "prefigurative politics" of participatory democracy, while the later phase, when the working class and lumpen rose to lead the movement, did not centrally contain this dimension. Many books characterize the early new left as peaceful and democratic and its later phase as undemocratic and violent. The myth of the "pure" participatory democracy of the upper-middle-class college students of the early 1960s was first given the lie by women who criticized the patriarchal control exerted by a few men. African

Americans simultaneously examined critically the presence of white activists as well as the strictures of non-violence imposed upon them by pacifists, whose mainstream media power made them larger than life. Studied ignorance of watershed events like the direct democracy practised in Philadelphia at the RPCC is an essential means of perpetuating the mythological superiority of the early 1960s.

In October 2006 I was privileged to attend the fortieth anniversary celebration of the Black Panther Party. At that event, many chapters had mini-reunions before reporting back to the group on what had happened in their cities four decades previously. FOUR DECADES! Because of the bitter internecine split in their ranks and the brutal repression they suffered from police and FBI, Panther members had not had an opportunity even to discuss what had happened. As we listened to reports from people who had been party activists in places such as New Bedford, Massachusetts, and Milwaukee, Wisconsin, I reflected on how many former college students active in the early 1960s had been given the opportunity to write their memoirs and imprint their perspective on the movement on future generations, while key activists from the movement's later phase were killed or remain imprisoned. The police and FBI came down so hard on the movement that former Philadelphia Panther Mumia Abu-Jamal, one of the key organizers of the Philadelphia RPCC, continues to be confined on death row.

# Universal Liberation as the Promise of 1968

The international resonance of the Black Panther Party led to groups with similar names being formed in at least five other countries, including among Dalits (untouchables) in India, Arab Jews in Israel, aborigines in Australia, and seniors in the United States. One of the papers delivered at the Queen's University New World Coming conference in 2007 was about the Black Panther Party in Israel, an organization about which I had waited many years to learn something substantive. The conference also had a Palestinian keynote speaker. (See chapter 1 here.) The presence of these activists reminded me that the new left was, if anything, a diverse and polycentric movement that did not respect anyone's rigid lines in the sand. It is impossible to characterize the new left as a movement that was unitary—rather, it was a global movement with a diverse membership that *acted* in unison against war and racism, against patriarchy and hierarchy, against hatred and for love.

It was not simply a movement for civil rights if you were an African American, a movement for women's liberation if you were a woman, a movement for gay rights if you were lesbian or gay, a movement for peace if you were against war; it was certainly all of those things, but it was also much more—and *that* is what was most interesting. The new left was a global movement that, at its best

Handbill for a
massive anti–
Vietnam War
demonstration,
London, England,
Spring 1968.

moments, contested the world capitalist system *as a whole*. For the first time, humans emerged as a species-being and rejected categories of existence imposed by the system. During the Vietnam War, for example, the patriotism of many Americans was superseded by solidarity with the people of Vietnam; in place of racism, many white Americans insisted that a Vietnamese life was worth the same as an American life (defying the continual media barrage to the contrary). According to many different opinion polls at that time, Vietnamese leader Ho Chi-Minh was more popular on U.S. college campuses than was U.S. president Nixon.

There were peace movements long before the 1960s and, unfortunately, there will need to be peace movements for years to come. Significant in the case of the new left was the way in which the global movement came together to oppose the war. In February 1972 the Vietnamese organized an international conference in Versailles, France, and activists from peace movements in more than eighty countries gathered. At that time, delegates agreed upon an action calendar designed to co-ordinate our demonstrations, to show the world how unpopular the U.S. war was. Something was supposed to happen around Easter in Vietnam, followed by demonstrations from East to West—from Moscow to Paris to New York and finally to San Diego, where Nixon was due to be renominated at the Republican National Convention in August. All over the world, activists were inspired when the Easter Offensive that led off the calendar involved, for the first time, tanks appearing among the arsenal of guerrilla forces in southern Vietnam. The Vietnamese military offensive in co-ordination with the global political movement was so well crafted that the Vietnamese simultaneously announced the formation of a provisional revolutionary government with a capital at Quang Tri. The U.S. response was increased barbarism. I have seen photos of Quang Tri after the United States bombed it. Scarcely a building's wall was left standing. It was said at the time that more destruction was done to the city than had been done to Hiroshima or Nagasaki.

The Vietnamese centrally orchestrated these actions in 1972, but in 1968 the global movement had a spontaneous synchronicity and international harmonization organized from the grassroots. Leading up to the French May events was a

Berlin conference in February 1968 to oppose the Vietnam War. Many French activists attended and returned to France prepared to confront the system that could produce such a barbarous war. The global movement was inspired by the Tet offensive in Vietnam, and animated by the Cultural Revolution in China, India's Naxalites, and the reform impetus in Czechoslovakia. After the strikes of May 1968 in France, people in many places modelled their actions on what French students had accomplished. Students in Yugoslavia, Senegal, and Mexico, as well as workers in Italy and Spain, were motivated to strike on their own. The French May events thus had what I call an "eros effect." In almost every country in the world, insurgent social movements intimately related to each other emerged in 1968. From Japan to Senegal, as in dozens of other countries, militant students were at the cutting edge, often detonating massive social explosions. In the United States the assassination of Martin Luther King Jr. led to riots in over 150 cities. More damage was done to Washington, D.C., than by the British when they captured it during the War of 1812. In Mexico hundreds of people were killed in protests against the coming Olympics, where the main sporting event in the media was the raised-fist, black-gloved salutes of the two U.S. Black athletes Tommie Smith and John Carlos as they stood on the medal podium. When the Prague Spring, the Czechoslovakian experiment of "socialism with a human face," was brought to an early end by half a million invading Soviets, people in Prague took down street signs and buildings' identification markers. It took the Russian army a week to find the post office. All these movements converged in a process of mutual amplification, or "eros effect."

The eros effect refers to moments of suddenly popular social upheavals that dramatically transform established social orders. When people identify with insurgent movements and massively rise up, the basic assumptions of a society—patriotic nationalism and the authority of the government; hierarchy, the division of labour, and specialization—vanish overnight. During moments of the eros effect, not only do popular movements imagine a new way of life and a different social reality, but millions of people live according to transformed norms, values, and beliefs. The conscious spontaneity of self-directed actions of hundreds of thousands of people—sometimes millions—who come together globally in beloved communities of struggle is a new tool in the struggle for freedom. The sixties' international insurgency defined a new level of struggle that continues to animate movements today.

# A World of Uprisings

After the heyday of the new left, a string of uprisings swept East Asian dictatorships and overthrew East European Soviet regimes. Immanuel Wallerstein and

Giovanni Arrighi called the movements of 1989 "the continuation of 1968."[3] The wave of Asian uprisings predated events in Eastern Europe and did not flow from decisions made by world leaders to end the Cold War. The new left's universal impetus for liberation was especially evident in the Gwangju uprising of 1980, which helped set off the chain reaction of revolts and uprisings throughout East Asia. Gwangju's "beautiful community" among the city's citizens—their spontaneous ability to drive out the military, to defend, govern, and manage their own affairs; the disappearance of crime and competition; and the rapid self-organization of the Citizens' Army and Citizen-Student Struggle Committee—is legendary. In the liberated city, daily rallies of tens of thousands of people directly made the most important decisions. Gwangju's participatory democracy illustrates concretely how the new left's vision, far from being peculiar to the sixties, remains globally central to insurgency. Other East Asian uprisings of the 1980s and 1990s demonstrated similar global awareness amid manifestations of the new left dimensions of autonomy, direct democracy, and solidarity: the Philippines (1986), Burma (1988), China (1989), Nepal (1990), Bangladesh (1990), Thailand (1992), and Indonesia (1998).

In the United States and Canada and Western Europe, spontaneous grass-roots movements for global economic justice and peace emerged after the 1960s, making such demands as cancelling the national debt of the world's poorest countries and organizing confrontations of elite summits. Well-intentioned celebrities like Bono have made famous the struggle against world starvation and human misery. Unfortunately, one day we will need to remind Bono that his brotherhood with IMF presidents Wolfensohn and Wolfowitz (and all the other wolves of high finance whose system gnaws at the bones of starving humanity) failed to end hunger. In the future, with continuing human misery and ecological devastation, people will realize that it is the system that is the problem. Bono is attempting to work with a failed system, while it is the system itself that must go.[4]

For many people, protests in Seattle in 1999 broke new ground when Teamsters and Turtles, workers and ecologists, Lesbian Avengers and Zapatista partisans all converged for unified action and stopped the WTO meetings. The worldwide synchronicity of protests that day involved actions in dozens of other cities around the world. Building up to Seattle's exhilarating victory, successful confrontations of attempted imposition of the corporate behemoth's domination were organized in Caracas (1987) and Seoul (1997). In Berlin in 1988, tens of thousands of people militantly confronted the global financial elite gathering and compelled the world's bankers to adjourn a day earlier than planned. After Seattle, as the "real axis of evil" took aim at pulling millions more people deeper into their exploitative system, ordinary people in places such as Cochabamba, Bolivia (2000), and Arequipa, Peru (2002), fought back against the attempted privatization of communal natural resources and won significant victories. On February 15, 2003, between fifteen and thirty million people around the world protested the U.S. war in Iraq even though it had not yet begun. No central organization called together these protesters.

In the future we can expect new uprisings against neo-liberalism and war. Ordinary people are capable of making far more intelligent decisions than is any elite—whether dictators like Saddam Hussein or "democratically" elected leaders like George Bush. People are sick and tired of elite greed and cruelty, of systematic injustice. While political leadership based upon authoritarian organizations has lost legitimacy, the power of example remains potent. Nation-states' and corporations' global quest for complete control and domination, to break down indigenous cultures and local autonomy, finds its most articulate negation in the Zapatista movement for dignity for the peoples of Chiapas. What began as an insurrection on the same day that the North American Free Trade Agreement was implemented—January 1, 1994—has turned into a worldwide focal point for grassroots actions against neo-liberal capitalism's systematic injustices—its perpetuation of billionaires' wealth alongside hundreds of millions of starving human beings. Zapatista *encuentros* (international gatherings of activists) in the jungle were instrumental in preparing the ground of the protests against the WTO in Seattle; in Europe they helped to inspire the actions of Reclaim the Streets, Carnival Against Capitalism, and EuroMayday.

To destroy the existing system of militarized nation-states, power-hungry political parties, and avaricious multinational corporations abetted by their international axis of evil, insurgent movements need to synchronize actions and goals internationally. Globally aware movements have already helped to defeat U.S. imperialism in Vietnam and to end apartheid in South Africa. By building on the legacy of these struggles, we can finally create a world fit for human beings and for all forms of life.

# 36 Lee Maracle

# RED POWER LEGACIES AND LIVES

## An Interview by Scott Rutherford

**Studies of** the 1960s have, for the most part, left unexplored the rise of indigenous decolonization struggles as part of the era's global consciousness. With the exception of sensational images from the occupation of Alcatraz Island outside of San Francisco and the dramatic standoff involving the American Indian Movement at Wounded Knee in South Dakota, little indigenous content—information or iconography—has made its way into the accounts of the period. Commonly known as "Red Power" in North America during the 1960s and 1970s, indigenous movements for sovereignty, land, cultural reclamation, and human rights carried with them a critical transnational imaginary connecting them to radical movements globally. These stories demand inclusion in the global sixties archive.

First Nations, Métis, and Inuit communities in Canada and elsewhere continue to live the legacies of colonialism as well as the multilayered efforts to decolonize. Lee Maracle has participated in, witnessed, and written about many of these moments. Of Salish and Cree descent, Maracle, a member of the Sto:lo Nation, became politically active in Indigenous decolonization movements in Canada during the 1960s and 1970s. Her first book, *Bobbi Lee: Indian Rebel* (1975), is a poignant account of life as a Red Power activist. Into the twenty-first century she continues to use written and oral accounts in her fight against racism, sexism, and economic oppression.

In spring 2008 we spoke about a number of wide-rangings issues, including Red Power, contemporary colonialism, and the place of feminism in decolonization.

**Scott Rutherford (SR)**: Can you describe how you became involved in the Red Power movement in Canada during the 1960s?

**Lee Maracle (LM)**: The first thing that I have to mention is that the sixties were preceded by the fifties, which was the anticolonial movements first of all and Tommy Douglas [of the New Democratic Party] working very hard to get Aboriginal people the vote. Unfortunately in getting us the right to vote, the Parliament of Canada arbitrarily declared us citizens, which I don't think we really wanted to be. There was a lot of loss. Our fishing and hunting rights, the ability to make decisions about our economy, including who to trade with—all those things that we normally did to survive in the forties, the thirties, and the twenties—became very restricted.

**SR**: How did these changes play out in your local community?

**LM**: In my area [Sto:lo Nation, West Coast of North America], Alfred Hope Jr. was arrested for fishing, I believe it was in 1956 or 1957, so sometime around there. I was a little kid anyway. He decided that, "Well, I'm not going to plead not guilty. I'm going to plead guilty and tell the judge go ahead put me in jail and fine me. I'm not paying the fine. I'd rather take the time in jail. You'll have to provide for my wife and six children—I think it was six children—and that will cost you something like $9,000 a month for every month that I spend in jail, or you can just drop the charge and let me feed my family, it's only two fish." The judge decided to dismiss the case because he didn't want to rule on it and the state had not clearly established the position that they had the right to curb our fishing rights. So it was sort of a first step that led to a kind of new initiative amongst the adults that perhaps we did have rights to do things.

My mother was involved specifically with the building of the Coqualeetza Fellowship Centre in Vancouver, which was the forerunner of the Native Friendship Centre. But also there was discussion on the authority over our reservation in terms of people driving through them, speeding, hitting kids; we were in the middle of the city. We had to get that clear in our minds over a number of summers. The women got together and tried to understand what the *Indian Act* actually meant. My mother is not status Indian, so she was part of that thought because, you know, I am. So that became part of my family history.

That really inspired a lot of youth to organize themselves and to do things and to find out what our situation really was. Some of our people were banned in the forties from speaking about Aboriginal rights. Then the African revolts occurred and our folks plugged into that and watched it on television together. We had one TV in our community and everyone would gather and kind of watch the news. Then Birmingham, Alabama, sort of erupted and it was clear that you were allowed to demonstrate whatever injustices existed. Then following all of that in 1968 Howard Adams came out with the Red Power movement in Canada and Black folks came out with the Black Power movement. People like Stokely Carmichael and Malcolm X became powerful influences,

Just after that was the publication of Frantz Fanon's *The Wretched of the Earth*, which we got a hold of. Like every other Third World person, we studied it and I remember we formed a study group to study it because we just couldn't understand it. But we thought, at least I did, that Fanon was actually a native guy from some reservation in Canada or maybe American or something, because he talks about "natives" [laughter]. So then our thinking got expanded beyond North America and that's when we found out about apartheid. I remember very clearly the Sharpeville massacre [South Africa, 1960] because it was reported on TV the very day we had a television, and my Ta'ah [great-grandmother] was there bellowing, "These people have no shame!" All of these things formed together to influence some young people, particularly the business of television. So we started to form the Native Alliance for Red Power.

**SR**: In your opinion, how did indigenous people in Canada experience the sixties?

**LM**: For a while the possibility of surviving led to us taking on the business of studying ourselves, our situation, studying colonization, studying feminism, studying radicalization, studying all kinds of things with one another and particularly rediscovering our history and our culture. That made a huge difference in our lives. At the same time we were fractured, much fractured people. At the same time we tried really hard to resist colonization and to fight for our rights, but we weren't really clear what that was. The internalization of the violence and the squabbling that still goes on in Aboriginal country impede our ability to look forward in the future. And that was the sixties for me as a young person.

But that whole period was a period of tremendous pain for all of us. I think of this little story that, I don't know if it is appropriate to tell it, but when I was a little girl I was helping my dad build boats and I remember him telling me not to stick my finger in the vise. I asked him, "Why?" He said, "When you take the vise off you'll be blind with pain." And of course I stuck my finger in the vise and he was absolutely right. It didn't hurt to squeeze my finger and I just thought, "Oh no." I took the vise off and was running around screaming. My sisters were trying to help me and I literally beat on them. I think that happened to us generally, the vise was off in the sixties.

From 1962 until 1973 we were just running around blind with pain. It was a period of tremendous internalization of the violence perpetrated against us. I think while the fifties was a period of sort of give up the fight, the sixties was a period of turn the fight in on ourselves. So while a lot of work that we were doing was also creating factionalism it was also fracturing us. I think that happened in the sixties, very much like in Black communities. The Panthers just sort of rose up and imploded in the same breath almost, and it happened so quickly, Eldridge Cleaver became a preacher and all sorts of crazy stuff happened. We were not different, we rose up and you know we started to implode, particularly urban Aboriginal people, not so much the reservation though. I think the reservations suffered from a mass exodus of youth to the cities.

**SR:** You mentioned earlier how through books and television you learned about the struggles of people globally. Were there movements or struggles outside of Canada that you felt were important to your own struggles?

**LM:** We struggled really hard against apartheid in South Africa because we were ourselves linked to that struggle. We struggled very hard for decolonization in the Portuguese colonies and we struggled hard against the Pinochet regime [in Chile] because the situation of the Mapuchis was similar to our own. We saw that supporting Third World liberation was in our own interests and to struggle against racism and to discover colonization and decolonization and to try and figure out some strategy for decolonizing Canada and the United States was on our minds.

I think quite a number of Aboriginal intellectuals or First Nations intellectuals believe that we have no hope of decolonizing in North America. I think that a lot of us feel that it is a fait accompli, that even in our struggle for sovereignty it is going to be very limited, more like minority rights vis-à-vis China where they have land rights and language rights and cultural rights but they are a part of the central government. I don't personally ascribe to that. I still believe that we're entitled to enough access to the land and its wealth unencumbered by Canada, and we're entitled to sovereignty unencumbered by Canada. I don't see why we can't do that.

However, as it stands Aboriginal people are not allowed to augment their land base the way a white person can, and cannot augment their rights beyond the land consigned to them. The smallness of the land base we were consigned to was intended to curb our growth and development as opposed to facilitating it.

**SR:** Were you successful in the attempt to link together Third World liberation and the situation of indigenous peoples in Canada?

**LM:** We had hopes that people would unite and effect collaborative decolonization. That was the hopefulness, the inspiration of youth, that maybe we could get Third World people together and do away with imperialism altogether. That didn't happen—in fact, the Right effected huge decimations of all kinds of people and Africa is experiencing its colonial implosion right now. For Black women and children it's extremely violent, and no one is doing anything to stop it. That is a colonial by-product—I know it is because we experienced that same implosion in the seventies, and the same kind of violence, and now we're struggling with it.

Some African people actually look to us, as well as Australians, to the work we've done to mitigate violence, colonial violence, really. It's not violence between each other, it's colonial violence. It's the business of being in the vise and then suddenly being blind with pain. We've done an awful lot to mitigate it.

I think the state is quite happy to see both Blacks and Aboriginal people, and Mexicans in North America, being violent to each other and being drug-addicted and alcohol-addicted and so on. I think that was one of the by-products of colonization that rendered our communities impotent. So they're not in a big hurry to deal with it, because if we sober up maybe we'll push back. It's very scary to have a sober Indian walking around in this country. That's one of the things that I think about.

But the idea was that we would have close collaboration between Third World people and Aboriginal people and that didn't happen. Partly because I think there is a parasitic consciousness within Aboriginal people as well. We are not exempt from it. North Americans have an overblown sense of entitlement and Aboriginal people want the same thing North Americans want.

**SR:** Are there instances where you see some success in the attempt to connect local struggles with global movements?

**LM:** What did happen was some of the indigenous people of the world got together and so indigeneity became a topic of discussion. And of course it's being voted on by the U.N. and the rights of Aboriginal people and indigenous people globally. That's a positive thing, but Canada's not signing it, and I don't expect it to. So, while it finger-points at other countries, it's not signing the basic rights to indigenous people here.

In the sixties a few Native people went to Cuba to cut sugar. I'm very proud we were part of sponsoring someone to go. I think that's the kind of thing we could do more.

**SR:** Can you tell me more about this?

**LM:** Well, it was the Venceremos Brigades and they asked—well, we had no relationship with Cuba, I don't want you to get the wrong idea here—but friends of Cuba asked if we would go cut sugar and David Hanuse of Alert Bay, says, "Well, I can swing a machete, it can't be that hard." So we put some money together, from each other, to send him to go cut sugar. And then some American Native people went. Not very many, it doesn't matter the numbers, but there was still a sense of collaboration with someone else that had no reward.

There was no reward for that. Cuba didn't write us letters and say "Thank you very much" and "Let's be friends forever." There was no communication after that. Once we did the brigade that was it more or less. You do things for your fellow human beings in the world. And if you're Salish or First Nations, we have inclusive cultures. We have cultures that require us to look at humanity in general. That means we have to look beyond what we want or what we even need at this moment and do right by the world.

It sort of came about later in my life, but it started in the sixties this whole business of supporting other struggles in the hope that we'd be able to collaborate some day. Well, the hope shouldn't be what determines whether we support other struggles. It should be our sense of humanity. I think Fanon taught some of us that, you know, that little *Wretched of the Earth*, that the struggle is one for humanity first and foremost, everything else is secondary.

I think that's true for me personally, although it wasn't true for all of us. But it is true for those people who started the little Red Power group way back in the sixties. It is true for us, in our own way, doing what we can, based on our sense of humanity. My sister went to Chiapas during that conflict between the government of Mexico and Chiapas, and so on and so forth. She went as a negotiator to help that situation resolve itself peacefully. I don't know how successful she was, but it doesn't matter. The thing was a sense of doing for others because you're part of a global system, a global arena, you're part of a planet and the planet itself is in trouble, and all of the people on it are in trouble, and you come from the parasitic centre of all of this and you come from the advantaged centre. I think time is a tremendous advantage which all North Americans have.

**SR:** Can you talk a bit more about inclusivity and indigenous cultures?

**LM:** Well, our cultures are inclusive. They say Earth, love the Earth and all of its children. Well the Earth is bigger than Canada, it's bigger than the United States, it encompasses the whole globe and all of its children. Excluding the Africans? No, including. It's an inclusive culture. It's a culture that speaks and addresses the Earth, it addresses caretaking the Earth and all of its children, it engages having relations with the Earth and all of its children. That's our cultures. And we're not doing that.

I think there are a few people like the Native Youth of Vancouver that are looking beyond themselves, and I'm really proud of them for being part of the No One Is Illegal movement. But it has to go beyond that. Even the new immigrants here, suffer as they do, are still privileged compared to a Pakistani piecemeal sewer for Wal-Mart, if you know what I mean. I'm not saying it's bad to want, but you have to balance it with your position in the world. I really believe that.

**SR:** In the different Red Power movements you were involved with, how did "looking beyond yourself" manifest?

**LM:** I think we talked a lot about the privilege of North Americans and discussed it a lot amongst ourselves. I think it comes a lot from writers like Samir Amin, and Kwame Nkrumah, and the relationship of welfare to imperialism generally. And that, you know, we were against further welfarization of Aboriginal people. We didn't stop it because that's basically what we are now, one massive welfare program, in exchange for not having sovereignty. I think that's the difference between ourselves and Canadians, Canadians are basically benefiting from the privilege of the rest of the world through not having to work so hard for the amount of wealth they get, but for Aboriginal people it's very clear you can have sovereignty and poverty or you can have welfare programs and be part of the parasitic privilege of the Imperial centre.

And that's what we spoke against, but we were unsuccessful in changing a lot of people's minds, partly because of our own inept articulation of it and our inability to do close work with Aboriginal people, but that's quite apart from the theory itself. The theory itself came about as a result of discussions with the Native Study Group in the sixties. And those people that are still alive still hold that we are a part of the privileged centre. We haven't forgotten that. So we are looking at how we relate to Africa, or South America. Well, certainly we don't ask them for stuff, I mean that's the least we can do. And the second thing is to have a look at where we put our time. Time is a privilege that only North Americans have, globally, you know, everybody else works and works and works ...

**SR:**  When you say your "own inept articulation," what are you referring to?

**LM:**  I think we did some great things and had some great influences, but we weren't able to really put a finger on the nature of imperialism and how resilient it was going to be, and how tremendously self-centred we were, as people. Not just us personally, but, you know, the rest of the North Americans.

I remember someone saying, "Tell me more about this diabolical and hysterical imperialism" [laughing]. We weren't dealing with people who had any clue whatsoever about what we were talking about and we weren't very good at speaking plain language and figuring out things that we could do, to engage people. I think we were a bunch of youth who wanted to show the world how smart we were. Just like every other young person [laughing]. So that becomes part of the dilemma of everybody that gets excited about a theory—"Okay, now how do we make it part of our praxis, part of our lives?" Well, I know I'm making it part of my life, you know, just generally, but I still don't have a clue how I go about organizing people to do it.

**SR:**  You mentioned really early on that you think you're becoming a global feminist. I want to know if you would have described yourself as a feminist when you were organizing around the Native Study Group and Native Alliance for Red Power?

**LM:**  No! Definitely not. I think I wrote in *I Am Woman* that I woke up one day and realized that I was a woman. No, I would have been against that and I was against feminism. I was like everybody else, "We don't need feminism, blah, blah, blah." No, I didn't see the effect of patriarchy within our communities. When we started actually looking at our communities and looking at our past societies and looking at how we came to be in the position that we are in, I realized that returning to how we were before is a feminist struggle. We didn't have societies that were patriarchal before, but reclaiming our colonial societies, which some people say is gender complementary, OK fine, it was, but it isn't now. We are not gender complementary now. So returning to the gender complementary societies would be a feminist act. We weren't violent to Aboriginal women before, but we are now. So stopping the violence is a feminist act. I just became very rational about what feminism is for me.

Most of my work has been around women and curbing lateral violence and dealing with that. It hasn't been specifically oriented towards any specific group. And I think it is one of the things Aboriginal women in this country are really struggling with, is how do we become human beings in the aftermath of this very fucked up and crazy colonization that occurred? And our societies—all of them— are still experiencing violence as we struggle with that question, and my big sort of emphasis in the last twenty years has been on that question. How do we deal with internalized violence? And then we can go out into the world and advocate something. But until we reduce the level of violence in our community—in the sixties and seventies it was 90 per cent, it's right now around 50 or 60 per cent— it's going down steadily, but we're not there yet. We are not in the place to say this is how we become a human being and this is what needs to happen and this is how human beings ought to behave.

**SR:** What do you mean by the term "gender complementary?"

**LM:** Oh, we had two chiefs before, a male and a female. And the female took care of the internal world and had a greater authority over the economy than the male chief did.

**SR:** In a way it's also redefining what feminism means too.

**LM:** Yeah, well, of course we have to redefine what feminism means because feminism for white women at the time was about equal pay for equal work of value, which I'm also for. I don't think anybody should get less for doing the same work. And of course a lot of Aboriginal women work at jobs and they get paid a lot less than their white counterparts do, so I would add regardless of your race, because if you're an immigrant you get a lot less than even Native people get for the same work. There's a hierarchy in capitalism's mind about who deserves to eat and who doesn't. I don't think that should be what it's based on. It shouldn't go from white down to the immigrant of colour, it shouldn't go that way, and it should all be equal pay for work of equal value regardless of your race or your gender. All that being said, we have very different histories, conditions, and claims than do Canadian women.

**SR:**  Can you tell me more about the struggles in the early seventies around indigenous women's status in relation to the *Indian Act*?

**LM:**  Well, those weren't feminist acts. It was for women who were married to white guys only. Aboriginal women, all of them, had to leave to join the men they married, whether [the men] were non-Native or Native; that was a patriarchal condition and that condition hasn't changed much. I'm registered at Seabird Island because that's where my husband is from. I had to leave my reserve to go to his. The first court case was [Jeannette] Corbière-Lavell, who wanted to change the whole thing: Native women should not have to leave their community to marry because traditionally the man came to our community.[1] That didn't change, because that would have been a whole reshuffling of all the reserves, and would have restored the power of Aboriginal women in their communities because your relatives are all there. Well, in Seabird my relatives are my husband's relatives so I don't have the same authority as I would in my own community, though his relatives do have a deep and abiding respect and love for me. The change was only for those women who married non-Natives. And in that sense it's not a feminist win. And there are some women who are trying to fight it again because of the double-mother clause, which I think is a feminist struggle because it fights on the basis of women generally, not of having to move from this community to that community and losing their place in the first community as a result.[2] The other thing they are trying to fight is the instances of your mother being dead. I think if your mother died before 1951 you can't get your status. But if your father died before 1951 it doesn't matter. You know, that sort of thing. So there's still some work to do around that and it gives me a lot of hope because I thought, well, this case now becomes part of a larger feminist struggle where women struggle to maintain their original place in their original societies. Okay. It will become part of a feminist struggle to restore rights to Aboriginal people as people take that law on over and over again. But it's still in the context of Canada, and so it becomes feminism as a Canadian as opposed to feminism as a Native women.

**SR:**  So feminism really is under the rubric of decolonization.

**LM:**  Well, not quite yet.

**SR:**  But you need it to be in order to decolonize?

**LM:**  Yes, feminism and decolonization have to come together. The same with the international perspective, the global feminist decolonizing perspective has to be a singular perspective. I'm trying to articulate that in an essay, and it's very very difficult, I think, to put it really simply. But I hope to launch some sort of discussion on it [laughing].

**SR:**  One last question. You mentioned the Native Youth Movement earlier. Are there other actions within local indigenous communities that you feel are interested in the "global"?

**LM:**   I think there are a number of Native people doing things globally that are interesting. The peace run, for instance, that goes on every year, that's a tremendous sacrifice for a lot of people. The elders asked my daughter to run and she did the thirty miles, I think, which is longer than a marathon, in the interests of peace globally. I think those kinds of actions are going on among Aboriginal people, and that's the kind of action I can get my soul behind because it allows us to talk about the world and the positions of ourselves vis-à-vis the world, and our obligations to the whole Earth and not just ourselves and that sort of thing. Those kinds of things I think are very powerful and very positive. Canadians and Aboriginal people and women generally have to look beyond what they want and look at the Earth and what it needs.

# 37 David Austin

# AN EMBARRASSMENT OF OMISSIONS, OR REWRITING THE SIXTIES

## The Case of the Caribbean Conference Committee, Canada, and the Global New Left

**Despite the** growing interest in sixties history, huge gaps exist in the historiography of those tempestuous times. While global accounts of the period generally ignore Canada, a cursory observation of the literature reveals another troubling trend. In spite of pleas to rethink the stark demarcations that have conventionally separated off immigrant, civil rights, and Black groups and movements from the new left,[1] the Caribbean and Black Canadian lefts have been routinely excluded from both global and Canadian studies of the sixties upsurge.[2] In the global North, the Caribbean remains synonymous with hedonistic tourist resorts and smiling, happy-go-lucky "locals" bent on attracting coveted tourist dollars by catering to the fanciful whims of foreigners. The Caribbean is not seen as a site of struggle.

Yet the Caribbean new left and Canada's Black left were intricate parts of the new left as a whole.[3] From the Montreal Congress of Black Writers and Walter Rodney's expulsion from Jamaica in 1968 through the founding of Abeng, the anglophone Caribbean's first new left group, to the 1979 Grenada Revolution, one does not have to look far to find a Caribbean-Canadian connection. This also holds true of the Sir George Williams Affair at what is now Concordia University in Montreal. This, the most destructive student protest of 1960s Canada,[4] was

sparked by Caribbean students who complained that they were being systematically failed by a science professor at the university. By the time the dust from
the protest settled, almost one hundred students had been arrested, and several
participants in the protest, including two of its ringleaders, Anne Cools and Rosie
Douglas, were given prison sentences, and in the streets of Trinidad the incident
inspired Black Power protests and a military mutiny that almost culminated in a
coup d'état.[5] In all of these events, members of a little-known group, the Caribbean Conference Committee (CCC), played central roles.[6]

    The stereotypical conception of the new left is one of a naive, starry-eyed
youth counterculture that purportedly eschewed Marxism, old left politics, and
traditional forms of left political organizing and political theory for more intuitive
and spontaneous forms of mass organization and protest.[7] While this depiction
of the new left is more apocryphal than real, not only did the CCC not conform
to that conception, but the group sat on its extreme opposite. Drawing on the
work of the prominent Trinidadian-born theorist and historian C.L.R. James,
CCC members grappled with some of the most important political events and
issues of the period.

## Caribbean Conference Committee

In the 1960s Montreal, as Canada's industrial and cultural capital, was particularly attractive to West Indians.[8] Many Anglophone Caribbean women entered
Canada under the domestic immigration scheme, which permitted them to work
in Canadian homes. Some would later go on to study and pursue professions in
Canada, while others arrived young enough to attend secondary school. Originally
from Barbados, Anne Cools arrived in Canada in her early teens. She finished her
secondary-school studies in Montreal and went on to become a core member of the
CCC, the only woman in that position. Cools was an avid reader of philosophy, politics, and history and an important contributor to the group's wide-ranging political
discussions. As a CCC member she travelled to Cuba, armed with the mission of
having C.L.R. James's classic study of the Haitian Revolution, *The Black Jacobins*,
translated into Spanish. Cools was also one of the key figures in the Sir George Williams Affair, for which she served a prison sentence, and she is credited with establishing one of the first, if not the first, women's shelters in Canada. But like many
women who experienced the stifling constraints of participating in groups that
were largely controlled by men, she became an active feminist who collaborated
with Selma James of the International Wages for Housework Campaign, credited
with influencing a new generation of women in Canada.[9] As Patricia Hill Collins
has written, "Social science research typically focuses on public, official, visible
political activity even though unofficial, private, and seemingly invisible spheres

of social life and organization may be equally important."[10] In relation to the CCC, this issue is further complicated because, according to my discussion with women who were involved in the group, they generally downplayed the significance of their role as organizers, despite its obvious importance. In Anne Cools's case, she was actively involved in the group's "visible political activity," but within this role she struggled to carve out a space for herself as the only woman in this position.

Sara Evans has remarked that by 1967, as a generation of women gained confidence in their leadership abilities and began to assert themselves within various movements, "They simultaneously experienced the increased male domination of the left." Unwilling to function in organizations controlled by men, many of these women, including Cools, went on to become active members in the women's movement.[11] Cools was painfully aware of the limitations of political groups largely dominated by men. In a short essay that no doubt reflected her experience within the CCC and Canada's Black Power movement, Cools argued that Black women carried "all the burdensome, backbreaking and stultifying labour of both black and white society" on their backs. Through their work and actions, Black women paved "the way towards economic independence for the women of the world." Cools suggested that perhaps "it is time that society in general, and black men in particular, take a careful look at black women." Cautious not to limit the problem to individual female-male relations, Cools concluded her essay by calling for the destruction of the economic and political system that limited the life chances of women and men, arguing: "Black women, the slaves of the slaves, can have no peace, no rest until they have evolved new social structures within which men can be Men, women can be Women, and their children, free-thinking total creative human beings."[12]

Although she no doubt had many occasions to reflect on gender relations and feminism, Cools was not a prolific writer, and she left no paper trail of her work within the CCC. Her case as an important actor in the women's movement—someone who collaborated with Selma James, Marlene Dixon, Quebec's Pauline Julien, and other prominent feminist activists—is not aided by her appointment as a Conservative Senator, which has in turn contributed to a kind of revisionism that has all but excluded her as an important sixties figure. Her absence, and that of Black women in general who actively participated in sixties social movements, have deprived us of much-needed insight into the inner workings of gender in Canadian-based Caribbean and Black sixties political groupings, into how these relationships shaped the politics of the groups in question, and into how gender relations within these groups inform our understanding of the dynamics of liberation.

Many Caribbean immigrants to Canada, taking advantage of the government's retraction of the "climate unsuitability" clause and other regulations that had previously restricted immigration to the country on the basis of "nationality, citizenship, ethnic group, occupation, class or geographical area of origin," migrated to Canada to work or study.[13] Many of these Caribbean newcomers were driven by the idea of returning home to participate in the Caribbean's social and economic development. That was certainly true of Cools and other CCC members, who found themselves caught not only in the maelstrom of the Quebec liberation struggle but also in the wave of social movements and anticolonial struggles that were sweeping the globe. They also found themselves immersed in lively discussions about Caribbean political economy spurred by Lloyd Best, Kari Polanyi Levitt, and other members of the Montreal chapter of the New World Group, one of the most important intellectual grouping the Caribbean has produced.[14]

Montreal, then, was a city full of Caribbean exiles. Referring to the experience of C.L.R. James, among others, Edward Said describes being an exile as "being liberated from the usual career, in which 'doing well' and following time-honored footsteps are the main milestones." Exile, for Said, also represents—and this was certainly true of CCC members—"a sort of freedom, a process of discovery in which you do things according to your own pattern, as various interests seize your attention, and as the particular goal you set for yourself dictates: that is a unique pleasure."[15] The exiles of the New World comprised highly trained intellectuals whose work consisted of economic and social analyses. The CCC's political core, on the other hand, was largely made up of young West Indian students who were oriented towards transforming the Caribbean from the bottom up. Between 1965 and 1967 CCC organized a series of conferences and activities that brought many of the Caribbean's leading thinkers and artists to the city.[16] The conferences were attended by West Indians living in Canada, the United States, Britain, and the West Indies and raised awareness about social, cultural, and political developments in the Caribbean. Nothing like these conferences had ever occurred, and the work, including publications, helped to politicize the public and raise awareness of Caribbean and global politics.[17] Moreover, working with the Detroit-based group Facing Reality, the CCC distributed James's various books and pamphlets and helped publish one of his most important works, *Notes on Dialectics* (1966).[18]

# Notes on Dialectics

In *If I Had a Hammer*, Maurice Isserman argues that James's influence as a member of Facing Reality, the group that James originally co-founded in the 1940s under the name of the Johnson-Forest Tendency, did not extend beyond Detroit.[19] The work of the CCC contradicts this claim. Indeed, through the work of CCC members, the influence of James and Facing Reality stretched from Canada to the Caribbean. The publication of *Notes on Dialectics* served the dual purpose of making the book available to members of the CCC for their own study while promoting James's work. More than any other James book, *Notes on Dialectics* shaped the CCC's view that the downtrodden and dispossessed of the world— Frantz Fanon's damned and condemned of the earth—were the driving force behind any meaningful process of social transformation. Kevin B. Anderson suggests that this idiosyncratic study of the evolution of socialism and the international socialist movement was part of a tendency in Marxism, which included the work of Henri Lefebvre in France and Raya Dunayevskaya and James in the United States, to "appropriate Lenin's writings on Hegel in a manner that made them central to their overall understanding of dialectics."[20] Along with James's caution against holding fast to fixed categories of thought long after events have passed them by, perhaps the book's most important contribution rests on its repudiation of the leadership of political elites, the intelligentsia, and the organized labour movement in favour of the self-organization of the working class. "You can organize workers as workers," declares James. "You can create a special organization of revolutionary workers. But once you have those two you have reached an end. The task is to abolish organization. The task today is to call for, to teach, to illustrate, to develop *spontaneity*—the free creative activity of the proletariat. The proletariat will find its method of proletarian organization."[21]

Adopting and adapting James's notion of self-organization, CCC members tackled some of the most pressing political preoccupations of the sixties—the Cuban Revolution, Vietnam, France 1968, and the relevance of Marxism and the theoretical musings of Louis Althusser. This work was not only a component part of the CCC's examination of sixties phenomena and of how social transformation might occur in the Caribbean, but also represents its lasting contribution to our understanding of the dynamics of liberation as a whole.

# Cuba

For the most part, CCC members embraced the Cuban Revolution, and none more enthusiastically than did Alfie Roberts, who eulogized Che Guevara[22] and admonished the editors of *Monthly Review* and other left groups for not playing close enough attention to the flourishing debate about bureaucracy in Cuba in the late 1960s.[23] But not all CCC members were enamoured of the Revolution. Tim Hector was quite critical of it, although it is noteworthy that he later became one of the Cuban Revolution's most avid supporters in the Caribbean. In 1966, echoing *Notes on Dialectics*, Hector declared, "ALL DEVELOPMENT TAKES PLACE AS A RESULT OF SELF-MOVEMENT, NOT ORGANISATION OR DIRECTION BY EXTERNAL FORCES."[24] According to Hector, Cuba failed to meet this basic criterion.

For Hector the crucial issue was the role played by the majority of the population in the Revolution. He cited a passage from volume seven of Lenin's *Selected Works*: "A revolution can be successfully carried out only if the majority of the toilers display independent historical CREATIVE SPIRIT."[25] For Hector, Cuba was not living up to this dictum. He did not believe that Cuba's was a genuine social revolution, but that, rather, it was a nationalist event in which the people were mobilized to make a clean break with the country's colonial legacy, only to have their creative potential stymied and snuffed out by a revolutionary vanguard poised to plan and administer over the heads of the population, having arrogated unto themselves the state apparatus. "Instead of cultivating, wholly and solely relying on the positive creative spirit of the Cuban toilers," he argued, "the Cuban leaders preferred to align themselves with the old Communist Party, which at first spurned the Revolution."[26]

## Vietnam

Hector was equally critical of the government of North Vietnam. From his own account, during his sojourn in Canada he became a somewhat prominent figure on the North American anti–Vietnam War circuit, someone who attempted to learn as much as he could about the struggle from the Vietnamese themselves.[27] He observed the Vietnamese struggle with a discerning eye, and in a way similar to his analysis of the Cuban Revolution, he saw the Vietnam War as neither a simple David and Goliath story nor a neat, clearly demarcated struggle between good and evil.

As Hector argued, it was not only the United States but also Russia and China that were exerting pressure on the North Vietnamese, under the guise of a policy of "peaceful co-existence," to accept the partition of Vietnam after their victory at Dien Bien Phu.[28] Whereas the communist historian Herbert Aptheker argued that China and the Soviet Union's support of North Vietnam was selfless—a position that Tom Hayden, co-founder of Students for a Democratic Society, appears to have endorsed—Hector believed that China and Russia were manipulating Vietnam for their own political ends.[29] Again contrary to Aptheker, Hector argued that the quality of life for North Vietnamese peasants did not fundamentally improve after the country gained independence and that they were still exploited by avaricious landlords.[30] When Northern opposition to the partition of Vietnam erupted in a peasant uprising in 1956, it was, in Hector's words, "as quickly suppressed [by the North Vietnamese government] as the Hungary Revolt of the same year," resulting in the exodus of close to a million North Vietnamese to South Vietnam.[31] More recently, historian Gareth Porter has raised questions about the centralized, authoritarian leadership of Vietnam's Communist Party and described how its grip on power shaped postwar Vietnamese society.[32] In 1968 such descriptions were rare among the new left and opponents of the war.

The exodus to the South sparked a "movement from below" that coalesced into the National Liberation Front (NLF). But Hector suggested that the NLF was viewed with scepticism and aloofness by the Communist bloc, even though Southern peasants flocked to the movement once it demonstrated its commitment to genuine land reform. Even his description of the process that led to civilian rule in South Vietnam made it clear that it was not due to the actions of the ruling class in the South or to the magnanimity of the United States; instead it was the result of the self-activity of the Vietnamese people—workers, peasants, Buddhists, Catholics—who demonstrated in the streets of Saigon and Hue and, in so doing, forced the hand of the military government.[33] Despite the devastation of the war, Hector was confident that the Vietnamese people would prevail against imperialism because, in addition to their valiant efforts, history itself, he triumphantly added, "has decreed the swift collapse of such a social order in the middle of this twentieth century."[34]

Hector's indictment of Cuba's and Vietnam's revolutionary governments has its flaws. It appears to downplay the role of foreign intervention and dismiss the weight of the geopolitics of the time. In the case of Cuba, he overlooks the role that the U.S. embargo played in Cuba's decision to develop close ties with the USSR. He also overlooks how U.S. hostility to Cuba influenced the country's centralized political structure and the imposition of stringent security measures. As Martin Glaberman, chairman of Facing Reality, asked in a letter to Alfie Roberts: how much of Cuba's problems are self-imposed and to what extent is the threat of U.S. intervention to blame for decisions made in the country?[35] And yet, consistent with the CCC's thinking, Hector clearly recognized that without the popular participation of the vast majority of the population, a revolution was destined to reinscribe the fundamental inequalities that it sought to overturn. It was this conception that animated the actions of students and workers in France in the same year that Hector penned his essay on Vietnam.

# France

Conventional accounts of France 1968 primarily focus on the role of students, and particularly the role of student leader Daniel Cohn-Bendit, thus reducing the events to what historian Mark Kurlansky describes as "simply an explosion" by students "against a suffocating, stagnant society."[36] But for Franklyn Harvey, France 1968 was much more than a rebellion by privileged or disgruntled students. As he observed, it was precisely because workers and students came together and mobilized the entire society that they were able to bring France to the brink of revolution. Nor can France 1968 be reduced to an attack against communism.[37] Echoing Daniel and Gabriel Cohn-Bendit's view, Harvey argued that the events demonstrated the potential for revolution in a highly industrialized country[38] and that it was the spontaneous self-activity of French students and workers, fighting against the state and what he described as the counterrevolutionary French Communist Party, and against the bureaucratic trade unions as well, that sparked the 1968 revolt.

Although the 1968 revolution succumbed to the forces of the wily General Charles de Gaulle, the emergence of action committees during the events signified a new form of political organization in which social movements shed hierarchical and elitist political parties, unions, and leaders in favour of a more collective mass movement. For Harvey this development represented the great legacy of the revolution, in which he observed the nucleus of an emerging social form: "Today in an advanced country, parliamentary government is not only obsolete. It is dead. The fact that the personificators [sic] of capital can only maintain the capitalist system and parliamentary government by naked organized violence is sufficient testimony to the death of an old an[d] antiquated social institution."[39] Once again echoing James, Harvey concluded that the "new [social order] exist all around us everywhere.[40] In every department of national life, the new social order was invading the old. Modern capitalism in its highest stage was pregnant with the new social order. But this new society could only begin its higher and unimpeded development by a LEAP, by a sudden JUMP." The leap signified a break with the old order, including the labour unions and the conservative old left. Harvey believed, "Modern society ... is approaching that critical point where a qualitative LEAP from the old to the new social organization will take place[,] and with that leap will come a quantitative increase in social production; thus making possible, for the first time in human history, the control of the productive forces of society by man." This would result in "the emancipation of man from man and the free development of the creative potentialities and capacities of the human species."[41] Moreover, the emergence of action committees represented the new society for Harvey, and just as the students and workers in France did not need Marx, Lenin, or Mao to demonstrate this—according to Harvey they learned from their own concrete experience—neither would the modern proletariat. "Either the working class takes power," he apocalyptically concluded, "or we are all DOOMED."[42]

# Althusser

My last example of the CCC's political-intellectual contributions to the new left comes in the form of an unpublished rejoinder that once again highlights the

CCC's emphasis on self-organization. In the mid- to late 1960s, philosopher Louis Althusser was one of France's leading intellectuals; his rise to fame was almost meteoric. He was a professor at the École Supérieur in Paris and taught both Régis Debray and Michel Foucault.[43] He had risen from relative obscurity to become one of the French Communist Party's leading theoreticians.[44] Having supplanted Jean-Paul Sartre, he was all but anointed as France's Marxist sage,[45] and in 1966, when the English translation of his famous essay "On Contradiction and Overdetermination" was published, he was riding a wave of popularity in French philosophical and left circles.

"On Contradiction and Overdetermination" was translated and published in the January-February 1967 issue of the British journal *New Left Review.* In the essay, Athusser attempts to divest Marxism of its Hegelian roots. Hegel's dialectic animated Marx's conception of the world, furnishing it with its sense of phenomenological movement and possibility, the idea that even with the deep recesses of conservatism or in the throes of capitalism, revolution is possible and that human beings, as subjects and as agents of their own destinies, can transform society and usher in a new social order. This arguably is the defining feature that separates Marxism from conventional political economy. But for Althusser, Hegel represented abstraction and idealism, and Marxism had to be shorn of this idealistic skin by applying it to concrete social phenomenon. The flaw was in the dialectic itself, and for Marxism to find its true form the dialectic had to be excised from dialectical materialism.[46]

Upon reading the essay, an obviously distraught C.L.R. James wrote a letter to Martin Glaberman, imploring him to write a timely rebuttal to Althusser's revisionism.[47] Glaberman partially took up the challenge in *Mao as a Dialectician.*[48] Prompted by Alfie Roberts, so too did Raya Dunayeskaya, James's erstwhile associate who was head of her own organization, News and Letters.[49] But while the others made allusions to Althusser, CCC member Robert Hill took on the titan of French philosophy by systematically dissecting and critiquing Althusser's "scientism." Like the work of his fellow CCC members, Hill's rebuttal was animated by *Notes on Dialectics*, from which he cites: "The negativity of the free activity of the proletariat can only come completely into play when it is in contradiction with the concrete obstacle, something which, to realise its own nature, it must overcome. It is the unbearable nature of the contradiction that creates negativity.... Thus it is not a blemish, a fault, a deficiency in a thing if a Contradiction is to be found in it. That is its life."[50] For Hill, the last lines of James's passages were almost tailor-made for Althusser, who in his attempt to substitute dialectics for his notion of overdetermination approaches the Hegel/Marx, economic structure/cultural superstructure contradictions as if they are in fact "blemishes and faults and deficiencies on the body politic of—scientific rigor."[51]

In Althusser's notion of overdetermination, society's elites are the lead actors who mould and transform society. Class struggle is not the motor force of history, as Marx argued, but more like a supporting cast, and the self-organization and spontaneity of the working class and the populace are all but absent from the stage. This absence is at the heart of Hill's critique of Althusser's essay: "Althusser[,] in enunciating the differences between Marx and Hegel, between economic structure and society and cultural superstructure, between backwardness of Russia and the advanced nature of its revolution[,] must leap out of his imagination with verbal inventions or trust that some words are meant merely as verbal romance."[52]

Central to Hill's argument is Hegel's notion of "understanding." According to James, unlike dialectical reasoning, the theory of understanding rigidly sticks to finite categories of thought and is unable to dissect and assess the manifold conceptual relations and contradictions that lurk behind it.[53] Whereas Althusser's understanding causes him to fix his gaze on the Bolshevism party structure, James argues that, in order to understand what happened in Russia after Lenin's death, Lenin's notion of organization must be assessed as a part of a symbiotic relationship between organization and spontaneity in which an attempt is made to reconcile the role of the party with the self-activity of the working class/underclass. This tension within the organization/spontaneity dialectic is the key to understanding what Lenin attempted to do in Russia, and why these efforts ultimately failed under Stalin.[54] For Hill, it is precisely this point that Althusser does not grasp in his attempt at separating Hegel from Marx.

# CCC members, then, grappled with some of the pressing events and issues

that were confronting the world, and particularly the global left, in the 1960s, and the writing of James, as their mentor, served as their guide. But this group of voracious readers also whetted their appetites on Fanon, Aimé Césaire, Herbert Marcuse, Dunaveyskaya, Sartre, Lenin, Marx, Hegel, Ortego y Gassett, and Malcolm X, among others. They collaborated with Rodney, Stokely Carmichael, and the members of Facing Reality and Students for a Democratic Society. Their theoretical "groundings" on Canadian soil provided the basis for their political work in the Caribbean, which in turn helped give birth to the Caribbean's new left and Canada's Black Power movements through a series of related developments that culminated in the Grenada Revolution—an event that, for a brief historical moment, demonstrated to the world that human possibility is not restricted to the limits of geographical size or resources.[55]

The CCC was not without weaknesses. The absence of gender praxis represents a gaping hole in their work. Moreover, like many sixties groups and writers, in asserting their belief that a New World was coming CCC members often oscillated between apocalyptic fatalism and zealous triumphalism. But ultimately their work symbolizes an abiding belief in the possible and represents an all-important reminder that social transformation is a human process in motion in which cook, scribe, and washer must play an active part. Surely a group, however small, that gave so much, and that played such an important role in the Caribbean and Canada while contributing to our global understanding of the dynamics of liberation, deserves—has earned—a place in annals of the sixties and the global new left.

Eric Zolov 38

# MEXICO'S ROCK COUNTERCULTURE (La Onda) IN HISTORICAL PERSPECTIVE AND MEMORY

The Mexican counterculture, called La Onda—roughly translated as "the wave"—evolved in the context of the push for modernization in the 1960s and helped to shape and was in turn shaped by the pro-democracy student demonstrations that took place in the summer and fall of 1968 as Mexico prepared for the Summer Olympics. The rock element of this countercultural movement peaked in the fall of 1971 at the Avándaro music festival, when over 200,000 youth from across the social spectrum gathered to experience two days of music, freedom, and *desmadre*—the subversion of social boundaries of propriety—before La Onda disappeared in the face of state repression, leftist denunciations of cultural imperialism, and pending middle-class economic collapse. As it turns out, Mexico was not alone in generating a vibrant countercultural scene linked to rock music: throughout Latin America, from Cuba to Chile, Brazil to Guatemala, Colombia to Argentina, each country in the Americas experienced its own version of La Onda.

Recovering this history, however, has been a slow process. Until fairly recently, Latin America's diverse countercultural movements had been completely ignored in the historiography of the 1960s, where the focus has been instead on the dynamics of Cuban-inspired insurgency, on one hand, and U.S.-directed counterinsurgency, on the other. This vast body of literature has had a tendency to reify the impact of the Cuban Revolution (and by extension the Cold War) as "the cause" for the breakdown and polarization of national politics and the socio-cultural transformations of the period. Bringing into this discussion a focus on countercultural, consumptive practices thus offers an opportunity to enrich our understanding of the complex cultural politics of the era, taking us beyond the more traditional narratives of political economy, militarism, and revolutionary struggle, thereby deepening our understanding of profound transformations whose reverberations are still unfolding today.

# Latin America's Countercultures

The trajectories of the various Latin American countercultural movements, despite tremendous diversity in national contexts, were remarkably similar even while local nuances made each movement distinctive. Each had its origins in the mid-1950s dissemination of rock 'n' roll culture via transnational recording companies working in tandem with U.S. film and television production companies to promote commodified versions of youth rebellion that travelled throughout the globe. By 1960 virtually every urban, middle-class teenager across the Americas (if not globally) knew who Elvis Presley was—what his music sounded like and what his gestures looked like, even if access to that music and imagery was widely uneven. Soon after, the earliest manifestations of rock 'n' roll in Latin America became apparent. These took the form of English-language and shortly thereafter Spanish-language covers of imported originals, as local bands sought to emulate their foreign idols. Many of these bands, which nearly always took anglicized names such as Los Flippers (Colombia), Apple Pie (Guatemala), or Los Teen Tops (Mexico), became widely popular, and not simply because they mimicked the gestures and sounds of foreign idols, but because of the unique sonic and lyric inflections they brought to their interpretations.

In Mexico the covers were called *refritos*, literally "refried" versions of the original, and the term's implicit associations of appropriation make it an apt label to describe the phenomenon more broadly. While some critics might see the work as mere mimicry, the sheer act of performance involved the reconfiguration of foreign reference points of rebellion for a local context. Writing about the Uruguayan group Los Shakers, which gained popularity through Spanglish hits modelled on songs by the Beatles, Abril Trigo points out that "the sound was Beatles-like" but that, according to one band member, the group "didn't quite know what the 'shake' was, it was just a gimmick." Still, Trigo says, "The songs were very good indeed. They were not mere imitation, but captured the flair of the Beatles while bringing to the surface a distinct style in a broken, tongue-in-cheek peripheral English."[1]

Then too, by the late 1960s each of these early cover movements had given rise to original rock performances that, while referenced in myriad ways to a globalized youth rebellion underway in the United States and abroad, formed the context for homegrown countercultural scenes and native hippie or so-called *jipismo* movements across the continent. These scenes evolved, moreover, into the highly politicized climate of student mobilization in many parts of Latin America and thus helped to shape the irreverent tone of street protests against governmental authority, protests often met with the violence of state brutality. In the face of such repression, for many youth the counterculture became a refuge for dissent, and "dropping out" became a strategy of protest politics.

A cover for an album by the Mexican rock band La Revolución de Emiliano Zapata, 1971. The group became famous for its name alone, which challenged the ruling political party's appropriation of Zapata in an effort to bolster its "revolutionary legitimacy." (Image courtesy of Arturo Lara.)

This was the case in Mexico, where the "La Onda Chicana"—the name given the homegrown rock movement that flourished there from roughly 1969 to 1972—channelled the defeated student energies in the wake of the fierce government repression of 1968. In Brazil the Tropicália movement, centred around performers such as Caetano Veloso, Gilberto Gil, and the band Os Mutantes, became a vanguard of countercultural dissent in the context of student protests against the military regime. The music of these native countercultural scenes was diverse, indeed, but they shared two important traits in common. First, they rejected the concept of the *refrito* as unoriginal and strove instead to create new rock sounds that fused those of the rock revolution happening abroad with a local vernacular, although Mexico presents an odd anomaly because most of the original music from this period was written and performed there solely in English. Second, the music directly incorporated images and references of national belonging—such as elements of a heroic national narrative—in turn subverting their original meanings. One of the clearest examples of this process comes from the Mexican rock band La Revolución de Emiliano Zapata. Although none of the group's songs had anything to do with agrarian reform, much less peasant (or student) rebellion—and the lyrics were written in English in any event—the sheer name of the band itself was a bold swipe at official efforts to dictate the terms of historical memory and national belonging. Placed in the context of countercultural rebellion, youth were now being encouraged to question the sacredness of such national discourses.

*Mexico's Rock Counterculture (La Onda) in Historical Perspective and Memory*

# The Cultural Politics of Latin American *Jipismo*

If a central theme of the 1960s is what one might term (quoting Homi Bhabha) a "longing for form"—that is, a pursuit of *more* nation-state by the left in the context of a perception of a window of opportunity created by the Cuban Revolution and the perceived crisis of U.S. hegemony globally—this longing for form was met by what might be called a "disillusionment with form" in the post-1968 period, expressed in the various countercultural movements that emerged throughout the Americas. Across the continent, by the late 1960s countercultural scenes were producing a complex cultural politics of *jipismo*: Mexican hippies, Chilean hippies, Uruguayan hippies, Colombian hippies, Cuban hippies. In many cases, moreover, these scenes culminated in massive rock festivals featuring local bands. There was, for instance, the Piedra Roja festival in Chile (1970), Avándaro in Mexico (1971), and Ancón in Colombia (1971); even Guatemala had a rock festival during this period. Linked to transnational, capitalist consumerism, these movements reflected a turning away from politics in all its forms, and they would lay the foundation for what sociologists later termed the "new social movements."

But the issue for Latin America was deeper still, because the turning away from politics represented a fundamental repudiation or, perhaps better, a reconfiguration of an ideologically sanctioned pursuit of a "national" identity, whether emanating from the left or the right. The transnational character of rock music embodied a transcendence of national form itself, and was part of a larger process of disillusionment with the nation-state and a search for alternatives outside of direct political action. This search became manifest in new forms of communication and living arrangements, alternative forms of spirituality, a search for meaning in indigenous epistemologies, the emergence of a drug culture (especially one linked to indigenous-derived drugs such as hallucinogenic plants and mushrooms), and other aspects of countercultural politics—about which much still needs to be researched and discussed.

Indeed, I would argue that we should expand our conceptual understanding of what constituted a Latin American "new left," a term used quite differently for Latin America in the 1960s than for the United States and Europe.[2] Rather than interpret the Latin American new left in the narrow, circumscribed sense as constituting a "new generation of vanguardist revolutionaries"[3] inspired by the success of the Cuban Revolution, we should broaden its definitional reach to encompass a wider spectrum of cultural and political practices. This broader approach is reflected in the work of scholars such as Jaime Pensado and Victoria Langland, for example, who write on the cultural politics of student protest in Mexico and Brazil, respectively (for Pensado, see chapter 33 here). Moreover, this would align the Latin Americanists' definition of a new left with that used by Americanists such as Van Gosse, who argues that the new left should be seen as a "movement of movements" (see chapter 3 here), a movement that spans from the political radicalism of groups such as the Black Panthers or Weather Underground to countercultural protest and church-based civil rights activism.

By the late 1960s, too, rock had become a target of both left and right across Latin America. It is not that rock lyrics were explicitly political per se; often, they were not. Instead, driving this confrontation was an important paradox, namely: in the early 1960s, rock 'n' roll coincided with the aesthetics and consumerist philosophy of capitalist modernization projects promoted by the United States and Latin American elites; yet by the end of the 1960s the rock counterculture was challenging the very social and ideological foundations of those same capitalist projects. For example, in the mid-1960s *El Club del Clan*, Colombia's equivalent of the *American Bandstand* TV program, featured domestic rock groups such as Los Flippers, who performed cover versions of Top 40 U.S. hits. At the same time that such bands were promoted by the mass media to Colombian youth, they were also provoking outrage within the historically traditional society of Bogotá. Something similar was occurring in Mexico, where Telesistema, the monopoly television conglomerate, promoted groups such as Los Yaki on its program *Yeah Yeah a Go Go*, to the consternation of religious conservatives.

Hence, from early on rock was caught in a fundamental contradiction. On one hand, rock was mistrusted and disparaged by the left for its association with U.S. consumerism, while on the other rock culture introduced a potential subversion of the Catholic, patriarchal values or *buenas costumbres* that sustained authoritarian politics throughout the region; thus for this reason rock would become a target for the right as well. While Caetano Veloso and Gilberto Gil (pillars of Brazil's Tropicália movement in the late 1960s) were exiled by the military government for their supposed threat to the social order, they were also denounced by Brazil's left-wing intellectuals for leading youth astray.

A central aspect of this polemic concerns the impact of the Cuban Revolution, which disseminated an ideological paradigm, embraced by many on the Latin American left, that identified rock and other forms of so-called frivolous consumption with "U.S. imperialism" and "bourgeois decadence." This paradigm in turn stimulated support for a new vision of popular music that emerged parallel with local countercultures. Known variously as Nueva Canción, Nueva Trova, Canción Protesta, and Canción Folklórica, this "counter-song," as it has been called, championed an indigenous-inspired concept of *música popular*—as opposed to *música pop*—rendered by artists such as Mercedes Sosa (Argentina), Víctor Jara (Chile), or Los Folkloristas (Mexico). Using native, non-amplified instruments—as opposed to electric guitars—these performers sought to reproduce and disseminate the traditional music and presumed political aspirations of the countryside, a place long regarded by the left as the embodiment of "authentic" national culture and thus a bulwark against the onslaught of urban, "foreign" culture. For socially conscious youth, this "political song" movement and the ideological rationale behind it were all but impossible to disregard. Indeed, many youth who had been rockers in the 1960s questioned their ideological positions by the early 1970s—were they in fact serving as agents of imperialism because they listened to rock?

In response to this ideological attack from the left, many Latin American rockers sought ways of strategically repositioning themselves, not only by incorporating elements of political song but also by attempting to redefine rock so that it would not necessarily be opposed to a revolutionary paradigm. Some sought to demonstrate through the syncretic musical forms they fashioned that a "dialogue" between rock and politicized song was possible, on both the aesthetic and ideological levels. The Chilean group Los Jaivas, whose music represented a fusion of indigenous instruments and rock styles, is a prime example of this effort to bridge the polemic that separated rock from political song. In Cuba, singer-songwriter Silvio Rodríguez, who was fired from his job at a state radio station for mentioning on the air that he was a fan of the Beatles, later joined forces with a short-lived band called Grupo de Experimentación Sonora del ICAIC, which included other Nueva Trova musicians such as Pablo Milanés.

Together these musicians insisted in the face of official opprobrium that revolutionary music could and should experiment freely with all available styles, including rock. As Deborah Pacini Hernandez and Reebee Garofalo write about Cuban rockers: "Many of these youth could see no contradiction between their revolution and rock. To them, rock should not be equated with U.S. cultural imperialism, but rather with the liberatory musical, cultural and political experiments youth elsewhere were engaging in. Indeed, some young rock fans were convinced that the cultural liberation movements taking place in the capitalist West were, in spirit, closely linked with the Cuban Revolution."[4] Thus, across Latin America rock was literally caught between *la espada y la pared* (the sword and the wall)—the sword of ideological purity inspired by the Cuban Revolution and Che Guevara's call to extirpate imperialism in all forms, and the wall of the old patriarchal order sustained by the brutal military authoritarianism that descended on numerous states across the region.

# Reconstructing Historical Memory

Recently, a combination of factors—the reassessment of rock's potential as a vehicle for political organization on the left; a renewed scholarly interest in the

1960s, especially by a new generation of academics (as evidenced by this collection); and the interconnectedness afforded by the Internet and email—has opened many new doors for the study of Latin American countercultures. Yet as our knowledge of rock music and performance continues to expand, it is important that researchers go beyond the study of a genealogy of rock bands and the "texts" of the counterculture—musical, literary, visual—to probe the ways in which those texts were received by urban middle and lower classes: how and why the music, language, styles, and gestures of countercultural performance informed everyday life and shaped the contours of individual, familial, and community relationships. There is much to research and many ways of exploring the diversity of *ondas* of countercultural expression and rebellion that became manifest across Latin America in the 1960s and 1970s.

Luis González-Reimann, 1972. (Photo courtesy of Luis González-Reimann.)

Perhaps the individual biographies of two figures of the time will help to illustrate the complexity of the 1960s Mexican counterculture. One of those people, Luis González-Reimann, was deeply immersed in the countercultural scene but was also the English announcer for the track and field events for the 1968 Mexico City Olympics—the very event at which Tommie Smith and John Carlos raised their fists in solidarity with African-American struggles for justice, a gesture of defiance that provided the definitive narrative framing of the Olympics for a U.S. audience. González-Reimann's participation in the Olympics did not contradict his protest sentiments against the regime, and ironically may have saved his life. This was because he inadvertently missed the infamous event of October 2, 1968, when government troops opened fire on a large gathering of student demonstrators and bystanders just ten days before the start of the Olympic games. The actual number of people killed and wounded has never been fully established, but was probably in the hundreds, and the massacre itself put an effective end to the student-led protests for democratic reform that began that summer. As González-Reimann related to me:

*Mexico's Rock Counterculture (La Onda) in Historical Perspective and Memory*

I was not in Tlatelolco the day of the massacre simply because I was late to catch the chartered bus that took students from my UNAM [National University] department (*facultad*) to the protest. I thought about taking my car, but I decided against it because in a previous demonstration—a huge one that went from the museum of anthropology to the Zócalo—I had left my car parked in the museum parking lot and when I returned the cars on either side had their windows smashed.... I did visit the site of the massacre the following day, though, with someone who had been there and was very shaken and said he had to go back. We couldn't enter the plaza, of course, because it was surrounded by soldiers, but he walked me through where he had ran once the firing started, and described how he saw people next to him fall as they were running and shots were heard. The reason why I was late for the bus is that I was at a rehearsal at the UNAM stadium for the Olympics.

Shortly after, González-Reimann opened an import record store, Yoko, in Mexico City's cosmopolitan district, the Zona Rosa. At the time Yoko was one of the only places available to purchase foreign rock music. His knowledge of music also landed him a position as rock critic for *Piedra Rodante*, Mexico's version of *Rolling Stone* magazine, and his coverage of the Avándaro music festival provides an essential documentary record of that event.

Following Avándaro, González-Reimann shifted away from rock and became deeply absorbed in religious philosophy. Many among the middle class in Mexico were going through a similar transformation, reflected in an embrace of esotericism and non-traditional religious practices. A number of youth joined religious cults, and many went to live in self-styled communes such as La Semilla de Amor, which lasted from 1971 to 1973.[5] We know very little about this other side of the counterculture, except what has been passed down anecdotally. González-Reimann was clearly part of this broader, generational shift. Because of his class background and academic inclinations, however, he chose to leave Mexico and pursue his interest in Eastern religious philosophies more seriously, going first to London and later to the University of California at Berkeley, where he received his doctorate in Sanskrit and South Asian studies. Today, in reflecting on his involvement in La Onda, González-Reimann refers to the period as "another lifetime." Yet those years were clearly an inextricable part of who he was and who he had become—as central to his identity as was the ideological impact of the Cuban Revolution or the experience of marching in student protest during 1968.

The other notable figure is José Luis Atristian, who during the 1960s similarly lived "another lifetime" as a countercultural rebel. Later he became a trade analyst with the Spanish Embassy in Toronto. We met not long ago at a conference on U.S.-Mexican relations and in the course of conversation about contemporary politics, it occurred to me—given his approximate age—to ask him if he had gone to the Avándaro rock festival. It turns out he had not, but only because the car he was travelling in to go to the festival broke down; he and his friends never made it. In fact, this well-dressed, mild-mannered, middle-aged man who crunched numbers for the Spanish Embassy and played an important role in mediating Canadian–Spanish–Latin American relations had once been the lead guitarist of a Mexican rock band. Somehow, I was not surprised. He told me about how his band had performed in Oaxaca during the solar eclipse in 1969—when thousands of Mexicans and foreigners converged on spiritually charged, pre-conquest indigenous sites. Moreover, he had consumed hallucinogenic mushrooms with the famous shaman María Sabina. Perhaps the most engrossing element of his narrative was that his rock group had been airlifted via army helicopter to see Sabina because members of the military stationed in Oaxaca had taken a liking to the band after hearing them play in a bar. His story thus complicates the ideological presumption that the military was "naturally" pitted against students, and that the counterculture was necessarily a refuge from the state. Here, instead, we find the experience of the Mexican counterculture being facilitated by the state itself.

Indeed, the history of Latin America in the 1960s is still in its infancy. I would like to suggest that, as the period recedes from lived memory, the process of a reconstruction of historical memory is presented to a new generation of academics who have come of age without the attachment of earlier ideological sentiments. This younger generation is perhaps more attuned to the rich historical sediment left by rock and countercultural experiences—sediment that earlier academics either ignored (choosing instead to focus on questions of diplomatic and political history) or disparaged as irrelevant to the larger ideological struggles taking place. By exploring the cultural terrain opened up by new areas of investigation, we can gain a glimpse into unexplored realms of the everyday and, moreover, obtain new vantage points from which to reassess the turbulent, impassioned, and highly contested nature of the 1960s as an epochal historical period.

Jim Harding

# CONTINUING ON

## Deepening the Anti-Nuclear Movement since the Sixties

**The mushroom cloud** does not have as compelling a place in the night-mares of children today as it once did. The threat of nuclear war has gone under-ground, literally and metaphorically. However, the weapons are still with us, in larger killing power and numbers, and among more countries than when the nuclear disarmament (ND) symbol was created. During a time when the Cold War that led to the arms race is over, when we have much more awareness of our fragile interdependence with all life, why are tens of thousands of these weapons of mass destruction (WMD) still with us?

The year 2008 saw the fiftieth anniversary of the ND symbol. Commis-sioned by the British Campaign for Nuclear Disarmament (CND) and composed of the semaphore for "N" and "D" within a circle designating the Earth, the sym-bol is universally recognizable. The revolt of the sixties had significant roots in the fifties, particularly the ban-the-bomb movement.[1] If we trace anti-nuclearism from the Cold War to the climate crisis we find that the passion for participatory democracy so central to the emergence of the new left remains front and centre in today's struggle for a new society.

In his introductory essay in *Protest and Survive*, Daniel Ellsberg reminds us, "Those who prepared it and carried it out ... regarded the effects of the first nuclear war as marvellously successful."[2] In popular culture the atomic bombing of Japan is said to have ended World War II and saved many American (though not Japanese) lives. But that bombing was not an isolated occurrence, and the flow of events chronicled by Ellsberg tells a different story. One year later, in 1946, the U.S. Pentagon created the Strategic Air Command (SAC) with the sole purpose of being able to carry out nuclear attacks on the Soviet Union. Soon after NATO's formation in 1949 SAC was "atomic capable." B-29s had already been placed in Germany and the United Kingdom by the start of the Berlin Blockade in June 1948. In 1950 U.S. president Harry Truman launched the "nuclear threat strategy" to keep the Soviet Union from becoming involved in the politics of oil in Iran, right on the USSR border.

For more than two decades the United States either had a monopoly on nuclear weapons or a massive nuclear advantage, but that is not how most people in the West understood the arms race. Anticommunism was so rampant that public reasoning about the dynamics of the nuclear arms race was nearly impossible. According to hard-nosed anticommunists, it was better to be "dead than Red." In the dualistic times, some nuclear disarmers countered that it was better to be "Red than dead," although that also did not represent the choices that we should have had. The peace movement searched for a "third way," outside the "either you are with us or against us" mentality,[3] stressing that war as an instrument of national policy was obsolete in the nuclear age.

After the frightening events of the Berlin Wall and Cuban Missile crises of 1961–62, the closest the United States came to using nuclear weapons was during the Vietnam War. Many of us active in the antiwar struggle of that time feared that the U.S. government might respond to ongoing military defeats at the hands of Vietnamese guerrilla fighters by escalating to nuclear weaponry. After all, the United States was already using Agent Orange and napalm chemical weapons. We now know that we weren't simply being paranoid, and that President Richard Nixon had his advisor Henry Kissinger secretly communicate with Hanoi in 1969 that nuclear weapons were being considered. In his memoirs Nixon called this the "November Ultimatum."[4]

So what stopped him? It clearly was not the threat of retaliation. While the Soviets supplied conventional arms to the North Vietnamese, they had no interest in seeing the colonial–civil war escalating into a nuclear catastrophe. But there was another deterrent. Nixon makes it clear that the ever-more militant antiwar demonstrations, especially in October and November of 1969, made it politically impossible to consider using nuclear weapons in Vietnam. The massive antiwar movement of the 1960s and early 1970s not only helped bring an end to U.S. military intervention in Southeast Asia; it played a critical role in keeping nuclear weapons from being used.[5]

*Continuing On*

# The Shift from the Antiwar to Ecological Critique of Nuclear Energy

The Canadian ban-the-bomb movement coalesced around keeping nuclear weapons off Canadian soil and advocating that Canada play a "positive neutralist" role between the superpowers.[6] Most peace activists opposed Canada staying in NATO and in the North American Aerospace Defence Command (NORAD), formed in 1958, because these organizations perpetuated the arms race.[7]

In 1963 the Pearson Liberal government reversed its position and agreed to locate the Bomarc nuclear missile in Canada.[8] Even some military analysts believed that such a missile, designed to attack a non-existent threat from Soviet bombers coming over the Arctic, was promoted to serve U.S. nuclear arms buildup propaganda. In 1964 some of us launched a Montreal–co-ordinated civil disobedience campaign in the economically depressed region near La Macaza, Quebec, where a missile pad was under construction. (Another site was at North Bay, Ontario.) Growing opposition to Canada directly joining the arms race led to a reversal of this policy, which was one of the Canadian peace movement's finer days, though the depth of Canadian complicity in the arms race had yet to be discovered.

While peace groups rallied opposition to nuclear weapons in Canada, the federal Crown corporation Atomic Energy of Canada Limited (AECL) was advancing its civil nuclear power program in Ontario and elsewhere. Most peace groups saw nuclear technology as primarily a weapons threat and uncritically accepted the notion of the "peaceful atom." An urgent goal was to stop preparations for nuclear war by getting international test-ban and non-proliferation treaties. This separation of the military from the industrial was sometimes tactical, that is, aimed at getting a large coalition supporting nuclear disarmament, and it was sometimes ideological. Otherwise differing capitalist and socialist-leaning peace groups often shared a belief that nuclear energy could be harnessed for the betterment of humankind.

The ban-the-bomb and early anti-nuclear power movements had no organizational links in Canada. The Combined Universities Campaign for Nuclear Disarmament (CUCND), founded in 1958, lasted only until 1964, and the Student Union for Peace Action (SUPA), which replaced it, existed only from 1964 to 1968. It was not until the environmental movement blossomed that the "peaceful atom" was directly challenged. The links between the issues became most clearly drawn with Greenpeace, which originated from Vancouver-based protests of U.S. weapons testing in the earthquake-prone area off Amchitka, Alaska.[9] While Greenpeace is primarily known for militant direct action against industrial whaling, it was also one of the first Canadian groups to overtly oppose nuclear power; it undertook civil disobedience against the Bruce Power complex in Ontario in 1977.

In Europe protests against nuclear power started much earlier, in 1971. The compartmentalized view that separated the military from the "peaceful atom" began to erode in Canada in 1974, when the Candu technology helped India develop its first nuclear bomb. Afterwards more peace groups explored the interconnection of the military and industrial nuclear systems. Fred Knelman's work played an important role in this, as did the Canadian Coalition for Nuclear Responsibility (CCNR), created in 1978 under the leadership of Gordon Edwards. We discovered that the Candu was intentionally designed using heavy water to enable it to produce plutonium for weapons, and that Canada had supplied both plutonium and refined uranium for the Manhattan Project.[10]

In 1974 the newly formed Organization of Petroleum Exporting Countries (OPEC) triggered the "energy crisis" by raising the price of oil. While the peace and ecology movements were integrating their critiques of the nuclear industry, the industry promoted itself as the energy alternative for oil. Nuclear power, however, can't replace the major uses of oil, and with energy efficiency and renewables already coming on stream, nuclear power did not expand to anywhere near what its proponents projected.[11] The industry continues to market itself erroneously, to the extent of now promoting itself as a panacea for global warming.[12] Without massive state subsidies linked to maintaining nuclear weapons, nuclear power probably would not have survived a half-century of such opportunistic promotion.

A huge generational paradigm shift, challenging Enlightenment-rooted instrumental rationality with its dualistic view of technology as being value-free, contributed to the shift in understanding the "peaceful atom." The name "Greenpeace" links the emerging ecological perspective with the peace movement. Indeed, it is not a huge leap from recognizing the destructive ecological consequences of nuclear weapons and war[13] to seeing the ecological devastation brought about by the whole nuclear fuel system. By the mid-1970s we knew that uranium mining increases radon-gas-induced lung cancers among workers and leaves long-lived radioactive tailings that will leach into watersheds and food chains forever. Recent research in India confirms an array of deadly diseases among those living near uranium mines. A rash of European studies directly links living near nuclear facilities with an increased incidence of childhood leukemia. Spent fuel—which will have to be contained from ecosystems for one million years—continues to accumulate at over four hundred reactors worldwide. Major nuclear reactor accidents will continue to occur about once every ten thousand reactor-years of operation (every twenty years with five hundred reactors).

*Continuing On*

Nevertheless, many "old left" activists in the ban-the-bomb peace movement remained sceptical of environmental and anti–nuclear power groups, which were seen as "liberal" or "politically incorrect." Some self-righteous religious peace groups with a singular focus on nuclear war saw these groups as Luddites who cared little for overcoming human poverty and despair. Even the new left manifesto, the 1962 Port Huron Statement of the Students for a Democratic Society, endorsed nuclear power.[14]

While environmentalism initially did not link the ecological crisis to international development, it exposed the growing environmental health and cancer crisis resulting from the drive for profitable accumulation. Soon "deep ecology" began to envisage "soft technology" to preserve ecological sustainability, and a socialist analysis that places capitalist economic growth at the centre of the crisis of ecological carrying capacity began to develop. The creation of this more encompassing political ecology was left to those who followed on the heels of the new left of the 1960s.[15]

# Another Nuclear Arms Race and the End of the Cold War

The United States was in domestic shock even before its defeat in Vietnam in 1975, and by the end of the 1970s the country's geopolitical influence was being challenged on many fronts.[16] The year 1979 was a particularly bad one for the American Empire. It saw the fall of the U.S.-backed Shah of Iran, and a series of events unfolded that can now be traced to the Persian Gulf War in 1991 and the U.S.-led occupation of Iraq in 2003. In 1979 the overthrow of Somoza, the pro-American dictator in Nicaragua, weakened the U.S.-backed counter-insurgency[17] and began a shift towards democratic, left-leaning governments in Latin America. The same year also saw the Soviets invade Afghanistan, where the United States armed and trained a national resistance that defeated the USSR and contributed to its downfall. U.S.-led NATO troops, fronted by Canada, now battle in vain for control of the country. It was also in this climate of shifting geopolitics in 1979 that the West German Green Party (Die Grunen) was formed.

After Ronald Reagan became president in 1981 the U.S. Congress approved hundreds of billions of dollars for the MX, Trident II, and Pershing and Cruise missile systems. Reagan threatened to use nuclear weapons in the Persian Gulf to ensure that oil supplies were not cut off from his country, and in 1983 the Pershing and Cruise missiles were deployed in West Germany and the United Kingdom, presumably to counter Soviet SS-20 missiles. The United States' willingness to risk a pre-emptive (first strike) nuclear war that would be fought on European soil sparked a mass movement that brought together the peace and environmental movements: those opposing nuclear weapons and nuclear power. Opposition to the placement of Pershing and Cruise missiles in West Germany was the main catalyst for the rise of the Green Party, which, after 1983, initially under the leadership of the late Petra Kelly,[18] began electing parliamentarians within West Germany's proportional representation system. The West German Greens have direct continuities with the German new left, which had opposed the capitalism and colonialism of the West as well as the authoritarian "socialism" behind the Iron Curtain. Amongst the Green Party's pillars of principle, two of them—"participatory democracy" and "non-violence"—came directly from the new left, and they were combined with "ecological preservation" and "anticolonialism."

The Soviet Union steadily imploded as dissident and Green formations gained ground within Eastern Europe. The dismantling of the Berlin Wall in 1989 marked the end of the Cold War, and many onlookers thought that development would bring an end to the arms race and deliver a "peace dividend" that would enable resources squandered on the military to be redirected for fundamental human development. The deeply repressed fear of a nuclear holocaust was prematurely lifted.

Some early signs of progress did appear. In 1995 180 countries, including the United States, extended the Nuclear Non-Proliferation Treaty (NPT).[19] In 1996 the five major nuclear powers and forty-four other countries that had the technology to construct nuclear weapons agreed to the Comprehensive Test-Ban Treaty (CTBT).[20] This was a response to the massive global opinion calling for an end to the dangerous and wasteful nuclear arms race. Those of us worn down from decades of anti-nuclear activism were, however, susceptible to wishful thinking. Perhaps we didn't want to believe our own analysis of how powerful the institutions that Eisenhower had warned us about—which he named the Military Industrial Complex (MIC)—had become during the decades of dangerous yet profitable nuclear brinkmanship. The United States insisted that its nuclear weapons labs be able to continue its Stockpile Stewardship and Management Program, which was defended as a means of ensuring the reliability and safety of its nuclear stockpile. Department of Energy documents indicate that the project also included the "ability to design new warheads."[21] Under the guise of "modernization," then, the United States continued to design and manufacture "completely new nuclear weapons."

Helen Caldicott calls this project Manhattan II, pointing out the irony that through the Cold War the United States had spent $3.8 billion a year on nuclear weapons, whereas after the Cold War was over it was spending $5 billion a year. Despite all the posturing about a peace dividend, the lone superpower continues with nuclear armament to help enforce its geopolitical goals, just as it did after World War II.[22]

In the aftermath of 9/11 these contradictions heightened. President George W. Bush not only withdrew from Kyoto and the International Criminal Court but also from the Anti-Ballistic Missile Treaty.[23] A question that perhaps only the next generation will be able to answer is: did the huge antiwar demonstrations prior to the U.S.-led invasion of Iraq act as a deterrent on the use of nuclear weapons? Or do U.S.-led military campaigns since the implosion of the Soviet Union perhaps signal a shift to a new type of nuclear weaponry?

Even if nuclear power is "peaceful," in the sense of not contributing to proliferation, there is nothing peaceful about its cancer-causing effects; and the spread of nuclear power has and will continue to contribute to proliferation. In 2006 George W. Bush proposed a Global Nuclear Energy Program to establish a monopoly on uranium enrichment and reprocessing among nuclear powers— requiring uranium-producing regions like Canada to take back spent fuel. This was an admission that the NPT was not stopping the spread of nuclear weapons, and it illustrates that the whole nuclear fuel system has to be a focus if we are to reverse the spread of nuclear weapons.

When I became active with the CUCND in the late 1950s, we had no idea how "the bomb" was made. When I asked Saskatchewan premier Tommy Douglas (now known as the father of Medicare) to speak at a Nuclear Disarmament rally, I had no idea that uranium was being shipped from the northern part of the province to fuel the U.S. nuclear arsenal. Nor do Canadians commonly realize that the same Lester Pearson who won the Nobel Peace Prize was the member of Parliament from Elliot Lake, Ontario, the other Canadian source of uranium for the U.S. nuclear arsenal. Even though we kept nuclear weapons from being stationed on Canadian soil, we now know that Canada was involved in the development of nuclear weapons from the start. Research at McGill University and later at Chalk River, Ontario, led to the separation of plutonium, which helped both the United Kingdom and United States with their weapons program. Canada supplied both plutonium and refined uranium to the Manhattan Project to help produce the first nuclear weapons.

Canada's place in the weapons' stream carries on. In Saskatchewan the New Democratic Party (NDP) government expanded uranium mining in the 1980s with assurances that the product would only be exported for nuclear reactors. However, though the uranium boom occurred, the boom in nuclear power did not. Meanwhile, the United States shut down its domestic low-grade uranium mines because of guarantees of Canadian uranium supplies under the Free Trade Agreement and later the North American Free Trade Agreement.[24] There is little doubt that Saskatchewan uranium played a role in the United States' nuclear arms buildup under Reagan in the 1980s; it freed up other sources for weapons, and it could make a further contribution through the direct use of depleted uranium (DU) left from the enriching process.

During the Manhattan Project the United States considered two streams of nuclear weaponry: atomic bombs and weapons that spread radioactivity. Though radioactive weapons were abandoned in 1954,[25] they returned with the development of DU weapons in the 1990s. As the heaviest element available, uranium can penetrate tanks, and such penetrator weapons were followed by the use of DU in Cruise, Tomahawk, and other missiles. These DU weapons were first used in the 1991 Persian Gulf War, and then in Bosnia, Afghanistan, and the 2003 invasion of Iraq. Upon explosion the DU weapons produce persistent, carcinogenic, alpha-emitting uranium aerosols that have been linked to increased birth deformations and childhood cancers. Because these DU weapons spread radioactivity, they are in effect weapons of mass destruction, and because they indiscriminately kill civilians returning to past war zones, their use can be considered a war crime. In November 2007 the U.N. process needed to ban these weapons won initial support from 122 countries, with the United States, United Kingdom, France, Israel, Netherlands, and Czech Republic opposing. Canada was among the thirty-five countries that abstained. The struggle for full and complete nuclear disarmament launched in the 1950s continues.

# Historical Reflection and Continuing Struggle

The events of the sixties are not abstract for my generation; they were deeply formative and created the backdrop for today's continuing anti-nuclear struggle. For instance, when I was attending the World Youth Festival in Helsinki, Finland, in 1961 I joined a new left protest of the USSR H-bomb test occurring at the time. It was my first experience with tear gas and the polarized, sometimes violent, politics stemming from World War II. The Finnish police were apparently trying to quell an anti-Soviet youth group, which I was later told had pro-fascist origins, that attacked our demonstration. These youth must have thought we were officially attached to the festival, with its pro-Soviet leanings, and were seemingly not aware that we were protesting a Soviet nuclear test. I learned that Cold War politics was not neat even at the local level.

At the World Disarmament Conference in Moscow in 1961 I witnessed the Chinese delegation leave and the Sino-Soviet split accentuate over whether the primary threat was nuclear war or colonialism. The new left had to overcome such reductionism, and learn to address both. (And we now have to also put "ecology" front and centre.)[26] While nuclear brinkmanship was racheting-up during the 1961 Berlin crisis, when I was on my way back from Moscow, I crossed Checkpoint Charlie, which separated East and West Berlin, both ways. I first

Continuing On

went into the U.S.-controlled zone, where I saw massive dumping of low-priced surplus consumer goods acting as propaganda for the "free enterprise" system. I then went back into the Soviet zone to continue my train travels to Southern Europe. I was treated aggressively by U.S. troops, who might have thought a Canadian coming into West Berlin from the Soviet bloc was a spy; and by Soviet troops, who suspected that such a quick trip involved contraband.[27]

With stampings from several Communist countries in my passport I was later interrogated and stalled from entering England at Dover, while all my papers, including address book, were taken and presumably copied. A quarter of a century later, in 1987—by which time I was a professor of human justice at the University of Regina—my family and I were stopped from flying through the United States en route to a sabbatical at the U.N. University for Peace in Costa Rica. When I appealed this travel ban at the U.S. Consulate in Vancouver, I found that they still had records of my 1961 trip into Eastern Europe. I was told that I was refused entry under the McCarran Act, which the Reagan administration had reactivated from the McCarthyism era. The U.S. government of the 1980s was, of course, deeply involved in counter-insurgency to destabilize the Sandinista government in Nicaragua. I never got to Costa Rica.[28]

I participated in U.S. civil rights activism during the summers of 1963–64, attending the March on Washington at which Martin Luther King Jr. gave his historic "Let Freedom Sing" speech, and I was on my way to help with the Student Nonviolent Coordinating Committee's voter registration campaign until the violent "summer of 64" in Mississippi led to us being turned away. I then joined the Quebec-Guantanamo march protesting the United States' retributive policies on Cuba. During these trips I realized just how unified the peace, human rights, and international development movements were becoming. The ND peace symbol was commonly worn by civil rights activists, who, I learned, had been inspired by and adopted tactics from the ban-the-bomb sit-ins. Activists understood that there would be no chance to expand human rights, or overthrow reactionary regimes holding back social development, if we fried in a nuclear war.

In 1964, when the United States was trying to expand nuclear weapons into Canada, I participated in the civil disobedience at La Macaza. Some of the non-violent training sessions were held at the Quaker-run peace camp at Grindstone Island in the Rideau Lakes district in Ontario. During morning meditation I began to realize the focused, spiritual commitment that was required for this kind of activist life. After that, the development of my "inner life," including learning to admit and reconcile with my fear, was part of my new left activism.

In 1968, at the apex of the new left revolt, I travelled to France, Czechoslovakia, and elsewhere in Europe as an observer for the Canadian Union of Students (CUS). I saw emerging in Europe the new left politics, which contrasted sharply in both theory and practice with what was happening in North America. In retrospect I recognize that "the long march though the institutions" promoted by German activist Rudi Dutschke was laying the ground for the Green Party.[29] At the World Youth Festival at Sofia, Bulgaria, I participated in a new left anti-Vietnam march staged at the U.S. Embassy. The unpredictable complexity of the Cold War hit home when we were charged by Bulgarian police on horseback, coming from one street, and by a "regiment" of Communist Party youth hostile to the presence of the dissident new left, from another. I was grateful to be among German and Spanish youth who were trained to disperse into affinity groups for self-defence. On that trip I left Prague, on advice from underground student activists, just hours before the Soviet tanks came into the city to squash the country's socialist reform movement. That year, when both Martin Luther King Jr. and Bobby Kennedy were assassinated, also marked the escalation of repressive forces in the United States and elsewhere in the West.[30]

I returned to Europe several times: in 1987, when I met with Green Party activists, starting to lay the ground for the hosting of the International Uranium Congress in Saskatoon, Canada, in 1988; in 1992, when I attended the World Uranium Hearings in Salzburg, Austria, and became convinced that I must document the central global role of the uranium industry in my home province, Saskatchewan;[31] in 1993, when I attended the first social anthropology meeting in a reunified Germany, and witnessed corporate ads flooding what had been Eastern Germany;[32] and in 2004, en route to the World Tribunal on Iraq (WTI), initiated by the Bertrand Russell Peace Foundation, which was holding its final session in Istanbul, Turkey.[33] These trips represented a kind of coming full circle from the 1950s, and after them there was no way of believing that what had started in the revolt of the 1950s and 1960s was not still with us historically.

It is revealing to look back at the 1964 Regina founding of Canada's main new left formation, SUPA, from the vantage point of a half-century's perspective. We were trying to replace the "bombcentric" perspective of the CUCND with a radical analysis of society that revealed the links between militarism, colonialism, and domestic injustice. In the process we began to unravel the realities and issues of race, gender, class, and empire that remain with us.[34] This shift was in part due to the pervasive impact of the U.S. civil rights movement and the rise of Black Power, from which the term "student power" developed.[35] It was also a response to the bankruptcy of liberalism and social democracy and ritualistic electoral politics in the face of the magnitude of the threat from the nuclear arms race.[36]

Our keynote speaker in 1964 was Robert Engler, author of the 1961 book *The Politics of Oil*.[37] We were even then, perhaps unknowingly, on to something for, once you look back at the basis of the United States' post–World War II "nuclear threat strategy" in the Middle East, and at the U.S.-initiated warfare in the Middle

*Continuing On*

East since the implosion of the USSR, the origins of the geopolitics of oil that is still with us become clearer. With the Cold War over, NATO's fiftieth-anniversary Washington Declaration altered the body's rhetoric: it went from being a defensive to an offensive alliance. Its revised mandate talks of launching "crisis response operations" over security risks like "terrorism." But it also talks of military interventions over "disruption of the flow of vital resources ... beyond the Allies' territory."[38] While NATO's intervention in Afghanistan is justified as spreading democratic development, the geopolitics of oil continues to play its part behind the scene.

Some SUPA activists focused more on the authoritarianism and militarism of the nation-state, while others looked more to the state's support for the dangerous imperial projects of "late capitalism." The debate was synergetic and held promise, and ultimately the new left was challenged to embrace anti-authoritarian, anticapitalism, and anti-imperialism principles.[39] But at the time none of the political tendencies had any particular ecological consciousness. Developing that approach became the task of the fledgling counterculture and burgeoning environmental movements, which began to deepen the awareness of our interconnectedness with all life in the biosphere and of the need to fundamentally alter the nature of energy and other technology. We went from the fear of nuclear annihilation to the discovery of our ecological home. This occurred *after* the 1960s had imploded from a combination of state repression and new left contradictions around gender and sectarianism. In that sense the end of the sixties constituted the beginning of something much more historically fundamental, revolutionary, and profoundly spiritual, something that remains with us to this day.

While the new left's revolutionary call to "participatory democracy" got somewhat sidetracked into vanguardism, the politics initiated during that time continued to grow with the feminist, environmental, human rights, and civil society movements from the 1970s on. These ventures, too, sometimes got sidetracked into identity politics. What we have experienced has been a long march through the institutions, and, in the wake of the anti-globalization protests of the 1990s and the deepening climate crisis, a new convergence of awareness is again upon us. The threat of nuclear proliferation is now deeply bound up with issues of energy and ecology. The same state-supported nuclear industry that fuelled the arms race, in part to protect oil for the United States and West, now wants to expand its radioactive hardware as a major energy source. This time the struggle is about ending the threat of nuclear war through nuclear disarmament and the phasing out of nuclear energy as we meet the urgent challenge to create a sustainable society. The struggle of the past fifty years or more shows that collective, non-violent, extraparliamentary activism makes a difference—and probably even helped to keep us alive—so let us continue on with it.

# "Tear it Down"

## Reflections of a Veteran

**While giving** credit to those who were known and symbolized for many the period known as the sixties, I will attempt to place a little spotlight and provide a different perspective on others who made that period truly dynamic. The historical emphasis is to shine a light on the thousands if not millions of activists who were unknown and unheralded but constituted the decisive mass critical in shaping and implementing a notable period of resistance.

Many of us have not really had time to reflect back on the 1960s because we have been, and still are, engaged in continuing struggles in different arenas, under different conditions, and with different perspectives. Yet we all realize how historically significant that time was. For many of us the sixties was a period of great diversity and complexity, with multiple contradictions and convergences around an idealism that, in its most positive aspect, continues to shape our lives and influence even the dominant culture in our respective societies.

It was a time when a young generation with little historical connection to previous oppositional movements or organizational frameworks took upon itself to present a defiant challenge to the status quo. The slogan of the day was "tear it down." We really believed in this slogan and set upon the path of bringing down the very foundations and institutions of capitalist society. For many, the slogan was not an abstract concept. It was discussed, debated, and acted upon by thousands of activists from various ideological and social perspectives and backgrounds. We did not tear down the system, obviously, but we did profoundly influence and propel changes that are still part of our lives today.

Many people who did not live during that period have only a one-dimensional, warped view of it. This misconception is deliberately fostered by the system and the mass commercial media, which have represented the period through distorted images of hippies, flower children, Woodstock, Hell's Angels, Abbie Hoffman, Tom Hayden, and the Students for a Democratic Society. While not diminishing or ignoring the various roles and contributions of those placed in this spotlight, I would argue that the 1960s was the sum of more than a period often depicted as anarchic or nihilistic. Rarely do we hear of the free speech movement at the University of California at Berkeley, or the 1968 Third World student-led strike at San Francisco State university. The revisionism of the sixties legacy flows from President Richard Nixon's claim to represent the "silent majority" as opposed to the unruly "minority" protesting the Vietnam War. More recently, when he was contending for the presidency, Barack Obama spoke dismissively of the need to overcome the "psychodrama" of the sixties.

As a young Latino coming of age politically at the time, I was also affected by this distorted image of the movement. When I participated in my first anti–Vietnam War demonstration in Washington, D.C., in 1971, I did so with great reluctance. My reservation stemmed from my doubts about smoking marijuana and taking my clothes off as symbolic of opposition to the system. As I told an organizer, "Listen, if that goes on, I am not going to be part of the show!" I viewed my participation as distinctly supportive of the Vietnamese in the struggle against imperialism, and I wanted to tear down the walls. Of course, I wound up joining hundreds who were arrested that day.

At that point in my political development, I also shared an immense misconception of the movement and in particular the multilayered mass antiwar movement. Even though I was a participant, I was nevertheless influenced by the dominant projection in the mass media. Yet beyond the diverting stories of alienation and general antagonism, fundamental shifts were occurring in society. It was a period of revolution, a period of altering social relationships and attitudes. Even *The New York Times* recognized the seismic shift in a poll conducted in 1970, which reported that four out of ten university students believed that a revolution was necessary.

It was kind of a long time ago. Our memories tend to diminish as time passes. Now the word "revolution" is a commercial demarcation, used to sell automobiles or the latest cellular phone accessory. The very music of the sixties, from Bob Dylan to Jefferson Airplane, has become a background for commercial advertising. When you think of the different context the music had in the sixties, you can only cringe at its commercial manipulation.

How we defined the movement of the sixties was a central issue at the time, and it continues to be the subject of debate today, long decades later. There is of course a debate among those who were prominent activists in the Students for a Democratic Society, the dominant student movement in the United States. The argument centres on the issue of the 1960s being divided between an early period—the Tom Hayden/Port Huron statement era, with its democratic social orientation—and the later, more radical, nihilistic, ultraleftist, combative, and militant phase that included the rise of the Weathermen faction within the SDS. The argument for that divide—for how the movement lost its democratic mass orientation—has been popularized by a number of writers, including Todd Gitlin, Christopher Hitchens, and, in Europe, the Fishers of Germany, Régis Debray of France, and Bernard Kushner, the new foreign minister under President Nicolas Sarkozy of France. Some of these people were prominent leftist radicals of the day. Many such people later shifted to the role of left-liberal cover for the anti-Islamic, pro-war agenda of the Bush-Cheney "War on Terror" doctrine.

Nevertheless, there was another layer of activists, in the millions, who were not well known, did not write, did not become intellectual authors, and in many cases did not fully realize their historical role. They were the people, largely youth, who were profoundly influenced by the cross-currents of the Black liberation struggle, Vietnam, and the explosive worldwide events of 1968. Examples of individual transformation are everywhere. A former prostitute in Selma, Alabama, for instance, saw fit to join Robert Moses and the Student Nonviolent Coordinating Committee (SNCC) when they were working to desegregate that city; she was radically reformed as an individual and today is a university professor. One can also think of the Yemeni labour organizer Naji Daifullah, who became a key organizer with César Chavez in the struggle of the United Farm Workers, and who died at the hands of the police during that historic struggle in 1973. This is an example of sacrifice unacknowledged even in the labour arena. Then there is the case of the United Arab Workers caucus in the United Auto Workers (UAW)—in 1974 they called upon the UAW to stop supporting Israeli policies in Palestine and argued for democratic reform within the union. The history is largely unknown, but reflective of the period. It coincides with issues and struggles raised by the League of Black Revolutionary Auto Workers. All were activists shaped and influenced by the decisive issues of the day: the Vietnam War, civil rights struggle, student activism, or police repression.

# I remember when I was a kid thinking that the world was going to end.

This was during the Cuban Missile Crisis of October 1962. The political crisis permeated the consciousness of masses of people and left indelible impressions that we were, as a song of the period phrased it, "on the eve of destruction." The whirlwind events unfolding during that period forced many of us to confront our ways of thinking, and to address issues beyond our immediate experiences.

My personal perspective was radically altered. Until 1967 my entire focus was on being the next great Puerto Rican baseball player after my hero Roberto Clemente. I had a shot with a couple of major league teams. Unfortunately I was also drafted by the U.S. army. During this period I slowly drifted from baseball and began to seriously question the political events of the period. A singular event for me was the stand of Black athletes during the 1968 Mexico Olympics—especially the Black Power salutes of U.S. medal winners John Carlos and Tommie Smith. That was a profound turning point in terms of my athletic perspective. The question of liberation, of community control, Black civil rights, and Black Power, and my identity as a Latino within the United States became my paramount concerns.

Like others I was influenced intellectually by the critical struggles of that time. The system was in crisis, and many of us were searching for analyses and ideological conceptions that could address the multitude of problems facing our communities. Overriding everything was the Vietnam War: thousands of Blacks, Latinos, Asians, Native Americans, and working-class whites were being sent off to fight and die. At the same time our communities were facing extreme discrimination, including segregated laws in the South and a profound lack of educational, housing, or employment opportunities. Martin Luther King Jr. drew this connection in his 1968 address at the Riverside Church in New York. The system was compelled to respond to this contradiction and expand the social programs in order to minimize it. Out of this came the Great Society program of President Lyndon B. Johnson, which funnelled millions of dollars into the communities. One of these programs was an expanded program called College Bound, with the goal of increasing college enrolment of Black, Latino, and other minority students. We were guaranteed college admission by fulfilling the required curriculum emphasis on reading and writing. Well, we did a lot of reading and writing: Malcolm X, Che Guevara, Richard Wright, Langston Hughes, Frantz Fanon, H. Rap Brown, Robert Williams, Mao, and every radical left publication we could get our hands on, from the Black Panther Party's newspaper to the Nation of Islam writings and Latin American and Palestinian literature. Personally, I think I read more then than I've read ever since. That was an intense period of awakening as we absorbed a great multitude of political perspectives and ideas.

No other group was as instrumental in shaping our perspective as the Black Panther Party. There were nuances, concerns, and distinct problems that differentiated the particular issues of Latinos from those of the Panthers. Nevertheless, by and large the Black Panthers were viewed as the vanguard and served as a nexus and heroic model for those of us who came of age during that period. Within the Latino community, militant Panther-style groups emerged, such as the Brown Berets in California and the Young Lords Party on the East Coast. We did not follow an exact model or formula. In fact, we were an eclectic blend of nationalism and cultural and ethnic identity with an array of new communist thinking. But we offered an alternative to the limitations of reforms and integration advocated by the traditional mainstream organizations in the Latino communities. Radical transformation through the dominant prism of Marxist-Leninist-Maoist ideology became the framework of a new generation of activists. It was a diverse adaptation of Guevara and Mao, symbolized especially by the slogan "Dare to struggle, Dare to win."

In the Puerto Rican community the Young Lords Party lasted from 1969 to 1973. It primarily comprised young Puerto Ricans born and raised in the United States. Many of us had never been to the island and did not have full command of Spanish. In Puerto Rico, many would derisively call us Nuyoricans. Among the cross-currents influencing our thinking as U.S.-born Puerto Ricans was Chicago Black Panther leader Fred Hampton, who helped to transform the Young Lords from a Chicago-based street gang to a national organization with a defined political perspective.

Puerto Rican nationalism and the struggle for Puerto Rican independence became our primary focus. Despite our lack of fluent Spanish, and our U.S. backgrounds, we became a critical component of the struggle connecting the island with the mainland. We became Puerto Rican nationalists who viewed ourselves as inseparable from the struggle of other communities, especially Black Americans. We identified ourselves with the global issues of the day, whether they involved the Vietnam War, China, Cuba, Africa, or the Middle East. Our bible of choice was Frantz Fanon's *Wretched of the Earth* and Mao's "Little Red Book." Our conception of the struggle was to bring down the system and end the colonial reality of Puerto Rico. What was unique within this framework was that we also incorporated people from all over Latin America and the Caribbean, as well as African Americans. One of the leading figures in the Young Lords was an African-American woman. The Young Lords Party was a multinational organization and reflected a conception of the struggle as a worldwide process. Our perspective was not limited to our immediate surroundings. Young people, many of whom had never ventured beyond their immediate neighbourhoods, adopted a worldview connecting their issues to the larger framework of worldwide struggle and radical transformation unfolding at the time. Our contextual understanding was based on mutual support and solidarity within the U.S. political arena and internationally.

In its short life the Young Lords Party made a significant contribution to the struggle of the sixties and raised issues of particular concern to the Latino community. We attempted to address the problems of inadequate health care, city services, welfare, unemployment, sweatshop exploitation, rampant drug abuse, and male chauvinism within the nationalist movement in Puerto Rico. We contested these issues and organized a presence throughout various Puerto Rican communities, especially on the East Coast but including areas of the West Coast.

I began my political involvement as a high-school student active in the 1967–68 struggle for community control of the educational system in Oceanhill-Brownsville, Brooklyn. Subsequently I helped organized around other issues, including "Free Angela Davis" events among high-school students.

While much has changed in the last forty years for many of us, especially those who were activists in the various Latino formations, there is a continuity in our present activities. This signals continuity between our experiences in the sixties and the struggles and concerns we are addressing decades later. Once again it is the case that many of us have continued on—not famous, not well known beyond our immediate corner of activism, but utilizing our experiences to make change. In today's antiwar movement, in the AIDS crisis, electoral politics, women's movement, academia, or the labour movement, you will find Black, white, and Latino veterans from the sixties.

The labour arena in the United States provides a clear example of continuity. The rupture in the traditional framework of the AFL-CIO, resulting in the creation of a second federation called Change to Win, was propelled by individuals who were largely shaped by their experiences during the sixties. Many were direct participants in struggles from civil rights to the women's, lesbian and gay, and Latino movements and of course the mass anti–Vietnam War mobilizations. These activists brought with them a history of grassroots organizing, and over the last thirty years they have introduced the most innovative, strategic changes, countering the old dinosaurs who used to proudly boast of never walking a picket line.

Today we do walk picket lines! We also organize mass community rallies and have organized on a mass level. In labour we have expanded the strategic concept of labour/community alliances. Some of this flows from our experiences of the sixties. Obviously not everything is applicable today. Nevertheless, a significant number of experienced, seasoned activists continue to shape the possibilities of social, progressive transformation in the future. In the United States many of us have helped to expand the possibilities because there are more women, Black, and Latino activists in the various arenas of struggle. In the case of labour, history has made it possible to raise issues of immigration, war, racism, and Palestine, and to fashion a greater receptivity to debate and discussion on these and other issues. Many of us to began to raise these issues during the sixties and continue to engage with them now.

Each generation has, of course, to come of its own. But we of the sixties, as activists, have a role to play in helping to shape and educate the next generation. As Fanon wrote, "Each generation must out of relative obscurity discover its mission, fulfill it, or betray it."[1] History has shown that each age has its particular historical moment and urgent missions. One could think of the generation shaped and moulded by the Spanish Civil War. As in the case of those activists and fighters, we of the sixties generation can and have continued to fulfil significant roles in the design and direction of social transformation. Today, given the period and context we are living in, it is more urgent than ever to provide continuity to the struggle. In so doing we can, I hope, get back to tearing down the wall.

# 41 Alice Echols

# ACROSS THE UNIVERSE
## Rethinking Narratives of Second-Wave Feminism

"Life is our cause."

—Joni Mitchell, "All I Want"

"We lived on distant shores
until we yearned for more."

—Labelle, "Chameleon"

**In October 2007,** less than six months after the Kingston, Ontario, New World Coming conference, Julie Taymor's giddy yet earnest evocation of the sixties, *Across the Universe*, hit the screens. At first viewing, Taymor's movie might seem like pure Hollywood schmaltz, with a storyline built around a conventional love story. But *Across the Universe* departs from the usual sixties narrative in significant ways. Women are central rather than ancillary figures in the movie. Audiences feel the generational angst, confusion, and rebelliousness of the sixties not just through the experiences of its male characters but also through the struggles of the antiwar Lucy, the lesbian Prudence, and the Joplinesque rocker Sadie.

The film is also unusual in its tacit acknowledgement of the permeability of national boundaries. In its insistence upon the absolute centrality of the war—for both Americans and the Vietnamese—its use of the Beatles' music to narrativize the period, and its repeated shots of the Atlantic Ocean, *Across the Universe* seems to be an echo of the conference's major theme: that is, the global dimension of the sixties. And yet the temptation to cast the era as peculiarly American was apparently irresistible to Taymor and her colleagues, who portray even the Beatles' Liverpool as curiously stagnant—a backwater, really—and New York as the epicentre of transformational grooviness.

Histories of second-wave feminism often proceed as if the movement was, like "the sixties" more generally, a primarily American phenomenon. Yet women's liberation was nothing if not transnational. As with the first wave, feminist ideas circulated globally, refusing national boundaries. While U.S. feminism is usually treated as the ur-feminism, many early women's liberationists in the United States (and Canada) were powerfully affected by examples of the women of North Vietnam, China, and Cuba. For example, Vivian Rothstein, one of the founders of the Chicago Women's Liberation Union, has said that her feminism was sparked in large measure by a trip she made to Vietnam in 1967 with a delegation of U.S. peace activists. Meeting with members of the Vietnamese Women's Union impressed upon her the importance of independent women's organizations.[1] That said, it is true that feminism burrowed very deeply into U.S. culture, where historically the legacy and strength of identity-based politics relative to class-based politics worked in its favour. So too did the absence of European-style social policies to support working mothers, which ratcheted up the tension between work and family obligations for many women.[2]

Here, though, I want to concentrate not on global feminism, but on what I know best—second-wave feminism in the United States—and, writing as a historian, touch on several broad areas: the relationship between the left and feminism; the idea that the Personal is Political; and the centrality of race to the U.S. women's movement.

At the 2007 New World Coming conference, the issues of feminism and gender came up time and again, usually from the floor. So quickly were questions about gender and feminism raised that I sometimes found myself wondering if the conference organizers, perhaps frustrated by how few proposals they received from women, had a pact of sorts to keep the issue alive. In any case, I appreciated the interventions—and find it fascinating that the conference apparently did not appeal to more feminist academics and activists. I was left wondering if that outcome was related to how the sixties is so often narrativized, with the new left and the civil rights movement providing the central stories and other movements—Black Power, women's, gay/lesbian, Chicano/a, Asian-American, and Native American—treated as pesky subplots that eventually overwhelm the sixties dream of the beloved community, that upend the dream of We-ness.

It may also be the case that the somewhat lukewarm response was the legacy of the fraught relationship between feminism and the left in the "long sixties." The new left's frequently uncomprehending, sometimes trivializing, even hostile stance towards feminism profoundly shaped both the second wave and the new left in the United States, and parenthetically I worry that their disputatious relationship gets lost when our histories too seamlessly fold feminism into the left. As for feminism, its autonomy from the left was to a great extent its strength—as it opened up for political analysis areas that had remained largely unexplored. Feminists delved into personal politics with a kind of ferocity that was unlike the left's more delimited discussions.

The P is P turned out to be, like "Black Power," both deliciously and dangerously labile. As originally formulated, it was meant to indicate the political dimensions of personal life, more specifically that women's oppression was embedded in the power dynamics of intimate life. But if feminism's independence from the left allowed it to see the world anew, without deference to old and familiar paradigms, over time that separation became a weakness, as the movement too often dismissed, as "male," concerns with economic class and with race. For some feminists, this rupture from the left would lead to a political stance that demonized the left and much of the "sixties" while celebrating so-called "female culture." "Goodbye to all that," ripped Robin Morgan in her incendiary 1970 essay, and she meant it as a kiss-off to the movement.[3] But as students of the sixties know, saying goodbye to *all that* proved impossible. Indeed, the way in which the P is P was moralistically deployed to impugn how people lived—sleeping with men, for example, or sleeping with women and men, or ... you get my point—could be traced to the persistent puritanism of U.S. culture, as Chris Stansell argues. And it could also be traced to the construction of normative femininity that encouraged the policing of the self and of other women.

Perhaps nowhere do we see the difficulty of breaking with hierarchies of power more than in the issue of race. Wrestling with the intersectionality of race, class, sexuality, and gender could prove uncomfortable for white feminists, for whom it meant dealing with their own embeddedness and complicity in systems of hierarchy. Very often white feminists were wedded to a false universalism in which their experiences stood in synecdochically for "woman's" experience. What was perhaps even more exasperating to many Black women was the eagerness with which white feminists appropriated the terms of racial oppression as analogous to their own—what was called the "racial analogy." To many Black women the notion that women were "the niggers of the world," a conception put forward in manifestos and in the John Lennon/Yoko Ono song, was offensive. Even more off-putting was the effort on the part of some white feminists to appropriate the "Black experience" for themselves. Indeed, to Toni Morrison it sometimes felt as if white women were involved in the shallowest sort of racial impersonation. Writing in 1971, she issued a stinging rebuke to the idea of sisterhood as she excoriated white feminists' appropriating of what she called "our thing," by which she meant Black cultural conventions. (This was a fascinating piece, even if Morrison ignored the underlying structural factors.) She included in her laundry list of hijacked cultural practices "common-law marriage (shacking)" and "children out of wedlock," which, she noted, "is even fashionable now if you are a member of the Jet Set (if you are poor and Black it is still a crime); families without men; right to work; sexual freedom, and an assumption that woman is equal to man."[4] That these practices and stances were heralded as liberatory in white women when Black women were still stigmatized for them (and had little choice but to engage in these practices) was the final insult for Morrison and some other Black women.

As Morrison's reaction suggests, the story of race and the women's movement is complicated. White movement women often emulated Black women, but in ways that did not usually engender cross-racial feelings of sisterhood on the part of Black women. Indeed, as sociologist Wini Breines demonstrated in her terrific book *The Trouble Between Us*, the history of the relationship between Black and white women in the movement was full of ironies.[5] For example, the supposed solipsism of women's liberation—its focus on analyzing and fighting against one's *own* oppression—was less the result of the therapeutic age or of class or racial privilege than it was the influence of Black Power, which treated political empathy and working on behalf of others as hopelessly compromised—the worst sort of liberal cop-out. The idea of organizing around one's own oppression rather than working on behalf of others less privileged than oneself became in the sixties a revolutionary commonplace that radical young whites took up seriously if apprehensively. The efforts to rethink revolutionary subjectivity can be seen in the transatlantic theorizing of white-collar workers as a "new working class," students as revolutionaries, and women as an oppressed caste. But if the principle of political separatism energized the mostly white, middle-class, college-educated women who made up the ranks of women's liberation, it was, when reworked as female separatism, usually a turnoff to women of colour, especially those who were involved in liberation movements of race and ethnicity. Also a turnoff was radical feminism's antagonism to men, the family, and religion. But the alienation that women of colour often felt went beyond this to include feminism's preoccupation with what came to be known as "process." At the New World Coming conference Sarita Srivastava argued that the "let's talk" orientation of white feminists privileges verbal processing in ways that can silence women of colour, who are accustomed to adopting strategies of silence in an interracial context.

That Black women (and women of colour more generally) were not especially active in the best-known parts of the women's liberation movement does not mean that they are not part of feminism's history. Recently, historian Ruth Feldstein has looked to the cultural arena and argued for the importance of Nina Simone, the singer-songwriter responsible for "Mississippi Goddam," "Four Women," and "New World Coming." Feldstein contends that in her music and self-presentation Simone "offered a vision of Black cultural nationalism within and outside the United States that insisted on female power." Feldstein also notes that this was "well before the apparent ascendance of black power or second-wave feminism."[6] Recent scholarship also suggests that Black women were not simply role models, that they were involved in shaping the agenda of the second wave in the years (sometimes decades) before 1968's Miss America protest put women's liberation on the map. In *The Other Feminists*, historian Susan M. Hartmann upends the usual periodization by pointing to the vitality of women's activism from the 1940s through the 1960s. Focusing on the International Union of Electrical Workers, American Civil Liberties Union, National Council of Churches, and Ford Foundation, she discovered that feminism was not nearly as race-specific or class-specific as often assumed.[7] Other scholars (among them Premilla Nadasen, who has published on the National Welfare Rights Organization) have studied groups that were feminist in practice if not in word, and in ways that illuminate the role of working-class women and women of colour. In my forthcoming book on disco I argue that one cannot understand the growth of Black feminism in the 1970s without taking account of the cultural work performed by Black women singers and songwriters of the period.

These revisionist studies have usefully de-centred white feminism, some of them without losing sight of what was distinctive in feminism's different strands—for example, the concern with motherhood that often powered Black feminism, and the hostility to the domestic that so often fuelled radical (white) feminists. For example, sociologist Benita Roth conceptualizes the second wave as one involving different strands or "roads" to feminism.[8] That said, I wonder if some of this revisionist work doesn't run the risk of rendering feminism hopelessly baggy, as everything—including strength in circumstances of hardship or, say, a particularly open approach to organizing—becomes understood as intrinsically feminist. There is also a way in which the new revisionism ironically allows feminism to retain its privileged position in the hierarchy of women's movements. Feminism is actually but one of many expressions of female (and gendered) activism, and I would like to see us tease out the dynamic relationship between it and other movements. As Rabab Abdulhadi points out (see chapter 1 here), it was a supposedly glamorous female revolutionary who mesmerized young Palestinian girls and discouraged them from leading conventional, domesticated lives.

Finally, I worry that the feminism-is-everything approach runs the risk of blunting differences between women. Difference is scary and uncomfortable, the big bogeyman that makes us want to be like others or, more typically, to make others over into versions of ourselves—a tendency I would hope we might resist so that there is room both for the less materialistic among us and for those who aspire to own houses, cars, and new—not second-hand—clothes.

# ENGAGING THE PAST AND MAPPING THE FUTURE

## Nuclear Weapons and Self-Determination— from Diego Garcia and Cuba to Iraq and Iran

**The 1960s** was a period of transition in human history at a global level—a period defined by the contestation of the verities of power across the entire globe: colonialism, apartheid, Jim Crow, superpower dominance, nuclear weapons, and the triumphalist advocacy of the "modern" over "tradition" in the shaping of human society. This contestation has continued into the present, and the contemporary context of the new millennium provides a way of thinking about the meaning of the 1960s as a period of transition. It also serves as a point from which we can examine the unresolved issues of the decade, and their impact upon global human society.

On February 3, 1960, in South Africa a speech delivered by British prime minister Harold Macmillan heralded a new era in international relations. Macmillan declared: "The wind of change is blowing through this continent, and whether we like it or not, this growth of national consciousness is a political fact. We must all accept it as a fact, and our national policies must take account of it."[1] The statement signalled Britain's recognition that its imperial sway in Africa was coming to an end. More important, Macmillan's words offered a recognition that European colonial rule in the non-European world had become an anachronism in international life. In effect, imperial retreat marked the consolidation of the influence of the emerging nuclear superpowers—the United States and USSR—within the international system and the struggle of those two nations to define their respective spheres of influence on the global stage.

The passage from European colonialism was further stimulated by a December 12, 1960, United Nations General Assembly resolution, which declared: "The subjection of peoples to alien subjugation, domination and exploitation constitutes a denial of fundamental human rights, is contrary to the Charter of the United Nations and is an important impediment to the promotion of world peace and co-operation"[2] The year thus represented a major turning point in the history of European colonialism and in the creation of new states that legitimized national independence as a cornerstone of the international order.

In the period between Macmillan's speech in March and the U.N. declaration in December, two other events occurred that illustrated the intensity of the struggle for a new international order: the Sharpeville massacre in South Africa, and the escalation of the Franco-Algerian conflict over the future of Algeria. The South African police decision to shoot unarmed peaceful demonstrators protesting against South African pass laws served as a powerful reminder of the brutality embedded in the construction of the Nazi-influenced apartheid regime in South Africa.[3] The escalation of the Algerian conflict with the French government under president Charles de Gaulle demonstrated why France, like Britain, would have to bring an end to its own formal empire in Africa.[4] This was, then, a time that did not just signal the transition away from colonialism but also opened further debate about the legacies of colonial rule and the intellectual deformations that colonialism had produced on a global scale.

This period of transition from direct and indirect colonial rule was not all-encompassing, and two cases in particular—Diego Garcia and the Chagos Islands in the Indian Ocean and Cuba in the Caribbean—provide extreme examples of the global struggle over colonialism and national self-determination in the 1960s.

**The case** of Diego Garcia and the Chagos Islanders offers a window into the survival of colonialism and its deleterious effects upon the colonized. The status of these islands and of their inhabitants illustrates the integration of European colonialism into the superpower struggle during the Cold War—a process that has had long-term consequences both for the local people and the wider global struggle for power among the major powers.

Diego Garcia, an island in the archipelago of Chagos Islands in the Indian Ocean, was part of the British colony of Mauritius until the mid-1960s, when the islands were separated from Mauritius, renamed the British Indian Ocean Territory, and placed under the direct rule of the Foreign and Colonial offices in

London. Earlier, in the wake of the 1956 Suez crisis and the expansion of U.S. influence in Asia and the Middle East, the United States had expressed interest in establishing a base in the Indian Ocean; and in 1966 Britain and the United States reached an agreement for Diego Garcia to be leased to the United States for fifty years. As a result of this agreement, and at the request of the U.S. government, the British government systematically pursued a policy of expelling the Chagos Islanders from their homes. To accommodate U.S. demands for complete control over the archipelago, the islanders were also denied the right of return. In return Britain received a subsidy of $11 million on its purchase of the Polaris submarine-launched nuclear missile system from the United States.[5] In effect the Chagos Islanders were in part deprived of their rights, their property, and their homeland, all to facilitate the British pursuit of a nuclear deterrent force that would allow the country to continue "punching above its weight" in the international arena.

Diego Garcia, then, is a symbol of the use of both colonialism and population displacement as part of the grand strategy of containment by the Western powers during the Cold War. The fate inflicted upon the Chagos Islanders illustrated the vulnerabilities of colonial populations to the machinations of Western imperial projects. Then too, after the end of the Cold War, the island acquired an even greater importance for the Anglo-U.S. alliance when it became a forward deployment base for the pursuit of wars on the mainland of Asia in Afghanistan and Iraq and a site for the use of torture beyond domestic law and international scrutiny. In light of the U.S. effort to establish military bases in Iraq, Diego Garcia emerged as part of a wider strategy for the reassertion of imperial rule in the Middle East. Diego Garcia is a reminder that colonialism remains an instrument of strategic power and a source of continuing abuses of human rights and crimes against humanity.[6] The occupation of Iraq accentuated the threat that colonialism poses to international peace and security in the new millennium.

# The role of Diego Garcia in the American grand strategy as a global power and in the development of Cold War and post–Cold War strategy serves as a reminder of the relationship between the struggle for national determination, conflict among the major powers, and the politics of nuclear weapons—and those same themes shaped the context within which the Cuban Missile Crisis of 1962 unfolded.

The Cuban Revolution of 1959 had resulted in the overthrow of the U.S. client government of Fulgencio Batista and the seizure of power by the guerrilla movement led by Fidel Castro. Confronted by a radical revolution in America's "backyard," and facing the gravest threat to the Monroe Doctrine since its enunciation in 1823, the Eisenhower and Kennedy administrations embarked upon a strategy aimed at the destabilization and overthrow of the Castro-led regime.[7]

For Castro and his supporters, the Revolution offered an opportunity to reconstruct the Cuban political system and minimize the influence of the U.S. economic, political, and military stakeholders whose influence had kept Cuba in a quasi-colonial relationship with the United States since 1898. For Castro, 1959 opened the way for the assertion of a genuine Cuban independence that had been denied by the Treaty of Paris, the Platt Amendment, and the growth of U.S. political, cultural, and economic influences that had shaped Cuba after the Spanish-American War.[8] Thus, the issue of national self-determination was key to the search for an alliance with the Communist bloc and the disruption of U.S. assumptions that the Monroe Doctrine, with its avowed aim of limiting European influence in the Americas, would govern the U.S. relationship with the revolutionary regime. Castro explicitly linked the challenges facing Cuba to the anticolonial struggle in Africa and the anti-apartheid struggle in South Africa.[9]

The Soviet decision to place nuclear missiles in Cuba was driven in part by the idea that the weapons could be used to counter the threat posed by U.S. nuclear missiles based in Turkey. Further, the deployment of the missiles created a security umbrella for the Cuban revolutionary regime as a symbol of Soviet support for national liberation in the non-European world. As well, in 1961 the United States had sponsored an invasion of the island by Cuban exiles at the Bay of Pigs. The attack, though easily defeated by the Castro government, left the revolutionary leaders with serious fears of U.S. intervention and made them receptive to the stationing of Soviet nuclear weapons on the island. Cuba had thus become a theatre of Cold War politics—with the Cuban Missile Crisis illustrating the volatility of superpower conflict when interwoven with the challenge of Third World nationalism. While commentators have tended to see the crisis as a product of competition between the superpowers in the early nuclear era, one of its most important consequences was an explicit pledge made by the Kennedy administration that the United States would not invade Cuba. In effect, Soviet nuclear diplomacy had placed limits on U.S. efforts to contain national self-determination and revolutionary change in Cuba.[10]

# Diego Garcia marked the failure of global consciousness to protect a vulnerable colonial population. In a sense, the story of the Chagos Islanders serves as a reminder that the past is not a foreign country. It is often an echo of human tragedy—a tragedy of indigenous dispossession that is being replicated today in Iraq. Hundreds of thousands of Iraqi refugees from the Anglo-U.S. invasion of 2003 and its aftermath have created the biggest population displacements in the

Middle East since the *naqba* of Palestinian dispossession that accompanied the creation of Israel.[11] Iraq now represents the legacy of incomplete transformation of the international order away from Euro-U.S. colonial rule in the 1960s. It also illustrates how the "threat" of nuclear weapons has become a *casus belli* and a strategy of colonial reassertion by the Western powers.

The U.S. effort to impose an occupation of Iraq and to create a client regime within that country represents a return to the policies that emerged out of the U.S. intervention and occupation of Cuba during the Spanish-American War of 1898.[12] That war signalled the United States' emergence as a full-fledged imperial power in both the Caribbean and the Pacific, a turn of events that transformed it into both a collaborator and competitor with its European counterparts. As the case of Diego Garcia reveals, the United States has continued the pattern of collaboration with its European partners on the maintenance of colonial rule as a strategy for projecting U.S. power well beyond its borders.[13] The invasion and occupation of Iraq represented a joint enterprise between the United States and Britain as the major partners, which suggests that the two parties still see colonialism as key to a long-term collaboration in projecting their influence at a global level. Similarly, the U.S. invasion of Afghanistan evolved into an effort to create a viable Afghan state, which is now a colonial responsibility assigned to the North Atlantic Treaty Organization, a configuration that links key European states with the United States and Canada.[14] In effect, NATO's colonial project in Afghanistan has become a joint enterprise among the traditional colonial powers and their newer partners. Further, in the case of Iraq, the United States and Britain apparently embarked upon an effort to re-create a Western-dominated order in the Middle East—along similar lines to the events that occurred in the aftermath of the First World War and the disintegration of the Ottoman Empire.

The effort to revive colonial rule in the service of great power strategy has been complicated by the spread of nuclear technology and weapons across the international system. In many ways the Cuban Missile Crisis was a precursor of a larger problem that emerged in the decades after 1962—how to ensure that the spread of nuclear weapons does not destabilize international relations, which would in turn lead to the outbreak of nuclear war. Just as important is the issue of how to guarantee the security of smaller non-nuclear states in a world that has seen the proliferation of "weapons of mass destruction." The Anglo-U.S. project in Iraq has undermined the United Nations as a guarantor of the system of international security that was fashioned over the course of the Cold War.

The wake of the U.S. occupation of Iraq clearly indicates the need for a concerted effort to re-establish national self-determination as a fundamental human right and a cornerstone of the international order. Failing such commitments on the part of the major powers, and assuming a further paralysis of the

United Nations, it would seem likely that nuclear weapons and technologies will continue to spread among or be developed in non-nuclear states—as occurred in India, Pakistan, Israel, North Korea, and South Africa during the Cold War era. Iran's commitment to develop a nuclear power industry with Russian support has become a major plank in that renewed debate and a potential flashpoint among the major powers.

The Cuban Missile Crisis of 1962 brought the world to the brink of nuclear confrontation over the island's right to self-determination; the invasion of Iraq in 2003, with the subsequent occupation, had its basis in efforts to mislead the international community about the existence of "weapons of mass destruction" in that country. In both instances the United Nations as a representative of the international community was largely reduced to the role of bystander in conflicts in which the threat of weapons of mass destruction was invoked—despite the organization's role as a champion of universal human rights and the right to self-determination for the peoples of the world.

The Cuban Missile Crisis ushered in an era of proliferation in which Britain, France, China, Israel, India, Pakistan, and South Africa developed nuclear weapons. In those years, too, the USSR and United States embarked upon the creation of a complex array of nuclear weapons systems grounded in the doctrine of Mutual Assured Destruction—MAD—a fitting acronym for the strategic concepts that underpinned the nuclear arms race. The major powers sought to develop even more sophisticated nuclear weapons with a diverse range of delivery systems. As they developed a wider range of weapons of even greater destructive capability—weapons that, in practical terms, could destroy the planet several times over—the United States and Soviet Union sought to create "a second-strike" capability that would allow them to engage in sustained nuclear exchanges. The (il)logic of MAD assumed a momentum that had crossed a critical threshold. Instead of Karl Clausewitz's formulation—"War is merely the continuation of politics by other means"—the calculus of nuclear war between nuclear superpowers was shaped by the assumption that war would represent the annihilation of politics and humanity itself.

In recent years the issue of nuclear proliferation in the Middle East has become urgent amid the effort to reassert Western imperial power in the region. The efforts by the Western powers, and Israel, to maintain an unchallenged Israeli monopoly on nuclear weapons in the region are tightly connected to the invasion and occupation of Iraq and the systematic campaign, including threats of military action, to destroy Iran's efforts to establish a nuclear industry. The Western campaign against Iran—where a civilian nuclear plant has been developed with Russian support—has been part of a broader NATO strategy to contain Russian power in Europe and the Persian Gulf region. Notwithstanding these threats, the Iranian government has continued the construction of its nuclear industry and its efforts to master the nuclear enrichment cycle. Significantly, Iran justifies its pursuit of nuclear technology by appealing to its basic right to national self-determination. Russia has not ended its support for the ongoing development of Iran's nuclear sector, and the pressure from the Western powers has led not only to increasing collaboration between Iran and Russia in energy development but also to Iran's purchases of Russian military technology. In addition, Iran has increasingly moved towards collaboration with China in the development of its energy resources and acquisition of missile and other military technology.[15] As a result of the divergent imperatives and agendas of the permanent members of the U.N. Security Council—United States, Russia, France, Britain, China—the organization has been less than coherent about the Iran nuclear dossier, leading to the periodic escalation of threats about military action against Iran and Iran's threats to respond in similar fashion.[16]

In effect, Iran has become a pivot of tensions between NATO and the resurgent Russia, as well as an arena for the growing strategic competition unfolding between NATO and the Russian-Chinese–dominated Shanghai Cooperation Organization in Central Asia. Given this context of overlapping strategic competition among the major powers of Europe and Asia, and Iran's assertion of its right to the development of nuclear technology as symbolic of its independence, the issue of nuclear proliferation has become a deep challenge to the idea of a global human community. Given, too, the importance of the Middle East as a major supplier of energy resources to the wider world, it would be catastrophic for the global community if Iran were to become a theatre of military confrontation based on the impasse surrounding its nuclear technology. Like Cuba in 1962, the geopolitics of Iran has elevated its importance as a source of global crisis and instability.

The Cuban Missile Crisis and Diego Garcia have their echoes, then, in the conflict between national self-determination and nuclear weapons proliferation in the Iran dossier—with enormous implications for the entire global community. Unless oppositional or alternative forces can mount effective and increasing pressure for a global consensus on nuclear weapons and the expansion of nuclear facilities for both military and civilian purposes, dangerous conflicts will inevitably erupt. The genie of nuclear weapons as instruments of military deterrence and diplomatic leverage has already left the bottle; and, if not astutely handled, it is likely to create immeasurable mischief as more states seek these weapons.

In the immediate aftermath of the Cuban Missile Crisis, Linus Pauling delivered the 1963 Nobel Peace Prize lecture, in which he asserted:

> Thousands of these superbombs have now been fabricated; and today, eighteen years after the construction of the first atomic bomb, the nuclear powers have stockpiles of

these weapons so great that if they were to be used in a war hundreds of millions of people would be killed, and our civilization itself might not survive the catastrophe.[17]

Pauling's words remain a stark recognition of the reality that continues to define the contemporary world. The spread of nuclear weapons since 1963 has done little to obviate the threat of nuclear war.

This reality suggests that an observation made by Albert Einstein in 1946 (and invoked by Pauling in 1963) is even more relevant today than when it was first uttered:

> Today the atomic bomb has altered profoundly the nature of the world as we know it, and the human race consequently finds itself in a new habitat to which it must adapt its thinking.... There is no defense in science against the weapon which can destroy civilization. Our defense is not in armaments, nor in science, nor in going underground. Our defense is in law and order.... Future thinking must prevent wars.[18]

The issues raised by Pauling and Einstein need to be reassessed in the contemporary context, with our immense need to forge a global consciousness and an inclusive social contract for all of humanity. Even without a resort to nuclear weapons, nuclear power poses a long-term threat to human life—as the Chernobyl reactor explosion of 1986 reminded us. Although the development of nuclear weapons and power has undoubtedly altered the nature of the world by conferring upon human beings the capacity to unleash premeditated cataclysmic damage upon the planet, it is by no means evident that human nature, including its penchant for war, has been transformed in the process. The conundrum of nuclear weapons has not disappeared. With the use of nuclear energy as an alternative to fossil fuels set to accelerate in the immediate future, the need for a global consensus on national self-determination and the politics of nuclear proliferation has become more acute than ever.

In the 1960s another important initiative, the Nuclear Test-Ban Treaty (1963), arose out of a growing recognition that the testing of nuclear weapons in the atmosphere was beginning to change the Earth through the release of increasing amounts of radiation in the atmosphere. The new levels of radiation posed a threat to the gene mutation rate among humans and increased the number of defective children born. In light of the success of that atmospheric Test-Ban Treaty, the negotiations that led to its establishment may provide contemporary advocates and policy-makers with a roadmap for dealing with international negotiations over climate change and its threat to humanity.

Yet another related issue is the accumulation of nuclear waste and the use of depleted uranium in weapons, which are by-products that have enormous consequences for health and environmental degradation—and across a wide spectrum of societies. Can the management of the nuclear industry and its by-products be left to national governments? Nuclear power has enormous implications for the entire human race—as a threat to human health and the environment posed by uranium mining, nuclear reactors, and weapons.

If the 1960s sparked the emergence of a growing sense of human commonality after the ravages fostered by the colonial order, we need to rethink the politics of human society to stem the damage unleashed by the struggles for national/communal survival. The global community needs to examine the fate of the Chagos Islanders to devise strategies to secure the rights of the subjects of continued colonial rule. The catastrophic damage unleashed upon Iraq by the Anglo-U.S. imperial war and occupation has emerged as a reminder of how colonialism had to be ended to ensure that national self-determination could be guaranteed as a fundamental human right. Similarly, we need to think about the development and expansion of nuclear power in the promotion of an international security regime that minimizes the resort to war. The global management of nuclear power needs to be extended to the management of nuclear waste and its by-products that threaten the global commons in an era of increasing concern about global environmental change.

The 1960s opened up new ways of thinking about a global human order, and we need to carry on with that rethinking now. Clearly, given the unfinished agendas of that decade, and the all too familiar problems that continue in its wake, the task of constructing a co-operative and sustainable global order continues. A key to this project is building an awareness of the relationship between national self-determination and nuclear weapons. If the 1960s helped to forge a global sensibility about the trauma of colonialism, now, for the future of humanity, we need an expansion of that sensibility to ensure that nuclear conflict does not emerge from the ongoing struggle for national self-determination.

Tina Mai Chen

# EPILOGUE

## Third World Possibilities and Problematics:
## Historical Connections and Critical Frameworks

**At the 2007** New World Coming conference, frequent iterations of Third Worldism, Third World status, and Third World solidarity became a shared topic for conversation across various papers and conference panels. Throughout the conference, references to the Third World not only functioned to call up political movements and strategies that countered the hegemonic projects of powerful states but were also used to examine the historical role of those movements and strategies in the 1960s. In many instances these examples also became part of thinking about how Third Worldism and its frameworks of solidarity might inform our contemporary politics and struggles.

Absent from these conversations was a discussion of the double bind in the politics of naming the Third World and in the radical rethinking of the world as promised by the term. On the one hand, invocation of the Third World often reinforces the authority of speakers located outside the designated geopolitical region and its people; it implicitly accepts a hierarchical framework that distances socialist states (the "Second World") and Asia-Africa-Latin America (the "Third World") from Euro-America (the "First World"). On the other hand, calls for solidarity with the Third World are part of an anti-imperialist politics that refuses U.S., Canadian, and other Western nation-state conceptualizations of citizenship in favour of globally inflected identifications and movements.

This tension between the Third World as an object of Euro-American knowledge and modernization theory and an active subject of alternative global formation and politics marks both the historic moment of the 1960s and the analytic frameworks through which we have studied the decade. Scholars such as Robert Young (in his oft-cited introduction to *Postcolonialism: An Historical Introduction*) and Kofi Buenor Hadjor have pointed to the political stakes of the term Third World. In Young's case, he elected to use terms such as "Tricontinental" or "Three Continents" rather than Third World.[1] At the New World Coming conference, the multiple contexts in which the Third World was discussed reinforced the concept's historical significance in the global trajectories of the 1960s, and how it was an important analytic category in attempts to understand the decade. Yet the collective taking up of the Third World as an object of historical inquiry, historical problematic, and analytic framework was complicated by the composition of panels. Despite the efforts of the organizing committee, a large proportion of the papers focused on peoples residing within the United States, Canada, and Europe; these discussions were only partially offset by a small number of papers on Latin America and even fewer on Asia and Africa.

As a historian of twentieth-century China I wondered why scholars in Chinese and Asian studies had not responded in significant numbers to the call for papers. After all, this was a conference on the "global sixties" that set out to explore "the international nature of Sixties protests, and the global circulation of politics and culture in the post-1945 period ... [by bringing] together scholars working on topics as diverse as the New Left, Third World decolonization and liberation movements, the politics of sex and race, and cultural studies, in the hopes of fostering a dialogue on the interconnected nature, and present day legacy, of the various forms of culture and movements which characterized 'The Sixties.'"[2] This is not a decade overlooked within the field of Chinese studies. First, the Cultural Revolution (1966–76) figures prominently in scholarly and popular works. Second, there is growing interest in the global engagements of Maoist China as well as in the importance of the 1955 Bandung conference (which brought together Asian and African nations in an effort to envision an alternative global world to the bipolar Cold War order) and in the ensuing "Bandung spirit" and its afterlives.[3] Third, Chinese studies itself as an academic field of inquiry that took shape through area studies programs[4]—and the field's key critical journals, such as the *Bulletin of Concerned Asian Studies*—is a product of the historic moment addressed by this conference. So why did a call for papers on the topic of the "global sixties" have greater appeal for other regional fields?

Searching for an answer to this question set me thinking about the very notion of "the sixties" as a specifically inflected historical periodization that implied particular forms of globality.[5] In an attempt to think through this question, at the closing plenary I suggested that we think more about the intertwined histories and multiple legacies for contemporary political projects of Third Worldism and the Third World, state formation, modernization theory, and their related epistemological projects, including scholarly periodization.

What I strive to do here is place into perspective the efforts made, both at the conference and in this book, to stretch the scholarly periodization beyond its conventional geopolitical referents and to interrogate the assumptions of this periodization. This book in itself foregrounds the multiple sites that gave meaning to the 1960s and that have contributed to the Third World as space and ideal. By encouraging comparative and transnational analyses of the 1960s the writers suggest new epistemological frameworks through which we might understand the sixties as historical moment and legacy. Still, as we work towards this goal, what are some of the assumptions and knowledge structures that may need to be revisited?

# Whose Third World? Modernization Theory, International Solidarities, or an Asian-American-Latin American Alternative

It is generally accepted that Albert Sauvy coined the term "Third World" in his 1952 article "Trois mondes, Une planète," published in Claude Bourdet's *L'Observateur*. Sauvy wrote, "Et peut-être, à sa vive lueur, le monde n°1, pourrait-il, même en dehors de toute solidarité humaine, ne pas rester insensible à une poussée lente et irrésistible, humble et féroce, vers la vie. Car enfin ce Tiers Monde ignoré, exploité, méprisé comme le Tiers Etat, veut, lui aussi, être quelque chose."[6] He suggested that the exploited, ignored, and mistreated peoples of the world would, like the Third Estate in the French Revolution, become a potent force in history.

The analogy to the Third Estate and the invocation of the French Revolution as a bourgeois revolution that led to the establishment of a nation-state concisely highlights the interconnected elements that converged in the Third World thus named. These elements included consciousness within particular segments of society of the structural dimensions of the inequalities that informed everyday life and the potential for people with such a consciousness to rise up collectively and become politically recognized as citizens. The term implied struggles against autocratic or feudal states in the name of democracy and equality; while the assumption of the French Revolution as the historic standard for progress and nation-state formation rendered the spatio-temporal differentiation of history as standard fare.

But to begin a discussion of the Third World and Third Worldism and its importance to the global sixties with Sauvy risks containing the Third World within a Cold War logic in which the Third World was a reaction to the major field of global politics in the decades following the Second World War. The Third World is then denied the agency required to challenge Euro-American global hierarchies. A genealogy of the Third World closely identified with the Cold War as dominant construction allows for the conflation of the progressive politics and alternative global imaginaries, to which Sauvy sought to draw attention, with the meaning conferred upon the Third World in the 1950s and 1960s by modernization theory. The conflation effects erasure of the tensions and historical processes that rendered the Cold War, modernization theory, and Third World the conditions for the existence of each other. It is precisely the complex relationships between these overlapping yet distinct discourses and movements that need to be mapped out in specific local, national, international, and transnational contexts. This would enable an understanding of how each—the Cold War, modernization theory, and the Third World—was more than a derivative category of a presumed primacy of the politics of superpowers.

Arif Dirlik suggests that when the world or globe operates as the ultimate frame of reference—as the Global Sixties conference proposed—we can "confront the contingencies and ground-level processes of human activity with the structures that are at once the products and conditions of that activity."[7] To foreground the contingencies and ground-level processes that took place in the 1960s would thus entail rethinking the temporal category of "the sixties" and how the category assumes meaning in relation to modernization theory and the Third World.

# Modernization Theory and Its Constitutive Role for "the Sixties"

Modernization theory emerged in the early decades of the post–Second World War era and was, in part, a response to the rise of so-called Third World societies as actors in world politics. U.S-based social scientists received funding from government and private agencies to consider what were a priori deemed "the problems" of economic development, political stability, and social and cultural change in the Third World. These projects tended to be rooted in developmentalist approaches and assumptions in which Euro-American capitalist nation-state formation and capitalist industrialization constituted the norm against which other societies were measured.[8] As such, as Dean C. Tipps puts it, "Modernization is not simply a process of change, but one which is defined in terms of the goals toward which it is moving."[9] Of course, the origins of the "Third World" came well before the postwar period, and so too did its relationship to developmentalist narratives and ecological poverty. Mike Davis argues that the Third World was being fashioned by Britain during the Late Victorian period, while Michael Adas notes that the intellectual underpinnings of modernization discourse can be traced to at least the Enlightenment era.[10] Yet the particular confluence of social science theorizing and U.S. foreign policy in the 1950s and 1960s shaped a new global order in which the familiar language of evolutionary change found expression in hierarchies that divided the "developed," "developing," and "underdeveloped" worlds and thus accrued a subordinate status to the category of Third World.

Critiques of modernization theory and its ethnocentric worldview have been sustained and numerous and therefore do not need to be rehearsed here. These critiques appeared alongside early advocates of various forms of modernization theory, including Talcott Parsons, Edward Shil, and Walt Rostow in the mid- to late 1960s, and have become standard fare in overviews of social-science methodologies.[11] But what is often missing in the critiques of modernization theory is a discussion of the interdependence of modernization theory and American understandings of post-colonial nations as "traditional" or "not-yet modern." Nils Gilman's analysis of modernization theory as an expression of American liberalism and nation addresses the role of the post-colonial nation in the development of modernization theory.[12] He does not, however, dwell on what this characterization does to disarticulate modernity from nation in particular geographic locations. Yet if we are to consider the ways in which the Third World operated simultaneously as a political category of radical promise and of Euro-American discipline in the 1960s, we need to consider the possibilities for the existence of a Third World nation that could lay claim to the historical trajectory implied by Sauvy, in which the Third World was "something"; that something being a global historical subject. The point to be made here is that at the turn of the twentieth century intellectuals and political leaders in Asia and other colonized regions of the world accepted the nation-state as the basis of modern subjectivity. While the specific nature of the relationship between people and state in the nation was the subject of debate and political struggle, with U.S. president Woodrow Wilson's fourteen points and the articulation of a right to national self-determination, non-Euro-American peoples acquired an internationally sanctioned (if unequally applied) language through which they could make claims to—and envision—global citizenship. Nation-state status and, in the post–World War II period, membership in the United Nations were to translate to recognition that they had become "something."

Yet at precisely the historical moment of the independence of India, Burma, Kenya, Ghana, and so on—a moment that initiated widespread and rapid (although not uncontested) decolonization—modernization theory acquired an analytic primacy in the U.S. social sciences. This theory effectively rendered the nation-state a necessary but insufficient condition of modernity and global participation. That is, as soon as national self-determination was successfully being claimed by non-Euro-Americans this status no longer in itself signified the joining of history (as suggested by Sauvy and by the numerous analogies to the French Revolution that circulated in the discourses of national liberation). Rather, by regrouping newly independent nations into regional constructs based on levels of development, modernization theory established new rules for global subjectivity in which nation-state status and membership in the United Nations did not suffice. In the act of naming the "Third World" and "underdeveloped nations," advocates of modernization theory and the policies that resulted created an undifferentiated category of existence to replace distinct newly independent nation-states. The result was a de-territorialization of the Third World.

We can see this in the collective meaning of the Third World as it appeared in the 1960s to North American readers of popular magazines, including *Time* magazine. At the beginning of the decade, in August 1960, the cover of *Time* featured "Cuba's Che Guevera." Showing Che dressed in black beret and green military jacket, set against a red background, and framed by Mao Zedong peering over his right shoulder and Nikita Khrushchev over his left, the cover announced the Argentinian-born revolutionary as "Communism's Western Beachhead." At the end of the decade, on September 12, 1969, *Time*'s cover depicted Ho Chi-Minh, whose yellow-tinted face and clothing were set against a black background with a wide red border. The headline was "New Era in North Vietnam." In the intervening years other Third World leaders appeared on the magazine's covers: Indira Gandhi (January 28, 1966), Fidel Castro (October 8, 1965), Benyoussef Ben Khedda (Algeria, March 16, 1962), Krishna Menon (India elections, February 2, 1962), and Moise Tshombe (struggle for Congo, December 22, 1961). Even as the magazine covers and articles introduced particular Third World leaders to the North American public, through colour associations, page layouts, and intertextual references the specificity of the national liberation movements featured was undermined by collective references to communism and socialism. These references rendered the movements interchangeable.

These critiques—of the making of the Third World as a homogeneous category rooted in modernization theory—and the assumptions of a Cold War bipolar world have become familiar to many of us over the years. Too often, however, critics counter this disciplining discourse of the Third World—a discipline that reinforced Euro-American hierarchies—by highlighting either the works, words, and associations of historical actors situated in the Third World, or the inspiration that those struggles provided for oppressed peoples within the First World. In the words of Jeremi Suri, the 1960s, and 1968 in particular, "marked a moment of 'global revolutions' because the cumulative effect of worldwide protest activities undermined basic assumptions about who rules, even in the eyes of the rulers themselves."[13] Yet, to take the common experience of these global revolutions to be a generalized challenge by youth to state power in various guises can be problematic, even if the challenges are further refined to prioritize anti-imperialist and anticolonial politics.

In such a framing of the globality of the revolutions and the Third World, it is the global that is privileged over the local or national. Robert Malley sums up this position: "For the vision of a world comprising a group of industrialized nations lending their civilizing and developing hand to less fortunate counterparts, Third Worldism sought to substitute the picture of a globe polarized between a revolutionary third world symbolizing the future and an imperialistic, exploitative, and decrepit West."[14] That substitution can only be a partial corrective to formulations of the Third World rooted in modernization theory because both sides of the polarity tend to share an assumption that the nation-state was/is an instrumental (and perhaps inconvenient) element in a broader vision; and neither, it seems, is able to configure a comfortable place in the global sixties for the People's Republic of China (PRC) as a nation-state (rather than as the geographic location of a de-territorialized Maoist Theory).[15]

# Third World Nation-States and Radical De-Territorialization

The assumption that U.S. state power, modernization theory, and related epistemological projects exist in an antithetical relationship to a Third Worldism that denies the bipolar Cold War world, and calls for new global identities and movements, has both opened up and foreclosed analyses of the 1960s. The global references through which people made sense of their lives and political projects in the 1960s have become increasingly evident in the development of world history courses and texts,[16] the rich body of scholarship concerned with cross-fertilization of movements,[17] or political projects based on solidarity movements. At the same time these studies tend to shy away from interrogating Third Worldist associations and identities in relation to nation-state aspirations and modernizing projects. In most cases, even when national liberation struggles are the focus of the scholarship, the nation-state aspirations of the Third World are attributed to a particular stage of development of colonized territory and peoples so that national liberation is presented as a "first step" in a broader anti-imperialist struggle that is the essence of a Third Worldism. In this framework, the Third World and Third Worldism appear as places of post-colonial and/or post-national promise.

But while we must take seriously the types of connections forged between national liberation struggles, Third World peoples, and political movements that extend well beyond Bandung and the Tricontinental, we must be careful about assumptions that the globality of the Third World necessarily transcends the nation-state. Such an assumption is perhaps at the root of the tenuous relationship between the People's Republic of China and the "global sixties." Specifically, in the genealogy of the Third World, the role of the PRC at the 1955 Bandung conference is often downplayed because of fears that China as an established nation was not a disinterested supporter of revolutionary struggles, and that Zhou Enlai used the meeting to shore up his nation's position vis-à-vis India. Moreover, the disaster of the Great Leap Forward that ushered in the decade of the 1960s within the PRC does not fit narratives of the 1960s. As a result China appears in accounts of the global sixties primarily during the period of the Cultural Revolution because of the attention that the anti-state Red Guards garnered internationally. But, and perhaps conveniently, there is little consideration in studies of Third Worldism as a global phenomena of the de-radicalization of the Red Guards in 1968 and the relationship of this to the rebuilding of the party and state. Nor, as this book attests, has much attention been given to the perhaps belated articulation of the "Three Worlds Theory" by Mao Zedong in 1974, because that formulation occurred as part of the process of the so-called normalization of relations between the PRC and the United States and the assumption of China's seat at the United Nations by the PRC.

Remapping the global sixties to include China more centrally proves difficult, in part, because of the ways in which the Third World has become the conceptual hinge for analysis and expression of the globality of the decade. The disarticulation of the Third World from established nation-states (distinct from national liberation struggles) leads to the dominance of questions about whether or not Third World nation-states upheld or betrayed the anti-imperialist politics and allegiances that bound them to the Third World and that had been advocated during national liberation struggles. This discursive construct of the fate of Third World ideals in the hands of Third World nation-states is evident where the PRC is concerned, and it is particularly dominant in critiques of the PRC's use of Third World associations to justify its historic and continuing support of Robert Mugabe and Zimbabwe. To explain the betrayals by Third World nation-states of the promise of the sixties and Third Worldism, the territorialized (regressive) nation-state is disarticulated from a de-territorialized (progressive) Third World. But this formulation has limited explanatory power because it fails to appreciate the place of the nation-state in Third World associations, and therefore tends towards a romanticized transnational Third World.

As Rebecca Karl argues in her analysis of the global referents through which Chinese intellectuals conceptualized people-state relations at the turn of the twentieth century, there is no inherent conflict between the territoriality of nation-states and de-territorialization. Karl states that if this moment in the social production of national space, understood broadly, is tied to its properly global moment and thence understood in terms of the emergence of a relationship between national territoriality and the deterritorialization of capital and labor, the apparent "paradox" of bounded space/unbounded people, far from appearing paradoxical, instead becomes an integral or even an inherent historical dimension of modern nationalism for China as elsewhere.[18]

Karl's theoretical intervention into debates over nationalism, and her analysis of the concept of "Asia" at the turn of the twentieth century as a historical cultural formation in which cultural heterogeneity is unified through a "synchronic spatio-temporal narrative of common historical experiences of modern imperialism," are equally as relevant to thinking about the Third World, Third Worldism, alternative geographies, and nation-states. Along with Aijaz Ahmad and others, Karl reminds us that radical solidarities do not rest upon a unitary experience of national oppression even as they construct solidarities rooted in perceived global structural commonality. Nor do these solidarities necessarily precede, follow upon, or co-exist with particular stages of nation-state formation.[19] In some instances, and very much within the contexts of the global sixties and Third World, the established nation-state was a vehicle for expressing such radical solidarities.[20]

I draw attention to the complex—and often underanalyzed—relationship between Marxist-inspired nationalist liberation movements, their subsequent states, and the internationalist or transnational historical connections because it seems that at the moment, when scholars are increasingly committed to "internationalizing (Euro)American history" and globalizing the periodizations of history common to these fields, it is easier to draw out the promises of transnational and global identifications against hegemonic orders than it is to make sense of the Third World as coeval with nation-state operations. Unless we take seriously this relationship by, first, insisting on the unevenness of global modernity and, second, refusing to deploy historical trajectories in which the Third World is a priori conceptualized as post-national or post-colonial promise, we will find ourselves mired in debates about the validity of nationalist liberation versus internationalist movements and whether or not particular nations *qua* nations betrayed Third World brothers and sisters.[21] This does not allow us to fully understand the Third World as a simultaneously unified and plural cultural, historical, and political formation of the global sixties. Nor does it allow us to globalize a historical periodization that takes as its inspiration the anti-establishment and anti-statist movements within European and North American states.

If we are to engage with the global historical processes and cultural formations in which, to invoke Sauvy once again, the Third World becomes "something," we need to ground our enthusiasm for transnational histories and accounts of the empowering politics of Third World identifications with considered analyses of Third World nation-state formation. This necessarily complicates the spatio-temporal dimensions, hierarchies, and global political identifications that we associate with the global sixties.

Notably, as Partha Chatterjee argues, those within the Third World did not have to reject the spatio-temporal hierarchies of nationalism or history for their own movements to gain followings and for these movements fundamentally to challenge the Euro-American ownership of democracy, equality, and the nation.[22] Whether taken up through Marxist or liberal frameworks, demands by the colonized for democracy and equality could and did result in new global geographies that empowered the disempowered—although never unproblematically. As a result, by the mid-1950s, when the term Third World acquired general acceptance within academia and public policy circles, key leaders in the regions of the world to which the term referred had also contributed to its meaning.

The Third World, as concept and entity, appropriated the language of nation formation for the non-Euro-American world; and it offered up forms of international and potentially transnational communities that challenged a global order premised on particular nation-state hierarchies. As we make the globe the ultimate frame of reference for the 1960s, we encounter the Third World as a metaphorical, physical, and imaginary space of action that is simultaneously re-territorialized and de-territorialized, that is both rendered coeval with history and denied such a coevalness. The collective project, then, must be to insist upon the coevality of all aspects of Third World participation in the 1960s—not to condone these aspects uncritically but to counter de-territorializations of the Third World that impose exclusionary global imaginaries. This approach entails recognizing that when the Third World is named as a form of radical solidarity by those outside Euro-American power it does so out of a much longer history of engagement with global subjectivity and modernity in which indigeneity, local vernaculars, and anti-imperialism have also been linked to nation-state projects.[23]

Such a conceptualization of the Third World offers up an alternative globality to modernization theory or a bipolar Cold War, yet it is still constituted in relation to these worlds. As such, our collective efforts to globalize the 1960s as historical period and legacy need to attend to the operation of nation-states, modernization theory, and Cold War bipolarity as conditions for the Third World and Third Worldism. To do so will help us to better understand the possibilities and problematics of the Third World and Third Worldism, and the global contexts within which those entities operated in the 1960s—and within which they operate today.

# notes

## 1 Whose 1960s? Gender, Resistance, and Liberation in Palestine
### RABAB IBRAHIM ABDULHADI

1 My use of the term "own" builds on that of Carolyn Dinshaw, who as director of the Center for the Study of Gender and Sexuality at New York University organized a 2002 roundtable discussion, "Who Owns Gender?"—posing the question of authority over gender studies to feminist theorists, women's studies scholars, and scholars of gender and sexuality.

2 At the three-day New World Coming conference, Kingston, Ont., June 2007, at which this paper was first presented, it was evident that multiple legacies of the 1960s existed and that no uniform assessment of that decade existed. Indeed, the first keynote plenary was titled "The Many Meanings of Liberation." Even though the organizers of the conference sought to stress the diverse readings of the 1960s by including keynote addresses and papers from many parts of the world and including discussions of class views and structural inequalities on the basis of gender, sexuality, race, ethnicity, ability, age, and more, the master narrative of U.S. white heterosexual males continued to dominate the discussion.

3 Frantz Fanon, *The Wretched of the Earth*, Preface by Jean-Paul Sartre, trans. Constance Farrington (New York: Grove Press, 1963).

4 I am not suggesting that other spaces are easy to define, but there is a peculiar way in which this space is perceived, constructed, and defined, especially in this day and age.

5 Almost half of the teachers refused to return to teach, citing the colonial curriculum as a reason for their action. As one teacher put it, "I can't teach that Palestine was always Jewish and we are parasites." Frank H. Epps, as cited in People's Press Palestine Book Project, *Our Roots Are Still Alive: The Story of the Palestinian People* (San Francisco: Institute for Independent Social Journalism, 1981), p. 128.

6 The Israeli control of border crossings with Jordan meant that no cars were allowed to travel between the West Bank and "the East Bank" (the name the Jordanian monarchy gave to Trans-Jordan after it annexed the West Bank and considered the area to be part of the Kingdom in 1950). Instead, Palestinians travelling from Nablus to Amman, for example, would have to take one form of public transportation from their own hometowns to the Israeli border control a short distance away from the bridge crossing. Then they had to take a bus that made the trip from the Israeli-controlled side to the Jordanian side. At the Jordanian side the passengers would take a third means of transportation to Amman or to wherever they wanted to go in the East Bank. The long wait, excessive search—including body cavities—exuberant cost, and high probability of being turned back made it almost impossible for anyone to travel except those in desperate need of crossing into Jordan, such as students, patients, or family members travelling for a funeral.

7 The Palestinian resistance movement adopted the modern form of guerrilla warfare in the early 1950s with the rise of the Arab National Movement in 1952, followed by the founding of the Al-Fatah movement a few years later. Earlier attempts at waging guerrilla warfare against Zionist settlers were evident in the 1930s, especially the movement of Sheikh Ezzedin Al Qassam, a Syrian peasant who joined the Palestinian resistance movement and the Great Palestinian Revolt in 1936–39 (the longest workers' strike in history) to fight alongside Palestinian peasants to defend their lands.

8 Felicia Langer, an Israeli Jewish lawyer, Holocaust survivor, and leading member of the Israeli Communist Party, was one of several Israeli lawyers who defended Palestinian prisoners.

9 On Feb. 22, 1969, two years after Saji was imprisoned, the DFLP split off the PFLP. Saji's ideas were more in line with the DFLP than with the PFLP.

10 Hamas and Islamic Jihad did not emerge as Palestinian political groups until the late 1980s.

11 See Simone de Beauvoir and Giselle Halimi, *Djamila Boupacha* (London: Cox and Wyman, 1962).

12 See, for example, T. Thornhill, *Making Women Talk: The Interrogation of Palestinian Women* (London: Lawyers for Palestinian Rights, 1992).

13 My forthcoming book, *Revising Narratives? Gender, Nation, and Resistance in Palestine*, explores questions of passing and gender performance more fully.

14 See Edward Said, *Orientalism* (New York: Vintage Books, 1979).

15 See, for example, Karin Andriolo, "Murder by Suicide: Episodes from Muslim History," *American Anthropologist*, 104, 3 (September 2002), pp.736–42; Maria Alvanou, "Hijab of Blood: The Role of Islam in Female Palestinian Terrorism," *ERCES Online Quarterly Review*, 1,3 (September–October 2004); Robin Morgan, *The Demon Lover: The Roots of Terrorism* (New York: Washington Square Press, 2001); Andrea Dworkin, "On Palestinian Suicide Bombers," letter to online journal *Feminista*, 2003; Barbara Ehrenreich, "A New Counterterrorism Strategy: Feminism," *Alternet*, Aug. 22, 2005 <www.alternet.org/story/21973>; Arlene Peck, "Arab Women and Farm Animals," Feb. 6, 2004 <www.arlenepeck.com/index.html>; Barbara Victor, *Army of Roses: Inside the World of Palestinian Women Suicide Bombers* (New York: Rodale, 2003); Eleanor Smeal, "Special Message from the Feminist Majority on the Taliban, Osama bin Laden, and Afghan Women," available on the Feminist Majority website at <www.feminist.org/news/pressstory.asp?id=5802>.

16 All of the women militants arrested in the late 1960s were released from Israeli jails through a prisoner exchange agreement between the Israeli government and Palestinian militant groups in 1985. By then some of them had spent at least seventeen years of their lives in prison.

17 People's Press Palestine Book Project, *Our Roots Are Still Alive*.

18 See James Scott, *Weapons of the Weak: Everyday Forms of Peasant Resistance* (New Haven, Conn.: Yale University Press, 1985); and Scott, *Domination and the Arts of Resistance* (New Haven, Conn.: Yale University Press, 1990).

19 Katherine Viner, "Beauty and the Bullets: What Became of Leila Khaled, the World's Most Famous Terrorist Pin-Up?" *The Guardian*, Jan. 26, 2001.

20 This is no different from the way in which the autobiography of Rigoberta Menchu was constructed. In it, she is described as "childlike." See Elisabeth Burgos-Debray, ed. and Introduction, *I, Rigoberta Menchú: An Indian Woman in Guatemala* (London: Verso, 1984), p.xiv.

21 Eileen MacDonald, *Shoot the Women First* (New York: Random House, 1991).

## 2 Sarnia in the Sixties (or the Peculiarities of the Canadians)
IAN MCKAY

1 E.P. Thompson, "The Peculiarities of the English," *Socialist Register* (London, 1965), pp.311–62.

2 William H. Sewell Jr., *Logics of History: Social Theory and Social Transformation* (Chicago and London: University of Chicago Press, 2005), pp.140–41, n.8. The second usage is closer to the French "transposer."

3 Ian McKay, *Rebels, Reds, Revolutionaries: Rethinking Canada's Left History* (Toronto: Between the Lines, 2005), Introduction.

4 With the ambiguous exception of semi-autonomous Greenland, Canada is the most thinly populated country in the Americas.

5 See especially Sean Mills, "The Empire Within: Montreal, the Sixties, and the Forging of a Radical Imagination," Ph.D.

thesis, Queen's University, Kingston, Ont., 2007.

6 See Peter H. Russell, *Constitutional Odyssey: Can Canadians Be a Sovereign People?* (Toronto: University of Toronto Press, 1992).

7 See Jean-Marc Piotte, *La communauté perdu: Petite histoire des militantismes* (Montréal: VLB éditeur, 1987).

8 See her memoirs in Betty Krawczyk, *Lock Me Up or Let Me Go: The Protests, Arrest and Trial of an Environmental Activist* (Vancouver: Press Gang, 2002).

### 3 Moving into "the Master's House": The State-Nation and Black Power in the United States
VAN GOSSE

1 Thomas McCormick, *America's Half-Century: United States Foreign Policy in the Cold War and After* (Baltimore: Johns Hopkins University Press, 1995).

2 Amiri Baraka, "Home Rule: An Interview with Amiri Baraka," in "Transnational Black Studies," Special Issue, *Radical History Review*, 87 (Fall 2003), pp.109–26. On Baraka's political journey, see Komozi Woodard, *A Nation Within a Nation: Amiri Baraka (LeRoi Jones) and Black Power Politics* (Chapel Hill: University of North Carolina Press, 1999).

3 See Peniel E. Joseph, *Waiting 'Til the Midnight Hour: A Narrative History of Black Power* (New York: Henry Holt, 2006), and Joseph, ed., *The Black Power Movement: Rethinking the Civil Rights-Black Power Era* (New York: Routledge, 2006).

4 See William W. Sales Jr., *From Civil Rights to Black Liberation: Malcolm X and the Organization of Afro-American Unity* (Boston: South End Press, 1994).

5 James and Grace Lee Boggs, "The City Is the Black Man's Land," *Monthly Review*, April 1966, reprinted in *Racism and the Class Struggle: Further Pages from a Black Worker's Notebook* (New York: Monthly Review Press, 1970).

6 Suzanne E. Smith, *Dancing in the Street: Motown and the Cultural Politics of Detroit* (Cambridge, Mass.: Harvard University Press, 1999).

7 The quotations are from *New York Herald*, June 14, 1856 and *State Gazette* (Trenton, N.J.), May 23, 1855. See also Senator Henry Wilson, quoted in *Boston Daily Atlas*, Sept. 29, 1855 ("Having witnessed the immolation of the American Party, at the shrine of the Black Power . . .") and *New York Tribune* editor Horace Greeley, quoted in *Ohio Statesman*, Feb. 29, 1856, as denouncing "the ever-shrewd Black Power."

8 *New York Evening Post*, review of book on U.S.-Haitian relations under President John Adams, quoted in *Ohio State Journal*, May 26, 1858. "Hayti" was a then-common spelling.

9 Richard Wright, *Black Power: A Record of Reactions in a Land of Pathos* (New York: Harper, 1954).

10 Carl T. Rowan, "Has Paul Robeson Betrayed the Negro?" *Ebony*, October 1957, p.39. See Penny M. Von Eschen, *Race Against Empire: Black Americans and Anticolonialism, 1937–1957* (Ithaca, N.Y.: Cornell University Press, 1997), p.184, for the context of this remarkable interview.

11 Cedric Johnson, *Revolutionaries to Race Leaders: Black Power and the Making of African American Politics* (Minneapolis: University of Minnesota Press, 2007), pp.74–79.

12 A good overview is Chandler Davidson and Bernard Grofman, eds., *Quiet Revolution in the South: The Impact of the Voting Rights Act, 1965–1990* (Princeton, N.J.: Princeton University Press, 1994).

13 Jacqueline Dowd Hall, "The Long Civil Rights Movement and the Political Uses of the Past," *Journal of American History* (March 2005), pp.1–66.

14 See Robin D.G. Kelley, *Hammer and Hoe: Alabama Communists during the Great Depression* (Chapel Hill: University of North Carolina Press, 1990).

15 George M. Fredrickson, *Black Liberation: A Comparative History of Black Ideologies in the United States and South Africa* (New York: Oxford, 1995), is the outstanding study.

16 The most useful study is Kevin Gaines, *American Africans in Ghana: Black Expatriates and the Civil Rights Era*

(Chapel Hill: University of North Carolina Press, 2006).

17 See, in particular, Winston James, *Holding Aloft the Banner of Ethiopia: Caribbean Radicalism in America, 1900–1932* (New York: Verso, 1997).

## 4  "The Malcolm X Doctrine": The Republic of New Afrika and National Liberation on U.S. Soil
DAN BERGER

Thanks to Andy Cornell and Matt Meyer for their help with and comments on this article.

1 The militant unionism and revolutionary nationalism characterizing Detroit's political landscape in the mid-twentieth century are well documented. The city was home to a slew of revolutionary figures, including James and General Baker, Grace Lee Boggs, Albert Cleage, Mike Hamlin, Luke Tripp, Max Stanford, and the Henry brothers. See, for instance, Grace Lee Boggs, *Living for Change: An Autobiography* (Minneapolis: University of Minnesota Press, 1998); Dan Georgakas and Marvin Surkin, *Detroit: I Do Mind Dying. A Study in Urban Revolution*, 2nd ed. (Cambridge: South End Press, 1998); Peniel E. Joseph, *Waiting 'Til the Midnight Hour: A Narrative History of Black Power in America* (New York: Henry Holt, 2006); and Heather Ann Thompson, *Whose Detroit? Politics, Labor, and Race in a Modern American City* (Ithaca, N.Y.: Cornell University Press, 2001).

2 Joseph, *Waiting 'Til the Midnight Hour*, pp. 168–69, 184.

3 After a trip to Africa in 1964, Ali told reporters, "I'm not an American; I'm a black man." Quoted in Melani McAlister, *Epic Encounters: Culture, Media, and U.S. Interests in the Middle East, 1945–2000* (Berkeley: University of California Press, 2001), p.92. At that time the boxer had been a member of the Nation of Islam.

4 Van Gosse, *Rethinking the New Left: An Interpretive History* (New York: Palgrave Macmillan, 2005), p.122.

5 At the convention and for several years after, the group spelled Africa with a "c," as is traditionally done in English. It ultimately switched to spelling it with a "k," as done here. Former Black Panther Sundiata Acoli explained the difference in an essay: "We of the New Afrikan Independence Movement spell 'Afrikan' with a 'k' as an indicator of our cultural identification with the Afrikan continent and because Afrikan linguists originally used 'k' to indicate the [hard] 'c' sound in the English language." See Sundiata Acoli, "An Updated History of the New Afrikan Prison Struggle," in *Imprisoned Intellectuals: America's Political Prisoners Write on Life, Liberation, and Rebellion*, ed. Joy James (Lanham, Md.: Rowman & Littlefield, 2003), p.138. Because this paper discusses the RNA and the self-proclaimed New Afrikan Independence Movement it helped launch—political formations that still command numerous adherents—I use the current spelling throughout, unless direct quotations use an alternate spelling.

6 Robert Sherill, "Birth of a Black Nation," *Esquire*, January 1969, pp.70–78.

7 Joseph, *Waiting 'Til the Midnight Hour*, pp. 276–83.

8 Quoted in "Black Group Explains 5-State Nation Dream," *Los Angeles Times*, June 7, 1968, p.A7.

9 Donald Cunnigen, "The Republic of New Africa in Mississippi," in *Black Power in the Belly of the Beast*, ed. Judson L. Jeffries (Urbana: University of Illinois Press, 2006), p.98. The RNA was not the only entity at the time to attempt establishing international relations; both the Black Panthers and the Yippies did as well, particularly in relation to the war in Vietnam.

10 Williams's statement is printed as a sidebar to Sherrill's 1969 *Esquire* story, "Birth of a Black Nation," p.73. For more on Williams, see Timothy B. Tyson, *Radio-Free Dixie: Robert F. Williams and the Roots of Black Power* (Chapel Hill: University of North Carolina Press, 1999), or Cynthia A. Young, *Soul Power: Culture, Radicalism, and the Making of a U.S. Third World Left* (Durham, N.C.: Duke University Press, 2006), pp.18–53.

11 Although Williams's departure was partially over political differences, it was also logistical: the legal battles he fled a decade

prior awaited him upon returning. The RNA helped make possible his homecoming. New Afrikan politics appealed to a much broader cross-section of the Black liberation movement than just Williams. Other early RNA officials included Muhammad Ahmad and Herman Ferguson of the Revolutionary Action Movement; Maulana Karenga of US (before he was expelled after members of US killed two Black Panthers at UCLA in 1969); Amiri Baraka, then of the Committee for a Unified Newark; H. Rap Brown of SNCC; and Malcolm X's widow, Betty Shabazz. The goal of an independent Republic also appealed to many in the Black Panther Party: Vietnam veteran turned Black Panther Geronimo ji Jaga helped the RNA build its ministry of defense, and many of the defendants of the Panther 21 conspiracy case acknowledged by 1971 that they considered themselves citizens of the Republic. Other ex-Panthers aligned themselves with the RNA or what became known as the New Afrikan Independence Movement more generally, including many political prisoners associated with clandestine outgrowths of the Panthers. The revolutionary nationalism of the RNA also appealed to a range of prisoners incarcerated for non-political and not-necessarily-political offences, especially as the Panthers collapsed. The most famous of these was "Monster" Kody Scott, a leader of the Los Angeles Crips incarcerated after a slew of brutal crimes. See Geronimo ji Jaga, "Every Nation Struggling to Be Free Has a Right to Struggle, a Duty to Struggle," in *Liberation, Imagination, and the Black Panther Party*, ed. Kathleen Cleaver and George Katsiaficas (New York: Routledge, 2001); Chokwe Lumumba, *The Roots of the New Afrikan Independence Movement* (Jackson, Ms.: New Afrikan Productions, n.d. [circa 1983]); and Kody Scott, *Monster: The Autobiography of an L.A. Gang Member* (New York: Grove Press, 1993).

12 Even after the move South, the RNA publishing house, House of Songhay, was based in Detroit for several years.

13 Lumumba, *Roots of the New Afrikan Independence Movement*, p.9. The Revolutionary Action Movement (RAM) also proved to be ideological mentors, with its strong focus on armed self-defence and the politics of internal colonialism. Milton Henry was elected RAM treasurer upon its 1964 founding, and the dissolution of RAM brought new members to both the PG-RNA and Black Panther Party. See Muhammad Ahmad, *We Will Return in the Whirlwind: Black Radical Organizations 1960–1975* (Chicago: Charles Kerr Publishers, 2007). By the time he passed away in September 2006, Milton Henry had become a Presbyterian reverend and had gone back to using his birth name.

14 Lumumba, *Roots of the New Afrikan Independence Movement*, p.9. See also Angela D. Dillard, "Religion and Radicalism: The Reverend Albert B. Cleage, Jr., and the Rise of Black Christian Nationalism in Detroit," in *Freedom North: Black Freedom Struggles Outside the South, 1940–1980*, ed. Jeanne F. Theoharis and Komozi Woodard (New York: Palgrave Macmillan, 2003); Joseph, *Waiting 'Til the Midnight Hour*, pp.51–57.

15 Brother Imari, *War in America: The Malcolm X Doctrine* (Chicago: Ujamaa Distributors, 1968). The creed is reprinted in Imari Abubakari Obadele, *Foundations of the Black Nation* (Detroit: House of Songhay Publishers, 1975), p.153.

16 Obadele, *Foundations of the Black Nation*, p.11. As Huey Newton's criticism of the RNA's plebiscite approach suggests, the Republic's Southern strategy had its own shortcomings relative to the ability of a numerical minority to stand off against the state on their own.

17 See, for example, Kevin Kruse, *White Flight: Atlanta and the Making of Modern Conservatism* (Princeton, N.J.: Princeton University Press, 2005); Matthew D. Lassiter, *The Silent Majority: Suburban Politics in the Sunbelt South* (Princeton, N.J.: Princeton University Press, 2006), Robert O. Self, *American Babylon: Race and the Struggle for Postwar Oakland* (Princeton, N.J.: Princeton University Press, 2005); and Thomas J. Sugrue, *The Origins of the Urban Crisis* (Princeton, N.J.: Princeton University Press, 1995).

18 Obadele, *Foundations of the Black Nation*, pp.xi, 134.

19 Lumumba, *Roots of the New Afrikan Independence Movement*, p.8.

20 The program is reprinted in Obadele, *Foundations of the Black Nation*, pp.73–106.

21 Obadele, *Foundations of the Black Nation*, p.71.

22 Milton Henry had publicly argued since 1964 that armed struggle would be a necessity in the Black struggle, and Imari had argued that political and financial support for clandestine Black insurgency through riots and sabotage was essential for all New Afrikans. See Sherill, "Birth of a Black Nation"; Joseph, *Waiting 'Til the Midnight Hour*, pp.107–8; and Brother Imari, *War in America*.

23 The centrality of international law can be seen throughout the RNA's foundational documents, including Brother Imari, *Revolution and Nation-Building: Strategy for Building the Black Nation in America* (Detroit: House of Songhay Publishers, 1970) and Obadele, *Foundations of the Black Nation*. Support for armed struggle among New Afrikan citizens is clear. In his pamphlet on the history of the New Afrikan independence movement, Chokwe Lumumba said the New Afrikan People's Organization is committed to a strategy of organizing toward eventual People's War. Many Black Liberation Army fighters in the late 1970s and 1980s also affirmed support to the Republic, and eight months after the Black Government Conference, someone hijacked a National Airlines flight and rerouted it to Cuba. The hijacker, whom press reports described as being dressed in the attire of a Black militant, dubbed the plane the Republic of New Africa. See UPI, "Hijacked Airliner Back from Havana," Nov. 5, 1968, p.38.

24 Obadele, *Foundations of the Black Nation*, p.120.

25 "Launch New Organization," *Chicago Defender*, Aug. 9, 1973, p.11; "New Africa Opens 1st New Site," *Chicago Defender*, March 27, 1971, p.15.

26 Obadele, *Foundations of the Black Nation*, p.132; "Reparations Plan Supported," *Chicago Defender*, March 26, 1974, p.9.

27 Brother Imari, *War in America*, p.2.

28 Lumumba, *Roots of the New Afrikan Independence Movement*, pp.11–13. For more on Moore, see Ahmad, *We Will Return in the Whirlwind*, pp.7–13. Indeed, the RNA made a splash upon its founding because reparations were the key ingredient to building the Black Nation; see Sherill, "Birth of a Black Nation." But the RNA's influence on the call for reparations manifested itself in other ways, most notably in helping found the National Coalition of Blacks for Reparations in America (N'COBRA). Although not exclusively focused on reparations, the RNA orbit also contributed to the founding of the New Afrikan People's Organization and the Malcolm X Grassroots Movement. See Adjoa A. Aiyetoro, "The National Coalition of Blacks for Reparations in America (N'COBRA): Its Creation and Contribution to the Reparations Movement," in *Should America Pay? Slavery and the Raging Debate on Reparations*, ed. Raymond A. Winbush (New York: Amistad, 2003); Martha Biondi, "The Rise of the Reparations Movement," *Radical History Review*, 87 (January 2003); and Conrad W. Worrill, "The National Black United Front and the Reparations Movement," in *Should America Pay?* ed. Winbush. The essays collected in Michael T. Martin and Marilyn Yaquinto, eds., *Redress for Historical Injustices in the United States: On Reparations for Slavery, Jim Crow, and their Legacies* (Durham, N.C.: Duke University Press, 2007), are also helpful in this regard.

29 Despite an articulated solidarity with the Palestinian struggle, RNA documents and rhetoric in its early years made consistent parallels to Israel and the role that German reparations played in building up that country.

30 Cunnigen, "Republic of New Africa in Mississippi," p.102. See also Brother Imari, *War in America*, and Obadele, *Foundations of the Black Nation*.

31 The plenary document is included in G. Louis Heath, ed., *Off the Pigs! The History and Literature of the Black Panther Party* (Metuchen, N.J.: Scarecrow Press, 1976), pp.377–82.

32 Newton, "To the Republic of New Africa," in Heath, ed., *Off the Pigs!* pp.383–86; quote p.384.

33 Brother Imari, *War in America*, p.39.

34 That the RNA advanced this term at a time when the designation of people of African descent was shifting was a strength and a weakness. On the one hand it presented a visionary approach to racial categories that was highly political and not limited by state boundaries or skin colour (prioritizing African ancestry over dark skin). On the other hand, the term has not been quick to catch on and represented an ideological commitment of its proponents rather than a commonly used designation (as Black or Afro-American were).

35 Lumumba, *Roots of the New Afrikan Independence Movement*, pp.42–43; Acoli, "Updated History of the New Afrikan Prison Struggle," p.198.

36 See Diane C. Fujino, *Heartbeat of Struggle: The Revolutionary Life of Yuri Kochiyama* (Minneapolis: University of Minnesota Press, 2005); and Yuri Kochiyama, *Passing It On: A Memoir* (Los Angeles: UCLA Asian American Studies Center Press, 2004).

37 The declaration and the New African creed are reprinted in Martin and Yaquinto, eds., *Redress for Historical Injustices in the United States*, pp.588–91.

38 Vijay Prashad, *The Darker Nations: A People's History of the Third World* (New York: New Press, 2007); Naomi Klein, *The Shock Doctrine: The Rise of Disaster Capitalism* (New York: Metropolitan Books, 2007).

39 On the essentialism, frontierism, and polygamy—ostensibly sanctioned because there were more New Afrikan women than men—see Obadele, *Foundations of the Black Nation*. On the relation of these issues to nationalist projects overall, see Benedict Anderson, *Imagined Community: The Birth of the Nation* (London: Verso, 1991); Laura Briggs, *Reproducing Empire: Race, Sex, Science, and U.S. Imperialism in Puerto Rico* (Berkeley: University of California Press, 2002); and Patricia Hill Collins, *Black Feminist Thought: Knowledge, Consciousness, and the Politics of Empowerment*, 2nd ed. (New York: Routledge, 2000).

40 Nikhil Singh, *Black Is a Country: Race and the Unfinished Struggle for Democracy* (Cambridge, Mass.: Harvard University Press, 2004), p.205. Singh defines this "projection of sovereignty" as "a set of oppositional discourses and practices that exposed the hegemony of Americanism as incomplete, challenged its universality, and imagined carving up its spaces differently." Such a definition fits with the discussion of reparations and land-based struggles in Robin D.G. Kelley, *Freedom Dreams: The Black Radical Imagination* (Boston: Beacon, 2002), pp.110–34.

41 Lumumba, *Roots of the New Afrikan Independence Movement*; Obadele, *Foundations of the Black Nation*, p.137. Contrary to traditional English grammar, most documents by RNA activists print the first-person pronoun "I" in lower case but capitalize "we" to eschew individualism and emphasize collectivity.

42 "Activists in Political Parley," *Chicago Defender*, May 5, 1975, p.30.

43 The RNA is often described as "territorial" nationalist relative to the "revolutionary" nationalism of the Panthers and similar groups. See, for instance, Cunnigen, "Republic of New Africa in Mississippi"; Gosse, *Rethinking the New Left*; and William L. Van Deburg, *New Day in Babylon: The Black Power Movement and American Culture, 1965–1975* (Chicago: University of Chicago Press, 1992). Cunnigen uses Raymond Hall's 1970s-era five-part classification schema to define the RNA as "territorial separatist" rather than "revolutionary nationalist."

44 See, for instance, Brother Imari, *War in America*; and Obadele, *Foundations of the Black Nation*.

45 Reprinted in Obadele, *Foundations of the Black Nation*, pp.151–52.

46 A 1969 conference in Detroit celebrating the first anniversary of the RNA's founding turned violent after a shootout between police and the RNA, leaving one officer dead (both sides accusing the other of having fired first). More than

one hundred activists were arrested as a result, though a Black radical judge freed most of the defendants and a jury acquitted the others. After the group moved to Mississippi, local, state, and federal governments utilized various mechanisms to repress the RNA, including a raid on the Republic's headquarters and an affiliated residence. Police opened fire during the raid. Besieged and surprised, the RNA returned fire, killing one police officer and wounding two others. Police then arrested eleven members of the group, who served time throughout the 1970s and 1980s. Two RNA citizens were arrested at the Democratic National Convention in 1972 on spurious charges of attempting to assassinate George McGovern. Several RNA citizens were also indicted by grand juries or tried on federal conspiracy charges in relation to the clandestine Black Liberation Army in the 1980s. For an RNA perspective on this repression, see Imari Obadele, *Free the Land!* (Washington, D.C.: The House of Songhay, 1987). See also Christian Davenport, "Understanding Covert Repressive Action: The Case of the U.S. Government against the Republic of New Africa," *Journal of Conflict Resolution*, 49,1 (2005), pp.120–40; and Ward Churchill and Jim Vander Wall, *The COINTELPRO Papers: Documents from the FBI's Secret War against Dissent in the United States* (Boston: South End Press, 1990). Several relevant legal documents are reprinted in Imari Obadele, *America the Nation-State: The Politics of the United States from a State-Building Perspective*, 3rd ed. (Baton Rouge, La.: House of Songhay, 1993), pp.357–75. For more on the 1980s repression, see Akinyele O. Umoja, "The Black Liberation Army and the Radical Legacy of the Black Panther Party," in *Black Power in the Belly of the Beast*, ed. Judson L. Jeffries (Urbana: University of Illinois Press, 2006); and Dan Berger, *Outlaws of America: The Weather Underground and the Politics of Solidarity* (Oakland, Cal.: AK Press, 2006).

47 Young, *Soul Power*, p. 205.

## 5  The Soviet Communist Party and 1968: A Case Study

KIMMO RENTOLA

1  Richard Reeves, *President Nixon: Alone in the White House* (New York: Simon & Schuster, 2001), p.51; Christopher Andrew, *For the President's Eyes Only: Secret Intelligence and the Presidency from Washington to Bush* (New York: Harper-Collins, 1995), p.554.

2  Jeremi Suri, *Power and Protest: Global Revolution and the Rise of Détente* (Cambridge, Mass.: Harvard University Press, 2003), pp.216, 261.

3  Arthur Marwick's big book has invited criticism, but I think at least he got the subtitle correct: *The Sixties: Cultural Revolution in Britain, France, Italy, and the United States c.1958–c.1974* (Oxford and New York: Oxford University Press, 1998).

4  Martin Wiklund, "Leninismens renässans i 1960-talets Sverige," in *Den jyske Historiker* (Aarhus), 101 (Oprud i 1960erne), July 2003, pp.95–119; Todd Gitlin, *The Sixties: Years of Hope, Days of Rage* (New York: Bantam Books, 1987), pp.383–84; Max Elbaum, *Revolution in the Air: Sixties Radicals Turn to Lenin, Mao and Che* (London: Verso, 2002); Carlo Feltrinelli, *Senior Service* (Feltrinelli, 2001), p.401; Martin Klimke and Joachim Sharloth, eds., *1968 in Europe: A History of Protest and Activism, 1956–1977* (London: Palgrave Macmillan, 2008).

5  Matthew J. Ouimet, *The Rise and Fall of the Brezhnev Doctrine in Soviet Foreign Policy* (Chapel Hill: University of North Carolina Press, 2003), p.58; Boris Kagarlitsky, *The Thinking Reed: Intellectuals and the Soviet State, 1917 to the Present* (London: Verso, 1988), pp.199–200; Anne de Tinguy, US-*Soviet Relations during the Détente* (New York: Columbia University Press, 1999), p.114; Brezhnev's speech for Czech party officials, Dec. 9, 1967; his letter to Dubček, April 11, 1968; Dubček's report on Kosygin's views, March 25, 1968; *The Prague Spring 1968: A National Security Archives Documents Reader*, ed. J. Navratil et al. (Budapest: Central European University, 1998), pp.18, 74, 98.

6   The Archives of the Security Police of Finland (Supo), personal file no. 11608, reports on A.P. Akulov's meetings with Johan von Bonsdorff from January 1969 on; J. von Bonsdorff, *Kun Vanha vallattiin* (Helsinki: Tammi 1988); National Archives (NA II, College Park), Department of State, Record Group 59, Central Foreign Policy Files 1967–69, Pol 12 Fin, Helsinki Embassy Airgram, no. 442, Nov. 26, 1969, J.P. Owens's report on his discussion with Akulov; Tore Forsberg, *Spioner som spionerar på spioner* (Stockholm: Hjalmarson & Högberg 2003), p.315. The CPSU CC International Department files contain KGB reports (in 1970 and in 1973) on Finnish Maoists (RGANI, f. 5, op. 62, d. 596; op. 66, d. 1199).

7   Maud Bracke, *Which Socialism, Whose Détente? West European Communism and the Czechoslovak Crisis, 1968* (Budapest: Central European University Press, 2007), pp.243, 250.

8   Boris Leibzon, "Communists in the Present World," in CPSU CC International Department Finnish-language bulletin, *Sosialismin teoria ja käytäntö* (hereafter STK), Dec. 27, 1968. The Soviets began this publication after the occupation of Czechoslovakia, when the Moscow line was no longer faithfully represented by the Finnish communist media. Article titles are my translation.

9   Odd Arne Westad, *The Global Cold War: Third World Interventions and the Making of Our Times* (Cambridge: Cambridge University Press, 2007), pp.202–6.

10  Anatoli Chernyaev, "Some Problems of the Labour Movement in Capitalist Countries," STK, April 3, 1969.

11  M.A. Suslov, "Leninizm i revolyutsionnoe pereobrazovanie mira," *Kommunist*, 15 (October 1969); Jon Lee Anderson, *Che: A Revolutionary Life* (New York: Grove Press, 1997), p.581; B.N. Ponomarev, "V.I. Lenin: velikii vozhd revolyutsonnoi epokhi," *Kommunist*, 18 (December 1969).

12  The CPSU CC theses were published in Finnish in STK, Jan. 15, 1970; originally in *Pravda*. Brezhnev's speech, April 21, 1970.

13  Kansan arkisto (KA, People's Archives, Helsinki), Erkki Kivimäki papers, notes by Kivimäki on discussions with Zagladin and Shaposhnikov, June 29, 1971; SAPMO BArch, DY 30/ J IV 2/202/347, Brezhnev to Ulbricht, Oct. 16, 1970; short information of the CPSU CC; DY 30/ J IV 2/2 J 3164, Brezhnev to Ulbricht, Oct. 21, 1970.

14  Arbetarrörelsens arkiv och bibliotek (ARAB), Swedish Social Democratic Party files (SAP), F 02 H: 2, report by Juan Bosch on his trip to Asia, Nov. 21, 1969; Ilya V. Gaiduk, *The Soviet Union and the Vietnam War* (Chicago: Ivan R. Dee, 1996), pp.216–17, quoting a political letter from the Soviet embassy in Hanoi, June 25, 1970; Hungarian State Archives (MOL), Foreign Ministry files (KÜM) XIX-J-1-j, 80 dobor (top secret, 1970), report on consultations with N.D. Belokhvostikov (Head of Department), by Ferenc Esztergályos (Head of Department), March 13, 1970, no. 144-001469.

15  A.P. Kositsyn, "On the Ways to Build up the Dictatorship of the Proletariat," STK, Jan. 22, 1970.

16  Politisches Archiv des Auswärtigen Amts (PAAA, Berlin), Ministerium für Auswärtige Angelegenheiten der DDR (MfAA), C1175/76, memo, Feb. 6, 1970.

17  Kekkonen's diary, May 11, 1970, *Urho Kekkosen päiväkirjat*, ed. J. Suomi, vol. 3, 1969–74 (Helsinki: Otava, 2003); PAAA MfAA C 1371/73, Heinz Oelzner's notes on discussion with Soviet Ambassador A.E. Kovalev, June 24, 1970.

18  Melvyn P. Leffler, "Bringing It Together: The Parts and the Whole," in *Reviewing the Cold War: Approaches, Interpretations, Theory*, ed. Odd Arne Westad (London: Frank Cass, 2000), p.44.

19  KA Aarne Saarinen papers, Box 8, Saarinen's notes on talks in Moscow, May 7, 8, 1970. Saarinen asked and got additional financial support for 400,000 roubles convertible. Direct connection between the position of Finland and the U.S. strength was similar to the one given by Zhdanov in January 1948. See Kimmo Rentola, "The Spring of 1948: Which Way Finland?" in *Jahrbücher für historische Kommunismusforschung 1998*, ed. Hrsg. Hermann Weber et al. (Berlin: Akademie Verlag, 1998).

20 Unusual features noted in the report by E.E. Orchard (Soviet Section, JRD), June 26, 1970; National Archives, UK (TNA), Foreign and Commonwealth Office (FCO) 33/1173.

21 Supo, information report no. 8/1964, Sept. 11, 1964.

22 A. Belyakov and F. Burlatski, "Leninskaya teoriya sotsialisticheskoi revolyutsii i sovremennost," *Kommunist*, 15 (September 1960), pp.10–17.

23 KA Files of the Communist Party of Finland (SKP), Secretariat minutes, Jan. 15, 1965, Hertta Kuusinen's report on talks with Belyakov; Belyakov in SKP politburo minutes, Feb. 10, 1965; KA Toivo Pohjonen papers, Pohjonen's notes on discussions with Belyakov, Oct. 14, 1965; KA SKP politburo minutes, Feb. 23, 1965, Brezhnev's remarks in the CPSU and SKP discussions, Feb. 19, 1965; KA Kivimäki papers, Kivimäki's notes on a discussion with Brezhnev, March 27, 1969.

24 On the hot autumn, Robert Lumley, *States of Emergency: Cultures of Revolt in Italy from 1968 to 1978* (London: Verso, 1990), pp.207–41; Erkki Kauppila's private papers, undated memo by Kauppila, October 1969.

25 The first comprehensive report by the security police, top secret bulletin no. 4/70, Aug. 28, 1970.

26 KA Kivimäki papers, Box 10, Erkki Kivimäki's notes on Belyakov's talk, June 10, 1970, in Moscow.

27 SAPMO-BArch, DY 30/IV A 2/20/1027, "Analyse über die Politik der Kommunistischen Partei Finnlands," a memo dated at the International Department of the SED Central Committee on Aug. 27, 1970, unsigned, probably written after consultations with the CPSU CC; Kauppila's memo on Belyakov's words, October 1969.

28 Sheila Rowbotham, *Promise of a Dream: Remembering the Sixties* (London: Verso 2001), p.234.

29 KA Kivimäki papers, Box 10, Erkki Kivimäki's notes on A. Kozlov's lecture in the CPSU CC, June 1970; Supo Special files on SKP for 1970, report by the chief of Pelshe's security guards on the CPSU visit, March 2–7, 1970.

30 Utrikesdepartementets arkiv (UD) HP 1 Af 290, Ambassador Hägglöf to Wachtmeister, Aug. 19, 1970.

31 KA SKP Central Committee minutes, March 21, 22, 1970, reports by Jorma Simpura and Aarne Saarinen on their talks with Belyakov; Bracke, *Which Socialism, Whose Détente?* pp.309–10.

32 This idea was hinted at by Yuri Krasin, interviewed by the author.

33 Raymond L. Garthoff, *Détente and Confrontation: American-Soviet Relations from Nixon to Reagan* (Washington, D.C.: Brookings Institution, 1985), p.175.

34 Kekkonen's diary, Nov. 8, 1968. Part of the increasing role of the CPSU International Department, Belyakov after 1965 met social democrats and President Kekkonen. His predecessors only dealt with communists. Also, Urho Kekkonen Archives (UKA), Yearbook 1970, memo by Lt.-Gen. L. Sutela on the visit of the generals in the Soviet embassy, Oct. 19, 1970.

35 In his memoirs, KGB political line officer Albert Akulov claims that the ambassador "downright showed off with this idea." Albert Akulov, *Vuodet Tehtaankadulla* (Keuruu: Otava, 1996), p.148.

36 KA Aarne Saarinen papers, Saarinen's notes on talks in Moscow, Aug. 4, 1969; KA Kivimäki papers, Box 10, Kivimäki's notes on Ponomaryov and Kapitonov, June 11, 1970.

37 SAPMO-BArch DY 30/ J IV 2/202/82, Ambassador P.A. Abrassimov's information to Ulbrict about discussions between Kosygin and Bahr, Feb. 13, 1970; M.E. Sarotte, *Dealing with the Devil: East Germany, Détente, and Ostpolitik, 1969–1973* (Chapel Hill: University of North Carolina Press, 2001), p.40. In June Kosygin even said that in a few weeks he would be free from government duties. TNA PREM 13/3490, report by Graham, to be forwarded to Harold Wilson, June 10, 1970. Also, UD HP 1 Af: 287, report by Ambassador Ingemar Hägglöf on discussions with Georgi Farafonov, Sept. 30, 1969.

38 See a carefully worded letter by Yuri Andropov to the CPSU CC, Dec. 31, 1970, RGANI, f. 89, per. 57, d. 20. Andropov's

KGB demonstrated a rather similar realistic approach in the contacts with the Brandt government. Wilfried Loth, *Overcoming the Cold War: A History of Détente, 1950–1991* (Basingstoke: Palgrave, 2002), p.107. In addition, there are two KGB memoirs, Akulov, *Vuodet Tehtaankadulla*, and Viktor Vladimirov, *Näin se oli . . .* (Helsinki: Otava, 1993). According to the latter (pp.202–4), in the Helsinki KGB the Belyakov approach was supported by the son-in-law of G. K. Tsinev, KGB deputy chairman and a close crony of Brezhnev.

39 Quotation from an intelligence report in Kekkonen's diary entry, Sept. 25, 1970. The moderate economic line was driven through in the SKP Central Committee on Sept. 25, 26, 1970.

40 KA Saarinen papers, Saarinen's notes on discussion with Belyakov, Oct. 31, 1970; partially published in Saarinen's memoirs *Kivimies* (Helsinki: Otava, 1995), pp.199–201. On pressure efforts in foreign policy, see Oelzner's report on Beljakov's meeting (Nov. 3) with GDR and Polish ambassadors, Nov. 12, 1970, PAAA MfAA C 1371/73. For Soviet criticism on Leskinen in Beljakov's meeting (Nov. 12) with five East European ambassadors, see Oelzner's memo signed on Nov. 19, 1970, PAAA MfAA 1371/73; on Leskinen's trip to Stockholm, see top secret, unsigned memo, Nov. 16, 1970, UD HP 1 Af 291.

41 UD HP 1 Af: 290, Ambassador Ingemar Hägglöf's lecture in Stockholm, Aug. 25, 1970.

42 NA RG 59 Subject-Numeric Files 1970–73 Political and Defence, Box 1728, Memcon between Semyonov and Nitze, Dec. 14, 1970.

43 Kekkonen's diary entry, Dec. 28, 1970; Chen Jian, *Mao's China and the Cold War* (Chapel Hill: University of North Carolina Press, 2001), pp.154–57; Garthoff, *Détente and Confrontation*, pp.146–47; Keith H. Nelson, *The Making of the Détente: Soviet-American Relations in the Shadow of Vietnam* (Baltimore: John Hopkins University Press, 1995), p.91.

44 UD HP 1 Af 292, Hägglöf to Wachtmeister, Feb. 8, 1971; TNA FCO 33/1578, Paul Lever's report, Feb. 3, 1971.

45 MOL M-KS-288 f. (Hungarian Socialist Workers' Party Political Committee), group 32, 12. dobor, Warsaw Pact foreign ministers' conference, Bucharest, Feb. 18, 19, 1971, Comrade Gromyko's speech.

46 KA SKP International Department H 29, papers of Moscow seminar 1971, including Krasin's lecture on July 2, 1971; KA Kivimäki papers, Box 10, notes on Zagladin and Shaposhnikov, June 29, 1971; KA Aimo Haapanen papers, Box 59, notes on Shaposhnikov and Zagladin, June 29, 1971.

47 KA Aimo Haapanen papers, Box 59, notes on Ponomarev, July 7, 1971. According to Ponomarev, the Soviets had advised Chilean communists to moderacy in the new leftist Allende government in Chile.

48 Bracke, *Which Socialism, Whose Détente?* p.2.

## 6 Interpretations of Third World Solidarity and Contemporary German Nationalism
JENNIFER RUTH HOSEK

1 Interview with Tom Morton. "Torn Curtain: The Secret History of the Cold War," ABC Radio National, May 14, 2006 <www.abc.net.au/rn/history/hindsight/features/torn/episode1.htm> (accessed February 2008).

2 Quoted in Stephan Brockmann, "'Normalization': Has Helmut Kohl's Vision Been Realized?" in *German Culture, Politics, and Literature into the Twenty-First Century: Beyond Normalization*, ed. Stuart Taberner and Paul Cooke (Rochester, N.Y.: Camden House, 2006).

3 For more on German normalization, see, for example, Ruth A. Starkman, *Transformations of the New Germany* (New York: Palgrave, 2006).

4 John Foster, "The Rise of the Intellectual Right in Germany," H-Net: Humanities & Social Sciences Online <www.h-net.org/reviews/showlist> (accessed March 2008); Glenn W. Smith, *The Politics of Deceit* (Hoboken, N.J.: John Wiley & Sons, 2004).

5 Ibid.

6 See also Jacob Heilbrunn, "Germany's New Right," *Foreign Affairs*, November/December 1996.

7   Michael Smith and J. Thompson, eds., *Confronting the New Conservatism: The Rise of the Right in America* (New York: New York University Press, 2007).

8   Roger Woods, *Germany's New Right as Culture and Politics* (New York: Palgrave, 2007).

9   In his new book, Grass admits his own participation in the SS as a youth. This admission is itself part of the normalization trend.

10  Horst Köhler, "Laudatio von Bundespräsident Horst Köhler auf der Festveranstaltung zum 80, Geburtstag von Günter Grass am 27. Oktober 2007 in Lübeck," *Bulletin 116-1*, Oct. 28, 2007 <www.bundesregierung.de/nn_1514/Content/DE/Bulletin/2007> (accessed April 2008). My thanks to Sonja Klocke. Translation by the author.

11  "'Menschenrechte achten—Vertreibungen ächten' Bundespräsident Köhler Festredner beim Tag der Heimat in Berlin," *BdV Nachrichten Mitteilungsblatt des Bundes der Vertriebenen*, December 2006/January-February 2007.

12  Stiftung Zentrum gegen Vertreibungen, "Erzwungene Wege: Flucht und Vertreibung im Europa des 20. Jahrhunderts," Berlin, 2006. See also the German Historical Museum's exhibit, "Flucht, Vertreibung, Integration, Heimat," Berlin, 2006.

13  Cursory examination of *Die Welt, BZ, Der Tagesspiegel, Die Frankfurter Allgemeiner Zeitung, Die Frankfurter Rundschau, Der Spiegel*, and *Die Zeit* and by Joan Gladwell, Steven Goodman, and Andrea Speltz. My thanks.

14  Belinda Davis, "Activism from Starbuck to Starbucks, or Terror: What's in a Name?" *Radical History Review*, 85 (Winter 2003), p.40.

15  Ulrich Chaussy, *Die drei Leben des Rudi Dutschke: Eine Biographie* (Berlin: Links, 1993). See also Gretchen Dutschke, *Wir hatten ein barbarisches, schönes Leben: Rudi Dutschke eine Biographie* (Cologne: Kiepenheuer und Witsch, 1996).

16  Gerd Langguth, *Mythos '68: Die Gewaltphilosophie von Rudi Dutschke—Ursachen und Folgen der Studentenbeweg* (Bonn: Olzog, 2001).

17  Michaela Karl, *Rudi Dutschke: Revolutionär ohne Revolution* (Frankfurt/M: Neue Kritik, 2003).

18  Wolfgang Kraushaar, "Rudi Dutschke und der bewaffnete Kampf," in *Rudi Dutschke Andreas Baader und die RAF*, ed. Wolfgang Kraushaar, Karin Wieland, and Jan Philipp Reemtsma (Hamburg: Hamburger Edition, 2005).

19  Peter Unfried, "'Wir alle diskutierten die Stadtguerilla,' Interview with Klaus Theweleit," *Taz Journal*, 2006, p.31.

20  Heide Berndt, "Afterthoughts on 'Student Unrest,'" *Psychoanalytic Quarterly*, 44,317 (1973); Wolfgang Kraushaar, ed., *Die RAF und der linke Terrorismus* (Hamburg: Hamburger Edition, 2006); Siegward Lönnendonker, Bernd Rabehl, and Jochen Staadt, eds., *Die antiautoritäre Revolte: Der Sozialistische Deutsche Studentenbund nach der Trennung von der SPD* (Wiesbaden: Westdeutscher Verlag, 2002); Butz Peters, *Tödlicher Irrtum: Die Geschichte der RAF* (Frankfurt/M: Fischer, 2007).

21  Jeffrey Herf, "An Age of Murder Ideology and Terror in Germany, 1969–1991," Opening Lecture at *The 'German Autumn' of 1977: Terror, State, and Society in West Germany* (German Historical Institute in Washington: 2007). This paragraph resulted from a discussion with Belinda Davis; she also points to recent alignments of the RAF and radical Islam in news articles. Tremendous thanks to her.

22  Langguth, *Mythos '68*, p.85.

23  Van Gosse, ed., *Radical History Review*, 85 (Winter 2003).

24  Davis, "Activism from Starbuck to Starbucks, or Terror."

25  Jennifer Ruth Hosek, "'Subaltern Nationalism' and the West Berlin Anti-Authoritarians," *German Politics and Society*, 85,26.1 (Spring 2008).

26  Bernd Rabehl, "Ein Volk ohne Kultur kann zu allem verleitet werden," *Junge Freiheit*, Dec. 18, 1998.

27  Bernd Rabehl, "Neue Linke und Gewalt," *Sezession* 5 (April 2004).

28  Bernd Rabehl, *Rudi Dutschke: Revolutionär im geteilten Deutschland* (Dresden: Edition Antaios, 2004).

29  Ibid., pp.7–8.
30  Ibid., p.112.
31  Ibid., p.8.
32  Ibid., p.114.
33  On the flawed comparison between the
    Nazis and the GDR, see Antonio Negri,
    *Goodbye Mister Socialism: Entretien avec
    Raf Valvola Scelsi*, trans. Paula Bertilotto
    (Paris: Edition du Seuil, 2006), p.15.
34  Jennifer Ruth Hosek, "Cuba and the Ger-
    mans: A Cultural History of an Infatua-
    tion," Ph.D. dissertation, University of
    California, Berkeley, 2004.
35  Wolfgang Kraushaar, "Rudi Dutschke und
    die Wiedervereinigung: Zur heimlichen
    Dialektik von Internationalismus und ·
    Nationalismus," *Mittelweg 36*, 2 (1992).
36  Hosek, "'Subaltern Nationalism' and the
    West Berlin Anti-Authoritarians."
37  Michael Hardt and Antonio Negri, *Empire*
    (Cambridge, Mass.: Harvard University
    Press, 2000).
38  Ibid.

## 7  The Canadian National Security War on Queers and the Left
GARY KINSMAN

Thanks to Tracy Gregory for making sense
of my notes from the conference session
that this chapter is based on; to Patrizia
Gentile for her collaboration in this
research; and to David and all the others
we have interviewed and learned from.

1   This chapter draws on work with Patrizia
    Gentile for *The Canadian War on Queers:
    National Security as Sexual Regulation*
    (Vancouver: UBC Press, forthcoming).
    For background on the national secur-
    ity campaigns against lesbian and gay
    men in Canada, see Gary Kinsman,
    "'Character Weaknesses' and 'Fruit
    Machines': Towards an Analysis of the
    Anti-Homosexual Security Campaign
    in the Canadian Civil Service," *Labour/
    Le Travail*, 35 (Spring 1995), pp.133–61;
    Kinsman and Patrizia Gentile with
    the assistance of Heidi McDonell and
    Mary Mahood-Greer, *"In the Interests of
    the State": The Anti-Gay, Anti-Lesbian
    National Security Campaigns in Can-
    ada, A Research Report* (Sudbury, Ont.:
    Laurentian University, 1998); Kinsman,

    "Constructing Gay Men and Lesbians as
    National Security Risks, 1950–70," in
    *Whose National Security? Canadian State
    Surveillance and the Creation of Enemies*,
    ed. Gary Kinsman, Dieter Buse, and
    Mercedes Steedman (Toronto: Between
    the Lines, 2000), pp.143–53; Kinsman,
    "Challenging Canadian and Queer Nation-
    alisms," in *In a Queer Country: Gay and
    Lesbian Studies in the Canadian Context*,
    ed. Terry Goldie (Vancouver: Arsenal
    Pulp Press, 2001), pp.209–34; Kinsman,
    "National Security as Moral Regulation:
    Making the Normal and the Deviant in
    the Security Campaigns against Gay
    Men and Lesbians," in *Making Normal:
    Social Regulation in Canada*, ed. Deborah
    Brock (Toronto: Thomson/Nelson, 2003),
    pp.121–45; and Kinsman, "The Canadian
    Cold War on Queers: Sexual Regulation
    and Resistance," in *Love, Hate, and Fear
    in Canada's Cold War*, ed. Richard Cavell
    (Toronto: University of Toronto Press,
    2004), pp.108–32. I use "queer" as a way
    of reclaiming a term of abuse used against
    us; as a term to bring together a series of
    sexual and gender practices in rupture
    with heterosexual hegemony and the two-
    gender binary way of doing gender; and as
    a place from which to critique heterosex-
    ual hegemony. On this see Gary Kinsman,
    *The Regulation of Desire: Homo and Hetero
    Sexualities* (Montreal; Black Rose, 1996);
    and Annamarie Jagose, *Queer Theory: An
    Introduction* (New York: New York Univer-
    sity Press, 1996).
2   Trotskyists are supporters of Leon Trot-
    sky who was one of the most significant
    figures in the Russian revolution in 1917.
    Later he became a major opponent of
    the rise of the Stalinist bureaucracy. On
    Trotsky, see Ernest Mandel, *Trotsky as
    Alternative* (London and New York: Verso,
    1995); Leon Trotsky, *The Revolution
    Betrayed* (New York: Merit, 1965); and
    Leon Trotsky, *History of the Russian Revo-
    lution* (London: Pluto Press, 1977).
3   On autonomist Marxism and cycles
    and compositions of struggle, see Harry
    Cleaver, *Reading Capital Politically* (Leeds/
    Edinburgh/San Francisco: AK Press,
    Antitheses, 2000); Nick Dyer-Witheford,

*Cyber-Marx: Cycles and Circuits of Struggle in High-Technology Capitalism* (Urbana and Chicago: University of Illinois Press, 1999); Steve Wright, *Storming Heaven: Class Composition and Struggle in Italian Autonomist Marxism* (London: Pluto Press, 2002); and Gary Kinsman, "The Politics of Revolution: Learning From Autonomist Marxism," *Upping the Anti, a Journal of Theory and Action*, 2005, pp.43–52.

4   See John D'Emilio, *Sexual Politics, Sexual Communities: The Making of a Homosexual Minority in the United States, 1940–1970* (Chicago and London: University of Chicago Press, 1983), pp.223–39.

5   See Lisa Duggan, *The Twilight of Equality? Neoliberalism, Cultural Politics and the Attack on Democracy* (Boston: Beacon, 2003); and *Radical History Review*, Queer Futures Issue, 100 (Winter 2008).

6   On memory and the social organization of forgetting, see Philip Corrigan and Derek Sayer, *The Great Arch: English State Formation as Cultural Revolution* (Oxford: Basil Blackwell, 1985); p.195; Roxanne Dunbar-Ortiz interview, "The Opposite of Truth Is Forgetting," *Upping the Anti*, 6 (Spring 2008), pp.47–58; Kristin Ross, *May '68 and Its Afterlives* (Chicago and London: University of Chicago Press, 2002); Susannah Radstone and Katherine Hodgkin, *Regimes of Memory* (London and New York: Routledge, 2007), and their companion volume *Contested Pasts: The Politics of Memory* (London and New York: Routledge, 2007).

7   Gary Kinsman, "'Responsibility' as a Strategy of Governance: Regulating People Living with AIDS and Lesbians and Gay Men in Ontario," *Economy and Society*, August 1996, pp.393–409.

8   George Smith, "The Ideology of 'Fag': Barriers to Education for Gay Students," *Sociological Quarterly*, 39,2 (1998), pp.309–35.

9   Dorothy E. Smith, "K Is Mentally Ill," in Smith, *Texts, Facts, Femininity: Exploring the Relations of Ruling* (London and New York: Routledge, 1990), pp.30–43.

10  In the United States, leftist and ex-Communist Party members were centrally involved in the formation of the Mattachine Society, established in the late 1940s as the first attempt at a homophile organization. In the context of the height of the Cold War frenzy against Communists and ex-Communists, these leaders were later thrown out by more conservative members of the groups. See D'Emilio, *Sexual Politics, Sexual Communities*, pp.57–91. Left-wing activists were also centrally involved in the formation of gay liberation fronts after the Stonewall riots in New York City in 1969, and the formation of the Gay Liberation Front in London, England. For some of the connections between the left and gay activism in Toronto in the 1970s see Deborah Brock, "'Workers of the World Caress,' an interview with Gary Kinsman on gay and lesbian organizing in the 1970s Toronto left," *Left History* website <www.yorku.ca/lefthist> (accessed June 10, 2008).

11  Patrizia Gentile and I use "war" as in "war on queers" in a way that is parallel to how antipoverty movements have used expressions like opposing the "war on the poor." Without in any way trivializing the experiences of actual warfare and colonialism, we want to point to the seriousness and systematic character of the national security campaigns against lesbians and gay men and the devastation that these crusades created in thousands of people's lives. At the same time, notions of "war," as in the Cold War, the war on drugs, and the war on terror, have often been inflected by and colonized by right-wing deployments of this term. Thanks to Dan O'Meara for raising this point in discussion at a security conference at Laurentian University, March 2008.

12  See references in note 1.

13  See John Sawatsky, *Men in the Shadows: The RCMP Security Service* (Toronto: Totem, 1980), pp.125–27.

14  "Prepolitical activities are social acts of resistance that have not yet crystallized into political institutions as opposed to isolated individual acts of resistance." Elizabeth Lapovsky Kennedy and Madeline D. Davis, *Boots of Leather, Slippers of Gold: The History of a Lesbian Community* (New York and London: Routledge, 1993), p.390, fn3.

15 Directorate of Security and Intelligence, RCMP, *Annual Report*, Ottawa, 1962–63, p.19.

16 Directorate of Security and Intelligence, RCMP, *Annual Report*, 1963–64, p.30.

17 This name is a pseudonym to protect confidentiality. A fictionalized and dramatized version of David's account is included in Nancy Nicol's video *Stand Together* (2002), on the history of lesbian and gay organizing in Ontario.

18 All male same-gender sexual acts were criminalized until 1969 in Canada.

19 Interview, May 12, 1994.

20 Interview, May 12, 1994.

21 On camp cultural formation, see Kinsman, *Regulation of Desire*, pp.226–27.

22 Steve Hewitt gave Patrizia Gentile and me our first set of documents released under Access to Information Act on RCMP surveillance of gay and lesbian groups in the 1970s. We thank him for this.

23 This was also partly the case for RCMP surveillance of high-school student activists in Toronto. See Christabelle Sethna, "High School Confidential: RCMP Surveillance of Secondary School Student Activists," in *Whose National Security?* ed. Kinsman, Buse, and Steedman, pp.121–28.

24 On the Socialist Workers Party, see Gary Kinsman, "From Anti-Queer to Queers as 'Peripheral,'" paper on the gay discussion in the U.S. Socialist Workers Party, History of American Trotskyism conference, New York, September 2000; David Thorstad, ed., *Gay Liberation and Socialism: Documents from the Discussions on Gay Liberation Inside the Socialist Workers Party (1970–1973)* (New York, 1976); and Steve Forgione and Kurt T. Hill, eds., *No Apologies: The Unauthorized Publication of Internal Discussion Documents of the Socialist Workers Party (SWP) Concerning Lesbian/Gay Male Liberation* (New York: Lesbian/Gay Rights Monitoring Group, 1980).

25 See Brock, "'Workers of the World Caress'"; "Statement of the Political Committee, Revolutionary Marxist Group, *Old Mole* (Toronto), 5 (July/August 1973), p.3. See also Socialist History Project website <www.socialisthistory.ca/Docs/1961-/RMG-GMR/Founding_of_RMG.htm> (accessed June 10, 2008).

26 On this see Christabelle Sethna and Steven Hewitt, "Staging Protest: The Abortion Caravan, Feminist Guerilla Theatre and RCMP Spying on Women's Groups," paper, New World Coming: The Sixties and the Shaping of Global Consciousness conference, Queen's University, Kingston, Ont., June 14, 2007.

27 Initially this campaign was more of a wages against housework campaign, and its theoretical basis was built from the autonomist Marxist notion of capital becoming a social factory that extended far beyond actual factory walls. Women doing domestic labour were labouring not only for individual men but also for capital. For the development of the theoretical perspective behind this campaign, see Mariarosa Dalla Costa and Selma James, *The Power of Women and the Subversion of the Community* (Bristol, Eng.: Falling Water Press, 1972); and Silvia Federici, *Wages Against Housework* (London: Power of Women Collective and Falling Wall Press, 1975). See also the account of the development of this perspective in relation to autonomist Marxism in Harry Cleaver, *Reading Capital Politically* (Leeds/Edinburgh/San Francisco: AK Press, Antitheses, 2000), pp.71–74.

28 National Archives of Canada (NAC), RG 146, v.3050, File: GATE-T: Unaligned Marxist and Pressure Groups, "Toronto Wages for Housework Committee," p.225 of file.

29 NAC, RG 146, v.3050, File: GATE-T: Unaligned Marxist and Pressure Groups, "Toronto Wages for Housework Committee," p.227 of file. In contrast there are no references to gay male "effeminacy" or gender inversion in any of the RCMP surveillance reports regarding gay male activists during these years.

30 On this, see Dorothy E. Smith, "Femininity as Discourse," in Smith, *Texts, Facts and Femininity: Exploring the Relations of Ruling*, pp.159–208.

31 On performances of lesbianism in relation to gender see Becki Ross, *The House*

That Jill Built: A Lesbian Nation in Formation (Toronto: University of Toronto Press, 1995); Joan Nestle, "Butch-Femme Relationships: Sexual Courage in the 1950s," in Nestle, *A Restricted Country* (Ithaca, N.Y.: Firebrand, 1987), pp.100–9; Kennedy and Davis, *Boots of Leather, Slippers of Gold*; and Aerlyn Weissman and Lynne Fernie, directors, *Forbidden Love*, National Film Board of Canada, 1993. Comments on the unfeminine appearance of feminists seems to have been common in RCMP reports from the early 1970s. On this see Sethna and Hewitt, "Staging Protest."

32 NAC, RG 146, v.3050, File: GATE-T: Unaligned Marxist and Pressure Groups, "Toronto Wages for Housework Committee," p. 230 of file.

33 RG 146, V. 3050, 21-6-1976, "Re: National Gay Rights Coalition (NGRC)," p.238.

34 NAC, RG 146, V. 3050, June 12, 1973, "Re: Gay Alliance Towards Equality–Vancouver," p.80.

35 NAC, RG 146, V. 3050, 21-6-1976, "Re: National Gay Rights Coalition (NGRC)," p.238.

36 See Trotsky, *Revolution Betrayed*.

37 On the Cuban Revolution and gays and lesbians, see Allen Young, *Gays under the Cuban Revolution* (San Francisco: Grey Fox Press, 1981); Lourdes Arguelles and B. Ruby Rich, "Homosexuality, Homophobia and Revolution: Notes Towards an Understanding of the Cuban Lesbian and Gay Male Experience," Part 1, *Signs*, 9, 4 (Summer 1984), pp.683–99; and Ian Lumsden, *Machos, Maricones, and Gays, Cuba and Homosexuality* (Philadelphia: Temple University Press, 1996).

38 NAC, RG 146, GATE-T, "Re: National Gay Rights Coalition (NGRC)," p.240.

39 On some of this see Jasbir K. Puar, *Terrorist Assemblages: Homonationalism in Queer Times* (Durham, N.C., and London: Duke University Press, 2007).

40 See Duggan, *Twilight of Equality?*; *Radical History Review*, Queer Futures Issue, 100 (Winter 2008); and Kinsman, "'Responsibility' as a Strategy of Governance."

41 See John Holloway, *Change the World Without Taking Power: The Meaning of Revolution Today* (London: Pluto, 2005).

## 8 Neo-Fascism, the Extraparliamentary Left Wing, and the Birth of Italian Terrorism

GUIDO PANVINI

The research in this article draws on the following texts:

"Azione collettiva, violenza e conflitto nella costruzione dell'Italia repubblicana," *Passato e Presente*, 26 (1991).

Baldelli, Pio. *Informazione e controinformazione*. Milano: Mazzotta, 1972.

Baldoni, Adalberto. *Noi rivoluzionari: la destra e il caso italiano. Appunti per una storia, 1960–1986*. Roma: Settimo Sigillo, 1986.

Baldoni, Adalberto and Sandro Provvisionato. *La notte più lunga della Repubblica: sinistra e destra, ideologie, estremismi, lotta armata (1968–89)*. Roma: Sesarcangeli, 1989.

Ballini, Piero and Maurizio Ridolfi, eds. *Storia delle campagne elettorali in Italia*. Milano: Bruno Mondadori, 2003.

Barbieri Paolo, Cucchiarelli Paolo, *La strage con i capelli bianchi, La sentenza per piazza Fontana*. Roma: Editori Riuniti, 2003.

Bianconi, Giovanni. *A mano armata: vita violenta di Giusva Fioravanti*. Milano: Baldini and Castoldi, 2002.

Bianconi, Giovanni. *Mi dichiaro prigioniero politico: storia delle Brigate rosse*. Torino: Einaudi, 2003.

Boatti, Giorgio. *Piazza Fontana, 12 dicembre 1969: il giorno dell'innocenza perduta*. Torino: Einaudi, 1999.

Cazzullo, Aldo. *Il caso Sofri: dalla condanna alla tregua civile*. Milano: Mondadori, 2004.

Cingolani, Giorgio. *La destra in armi: neofascisti italiani tra ribellismo ed eversione (1977–82)*. Roma: Editori Riuniti, 1996.

Colarizi, Simona. *Storia politica della Repubblica: partiti, movimenti e istituzioni, 1943–2006*. Roma-Bari: Laterza, 2007.

Crainz, Guido. *Il Paese mancato: dal miracolo economico agli anni ottanta*. Roma: Donzelli, 2003.

Della Porta, Donatella and Mario Rossi. *Cifre crudeli: bilancio dei terrorismi italiani*. Bologna: Il Mulino, 1984.

Della Porta, Donatella. *Il terrorismo di sinistra*. Bologna: Il Mulino, 1990.

Della Porta, Donatella. *Movimenti collettivi e sistema politico in Italia, 1960–1995*. Roma-Bari: Laterza, 1996.

Eco, Umberto and Paolo Violi. "La contro-informazione," in *Storia della stampa italiana: la stampa italiana del neocapitalismo*, vol.5, ed. Valerio Castronovo and Nicola Tranfaglia. Roma–Bari: Laterza, 1976.

Ferraresi, Franco. *Minacce alla democrazia: la destra radicale e la strategia della tensione in Italia nel dopoguerra (1945–1984)*. Milano: Feltrinelli, 1995.

Galleni, Mauro. *Rapporto sul terrorismo*. Milano: Rizzoli, 1981.

Gasparetti, Alessandro. *La destra e il '68*. Roma: Settimo Sigillo, 2006.

Giannuli, Aldo. *Bombe ad inchiostro*. Milano: Rizzoli, 2008.

Ginsborg, Paul. *Storia d'Italia dal dopoguerra a oggi: società e politica, 1943–1988*. Torino: Einaudi, 1989.

Ignazi, Piero. *Il polo escluso: profilo storico del Movimento Sociale Italiano*. Bologna: Il Mulino, 1998.

Klatch, R.E. *A Generation Divided: The New Left, the New Right and the 1960s*. Berkeley: University of California Press, 1999.

Lupo, Salvatore. *Partito e antipartito: una storia politica della prima Repubblica*. Roma: Donzelli, 2004.

Manconi, Luigi. "Il nemico assoluto: antifascismo e contropotere nella fase aurorale del terrorismo di sinistra," in *La politica della violenza*, ed. Raimondo Catanzaro. Bologna: Il Mulino, 1990.

Ortoleva, Peppino. *Saggio sui movimenti del 1968 in Europa e in America*. Roma: Editori Riuniti, 1988.

Panvini, Guido. "Alle origini del terrorismo diffuso. La schedatura degli avversari politici negli anni della conflittualità. Tracce di una fonte," *Mondo Contemporaneo*, 3 (2006).

Rapini Andrea. "Antifascismo sociale, soggettività e strategia della tensione," *Novecento*, 1 (July–December 1999).

Rapoport, David C. and Leonard Weinberg. "Elections and Violence," in *The Democratic Experience and Political Violence*, ed. David C. Rapoport and Leonard Weinberg. London and Portland, Ore: Frank Cass, 2001.

Ridolfi, Maurizio. "La contrapposizione amico/nemico nella celebrazione delle festività nazionali," in *L'ossessione del nemico: memorie divise nella storia della Repubblica*, ed. A. Ventrone. Roma: Donzelli, 2006.

Schelling, Thomas C. *La strategia del conflitto*. Milano: Bruno Mondadori, 2006.

Schnur Roman. *Rivoluzione e guerra civile*. Milano: Giuffrè, 1986.

Scoppola, Piétro. *La repubblica dei partiti: evoluzione e crisi di un sistema politico, 1945–1996*. Bologna: Il Mulino, 1997.

Tarrow, Sydney. *Democracy and Disorder: Protest and Politics in Italy 1965–1975*. New York: Oxford University Press, 1989.

Tessandori, Vincenzo. *Br: imputazione banda armata*. Milano: Baldini and Castoldi, 2002.

## 9  Resisting the Sixties: A Dutch Reaction in a Global Perspective
TITY DE VRIES

1  A.P.M. Lucardie, "De stiefkinderen van de social-democratie. DS'70 vergeleken met zusterpartijen elders in Europa," *Jaarboek DNPP*, 1990, p.117.

2  As cited in J.H. Scheps, *Kink in de Kabel: Scheuring en Polarisatie PvdA-DS'70* (Apeldoorn: Semper Agendo, 1972), p.73.

3  Lucardie, "Stiefkindern van de social-democratie," p.118.

4  In the 1971 elections 1 per cent of the Labour Party voters switched to DS70. Willem Drees, *Gespiegeld in de Tijd. De Nagelaten Autobiografie* (Amsterdam: Balans, 2000), p.159.

5  As cited by vice-chairman J.H.Gootjes in 1978. G. Voerman, "Een Geval van Politieke Schizofrenie. Het Gespleten Gedachtengoed van DS'70," *Jaarboek DNPP*, 1990, p.102.

6  As cited in Scheps, *Kink in de kabel*, p.77.

7  As cited in Voerman, "Een Geval van Politieke Schizofrenie," p.103.

## 10  Transpacific Revolutionaries: The Creation of Latin American Maoism
MATTHEW ROTHWELL

1  José Sotomayor Pérez, *¿Leninismo o maoismo?* (Lima: Editorial Universo, 1979), p.24. The original Spanish quotation reads "¿Ya ven?—prosiguió Mao—así se puede comenzar una guerra popular;

no es difícil. ¿Quieren ustedes hacer la guerra? Es cuestión de decidirse." All translations are by the author.

2   For a full examination of this phenomenon (and a full documentation of sources), see Matthew Rothwell, "Transpacific Revolutionaries: The Chinese Revolution in Latin America," Ph.D. dissertation, University of Illinois at Chicago, forthcoming.

3   The first wave of scholarship on Maoism in Latin America, on whose shoulders this work stands, took place in the context of the Cold War and was mainly concerned with how the Chinese were seeking to spread their influence in Latin America. See, for example, Daniel Tretiak, "China and Latin America: An Ebbing Tide in Transpacific Maoism," *Current Scene: Developments in Mainland China*, 4, 5 (March 1, 1966), pp.1–12; or Ernst Halperin, "Peking and the Latin American Communists," *China Quarterly*, 29 (January–March 1967), pp.111–54.

4   The two essays, originally dated April 5 and December 29, 1956, have been published together as Chinese Communist Party, *The Historical Experience of the Dictatorship of the Proletariat* (Peking: Foreign Languages Press, 1959).

5   The request was ignored. Sotomayor, *¿Leninismo o maoísmo?*, pp.47–48; José Sotomayor Pérez, *Revolución cultural proletaria* (Lima: Ediciones Nueva Democracia, 1967), p.71.

6   Sotomayor, *¿Leninismo o maoísmo?*, pp.48–49.

7   After the victory of the Chinese Revolution in 1949, the Soviet Union and the People's Republic of China were close allies. But serious political differences came to the fore as the leaders of both countries drew differing lessons from the period of Stalin's rule in the Soviet Union, which had served as an initial model for the Chinese socialist state and its economic development. The split is commonly understood to have begun with Khrushchev's denunciations of Stalin in 1956, but only erupted into public polemics between the ruling Communist parties of each country in 1963. The split reached its highest point of tension in 1969, when the Soviets and Chinese fought a series of border skirmishes.

8   Carlos De la Riva, *Donde nace la aurora* (Arequipa: Ediciones Nueva Era, 1961), p.5.

9   It is not clear whether this translator just happened to be in Bern, or whether he travelled there for this meeting.

10   Sotomayor, *¿Leninismo o maoísmo?*, pp.15–18.

11   For background information on Medrano and the details of his trip to China, see Elena Poniatowska, *Fuerte es el silencio* (Mexico City: Ediciones Era, 1980), pp.244–45, 251; Ramón Pérez, *Diary of a Guerrilla* (Houston: Arte Público Press, 1999), pp.107–8; Fiscalía Especial para Movimientos Sociales y Políticos del Pasado, "La guerrilla se extiende por todo el país," National Security Archive, George Washington University <www.gwu.edu/~nsarchiv> (accessed July 7, 2006), p.9. There are discrepancies in the sources regarding the details of Medrano's trip to China, and the Fiscalía Especial document claims that Medrano travelled to China in 1970, not 1969. Because of the discrepancies in the sources, the dates given in this paragraph should be taken as approximations. Also, while the Fiscalía Especial document places Medrano's hometown in Tlatlaya, Estado de México, Poniatowska gives his birthplace as Guerrero; see Poniatowska, *Fuerte es el silencio*, p.251.

12   Poniatowska, *Fuerte es el silencio*, pp.197, 252, 259.

13   See, for example, Juan Manuel Ramírez Sáiz, *El movimiento urbano popular en México* (Mexico City: Siglo Veintiuno Editores, 1986).

14   Poniatowska, *Fuerte es el silencio*, pp.181–83, 185, 191–92, 197–98. At the same time as Poniatowska gives the number of squatters as 10,000, she claims there were 5,000 families.

15   Ibid., 190–95, 197–200, 262–63.

16   Pérez, *Diary of a Guerrilla*, p.49. This quote almost certainly relies on Pérez's memory of what Medrano said.

17   Ibid., p.67.

18 On the idea of revolutionary asynchronicity see John Lewis Gaddis, *We Now Know: Rethinking Cold War History* (New York: Oxford University Press, 1997), pp.212–13, 362, n39.

## 11 On Digging It: Correspondences between Dineh Uranium Miners and the Health and Safety Program of the Oil, Chemical and Atomic Workers
JULIE BODDY

1 Stan Steiner, *The New Indians* (New York: Harper and Row, 1968), p.33.
2 Les Leopold: *The Man Who Hated Work and Loved Labor: The Life and Times of Tony Mazzocchi* (New York: Chelsea Green Publishing, 2007).
3 Ibid.
4 Barbara Garson, *All the Livelong Day: The Meaning and Demeaning of Routine Work*, rev. ed. (New York: Penguin, 1994), p.78.
5 Leo Goodman Papers, Box143, Library of Congress.
6 Doug Brugge et al., *Memories Come to Us in the Wind and Rain: Oral Histories and Photographs of Navajo Uranium Miners and Their Families*, Navajo Uranium Miners Oral History and Photography Project, 1997.

## 12 Liberation Support and Anti-Apartheid Work as Seeds of Global Consciousness: The Birth of Solidarity with Southern African Struggles
JOHN S. SAUL

1 These first pages parallel the first pages of John S. Saul, *Decolonization and Empire: Contesting the Rhetoric and Practice of Resubordination in Southern Africa and Beyond* (Delhi and London: Three Essays Collective and Merlin Press, 2007), in order both to situate a detailed critique of the present situation of an ostensibly "liberated Southern Africa" and, as here, to evaluate the strengths and weaknesses of the global support movement, which also played some role in producing this "liberated" outcome.
2 The five countries that thus became the hostages of a "late decolonization" process—and sites of dramatic "liberation struggles"—were Angola, Mozambique, Rhodesia (now Zimbabwe), South-West Africa (now Namibia), and South Africa. Other countries in the region were either small and had their decolonizations linked, somewhat earlier and more or less by historical accident, to the general processes of British decolonization on the continent (Botswana, Swaziland, Lesotho); or they were situated on the borders of the region (Malawi, Zambia), where their own (relatively peaceful) decolonization became an early phase in the complex process that would eventually produce Zimbabwe.
3 Du Bois, quoted in Ronald Segal, *The Race War: The World-Wide Clash of White and Non-White* (New York: New Bantam, 1967).
4 Henning Melber, "Namibia's Post-Colonial Socio-Economic (Non) Transformation: Business as Usual," *Nord-Sud actuel* (3/4 Quarter 2005), p.306.
5 See, for various startling statements by Thabo Mbeki, the following (inter alia): Mbeki, "The Fatton Thesis: A Rejoinder," *Canadian Journal of African Studies*, 18, 3 (1984), p.609; his interview in the ANC journal *Mayibuye*, March, 1991, p.2; and as quoted by Pippa Green, "The Outsider Who Has Measured Vision against Reality," *Business Report*, Feb. 16, 2006.
6 Colin Leys and John Saul, "Sub-Saharan Africa in Global Capitalism," ch.1 in Saul, *The Next Liberation Struggle: Capitalism, Socialism and Democracy in Southern Africa* (Toronto, New York, London, and Durban: Between the Lines, Monthly Review Press, Merlin Press, and University of KwaZulu/Natal Press, 2006), p.21.
7 John S. Saul, "The Strange Death of Liberated Southern Africa," ch.5 in Saul, *Decolonization and Empire*.
8 Penny Von Eschen, *Race Against Empire: Black Americans and Anticolonialism, 1937–1957* (Ithaca, N.Y.: Cornell University Press, 1996).
9 Ibid., p.187; also Brenda Gayle Plummer, *Rising Wind: Black Americans and U.S. Foreign Affairs, 1935–1969* (Chapel Hill: University of North Carolina Press, 1996).
10 Von Eschen, *Race Against Empire*, p.185.

11 Von Eschen, *Race Against Empire*, pp.188–89, where she also quotes, tellingly, from King's February 1968 address, "Tribute of Du Bois by Martin Luther King Jr," in *W.E.B. Du Bois Speaks: Speeches and Addresses, 1890–1919*, ed. Phillip Foner (New York: Pathfinder Press, 1970), pp.14, 19.

12 Rhoda Howard, "Reparations for Colonialism," ch.5 of her forthcoming book, which she made available to me.

13 Robert Kinlock Massie, *Loosing the Bonds: The United States and South Africa in the Apartheid Era* (New York: Doubleday, 1997); Francis Njubi Nesbitt, *Race for Sanctions: African Americans against Apartheid* (Bloomington: Indiana University Press, 2004); Roger Fieldhouse, *Anti-Apartheid: A History of the Movement in Britain* (London: Merlin, 2005).

14 Many of them are admirably canvassed in the volumes by Massie, *Loosing the Bonds*; and Nesbitt, *Race for Sanctions*.

15 See Gay Seidman, "Monitoring Multinationals: Lessons from the Anti-Apartheid Era," *Politics and Society*, 31 (2003); despite a two-decade struggle to pressure corporations to adopt the code, "the Sullivan Principles had little demonstrable effect on the ending of apartheid and were open to abuse" (p.26).

16 Nesbitt, *Race for Sanctions*.

17 Ibid.

18 Bill Fletcher, "My Friends Are Being Tortured in Zimbabwe, " *Black Commentator*, Nov. 16, 2006.

19 Fieldhouse, *Anti-Apartheid*, pp.465–66.

20 Garth Legge, Cranford Pratt, Richard Williams, and Hugh Winsor, *The Black Paper: An Alternative Policy for Canada towards Southern Africa* (Toronto: Committee for a Just Policy Towards Africa, 1970).

21 Legge et al., *Black Paper*. The four authors were Garth Legge of the United Church of Canada, Cranford Pratt of the University of Toronto, Richard Williams and Hugh Winsor, both returned CUSO volunteers but with Williams now (as of 1970) an active member of the International Education Project and Winsor a journalist with Toronto's *Globe and Mail*.

22 YWCA, *Investment in Oppression: Report of the Study and Action Committee of the World Relationships Committee of the YWCA of Canada on Canadian Economic Links with South Africa* (Toronto, 1973).

23 Renate Pratt, *In Good Faith: Canadian Churches against Apartheid* (Waterloo, Ont.: Wilfrid Laurier University Press, 1997).

24 See Linda Freemen, *The Ambiguous Champion: Canada and South Africa in the Trudeau and Mulroney Years* (Toronto: University of Toronto Press, 1997); but also, for a critique and brief complementary analysis of Canada's role vis-à-vis Southern Africa over the years, John S. Saul, "A Class Act: Canada's Anti-Apartheid Record," in Saul, *Decolonization and Empire*.

25 Saul, "A Class Act."

26 As cited in Legge et al., *Black Paper*, p.1, quoting Trudeau's original statement in Claude Henault, "Canada Must Cut Trade Links with South Africa," *The Telegram* (Toronto), Feb. 25, 1970, p.70.

27 See also, inter alia, Peter Limb, "Apartheid, Solidarity and Globalisation: Lessons from the History of the Anti-Apartheid Movements," paper presented to "Apartheid, Solidarity, and Globalisation: Lessons from the History of the Anti-Apartheid Movements," a conference held in Durban, South Africa, Oct.10–13, 2004, for Australia; the series of volumes, one for the each of the Scandinavian countries, published by the Nordiska Africkainstitutet; for Switzerland, Georg Kreis, *Switzerland and South Africa, 1948–1994* (Bern: Peter Lang, 2007).

28 Hakan Thorn, *Anti-Apartheid and the Emergence of a Global Civil Society* (London: Palgrave, 2006); Limb, "Apartheid, Solidarity and Globalisation."

29 Thorn, *Anti-Apartheid and the Emergence of a Global Civil Society*, as summarized in Limb, "Apartheid, Solidarity and Globalisation," pp.3–4.

30 Ibid.

31 However important such a "reform" might be considered to be.

32 Saul, "Strange Death of Liberated Southern Africa."

### 13 Upon the Long Avenues of Sadness: Otto René Castillo and Transnational Spaces of Exile

MICHAEL D. KIRKPATRICK

Special thanks to Ana Vialard, Jim Handy, Angel González Abreu, and Charlotte Kirkpatrick for their insights and assistance with this project. As well, I would like to thank the late Octavio Cortázar Jiménez—a wonderful storyteller and filmmaker—who graciously shared his time with me. His death reminds us of the need to listen carefully to those who made the 1960s the 1960s.

1 Karlheind Mund, *Erinnerungen an Otto René Castillo*, DEFA-Studio, German Democratic Republic, 1979.

2 For more on the 1944–54 period, see Jim Handy, *Gift of the Devil* (Toronto: Between the Lines, 1984); and Susanne Jonas, *The Battle for Guatemala: Rebels, Death Squads, and US Power* (Boulder, Col.: Westview Press, 1991).

3 Two such figures were Ernesto Che Guevara—who later travelled to Mexico City, where he joined Fidel Castro's expedition to Cuba—and Miguel Mármol—a lifetime Salvadoran communist whose testimony was given to poet Roque Dalton. For more on these figures and their time in Guatemala, see Jon Lee Anderson, *Che Guevara: A Revolutionary Life* (New York: Grove Press, 1997); and Roque Dalton, *Miguel Mármol*, trans. Kathleen Ross and Richard Schaaf (Willimantic, Conn.: Curbstone Press, 1987).

4 John Beverley and Marc Zimmerman, *Literature and Politics in the Central American Revolutions* (Austin: University of Texas Press, 1990), pp.152–54.

5 The most satisfying accounts of the agrarian reform process and the overthrow of Jacobo Arbenz are Cindy Forster, *The Time of Freedom: Campesino Workers in Guatemala's October Revolution* (Pittsburgh: University of Pittsburgh Press, 2001); Greg Grandin, *The Blood of Guatemala: A History of Race and Nation* (Durham, N.C.: Duke University Press, 2000); and Jim Handy, *Revolution in the Countryside: Rural Conflict and Agrarian Reform in Guatemala, 1944–1954* (Chapel Hill:

University of North Carolina Press, 1994).

6 See Dalton, "Su ejemplo y nuestra responsabilidad," in Otto René Castillo, *Informe de una injusticia* (Guatemala: Editorial Cultura, 1993).

7 "Tragedy in Guatemala," *The New York Times*, July 28, 1957, p.2; and Augusto Cazali Avila, *Historia de la Universidad de San Carlos de Guatemala: Epoca Republicana (1821–1994)* (Universidad de San Carlos de Guatemala: Editorial Universitaria, 2001), p.365.

8 "A Cuba que lucha," *El Estudiante*, Epoca II, 46 (July 26, 1958), p.4.

9 He writes, in part, "your dawn, Algeria,/ opens its radiant wings/to defend/the liberty won by your people." The poem was later published in Spanish in Castillo, "Mensaje para Argelia," *Alero*, Epoca IV, 3 (September–October 1979), pp.5–7.

10 Electronic correspondence with Octavio Cortázar Jiménez, Feb. 15, 2008.

11 Here, the name Third World is used not in a pejorative sense associated with ideas of arrested economic development but as a phrase of empowerment, as envisioned by those who adopted the concept of the Third World at the Bandung Conference in 1955.

12 For more on Ivens's account of his early career and the associated changes in technology, see Joris Ivens, *The Camera and I* (New York: International Publishers, 1969). For Ivens in Cuba, see chapter 14 here.

13 See Julianne Burton, "The Camera as 'Gun': Two Decades of Culture and Resistance in Latin America," *Latin American Perspectives*, 5,1 (Winter 1978); Fernando Solanas and Octavio Getino, "Towards a Third Cinema," in *Movies and Methods: An Anthology*, ed. Bill Nichols (Berkeley: University of California Press, 1976); and Alfredo Rostgaard's poster print for the tenth anniversary of ICAIC, found in Lincoln Cushing, *Revolución! Cuban Poster Art* (San Francisco: Chronicle Books, 2003), p.109.

14 For accounts of the first phase of guerrilla struggle in Guatemala, see Régis Debray, *A Critique of Arms*, vol.2, *The Revolution on Trial*, trans. Rosemary

Sheed (London: Penguin Books, 1978);
Eduardo Galeano, *Guatemala: Occupied
Country* (New York: Monthly Review Press,
1969); and Richard Gott, *Guerrilla Movements in Latin America* (London: Nelson,
1970).

15 Dalton, "Su ejemplo y nuestra
responsabilidad."

16 For example, see the memoirs of a former
Guatemalan president: Miguel Ydigoras
Fuentes, *My War with Communism* (Engle-
wood Cliffs, N.J.: Prentice Hill, 1963).

17 The conference made use of many of the
maxims found in Castro's *Second Declaration of Havana*, February 1962. Castro
argued that the three continents shared
the experience of colonialism, which
served as justification for a unified future.

18 Historian Robert Young has noted the
historical importance of the Tricontinental Conference and its magazine, which
he regards as the founding moment of
post-colonial theory. See Robert Young,
*Postcolonialism: An Historical Introduction*
(Oxford: Blackwell Publishing, 2001), p.5.

19 For more on Turcios Lima's activities
at the Tricontinental Conference, see
Orlando Fernández, *Turcios Lima* (Havana:
Tricontinental, 1970).

20 Castillo, "Comandante Cuba," *Vocero Estudiantil*, Epoca VI, 3, (August 1964), p.3.

21 See Régis Debray, *Revolution in the Revolution? Armed Struggle and Political Struggle in Latin America*, trans. Bobbye Ortis
(New York: Monthly Review Press, 1968);
and Anderson, *Che Guevara*.

22 Mario Roberto Morales, *La ideología y la
lírica de la lucha armada* (Ciudad de Guatemala: Editorial Universitaria de Guatemala, 1994), pp.263–65.

23 Otto René Castillo, *Let's Go!*, trans. Margaret Randall (Willimantic, Conn.: Curbstone Press, [1984], 1971), pp.14–17.

24 Bertolt Brecht, "Señora Carrar's Rifles,"
in *Collected Plays*, vol.4, Part 3, ed. John
Millet and Ralph Manheim (London:
Methuen, 1970); and Mund, *Erinnerungen
an Otto René Castillo*.

25 For more on Castillo's time in the FGEI
and his death, see Morales, *La ideología
y la lírica de la lucha armada*; and Julio
César Macías, *La guerrilla fue mi camino:*

*epitafio para César Montes* (Guatemala:
Editorial Piedra Santa, 1997).

26 Castillo, *Let's Go!*, p.50.

## 14 Cuban Film and the Burden of Revolutionary Representation
MARÍA CARIDAD CUMANÁ GONZÁLEZ

1 See Alfredo Guevara-Cesare Zavattini,
*Ese diamantino corazón de la verdad*,
2nd ed. (Madrid: Iberautor Promociones
Culturales S.L., 2002). In this there was
an excessive and intense exchange of
correspondence between the founding
president of ICAIC and the notable Italian
scriptwriter.

2 This meeting corresponds with the information in Silvia Oroz, *Los filmes que no
filme* (Havana: ediciones unión, 1989),
pp.40–43 and was taken from Jose Antonio
Evora, *Tomás Gutiérrez Alea* (Madrid: Ediciones Catedra, S.A, 1996), p.24.

3 *Cuban Cinema*, 11, p.1.

4 Michael Chanan, *Cuban Cinema* (Minneapolis and London: University of Minnesota Press, 2004), pp.214–15.

5 Tomás Gutiérrez Alea, *Dialéctica del
espectador* (Havana: Editorial José Martí,
1988), pp.29–30.

6 An example of ideological polarization was
the whole debate around the closing of
*Lunes de Revolución*, and the screening
on the Lunes channel of the documentary
filmed by Saba Cabrera Infante y Orlando
Jimenez Leal, *P.M.*, after it was banned by
ICAIC.

7 An activist of the French Communist
Party who developed part of his political
activism in Latin America (he visited Cuba
in the 1960s) and was a close friend of
Sara's.

## 15 The Japanese Sixties: Kon Ichikawa's "Tokyo Olympiad"
KYOKO SATO

1 Kojin Karatani, "The Discursive Space of
Modern Japan," *Boundary 2*, 18, 3 (Fall
1991), p.193.

2 Ibid., p.192.

3 Fredric Jameson, "Periodizing the 60s,"
in Jameson, *The Ideologies of Theory:
Essays, 1971–1986* (Minneapolis: University of Minnesota Press, 1988), p.180.

4 Victor Koschmann, "Intellectuals and Politics," in *Postwar Japan as History*, ed. Andrew Gordon (Berkeley: University of California Press, 1993), p.402.

5 By 1960 the U.S. military presence on Japanese soil "amounted to forty-six thousand troops stationed on several hundred military installations on Japan's four main islands, and another thirty-seven thousand soldiers on Okinawa." Andrew Gordon, *A Modern History of Japan: From Tokugawa Times to the Present* (Oxford: Oxford University Press, 2003), p.274. Okinawa remained under the jurisdiction of the U.S. government until its "reversion" to Japan in May 1972. To this day Okinawa remains the most heavily militarized zone on the Japanese archipelago.

6 Koschmann, "Intellectuals and Politics," p.401.

7 Ibid.

8 Ibid., p.403.

9 Article V of the treaty "emphasized the bilateral nature of the contract." The articles in the original treaty that were considered particularly offensive to the Japanese—including "Article I, which gave the United States the right to intervene in Japan's domestic disturbances, and Article II, which prohibited Japan from granting bases to other countries without prior U.S. consultation" —were eliminated. In addition, the 1960 revision "specified that the term of the treaty would be ten years" and that "either party could terminate the treaty with one-year notice of such an intention." Furthermore, the revised treaty "promoted close economic mutual assistance between the two countries." Yoshikuni Igarashi, *Bodies of Memory: Narratives of War in Postwar Japanese Culture, 1945–1970* (Princeton, N.J.: Princeton University Press, 2000), p.133.

10 Gordon, *Modern History of Japan*, p.276.

11 Igarashi, *Bodies of Memory*, p.136.

12 Ibid., pp.136, 132, 139, 140.

13 Koschmann, "Intellectuals and Politics," p.412.

14 Eiji Oguma, *"Minshu" to "Aikoku": Sengo Nihon no Nashonarizumu to Kokyosei* ["Democracy" and "patriotism": postwar Japanese nationalism and the public]

(Tokyo: Shinyosha, 2003), p.554. Zenkyôtô is a shorthand name for *Zengaku Kyôtô Kaigi* (university-wide joint struggle councils). The Japanese radical student movement began to form in 1968 "in the wake of African-American struggles in the United States, expansion of the war in Southeast Asia, and the events of May in France." Koschmann, "Intellectuals and Politics," p.416. Broadly speaking, this movement opposed structures of over-management and mass culture.

15 The Japanese government used the Tokyo Olympics "as an occasion for a variety of social reform campaigns." According to Gordon, it urged "citizens to improve public hygiene and sanitation and exhorted shopkeepers to curtail shady retail sales tactics." The Ministry of Education advocated "patriotism" and increased "the compulsory character of 'moral education' or 'civics' courses in the schools." Moreover, the impact of mass media cannot be underestimated. As Gordon states, "The presence of seventy-five hundred athletes from ninety-four countries, Kenzō Tange's monumental architecture of the stadium and pool, the opening of the bullet train to Osaka and a parallel network of expressways, and the success of Japanese athletes, who won an unprecedented sixteen gold medals (twenty-nine overall), sparked a media-induced surge of national pride in peaceful collective achievements in economy, technology, sports, and culture." Gordon, *Modern History of Japan*, p.266.

16 David Apter and Nagoyo Sawa, *Against the State: Politics and Social Protest in Japan* (Cambridge, Mass.: Harvard University Press, 1984).

17 Ibid., p.5.

18 Louis Althusser, "Ideology and Ideological State Apparatuses (Notes towards an Investigation)," in Althusser, *Essays on Ideology*, trans. B. Brewster and G. Lock (London: Verso, 1993). Here I am following Althusser in the use of the term "interpellation." Althusser suggested in this influential piece, "Ideology and Ideological State Apparatuses," p.47, that *"all ideology hails or interpellates concrete individuals as concrete subjects,*

by the functioning of the category of the subject."

19 In a manner reminiscent of Kishi's in 1960, Koizumi pushed through a bill to privatize the Japanese postal service (JPS) so as to make available a huge reserve of capital that the JPS held to the private and overseas investors, ensuring that, once the JPS is fully privatized in 2017, "global finance capital will have a powerful new say in the direction of Japanese savings, interest rates and public expenditure." Gavan McCormack, "Koizumi's Coup," *New Left Review*, 35 (September/October 2005), p.16.

20 Against fierce domestic oppositions, Koizumi's government sent armed troops to Iraq. As McCormack states, "In dispatching an armed body of men to Iraq, Japan was committing itself for the first time in sixty years, albeit in a subordinate and non-combat role, to an illegal and aggressive war. Koizumi was leading his country into uncharted constitutional waters." Gavan McCormack, "Remilitarizing Japan," *New Left Review*, 29 (September/October 2004).

21 Tomiko Yoda, "A Roadmap to Millennial Japan," in *Japan after Japan: Social and Cultural Life from the Recessionary 1990s to the Present*, ed. Tomiko Yoda and Harry Harootunian (Durham, N.C.: Duke University Press, 2006).

## 16 Consuming and Contesting "Soul" in Tanzania
ANDREW M. IVASKA

1 J.K. Obatala, "U.S. 'Soul' Music in Africa," *The African Communist*, 41 (1970), p.80.

2 Ibid., pp.81–82.

3 "Songambele Bans 'Soul' Music," *The Standard* (Dar es Salaam), Nov.13, 1969, p.1.

4 A.A. Riyami, "Government Backs Ban," letter to *The Standard*, Nov. 20, 1969.

5 Message from the editor, *The Standard*, Nov. 20, 1969.

6 For more on this series of bans, see Andrew M. Ivaska, *Cultured States: Youth, Gender and Modern Style in 1960s Dar es Salaam* (Durham, N.C.: Duke University Press, forthcoming). On Tanzanian national culture as it related to music and

performance, see Kelly Askew, *Performing the Nation: Swahili Music and Cultural Politics in Tanzania* (Chicago: University of Chicago Press, 2002).

7 Andrew M. Ivaska, "'Anti-Mini Militants Meet Modern Misses': Urban Style, Gender, and the Politics of 'National Culture' in 1960s Dar es Salaam, Tanzania," *Gender and History*, 14,3 (2002).

8 On the urban policies of colonial and post-colonial states in Tanzania, see Andrew Burton, *African Underclass: Urbanization, Crime and Colonial Order in Dar es Salaam, 1919–61* (Athens: Ohio University Press, 2005); and James R. Brennan, "Nation, Race and Urbanization in Dar es Salaam, Tanzania, 1916–1976," unpublished doctoral thesis, Northwestern University, Chicago, 2002. For Tanzania's villagization policies of the 1970s, see Michaela von Freyhold, *Ujamaa Villages in Tanzania: Analysis of a Social Experiment* (London: Heinemann, 1979); and Leander Schneider, "Developmentalism and Its Failings: Why Rural Development Went Wrong in 1960s and 1970s Tanzania," unpublished doctoral thesis, Columbia University, New York, 2003.

9 For an insightful portrait of the African-American expatriate community in Nkrumah's Ghana, see Kevin Gaines, *American Africans in Ghana: Black Expatriates and the Civil Rights Era* (Raleigh: University of North Carolina Press, 2006).

10 On struggles involving the student and faculty left at the University of Dar es Salaam during this time, see Ivaska, *Cultured States*, ch.4.

11 Hadji Konde, "Air Bantou—Dar's Top Soul Songsters," *Sunday News* (Dar es Salaam), Sept. 21, 1969.

12 The quotation is from an article on the Rifters: "If You Dig Soul You Won't Be Alone," *The Standard*, Nov. 2, 1969.

13 Bob Eubanks, letter to *The Standard*, Nov. 20, 1969.

14 Unsigned letter to *The Standard*, Nov. 14, 1969.

15 A.A. Riyami, letter to *The Standard*, Nov. 20, 1969.

16 Abdon D. Mally, letter to *The Standard*, Nov. 20, 1969.

17 Eubanks, letter to *The Standard*, Nov. 20, 1969.

18 "Fairness," letter to *The Standard*, Nov. 19, 1969.

19 "Ungando," letter to *The Standard*, Nov. 20, 1969.

20 See letters by Salum Hemedi, Flavian Mwingira, and "Pilly," all in *The Standard*, Nov. 19, 1969.

21 Mike P. Francis, letter to *The Standard*, Nov. 20, 1969.

22 See also letters from K.M. Songwe (Nov. 13), Salum R.H. Hemedi (Nov. 19), "Soul-man" (Nov. 19), Flavian C. Mwingira (Nov. 19), P.A.L. (Nov. 19), Charles M. Njau (Nov. 20), and the statement by the editor (Nov. 14), all in *The Standard*, 1969.

23 A.J. Kanoni, letter to *The Standard*, Nov. 19, 1969.

24 Editorial statement, *The Standard*, Nov. 14, 1969.

25 "Soulman," letter to *The Standard*, Nov. 19, 1969.

26 "P.A.L.," letter to *The Standard*, Nov. 19, 1969.

27 Letters from "Soulman" (Nov. 19) and Mike P. Francis (Nov. 20), to *The Standard*, 1969.

28 "Ungando," letter to *The Standard*, Nov. 20, 1969.

29 Maganja-Stone Chimlo, letter to *The Standard*, Nov. 20, 1969.

30 "Pilly," letter to *The Standard*, Nov. 20, 1969.

31 A.J. Kanoni, letter to *The Standard*, Nov. 19, 1969.

32 Charles M. Njau, letter to *The Standard*, Nov. 19, 1969.

33 Tanzania African Nationalist Union (TANU), *Azimio la Arusha na Siasa ya TANU juu ya Ujamaa na Kujitegemea* (Dar es Salaam: Idara ya Habari, TANU, 1967), pp.12–15.

34 TANU, *Azimio la Arusha*, p.15.

35 Obatala, "U.S. 'Soul' Music in Africa."

36 *Nchi Yetu*, October 1973, p.1.

37 Lawrence A. Mtawa, "Mavazi ya Heshima," *Nchi Yetu* (October 1973), p.3.

38 A. Likoko, "Mgigania haki sawa za Binadamu," *Nchi Yetu* (October 1973), pp.12–13.

39 The caption to this photo of two women portrayed as examples of "indecent" dressing: "They aren't bad, these young sisters. Because of their dress they have lowered their respectability as well as their natural beauty." *Nchi Yetu*, November 1973, p.7.

40 Kennell Jackson, "Introduction," in *Black Cultural Traffic: Crossroads in Global Performance and Popular Culture*, ed. Harry Elam Jr. and Kennell Jackson (Ann Arbor: University of Michigan Press, 2005).

41 Brent Hayes Edwards, *The Practice of Diaspora: Literature, Translation, and the Rise of Black Internationalism* (Cambridge, Mass.: Harvard University Press, 2003); Paulla A. Ebron, *Performing Africa* (Princeton, N.J.: Princeton University Press, 2002); and Catherine Cole, "When Is African Theater 'Black'?" in *Black Cultural Traffic*, ed. Elam Jr. and Jackson.

## 17 Exhibiting a Global Blackness: The First World Festival of Negro Arts
TOBIAS WOFFORD

1 Stuart Hall, "Cultural Identity and Diaspora," in *Diaspora and Visual Culture: Representing Africans and Jews*, ed. Nicholas Mirzoeff (London: Routledge, 2000).

2 Paul Cooke, "The Art of Africa for the Whole World: An Account of the First World Festival of Negro Arts in Dakar, Senegal—April 1–24, 1966," *Negro History Bulletin*, 29, 7 (April 1966), p.171.

3 Leopold Sedar Senghor, "The Function and Meaning of the First World Festival of Negro Arts," *African Forum*, 1,4 (Spring 1966), p.6.

4 Engelbert Mveng, "The Function and Significance of Negro Art in the Life of the Peoples of Black Africa," in *Colloquium: Function and Significance of African Negro Art in the Life of the People and for the People* (Paris: Présence Africaine, 1968), p.24.

5 According to Harney, 25 per cent of the state budget was dedicated to culture. Elizabeth Harney, "'Les Chers Enfants' sans Papa," *Oxford Art Journal*, 19,1 (1996), p.43. See also Harney, *In Senghor's Shadow: Art, Politics and the Avant-Garde in Senegal, 1960–1995* (Durham, N.C., and London: Duke University Press, 2004).

6  Harney, *In Senghor's Shadow*, p.68.

7  See Ima Ebong, "Negritude Between Mask and Flag—Senegalese Cultural Ideology and the École de Dakar," in *Africa Explores: 20th Century African Art*, ed. Susan Vogel (New York: Center for African Art, 1991); Ousmane Sow Hutchard, "The First International Festival of Black Arts, Dakar, 1966," in *An Anthology of African Art: The Twentieth Century*, ed. N'Goné Fall and Jean Loup Pivin (New York: Distributed Art Publishers, 2002); and Harney, "'Les Chers Enfants' san Papa."

8  See Harney, *In Senghor's Shadow*, pp.69–75.

9  Lloyd Garrison. "Debate on 'Negritude' Splits Festival in Dakar," *The New York Times*, April 24, 1966, p.17.

10  Ibid.

11  Ibid.

12  Hale Woodruff, "Foreword," in *Dix Artistes Negres des Etats-Unis*," ed. Joseph Lawe (New York: United States.Committee for the First World Festival of Negro Arts, 1966), no pagination.

13  First World Festival of Negro Arts, United States Committee, "Press agent's files, 1965–1966," Schomburg Center for Research in Black Culture.

14  Jeanne Siegel, "Why Spiral?" *ArtNews*, 65,5 (September 1966), p.67.

15  See Albert H. Berrain and Richard A. Long, eds., *Negritude: Essays and Studies* (Hampton, Va.: Hampton University Press, 1967).

16  See Eva Crockoft, "Abstract Expressionism—Weapon of the Cold War," *Artforum*, 15,10 (June 1974), pp.43–54; and Serge Guilbaut, *How New York Stole the Idea of Modern Art: Abstract Expressionism, Freedom and the Cold War*, trans. Arthur Goldhammer (Chicago: University of Chicago Press, 1983).

17  Lloyd Garrison, "A Gentle Cold-War Wind Wafts through Senegal's Festival of Negro Arts," *The New York Times*, April 19, 1966, p.14.

18  Charles Sanders, "Africans Disappointed in U.S. Negro Festival Showing," *Jet*, 30, 4 (May 5, 1966), p.18.

19  Ibid., p.34.

20  Hoyt W. Fuller, "Festival Postscripts," *Negro Digest*, 15, 8 (June 1966), p.86.

## 18  Rock 'n' Roll, Politics, and Society during the Italian Economic Boom
MARILISA MEROLLA

1  P.G. Martellini, "Il setaccio," *Radiocorriere TV*, 11 (1961).

2  S.G. Biamonte, "Una nuova rubrica radiofonica: Musica sprint," *Radiocorriere TV*, 17 (1959).

3  B.B., "Dopo quattro settimane puntata d'addio per Alta Pressione," *Radiocorriere TV*, 42 (1962), p.21.

## 19  Popular Culture as a Tool for Change: Rural Working-Class Theatre in Sweden
STEFAN BACKIUS

1  Tom Hayden, "The Future of 1968's Restless Youth," in *1968 in Europe: A History of Protest and Activism, 1956–1977*, ed. Martin Klimke and Joachim Scharloth (Basingstoke, Eng.: Palgrave Macmillan, 2008).

2  Arthur Marwick, *The Sixties: Cultural Revolution in Britain, France, Italy, and the United States, c.1958–c.1974* (Oxford: Oxford University Press, 1998).

3  Gerd-Rainer Horn, *The Spirit of '68: Rebellion in Western Europe and North America, 1956–1976* (Oxford: Oxford University Press, 2007).

4  Klimke and Scharloth, eds., *1968 in Europe*.

5  The empirical study is based on material from a local archive in Norberg, the Swedish national labour movement archive, and newspapers and interviews.

6  For a qualitative study focusing how the script and performance were influenced by the progressive ideas and working-class experiences, see Gunnel Testad, "The Play about the Norberg Strike—A Study in Working Class Culture," dissertation, Stockholm University, forthcoming.

7  Leif Dahlberg, "Experimentet som kom för att stanna. Hur arbetarspelen bröt finteatervallen," in *Kulturen—möten och mödor: bidrag till studiet av kulturens villkor*, ed. Holger Värnlund (Stockholm: Carlsson, 1995).

8   The conception of "labouring of American culture" comes from Michael Denning, "Introduction," *The Cultural Front: The Laboring of American Culture in the Twentieth Century* (London: Verso, 1997).

9   Ralph Yarrow, ed., *European Theatre 1960–1990: Cross-Cultural Perspectives* (London and New York, Routledge, 1992). Its interesting articles in this perspective are on France (David Jeffery), West Germany (Theo Girshausen), Switzerland (Ralph Yarrow), Italy (Christopher Cairns), Spain (Gwynne Edwards), and to some extent Poland (George Hyde). For a complementary picture of the present case, see Sweden (Margareta Wirmark).

10  The connection between both individual security and growth, mutually reinforcing objectives and coherent ends, was a successful ideological articulation and one important aspect of the hegemonic position of the Social Democracy Party. Jenny Andersson, *Between Growth and Security: Swedish Social Democracy from a Strong Society to a Third Way* (Manchester, Eng.: Manchester University Press, 2006). For a comprehensive and conventional historical description of the Social Democratic Party, see Klaus Misgeld, Karl Molin, and Klas Åmark, eds., *Creating Social Democracy: A Century of the Social Democratic Labor Party in Sweden*, trans. Jan Teeland (University Park: Pennsylvania State University Press, 1992).

11  Fortified already in 1936 through Marquis W. Childs, *Sweden: The Middle Way* (New Haven, Conn.: Yale University Press, 1936); Bo Stråth, *Mellan två fonder: LO och den svenska modellen* (Stockholm: Atlas, 1998).

12  About Social Democratic hegemony and its relation to the state, see Esping-Andersen, "The Making of a Social Democratic Welfare State," and Tilton, "The Role of Ideology in Social Democratic Politics"; about the party's internationally unique position of power see Therborn, "A Unique Chapter in the History of Democracy: The Social Democrats in Sweden," all in *Creating Social Democracy*, ed. Misgeld. Molin, and Åmark.

13  Kjell Östberg, *1968 när allting var i rörelse: sextiotalsradikaliseringen och de sociala rörelserna* (Stockholm: Prisma, 2002); and Michael Frey, "The International Peace Movement," in *1968 in Europe*, ed. Klimke and Scharloth. Compare with the perspective from Thomas Ekman Jörgensen, "Scandinavia," also in *1968 in Europe*, ed. Klimke and Scharloth.

14  Östberg, *1968 när allting var i rörelse*.

15  Anders Frenander, *Debattens vågor: om politisk-ideologiska frågor i efterkrigstidens svenska kulturdebatt* (Göteborg: Arachne, 1999).

16  For one perspective on Swedish cultural policy, see Tobias Harding, *Nationalising Culture: The Reorganisation of National Culture in Swedish Cultural Policy 1970–2002* (Linköping: Department for Studies of Social Change and Culture, Linköping University, 2007) <www.ep.liu.se/abstract>.

17  One important result of this was the establishment of new regional institutional theatres, governed locally but financed nationally. Rikard Hoogland, *Spelet om teaterpolitiken. Det svenska regionteatersystemet—från statligt initiativ till lokal realitet* (Stockholm: Teatertidningens bokförlag, 2005).

18  Håkan Lahger, *Proggen: musikrörelsens uppgång och fall* (Stockholm: Atlas, 2002).

19  Hoogland, *Spelet om teaterpolitiken*; Willmar Sauter, "60-talets optimistiska revolt: en länk i teaterns avantgarde," in *Svenska teaterhändelser 1946–1996*, ed. Lena Hammergren, Karin Helander, and Willmar Sauter (Stockholm: Natur och kultur, 1996).

20  Sven Lindqvist, *Gräv där du står: hur man utforskar ett jobb* (Stockholm: Bonnier, 1978).

21  Annica Alzén, *Fabriken som kulturarv: frågan om industrilandskapets bevarande i Norrköping 1950–1985* (Stockholm; Stehag: B. Östlings bokförl. Symposion, 1996).

22  Johan Fornäs, *Tältprojektet: musikteater som manifestation* (The tent project: music theatre as a manifestation) (Stockholm/ Göteborg: Symposion, 1985).

## 20 A "Bubbling Volcano": Edinburgh, the Festivals, and a Cultural Explosion
ANGELA BARTIE

This chapter is based on research conducted for my doctoral thesis, which explored the various theoretical definitions of culture that were expressed in postwar Britain and the shifts that occurred in them by using the Festivals as a "lens." A Bartie, "Festival City: the Arts, Culture and Moral Conflict in Edinburgh, 1947–1967," Ph.D. thesis, University of Dundee, 2007. Grateful thanks to my partner, Andy Perchard, for his constructive criticism and warm enthusiasm, and to Lucy Robinson and Sam Carroll for their feedback and comments on the conference paper on which this chapter is based.

1   Robert Hewison, *Too Much: Art and Society in the Sixties, 1960–1975* (London: Methuen London, 1986), cover.

2   Bart Moore-Gilbert and John Seed, eds, *Cultural Revolution? The Challenge of the Arts in the 1960s* (London: Routledge, 1992), p.1.

3   Arthur Marwick, *The Sixties: Cultural Revolution in Britain, France, Italy, and the United States, c.1958–c.1974* (New York: Oxford University Press, 1998), p.117.

4   Jeremy Varon, Michael S. Foley, and John McMillan, "Time Is an Ocean: The Past and Future of the Sixties," *The Sixties: A Journal of History, Politics and Culture*, 1,1 (June 2008), pp.1–3.

5   Matthew Arnold, *Culture and Anarchy*, ed. J. Dover Wilson (Cambridge: Cambridge University Press, 1996), p.6.

6   Dennis Dworkin, *Cultural Marxism in Postwar Britain: History, the New Left and the Origins of Cultural Studies* (Durham, N.C.: Duke University Press, 1997), pp.3, 79.

7   Raymond Williams, *Keywords: A Vocabulary of Culture and Society* (London: Fontana, 1985), p.92.

8   By the 1970s the festival had developed to combine the arts and sport with social action; its slogan was "Community concern, care and action for social change through culture."

9   Joyce McMillan, *The Traverse Theatre Story, 1963–1988* (London: Methuen Drama, 1988), p.10.

10  Jim Haynes, *Thanks for Coming! An Autobiography* (London: Faber and Faber, 1984), p.70.

11  Haynes has said that at the time he set up the Paperback he "knew *nothing* about City Lights." Jim Haynes, interviewed by author, Aug. 17, 2003.

12  Jonathon Green, *Days in the Life: Voices from the English Underground 1961–1971* (London: Plimico, 1998), pp.22–23.

13  Nuttall was an artist, CND activist, author of *Bomb Culture*, and founder of the fringe theatre group The People Show; Miles co-founded and ran Indica Bookshop, the "command centre" for the London underground scene, and co-founded (with Haynes and others) *International Times (IT)*.

14  International Writer's Conference, original transcript, Edinburgh, August 1962 (copy donated from Jim Haynes's personal archives), Nicka Tucci on Day 1, p.19.

15  It remained a criminal offence until 1968 in England and Wales, 1980 in Scotland, 1982 in Northern Ireland, and 2000 in the armed forces and navy. Research in this area is still in its infancy in Britain; see, for example, Lucy Robinson, *Gay Men and the Left in Britain: How the Personal Got Political* (Manchester, Eng.: Manchester University Press, 2007).

16  *The Times* (London), Aug. 24, 1962.

17  International Writer's Conference, original transcript, Day 5, pp.32–33; Day 3, p.22.

18  For more information on Trocchi's fascinating life, see Andrew Murray Scott, *Alexander Trocchi: The Making of the Monster* (Edinburgh: Polygon, 1991).

19  This informal network helped when Trocchi helped to organize the seminal Albert Hall Poetry Reading of 1965. Letter written by Edwin Morgan, January 2002, in *Justified Sinners: An Archaeology of Scottish Counter-Culture (1960–2000)*, ed. Ross Birrell and Alec Finlay (Edinburgh: Pocketbooks, 2001).

20  John Calder, *Pursuit: The Uncensored Memoirs of John Calder* (London: Calder Publications, 2001), p.255.

21  Green, *Days in the Life*, p.43; Charles Marowitz, Tom Milne, and Owen Hale, eds., *New Theatre Voices of the Fifties*

and Sixties: Selections from Encore Magazine 1956–1963 (London: Eyre Methuen,
1965), pp.211–12.

22 Barry Curtis, "A Highly Mobile and Plastic
Environ," in Art and the 60s: This Was
Tomorrow, ed. Chris Stephens and Kath-
arine Stout (London: Tate Publishing,
2004), p.52.

23 Tom Normand, "55° North 3° West: A
Panorama from Scotland," in Remapping
British Art and Architecture, p.25. I am
grateful to Tom for sending me a draft of
this chapter.

24 John Haynes, "C'est Ma Vie Folks! Bits
from a Participatory Autobiography,"
vol. 1, 1933–69, unpublished manuscript, Handshake Editions, 1982, p.173
(Jim Haynes's personal copy consulted);
shortened version published as Haynes,
Thanks for Coming!

25 Mark Kurlansky, 1968: The Year That
Rocked the World (New York: Random
House, 2004), p.75.

26 Marwick, The Sixties, p.348.

27 Catherine Itzin, Stages of the Revolution:
Political Theatre in Britain since 1968 (London: Methuen, 1980), p.9.

28 Ibid.

29 Shawn Levy, Ready, Steady, Go! Swinging
London and the Invention of Cool (London:
Fourth Estate, 2002), p.7.

30 Interview with Jim Haynes, June 17, 2005.

31 The Herald (Glasgow), Oct. 4, 2004.

32 Marwick, The Sixties, p.7.

### 21 Constructing Pariah Spaces: Newspaper Representations of Slums, Ghettos, and Favelas in São Paulo and Chicago
SEAN PURDY

1 Loïc Wacquant, Os Condenados da cidade
(Rio de Janeiro: Revan, 2001), p.1.

2 Peter Marcuse, "The Divided City in History," in Of States and Cities: The Partitioning of Urban Space, ed. Peter Marcuse
and Ronald van Kempen (Oxford: Oxford
University Press, 2002).

3 Bryan D. Palmer, Dark Cultures: Night
Travels in the History of Transgression
(New York: Monthly Review Press, 2000),
p.5.

4 Janice Pearlman, The Myth of Marginality
(Berkeley: University of California Press,
1976); Manuel Castells, The City and
the Grassroots (Berkeley: University of
California Press, 1983); Julio César Pino,
Family and Favela: The Reproduction of
Poverty in Rio de Janeiro (Westport, Conn.:
Greenwood Press, 1997); Alicia Ziccardi,
"Villas Miseria and Favelas: State Institu-
tions and Working-Class Organizations,"
Comparative Urban Research, 11 (1985);
Fernanda Pedrosa, Francisco Luis Noel,
Luarlindo Ernesto, and Sergio Pugliese,
A Violência que Oculta a Favela (Rio de
Janeiro: Jornal do Brasil, 1990); Carlos
Nelson Ferreira Dos Santaos, Movimentos
Urbanos no Rio de Janeiro (Rio de Janeiro:
Zahar, 1981); Jane Roessner, A Decent
Place to Live: From Columbia Point to Har-
bor Point, A Community History (Boston:
Northeastern University Press, 2000);
Rhonda Y. Williams, "Living Just Enough
in the City: Change and Activism in Bal-
timore's Public Housing, 1940–1980,"
Ph.D. thesis, University of Pennsylvania,
Philadelphia, 1998; David Ley, "The Inner-
City," in Canadian Cities in Transition, ed.
Trudi Bunting and Pierre Filion (Toronto:
Oxford University Press, 1991); and Gerry
Mooney, "Urban Disorders," in Unruly Cit-
ies? ed. Steve Pile, Christopher Brook, and
Gerry Mooney (London: Routledge, 2000.

5 Herbert Gans, "The Dangers of the Underclass: Its Harmfulness as a Planning
Concept," in Gans, People, Plans and Policies: Essays on Poverty, Racism, and Other
National Urban Problems (New York: Columbia University Press, 1991), pp. 85–93.

6 Here, drawing on recent literature in
urban history, cultural geography, and
media and transnational studies and
focusing on the post–Second World War
period in Chicago, Toronto, and São
Paulo, I am presenting the early results
of a larger transnational research project exploring social constructions of
urban marginality in the media, cinema,
academic, and political discourse in the
transnational context. Further studies will
consider the textual representation of the
urban poor as dangerous social and cultural "outcasts."

7 Peter Marcuse, "The Divided City in
History," in Of States and Cities: The

*Partitioning of Urban Space*, ed. Peter Marcuse and Ronald van Kempen (Oxford: Oxford University Press, 2002); and Larry Bennett, "Ghettoization," *Chicago Encyclopedia* online <www.encyclopedia.chicagohistory.org> (accessed June 15, 2008).

8  Nabil Bonduki, *Origens da habitação social no Brasil: Arquitetura Moderna, Lei do Inquilinato e Difusão da Casa Própria* (São Paulo: Estação Liberdade, 1998), p.264.

9  Bryan D. Palmer, *Working-Class Experience: Rethinking the History of Canadian Labour 1880–1991* (Toronto: McClelland and Stewart, 1992), pp.152, 155–56.

10  John Walton, "Urban Conflict and Social Movements in Poor Countries: Theory and Evidence of Collective Action," *International Journal of Urban and Regional Research*, 22 (September 1998), pp.463–65.

11  Magnus Morner, Julia Fawaz de Viñuela, and John French, "Comparative Approaches to Latin American History," *Latin American Research Review*, 17,3 (1982), p.57. See also Licia Valladares Valladares and Magda Prates Coelho, "Urban Research in Latin America: Towards a Research Agenda," Discussion Paper Series No. 4, "Management of Social Transformations" (MOST), UNESCO <www.unesco.org/most/valleng.htm> (accessed June 15, 2008); and Peter H. Smith, "The Changing Agenda for Social Science Research on Latin America," in *Latin America in Comparative Perspective: New Approaches to Methods and Analysis*, ed. Peter H. Smith (Boulder, Col.: Westview Press, 1995), pp.1–30. For enlightening syntheses of the debates surrounding transnational history, with full references to the burgeoning literature, see the Introduction by Cañizares-Esguerra and Seeman and Preface by Bender in *The Atlantic in Global History*, ed. Jorge Cañizares-Esguerra and Erik Seeman (New York: Prentice-Hall, 2007); Boris Fausto and Fernando Devoto, *Brasil e Argentina: Um ensaio de história comparada* (São Paulo: Editora 34, 2004), pp.9–28; Maria Ligia Coelho Prado, "Repensando a História Comparada da América Latina," *Revista*

*da História da USP*, 153 (2005), pp.11–34; and David Thelen, "Of Audiences, Borderlands, and Comparisons: Toward the Internationalization of American History," *Journal of American History*, 79,2 (September 1992), pp.432–62.

12  Alan Mayne, *The Imagined Slum: Newspaper Representations in Three Cities, 1870–1914* (London: Leicester University Press, 1993); Mooney, "Urban Disorders"; Kay Anderson, *Vancouver's Chinatown: Racial Discourse in Canada, 1875–1980* (Montreal and Kingston, Ont.: McGill-Queen's University Press, 1991).

13  Licia do Prado Valladares, *A invenção da favela: do mito de origem a favela.com* (Rio de Janeiro: FGV, 2005). See also Tamara Tania Cohen Egler, "Interação social no espaço urbano: encontros e confrontos," in *Repensando a Experiencia Urbana da Americana Latina: Questões, Conceitos e Valores*, ed. Clara Torres Ribeiro (Buenos Aires: Consejo Latinoamericano de Ciencas Sociales, 2001), pp.205–21; Ana Maria Mauad, "Janelas que se abrem para o mundo: fotografia de imprensa e distinção social no Rio de Janeiro, na primeira metade do século XX," *Estudios Interdisciplinarios de America Latina y el Caribe*, 10 (July–December 1999).

14  Ney dos Santos Oliveira, "Favelas and Ghettoes: Race and Class in Rio de Janeiro and New York City," *Latin American Perspectives*, 23 (Fall 1996), pp.71–89.

15  Steve Macek, *Urban Nightmares: The Media, the Right, and the Moral Panic over the City* (Minneapolis: University of Minnesota Press, 2006), pp.xiv–xv.

16  The study was conducted by SAGMAS and published in *Estado de São Paulo* in two parts: April 13, 1960, supplement pp.1–40; and April 15, 1960, supplement pp.1–48.

17  Brian Owensby, *Intimate Ironies: Modernity and the Making of Middle-Class Lives in Brazil* (Stanford, Cal.: Stanford University Press, 1999).

18  "Favela é também estado de espírito," *Estado de São Paulo*, Aug. 13, 1968. For a review of two documentary films about favelas in São Paulo and Rio that

repeat this spurious pride, see the blog by *Estadão* columnist Paulo Moreira Leite <blog.estadao.com.br/blog/paulo/?cat=167> (accessed June 15, 2008).

19  Bonduki, *Origens da habitação social no Brasil*, p.294.

20  Ibid., p.262.

21  Sandro Anselmo Coelho, "O Partido Democrata Cristão: teores programáticos da terceira via brasileira (1945–1964)," *Revista Brasileira de História*, 23,46 (2003).

22  "Favelas em São Paulo," editorial, *Estado de São Paulo*, July 31, 1966.

23  "5% dos paulistanos moram em favelas," *Folha de São Paulo*, Jan. 3, 1968.

24  "Favela é também estado de espírito," *Estado de São Paulo*, Aug. 13, 1968.

25  "Mais uma favela de S. Paulo com os dias contados: agora é Barra Funda," *Folha de São Paulo*, Nov. 11, 1970.

26  Suzanna Pasternak, "Espaço e População nas Favelas de São Paulo," paper presented to the XIII Encontro da Associação Brasileira de Estudos Populacionais, Ouro Preto, Minas Gerais, Nov. 4–8, 2002. See also Bonduki, *Origens da habitação social no Brasil*, p.264.

27  On MOV's policies, see "Mais uma favela de S.Paulo com os dias contados: agora é Barra Funda," *Folha de São Paulo*, Nov. 11, 1970.

28  "Duas idéias para eliminar favelas," *O Estado de São Paulo*, Oct. 9, 1967.

29  See the interviews in Marta Tanaka, ed., *A Vivência da Realidade e a Prática do Fazer Movimento Universitário de Desfavelamento*. Cadernos do LAP (São Paulo: Editora: FAU USP, 1997).

30  Thomas Buck, "Daley Tells Harvard about Urban Renewal," *Chicago Tribune*, Feb. 8, 1964.

31  "Chicago Has No Ghettos, Says Mayor," *Chicago Tribune*, July 3, 1963.

32  "Seek Racial Policy for Real Estate, " *Chicago Tribune*, Aug. 10, 1962. For civil rights in quotation marks see the editorial "Offensive Threats," *Chicago Tribune*, April 7, 1965. For other stories in which studies of racial discrimination are presented as "accusations" or merely "claims," see "Housing Plight of Negro Cited," *Chicago*

*Tribune*, March 4, 1963; Philip Warden, "Negroes Pay Color Tax—King," *Chicago Tribune*, Dec. 16, 1966; C.O.R.E. Plans Negro Attack on Food Costs, *Chicago Tribune*, June 20, 1967; "Charge City Helps to Build Ghetto," *Chicago Tribune*, Nov. 19, 1967.

33  Aldo Beckman, "Ghetto Negro Survey Gives New Picture," *Chicago Tribune*, Sept. 4, 1966.

34  See Casey Burko, "Bare Ghetto Facts, Panel Advises," *Chicago Tribune*, March 24, 1968; and James Ritch, "2 U.C. Profs Finish 3-Year Study of Bias," *Chicago Tribune*, May 24, 1965.

35  "Offensive Threat," editorial, *Chicago Tribune*, April 7, 1965.

## 22  "No Axe to Grind in Africa": Violence, Racial Prejudice, and Media Depictions of the Canadian Peacekeeping Mission to the Congo, 1960–64

COLIN MCCULLOUGH

1   Associated Press, "Cannibalism Making Comeback," *The Globe and Mail* (Toronto), Nov. 28, 1960, p.17; Associated Press, "Congo Cannibals Eat U.N. Troops," *The Toronto Daily Star*, Nov. 28, 1960, p.1.

2   AP, *The Globe and Mail*, Nov. 28, 1960, p.17.

3   For an excellent analysis of what did go on, see Sean Maloney, *Canada and U.N. Peacekeeping: Cold War by Other Means 1945–1970* (St. Catherines, Ont.: Van Well Publishing, 2002), pp.103–31.

4   Donald Gordon, "News and Foreign Policy," *Behind the Headlines*, 24,2 (Toronto: Canadian Institute for International Affairs, October 1964), p.4.

5   Ibid.

6   Examples of works that briefly mention the influence of the press on the mission to the Congo are Joseph Jockel, *Canada and International Peacekeeping* (Toronto: Canadian Institute of Strategic Studies, 1994), p.12; Andrew F. Cooper, *Canadian Foreign Policy: Old Habits and New Directions* (Scarborough, Ont.: Prentice Hall Allyn and Bacon, 1997), p.175; Pierre Martin and Michel Fortmann, "Canadian Public Opinion and Peacekeeping in a Turbulent World," *International Journal*,

1,2 (Spring 1995), p.381; Norman Hillmer and J.L. Granatstein, *Empire to Umpire* (Toronto: Irwin Publishing, 1994), p.255.

7   John Thompson, *The Media and Modernity: A Social Theory of the Media* (Cambridge: Polity Press, 1995), p.29.

8   Kevin Spooner, "Race, (De)colonization, and Canadian Peacekeeping in the Congo," paper given at CHA Annual Conference, 2008, p.9. Spooner's work provides an interesting counterpoint to the views revealed in the *Globe* and *Star*.

9   Albert Memmi, *The Colonizer and the Colonized* (Boston: Beacon Press, 1965), pp.7, 38.

10  Edward Said, *Orientalism* (New York: Vintage Books, 1994), p.41.

11  Ibid., p.204.

12  Ibid., p.207.

13  Editorial, *The Toronto Star*, Jan. 9, 1959, p.6.

14  Ibid.

15  Ibid.

16  Robert B. Edgerton, *The Troubled Heart of Africa: A History of the Congo*, 1st ed. (New York: St. Martin's Press, 2002), p.171.

17  Associated Press, "New Congo Terror; Two Whites Slain," *The Toronto Star*, July 9, 1960, p.1.

18  Ray Moloney, "Congo Women Pay Terrible Price," *The Toronto Star*, July 18, 1960, p.1.

19  Ibid.

20  Editorial, *The Toronto Star*, July 7, 1960, p.6.

21  Editorial, *The Toronto Star*, Nov. 2, 1956, p.6; editorial, *The Toronto Star*, Nov. 26, 1956, p.6.

22  Editorial, *The Toronto Star*, July 11, 1960, p.6.

23  Spooner, "Race, (De)colonization, and Canadian Peacekeeping in the Congo," p.9.

24  Editorial, *The Toronto Star*, July 7, 1960, p.6.

25  Editorial, *The Toronto Star*, July 13, 1960, p.6.

26  Editorial, *The Toronto Star*, July 20, 1960, p.6.

27  Associated Press, "Russians Warn Canada to Stay out of Congo," *The Toronto Star*, Aug. 8, 1960, p.1.

28  Smith Hempstone, "Congo Leaders Burst into the Light of Freedom," *The Toronto Star*, June 3, 1960, p.7.

29  Ron Haggert, "Thought They Would Eat Me Alive, Canuck Tells Haggert," *The Toronto Star*, Aug. 28, 1960, p.1.

30  Ibid.

31  Editorial, *The Globe and Mail*, July 21, 1960, p.6.

32  Ibid; and editorial, *The Globe and Mail*, July 14, 1960, p.6.

33  Editorial, *The Globe and Mail*, July 14, 1960, p.6.

34  Editorial, *The Globe and Mail*, Aug. 2, 1960, p.6.

35  Editorial, *The Globe and Mail*, July 19, 1960, p.6.

36  Ibid.

37  "Bingo, Bango, Bongo, I Don't Wanna Leave the Congo!" *The Globe and Mail*, Aug. 2, 1960, p.6.

38  "Clothes Don't Make the Man," *The Globe and Mail*, July 20, 1960, p.6.

39  Donald R. Gordon, "Primitives Loose in Technology's China Shop," *The Globe and Mail*, Aug. 17, 1960, p.7. Other articles included "Men of the Jungle Reverting to their Savage Pasts," *The Globe and Mail*, Oct. 17, 1960, p.7.

40  Ibid.

41  Ibid

42  Gordon, "News and Foreign Policy," p.4.

43  Spooner, "Race, (De)colonization, and Canadian Peacekeeping in the Congo," p.18.

44  Scholarly works that did this include the essays in Alastair Taylor, ed., *Peacekeeping: International Challenge and Canadian Response* (Toronto: Canadian Institute of International Affairs, 1968); and Donald Gordon, "Canada as Peacekeeper," in *Canada's Role as Middle Power*, ed. J. King Gordon (Toronto: Canadian Institute for International Affairs, 1966).

## 23  Trip to Hanoi: Antiwar Travel and International Consciousness

FRANNY NUDELMAN

I am grateful to Dave Cannon, who helped me to research this essay, and to David Holton, Mark Philips, and Victoria

Olwell for their astute comments and suggestions.

1 Rennie Davis, "Behind Enemy Lines," in Davis, *The Conspiracy* (New York: Dell Publishing, 1969), pp. 189, 178–80, 182.

2 For a comprehensive account of Americans who travelled to Hanoi during the war, see Mary Hershberger, *Traveling to Vietnam: American Peace Activists and the War* (Syracuse, N.Y.: Syracuse University Press, 1998).

3 The right to travel, threatened by Cold War restrictions, was highly politicized by the mid-1960s. See Alan Rogers, "Passports and Politics: The Courts and the Cold War," *Historian*, 47 (1985).

4 Thomas Hayden and Staughton Lynd, *The Other Side* (New York: New American Library, 1966), p.234.

5 Van Gosse argues for the formative influence of the Cuban Revolution, and North American fascination with it, on the developing transnational politics of the new left. See Van Gosse, *Where the Boys Are: Cuba, Cold War America and the Making of the New Left* (London and New York: Verso Press, 1993). Examining the relationship between the politics of solidarity and the practice of consciousness-raising, my essay attempts to build on Gosse's assertion that the effort to create coalition played an important part in shaping radical political practice. On the impact of emerging anti-colonial movements for national autonomy on Black radicalism, see also Kevin Gaines, *American Africans in Ghana: Black Expatriates and the Civil Rights Era* (Chapel Hill: University of North Carolina Press, 2006); Nikhil Singh, *Black Is a Country: Race and the Unfinished Struggle for Democracy* (Cambridge, Mass.: Harvard University Press, 2004); and Cynthia Young, *Soul Power: Culture, Radicalism, and the Making of a U.S. Third World Left* (Durham, N.C.: Duke University Press, 2006).

6 Hershberger, *Traveling to Vietnam*, p.xxii.

7 "4 U.S. Women Get Visas," *The New York Times*, Dec. 17, 1966, p.5.

8 According to Hershberger, Salisbury's reports produced a change in official rhetoric at the same time as they were attacked by military personnel. Noting that Salisbury's conclusions are identical to those that had been published in the antiwar press during the previous year, Hershberger maintains that the antiwar press provided the most reliable reporting of the war during its early phases. See *Traveling to Vietnam*, pp.80–81, 30.

9 Harrison E. Salisbury, *Behind the Lines–Hanoi* (New York: Harper and Row, 1967), p.5.

10 Ibid., pp.68–71.

11 Ibid., pp.103–4.

12 David Dellinger, "North Vietnam: Eyewitness Report," *Liberation*, 11, 9 (December 1966), pp.6–8.

13 John Gerassi, "Report from North Vietnam," *The New Republic*, March 4, 1967, p.14.

14 Dellinger, "North Vietnam: Eyewitness Report," p.11.

15 Marilyn B. Young, *The Vietnam Wars, 1945–1990* (New York: HarperCollins Publishers, 1991), p.197.

16 Mary McCarthy, *Hanoi* (New York: Harcourt, Brace & World, 1968), pp.123–24.

17 McCarthy's isolation increases over the course of her visit, as her sense of political effectiveness wanes. Deborah Nelson has observed that McCarthy's "preference for solitude over solidarity" makes her political perspective "difficult to categorize." In contrast to other narratives that describe the trip as an opportunity for positive self-transformation, in *Hanoi* McCarthy gains painful self-knowledge that hobbles her activism. Deborah Nelson, "The Virtues of Heartlessness: Mary McCarthy, Hannah Arendt, and the Anesthetics of Empathy," *American Literary History*, 18,1 (2006), pp.86–87.

18 Focusing on McCarthy and Sontag, Rabinowitz argues that women writers who travelled to Vietnam reject the authoritative role of reporter as well as the value of objectivity. She maintains that this "new kind of war writing," which openly expresses partisanship, dates from the Spanish Civil War. Paula Rabinowitz, *They Must Be Represented: The Politics of Documentary* (London and New York: Verso Press, 1994), pp.128, 119.

19  Mary Louise Pratt discusses the role of natural science in the evolution of travel writing: collecting data about the environment and cataloguing it, the amateur botanist brings order to the world while not seeming to interfere with it. She argues that the benign appearance of the "'herborizer' ... desiring nothing more than a few peaceful hours alone with the bugs and flowers" helped to naturalize the "bourgeois European's own global presence and authority." McCarthy anticipates this critique, and applies it to her own role in North Vietnam. McCarthy, *Hanoi*, pp.16, 82; Mary Louise Pratt, *Imperial Eyes: Travel Writing and Transculturation* (New York: Routledge, 1992), pp.27–28.

20  Grace Paley, *Just As I Thought* (New York: Farrar, Straus and Giroux, 1998), p.56.

21  Noam Chomsky, "A Special Supplement: In North Vietnam," *The New York Review of Books*, 15,3 (Aug. 13, 1970).

22  Davis, *Behind Enemy Lines*, pp.186, 180, 186. Paley regards the relative absence of wounded or dead bodies amidst the ravaged landscape more sceptically. She remarks, "I think they hid the cost—they did not, except in two or three cases, introduce us to the severely wounded or ill." Yet even when visitors recognize that their exposure to the reality of war is circumscribed, they do not, by and large, distrust the spectacle of resistance. Paley, *Just As I Thought*, p.70.

23  Susan Sontag, *Trip to Hanoi* (New York: Farrar, Straus and Giroux, 1968), pp.65–66, 61.

24  McCarthy, *Hanoi*, pp.48–49.

25  Davis, *Behind Enemy Lines*, p.179.

26  Sontag, *Trip to Hanoi*, p.87.

27  Michael Renov, "Imagining the Other: Representations of Vietnam in Sixties Political Documentary," in *From Hanoi to Hollywood: The Vietnam War in American Film*, ed. Linda Dittmar and Gene Michaud (New Brunswick, N.J.: Rutgers University Press, 1990), pp.261, 268.

28  Sontag, *Trip to Hanoi*, p.87.

29  Ibid., pp.3, 6, 8.

30  Herbert Marcuse, *Essay on Liberation* (Boston: Beacon Press, 1969), p.37.

31  For an analysis of countercultural travel in a very different context, see Brian Edwards's discussion of "hippie orientalism." Arguing that during the U.S. war in Vietnam popular representations of Morocco reflect the urge to escape "another more troubling Orient, that of Southeast Asia," Edwards reminds us that the processes of identification are multiply determined as they unfold across national and regional cultures. Brian Edwards, *Morocco Bound: Disorienting America's Maghreb from Casablanca to the Marrakech Express* (Durham, N.C.: Duke University Press, 2005), p.254.

32  Sontag, *Trip to Hanoi*, p.72.

## 25   1968: Springboard for Women's Liberation
SHEILA ROWBOTHAM

1   See Helene Curtis and Mimi Sanderson, eds., *The Unsung Sixties: Memoirs of Social Innovation* (London: Whiting & Birch, 2006).

2   See David Cooper, ed., *The Dialectics of Liberation* (London: Penguin Books, 1968).

3   Wini Breines, *The Great Refusal: Community and Organization in the New Left: 1962–1968* (Cambridge, Mass: J.F. Bergin,1982), p.83.

4   Greg Calvert, quoted in Breines, *Great Refusal*, p.48.

5   Breines, *Great Refusal*, p.170, n.35.

6   Ben Harker, *Class Act: The Cultural and Political Life of Ewan MacColl* (London: Pluto Press, 2007), pp.133–35, 141–43, 147–53.

7   Ibid., p.70.

8   Ibid., p.102.

9   Robert Hewison, *Too Much: Art and Society in the Sixties, 1960–75* (London: Methuen, 1986), p.116.

## 26   Group Consciousness in Brazil: Appropriation (1964–89)
JOANA MARIA PEDRO

My findings in this article derive from a larger study that I am currently undertaking, which consists primarily of thirty-three interviews with Brazilian women who became involved in feminism and the women's movement between 1964 and 1985.

1  Moema Toscano and Miriam Goldenberg, *A revolução das mulheres: um balanço do feminismo no Brasil* (Rio de Janeiro: Revan, 1992), p.55.

2  Amy Erdman Farrell, *Ms. Magazine e a promessa do feminismo popular* (São Paulo: Editora Barracuda, 2004), pp.37–38.

3  Juliet Mitchell, *A condición de la mujer* (Barcelona: Editorial Anagrama, 1977), pp.63–66.

4  Maria Odila Leite da Silva Dias, interviewed by Roselane Neckel, São Paulo, June 24, 2005.

5  Annete Goldberg, "Eminismo e Autoritarismo: A Metamorfose de uma Utopia de Liberaço em Ideologia Liberalizante," Master's thesis, IFCS, UFRJ, Rio de Janeiro, 1987, pp.101–9.

6  Maria do Espírito Santo Tavares dos Santos, interviewed by Roselane Neckel, Rio de Janeiro, Feb. 14, 2005.

7  Suely Gomes Costa, interviewed by Joana Maria Pedro, Florianópolis, Feb. 17, 2004.

8  Jaqueline Pitanguy, Maria Amélia Telles, Albertina Costa, and Marta Suplicy are among the best known.

9  Joana Maria Pedro, "Narrativas fundadoras do feminismo: poderes e conflitos (1970–1978," *Revista Brasileira de História* (São Paulo, Anpuh), 52, 26 (2006).

10  Féliz Guattari and Suely Rolnik, *Micropolítica: Cartografias do desejo*, 4th ed. (Petrópolis, RJ: Vozes, 1996).

11  Julia Silvia Guivant, interviewed by Janine Petersen, Florianópolis, Aug. 1, 2003.

12  This group is similar to the CFFC (Catholics for a Free Choice) in the United States.

13  Júlia Matias de Albuquerque, interviewed by the author, Rio Branco, Acre, May 5, 2006; Mara Vidal, interviewed by the author, Acre, May 5, 2006.

14  Maria Amélia de Almeida Teles, interviewed by the author, São Paulo, Aug. 24, 2005.

15  Sônia Weider Maluf, interviewed by the author and Maise C. Zucco, Florianópolis, July 6, 2006.

16  Françoise Collin, "Nuevo Feminismo: Nueva sociedad ou el advenimiento de outra," *Boletim Nosotras—Grupo Latinoamericano de Mujeres*, 2,21–22 (September/October 1975), pp.9–12.

17  Mitchell, *Condición de la mujer*, pp.62–63.

18  Jo Freeman, *Tirania das organizaçes sem estrutura* (São Paulo: Index Editora Prohibitorum, July 2002), p.7.

19  The play was written by Rose Marie Muraro and Heloneida Studart, two well-known Brazilian feminists.

20  Eve Ensler's play was published in Brazil by Bertrand Russel Co. It has been staged in Brazil in a version adapted by theatre director Miguel Falabella.

21  Rose Marie Muraro, *Memórias de uma mulher impossível* (Rio de Janeiro: Ed. Rosa dos Tempos, 1999).

22  Sonia E. Álvares, *A globalização dos feminismos latino-americanos: Tendências dos anos 90 e desafios para o novo milênio in Alvares*, in *Cultura e política nos movimentos sociais latino-americanos: novas leituras*, ed. Sonia Álvares, Evelina Dagnino, and Arturo Escobar (Belo Horizonte: Ed. UFMG, 2000), pp.383–426.

23  As related by Sonia Maluf, in her interview.

24  Stuart Hall, *A identidade cultural na pós-modernidade* (Rio de Janeiro: DP&A, 1999), p.21.

## 27  Reframing the "Whiteness" of U.S. Feminism: The Protest Movement, Radical Feminism, and the Abjection of Whiteness
AMANDA THIRD

1  See Ellen Willis, "Foreword," in Alice Echols, *Daring to Be Bad: Radical Feminism in America 1967–1975* (Minneapolis: University of Minnesota Press, 1989), p.vii; Barbara A. Crow, "Introduction," in *Radical Feminism: A Documentary Reader*, ed. Barbara A. Crow (New York: New York University Press, 2000), p.2; and Echols, *Daring to Be Bad*, p.243. As radical feminism emerged in the late 1960s, a heated debate between "politicos" and "feminists" took place: "feminists" argued that women needed to organize separately from the new left; "politicos" insisted that women's liberation was an important part of the new left struggle and remained committed to collaborating with the men on the left until the early 1970s.

2 Todd Gitlin, *The Sixties: Years of Hope, Days of Rage* (Toronto: Bantam, 1987), p.376; emphasis added.

3 Full elaboration of the argument is in Amanda Third, "Terrorising Women: (Radical) Feminism and the Discourse of the Female Terrorist," Australasian Digital Theses Program, 2006, ch.6, pp.302–43 <adt.caul.edu.au/>.

4 Sara Evans, *Personal Politics: The Roots of Women's Liberation in the Civil Rights Movement and the New Left* (New York: Alfred A. Knopf, 1979), p.102.

5 Ibid.

6 John Muncie, *The Trouble with Kids Today* (London: Hutchison, 1984), p.117.

7 See respectively Evans, *Personal Politics*, p.200; Ted Robert Gurr, ed., *Violence in America: Protest, Rebellion, Reform* (Newbury Park, Cal.: Sage, 1989), p.17; and Jonah Raskin, *For the Hell of It: The Life and Times of Abbie Hoffman* (Berkeley: University of California Press, 1998), p.255.

8 I use the word "white" here advisedly. Of course, whiteness is always a highly contingent category—see, for example, Richard Dyer, *White* (London and New York: Routledge, 1997)—and, in the U.S. context, it was, and still is, a discursive construction legitimated by a reductionist politics of race that produces identity through the oppositional dichotomy of "Black" and "white." By "white" radicals then, I mean those positioned in the context of the shift within the civil rights movement towards Black Power, and on that basis excluded from leadership and participation in the movement. Whilst the Black/white dichotomy operated with discursive power in the movement, it simplified a very complex "racial" politics. Many of the white activists were, in fact, Jewish, and therefore only problematically "white." For a full discussion of the problematic status of these radicals, see Third, "Terrorising Women," pp.312–13.

9 Andrew Kopkind as cited in Echols, *Daring to Be Bad*, p.41.

10 On Black leaders' antagonism towards whites, see Evans, *Personal Politics*, p.197; and Echols, *Daring to Be Bad*, p.47. On white activists' difficulties organizing the poor, see Third, "Terrorising Women," pp.314–16.

11 Echols, *Daring to Be Bad*, p.29.

12 Evans, *Personal Politics*, p.197. This example draws attention not only to the problematic positioning of whiteness, but also to the ambiguities that structure the categorization of whites within the movement. See Third, "Terrorising Women," pp.317–19.

13 Echols, *Daring to Be Bad*, p.45.

14 Todd Gitlin, "The Implosion," in *The Sixties*, ed. Peter Stines (Detroit: Wayne State University Press, 1988), p.218.

15 Echols, *Daring to Be Bad*, p.29. See also Jeremy Rabkin, "Feminism: Where the Spirit of the Sixties Lives On," in *Reassessing the Sixties: Debating the Political and Cultural Legacy*, ed. Stephen Macedo (New York: W.W. Norton, 1997), p.54.

16 See, for example, Anne McClintock, *Imperial Leather: Race, Gender and Sexuality in the Colonial Contest* (New York: Routledge, 1995).

17 For radical feminist accounts of their decision to organize on behalf of women as a result of their experiences of the sexism of the left, see Robin Morgan, "Goodbye to All That," in *Going Too Far: The Personal Chronicle of a Feminist* (New York: Vintage, 1978), pp.121–30; and Marge Piercy, "The Grand Coolie Damn," in *Sisterhood Is Powerful: An Anthology of Writings from the Women's Liberation Movement*, ed. Robin Morgan (New York: Vintage, 1970), pp.473–92.

18 Evans, *Personal Politics*, p.221.

19 Shulamith Firestone, "The Dialectic of Sex" (1970), in *Radical Feminism*, ed. Crow, p.90; Valerie Solanas, *The SCUM Manifesto* (Edinburgh, San Francisco: AK Press, 1997), p.5; Ti-Grace Atkinson, "Radical Feminism" (1969), in *Radical Feminism*, ed. Crow, p.87 (emphasis added); Roxanne Dunbar et al., "What Is Liberation?" (1970), in *Radical Feminism*, ed. Crow, p.81 (emphasis added).

20 As Rabkin, "Feminism," p.66, points out, radical feminists "regularly compared the plight of women with that of Blacks in

the segregated South, oppressed colonial peoples, starving masses in the Third World."

21 Solanas, *SCUM Manifesto*, p.1.

22 Ibid.

23 Ibid., p.46.

24 Dunbar as paraphrased in Echols, *Daring to Be Bad*, 104; Atkinson cited in Freddie Baer, "About Valerie Solanas," in Solanas, *SCUM Manifesto*, p.54.

25 Firestone, "Dialectic of Sex," p.95.

26 Robin Morgan, *The Demon Lover: The Roots of Terrorism* (London: Piatkus, 2001), p.224.

27 Elizabeth Grosz, "The Body of Signification," in *Abjection, Melancholia and Love: The Work of Julia Kristeva*, ed. John Fletcher and Andrew Benjamin (London: Routledge, 1990), p.89 (emphasis added).

28 In other words, Morgan's whiteness defines a boundary, a border. Again, this is characteristic of the abject. As Kristeva suggests, "We may call it a border." Julia Kristeva, *Powers of Horror: An Essay on Abjection* (New York: Columbia University Press, 1982), p.9.

29 Grosz, "Body of Signification," p.87.

30 Kristeva, *Powers of Horror*, p.3.

31 Grosz, "Body of Signification," pp.80–103 (emphasis added).

32 Kristeva, *Powers of Horror*, p.4.

33 Grosz, "Body of Signification," p.86 (emphasis added). See also Kristeva, *Powers of Horror*, p.3.

34 For example, Sigmund Freud's story of the primal horde in *Moses and Monotheism*, in *The Standard Edition of the Complete Psychological Works of Sigmund Freud*, vol. 23, ed. James Strachey (London: Hogarth, 1955), and in *Totem and Taboo*, in *Standard Edition*, vol. 13, ed. Strachey.

35 Kristeva, *Powers of Horror*, p.10.

36 Ibid., p.2.

37 Jane Gerhard, *Desiring Revolution: Second-Wave Feminism and the Rewriting of American Sexual Thought, 1920–1982* (New York and Chichester: Columbia University Press, 2001), p.155; and Cynthia Washington, "We Started from Different Ends of the Spectrum," excerpted in Evans, *Personal Politics*, pp.239–40.

38 Evans, *Personal Politics*, p.196n.

## 28 Cuban Women and the Time of Transformation
### SONIA ENJAMIO EXPÓSITO, LOURDES PÉREZ MONTALVO, AND INÉS RODRÍGUEZ PEDROSO

1 Fernando Portuondo, *Historia de Cuba de 1492 a 1898* (Havana: Instituto Cubano del Libro, 1965), p.41.

2 Manuel Moreno Fraginal, *El ingenio, complejo económico social cubano del azúcar*, vol.1 (Havana: Editorial de Ciencias Sociales, 1978), p.43.

3 Eduardo Torres Cuevas and Oscar Loyola Vega, *Historia de Cuba 1492–1898: Formación y liberación de la Nación* (Havana: Editorial Ciencias Sociales, 1965), p.360.

4 Ibid., p.361.

5 José Luis Rodríguez and George Carriazo Moreno, *La erradición de la pobreza en Cuba* (Havana: Editorial Ciencias Sociales, 1987), p.14.

6 On Sept. 26, 1960, Fidel Castro reported to the United Nations General Assembly: "Cuba will be the first American country that within a few months will be able to say that it does not have a single illiterate person.... From that date and until December, the preparatory phase for the Literacy Campaign will be developed." During the campaign 493,177 women learned reading and writing.

7 Fondo Registro de Asociaciones, File 012666, National Archives, Havana.

8 Ibid., File 012693.

9 Ibid., File 000766.

10 Ibid.

11 "Puntadas," *Revolución*, Aug. 26, 1960, p.7. National associations included Revolutionary Women's Unit, Congress of Cuban Women for the Liberation of Latin America (which later became the Federation of Cuban Women), Women's Section of the Integration and Orientation National Movement, and Women's Committee of the organization "With Cross and Country." Provincial associations included the Sisterhood of Mothers (Havana), Agricultural Column José Martí (Matanzas), Women's Brigade and Humanitarian Women (Santiago de Cuba), Women's Medical Revolutionary Association (Havana), and Women's Section of Families of Martyrs (Santiago de Cuba).

12  Testimony of Maria Bosch, Director of América Libre School, in Margaret Randall, *Mujeres en la Revolución* (Mexico,1978), pp.164–68.

13  Fidel Castro Ruz, Speech to the V Plenaria, FMC, Santa Clara., Dec. 9, 1966.

## 29  Shamans of the Spring: Environmentalism and the New Jeremiad
MICHAEL EGAN

1   Ulrich Beck, *Risk Society: Towards a New Modernity* (London: Sage Publications, 1992); Frederick Buell, *From Apocalypse to Way of Life: Environmental Crisis in the American Century* (New York: Routledge, 2003), p.193.

2   Donald Worster, *Nature's Economy: A History of Ecological Ideas*, 2nd ed. (New York: Cambridge University Press, 1994), p.22.

3   Joseph M. Petulla, *American Environmentalism: Values, Tactics, Priorities* (College Station: Texas A & M University Press, 1980), p.xii.

4   Barry Commoner, interview with author, July 17, 2003.

5   Paul R. Ehrlich, *The Population Bomb* (New York: Ballantine Books, 1968).

6   René Dubos, *So Human an Animal: How We Are Shaped by Surroundings and Events* (New York: Scribner Book Company, 1968).

7   Barry Commoner, "A Scientist Views Pollution," address to National Industrial Conference Board, New York City, Dec. 15, 1966, p.15; Barry Commoner Papers, Library of Congress, box 493.

8   The Committee for Nuclear Information's Baby Tooth Survey is a key example of science information in practice. See Michael Egan, *Barry Commoner and the Science of Survival: The Remaking of American Environmentalism* (Cambridge, Mass.: MIT Press, 2007), pp.47–78.

9   Barry Commoner, *Science and Survival* (New York: Viking Press, 1966), p.108.

10  Paul Brooks, *The House of Life: Rachel Carson at Work* (Boston: Houghton Mifflin, 1972), p.128.

11  Commoner, *Science and Survival*, p.108.

12  Barry Commoner, "Fallout and Water Pollution—Parallel Cases," *Scientist and Citizen*, 6 (December 1964), p.2.

13  Sarah L. Thomas, "A Call to Action: *Silent Spring*, Public Disclosure, and the Rise of Modern Environmentalism," in *Natural Protest: Essays on the History of American Environmentalism*, ed. Michael Egan and Jeff Crane (New York: Routledge, 2008).

14  Perhaps the most famous instance of divisions within the movement involved the population vs. pollution debate between Ehrlich and Commoner. Ehrlich argued that population growth was responsible for the environmental crisis, while Commoner claimed that pollution from new technologies was the key element that required repair. This debate is discussed in some detail in Egan, *Barry Commoner and the Science of Survival*, pp.116–38.

15  Kelly Moore, *Disrupting Science: Social Movements, American Scientists, and the Politics of the Military, 1945–1975* (Princeton, N.J.: Princeton University Press, 2008), p.134.

16  Ronald Bailey, "Earth Day, Then and Now," *Reason*, May 2000.

17  *Time*, Feb. 2, 1970.

18  Commoner, *Science and Survival*, p.27.

19  Ibid., p.126.

20  Ehrlich, *Population Bomb*, p.xi.

21  Stephen Fox, *The American Conservation Movement: John Muir and His Legacy* (Madison: University of Wisconsin Press, 1985), p.311.

22  Robert Gottlieb, *Forcing the Spring: The Transformation of the American Environmental Movement* (Washington, D.C.: Island Press, 1993), p.85.

23  Buell, *From Apocalypse to Way of Life*.

24  The popular acceptance of scientists among environmentalists adds some fuel to arguments that the environmental movement was a conservative rather than a countercultural movement, but the emphasis on health and pollution—and not just natural resource conservation— through 1960s and the rise of more politically engaged scientists who devoted their expertise to public interests suggests that American environmentalism experienced a significant transition of its own during this decade. See, for example, Thomas,

"Call to Action"; Egan, *Barry Commoner and the Science of Survival*; and Maril Hazlett, "The Story of *Silent Spring* and the Ecological Turn," Ph.D. dissertation, University of Kansas, 2003.

## 30  More Dangerous Than Bombs or Bullets: Agent Orange, Dioxin, and the Environmental Imaginary
### EDWIN MARTINI

1   Jeanne Stellman et al., "The Extent and Patterns of Usage of Agent Orange and Other Herbicides in Vietnam," *Nature*, 422 (April 2003).

2   Ibid. For more on Bliss, see Alistair Hay, *The Chemical Scythe: The Lessons of 2,4, 5-T and Dioxin* (New York: Plenum Press, 1982); and Aaron Wildavsky and Brendan Swedlow, "Dioxin, Agent Orange, and Times Beach," in *But Is It True? A Citizen's Guide to Health and Safety Issues*, ed. Aaron Wildavsky (Cambridge, Mass.: Harvard University Press, 1995).

3   "Dioxin: Quandary for the 80s," *St. Louis Post-Dispatch*, Nov. 14, 1983, p.6.

4   Christopher Sellers, "Body, Place and the State: The Makings of an 'Environmentalist' Imaginary in the Post-World War II U.S.," *Radical History Review*, 74 (Spring 1999), p.58.

5   All of the RAND interviews are available at the National Agricultural Library, Beltsville, Md., Alvin Young Collection (AYC), Series II, Boxes 13–14; hereafter I will simply cite them by their number followed by the page citation.

6   NLF Interview Five, p.9; Interview Eleven, p.6.

7   NLF Interview Seven, p.3.

8   NLF Interview Thirty-Four, p.3.

9   NLF Interview Eighteen, p.3.

10  NLF Interview Eighteen, p.2.

11  NLF Interview Five, p.9.

12  NLF Interview Thirteen, pp.5, 8.

13  NLF Interview Twelve, p.11.

14  On the veterans lawsuit and the legal fallout from the case, see Peter Schuck, *Agent Orange on Trial* (Cambridge: Belknap Press, 1986).

15  "Jury Awards $58 Million to 47 Railroad Workers Exposed to Dioxin," *The New York Times*, Aug. 27, 1982, p.A9.

16  "Dioxin Threat Puts U.S. under Fire," *The New York Times*, Dec. 26, 1982, p.A22.

17  "Town Struggles with Toxic Legacy," *Washington Post*, Jan.10, 1983, p.A8.

18  "Dioxin Threat Puts U.S. under Fire."

19  "In Dioxin-Tainted Town, No 'Welcome' Signs," *The New York Times*, Jan. 10, 1983, p.A1.

20  "Orange Lining in Dioxin Cloud," *St. Louis Post Dispatch*, Feb. 28, 1983; "Environmental News," Dec. 8, 1982 (Washington, D.C.: EPA, 1982), ALY Collection on Agent Orange, Series Four, Box 85, Folders 2113, 2114.

21  "Town Struggles with Toxic Legacy." For several other quotes about the fear of the unknown, see *St. Louis Globe*, Dec. 9, 1982, p.A1.

22  "Town Struggles with Toxic Legacy."

23  "Concern Growing over Unclear Threat of Dioxin," *The New York Times*, Feb. 15, 1982, p.A21.

24  According to two accounts, Bliss's claim that he was unaware that the waste oil contained hazardous chemical waste was belied by the fact that he was paid by the Northeastern Pharmaceutical and Chemical Company (NEPACCO) to remove the waste. Under Missouri law at the time, haulers would pay for non-hazardous oil, while manufacturers would pay to have hazardous waste removed.

25  "Ignorance is Bliss." For the bumper sticker, see "Dioxin, Quandary for the '80s," p.8.

26  For information about the Vietnam Victims of Agent Orange lawsuit, still pending at the time of writing, see <www.ffrd.org/Lawsuit/Lawsuit.htm>.

## 31  Sex Reassignment Surgery in Ontario: Adrift in a Political and Cultural Climate
### KRISTIN IRELAND

1   Razack then critiques this imagining by exploring the incidents in 1993 when two Somalis were shot, one fatally, in the back of the head by Canadian peacekeepers and another sixteen-year-old was tortured to death. Sherene H. Razack, *Dark Threats & White Knights: The Somalia Affair, Peacekeeping, and the New Imperialism* (Toronto: University of Toronto Press, 2004), p.9.

2 For a more detailed discussion of Gender Identity Clinics in the United States, see Joanne Meyerowitz, *How Sex Changed: A History of Transsexuality in the United States* (Cambridge, Mass.: Harvard University Press, 2002).

3 See Viviane K. Namaste, "Sex Change, Social Change: Reflections on Identity and Institutions," in Namaste, *Sex Change, Social Change: Reflections on Identity, Institutions, and Imperialism* (Toronto: Women's Press, 2005). For more on the operation of the clinic in Vancouver see Stephanie Castle, *The Zenith Experience: Encounters and Memories in a Transgender Setting* (Vancouver: Perceptions Press, 2005).

4 The Alberta Health Care Insurance Plan (AHCIP) offers financial support for certain sex reassignment procedures. The surgeries are performed in a clinic in Montreal while AHCIP pays the physicians. For a more detailed description of SRS in Canadian provinces and territories, see Egale Canada, "Sex Reassignment Surgery (SRS) Backgrounder" <www.egale.ca> (accessed July 28, 2008).

5 Castle, *Zenith Experience*, p.19.

6 The concept of *choice* here refers not to the experience of *being* transsexual but to the possibility of *choosing* sex reassignment surgery.

7 "OHIP Covered Cost of Sex-Change Surgery," *The Toronto Star*, Jan. 28, 1974, Clarke Institute of Psychiatry fonds, 5-10, A-2, Scrapbook: 1974, Centre for Addiction and Mental Health, Archives, Toronto (hereafter cited as CAMH).

8 See "So Womanly, Glad Hair Is Blonde, Christine Says," *The Toronto Daily Star*, Dec. 2, 1952.

9 Eric Nicol, *Shall We Join the Ladies?* (Toronto: Ryerson Press, 1955), p.31.

10 Ibid.

11 "Discussion: Trans-Sexualism at Journal Club. T.P.H. October 25, 1960," 1960, Clarke Institute of Psychiatry fonds, 4-04, E-1, Medical Literature, CAMH.

12 Torontonian Dr. Ball collected twenty-three cases, but it is unclear how many individuals were seen by the other doctors participating in this meeting. "Discussion: Trans-Sexualism at Journal Club. T.P.H. October 25, 1960," CAMH.

13 "U of T Studying Trans-Sexualism," *The Toronto Star*, Oct. 20, 1969, Clarke Institute of Psychiatry fonds, 5-10, A-2, Scrapbook: 1969, CAMH.

14 Ibid.

15 B. Steiner and D. Paitich, "The Toronto Gender Identity Project: A Preliminary Report," in *Proceedings of the Second Interdisciplinary Symposium on Gender Dysphoria Syndrome*, ed. Donald Laub and Patrick Gandy (Stanford, Cal.: Stanford University Medical Center, 1973), p.73.

16 Ibid.

17 Ibid.

18 Ibid.

19 Ibid., p.74.

20 Kurt Freund, "A Comparison of Transsexuals and Non-Transsexual Homosexual Males," in *Proceedings of the Second Interdisciplinary Symposium*, ed. Laub and Gandy, p.28.

21 Ibid.

22 Dianna [pseud.], *Once I Was a Man: Behold I Am a Woman*, as told to Felicity Cochrane (New York: Pyramid Books, 1972), p.203.

23 Ibid.

24 Robert Gilder, *Transsexual and Lesbian Couples*, with commentary by Daniel Paitich and Betty W. Steiner (Toronto: Faculty of Medicine, University of Toronto, 1975).

25 Ibid.

26 Ibid.

27 "Transsexualism or Eonism: A Morphological, Psychiatric and Psychological Study," 1960, Clarke Institute of Psychiatry fonds, 4-04, E-1, Medical Literature, CAMH.

28 Ibid. Emphasis in original.

29 Ibid.

30 Robert Gilder, *Changing Faces: Disorders of Gender Identity*, with commentary by Betty W. Steiner (Toronto: Faculty of Medicine, University of Toronto, 1979).

31 Ibid.

32 Ibid.

33 Viviane K. Namaste, *Invisible Lives: The Erasure of Transsexual and*

*Transgendered People* (Chicago: University of Chicago Press, 2000), p.196.

34 "Question Period," 1960, Clarke Institute of Psychiatry fonds, 4-04, E-1, Medical Literature, CAMH.

35 Ibid. Emphasis in original.

36 Anonymous Letter, 1972, Association for Canadian Transsexuals, 284, Canadian Lesbian and Gay Archives, Toronto.

37 Ira M. Dushoff, "Economic, Psychological and Social Rehabilitation of Male and Female Transsexuals Prior to Surgery," in *Proceedings of the Second Interdisciplinary Symposium*, ed. Laub and Gandy, p.200.

38 Alexandra Gill, "Ontario Decision to Halt Sex-Change Surgery Payments Challenged," *The Globe and Mail* (Toronto), May 4, 1999.

39 The cost of sex reassignment surgery varies. According to the Ontario Human Rights Commission's working policy on gender identity, in Toronto female-to-male surgery costs about $10,000 to $12,000 and male-to-female surgery about $18,000. The 1996 British Columbia law reform project on human rights and the transgendered community estimates that SRS for MTFs is between $5,000 and $10,000, and FTM SRS ranges from $20,000 to more than $60,000. See Ontario Human Rights Commission, "Towards a Commission Policy on Gender Identity," Queen's Printer for Ontario, 2005 <www.ohrc.on.ca/en_text/ consultations/gender-identity-discussion-paper> (accessed Jan. 15, 2009). However, it is unclear here what surgeries are being incorporated. See Egale Canada, "Sex Reassignment Surgery (SRS) Backgrounder," Egale Canada <www.egale.ca> (accessed Jan. 15, 2009).

40 Ian McKay, "The Liberal Order Framework: A Prospectus for a Reconnaissance of Canadian History," *The Canadian Historical Review*, 81,4 (2000), p.630.

41 Such a statement does not mean that these experts were necessarily working outside of the liberal order, since it may be argued that they saw transsexual people as not *true individuals*; in this case denying their bodily integrity would not be in conflict with maintaining the liberal order.

42 Patrick Califia, *Sex Changes: Transgender Politics*, 2nd ed. (San Francisco: Cleis Press, 2003), p.263.

43 McKay, "Liberal Order Framework," p.623.

44 It is also important to note here that it was not until 1969 that homosexuality became (at least partially) decriminalized in Canada. For more on the 1969 Criminal Code reform, see Gary Kinsman, *The Regulation of Desire: Homo and Hetero Sexualities*, 2nd ed. (Montreal: Black Rose Books, 1996), pp.264–87.

**32  At the Point of the Lance: Gender, Development, and the Peace Corps**
MOLLY GEIDEL

Thanks to Nancy Braus, Aaron Lecklider, Rachel Rubin, Bruce Schulman, Nina Silber, Judith Smith, Patricia Stuelke, and the students in Honors 290 at U Mass Boston.

1  Frank Zappa, *We're Only in It for the Money* (Verve, Bizarre Rykodisc, 1968).

2  See Arturo Escobar, *Encountering Development: The Making and Unmaking of the Third World* (Princeton, N.J.: Princeton University Press, 1995); Michael Latham, *Modernization as Ideology: American Social Science and "Nation Building" in the Kennedy Era* (Chapel Hill: University of North Carolina Press, 2000); and Maria Josefina Saldaña-Portillo, *The Revolutionary Imagination and the Age of Development in the Americas* (Durham, N.C.: Duke University Press, 2003).

3  Daniel Lerner, *The Passing of Traditional Society: Modernizing the Middle East* (New York: Free Press, 1958).

4  Walt Whitman Rostow, *Stages of Economic Growth: A Non-Communist Manifesto* (Cambridge, Mass.: Cambridge University Press, 1960).

5  Sargent Shriver, *Point of the Lance* (New York: Harper & Row, 1964), p.1.

6  See Barbara Ehrenreich, *The Hearts of Men: American Dreams and the Flight from Commitment* (New York: Doubleday, 1983).

7  Sargent Shriver, "Memorandum to the President," Shriver Papers, John F. Kennedy Library (JFKL).

8  Coates Redmon, *Come As You Are: The Peace Corps Story* (New York: Harcourt Brace, 1986), p.396.

9  Letter from Jack Vaughn to Sargent Shriver, Shriver Papers, JFKL.

10  Redmon, *Come As You Are*, p.397. *Campesino* means *peasant*.

11  See Eve Sedgwick, *Between Men: English Literature and Male Homosocial Desire* (New York: Columbia University Press, 1985), esp. the introduction. Eunice Kennedy Shriver's marriage and her family connections linked her husband to the highest echelons of power and helped shape the image of the Peace Corps as elite brotherhood.

12  Moritz Thomsen, *Living Poor: A Peace Corps Chronicle* (Seattle: University of Washington Press, 1969), p.165.

13  Daniel Patrick Moynihan, *The Negro Family: The Case for National Action* (Washington, D.C.: U.S. Government Printing Office, 1965).

14  Thomsen, *Living Poor*.

15  *So That Men Are Free*, dir. Willard Van Dyke, McGraw-Hill Films, 1962.

16  "Vicos: A Hard Lesson," *Peace Corps Volunteer*, 4,3 (January 1966), pp.10–13.

17  "Sex Makes an Impact," *Peace Corps Volunteer*, January 1966, p.17.

18  Kopkind, "The Peace Corps' Daring New Look," *New Republic*, 6 (Feb. 5, 1966), p.17.

19  Jorge Sanjinés, "Revolutionary Cinema: The Bolivian Experience," in *Cinema and Social Change in Latin America*, ed. Julianne Burton (Austin: University of Texas Press, 1986), p.40.

20  Barack Obama, "Commencement address at Wesleyan University," May 25, 2008 <thepage.time.com/obamas-commencement-address-at-wesleyan-university>.

## 33  Student Politics in Mexico in the Wake of the Cuban Revolution
JAIME PENSADO

1  In a more comprehensive study I examine the influence of the Cuban Revolution on student politics in Mexico as evident in: (1) the polarization of both leftist and conservative students throughout the long 1960s; (2) the re-evaluation of the importance of ideology by this new generation of politicized students (and intellectuals); and (3) the rise of reactionary politics and political violence. See Jaime Pensado, "Political Violence and Student Culture in Mexico: The Consolidation of *Porrismo* during the 1950s and 1960s," Ph.D. dissertation, University of Chicago, 2008.

2  The literature on the Mexican student movement of 1968 is too thick to list in one citation. For an excellent review of the major trends and political debates that have dominated this historiography over the past three decades, see Vania Markarian, "El movimiento estudiantil mexicano de 1968: Treinta años de debates públicos," *Anuario de Espacios Urbanos, Historia, Cultura, Diseño*, 2001. For a bibliographical list of the major works published on 1968, see Ana Maria Sánchez Saénz, "Bibliografía sobre el movimiento estudiantil mexicano de 1968," in *Diálogos sobre el 68*, ed. Silvia González Marín (Mexico: UNAM, 2003).

3  Some of the student organizations that emerged inside the university with the support of the PCM included Grupo Julio Antonio Mella, Grupo Renacimiento, Grupo César Vallejo, Partido Estudiantil Socialista (PES), and Partido Estudiantil Socialista Universitario (PESU). See, for example, Pensado "Political Violence and Student Culture in Mexico"; and René Rivas Ontiveros, *La izquierda estudiantil en la UNAM: organizaciones, movilizaciones y liderazgos (1958–1972)* (Mexico: UNAM, 2007).

4  On student activism in the 1950s, see Pensado "Political Violence and Student Culture in Mexico"; and Antonio Gómez Nashiki, "El Movimiento y la Violencia Institucional: La Universidad Michoacana de San Nicolás de Hidalgo, 1956–1966," *Revista de Investigaciones Educativa*, 12,35 (October-December 2007).

5  On CNED, see Sergio Zermeño, *México: una democracia utópica* (Mexico: Siglo XXI, 1978).

6  See, for example, Gilberto Guevara Niebla, *La libertad nunca de olvida: Memoria*

*del 68* (Mexico: Cal y Arena, 2004), pp.149–50.

7 For a detailed discussion of the emergence of the new left in Latin America, see Eric Zolov, "Expanding Our Conceptual Horizons: The Shift from an Old to a New Left in Latin America," *Contra-corriente: A Journal on Social History and Literature in Latin America*, 5,2 (Winter 2008).

8 See, for example, José Revueltas, *Ensayo de un proletario sin cabeza* (Mexico, 1962). For a broad discussion on the labour strikes of the late 1950s and their impact on student politics, see Elaine Carey, *Plaza of Sacrifices: Gender, Power and Terror in 1968 Mexico* (Albuquerque: University of New Mexico Press, 2005).

9 For early critiques of the Mexican Revolution, see the collection of essays in Stanley R. Ross, ed., *¿Ha muerto la revolución?* (Mexico: Red de Jonás, 1979). In addition to Revueltas, *Ensayo de un proletario sin cabeza*, see also his *México 1968: juventud y revolución* (Mexico: Era, 1978).

10 See, for example, Guevara Niebla, *Libertad nunca de olvida*, pp.145–52.

11 See, for example, Marco Bellingeri, "La imposibilidad del odio: la guerrilla y el movimiento estudiantil en México, 1960–1974," in *La Transición interrumpida: México, 1968-1988*, ed. Ilán Semo et al. (Mexico: Nueva Imágen, 1993), pp.49–73; and Alberto Ulloa Bornemann, *Surviving Mexico's Dirty War: A Political Prisoner's Memoir*, ed. and trans. Arthur Schmidt and Aurora Camacho de Schmidt (Philadelphia: Temple University Press, 2007). On the 1968 and 1971 student massacres, see Sergio Aguayo Quezada, *1968: Los archivos de la violencia* (Mexico: Grijalbo, 1998); Carey, *Plaza of Sacrifices*; Julio Scherer García and Carlos Monsiváis, *Los patriotas: de Tlatelolco a la guerra sucia* (Mexico: Nuevo Siglo, 2004); Raúl Jardón, *El espionaje contra el movimiento estudiantil: Los documentos de la Dirección Federal de Seguridad y las agencias de inteligencia estadounidense en 1968* (Mexico: Itaca, 2003); and Kate Doyle, "The Corpus Christi Massacre: Mexico's Attack on Its Student Movement, June 10, 1971," National Security Archive <www.gwu.edu/~nsarchiv/NSAEBB/NSAEBB91/> (accessed May 10, 2008).

12 The "law of social dissolution" refers to an article of Mexico's penal code. It was originally enacted in 1941 to protect Mexico from Fascists and Nazis, but expanded in the following two decades to prohibit any activity that might undermine national sovereignty, including acts of subversion, treason, and disorder. For a detailed discussion on the law of social dissolution, see Evelyn P. Stevens, *Protest and Response in Mexico* (Boston: MIT Press, 1974).

13 In Mexico, the term "economic miracle" is frequently used to describe a period of prosperity in the 1940s that began to wane during the late 1950s and early 1960s.

14 See, for example, Eric Zolov, *Refried Elvis: The Rise of the Mexican Counterculture* (Berkeley and Los Angeles: University of California Press, 1999); Zolov, "Expanding Our Conceptual Horizons"; and Deborah Cohn, "The Mexican Intelligentsia, 1950–1968: Cosmopolitanism, National Identity, and the State," *Mexican Studies/Estudios Mexicanos*, 21,1 (Winter 2006).

15 Gabriel Careaga, "La vida cultural y política de los sesentas," *Revista Mexicana de Ciencias Políticas y Sociales*, 108 (October–December 1994), p.178.

## 34  "Women United Against the War": Gender Politics, Feminism, and Vietnam Draft Resistance in Canada
LARA CAMPBELL

1 Estimates on the number who arrived in opposition to the war vary. The number of 100,000 is borrowed from John Hagan, *Northern Passage: American Vietnam War Resisters in Canada* (Cambridge, Mass: Harvard University Press, 2001), pp.3, 184. About 250,000 Americans immigrated to Canada in the period of the Vietnam War, although not all were war resisters. David Churchill, "An Ambiguous Welcome: Vietnam Draft Resistance, the Canadian State, and Cold War Containment," *Histoire Sociale/Social History*, 27,73 (May 2004), p.3. For more details

on calculating numbers, see Hagan, *Northern Passage*, p.241, Table B.5. While the term draft dodger is contentious, I do not understand it in a pejorative way. Draft dodger was the most commonly used term in the time period under study; and I explicitly position draft dodging within the framework of war resistance because most dodgers made a political choice to risk exile in protest against the war.

2 This article is part of a larger study that looks at how antiwar activism in Canada was a gendered social movement, shaped not only by nationalist tensions surrounding critiques of U.S. political hegemony but also by the development of a Canadian women's liberation movement that critiqued the subordinate position of women within radical activism. The project takes a transnational approach, emphasizing the interconnected relationships between U.S. and Canadian activists and feminists while acknowledging the independent nature of Canadian social movements in the 1960s.

3 See Leslie Cagan, "Women and the Anti-Draft Movement," *Radical America* (September-October 1980), pp.9–11; Michael Foley, "The 'Point of Ultimate Indignity' or a 'Beloved Community'? The Draft Resistance Movement and Gender Dynamics," in *The New Left Revisited*, ed. John McMillian and Paul Buhle (Philadelphia: Temple University Press, 2003).

4 Perhaps the most famous U.S. manifesto was the memo in 1965 by Casey Hayden and Mary King, "A Kind of Memo to Women in the Peace and Freedom Movements," reprinted in *Major Problems in American Women's History*, 2nd ed., ed. Mary Beth Norton and Ruth M. Alexander (Lexington, Mass.: D.C. Heath, 1996), pp.443–44.

5 Melody Kilian, *Georgia Straight*, Dec. 20–Jan. 2, 1969, p.12. Regarding the experiences of sexism within sixties-era social movements, see Alice Echols, *Daring to Be Bad: Radical Feminism in America, 1969–75* (Minneapolis: University of Minnesota Press, 1989); and Sara Evans, *Personal Politics: The Roots of Women's Liberation in the Civil Rights Movement*

and the New Left (New York: Alfred A. Knopf, 1979).

6 *Georgia Straight*, June 17-24, 1970, p.2.

7 Melody Kilian, *Yankee Refugee*, 4 (1969), p.1.

8 *The Pedestal*, 2,2 (March 1970), 2,3 (April 1970), 2,4 (May 1970), 5,2 (February 1973).

9 Hagan, *Northern Passage*; *The Globe and Mail* (Toronto), Aug. 4, 1967, p.1, Sept. 23, 1967, p.5.

10 Vietnam Action Committee, Boxes 1–5, Special Collections, University of British Columbia, Vancouver.

11 Nancy Knox, "Women United against the War," Vancouver Vietnam Actions Committee fonds, Folder 5-2, n.d., Special Collections, University of British Columbia.

12 *The Pedestal*, 3,5 (May 1971), 3,2 (February, 1971), 2,2 (March 1970), 3,3 (April 1970).

13 City of Vancouver Archives, VVAC fonds, folder 5-2, n.d. possibly 1970, "Women United Against the War, Nancy Knox, for the women of the Vietnam Action Committee. Note also that the bulk of the pamphlet is about women's position in Canada, not women in Vietnam.

14 *The Pedestal*, 3,5 (May 1971).

15 *The Vancouver Sun*, Dec. 7, 1969, April 25, 1968. See also Amy Swerdlow, *Women Strike for Peace: Traditional Motherhood and Radical Politics in the 1960s* (Chicago: University of Chicago Press, 1993).

16 *The Pedestal*, 3,5 (May 1971).

17 *Everywoman*, May 28, 1971.

18 Hagan, *Northern Passage*; Robert Bothwell, *Alliance and Illusion: Canada and the World, 1945–1984* (Vancouver: University of British Columbia Press, 2007).

19 *The Globe and Mail*, Feb. 17, 1968, p.1; *The New York Times*, Jan. 22, 1969, p.11. See also Ryan Edwardson, "Kicking Uncle Sam out of the Peaceable Kingdom: English-Canadian 'New Nationalism' and Americanization," *Journal of Canadian Studies*, 37,4 (Winter 2002/3), pp.131–50.

20 *The Pedestal*, 3,5 (May 1971); *Everywoman*, 2,8, issue 19 (May 28, 1971).

21 This has happened in part because the military and the draft formed a male sphere, and nominally heterosexual.

Although see Paul Jackson, *One of the Boys: Homosexuality in the Military during World War II* (Montreal and Kingston: McGill-Queen's University Press, 2004).

22 *The Globe and Mail*, Dec. 23, 1967, pp.1–2.

23 *Georgia Straight*, Dec. 20–Jan. 2, 1969, p.12.

24 *Georgia Straight*, Feb. 24–March 4, 1970, p.11.

25 See Van Gosse, *Rethinking the New Left: An Interpretive History* (New York: Palgrave, 2005); Ian Lekus, "Losing Our Kids: Queer Perspectives on the Chicago Seven Conspiracy Trial," in *New Left Revisited*, ed. McMillian and Buhle.

26 Yankee Refugee Staff, "Americans in Canada," Position paper, 1969.

27 *The Globe and Mail*, March 6, 1968.

28 See *The Globe and Mail*, Aug. 14, 1967, p.5, Feb. 23, 1971, p.6.

29 Michael Foley, *Confronting the War Machine: Draft Resistance during the Vietnam War* (Chapel Hill: University of North Carolina Press, 2003); Scott Young, "How Rigidity Taints a Free Spirit," *The Globe and Mail*, March 27, 1967, p.3; *The Globe and Mail*, Feb. 16, 1968, p.7. See also Doug Rossinow. *The Politics of Authenticity: Liberalism, Christianity and the New Left in America* (New York: Columbia University Press, 1998); and Tim O'Brien, *If I Die in a Combat Zone: Box Me Up and Ship Me Home* (New York: Broadway, 1999).

30 *The Globe and Mail*, Feb. 16, 1968, p.7, Feb. 16, 1968, Oct. 12, 1967, March 27, 1967.

31 *The Globe and Mail*, letter to the editor, March 6, 1968, p.6.

32 *The Globe and Mail*, Oct. 12, 1967, p.5.

33 For a brief overview, seee Hagan, *Northern Passage*, p.27. Future oral histories with men who chose to leave the United States for Canada will help to illuminate how individual men felt about such characterizations of draft dodgers, and how they negotiated the criticism from family, friends, and fellow activists in both countries.

34 See J. McRee Elrod Collection, 1968–76, Box 1, Special Collections, University of British Columbia.

35 Ibid., letter to Elrod from Kanter, March 6, 1968, March 24 1968, April 9, 1968, Oct. 29, 1968.

36 Ibid., letter to Elrod from Hurwitt, Feb. 24, 1968.

37 Melody Kilian, *Yankee Refugee*, 4 (1969), p.1.

38 Renée Kasinksy, *Refugees from Militarism: Draft Age Americans in Canada* (New Brunswick, N.J.: Transaction Books, 1976), p.134. Hagan, quoting Evangeline Mix, *Northern Passage*, p.163.

39 *Yankee Refugee*, 3 (1968), p.3.

40 "Draft Dodgers Find Life in Canada Is Not Easy," *The New York Times*, April 10,1968, p.49.

## 35 The Global Imagination of 1968: The New Left's Unfulfilled Promise
### GEORGE KATSIAFICAS

1 Katsiaficas, "The Real Axis of Evil," p. 343.

2 These documents are contained in George Katsiaficas, "The Real Axis of Evil," in *Masters of War: Militarism and Blowback in the Era of American Empire*, ed. Carl Boggs (New York and London: Routledge, 2003), pp. 287–300.

3 Giovanni Arrighi, Terence K. Hopkins, and Immanuel Wallerstein, "1989: The Continuation of 1968," in *After the Fall: 1989 and the Future of Freedom*, ed. George Katsiaficas (New York and London: Routledge, 2001), p. 35.

4 <www.eroseffect.com/articles/systemisproblem.htm> (accessed June 6, 2008).

## 36 Red Power Legacies and Lives: An Interview by Scott Rutherford
### LEE MARACLE

1 In 1971 Jeannette Corbière-Lavell, a Native woman who lost her status through marriage, challenged sections of the *Indian Act* that disempowered Native women. As Joyce Green notes, the *Indian Act*, "a piece of federal legislation passed under the constitutional aegis of s91(24) of the Constitution Act 1867, governs most aspects of life on Indian reserves in Canada. 'Status' is the term used to refer to those who are recognized by the federal (national) government as 'Indian' for the purposes

of the *Indian Act*. Prior to 1985 the act's membership provisions stripped status from any Indian woman who married anyone other than a status Indian man. Their children were not recognized as Indian, and non-status Indians could not reside on reserves or participate in the political life of reserve communities. Status Indian men, however, retained their status upon marriage and conferred it upon their wives; thus, non-Indian women acquired status upon marriage to status Indian men, and the children of these marriages were recognized as Indian." Joyce Green, "Balancing Strategies: Aboriginal Women and Constitutional Rights in Canada," in *Making Space for Indigenous Feminism*, ed Joyce Green (Halifax: Fernwood Publishing, 2007), p.155.

2   Maracle is referring to an amendment to the 1951 *Indian Act*, "Section 12(1)(a)(iv), known as the "double mother" clause, which "provided that a person whose parents married on or after 4 September 1951 and whose mother and paternal grandmother had not been recognized as Indians before their marriages, could be registered at birth, but would lose status and band membership on his or her 21st birthday." See <www.parl.gc.ca/information/library/PRBpubs/bp410-e.htm>.

## 37   An Embarrassment of Omissions, or Rewriting the Sixties: The Case of the Caribbean Conference Committee, Canada, and the Global New Left
DAVID AUSTIN

1   See Elizabeth Martinez, *De Colores Means All of Us: Latina Views for a Multi-Colored Century* (Cambridge, Mass.: South End Press, 1998), pp.22–23, 28; Paul Buhle and Dan Georgakas, *The Immigrant Left in the United States* (Albany, N.Y: State University of New York Press, 1996), pp.4–5; Van Gosse, *Rethinking the New Left: An Interpretive History* (New York: Palgrave Macmillan, 2005), p.5.

2   For example, Mark Kurlansky, *1968: The Year That Rocked the World*—arguably the most comprehensive assessment of the global 1960s—does not treat a single anglophone Caribbean group or movement and, with the exception of "Trudeaumania" and a few fleeting references to Quebec, Canada is not mentioned. Kurlansky, *1968: The Year That Rocked the World* (New York: Random House, 2005), p.351.

3   For an example of how the Black left remains excluded from new left recent historiography, see Myrna Kostash, *Long Way from Home: The Story of the Sixties Generation in Canada* (Toronto: James Lorimer and Company, 1980); and Pierre Berton's popular history, *1967: The Last Good Year* (Toronto: Doubleday Canada, 1997). Ian McKay, *Rebels, Reds, Radicals: Rethinking Canada's Left History* (Toronto: Between the Lines, 2005), is an important introduction to the Canadian left written by someone with an acute appreciation for theory, but nonetheless ignores Canada's Black left.

4   In her journalistic account of the incident, author Dorothy Eber quotes the damage to the university at $2,000,000, twice the amount of a previous student rebellion in Tokyo, Japan. See Eber, *The Computer Centre Party: Canada Meets Black Power: That Sir George Williams Affair* (Montreal: Tundra Books, 1969), p.8. Although Eber refers to Rosie Douglas and Anne Cools as ringleaders of the Sir George Williams Affair, she also appears to be unaware that Douglas and Cools were former CCC members.

5   Brian Meeks, *Radical Caribbean: From Black Power to Abu Bakr* (Kingston, Jamaica: The Press, University of West Indies, 1996), pp.31–32.

6   For an overview of the CCC's work and influence in North America and the Caribbean, see David Austin, "All Roads Led to Montreal: Black Power, the Caribbean, and the Black Radical Tradition in Canada," *Journal of African American History*, 92,4 (Fall 2007), pp.516–39.

7   For an analysis of the link between the old left and the new left, see Maurice Isserman, *If I Had a Hammer: The Death of the Old Left and the Birth of the New Left* (New York: Basic Books, 1987).

8   Estimates for Montreal's Black population vary between 7,000 residents in 1961

and 50,000 in 1968 (the latter figure is believed to be a serious overestimation). Dorothy Williams, *The Road to Now: A History of Blacks in Montreal* (Montreal: Véhicule Press, 1997), p.65.

9   For a brief reference to Anne Cools's influence as a member of the woman's movement, see Judy Rebick, *Ten Thousand Roses: The Making of a Feminist Revolution* (Toronto: Penguin Canada, 2005), pp.9–10. Cools's relationship to feminism is complicated and conflicted, but deserves considerably more attention than it has thus far been given.

10  Patricia Hill Collins, *Black Feminist Thought: Knowledge, Consciousness, and the Politics of Empowerment* (New York: Routledge, 1991), pp.140–41.

11  Sara Evans, *Personal Politics: The Roots of Women's Liberation in the Civil Rights Movement and the New Left* (New York: Vintage Books, 1980), pp.193–94.

12  Anne Cools, "Womanhood," in Black Spark Edition, *McGill Free Press*, February 1971, p.8.

13  Robin Winks, *The Blacks in Canada* (Montreal and Kingston: McGill-Queen's University Press, 1997 [1971]), p.438; and Williams, *Road to Now*, p.105.

14  See Alfie Roberts, *A View for Freedom: Alfie Roberts Speaks on the Caribbean, Cricket, Montreal, and C.L.R. James* (Montreal: Alfie Roberts Institute, 2005), pp.58, 62; see also Kari Levitt, "The Montreal New World Group," unpublished paper, Montreal. For a general account of New World's activities, see Denis Benn, *The Caribbean: An Intellectual History, 1774–2003* (Kingston and Miami: Ian Randle Publishers, 2004), pp.122–51.

15  Edward Said, *Representations of the Intellectual* (New York: Vintage Books, 1996), p.62.

16  Roberts, *View for Freedom*, p.76. Guests included George Lamming, C.L.R. James, Jan Carew, Norman Girvan, Austin Clarke, Orlando Patterson, Lloyd Best, Richard B. Moore, M.G. Smith, and calypso singer The Mighty Sparrow.

17  George Lamming, "West Indian People," *New World*, 2, 2 (1966), p.63. This edition of *New World* also includes a resumé of the October 1965 conference. Publications include: *Caribbean Symposium: The West Indian Nation in Exile*, Oct. 6-8, 1967; *Caribbean Conference Bulletin*, 1,2 (September 1967); and *Caribbean Conference*, October 1967, Alfie Roberts Papers, Alfie Roberts Institute; *Caribbean International Opinion: The Dynamics of Liberation* (October 1968). CCC members also published in *Speak Out*, Facing Reality's weekly paper, and circulated several unpublished documents that they wrote.

18  Robert Hill to Franklyn Harvey, Jan. 11, 1970, Alfie Roberts Papers, Alfie Roberts Institute. For James's opinion on *Notes on Dialectics*, see C.L.R. James, "Interview," in *C.L.R. James: His Life and Work*, ed. Paul Buhle (London: Allison and Busby, 1986), p.164.

19  Isserman, *If I Had a Hammer*, p.xvi.

20  See Kevin B. Anderson, "The Rediscovery and Persistence of the Dialectic in Philosophy and in World Politics," in *Lenin Reloaded: Towards a Politics of Truth*, ed. Sebastian Budgen, Stathis Kouvelakis, and Slavoj Žižek (Durham, N.C., and London: Duke University Press, 2007), p.137.

21  C.L.R. James, *Notes on Dialectics* (Detroit: 1966), p.96 (emphasis in original).

22  Antillean [Alfie Roberts], "On Guevara's Message to the People of the World," *Speak Out*, 16 (November 1967).

23  Alfie Roberts to Martin Glaberman, April 21, 1967; and Alfie Roberts to *Monthly Review*, April 24, 1967.

24  Tim Hector to Alfie Roberts, July 1966, 1, 2, Alfie Roberts Papers, Alfie Roberts Institute (emphasis in original).

25  Lenin in Hector to Roberts, p.2 (emphasis in original).

26  Hector does not deny that much of the talent required for the reconstruction of Cuba was to be found among the communists. But, as he asserts, "Against the Cuban Revolutionary masses and their independent institutions, the Cuban Communist Party would have been reduced to the shambles and hoax it really is." Hector to Roberts, p.4.

27  Tim Hector, "My Grandmother in Time and Place and Luck," Fan the Flame, *Outlet*, Aug. 30, 2002.

28 Tim Hector, "Vietnam: The Struggle Against Imperialism," *Caribbean International Opinion*, October 1968, p.57. Che Guevara was also critical of the Soviet unwillingness to throw the weight of its support behind the Vietnamese struggle and embrace Vietnam into the socialist fold. See Guevara, *On Vietnam and World Revolution* (New York: Merit Publishers, 1967), p.6.

29 Herbert Aptheker, *Mission to Hanoi* (New York: International Publishers, 1966), p.91; Hector, "Vietnam: The Struggle Against Imperialism," p.57.

30 Aptheker, *Mission to Hanoi*, pp.21–26; and Hector, "Vietnam: The Struggle Against Imperialism," p.57.

31 Hector, "Vietnam: The Struggle Against Imperialism," p.57.

32 Gareth Porter, *Vietnam: The Politics of Bureaucratic Socialism* (Ithaca, N.Y: Cornell University Press, 1993).

33 Hector, "Vietnam: The Struggle Against Imperialism," pp.57–59.

34 Ibid., p.59.

35 Martin Glaberman to Alfie Roberts, May 4, 1967, Alfie Roberts Papers, Alfie Roberts Institute.

36 Kurlansky, *1968*, p.236.

37 See Kristin Ross, who in *May '68 and Its Afterlives* challenges attempts to situate the events within a historical trajectory that begins with opposition to the French Communist Party and the organized labour movement in 1968, and ends with the collapse of the Soviet Bloc. Ross, *May '68 and Its Afterlives* (Chicago: University of Chicago Press, 2002), p.20.

38 Daniel and Gabriel Cohn-Bendit, *Obsolete Communism: The Left-Wing Alternative* (Edinburgh, London, and San Francisco: AK Press, 2000 [1968]), p.18.

39 Ibid., p.20.

40 Grace C. Lee, Pierre Chaulieu, and J.R. Johnson (C.L.R. James), *Facing Reality* (Detroit: Facing Reality, 1958), pp.67, 107.

41 Franklyn Harvey, "French Revolution '68," *Caribbean International Opinion*, October 1968, p.20.

42 Ibid., pp.21–22, 23.

43 See Keith Reader, *Regis Debray: A Critical Introduction* (London: Pluto Press, 1995),

p.2; and Robert Young, *White Mythologies: Writing History and the West* (London: Routledge, 1990), p.48.

44 Reader, *Regis Debray*, p.2.

45 Anon., "The Structure of Capital," *Times Literary Supplement*, Dec. 15, 1966, p.1162.

46 Louis Althusser, "Contradiction and Overdetermination," *New Left Review*, 41 (January-February 1967), p.18.

47 C.L.R. James to Martin Glaberman, Feb. 27, 1967, Glaberman Collection, pp.8–7.

48 Martin Glaberman, *Mao as a Dialectician* (Detroit: Bewick/ed, 1971).

49 Raya Dunayevskaya letter to Alfie Roberts, Jan. 29, 1968, p.1; and Alfie Roberts to Raya Dunayevskaya, Feb. 9, 1968, Alfie Roberts Papers, Alfie Roberts Institute. See also Raya Dunayevskaya, *Philosophy and Revolution: From Hegel to Sartre and from Marx to Mao* (Atlantic Highlands, N.J.: Humanities Press 1982 [1973]), p.257.

50 C.L.R. James, cited in Robert Hill, "Draft of Article on L. Althusser (based mainly upon reading his "On Contradiction" in *New Left Review* of January-February, 1967)," n.d., unpublished, p.10, Alfie Roberts Papers, Alfie Roberts Institute.

51 Hill, "Draft of Article on L. Althusser," p.10.

52 Athusser, p.34, cited in Hill, "Draft of Article on L. Althusser," p.9.

53 James, *Notes on Dialectics*, p.72.

54 James, in Hill, "Draft of Article on L. Althusser," p.11.

55 Meeks, *Radical Caribbean*, pp.1–2.

## 38 Mexico's Rock Counterculture (La Onda) in Historical Perspective and Memory
ERIC ZOLOV

Certain ideas and passages in this essay are drawn from a previously published, co-authored chapter by Deborah Pacini Hernandez, Héctor Fernández L'Hoeste, and Eric Zolov, "Mapping Rock Music Cultures across the Americas," in *Rockin' Las Américas: The Global Politics of Rock in Latin/o America*, ed. Deborah Pacini Hernandez, Héctor Fernández L'Hoeste, and Eric Zolov (Pittsburgh: University of Pittsburgh Press, 2004).

1 Abril Trigo, "The Politics and Anti-Politics of Uruguayan Rock," in *Rockin' Las Américas*, ed. Pacini Hernandez, Fernández L'Hoeste, and Zolov, p.119.

2 Eric Zolov, "Expanding Our Conceptual Horizons: The Shift from an Old to a New Left in Latin America," *A Contracorriente: A Journal of Social History and Literature in Latin America*, Spring 2008, pp.47–73.

3 Gilbert Joseph, "What We Now Know and Should Know: Bringing Latin America More Meaningfully into Cold War Studies," in *In from the Cold: Latin America's New Encounter with the Cold War*, ed. Gilbert Joseph and Daniela Spenser (Durham, N.C.: Duke University Press, 2007), p.23.

4 Deborah Pacini Hernandez and Reebee Garofalo, "Between Rock and a Hard Place: Negotiating Rock in Revolutionary Cuba, 1960–1980," in *Rockin' Las Américas*, ed. Pacini Hernandez, Fernández L'Hoeste, and Zolov, p.54.

5 Julia Palacios and Tere Estrada, "'A contra corriente': A History of Women Rockers in Mexico," in *Rockin' Las Américas*, ed. Pacini Hernandez, Fernandez L'Hoeste, and Zolov, p.150.

### 39 Continuing On: Deepening the Anti-Nuclear Movement since the Sixties
JIM HARDING

1 Deep psycho-cultural changes occurring in the 1950s laid the basis for the 1960s counterculture. See Barbara Ehrenreich, *The Hearts of Men: American Dreams and the Flight from Commitment* (Garden City, N.Y.: Anchor Books, 1983). This background and sixties activism is discussed in James Pitsula, *New World Dawning: The Sixties at Regina Campus* (Regina: Canadian Plains Research Centre, 2008); see my review of this title in *Topia-Canadian Journal of Cultural Studies*, Spring 2009.

2 Daniel Ellsberg, "Call to Mutiny," in *Protest and Survive*, ed. E.P. Thompson and Dan Smith (London: Monthly Review Press, 1981), p.i. This book helped jumpstart the trans-Atlantic anti-nuclear peace movement in the 1980s.

3 This polarizing mentality was resurrected in George W. Bush's "War on Terror" after 9/11.

4 Ellsberg, "Call to Mutiny," p.xv.

5 It was during this frightening and desperate time that many new left formations became more militantly anti-imperialist and abandoned the remnants of nonviolence inherited from the earlier peace movement.

6 Some of this early anti-nuclear history is discussed in Ronald Babin, "Origins of Antinuclear Protest," in Babin, *The Nuclear Power Game* (Montreal: Black Rose, 1985), pp.141–48. The Voice of Women (VOW) is often ignored as one precursor to the later feminist movement and its rejection of patriarchal violence.

7 This question polarized the left-leaning Co-operative Commonwealth Federation (CCF)–New Democratic Party (NDP), but the establishment stayed loyal to Cold War institutions. Pro-NATO British Labour leader Hugh Gaitskell was even brought in as keynote speaker at the founding convention of the NDP in Ottawa in 1961. When those of us who were delegates with involvement in the CND tried to protest his appearance we were strong-armed out of the Ottawa arena.

8 See Fred Knelman, *Nuclear Energy: The Unforgiving Technology* (Edmonton, Alta.: Hurtig, 1976), ch.3.

9 At the largest demonstration, of several thousand, in 1969, several hundred of us broke off from the general protest and blockaded the U.S.–Canada border as a protest of U.S. weapons testing and military intervention in Vietnam.

10 See CCNR website and Jim Harding, *Canada's Deadly Secret: Saskatchewan Uranium and the Global Nuclear System* (Halifax, N.S.: Fernwood Publishing, 2007), ch.18, for more background on the weapons connection.

11 In 1972 the Nuclear Energy Agency (NEA) predicted that by 1990 there would be 1,000 gigawatts (GW) of nuclear electricity globally. The actual capacity in 1990 was 260 GW. See Harding, *Canada's Deadly Secret*, p.207. Today's 439 nuclear reactors have a 372 GW capacity and produce

only 14 per cent of the world's electricity. Even with talk of a nuclear renaissance, the IAEA projects only between 447 and 679 GW over the next decades.

12 See Jim Harding, "Saskatchewan's Critical Choice: Nuclear Power Is Dirty, Dangerous and It Won't Solve Global Warming Either," *Straight Goods*, Jan. 17, 2008.

13 The dangers of Nuclear Winter became more widely known with the publication of Jonathan Schell, *The Fate of The Earth* (New York: Alfred A. Knopf, 1982).

14 Gregory N. Calvert, "Democratic Idealism: SDS and the Gospel of Participatory Democracy," in *The New Left: Legacy and Continuity*, ed. Dimitrios Roussopoulos (Montreal: Black Rose, 2007), p.122. A pamphlet located in the archives of past Saskatchewan premier Woodrow Lloyd, which was mailed widely to supporting study groups soon after the CCF was elected in 1944, confirms that this generation of social democrats enthusiastically supported "atomic power." The pamphlet, which has no language about "environment" or "ecology," sees atomic science as liberating workers from capitalism by creating an abundance of energy.

15 See, for example, the work of French writer André Gorz and U.S. writer Joel Kovel. I have attempted a left green synthesis in the Canadian context.

16 It was during this period that the United States began to envision policies that we have come to know as part of "globalization." See John Ralston Saul, *The Collapse of Globalism: and the Reinvention of the World* (Toronto: Viking, 2005).

17 U.S.-supported counter-insurgency intensified after the 1958 overthrow of the Batista regime in Cuba by the Castro-led Revolution, and was shown most blatantly with Augusto Pinochet's overthrow of Salvador Allende in Chile in 1973. After this coup some new leftists joined authoritarian Marxist-Leninist groups.

18 We are all indebted to Petra Kelly. See Sara Parkin, *The Life and Death of Petra Kelly* (London: Pandora, 1994).

19 Accordingly, the parties undertook "to pursue negotiations in good faith on effective measures relating to cessation

of the nuclear arms race at an early date and to nuclear disarmament, and on a treaty on general and complete disarmament under strict and effective international control." Israel, India, and Pakistan did not sign on to the original NPT or to its extension.

20 The Preamble states, "The cessation of all nuclear weapons test explosions and all other nuclear explosions, by constraining the development and qualitative improvement of nuclear weapons and ending the development of advanced new types of nuclear weapons, constitutes an effective measure of nuclear disarmament and non-proliferation in all its aspects." See Helen Caldicott, *The New Nuclear Danger* (New York: New Press, 2002), pp.43–44.

21 Caldicott, *New Nuclear Danger*, p.44.

22 It remains to be seen whether the administration of Barack Obama wants to and can fundamentally alter this. There are some encouraging signs. See Ernie Regehr, "Obama on Nuclear Disarmament," *The Ploughhares Monitor*, Winter 2008, pp.17–19.

23 See Jim Harding, *After Iraq: War, Imperialism and Democracy* (Halifax, N.S.: Fernwood Publishing, 2004), p.36.

24 See Harding, *Canada's Deadly Secret*, ch.6.

25 Robert Burns, "US Considered Radiological Weapon," reprinted in *Common Dreams* from Associated Press, Oct. 9, 2007.

26 My activist credo has become "There is no positive peace without distributive justice and no such justice without preserving ecology."

27 In the highly polarized and charged period you might be considered a "CIA agent" if you protested Soviet tests, and a "KGB agent" if you protested U.S. tests.

28 See Jim Harding, "Forbidden Journey: Barred from the USA," *CAUT Bulletin*, June 1987, pp.17–18.

29 This tendency, which I supported in Canada, saw participatory democracy developing in the process of revolutionizing society, and was in opposition to those who formed the Red Army faction in the German SDS.

30 At the time King was becoming more vocal in his criticism of U.S. foreign policy and Kennedy was reaching out to a broad-based coalition of the marginalized. Earlier, in 1965, Malcolm X was assassinated soon after he renounced the Black Muslim ideology and began to embrace human rights.

31 See Harding, *Canada's Deadly Secret*.

32 I spent a week in Berlin studying the dismantling of the East German legal system. See Jim Harding, "Test the West: The Social and Legal Crisis in Germany since Unification," *Prairie Justice Research*, University of Regina, January 1994.

33 See Muge Gursoy Sokmen, ed., *World Tribunal on Iraq: Making the Case against War* (Northampton, Ill: Olive Branch Press, 2008).

34 After I returned from working in the U.S. civil rights movement, and SUPA was formed, I worked with mentor and Métis leader Malcolm Norris to initiate the Student Neestow Partnership Project (SNPP). This brought activist students from across Canada into Indian and Métis communities in Saskatchewan, and helped link the struggle for Aboriginal self-determination into new left understanding and practice.

35 Student syndicalism, coming from France via Quebec, also had some influence on how students self-organized across Canada, including in the Canadian Union of Students (CUS).

36 I was a federal candidate for the NDP in Saskatoon in 1964, was president of the Saskatchewan New Democratic Youth and on the Federal NDP Council in 1965, but quit the party over its Cold war policies.

37 Robert Engler, *The Politics of Oil* (New York: Macmillan, 1961).

38 Jim Harding, "The Doctrine of Humanitarian Intervention and the Neo-Colonial Implications of Its Revival in a Unipolar World," in Sokmen, *World Tribunal on Iraq*, p.57.

39 See Jim Harding, *Student Power and National Liberation: Essays on the 'New Left' Revolt in Canada—1964–74* (Fort Qu'Appelle, Sask.: Crows Nest Publishing, 2006).

## 40 "Tear It Down": Reflections of a Veteran
JAIME VEVE

1 Frantz Fanon, *The Wretched of the Earth* (New York: Grove Press, 1968), p.206.

## 41 Across the Universe: Rethinking Narratives of Second-Wave Feminism
ALICE ECHOLS

1 Amy Kesselman, with Heather Booth, Vivian Rothstein, and Naomi Weisstein, "Our Gang of Four: Friendship and Women's Liberation," in *The Feminist Memoir Project: Voices from Women's Liberation*, ed. Rachel Blau DuPlessis and Ann Snitow (New York: Three Rivers Press, 1998), p.39.

2 Christine Stansell makes this argument in her forthcoming book, *The Feminist Promise* (New York: Random House, 2010).

3 Robin Morgan, "Goodbye to All That," was originally published in *Rat*, January 1970, and has since appeared in anthologies of radical feminist writing, including Morgan, *The Word of a Woman: Feminist Dispatches, 1968–1992* (New York: W.W. Norton, 1994).

4 Toni Morrison, "What the Black Woman Thinks about Women's Lib," reprinted in *Public Women, Public Words: A Documentary History of American Feminism*, ed. Dawn Keetley and John Pettegrew (New York: Rowman & Littlefield, 2005), p.76. This essay was originally published in *The New York Times Magazine*, Aug. 22, 1971.

5 Wini Breines, *The Trouble Between Us: An Uneasy History of White and Black Women in the Feminist Movement* (New York: Oxford University Press, 2006).

6 Ruth Feldsein, "'I Don't Trust You Anymore': Nina Simone, Culture, and Black Activism in the 1960s," *Journal of American History*, 91,4 (March 2005).

7 Susan M. Hartmann, *The Other Feminists: Activists in the Liberal Establishment* (New Haven, Conn.: Yale University Press, 1998).

8 Benita Roth, *Separate Roads to Feminism: Black, Chicana, and White Feminist Movements in America's Second Wave* (Cambridge: Cambridge University Press, 2004).

## 42 Engaging the Past and Mapping the Future: Nuclear Weapons and Self-Determination—from Diego Garcia and Cuba to Iraq and Iran
CARY FRASER

1 Cited in Frank Myers, "Harold Macmillan's 'Winds of Change' Speech: A Case Study in the Rhetoric of Policy Change," *Rhetoric & Public Affairs*, 3,4 (2000), pp.555–75.

2 United Nations, General Assembly Resolution 1541 (XV), 1960, New York.

3 "50 Killed in South Africa as Police Fire on Rioters, *The New York Times*, March 22, 1960; for the political context of South Africa in 1960, see Robert Kinloch Massie, *Loosing the Bonds: The United States and South Africa in the Apartheid Years* (New York: Doubleday, 1997), pp.55–94.

4 See Alistair Horne, *A Savage War of Peace: Algeria 1954–1962* (New York: Penguin, 1987), pp.330–435.

5 Neil Tweedle, "Britain Shamed as Exiles of the Chagos Islands Win the Right to Go Home," *The Daily Telegraph* (London), May 12, 2006 <www.telegraph.co.uk>; "The Chagos Islands: A Sordid Tale," *BBC News*, Nov. 3, 2000 <news.bbc.co.uk>; and Marjorie Miller, "Britain Illegally Expelled Chagos Islanders for U.S. Base, Court Rules," *Los Angeles Times*, Nov. 4, 2000.

6 Clive Stafford Smith, "A Shameful Anniversary," *The Guardian* (London), Jan. 11, 2007 <commentisfree.guardian.co.uk>.

7 See Morris H. Morley, *Imperial State and Revolution: The United States and Cuba, 1952–1986* (New York: Cambridge University Press, 1987).

8 Fidel Castro, "The Revolution Begins Now," speech, Jan. 3, 1959, Cospedes Park, Santiago de Cuba, online version, Castro Internet Archive (marxists.org) 2002: "... in the four centuries since our country was founded, this will be the first time that we are entirely free and that the work of the first settlers will have been completed."

9 See Fidel Castro, "The Problem of Cuba and Its Revolutionary Policy," address to the United Nations General Assembly, New York, Sept. 26, 1960: "We are, therefore, on the side of the Algerian people, as we are on the [side of the] remaining colonial peoples in Africa, and on the side of the Negroes who are discriminated against in the Union of South Africa."

10 See Raymond L. Garthoff, *Reflections on the Cuban Missile Crisis* (Washington, D.C.: Brookings Institution, 1989).

11 Hani Mowafi and Paul Spiegel, "The Iraqi Refugee Crisis: Familiar Problems and New Challenges," *Journal of the American Medical Association*, 299,14 (April 2008), pp.1713–15.

12 See Robert Burns, "US-Iraq Talks to Start Saturday," *Washington Post*, March 8, 2008, for an outline of U.S. goals. In negotiating the end of the U.S. occupation of Cuba, the Cuban government was constrained to include the Platt Amendment guaranteeing U.S. intervention in Cuba and the rights to the Guantánamo naval base.

13 See Cary Fraser, "Understanding American Policy towards the Decolonization of European Empires, 1945–64," *Diplomacy and Statecraft*, 3,1 (1992), pp.105–25.

14 The Anglo-U.S. occupation of Iraq and the NATO military presence in Afghanistan offer striking similarities with the assessment by Robinson and Gallagher of the British occupation of Egypt: "The British expedition was intended to restore a stable Egyptian government under the ostensible rule of the Khedive and inside the orbit of informal British influence. When this was achieved, the army, it was intended, should be withdrawn. But the expedition had so crushed the structure of Egyptian rule that no power short of direct British force could make it a viable and trustworthy instrument of informal hegemony and development.... The perverse effect of British policy was gloomily summed up by Gladstone: 'We have done our Egyptian business and we are an Egyptian government.'" See John Gallagher and Ronald Robinson, "The Imperialism of Free Trade," in *Imperialism: The Robinson and Gallagher Controversy*, ed. and with an Introduction by Wm. Roger Louis (New York: New Viewpoints, 1976), pp.53–72.

15 For an account of Iran's strategy in dealing with the major powers, see M.K.

Bhadrakumar, "Energized Iran Builds More Bridges," *Asia Times Online*, May 6, 2008 <www.atimes.com>.

16 The search for a negotiated solution to the impasse over Iran's nuclear programs has been conducted in the shadow of the United Nations. See William Luers, Thomas R. Pickering, and Jim Walsh, "A Solution for the US-Iran Nuclear Stand-off," *The New York Review of Books*, 55,4 (March 2008).

17 Linus Pauling, "Science and Peace," Nobel Lecture, Dec. 11, 1963 <nobelprize.org/>.

18 From "Only Then Shall We Find Courage," interview with Michael Amrine, *The New York Times Magazine*, June 23, 1946, cited by Pauling, "Science and Peace."

## Epilogue   Third World Possibilities and Problematics: Historical Connections and Critical Frameworks
TINA MAI CHEN

1 Robert J.C. Young, *Postcolonialism: An Historical Introduction* (Oxford: Blackwell Publishing, 2001), pp.6–7; Kofi Buenor Hadjor, *Dictionary of Third World Terms* (London: I.B. Tauris and Co., 1993).

2 "New World Coming: The Sixties and the Shaping of Global Consciousness, Call for Papers" <www.queensu.ca/history/News/CallForPapersEng.htm> (accessed July 18, 2008).

3 See the special issue of *Inter-Asian Cultural Studies* (December 2005) on Bandung and Third Worldism. The conference held in Bandung, Indonesia, in April 1955 brought together twenty-nine newly independent Afro-Asian nations in an attempt to distance themselves from superpower rivalry. Also, on Bandung and the Third World, see Vijay Prashad, *Darker Nations: History of the Third World* (New York: New Press, 2008), p.4.

4 See, for example, Harry Harootunian and Naoki Sakai, "Japan Studies and Cultural Studies," *Positions: East Asia Cultures Critique*, 7,1 (1999), pp.593–647.

5 Globality, in this instance, refers to the multiple global processes, imaginaries, and ways of "thinking the globe" operating at a given moment for particular persons, regions, and knowledge paradigms.

6 Albert Sauvy, "Trois mondes, Une planète," *L'Observateur*, 18 (Aug. 14, 1952), p.14. Translation: "Yet even aside from all questions of human solidarity the shining brilliance of the First World perhaps cannot remain indifferent to this slow yet irresistible, this humble but still ferocious, impulse towards life. For finally this ignored, exploited, and despised Third World—like the Third Estate—wishes to be something." (Trans. Henry Heller.)

7 Arif Dirlik, "Performing the World: Reality and Representation in the Making of World Histor(ies)," *Journal of World History*, 16,4 (2005).

8 Joyce Appleby, Lynn Hunt, and Margaret Jacob, *Telling the Truth about History* (New York: W.W. Norton & Company, 1994).

9 Dean C. Tipps, "Modernization Theory and the Comparative Study of Societies: A Critical Perspective," *Comparative Studies in Society and History*, 15,2 (March 1973), p.204.

10 Mike Davis, *Late Victorian Holocausts: El Niño Famines and the Making of the Third World* (London: Verso, 2001); Michael Adas, *Dominance by Design: Technological Imperatives and America's Civilizing Mission* (Cambridge, Mass.: Harvard University Press, 2006).

11 For example, Richard Peet with Elaine Hartwick, *Theories of Development* (New York: Guilford Press, 1999); Susanne Schech and Jane Haggis, *Culture and Development: A Critical Introduction* (Oxford: Blackwell Publishing, 2000).

12 Nils Gilman, *Mandarins of the Future: Modernization Theory in Cold War America* (Baltimore: Johns Hopkins University, 2007).

13 Jeremy Suri, *The Global Revolutions of 1968* (New York and London: W.W. Norton & Company, 2007), p.xiii.

14 Robert Malley, "The Third Worldist Movement," *Current History*, November 1999, p.361.

15 For example, see Robeson Taj. P. Frazier, "The Congress of African People: Baraka, Brother Mao, and the Year of '74," *Souls: A Critical Journal of Black Politics, Culture, and Society*, 8,3 (2006), pp.142–59.

16  See the critical commentary of Daniel A. Segal, "'Western Civ' and the Staging of History in American Higher Education," *The American Historical Review*, 105,3 (June 2000); also Li Anshan, "African Studies in China in the Twentieth Century: A Historiographical Survey," *African Studies Review*, 48,1 (April 2005), pp.59–87; and Luo Xu, "Reconstructing World History in the People's Republic of China since the 1980s," *Journal of World History*, 18,3 (2007), pp.325–50.

17  In addition to this volume, see Cheng Yinghong, "Sino-Cuban Relations during the Early Years of the Castro Regime, 1959–1965," *Journal of Cold War Studies*, 9,3 (Summer 2007), pp.78–114.

18  Rebecca Karl, *Staging the World: Chinese Nationalism at the Turn of the Twentieth Century* (Durham, N.C.: Duke University Press, 2002), p.56.

19  Ibid., pp.170–72.

20  Partha Chatterjee discusses these issues in terms of the notion of colonial exception and the interconnection between the normative nature of nation-state, Bandung, and Third World. See Chatterjee, *Nationalist Thought and the Colonial World: A Derivative Discourse* (Minneapolis: University of Minnesota Press, 1993).

21  See the special issue of *Inter-Asian Cultural Studies* (December 2005) on Bandung and Third Worldism, including Hee-Yeon Cho, "'Second Death,' or Revival of the 'Third World' in the Context of Neoliberal Globalization," *Inter-Asia Cultural Studies*, 6,4 (December 2005).

22  Chatterjee, *Nationalist Thought and the Colonial World.*

23  Consider Gauri Viswanathan, "Ireland, India, and the Poetics of Internationalism," *Journal of World History*, 15,1 (March 2004).

# SELECTED BIBLIOGRAPHY

Adams, Howard. *Prison of Grass: Canada from a Native Point of View*. Calgary: Fifth House Publishers, 1975.

Ahmad, Muhammad. *We Will Return in the Whirlwind: Black Radical Organizations 1960–1975*. Chicago: Charles Kerr Publishers, 2007.

Ali, Tariq and Watkins, Susan. *1968: Marching in the Streets*. New York: Free Press, 1998.

Berger, Dan. *Outlaws of America: The Weather Underground and the Politics of Solidarity*. Oakland, Cal.: AK Press, 2006.

Berrain, Albert H. and Richard A. Long, eds. *Negritude: Essays and Studies*. Hampton, Va.: Hampton University Press, 1967.

Berrigan, Daniel. *Night Flight to Hanoi: War Diary with 11 Poems*. New York: Macmillan Company, 1968.

Billingsley, William J. *Communists on Campus: Race, Politics, and the Public University in Sixties North Carolina*. Athens: University of Georgia Press, 1999.

Braunstein, Peter and Michael William Doyle. *Imagine Nation: The American Counterculture of the 1960s and '70s*. New York: Routledge, 2002.

Carson, Rachel. *Silent Spring*. New York: Houghton Mifflin Harcourt, 1962.

Cavallo, Dominick. *Fiction of the Past: The Sixties in American History*. New York: Palgrave, 1999.

Chomsky, Noam. "A Special Supplement: In North Vietnam." *The New York Review of Books*, 15, 3 (Aug. 13, 1970).

Cleaver, Eldridge. *Soul on Ice*. New York: Delta Trade Paperbacks, 1992.

Commoner, Barry. *Science and Survival*. New York: Viking Press, 1966.

Cox, Craig. *Storefront Revolution: Food Co-Ops and the Counterculture*. Piscataway, N.J.: Rutgers University Press, 1994.

Curtis, Helene and Mimi Sanderson, eds. *The Unsung Sixties: Memoirs of Social Innovation*. London: Whiting and Birch 2006.

Cushing, Lincoln. *Revolución! Cuban Poster Art*. San Francisco: Chronicle Books, 2003.

Davis, Belinda, Martin Klimke, Carla MacDougall, and Wilfried Mausbach, eds. *Changing the World, Changing Oneself: Political Protest and Collective Identities in the 1960s/70s West Germany and U.S.* New York/Oxford: Berghahn Books, forthcoming, 2009.

De Beauvoir, Simone and Halimi, Giselle. *Djamila Boupacha*. London: Cox and Wyman, 1962.

Debray, Régis. *Revolution in the Revolution? Armed Struggle and Political Struggle in Latin America*. Trans. Bobbye Ortis. New York: Monthly Review Press, 1968.

DeGroot, Gerard J., ed. *Student Protest: The Sixties and After*. New York: Wesley Longman, 1998.

Deloria Jr., Vine. *Custer Died for Your Sins: An Indian Manifesto*. New York: Macmillan, 1969.

DuPlessis, Rachel Blau and Ann Snitow, eds. *The Feminist Memoir Project: Voices from Women's Liberation*. New York: Three Rivers Press, 1998.

Duran, Eduardo, Bonnie Duran, Maria Yellow Horse Brave Heart, and Sandra Yellow Horse-Davis. "Healing the American Indian Soul Wound," in *International Handbook of Multigenerational Legacies of Trauma*, ed. Yael Danieli. New York: Plenum Press, 1998.

Echols, Alice. *Shaky Ground: The Sixties and Its Aftershocks*. New York: Columbia University Press, 2002.

----------. *Daring to Be Bad: Radical Feminism in America 1967–1975*. Minneapolis: University of Minnesota Press, 1989.

Egan, Michael. *Barry Commoner and the Science of Survival: The Remaking of American Environmentalism*. Cambridge, Mass.: MIT Press, 2007.

Elbaum, Max. *Revolution in the Air: Sixties Radicals Turn to Lenin, Mao and Che*. London: Verso, 2002.

Enke, Anne. *Finding the Movement: Sexuality, Contested Space, and Feminist Activism*. Durham, N.C. and London: Duke University Press, 2007.

Erdberg, Lisa and Passerini, Luisa. *Autobiography of a Generation: Italy*. Hanover, N.H.: Wesleyan University Press, 1968.

Evans, Sara. *Personal Politics: The Roots of Women's Liberation in the Civil Rights Movement and the New Left*. New York: Alfred A. Knopf, 1979.

Fanon, Frantz. *The Wretched of the Earth*. Preface by Jean-Paul Sartre, trans. Constance Farrington. New York: Grove Press, 1968. Originally published as *Les damnés de la terre* by François Maspéro éditeur, 1961.

Farber, David., ed. *The 60s: From Memory to History*. Chapel Hill: University of North Carolina Press, 1994.

Foucault, Michel. *Madness and Civilization: A History of Insanity in the Age of Reason*. New York: Pantheon Books, 1965.

Frazier, L.J. and Cohen, D. *Gender and Sexuality in 1968: Transformative Politics in the Cultural Imagination*. Houndsmill, Basingstoke, Eng.: Palgrave Macmillan, forthcoming 2009.

Friedan, Betty. *The Feminine Mystique*. New York: W.W. Norton, 1997.

Freire, Paulo. *Pedagogy of the Oppressed*. New York: Seabury Press, 1970.

Gaines, Kevin. *American Africans in Ghana: Black Expatriates and the Civil Rights Era*. Chapel Hill: University of North Carolina Press, 2006.

Galeano, Eduardo. *Open Veins of Latin America: Five Centuries of the Pillage of a Continent*. New York: Monthly Review Press, 1973.

Georgakas, Dan and Surkin. Marvin. *Detroit, I Do Mind Dying*. Boston: South End Press, 1998.

Gerd-Rainer Horn. *The Spirit of '68: Rebellion in Western Europe and North America, 1956–1976*. Oxford: Oxford University Press, 2007.

Gitlin, Todd. *The Whole World Is Watching: Mass Media in the Making and Unmaking of the New Left*. Berkeley: University of California Press, 1980.

---------. *The Sixties: Years of Hope, Days of Rage*. Toronto: Bantam, 1987.

Gosse, Van. *Rethinking the New Left: An Interpretive History*. New York: Palgrave Macmillan, 2005.

Grandin, Greg. *The Last Colonial Massacre: Latin America in the Cold War*. Chicago: University of Chicago Press, 2004.

Heale, M.J. *The Sixties in America: History, Politics and Protest*. Fitzroy, Scotland: Edinburgh University Press, 2001.

Hewison, Robert. *Too Much: Art and Society in the Sixties, 1960–1975*. London: Methuen London, 1986.

Iacovetta, Franca. "Recipes for Democracy? Gender, Family, and Making Female Citizens in Cold War Canada," in *Moral Regulation and Governance in Canada*, ed. Amanda Glasbeek. Toronto: Canadian Scholars Press, 2006.

Igarashi, Yoshikuni. *Bodies of Memory: Narratives of War in Postwar Japanese Culture, 1945–1970*. Princeton, N.J.: Princeton University Press, 2000.

Isserman, Maurica and Michael Kazin. *America Divided: The Civil War of the 1960s*. New York: Oxford University Press, 2000.

Ivens, Joris. *The Camera and I*. New York: International Publishers, 1969.

Jameson, Fredric. "Periodizing the 60s," in Jameson, *The Ideologies of Theory: Essays, 1971–1986*. Minneapolis: University of Minnesota Press, 1988.

Joseph, Peniel E. *Waiting 'Til the Midnight Hour: A Narrative History of Black Power in America*. New York: Henry Holt, 2006.

Katsiaficas, George. *The Imagination of the New Left: A Global Analysis of 1968*. Boston: South End Press, 1987.

Kelley, Robin D.G. *Freedom Dreams: The Black Radical Imagination*. Boston: Beacon Press, 2002.

Khaled, Leila and George Hajjar, eds. *My People Shall Live: The Autobiography of a Revolutionary*. London: Hodder and Stoughton, 1975.

Klatch, R.E. *A Generation Divided: The New Left, the New Right and the 1960s*. Berkeley: University of California Press, 1999.

Kostash, Myrna. *Long Way from Home: The Story of the Sixties Generation*. Toronto: James Lorimer and Company, 1980.

Kurlansky, Mark. *1968: The Year That Rocked the World*. New York: Random House, 2005.

Laffan, Barry. *Communal Organization and Social Transition: A Case Study from the Counterculture of the Sixties and Seventies.* New York: Peter Lang, 1997.

Levitt, Kari. *Silent Surrender: The Multinational Corporation in Canada.* Toronto: Macmillan of Canada, 1970.

Marcuse, Herbert. *Essay on Liberation.* Boston: Beacon Press, 1969.

Marqusee, Mike. *Redemption Song: Muhammad Ali and the Spirit of the Sixties.* London/New York: Verso 2000.

Marwick, Arthur. *The Sixties: Cultural Revolution in Britain, France, Italy, and the United States, c.1958–c.1974.* New York: Oxford University Press, 1998.

McCarthy, Mary. *Hanoi.* New York: Harcourt, Brace and World, 1968.

McKay, Ian. *Rebels, Reds, Radicals: Rethinking Canada's Left History.* Toronto: Between the Lines, 2005.

Meeks, Brian. *Radical Caribbean: From Black Power to Abu Bakr.* Kingston, Jamaica: University of West Indies Press, 1996.

Meier, August and Elliott M. Rudwick. *Black Protest in the Sixties.* New York: Markus Wiener, 1991.

Miller, Timothy. *The 60s Communes: Hippies and Beyond.* Syracuse, N.Y.: Syracuse University Press, 1999.

Morgan, Robin, ed. *Sisterhood Is Powerful.* New York: Vintage, 1970.

Prashad, Vijay. *The Darker Nations: A People's History of the Third World.* New York: New Press, 2007.

Maracle, Lee. *Bobbi Lee: Indian Rebel.* Toronto: Women's Press, 1990.

Muñoz, Carlos, ed. *Youth, Identity, Power: The Sixties Chicano Movement.* New York/London: Verso, 2002.

Ogbar, Jeffrey O.G. *Black Power: Radical Politics and African American Identity.* Baltimore and London: Johns Hopkins University Press, 2004.

Perkins, Margo V. *Autobiography as Activism: Three Black Women of the Sixties.* Jackson: University Press of Mississippi, 2000.

Piotte, Jean-Marc. *La communauté perdue: petite histoire des militantismes.* Montreal: VLB, 1987.

Randall, Margaret. *Cuban Women Now.* Toronto: Woman's Press, 1974.

Rodney, Walter. *How Europe Underdeveloped Africa.* London and Dar-es-Salaam: Bogle-L'Ouverture Publications and Tanzania Publishing House, 1972.

Ross, Kristin. *May '68 and Its Afterlives.* Chicago and London: University of Chicago Press, 2002.

Rossinow, Doug. *The Politics of Authenticity: Liberalism, Christianity, and the New Left in America.* New York: Columbia University Press, 1998.

Rowbotham, Sheila. *Women, Resistance and Revolution.* New York: Pantheon Books, 1972.

----------. *Woman's Consciousness, Man's World.* New York: Penguin, 1973.

----------. *Promise of a Dream: Remembering the Sixties.* London: Verso, 2001.

Ryan, William. *Blaming the Victim.* New York: Vintage Books, 1972.

Saldaña-Portillo, Maria Josefina. *The Revolutionary Imagination and the Age of Development in the Americas.* Durham, N.C.: Duke University Press, 2003.

Smith, Patricia Juliana, ed. *The Queer Sixties.* New York: Routledge 1999.

Solanas, Fernando and Octavio Getino. "Towards a Third Cinema." In *Movies and Methods: An Anthology,* ed. Bill Nichols. Berkeley: University of California Press, 1976.

Solanas, Valerie. *SCUM Manifesto.* New York: Olympia Press, 1968.

Sontag, Susan. *Trip to Hanoi.* New York: Farrar, Straus and Giroux, 1968.

Springer, Kimberly. *Living for the Revolution: Black Feminist Organizations, 1968–1980.* Durham, N.C.: Duke University Press, 2005.

Stephens, Julie. *Anti-Disciplinary Protest: Sixties Radicalism and Postmodernism.* Cambridge: Cambridge University Press, 1998.

Suri, Jeremy. *Power and Protest: Global Revolution and the Rise of Detente.* Cambridge, Mass.: Harvard University Press, 2003.

----------. *The Global Revolutions of 1968.* New York and London: W.W. Norton and Company, 2007.

Wagner, Sally Roesch. *Sisters in Spirit: Haudenosaunee (Iroquois) Influence on Early American Feminists.* Summertown, Tenn.:

Native Voices Book Publishing Company, 2001.

_____. "The Iroquois Influence on Women's Rights," in *Indian Roots of American Democracy*, ed. José Barreiro. Ithaca, N.Y.: Akwe:kon Press, 1992.

Warren, Jean-Philippe. *Une douce anarchie: les années 68 au Québec*. Montreal: Boréal, 2008.

Young, Cynthia A. *Soul Power: Culture, Radicalism, and the Making of a U.S. Third World Left*. Chapel Hill: The University of North Carolina Press.

Young, Robert. *Postcolonialism: An Historical Introduction*. Oxford: Blackwell Publishing, 2001.

Zolov, Eric. *Refried Elvis: The Rise of the Mexican Counterculture*. Berkeley: University of California Press, 1999.

# CONTRIBUTORS

**Dr. Rabab Abdulhadi** was born and raised in the West Bank City of Nablus, Palestine, and joined the College of Ethnic Studies at San Francisco State University in January 2007. Her publications include newspaper, magazine, and scholarly articles in Arabic and English that take up questions of Palestinian feminisms, gender and exilic existence, racial and ethnic profiling post-9/11, social movements and social change, and the dynamics of race, class, nation, and citizenship as they interact with gender and sexuality. Her projects include "Cultures of Resistance and the 'Post-Colonial' State: Altering the Question of Palestine" and "Revising Narratives: Gender, Nation, and Resistance in Palestine" (working titles). Another work in progress focuses on "Carving Spaces, Building Communities: Palestinian Women's Activism in North America 1983–1995."

**Lillian Allen** teaches at the Ontario College of Art and Design, Toronto. Known internationally as a pioneer of dub poetry and a groundbreaker for women in the field, she is also recognized for her work and activism on issues of diversity in culture, cross-cultural learning, and the arts in education. She is a published author and playwright and a Juno Award winner for her albums of poetry set to music: *Revolutionary Tea Party* (1986) and *Conditions Critical* (1988).

**David Austin**, the co-founder of the Alfie Roberts Institute, Montreal, is the editor of *A View for Freedom: Alfie Roberts Speaks on the Caribbean, Cricket, Montreal, and C.L.R. James* (2005) and *You Don't Play with Revolution: The Montreal Lectures of C.L.R. James* (forthcoming). He has contributed to *Labour, Capital and Society*, *Small Axe*, *The Journal of African-American History*, and *Race and Class*; and he has completed documentaries for CBC-Radio's *Ideas* on the life and work of C.L.R. James (*C.L.R. James: The Black Jacobin*, 2005) and Frantz Fanon (*The*

*Wretched of the Earth*, 2006). His other work includes "The Unfinished Revolution: Linton Kwesi Johnson, Poetry, and the New Society" and "Liberation from Below: The Caribbean Conference Committee and the Making of the Caribbean Radical Tradition" (working title).

**Stefan Backius** is a Ph.D. student in History and works in the Centre of Urban and Regional Studies, Örebro University, Sweden. His thesis focuses on cultural activities in the Swedish industrialized area of Bergslagen, starting in the 1970s.

**Angela Bartie** is a Research Assistant at the University of Edinburgh (where she is working on a project on the policing of youth in postwar Britain) and a Research Fellow at the Scottish Oral History Centre, University of Strathclyde. She was awarded her Ph.D. from the University of Dundee in 2007 and plans to rework her dissertation, "Festival City: The Arts, Culture and Moral Conflict in Edinburgh, 1947–1967," into a book. She is writing an article on the "moral panic" over youth gangs in Glasgow in the 1960s, part of a larger study of the experiences of Scottish youth in that decade.

**Dan Berger** is the author of *Outlaws of America: The Weather Underground and the Politics of Solidarity* (2006), co-editor of *Letters from Young Activists: Today's Rebels Speak Out* (2005), and co-editor of *Seventies Confidential: Hidden Histories from the Sixties' Second Decade* (forthcoming). He is a Ph.D. candidate at the University of Pennsylvania's Annenberg School for Communication, where he is also earning a certificate in Africana Studies. His dissertation traces the political battles over crime and prison in 1970s United States.

**Julie Boddy**, based in Takoma Park, Md., is an independent social and cultural historian of the twentieth-century United States who has been on the staff of the Library of Congress since 1982; in recent years she has also served as an Observer at the United Nations Permanent Forum on Indigenous Issues. She has been involved as an activist in social justice, environmental, and health issues. Her research agenda explores the relationship of changing political economy and related technologies with cultural and personal agency.

**Lara Campbell** is an Assistant Professor of Women's Studies at Simon Fraser University, Burnaby, B.C. She is researching gender and sexual politics in the Vietnam draft resistance movement in Canada and completing a manuscript, "Respectable Citizens: Gender, Family, and Unemployment in the Great Depression, Ontario, 1929–1939."

**Tina Mai Chen** is Associate Professor of History and Co-coordinator of the Interdisciplinary Research Circle on Globalization and Cosmopolitanism at the University of Manitoba, Winnipeg. Her research centres around the intellectual and cultural history of twentieth-century China and its global reference points. Other major projects include examinations of Soviet film in Maoist China and migration of overseas Chinese between Burma, China, and India during the 1930s and 1940s.

**María Caridad Cumaná González** is a film critic and programmer who teaches Latin American Film at the University of Havana, where she is an Adjunct Professor in the Department of Art History. Her writing on Cuban and Latin American cinema has been published in film journals and anthologies. Her book *Latitudes del margen: El cine latinoamericano ante el tercer milenio*, co-written with Joel del Río, was awarded a special jury prize from the Fundación del Nuevo Cine Latinoamericano jointly with the Alcalá de Henares University (Spain). She has also been a member of juries at national and international film festivals, including the Regina Festival of Cinematic Arts.

**Lincoln Cushing** has been a printer, artist, librarian, archivist, and author. At the University of California at Berkeley he was the Cataloging and Electronic Outreach Librarian at Bancroft Library and the Electronic

Outreach Librarian at the Institute of Industrial Relations. He is involved in several projects to document, catalogue, and disseminate oppositional political culture of the late twentieth century. He is the author of *Revolucion! Cuban Poster Art* (2003), editor of *Visions of Peace and Justice: Over 30 Years of Political Posters from the Archives of Inkworks Press* (2007); author of *Chinese Posters: Art from the Great Proletarian Cultural Revolution* (2007); and co-author of *Agitate! Educate! Organize! American Labor Graphics* (forthcoming, 2009).

**Karen Dubinsky** is a Professor in Global Development Studies and the Department of History at Queen's University, Kingston, Ont. She is the author of *Improper Advances, Rape and Heterosexual Conflict in Ontario, 1880–1929* (1993), *The Second Greatest Disappointment: Honeymooning and Tourism at Niagara Falls* (1999), and a forthcoming book on the history of children and migration and adoption conflicts in Guatemala, Cuba, and Canada.

**Alice Echols** teaches at the University of Southern California, Los Angeles, and is the author of *Daring to Be Bad: Radical Feminism in America, 1967–75 (1989)*; *Scars of Sweet Paradise: The Life and Times of Janis Joplin* (1999); *Shaky Ground: The Sixties and Its Aftershocks* (2002); and *Upside Down: Disco and the Remaking of American Culture* (forthcoming, 2010).

**Michael Egan** is an Assistant Professor in the History Department at McMaster University, Hamilton, Ont. He is the author of *Barry Commoner and the Science of Survival: The Remaking of American Environmentalism* (2007).

**Sonia Enjamio Expósito** is an Assistant Professor in the School of Philosophy and History at the University of Havana in Cuba, with a degree in history. She specializes in studies of the Cuban Revolution from 1950 to 1975. She has published work on Gallegan immigration in Cuba for the la Junta de Galicia and the Universidad de Santiago de Compostela. She is a member of the Cátedra de Estudios Gallegos en Cuba and Cátedra de la Mujer de la Universidad de La Habana.

**Cary Fraser** teaches in History and African and African American Studies at Pennsylvania State University, University Park. He is a historian of international relations in the twentieth century and author of *Ambivalent Anti-Colonialism: The United States and the Genesis of West Indian Independence, 1943–1964* (1994). His essays have been published in Canada, the Caribbean, the United Kingdom, and the United States. His publications explore American political history and foreign policy, issues in twentieth-century Caribbean history, the international relations of the contemporary Middle East, and the politics of imperialism and decolonization in the global context. He received his Ph.D. from the Graduate Institute of International Studies at the University of Geneva.

**Molly Geidel** is a Doctoral Candidate in American Studies at Boston University. Her dissertation is entitled "At the Point of the Lance: Gender, Development, and the 1960s Peace Corps."

**Van Gosse** is Associate Professor of History at Franklin and Marshall College in Lancaster, Penn. He is the author of *Where the Boys Are: Cuba, Cold War America and the Making of a New Left* (1993) and *Rethinking the New Left: An Interpretative History* (2005), as well as many articles, including "Postmodern America: A New Democratic Order in a Second Gilded Age," in Van Gosse and Richard Moser, eds., *The World the Sixties Made: Politics and Culture in Recent America* (2003); and "'As a Nation, the English Are Our Friends': The Emergence of African American Politics in the British Atlantic World, 1772–1861," *American Historical Review* (October 2008). His latest book is *We Are Americans: The Emergence of African American Politics from the Revolution to the Civil War* (forthcoming, Fall 2009).

**Jim Harding** is a retired Professor of Environmental and Justice Studies. He helped found the Combined Universities Campaign for Nuclear Disarmament (CUCND) at the universities of Regina and Saskatchewan during the 1960s and was Chairman of the National Council of Student Union for Peace Action (SUPA). He also helped found the Students

for a Democratic University (SDU) at Simon Fraser University. Since the 1960s he has remained active in ecological preservation, environmental health, inner-city issues, and anti-nuclear organizing. He is the editor of *Social Policy and Social Justice* (1995) and author of *After Iraq: War, Imperialism and Democracy* (2004) and *Canada's Deadly Secret: Saskatchewan Uranium and the Global Nuclear System* (2007). Some of his writings from the sixties are in an out-of-print volume, *Student Radicalism and National Liberation: Essays on the "New Left" Revolt in Canada, 1964–74* (2006).

**Jennifer Ruth Hosek** is Assistant Professor in the Department of German, Queen's University, Kingston, Ont. After taking a Comparative Literature Ph.D. from the University of California, Berkeley, she was Stanford Fellow in the Humanities before accepting the position at Queen's. She has published on literature, film, critical theory and neuroscience, and the women's movement, and is working on a manuscript analyzing the cultural influences of the global South on the North through Cuba and Germany.

**Kristin Ireland** is a Doctoral Candidate in the Department of History, Queen's University, Kingston, Ont., where she also teaches a fourth-year seminar on the history of sexuality. Her dissertation examines the histories of transsexuality in postwar Canada.

**Andrew M. Ivaska** is Associate Professor of History at Concordia University, Montreal, and specializes in the cultural history of postcolonial urban Africa. He received his Ph.D. in African History at the University of Michigan (2003) after completing an M.A. in Arab Studies at Georgetown University. His research focuses on struggles around gender, global culture, youth, and the state in twentieth-century Tanzania. In addition to several articles and book chapters, his publications include *Cultured States: Youth, Gender, and Modern Style in 1960s Dar es Salaam* (forthcoming). He is also undertaking a project exploring Tanzanian engagements with various manifestations of African-American style and politics in the late 1960s and early 1970s.

**George Katsiaficas** has been active in social movements since 1969. He is the author of two books: *The Imagination of the New Left: A Global Analysis of 1968* (1987) and *The Subversion of Politics: European Autonomous Social Movements and the Decolonization of Everyday Life* (1997). With Kathleen Cleaver he co-edited *Liberation, Imagination and the Black Panther Party* (2001). He is based at Chonnam National University in Gwangju, South Korea, where he is finishing a book on Asian uprisings.

**Gary Kinsman** is a long-time queer, antipoverty, antiwar, and anticapitalist activist. He teaches Sociology at Laurentian University, Sudbury, Ont. He is the author of *The Regulation of Desire: Homo and Hetero Sexualities* (1996) and, with Patrizia Gentile, of *The Canadian War on Queers: National Security as Sexual Regulation* (forthcoming); and a co-editor of *Whose National Security? Canadian State Surveillance and the Creation of Enemies* (2000), *Mine Mill Fights Back: Mine Mill/CAW Local 598 Strike 2000–2001* (2005), and *Sociology for Changing the World: Social Movements/Social Research* (2006).

**Michael D. Kirkpatrick** is a Doctoral Candidate at the University of Saskatchewan, Saskatoon. His academic interests include cultural production in Guatemala City and perceptions of urban space.

**Catherine Krull** is an Associate Professor in the Department of Sociology, Queen's University, Kingston, Ont., and is cross-appointed with Women's Studies and Cultural Studies. Her research interests include reproductive/body politics, family relations, social movements, and community development. She is now working on a generational analysis of women living in Havana, Cuba.

**Susan Lord** teaches in the Department of Film and Media at Queen's University, Kingston, Ont. She has written about Cuban culture of the 1960s and today, new media, and international women's cinema cultures. She co-edited, with Janine Marchessault, *Fluid Screens/Expanded Cinema* (2007) and, with Annette Burfoot, *Killing Women: The Visual Culture of Gender and Violence* (2006). She is co-director of The Visible City Project <visiblecity.ca> and is on the editorial collective of *Public: Art/Culture/Ideas*.

**Colin McCullough** is a Ph.D. student in his third year of study at York University, Toronto. His dissertation looks at the cultural history of peacekeeping in Canada, emphasizing how the state, media, and school curricula all helped to turn peacekeeping into a Canadian icon. His other publications include "Chloe Cooley and the Limitation of Slavery in Ontario," in *Heritage Matters* (August 2007).

**Ian McKay** teaches history at Queen's University, Kingston, Ont., and is the author of *Reasoning Otherwise: Leftists and the People's Enlightenment in Canada, 1890–1920* (2008) and *Rebels, Reds, Radicals: Rethinking Canada's Left History* (1995).

**Lee Maracle** is the author of many novels and books. She is Associate Professor in the Department of English at the University of Toronto, Writer in Residence for the university's Aboriginal Studies Programme, and Traditional Cultural Director for the Indigenous Theatre School.

**Edwin Martini** is Assistant Professor of History at Western Michigan University. He is the author of *Invisible Enemies: The American War on Vietnam, 1975–2000* (2007) and numerous articles and book reviews. He is now working on an international history of Agent Orange. The research for the article in this book was supported by the Faculty Research and Creative Activities Support Fund, Western Michigan University, Kalamazoo.

**Marilisa Merolla** is Assistant Professor in Contemporary History and Mass Communication History in the Faculty of Sociology, University of Rome "La Sapienza." Her field of studies concerns media politics and society in the postwar period. She is a member of the committee of the international research group EURO-HISMEDIA, Médias, guerre et imaginaires de guerre en Europe XXè–XXIè siècles, and is the author of *Italia 1961: I media celebrano il Centenario della nazione* (2004).

**Sean Mills** is a Postdoctoral Fellow at New York University. He holds a Ph.D. from Queen's University, Kingston, Ont., and has published many articles on Quebec and Canadian history. His dissertation is entitled "The Empire Within: Montreal, the Sixties, and the Forging of a Radical Imagination, 1963–1972."

**Franny Nudelman** is Associate Professor in the Department of English and Institute for the Comparative Study of Literature, Art and Culture at Carleton University, Ottawa. She is the author of *John Brown's Body: Slavery, Violence, and the Culture of War* (2004) and is writing a book about radical documentary in the post–Second World War United States.

**Guido Panvini** received a Ph.D. in Modern History from the University of Tuscia, Viterbo, Italy. He studies political violence in the 1970s in Italy and is the author of many essays and articles.

**Joana Maria Pedro** is Professor of History at the Universidade Federal de Santa Catarina in Southern Brazil, where she has been teaching since 1983. She teaches in undergraduate and graduate programs in History as well as in the Interdisciplinary Doctoral Program in Human Sciences. She completed a doctorate in Social History at the University of São Paulo in 1992, and did a post-doctorate in France in 2001–02. She is a CNPq (National Research Council)–financed researcher whose work focuses on gender and feminist issues.

**Jaime Pensado** is Assistant Professor of History at the University of Notre Dame, Indiana, and is revising his doctoral dissertation for a book manuscript.

**Lourdes Pérez Montalvo** is an Assistant Professor in the School of Philosophy and History at the University of Havana in Cuba and holds degrees in philosophy, consultation and organizational development, and applied political studies. She is a member of the Junta Directiva Nacional de la Sociedad Cubana de Investigaciones and Asociación de Estudios Latinoamericanos (LASA). Her publications include articles in the book *Ciudad y Cambio Social en los 90s* (1998)

and in *Servicios Sociales y Política Social* 56 (Spain, 2001) and *La Alborada*, 2 (United States, 2002).

**Sean Purdy** teaches the History of the Americas at the University of São Paulo, Brazil. He was visiting researcher in the Department of History and the Center for Latin American Studies at the University of Chicago from January to June 2009.

**Kimmo Rentola** is a Historian and Professor of Contemporary History, University of Turku, Finland. She has published several books and articles on European communism, Finnish-Soviet relations, and the 1968 movements.

**Inés Rodríguez Pedroso** is an Assistant Professor in the School of Philosophy and History at the University of Havana in Cuba, with degrees in history and development studies. She is a specialist in gender studies and a member of the Consejo Científico de la Cátedra de la Mujer de la Universidad de La Habana, Tribunal de Categorías Docentes de la Facultad de Filosofía e Historia, and Sociedad Cubana de Investigaciones Filosóficas.

**Sheila Rowbotham** helped to develop women's history with early works such as *Women, Resistance and Revolution* (1972) and *Hidden from History: 300 Years of Women's Oppression and the Fight Against It* (1973). Her more recent work includes *Promise of a Dream: Remembering the Sixties* (2000) and *Edward Carpenter: A Life of Liberty and Love* (2008). During the early 1980s she worked at the Greater London Council in the Economic Policy Unit. She has taught in schools in further education and adult education and is a Simon Professor at Manchester University.

**Matthew Rothwell** is a Ph.D. Candidate in History at the University of Illinois at Chicago. His dissertation is entitled "Transpacific Revolutionaries: The Chinese Revolution in Latin America."

**Scott Rutherford** is a Ph.D. Candidate in the Department of History, Queen's University, Kingston, Ont. His dissertation subject is "Canada's Other Red Scare: Indigenous

Anti-Colonial Politics and Culture, Global Consciousness, and the 'Sixties.'"

**Kyoko Sato** teaches in the Department of East Asian Studies, University of Toronto. She graduated from the Ontario Institute for Studies in Education of the University of Toronto, where she conducted research on the institutional history of the Japan Foundation, a state-sponsored cultural institution of Japan. Her research investigates how the political and economic processes that took hold in the 1960s were mediated in cultural representations of the 1964 Tokyo Olympics.

**John S. Saul** has taught for many years both at York University, Toronto, and in Africa: in Tanzania, Mozambique, and South Africa. He is the author of some eighteen books on Southern Africa and on development issues more generally. He has also worked through the years as a liberation support and anti-apartheid activist, notably with the Toronto Committee for the Liberation of Southern Africa (TCLSAC) and with *Southern Africa Report* magazine. He remains committed to an anti-capitalist/anti-imperialist politics.

**Amanda Third** is Senior Lecturer and Director of the Centre for Everyday Life in the School of Media, Communication and Culture, Murdoch University, Western Australia, where she teaches in Gender and Cultural Studies. Her research has been published by Duke University Press, Peter Lang, Cambridge Scholars Press, and journals such as *Hecate*, *Social Alternatives*, and *Current Issues in Criminal Justice*. Her recent work includes a study of popular cultural representations of female terrorists, which discusses how second-wave feminism was "cross-wired" with terrorism within the U.S. popular imagination in the late 1960s and early 1970s.

**Jaime Veve** is a long-time U.S. labour activist, educator, and organizer. He has been active in various struggles since the sixties, including the Vietnam War, civil rights, and Pro–Puerto Rican independence movements. He was a founder of the New Direction reform movement within the Transit Workers Union (TWU) of New York City.

**Tity de Vries** is Assistant Professor in Contemporary and American History at the University of Groningen in The Netherlands. In 1996 she received her Ph.D. at the University of Amsterdam with a dissertation on the consensus climate of opinion in the United States and the Netherlands during the 1950s. She has published works on Dutch intellectuals of the 1950s and 1960s, Dutch-American cultural and intellectual relations, documentary film history, and the representation of history in Alaska. She is one of the editors of the Dutch journal of media history *Tijdschrift voor Mediageschiedenis*. She is working on a biography of the internationally known journalist Sal Tas, one of the most colourful and controversial reporters of his time.

**Tobias Wofford** is a Doctoral Candidate in the Department of Art History, University of California, Los Angeles, and is the 2008–10 Wyeth Fellow at the Center for Advanced Study in the Visual Arts at the National Gallery. His research interests include the contemporary art of Africa and the African diaspora. He is working on a dissertation exploring the visualization of Africa in African-American art of the 1960s and 1970s.

**Eric Zolov** is Associate Professor in the Department of History, Franklin and Marshall College, Lancaster, Penn. He received his Ph.D. in Latin American history from the University of Chicago (1995), from which he also holds Masters degrees in Latin American Studies (1990) and International Relations (1990). He is the author of *Refried Elvis: The Rise of the Mexican Counterculture* (1999) and *Rebeldes con causa: La contracultura mexicana y la crisis del estado patriarcal* (2002); and co-editor of *Fragments of a Golden Age: The Politics of Popular Culture in Mexico since 1940* (2001), *Rockin' Las Américas: The Global Politics of Rock in Latin/o America* (2004), and *Latin America and the United States: A Documentary History* (2000). He is Senior Editor for *The Americas: A Quarterly Review of Inter-American Cultural History*, and is now researching and writing on the impact of the Cuban Revolution on Mexican political culture and U.S.-Mexican relations during the "long 1960s."

# INDEX

cowardice, draft and, 343–44
Cowley, Sue, 261
Crepax, Franco, 191
crime, 220, 222
Cronkite, Walter, 324
Crummy, Helen, 212
Cruse, Harold, 39
Cuba, 1, 29, 36, 99, 148–50, 152, 251, 335–36, 337, 362, 369, 379, 382, 403, 407, 415, 417; education programs, 290–94; film, 153–60; history of, 285–88; homosexuality, 85; literacy, 290–91; revolution, 2, 36, 76, 144, 146–47, 149–50, 152, 153–60, 284–85, 288–94, 330–38, 372–73, 374, 379, 382, 384, 386, 413–14, 448n37, 482n17; Soviet Union and, 374; women, 284–95
Cuban Missile Crisis, 285, 389, 401, 413–17
cultural activities, politicization of, 196, 202–4, 206–8
culture: eradication of, 327; explosion of in Edinburgh, 209–18; popular, 196–208
Curtis, Barry, 215
Curtis, Betty, 192
Czechoslovakia, 61, 355; Soviet invasion of, 2, 57–58, 64, 355

Daifullah, Naji, 401
Daley, Richard, 225–26
Dallara, Tony, 190, 192
Dalton, Roque, 146, 453n3
Dar es Salaam (Tanzania), 170–76, 178
Davin, Anna, 264
Davis, Angela, 172, 177
Davis, Belinda, 73
Davis, Mike, 425
Davis, Rennie, 237, 242, 243
de Albuquerque, Júlia Matias, 270
de Beauvoir, Simone, 262
Debray, Régis, 151, 334, 376, 401
decolonization, 29, 30, 91, 162, 167, 230–31, 234, 361, 425, 451n2(ch.12); feminism and, 366; indigenous, 358, 361
DEFA (East German film company), 143, 148, 149
de Gaulle, Charles, 250, 375, 412
Delaney, Shelagh, 263
Dellinger, David, 239, 240
Deloria, Vine, 120
democracy: direct, 25, 260, 349–50, 353, 356; grassroots, 48, 103; parliamentary, 89, 103; participatory, 259, 264, 352,

388, 393, 398, 356; representative, 145, 259; social, 59, 60, 62–63, 65, 208, 265, 397
Democratic Appeal (Netherlands), 99
Democratic Front for the Liberation of Palestine (DFLP), 17
democratization, 43, 336
Dene peoples, 117
Deng Xiaoping, 110, 114
Denmark, 98
de Sica, Vittorio, 155
détente, 56, 59–61, 64, 66–67
development: as alienation and genocide, 328; Peace Corps and, 320–29
Dewet, Kenneth, 215
Dialectics of Liberation conference (London), 261
Dias, Maria Odila Leite da Silva, 268
Diefenbaker, John, 135, 231, 234
Diego Garcia, 412–15, 417
Diggs, Charles, Jr., 42
Dineh Navajo, 115–26; mobilization of, 119–21; sovereignty of, 120
Dinshaw, Carolyn, 433n1
Diop, Alioune, 186
Diouf, Ibou, 182
dioxin, 304–12; Times Beach disaster, 308–11
direct action, 121, 237, 260, 391
Dirlik, Arif, 424
dissent, 68–70, 73–74, 76, 149, 275, 381
Dixon, Marlene, 370
Douglas, Emory, 252
Douglas, Rosie, 369
Douglas, Tommy, 359, 394
Dow Chemical, 25, 31
Drabble, Margaret, 263
draft resistance, women and, 339–46
Drees, Willem, Jr. and Sr., 102
drug use, 214, 244–45, 382
DS70 (Democratic Socialists '70) (Netherlands), 98, 105; origins of, 98–102; political agenda of, 102–4
Du Bois, W.E.B., 37, 45, 128, 130, 134
Dubos, René, 124, 298–300
Dunayevskaya, Raya, 372, 376, 377
Dunbar, Roxanne, 278–79
Dunham, Katherine, 182–83
Dunn, Nell, 263
Dushoff, Ira M., 318
Dutschke, Rudi, 70, 73–76, 397
Dworkin, Andrea, 13, 15
Dworkin, Dennis, 211

resistance, 30, 31, 34, 53, 60, 64, 86, 100–102, 138, 145, 260, 268, 278, 326, 392; in Cuba, 150, 152; draft, 339–46; gay and lesbian, 77, 81; in Germany, 74; in the Netherlands, 97–105; in Palestine, 13–23; in Vietnam, 243–44, 246; women's 22–23
Revolutionary Action Movement (RAM), 39, 437n13
Revolutionary Left Movement (MIR), 19
Revolutionary Party of the Proletariat (PRP) (Mexico), 111
Revueltas, José, 333–34, 335
Rhodesia, 128, 451n2(ch.12); *see also* Zimbabwe
Rice, Condaleeza, 140
Ricks, Willie, 39
Ricordi, Nanni, 191
Rio de Janeiro, 222–23
risk assessment, 297, 299
Riva, Carlos de la, 108–9
Riyami, A.A., 170, 173
RMG. *See* Trotskyist Revolutionary Marxist Group.
Roberts, Alfie, 372, 374, 376
Robeson, Paul, 40, 130, 134
rock 'n' roll music: in Italy, 188–95; in Latin America, 379–87
Rodney, Walter, 368, 377
Rodríguez, Silvio, 384
Rossellini, Roberto, 155
Rossman, Michael, 248
Rostow, Walt Whitman, 321, 322, 425
Roth, Benita, 410
Rothstein, Vivian, 407
Rowbotham, Sheila, 263–64
Royal Canadian Mounted Police (RCMP): surveillance by, 77, 79–83, 85; non-cooperation with, 79–80
Rubin, Jerry, 249
Ruskin History Workshop, 264
Russia, 377, 416–17; revolution in, 109; *see also* Soviet Union

Saarinen, Aarne, 65
Sabina, Maria, 387
Said, Edward, 231–32, 371
Saínz, Gustavo, 336
Salazar, Othón, 335
Saldaña-Portillo, Maria Josefina, 326
Salisbury, Harrison, 239–41, 244
same-sex marriage, 34, 86
Samuel, Raphael, 264

Sandinistas, 31, 396
Sandino, A.C., 37
San Francisco State University, 400
Sanjinés, Jorge, 326–29
São Paulo (Brazil), 268; favelas in, 220, 221, 222–25, 227–28
Sarkozy, Nicolas, 401
Sarnia (Ontario), 24–35
Sartre, Jean-Paul, 36, 261, 376, 377
Saul, John, 3
Sauvy, Albert, 423–26, 429
Sawa, Nagoyo, 166
School of Revolutionary Instructors ("Conrado Benítez"), 290
science information movement, 300
scientism, 376
scientist-activists, 297–303
Scientists' Institute for Public Information (SIPI), 300
Seattle protests, 356–57
Second International, 37
sectarianism, 335
secularization, 188
Seidman, Gary, 132
self-determination, 37, 47, 53, 55, 117, 120, 252, 276, 426; nuclear weapons and, 411–19
self-management, 350
self-organization, 372, 376
Sellers, Christopher, 305
Senegal, 179–86, 355
Senghor, Léopold, 180–83
Sentieri, Joe, 192
September 11 attacks, 394
sexism, 78, 84, 259, 278, 340
"sexocide," 279
sex reassignment surgery (SRS), 313–19; cost of, 473n39
sexual mores, 259, 338
sexual politics, draft resistance and, 339–46
Shabazz, Betty, 437n11
Shanghai Cooperation Organization, 417
Sharpeville massacre, 360, 412
Sherman, William Tecumseh, 44
Shil, Edward, 425
Shining Path, 107, 114
Shriver, Eunice Kennedy, 323, 474n11
Shriver, R. Sargent, 321–23
Simon Fraser University, 26
Simone, Nina, 409
Singh, Nikhil, 53
Sir George Williams University, 26, 368, 369

Suplicy, Marta, 272
Suri, Jeremi, 56, 426
Suslov, Mikhail, 59, 62
Swaziland, 451n2(ch.12)
Sweden, 57, 59, 60, 65; rural working-class theatre in, 196–208; welfare state in, 204–5
Swedish National Touring Theatre (Riksteatern), 201
Sylvania plant, 123

Tajoli, Luciano, 190
Tall, Papa Ibra, 182
Taller de Gráfica Popular (TGP), 251
Tambroni, Fernando, 193
Tanzania, 45, 50, 326; soul music in, 169–78
Tanzania African Nationalist Union (TANU), 172, 176–77
Tavares dos Santos, Maria do Espirito Santo, 269
Taylor, Barbara, 264
Telegraaf, De, 98, 104
Teles, Maria Amélia de Almeida, 270–71
Tenco, Luigi, 190
Tent Project, 207
terrorism, 18, 73, 74, 277, 285, 398; birth of in Italy, 87–96
theatre, rural working-class in Sweden, 196–208
Third International, 37
Third World: coinage of term, 423; possibilities and problematics of, 421–30
Third Worldism, 162; American, 133; German, 75; Soviet, 58
Third World liberation, 53, 332, 414: Aboriginal people and, 361–62
Third World solidarity, 36, 68–76, 77
Thomas, Edith, 262
Thompson, E.P., 26
Thomsen, Moritz, 323–24
Thorn, Hakan, 138
Time magazine, 426
Times Beach dioxin disaster, 308–11
Tipps, Dean C., 424
Tokyo Olympiad (Kon Ichikawa), 161, 165–68
Tokyo Olympics, 165–68
Tome, Harry, 121
Toronto Anti-Draft Program (TADP), 343
Toronto Committee for the Liberation of Portugal's African Colonies/Southern Africa (TCLPAC/TCLSAC), 136, 138

Toronto Daily Star, 229–30, 232–34
Toronto Wages for Housework campaign (TWHC), 83–84; Wages Due (WD), 84
Torres, Oscar, 154
Torres Cuevas, Eduardo, 286
totalitarianism, 69, 100
trade union movement, 26–27, 32, 34, 61–62, 116, 120, 123–25, 135, 197–98, 207, 253, 259, 350, 375
TransAfrica, 133
transnationalism, 27, 36, 70, 172, 178, 211, 223, 354, 388, 390, 415, 431–32, 436–38; communist movement, 202; cultural movement, 197; environmentalism, 25; feminism, 32; identity, 54, 74, 76; imaginary, 176, 366; media representation, 221–28; networks, 171, 203; social movement, 138; spaces of exile, 143–52
transsexuality, 313–19
Traverse Theatre Club (Edinburgh), 215–17
Treaty of Paris, 414
Tricontinental Conference, 115–16, 150
Tricontinental magazine, 150, 251
tricontinentalism, 115–16, 422, 428
Trigo, Abril, 380
Trinidad, 369
Trocchi, Alexander, 213–14
Trotskyism, 19, 58, 77, 85, 333, 445n2
Trotskyist League for Socialist Action (LSA), 81–82, 85
Trotskyist Revolutionary Marxist Group (RMG), 82, 85
Trotskyist Socialist Workers Party, 81
Trudeau, Pierre Elliott, 137–38
Truman, Harry, 130–31, 389
Tshombe, Moise, 426
Tupamaros, 19
Turcios Lima, Luis, 149–51
Turkey, 326, 414
Turner, Henry M., 45

Udall, Stewart, 120
ujamaa, 50, 171–72, 177
underclass, 220, 377
underground press, 340
United Auto Workers (UAW): United Arab Workers caucus, 401
United Farm Workers, 401
United Fruit Company, 146
United Gas, Coke and Chemical Workers Union, 122
United Mine Workers of America, 27

Willis, Raymond, 48
Wilson, Woodrow, 425
Winsor, Hugh, 452n21
"With the Cross and the Country," 289
Wolf, Christa, 72
women: Black, 282–83, 370, 408–10;
    Canadian, 370; in Congo, 232–33; con-
    sciousness of, 18; creating community
    among, 345–46; in Cuba, 284–95; draft
    resistance and, 339–46; equality of, 18;
    indigenous, 366; labour market and, 103;
    oppression of, 408; organizations for,
    289–90; in Palestine, 18–19; resistance of,
    22–23; rights of, 249; subordination of,
    258, 274, 278–79
Women's Leadership Program (Cuba), 290
women's liberation, 25, 29, 32–33, 257–65,
    301, 338, 349, 353, 370, 404; antiwar
    work and, 340–43; in Brazil, 266–73;
    whiteness and, 274–83; see also
    feminism
Women's Revolutionary Unity (Cuba), 289
Women Strike for Peace, 121, 342
Woodruff, Hale, 183
Woods, Roger, 70–71, 75
Woolf, Virginia, 22, 23
Workers' Party (PT) (Brazil), 271
working class, 33, 95, 193, 221, 260, 264,
    287, 333–34, 352, 409; insurgencies of,
    77–78; self-organization of, 372, 377;
    theatre in Sweden, 196–208; women, 83,
    286, 410
Works Progress Administration (WPA), 248
World Bank, 349
World Disarmament Conference, 395, 397
World Trade Organization (WTO), 349, 356–57
World Youth Festival, 395
Worster, Donald, 298
Worthy, William, 39
Wortis, Sheli, 261
Wounded Knee standoff, 358
Wright, Richard, 40, 402

Yazzie, Esther, 121
Yemen, 14
Young, Marilyn, 240
Young, Robert, 422
Young, Whitney, 42
Young Lords Party, 403
Young Socialists (YS), 26, 82, 85
youth, laicization/secularization of, 188
youth culture, 197; global, 176, 189

youth movements, 56, 58, 63, 65, 75, 78, 88,
    153, 369, 380–81, 384, 395
Yugoslavia, 355

Zagladin, Vadim, 58, 66
Zambia, 451n2(ch.12)
Zapatista movement, 357
Zappa, Frank, 320
Zavattini, Cesare, 155
Zenkyôtô, 165
Zhou Enlai, 111, 428
Zhou Ruizhuang, 249
Zimbabwe, 36, 133, 139, 251, 428
Zionism, 74